Samurai among Panthers

Critical American Studies Series

George Lipsitz, University of California–Santa Barbara, Series Editor

Samurai among Panthers

RICHARD AOKI ON RACE, RESISTANCE,
AND A PARADOXICAL LIFE

Diane C. Fujino

Critical American Studies

University of Minnesota Press
Minneapolis • London

All royalties from the sale of this book will be donated to the Richard Aoki Freedom Fund.

Published by the University of Minnesota Press
111 Third Avenue South, Suite 290
Minneapolis, MN 55401-2520
http://www.upress.umn.edu

Library of Congress Cataloging-in-Publication Data

Fujino, Diane Carol.
    Samurai among panthers : Richard Aoki on race, resistance, and a paradoxical life / Diane C. Fujino.
       (Critical American Studies)
    Includes bibliographical references and index.
    ISBN 978-0-8166-7786-3 (hc : alk. paper)
    ISBN 978-0-8166-7787-0 (pb : alk. paper)
1. Aoki, Richard, 1938–2009. 2. Black Panther Party—Biography.
3. Asian American Political Alliance (Berkeley, Calif.)—Biography.
4. Civil rights movements—United States—History—20th century.
5. Asian Americans—Civil rights—History—20th century. 6. African Americans—Civil rights—History—20th century. 7. Political activists—California—Biography. 8. Japanese Americans—California—Biography.
9. United States—Race relations. I. Title.
    F870.J3F87 2012
    323.092—dc23
    [B]
                                                    2012000476

Printed in the United States of America on acid-free paper

The University of Minnesota is an equal-opportunity educator and employer.

20 19 18 17 16 15 14 13   10 9 8 7 6 5 4 3 2

Contents

Abbreviations

AAM	Asian American Movement
AAPA	Asian American Political Alliance
AAS	Asian American Studies
AASU	Afro-American Student Union
AFL	American Federation of Labor
BPP	Black Panther Party
CAP	Community Action Patrol
CORE	Congress of Racial Equality
CPUSA	Communist Party of the United States of America
CWRIC	Commission on Wartime Relocation and Internment of Civilians
FPCC	Fair Play for Cuba Committee
IWW	International Workers of the World
JACL	Japanese American Citizens League
MASC	Mexican American Student Confederation
NAACP	National Association for the Advancement of Colored People
PACE	Pilipino American Collegiate Endeavor
RNA	Republic of New Africa
SNCC	Student Nonviolent Coordinating Committee
SWP	Socialist Workers Party
TWLF	Third World Liberation Front
VDC	Vietnam Day Committee
YSA	Young Socialist Alliance

Introduction

Demystifying the Japanese Radical Cat

An Asian American Movement Icon

At his memorial service in May 2009, there were signs that Richard Aoki's image could rival that of Che Guevara—in style that is, though of course not in fame.[1] The memorial, held at UC Berkeley's Wheeler Auditorium, began with a processional of former Black Panther Party (BPP) members holding a large painted banner that proclaimed Aoki to be a "People's Warrior" and identified him as a "BLACK PANTHER AND TWLF MEMBER."[2] A large black panther leaped out from the center of the banner, across a red star symbolizing revolution; black lettering against a light blue background echoed the colors of the Black Panther uniform. The black cat was flanked by two portraits of Aoki, a recent one showing a slightly puffy-faced older man and a 1960s image of Third World militancy, created by a Panther-inspired beret, dark shades, and the menacing scowl. It was the latter image that was captured again and again that weekend, on bright orange buttons distributed generously, on free silk-screened T-shirts, and on literature. This is the Che-esque image that is becoming equated with Asian American militancy and Afro–Asian solidarity.

The banner, sponsored by a Black Panther alumni organization, highlighted Aoki's most famous historic connection. Although Aoki by and large stayed under the radar during his time in the party, his association was broadcast in Bobby Seale's 1968 book, *Seize the Time*. Aoki, a military veteran and a gun collector, is the "Japanese radical cat," Seale relays, who gave the BPP their first guns to start their legendary police patrols.[3] Much more than a weapons supplier, Aoki was an experienced activist and well read in revolutionary theory. Still, the sensationalism of guns is alluring. It is the image captured in Mario Van Peebles's 1995 Hollywood film, *Panther,* with the Aoki figure, in a moment of ethnic interchangeability, represented as a Chinese American gun supplier.

The banner unveiled at Aoki's memorial includes only one sign of his involvement with the Asian American Movement (AAM). On his black beret is a small button with the Chinese character, or *kanji* in Japanese, for "east" adopted by the Asian American Political Alliance in Berkeley. The AAPA, formed in May 1968, was one of the first political organizations of the Asian American Movement. The AAPA viewed itself as "a people's alliance to effect political and social change" and characterized "American society [as a] historically racist" society built on "social discrimination" and "economic imperialism" that "exploit[ed] all non-white people in the process of building up their affluent society."[4] This analysis and language appealed to Aoki, who had already been working for a few years in the Old Left, the antiwar movement, and of course, the BPP. When Aoki was put forth as one of the most visible Asian American leaders of the 1969 Third World Liberation Front strike at UC Berkeley, it was his work with AAPA, his militant style (an outward expression of his hidden Panther membership), and his known connections with Black Power that bolstered his activist credentials. During the strike in winter 1969, he simultaneously chaired AAPA and sat on the TWLF Central Committee.

The memorial banner captured Aoki's connections with the Black Power and Third World movements, but its subtle reference to Asian American activism reflects the general amnesia in U.S. society toward AAPA and the larger Asian American Movement. Yet, AAPA made at least two significant contributions worthy of historic attention. First, AAPA and its founder, Yuji Ichioka, coined the very term, "Asian American," that has since become common nomenclature in U.S. society.[5] In 1968, however, it was unusual to see pan-Asian unity, which AAPA expressed in its membership, program, and activities. The group, among other projects, was one of the earliest proponents of Japanese American redress, supported draft counseling in Chinatown, and forged solidarity with Filipino farmworkers. Second, Berkeley's AAPA inspired the formation of a loose network of AAPA groups throughout the United States and thereby helped build the early AAM. The AAPA at San Francisco State College, instrumental in that campus's TWLF strike, helped birth the first school of Ethnic Studies in the nation. The AAPA at Yale University helped create *Amerasia Journal,* the first and longest-running journal in the field of Asian American Studies. The AAPA at Columbia University helped form I Wor Kuen in New York's Chinatown, which later became the first nationwide revolutionary Asian American organization. Many former Berkeley AAPA members joined the Asian American revolutionary group Wei Min She, based in San Francisco.[6]

Richard Aoki is one of the most important political leaders bridging the Asian American, Black Power, and Third World movements. Aoki was a founding member of one of the most influential, though understudied, organizations of the AAM. He was the most prominent non-Black member of the Black Panther Party. He provided tremendous leadership to the Third World strike at Berkeley, which, together with the San Francisco State College strike, helped launch a new academic field. Following the strike, he served as one of the first coordinators and instructors to help build Berkeley's nascent Asian American Studies program. Through his grassroots activism and professional work in ethnic studies, Aoki was among the many people who worked to rearticulate the nation's ideological constructions of race. While these ideas are continuously challenged and renegotiated to the present, there has been an undeniable shift in racial politics in the United States.[7] Aoki combined radical theory with military strategies to produce a combustible form of activism that had the teeth to fight back against power and police repression, the creativity to devise and implement strategies to gain rights and freedoms for ordinary people, the revolutionary vision of a liberatory society, the humility to work in service to others, and the militancy to inspire. Today, he is represented as the most iconic figure of the Asian American Movement.

Creating a Life: History and Biography

Aoki's historic significance stems from his social justice work, but his life's story holds meaning beyond the strictly political. Born on November 20, 1938, he was three and a half years old when his family was forced to relocate, first to the Tanforan Assembly Center in San Bruno, twelve miles south of San Francisco near the San Francisco Municipal Airport, and then to the Topaz, Utah, concentration camp. That experience shaped Aoki's life in complex ways. With his father's previously patriotic views challenged, Richard, even at such a tender age, learned about race discrimination and lost a measure of faith in his nation's ability to uphold democracy and justice for all. His parents separated in the fishbowl atmosphere of the Topaz concentration camp, and unexpectedly Richard and his younger brother David lived with their father in Topaz and upon their return to West Oakland. Shozo Aoki was an involved father who homeschooled his sons decades before most people had ever heard of the concept. But he also was an erratic father whose growing illegal activities left him unpredictable, until one day when Richard was in his early teens, his father left town without so much as a word to his sons. Between his father's outlaw activities, his mother's absence, and the later development of his own radical activism, Richard saw his immediate family as the "bad" apples in an otherwise successful and noble Aoki extended family. But my own research uncovers a much more convoluted story of "respectable sons" and "unworthy sons" that complicates the simplistic dichotomy between good and bad.

A year or two before their father left town, Richard and David had moved into their mother's home in nearby Berkeley and began to reconcile tenuous mother–son relationships. His mother's sacrifices—the giving up of her single bedroom to her sons; the ability to feed and care for two growing and hungry teenage boys on, as Richard stated, "a $1.25 per hour minimum wage job"; and the haunting, but unfathomable and unspoken eight-year maternal separation—and her great delight at having her sons with her helped facilitate a process of healing and forgiveness. When I interviewed Richard in 2003, he was the primary familial caregiver for his aging mother, as she had been for him many years earlier. He had also retired from a twenty-five-year career as a counselor, instructor, and intermittent administrator in the East Bay community college system. Even as the hurts of history remain just under the surface of Richard's story, he also managed to create a life of joy and community filled with many close friends, with enthusiastic responses as he got to know his extended family, and with many meaningful—and frivolous—activities.

Samurai among Panthers

In titling this book *Samurai among Panthers,* I am guilty of overemphasizing the masculine—of focusing on Aoki's lifelong fascination with weaponry, his attraction to military maneuvers, and the militancy of his politics. Aoki, like the samurai and the Black Panther, was much more complex than the iconic image suggests. Still, the title aptly captures Aoki's story, that is, the story he constructed for public consumption. While some people are candid, open, impulsive even, Aoki struck me as careful and planned. He had figured out most of the story he wanted to tell before we sat down for each three-day interview marathon. During our conversations, he regularly paused to think about what he wanted to say and how to say it. Each word was measured, but not in the way of a hesitant or tentative speaker. To the contrary, Aoki was a lively and dramatic storyteller. Once he got on a roll, it was difficult for him to stop until he finished the story. These were stories that he liked to tell repeatedly. Like all narrators, Aoki was constructing a story about his life. His had a particular emphasis. He focused on military exploits, whether talking about his time in the U.S. Army, with AAPA, or in the Third World strike. He also promoted a masculine gaze on public life, focusing on activism and professional work and shying away from more intimate relationships. "Oh, he's telling his macho warrior story," one of his female friends commented wryly.[8]

Of the two icons in this book's title, the Black Panther Party is discussed at length in chapter 6, so I focus here on the samurai, imagined as noble warriors, the military elite of feudal Japan. I suggest that this is a generative metaphor and one that Aoki himself embraced, despite its clear limitations. In Aoki's activist days and to the present, many Japanese Americans glorified the samurai to claim roots in the fierce, fighting brigades of their cultural heritage. But the samurai possessed both the noble qualities that I discuss here as well as the vicious qualities of killing for their lord or for more arbitrary reasons and working to uphold a cruelly hierarchical feudal system that granted them a certain status and privileges.[9] Aoki's identification as a modern-day samurai stems not only from a generalized cultural inheritance but also from his genealogical connection to the samurai class in Japan. A samurai carried two swords, one long and one short, as part of his intricately decorated armor. Because only the samurai class was allowed to carry swords, the swords came to symbolize power and military might as well as the position of the samurai as a class separate and superior to the common people.[10] During one interview session, Aoki proudly showed me two swords that he had acquired from his recently deceased father's estate. The Aoki family was able to retain these swords, and others as well, by burying them in their backyard during World War II.[11] Around 1970, when Aoki entered the house of an academic mentor and Japanese American father figure, he would remove his guns and place them on the console. "This is what a warrior does. He takes off weapons in a friend's house," Aoki remarked. That professor interpreted Aoki's actions as that of a samurai, removing his modern-day swords to show proper respect to his teacher.[12]

But military prowess was not the singular characteristic of the samurai. At the center of the samurai ethic was *bushido,* or the Way of the Warrior. As it originated, bushido was not a written code but rather a few orally transmitted maxims. More often, it was "unuttered and unwritten, possessing all the more powerful sanction of veritable deed, of a law written on the fleshly tablet of the heart."[13] Its main precepts have since been explained in writing, notably in Inazo Nitobe's book *Bushido: The Soul of Japan*. A few years ago, Aoki gave me his copy of Nitobe's book; its yellowing and unmarked pages provided no clues about important passages. But many elements of the bushido code are evident in Aoki's thoughts and actions. Bushido stressed righteous action and service to others, especially impoverished commoners, regardless of personal risk or sacrifice. Honor, duty, loyalty, courage, and self-control were central to the samurai code. Influenced by Confucianism, duty was the fulfillment of one's loyalties and obligations in the five moral (and patriarchal) relations: between master and servant, father and son, husband and wife, older and younger brother, and friends. Violence was not to be dispensed indiscriminately, and courage and duty were to be called forth in service to righteousness and justice. The ultimate act of bushido was embodied in dying, famously associated with *seppuku* (or *hara-kiri* as it is popularly known), or suicide by disembowelment. This death is not to be gained through recklessness or resorted to inappropriately. But when used to avenge an injustice done to a parent or master, to rectify one's own wrongs, to avoid falling into the enemy's hands, or to atone for defeat in battle, seppuku was regarded as the noblest of deeds.[14]

The duality of the samurai, the brave warrior and the gentle cultured scholar, is depicted in a woodblock print by famed Japanese artist Tsukoika Yoshitoshi. The serene scene shows a samurai playing the *biwa* or Japanese flute, but a menacing long sword attached to his elaborate armored suit looms large in the foreground and reveals his readiness for battle.[15] It was during the Tokugawa period's two-and-a-half centuries of isolation (1600–1868) that the samurai, especially the elite samurai, was transformed from a regional fighter to an administrator–scholar–warrior. After all, in the long absence of war and foreign invasion, as was the defining characteristic of the Tokugawa period, what productive labor did the warrior perform? The bushido code, perfected in this period, mandated the samurai to become both learned and cultured ("bun" or the pen) and skilled in military arts ("bu" or the sword). While seemingly contradictory, these two sides in fact represented the harmony of fighting and learning, of theory and practice.[16] Aoki prided himself on being a warrior–scholar. He read voraciously. By his own account, he read six hundred library books in a single year in his youth. A close friend of Aoki's, himself a university professor, commented that he had never met anyone more widely read than Aoki. Bobby Seale viewed Aoki as the most well versed in the Marxist–Leninist classics in the early years of the BPP.[17] To Aoki, being a warrior meant being a thinking person *and* a person of action; it meant sharpening one's political analysis and fighting skills.

It was this bushido code of the warrior–scholar that attracted Aoki and inspired his filial loyalties and political commitments. Aoki's narrative is filled with examples of familial obligations, especially caring for his younger brother, only fifteen months his junior. He lamented getting in trouble as a young boy, even when his brother was the instigator. He relayed his father's admonition: "You are responsible for your younger brother. Even if he does wrong, you are the oldest. Therefore you are responsible." The role of older brother and the concomitant duties to family and community formed a core part of his identity. Aoki likewise exhibited a fierce loyalty to Huey Newton, his greatest political mentor. I tried, quite unsuccessfully, to get Aoki to provide a political assessment of the BPP and Newton's controversial role within it. But he would not, even off the record, although he shared his private thoughts with me on many other topics. The strongest criticism Aoki offered was that he refused to visit Newton's penthouse, an understated remark that revealed his views on Newton's lavish lifestyle and changed politics. Aoki's loyalty evokes the image of the samurai, who, at least in theory, would remain loyal to his "master," even to the point of committing suicide, or seppuku, to bring honor to his master.[18]

Aoki's political activism can also be seen as a fulfillment of a samurai's duty to serve the downtrodden with righteous service. By being willing to place oneself in danger in service to justice, one exhibited courage, self-discipline, and honor. Aoki's narrative is filled with many stories involving great personal risk. He faced down the police to fulfill his duty as BPP security at a rally in Richmond, California. In the midst of antiwar struggles, he risked charges of treason and sedition, not to mention academic punishment, by helping to organize an event that featured outspoken anti-imperialist speakers and raised funds for the National Liberation Front for South Vietnam (also known as the Vietcong). During that Third World strike, he stood by a friend who was getting beaten by the police, risking his own bodily harm and arrest. On a particularly cold morning on the strike picket line, a student complained about the freezing weather. Aoki's response evoked the self-discipline and duty required of a samurai: "We invited cold weather just to test out the intestinal fortitude of everybody here. If you're complaining about a little cold weather, I think you should go." Certainly a samurai would not complain about such a minor discomfort as he performed his duties.

Aoki also meticulously strategized militant political actions, was a stickler for being on time, and prided himself on being organized and self-disciplined.

This book's title, *Samurai among Panthers,* while reflecting the warrior themes contained in Aoki's narrative, also points to different cultural manifestations of the combatant. The Black Panther and the samurai come from different time periods, represent different racial and cultural genealogies, and had different political goals. The BPP, one of the key symbols of 1960s Black Power, used the gun to stop police brutality and provided direct services to the poor. By contrast, the samurai reached their zenith during the Tokugawa period. Their allegiances rested with individual aristocratic families or at times the imperial court. Significantly, the Panthers embraced a radical vision of society and raised a twentieth-century critique of capitalist and imperialist development. Even as they structured their organization along a hierarchical military chain of command, they sought to eradicate economic, racial, and national inequalities, created and maintained artificially through the inheritance of wealth, property, and unequal access to power. The BPP emerged largely from working-class Black communities and aligned themselves with common people. They went so far as to advocate redeeming qualities in the lumpenproletariat, or those on the margins of society and productive work, including gang members, criminals, and prostitutes. In stark contrast, the samurai enjoyed a hereditary linkage to power and privilege. Samurai status was passed from father to son, especially among higher-ranking samurai. Although there was some room for upward mobility based on meritocracy, this factor was of limited influence. Moreover, after Japanese commoners were deprived of their swords, the samurai class became "like an army of occupation that stayed in place from generation to generation."[19] The function of the samurai diverged sharply from that of the BPP, who saw themselves as the eradicators of the police as an "occupying army" within the Black ghettos of America. Despite these significant differences between samurai and Black Panthers, both figures signify a warrior's struggle and call to service. The book's title, quite obviously, also signifies Aoki's Afro–Asian solidarities.

In addition, *Samurai among Panthers* references the insider–outsider location that Aoki occupied throughout most of his life. He was a Japanese American living in the predominantly Black community of West Oakland. He gained activist credentials as the leading Asian American in the BPP. His rise to leadership in the Third World strike stemmed, in part, from his link to Black Power. His whole style—his oratorical skills, his dress, his politics, the ever-present gun—oozed militancy and Black Power and created an iconic symbol of Asian American militancy and manhood. But there are two sides to this sword—admiration and isolation. In fact, his isolation resulted, in part, from the very respect given him because of his iconic stature. A former colleague of Aoki's in the early years of the Asian American Studies program at UC Berkeley told me a revealing story. This colleague had taken a drink from a faulty water fountain. He knew that one needed to turn the handle carefully to allow for a gentle flow of water. But Aoki didn't know this. So when he placed his mouth above the spout and turned the handle, a blast of water hit him in the face, knocking off his sunglasses and drenching him. This colleague expected Aoki to respond with anger. But instead Aoki began laughing, assuming incorrectly that he was the target of a practical joke. No one dared do such a thing, for fear that Aoki, viewed by some as a "scary and shadowy" figure, might go off on them.[20] But Aoki laughed—to be the recipient of such a prank means that you're one of the gang, someone people joke with. There is a feeling of belonging inscribed in joshing, something that often eluded him.

Aoki felt the sting of marginalization in other ways as well. He grew up in, as he put it, a "broken home" in a Japanese American community that shunned divorce. He never married or had children in a society that idealizes the nuclear family. His father's outlaw activities and his own radicalness created a distance from the mainstream Japanese American community. I write elsewhere of how, in the period before the onset of the Asian American Movement, a social or geographic distance from the mainstream community enabled "premovement" activists like Aoki to develop Left politics and/or to ally with Black radicalism.[21] The Japanese American mainstream community exerted social control over behaviors that might bring shame or negative attention, especially after being the targets of virulent anti-Japanese activities throughout the first half of the twentieth century.[22] Contrary to conventional wisdom, I am not associating political conformity with Japanese culture. There was, in fact, a strong undercurrent of radicalism in the prewar Japanese American community, which included Sen Katayama, leader of the Communist Party USA and father of the Japanese labor movement, and widespread protest inside the concentration camps as well.[23] But the long years of anti-Japanese racism, culminating in incarceration, inspired an assimilationist drive by Japanese Americans, particularly the elite, as a counter to racial exclusion.[24] By the early 1960s, after the concentration camps, global Cold War relations, and McCarthyism smothered Japanese

American radicalism, assimilationism and model minority aspirations dominated mainstream Japanese America. But Aoki, having grown up with a
nonconforming father and in a working-class Black community, identified,
as he put it, "with the aspirations of the masses more than with integrationism." In particular, he linked his oppositional consciousness with being
"alienated culturally."[25]

Aoki's narrative about his role in the BPP shows an awareness of his
insider–outsider position. In some ways, he was respected for his Afro–Asian
linkages and was treated like one of the brothers. Aoki was honored, for
example, to have been the only non-Black (or one of the few) invited to participate in the Black nationalism conference held in San Francisco in 1966.
There, he raised the idea of "double genocide" of Black American soldiers
and the Vietcong, and he warned about the continuing existence of concentration camps to detain radicals, particularly Black militants. That he
made such Afro–Asian connections illustrated the ways in which Asian and
Asian American experiences were intertwined with Black history; racism
and imperialism forged that common bond. But there remained a pervasive
feeling of being an outsider to the Black movement, especially in a period of
heightened nationalism. Aoki's reluctance to offer a candid political assessment of the BPP or Huey Newton stems, in part, from his deference to Black
leadership and Black self-determination.

Historiography of the "Long Freedom Movement"

A plethora of studies—"perhaps the most important development in recent
years"[26]—compels our attention toward a "long Civil Rights Movement"
(or less commonly, a "long movement" or "long Black Power Movement")
framework that extends the sixties decade backward and forward in time and
across the geography of place.[27] Martha Biondi, Rod Bush, Mary Dudziak,
Kevin Gaines, Glenda Gilmore, Van Gosse, Gerald Horne, Robin Kelley,
Brenda Plummer, Barbara Ransby, Nikhil Singh, Penny Von Eschen, and
others argue that the Civil Rights Movement (CRM) did not suddenly emerge
in 1954 with *Brown v. Board of Education* or in 1955–56 with the Mont-
gomery bus boycott, but had its roots in the radical social upheavals of an
earlier period, particularly the 1930s.[28] Jacquelyn Dowd Hall posits that this
earlier period was "not just a precursor of the modern civil rights movement"
but was "its decisive first phase."[29] The long movement approach shows that
racism was not limited to a particular region (the South), but was a universal feature of the nation as a whole. Moreover, U.S.-based movements

were not contained within national boundaries but were influenced by and in turned shaped Third World anticolonial struggles.

Critics of the "long CRM" state that this approach flattens differences across time and space, blurring analytic distinctions between civil rights and Black Power and important articulations of ideologies, strategies, tactics, and goals.[30] Whether to emphasize continuities or differences remains a key element of the debate. When Aoki stated that his "identification went with the aspirations of the masses more than with the integrationism of the incipient middle class," or when he insisted on carrying a gun to the Freedom Rides, he was articulating differences between civil rights and Black Power. The analytic distinction is useful, even as the actual workings of these movements and activists were much more complex. In Mississippi in the mid-1950s, the president of the state's NAACP (National Association for the Advancement of Colored People) kept weapons in his home and on his person. Another Southern civil rights activist, known to be "a very gentle woman," never left home without a brown paper bag that no one suspected contained a pistol for self-defense.[31] Charles Payne reminds us that the central place given to the violence–nonviolence binary in discussions of the CRM "probably tells us much more about the anxieties of white commentators . . . than it does about the priorities of black people."[32]

A major point of the long freedom movement approach focuses on how historical forces shape the development of social movements and the writing of such history.[33] In particular, long movement studies show how Cold War politics narrowed the earlier movement's vision for a radical restructuring of society. As Penny Von Eschen shows, under Cold War constrictions, many civil rights leaders abandoned critiques of colonialism and reframed their antiracist arguments in terms of how U.S. racism undermined the nation's global moral authority and efforts at empire building.[34] Even so, a dynamic discussion about imperialism, internationalism, and White supremacy continued into the postwar years.[35] Japanese American radicals, though constricted by Cold War politics, boldly advocated Leftist positions such as opposing the 1952 Immigration and Nationality Act. This act was celebrated in the mainstream community for granting naturalized citizenship to Japanese immigrants, but it also targeted alleged subversives for deportation. As a result, these radicals rejected the transformation of Asian Americans into "good minorities" who could assimilate into the nation, at the expense of Communists.[36] In addition, recent studies of Black Power by Peniel Joseph, Muhammad Ahmad, Cedric Johnson, Jeffrey Ogbar, James Smethurst, Timothy

Tyson, Komozi Woodard, and others have argued that it was in response to the victories of the CRM and to changes in the Cold War milieu that Black Power activists advanced changes in methods, goals, and ideologies as well as consciousness and identity.[37] Thus, the long movement analysis offers a framework for recognizing differences and illuminating how historical context, political economy, and culture shape specific ideologies and strategies. Van Gosse's discussion of "a movement of movements" provides a useful analytic for understanding how the Black Power, New Left, Asian American, antiwar, and other movements, rather than being collapsed as a single formation, were a "'polycentric' left encompassing a series of overlapping, contingent social movements, each with its own centers of power, that related to each other through a series of strategic arrangements."[38]

Richard Aoki's story fits within, and also expands, the newer scholarship on the long movement in at least five ways. First, Aoki's story showcases the Third World solidarities and the local–global linkages emphasized in long movement studies. Second, by exploring how Aoki's work in the Socialist Workers Party links the Old Left to the Black Panthers and the Asian American Movement, his story illuminates continuities between the 1930s and 1960s and compels "the need to rethink 'the Sixties' as a radical break."[39] Third, Aoki's activism responds to calls by John Dittmer, Charles Payne, Jeanne Theoharis, and Komozi Woodard for local studies and alternative leadership models.[40] By contrast to the early CRM scholars' emphasis on the "Great Man" paradigm and media-spotlighted national events, attention to the local makes visible the leadership of the working class, women, and the rural poor.[41] It also shifts the gaze from judicial and legislative strategies to grassroots organizing. Aoki's story exemplifies the Asian American Movement's focus on the power of ordinary people and the multitude of methods involved in creating social change. Fourth, the study of activism in the North and West debunks the myth of the South as the particular region of White supremacy separate from the practices of the nation. Fifth, Aoki's narrative spotlights Asian American activism. While this history suffers from national amnesia and severe understudy by both social movement scholars and U.S. historians, recent studies by Fred Ho; Daryl Maeda; Estella Habal; Steve Louie and Glenn Omatsu; Michael Liu, Kim Geron, and Tracy Lai; Laura Pulido; and Diane Fujino show the Asian American Movement's focus on anti-imperialist critiques, internationalism, Afro–Asian and Third World solidarities, and local, grassroots, and collective leadership.[42] In all these ways, the study of Aoki's life fits in with the long movement's framework that examines continuities and discontinuities across time and space and produces a richer, more nuanced history of U.S. social movements and of U.S. society itself.

The Dance of Methodology

As a feminist scholar, I wanted to explore how the personal and political intersected in Richard Aoki's life by looking at his relationships with his parents and brother, as well as long-term romantic relationships he had with women. It was particularly difficult to get him to talk about his mother in the postwar years. I knew his parents had split up inside the Topaz, Utah, concentration camp and that the shame and stigma of that rare separation in the 1940s Japanese American community were exacerbated by the camp's fishbowl atmosphere. Aoki regularly used the term "broken home" to refer to his family, reflecting not only the vocabulary of his generation but also his views on what a "normal" family ought to look like. But he knew many single-parent families growing up in West Oakland, and being raised by one parent was of lesser concern to him. What disturbed him most was the unspoken act of maternal separation, or what must have seemed, through the eyes of a young boy, like maternal abandonment. Aoki's decadelong separation from his mother from about age five to fourteen was a topic he never discussed in any detail with me, not even off the record. I doubt he ever uncovered the reasons for her leaving, nor did he necessarily want to know. Throughout hours of interviewing, Aoki repeatedly diverted the conversation away from his mother. Finally, toward the end of one multiday session, I commented on the process of our interview—on how he repeatedly switched to innocuous topics to avoid this painful one. I recalled Alex Haley's efforts to get Malcolm X to discuss his mother. Malcolm wouldn't talk about his mother until one night Haley asked a question—"Could you tell me something about your mother?"—that opened the floodgates.[43] I can't say that my comment unleashed any raging torrent, but it did open the door to a still-safe conversation about his mother. He talked about her work and how stunned he was that she could raise two teenage sons on minimum wage. Upon my inquiry, he revealed that he saw his mother about a dozen times in the eight years following their return from Topaz, despite her proximity in nearby Berkeley. He ended this subject by relaying his mother's words, stated many times over, that the four or five years that her sons lived with her were "the happiest period of her life." Aoki had reconciled, in his own way, his relationship with his mother.

Aoki never married. He explained that he prioritized the struggle for justice above his personal pleasures and that few women could put up with his single-minded focus on politics and liberation. But he wanted me to know that he had had a number of girlfriends and had enjoyed their sexual intimacies. He showed me pictures of a few women and was particularly proud to show me one of an attractive buxom blond. But virtually all these details were to remain off the record. I tried, rather unsuccessfully, to encourage him to discuss the ways the personal and political intersected. One woman, in particular, had been active in the Asian American and Black freedom movements during the time they lived together in the late 1960s and early 1970s. I was interested in how their politics and practices affected one another. Three decades after they broke up, they remained close friends and Aoki initiated a lunch for us to meet. After the meal, he went outside, providing space for us to talk, knowing full well that I would ask her for an interview. She readily agreed. But Aoki grew increasingly anxious as the date of our scheduled interview approached, and his former partner canceled our interview out of her respect for him. Aoki had been confident that she would turn me down and thus it felt safe to him for us to meet. Throughout his life, Aoki compartmentalized his life. He didn't tell girlfriends, even those he was living with, much about his political activities. His coworkers knew little about his personal life or political history. Even his political comrades knew little about his other political activities.

In telling me his narrative, Aoki wanted me to convey *his* story to the world, unfettered by other interpretations, including my own. One way he sought to control the narrative of his life was to limit whom I interviewed. He initially stated that I needed to talk with three people. Two were longtime close friends, but the third person, I was surprised to learn, was not. Instead, she had gained his confidence enough for him to grant the first extended interview about his life—no small accomplishment indeed. Her life did intersect with his, beginning with her student days in Aoki's class at UC Berkeley, but many parts of his life were unknown to her. Aoki allowed me to speak to these three people because he felt assured of their positive assessment of his life. At one point, I told him that I wanted to interview Bobby Seale, cofounder of the BPP; the other cofounder, Huey Newton, had passed away. My request raised Aoki's anxiety. After much prompting, he finally agreed. But even then, he called Bobby Seale's home at the beginning of our interview and then stopped by toward the end of session. Given years of intense BPP intraparty conflict, even in 2003, Aoki wasn't sure where he stood with party figures. After I shared Seale's fond memories and glowing report, Aoki expressed a sense of knowing all along what Seale would say, but his relief was obvious.[44] Thereafter, Seale began speaking at events about Aoki, including a sneak preview of a documentary film about Aoki, thus cementing Aoki's place in BPP history.

It is difficult to know how a relationship will develop. It takes time to understand the patterns of narrative telling and of listening to unspoken or coded messages and truths. For the historical actor, it takes time to develop trust in his or her biographer, especially for someone as private and paranoid as Aoki. All along I had been gathering archival sources from libraries and people's personal archives as well as court records, census data, newspapers, and birth, death, and marriage licenses to augment, as I understood it, Aoki's expressed desire to have me research his life. After my auspicious interview with Bobby Seale, I began interviewing more people and in the end, interviewed twenty-six political associates, friends, and family members of Aoki's. I always let Aoki know whom I was interviewing, not to get his permission, as I saw it, but out of respect to him and also to those I interviewed, many of whom checked with Aoki to make sure I was legitimate, if they didn't already know about our project. So, our dance of talking, researching, interpreting, and reassessing unfolded. From the start, Aoki's dramatic storytelling had me in stitches, but it also aroused my suspicions. Did the events really occur as described, or was this a performer's use of hyperbole and theatrical license? Aoki also had a way of framing events through allusion. On his involvement in the BPP, for example, another interviewer inquired, "You, Huey and Bobby sat down and wrote the 10-point program?" Knowing the interview was to be published, Aoki responded: "I recall we did with a bottle of scotch, but there are different interpretations of it. . . . The 10 point program was the result that we got to have a program. We all knew that you can't get nowhere without a program."[45] Naturally, many readers believed Aoki coauthored the BPP's famous Ten-Point Platform and Program. But when I questioned him, Aoki readily acknowledged that he did not help write the document, but rather helped reproduce and distribute it and, I will add, influenced Newton's and Seale's politics in the years preceding the formation of the BPP.

Did Aoki use vague and indirect language to insinuate a greater involvement in the BPP than he actually had? Was Aoki committed to factual accuracy? "Probably yes" is the answer to both questions, suggesting that narratives are more than simple truths or falsehoods. As Norman Denzin argues, all stories are fiction.[46] It is my job as biographer–scholar to sift through Aoki's narrative to reconstruct a perspective on history from available sources and to interpret the meaning of Aoki's story. When a factual discrepancy emerges, Alejandro Portelli teaches us not to simply write it off as a distortion of memory or as a calculated misrepresentation, but rather to find its social meaning.[47] Aoki's statement, "I recall we did with a bottle of scotch," quite obviously serves to magnify the significance of his involvement in the BPP. Why might he do this? For one thing, he was among the unsung heroes who made tremendous personal sacrifices to advance liberation but rarely received recognition. In this he was not alone. Only a few charismatic movement leaders have become widely known. Their very fame reinforces the notion that a few "great men" make history and eclipses the involvement of masses of ordinary people in liberation struggles, as Charles Payne observed and Ella Baker railed against.[48] In light of their relative obscurity, these makers of history may also find ways to be heard and seen.

In addition, Aoki exhibited an uncertainty about the meaning of his activist contributions. Events do not simply happen, but rather, as symbolic interactionists posit, people construct their social meanings through interpretations derived from social interactions. In other words, how people decipher events helps signify the importance of those events. The "looking-glass self," a phrase coined by Charles Cooley, refers to the ways we construct our sense of self through the meanings reflected back by others. But what happens when the political movements one works in remain obscure? The Asian American Movement, in particular, suffers from a general amnesia in U.S. society. There has also been limited attention paid to Berkeley's Third World strike, with the Free Speech movement and antiwar movement towering over the histories of Berkeley in the 1960s and with the San Francisco State College strike overshadowing the literature on Ethnic Studies struggles. Moreover, what happens when one's own personal practice was to stay below the radar, as Aoki did in the BPP? The combination of Aoki's relative obscurity and the invisibility of the social movements with which he was involved meant there was scant looking-glass reflection back to him to help give wider social meaning to his political activities.[49]

In this context, the thirtieth- and fortieth-anniversary reunions of the BPP, TWLF, and AAPA have provided an important looking-glass lens through which to reflect on and assess activist contributions and to draw connections to today's social movements. The gatherings brought together veteran organizers, many of whom hadn't seen each other in decades. The accompanying commemoration events served to educate younger generations about these often-obscure histories and to make relevant the lessons of the 1960s for current liberation struggles. For activists like Aoki, these events provided a forum in which to dialogue about the old days, to feel the respect of young people, to reactivate political engagement, and significantly, to place their own activist contributions in a larger historical framework. The social interactions among veteran activists, current activists, young people, and scholars have generated information about the meaning and significance of these more obscure '60s social movements, with Aoki emerging as a respected leader. For Aoki, and no doubt countless others, this provided the necessary looking glass to reflect on his own activities, contributions, and sacrifices.

Aoki's growing sense of his own historic significance, coupled with an epiphany at a former AAPA member's memorial, reversed his earlier objections to my documenting his life history. I was surprised to receive a phone call from him in late 2002 asking me to write his life's story.[50] Three years earlier, Aoki had allowed me to interview him for a larger research project on Asian American activism. After he conducted his usual "security checks," I was given the green light. Dolly Veale generously made the formal introduction and, at Aoki's request, stayed throughout the interview. Still, it took a huge leap of trust for Aoki to invite me to write his story. He expressed this confidence based on my writing of Yuri Kochiyama's biography.[51] He also noted that my doctoral-level training in psychology and my gender might be a good complement to his own background. My being Japanese American, an activist, and a generation younger allowed him to pass on the '60s legacy to future generations.

The Format and Organization of the Book

Aoki's narrative was constructed from the eleven multiday interview sessions, lasting from late morning until well after dinner, conducted from January 2003 through March 2004, as well as a shorter interview in 1999 and follow-up telephone interviews. In total, we gathered one hundred hours of tape-recorded interview material. My extensive research enabled me to check facts, to place his story within a historical and social context, and to interpret his narrative. As with any narrative, differences emerged between the subject's story and other sources. I was faced with the dilemma of how to present the various perspectives. Some scholars include only material that can be collaborated by at least one other source. But a narrative is important

not only for what it tells but also for what it does not say, for what it dis-
torts, and for what it says about issues important to the narrator. So I
included Aoki's narrative in the book when it revealed a larger social meaning, even when I could not fully verify its occurrence or it was inconsistent
with other sources. Aoki stated, for example, that in 1964 he started his
full-time studies at Merritt College and joined the Vietnam Day Committee.
His transcripts, however, show he returned full-time to Merritt College in
fall 1963 and archival materials indicate that the Vietnam Day Committee
began in 1965. But Aoki's memories are consistent: "The year 1964 was big
for me, though I didn't realize it at the time." By distilling into a single year
his full-time studies, his discharge from the military, and his antiwar work,
he could make sense of his activist development. For the interested reader,
the endnotes describe my research efforts and discuss other sources and
interpretations.

Many different formats are appropriate for a biographical project. A traditional biography, written in the third person, would allow me to construct
his life's story around my interpretations and to integrate various sources
into Aoki's narrative. But this approach would disrespect Aoki's desire to
tell his own story, not to mention lose the strength of his captivating voice
and style. A traditional oral history narrative would allow for the telling of
Aoki's own story uninterrupted by other voices. But both Aoki and I felt
compelled to conduct additional research, even if for different reasons. The
question became, how and where should I integrate my research and interpretations? I could place my views and research in endnotes and in lengthy
essays at the beginning and end of the book. But doing this rendered alternative views, analysis, and social context quite distal to Aoki's narrative. I
could intersperse archival sources and my interpretations throughout Aoki's
story. But this felt too intrusive and made it impossible to read Aoki's story
uninterrupted, if one so desired.[52]

I decided to place my commentary at the end of each chapter, in addition
to the endnotes, introduction, and epilogue. While this option detracts from
a straightforward and uninterrupted reading of Aoki's narrative, in many
ways it also strengthens his story. I sensed that Aoki felt his story would be
accepted at face value, especially if facts had been checked. But as a scholar,
I understand the multiple views a readership can bring to a narrative, including questioning perspectives and reading for signs of bias. Aoki, never
bland or middle-of-the-road, was certain to raise people's suspicions. In
addition, his tendency to compartmentalize his life and to shy away from

deep self-reflection left holes in an understanding of his life. I also worried that Aoki's preference for militaristic maneuvers and distance from the participatory style of grassroots organizing would shape the historical perspective on social movements. I wasn't troubled by adding another voice to the already multifaceted history of the BPP. But I was concerned about biasing the largely hidden histories of AAPA and Berkeley's TWLF. The space at the end of each chapter allowed me to comment on Aoki's narrative, including researching the sparse history of his family known to Aoki; discussing militarism, citizenship, and racialized masculinity in the context of the Cold War; and exploring his insider–outsider position within the BPP. My commentaries would thus serve to complicate Aoki's story, to contextualize his life within historic social forces and political economies, and to raise alternative perspectives on Aoki and ultimately on the meaning of political agency. While the placing of my commentaries at the end of Aoki's account is unusual, it allows for a conversation to occur between the historical actor and his biographer. This unique format might well prove useful to those interested in the study of narrative construction or research methodology.

Aoki's story is presented in a chronological format common to the biographical genre. From the moment of his birth, there are hints of the unconventional and colorful life he would lead (chapter 1). His "happy" childhood was cut short by the forced incarceration of Japanese Americans during World War II and by the demise of his parents' marriage (chapter 2). My study of the Aoki family reveals a complex and convoluted history that disrupts the dichotomy established in Richard's mind between the "noble" Aoki extended family and the "deviant" behaviors of his immediate family. The positioning of the incarceration as an "absent presence" in U.S. history has left many, including Richard, to deal with the legacy of the camps—a monumental trauma that has been neither fully articulated nor represented in history.

The story follows Aoki's life growing up in the Cold War period in Black West Oakland and in a household predominated by men (chapter 3). Even before graduating from high school, Aoki rushed to join the army. He was to serve six months in active duty, followed by seven and a half years in the reserve, according to the Universal Military Training and Service Act of 1951 and 1955 (chapter 4). Richard's manhood was shaped by the divergent masculinities represented by his grandfather, a successful immigrant entrepreneur and church leader; his uncles, one a Boy Scout leader and another a paragon of U.S. citizenship who was selected as the keynote speaker for Citizens Day in Oakland; and his own father, a complex mixture of involved parenting and of failed manhood in abdicating his responsibilities as father and economic provider (chapter 3). In addition, the paradox of the Cold War, of the nation's anxiety about threats to its newly acquired world dominance amid material abundance, represented the historic context in which Richard developed his ideas about militarism, manhood, and nation (chapter 4).

Through a series of blue-collar jobs, Aoki was introduced to the workings of capitalism and the class analysis of labor organizers and socialist activists. By the early 1960s, he was involved with the Socialist Workers Party and its youth group, the Young Socialist Alliance. I argue that the predominantly White Old Left, through the SWP and YSA, were pivotal in moving Aoki not only to Marxism–Leninism but also ironically toward Black nationalism. The pages of the *Militant,* the SWP's newspaper, reveal a heavy focus on the radicalization of the Negro struggle, as it was then called, and strong support for Black self-determination and Black nationalism. The *Militant* also printed many of Malcolm X's speeches, revealing the development of Malcolm X's radical and international perspectives during his last year (chapter 5). Having worked in the antiwar and Third World solidarity movements and with BPP cofounders Huey Newton and Bobby Seale in the mid-1960s, Aoki was politically ready to join the BPP when it started in Oakland in 1966. I contend that in this period of heightened nationalism, Aoki's BPP experiences were marked by both racial solidarity and racial ambiguity. While he himself chose solidarity, he, like everyone else, could not completely escape the ideological and social organization of race in the United States (chapter 6).

Still, Aoki was not a mere recipient of structural forces. He also helped shape ideas about racial equality and economic justice through his activism in the Black, Asian American, and U.S. Third World movements. He became a founding member and chair of AAPA in Berkeley, an organization that not only coined the very term "Asian American" but also helped launch numerous Asian American student groups nationwide that formed the incipient Asian American Movement (chapter 7). He was also a leader of the Third World strike at UC Berkeley that developed the new academic field of Ethnic Studies and sought to restructure education. In these struggles in the mid- to late 1960s, activists like Aoki were developing new ideologies and militant strategies to achieve radical social change. Aoki displayed the courage, and even an arguably necessary macho bravado, to defy powerful institutions as he "learned to fly on the way down" during a time of intense political struggle and repression (chapter 8).[53]

As one of the first coordinators and instructors, Aoki was instrumental in developing UC Berkeley's nascent Asian American Studies program and in striving to insert community connections and student power into the new department (chapter 9). He went on to have a twenty-five-year career in the East Bay community college system, using his positions as counselor, instructor, and intermittent administrator to help the working-class students and staff around him achieve some measure of equality and fulfillment (chapter 10). The twentieth and thirtieth anniversaries of the Third World strike and the launching of BPP commemorations, the growing social movements of the 1990s, and his own retirement in the late 1990s, facilitated his return to grassroots activism (chapter 11). In the last dozen years of his life, Aoki, for the first time, gained public recognition of his social justice contributions and came to see his life as historically significant and personally fulfilling.

1   "My Happy Childhood That I Don't Remember"

I've been told that my early years, before the war, were the happiest period of my childhood. I was adored by my extended family. Yet I don't remember it. I was born on November 20, 1938, in the year of the tiger and in the European zodiac, Scorpio. I've heard rumors that my birth was a bit of a surprise. My father was a big man on campus. He was, my mother's sister Decky tells me, the only Japanese American student at UC Berkeley before the war who had his own car and I'm sure it was a sporty car. My father was smooth talking, well dressed, and from a good family. I guess my mother got smitten. I'm not exactly sure how the family history goes, I came along just in time for the marriage or whatever. At first I thought they were rumors and then I started jamming people in the family: "Look, I heard about an incident. I need to know the truth. We're adults now. I can take the truth." Then I'd have the story verified.[1]

My mother's parents weren't happy about the marriage or the relationship. One would think that my father's family would be more opposed because they were from a higher class—from samurai stock, according to family myth. By the time I was born, my paternal grandfather had amassed a noodle factory and two houses, all on the same block in West Oakland. It was a big factory, probably made all the noodles in Oakland. My mother's father had to work like a dog to support four kids, but by the time I was born, he had been able to purchase a house with a big lot, twice of the size of an ordinary lot, right there on Stuart Street in Berkeley. Still, the Aokis were much wealthier. When I think something is logical but find the opposite, I have a tendency to keep throwing it out just to see if there's consistency and if there is, then I have to rethink my assumptions. All of the info I've gotten is that my mother's parents were more hostile toward their marriage than my father's parents. They seem to think my father was a bit of a rake. During Victorian times in England, rakes were dandies, the spoiled sons of the bourgeois aristocracy, a little loose on the moral side. So from the very beginning, there was some discord.[2]

But along comes Richard. Then fifteen months later, my brother, David Tatsuo Aoki, was born in February 1940. The closeness of his birth to mine at times enhanced our relationship. The sad news is that the one relative who's been with me the most is my younger brother. I'm sorry he's gone. He left a big void in my life. My mother was a stay-at-home mom. My father was listed on my birth certificate as laundry help, which might have been a bit demeaning because he was the youngest of six children and one of two siblings that went to the University of California. The Aokis had a reputation of being smart and my father lived up to that. Now my father had to drop out of school to get a job to support his family. He never talked to me about the would haves, could haves and should haves. I never heard him whine and he didn't encourage that in me. In fact, he never told me anything about that particular period.[3]

I think my father went to work for Ashby's cleaners in Berkeley. It must have been months after I was born that my mother and father and I moved from San Leandro to Berkeley [about fifteen miles north]. There were a lot of Japanese living in Berkeley at the time. But because of residential segregation that existed at the time and well into the sixties, people of minority ancestry couldn't buy houses north of the University Avenue. Davis McEntire, a social welfare professor at UC Berkeley got his professional recognition writing about residential segregation in the city of Berkeley, focusing primarily on the Japanese.[4] So we lived south of University Avenue, on Stuart Street, near Sacramento Avenue. We lived in the same neighborhood, almost the same block, as my maternal grandparents, and my paternal grandparents were living nearby in West Oakland. In fact, practically all my uncles and aunts were in Oakland or Berkeley. It's kind of significant because within the local Japanese American community, your status somewhat depended on where you lived. Oakland was an industrial city, the third-largest industrial city in the state, and so was working class. Berkeley was connected to the university, so was a little more genteel. I think all ethnic groups are like this, that the physical location of the residence will somewhat determine their socioeconomic status within the community. I had a feeling that the Japanese American community in Berkeley looked down their noses at those in Oakland.

So how did my family end up in Oakland and Berkeley? Here's what happened. My grandparents on both sides immigrated to the United States around the turn of the twentieth century. This was during the high point of Japanese immigration, with most Japanese immigrating between 1890 and 1907. Most came as cheap labor.[5] The year 1902 sticks on me because not only do I have other relatives' narratives but I do have correspondence. I used to be a stamp collector and I had some postcards from that period of time. I don't know much about my father's family's history—and almost nothing about my mother's—but I was told that my Aoki grandfather was disturbed by the militarization of Japan and decided to come to the United States. My paternal grandparents married in Japan and three of their six children were born in Japan—my aunt Sadae, my aunt Minoru, and my uncle Shigeo. My uncle Riuzo was born here, then my aunt Haruko, and my father Shozo was the youngest. My father was born in Oakland in 1914.[6] My mother was the third of four children. In birth order, my uncle Hideo was the firstborn, then my aunt Yoshiko, then my mother, and then my aunt Decky. They are typical Nisei (second generation, the children of immigrants) in that they were all born before the war, mostly in the 1910s and 1920s. My mom was born in 1916 and grew up in Berkeley.[7]

That my uncle Riuzo was the first child born in the United States is important because when it came to the property and legal financial affairs of my grandfather, he had to bring Riuzo in as the official owner of the house and all the property. I always knew when I was a kid that because of the Alien Land Law my grandfather didn't own the property, but that Riuzo was the boss in a way. That's rather disrespectful and undercuts parental authority when a young kid ends up being the interpreter and owner. Poor Riuzo, too, because he must have felt the burden of the whole family depending on him.[8]

Despite the discrimination and humiliation my grandfather faced, he started that noodle business and within a short period was able to acquire two houses and a factory. Can you imagine that? The noodle factory still stands, but it's a skateboarding company now.[9] Because my older uncles and aunts had to work in my grandfather's business, they weren't able to attend college. But my uncle Shigeo, the oldest son, and my father, the youngest son, were able to go to UC Berkeley. On my mother's side, my aunt Decky was the only one to attend UC Berkeley. She got her master's degree in social work. I found out years later that the very dean that I had a conflict with in the 1960s was the person who helped my aunt get her degree after the war broke out. Before that, my father graduated from McClymonds High School, which was the main high school for residents of West Oakland. I have a picture of him that I've managed to retain over the years. This is a photograph of my father in his ROTC uniform marching with other members of his high school ROTC group.[10]

My mother grew up in Berkeley, where her father was a gardener and her mother, a housewife. I suspect my grandfather worked for the hill people.

That's the only way you can make money here. Berkeley's pretty geographically distinct. There's the flatlands, where the lower and middle classes reside, and then the hill portion of the city, where the more economically affluent reside and they would require services. During high school, I did work as a gardener's helper and traveled all over those Berkeley and Oakland hills helping the gardener. That was a revealing experience—big houses, big lots, lots of vegetation.[11] My mother went to Longfellow, which is the major elementary school for the southwest district of Berkeley. She graduated from high school here in Berkeley, but before that, probably in her teens, she was sent back to Japan for study. She didn't stay there long enough to identify as a Kibei.[12] She was rather unhappy about being in Japan and away from the family. So with her innate individual single-minded firmness, she was able to convince her parents it wasn't a good idea and she returned to Berkeley after spending only a short time in Japan. While she was in high school, she took a variety of vocationally geared classes. It sounds reasonable for a female at that time. She did well in high school. According to her, her strongest points in high school were typing and Spanish. She started working in a cleaners as a counter girl, that's what they called them, counter girls. The cleaners was owned by Japanese, so that she was bilingual probably helped. I imagine her social life was probably restricted a bit because of her occupation. There's nothing wrong with it; it's just a typical working-class set.

So I'm bebopping along. I had nothing to complain about. I had a mother. I had a father. I had a younger brother. I had doting grandparents who adored me. There's one incident that my mother mentioned a lot. She wondered how I was able to get out of the yard and go down the street to my aunt's place. I must have been two or three, old enough to walk. The latch on the gate was at the top and there was no way I could reach it. So one day she spied on me to see how I was able to get the gate open and scoot down the way. I took a stick and moved the latch up, then scooted. The inducement was my relatives loved me and I knew whenever I showed up, I would get candy or something. That's one of her favorite stories regarding how bright I was. The fact that I was able to pick up Japanese as fast as English also astounded my mother. However, I spoke Japanese fluently because I had to communicate with my grandparents, especially my two grandmothers. My grandparents on both sides, especially my grandfathers, doted on me. They were the ones who said, "Oh, he's a bright little boy." But then their opinions are suspect anyway. I was also given the nickname of Chatterbox. I don't know why. It's not me, it's not me.

But the American Dream shatters and the Japanese American nightmare takes over. What was this Japanese American nightmare? It was the exclusion, evacuation, and internment of the national Japanese American community on the West Coast. Now comes the end of Richard's happy childhood, which Richard doesn't even remember.

DISRUPTING THE DEVIANT–NOBLE BINARY

This is an atypically short chapter. I considered combining it with the next, but its very brevity speaks volumes about Richard's limited knowledge of his early childhood years and family history. Because he lived in his paternal grandparents' home until his early teen years, I wondered why he hadn't heard more family stories. Was this a family that didn't tell stories? Or was this about his forgetting, and if so, why? Or was there something else going on? As I researched Richard's family history, I discovered that other relatives, particularly his cousin James T. Aoki, had been gathering substantial materials on the family history. To be fair, Richard did know more than I placed in his narration. But most of the omitted material focused on his recounting the histories of Japan and Japanese America, with only limited reference to his own family. His parents' tense relationship and the meager contact he had with his extended family during and after their World War II internment constrained his knowledge. Indeed, Richard had an ambivalent relationship with his extended families, enjoying the sense of belonging they provided but never quite knowing how they perceived him and the "deviant" behaviors of his nuclear family. These are issues I address in subsequent chapters. My purpose here is to fill in the skeletal family history relayed by Richard and, in doing so, to complicate the dichotomy established in Richard's mind of his problematic nuclear family in the midst of the noble Aoki extended family. Here I focus on Richard's paternal family. Although both sides of his family are personally meaningful to Richard, the weight of history rests with the Aokis.

Richard's grandfather, Jitsuji Aoki, immigrated to the United States in 1902.[13] The majority of Japanese immigrants in that period came as sojourners who expected to return to their homelands with savings from overseas work to establish themselves in Japan or to help in Japan's modernization efforts.[14] That Jitsuji left his wife and children in Japan might suggest that he too came with a sojourner mentality. But three significant factors distinguish Jitsuji's migration from that of most Japanese immigrants and hint at an early decision to remain in the United States. First, the Aoki family was Christian in an overwhelmingly Buddhist society.[15] Chojiro Aoki, the first of the three Aoki brothers to immigrate to the United States, apparently came to attend divinity school in a modern Christian society. He subsequently worked as a minister in the Episcopal Archdiocese of San Francisco and later founded the Japanese Episcopal Mission in Oakland.[16]

Second, the Aokis were a family of some financial means. Most Japanese immigrants came as laborers, working in the sugarcane plantations in Hawaii or in agriculture, salmon canneries, or railroad maintenance on the West Coast. The typical immigrant had to work many long years to save sufficient funds to cover transportation for his new bride, who had to travel unescorted as a "picture bride."[17] By contrast, a relatively short five years after Chojiro and Jitsuji immigrated, the Aokis could afford to cover travel expenses for Chojiro to escort his mother and Jitsuji's wife, Fusa, and three children to the United States. Fusa Aoki's "father," or perhaps it was her father-in-law, was listed as the person paying for her passage.[18] Jitsuji, the eldest son who inherited the entirety of the family's wealth according to Japan's system of primogeniture, was able to start a noodle manufacturing business in Oakland the year after he entered the United States.[19] Jitsuji may have been too busy establishing his business to travel to Japan in 1907, so instead asked his brother, the minister, to accompany his family to the United States and presumably covered his travel expenses.

Aoki's company was unusual among Japanese immigrant businesses in two respects. First, to have started one's own business, no matter how small, would have required the kind of financial capital that eluded most Japanese immigrants. In the early twentieth century, most Japanese immigrants were laborers, few owned businesses, and even fewer participated in manufacturing of any kind.[20] Second, Jitsuji Aoki promoted ideas more often seen in the post–World War II period. He engaged in pan-Asian and assimilationist practices, making Chinese-style noodles and advertising to a mainstream American clientele at a time when virtually all Japanese immigrant businesses catered to Japanese American customers. Moreover, he publicized his trademark "Chop Suey" brand noodles, registered with the U.S. Patent Office, as providing the quick convenience of processed foods and appealing to modernity and nutrition: "Why waste your time rolling out noodles, when by asking for the Chop Suey brand . . . you can obtain the very highest quality, all ready for use, rich in flavor and nutriment [sic], easily prepared and adaptable to many combinations"; "cooks in five minutes"; and "The wise housewife keeps half a dozen packages of them on her pantry shelf."[21] American-style recipes using Jitsuji Aoki's "Chop Suey Noodles" brand were regular features of the *Oakland Tribune* food section. The business apparently did well, growing from noodles "made by hand" to establishing a fully equipped factory, adding salespeople and an automobile, and by 1930, manufacturing more than a ton of noodles daily and distributing them from coast to coast.[22]

The Aoki family's acquisition of wealth seems to have stemmed from their position in Japan as descendants of samurai. There is some contestation about this lineage. "Everyone knows the Aoki clan started out as dirt-poor sharecroppers," relayed Brenda Wong Aoki, Chojiro's granddaughter.[23] But as she conducted research for her play about a shocking event in her family's history, she discovered that Chojiro's father was reported to have been "a Japanese General and one of the noble Samurai families of Japan."[24] Another family member recounted that Jitsuji had consistently claimed that they were poor peasants in Japan. But this was told, family members speculate, to cover up the Aokis' illegal retention of land in Japan, in violation of the new Meiji government's mandate to reclaim samurai property in an effort to transform feudal Japan into a global capitalist power.[25] That the Aoki family has five or more swords, including two that Richard received when his father died, further points to a samurai past. In any case, that Jitsuji Aoki had access to financial capital alludes to some sort of privileged position in Japan.[26]

Third, that Jitsuji, his two brothers, his mother, and his wife and children all immigrated to the United States suggests that the family planned to put down roots in the United States, rather than coming with the more common sojourn mentality. Moreover, the actions of Jitsuji's youngest brother, Gunjiro Aoki, displayed an unusual relationship with White America. In what was a rarity among Japanese immigrants, Gunjiro married a White American woman. The union caused a scandalous stir and made front-page headline news in the *San Francisco Chronicle, Oakland Tribune,* and *New York Times.* His bride, Helen Gladys Emery, was no less than the daughter of the archdeacon of the Episcopal Church in San Francisco; she and Gunjiro met while Gunjiro worked as a servant in the Emery home. In marrying Helen, Gunjiro dared to cross both racial and class lines. In 1909, when they married, California and most other states had antimiscegenation laws in effect, reflecting widespread popular and legal condemnation of White–"minority" unions and support for White "racial purity."[27] In fact, to get married, Gunjiro and his bride had to travel eight hundred miles north to the state of Washington, the only western state in which White–minority marriages were legal.[28] Throughout their journey, with Helen accompanied by her mother and Gunjiro joining them at a later destination, they braved harassment and violence. En route to Helen's home in San Francisco, Gunjiro had previously been attacked by three men, to whom he "gave a beating" by using jujitsu.[29] Helen and her mother left for Seattle amid "the beating of tin cans and the throwing of rice, rocks, and flowers" and faced a belligerent crowd at the train depot.[30] In Portland, the district attorney announced that "should they appear on the streets of Portland arm in arm, as is wont of true lovers," they would be "arrested as common nuisances."[31] The mayor of Tacoma warned all clergy against marrying them and refused their stay in his city.[32] Finally, they were able to marry in Seattle on March 27, 1909, and became a rare Japanese–White married couple in California.[33]

It took tremendous courage to cross miscegenation lines in 1909. Gunjiro, age twenty-five, is reported to have rejected a thousand-dollar bribe to call off the wedding: "Not for two million dollars," he proclaimed.[34] He expressed a post–civil rights color blindness, stemming from his Christian upbringing: "To the Christian spirit all things are equal. If you understand about love, you know it is the same in all nationalities. What is the color of love?"[35] Helen, age twenty-one, expressed similar beliefs in a written statement published in the *Oakland Tribune:* "As Christians, we believe that nothing counts but the character of the individual."[36] In her quest, she appealed to the noblest ideals of America and chastised the public for falling short: "If America ever stood for freedom that freedom has been debased. If America ever stood for free thinking, that free thinking has disappeared."[37] Still, her ideas were constrained by the racial context of the times: "That the two races will ever mix, I do not believe possible, but individuals may find happiness in marriage."[38] Indeed, the races did not mix and there were high costs for everyone involved. Under the law, Helen lost her U.S. citizenship when she married an "alien ineligible for citizenship."[39] Helen filed for divorce and then reunited with Gunjiro, all in their first year of marriage.[40] Helen's parents split up.[41] Gunjiro's brother, the Reverend Peter Chojiro Aoki, was asked to resign by his own congregation and left Oakland for Salt Lake City, Utah.[42] In the end, Gunjiro and Helen raised five children together.[43]

Gunjiro and Helen Aoki made headline news a second time in 1923, when the Japanese Exclusion League of San Francisco and former senator James D. Phelan launched an investigation to reclaim White superiority. The Aoki children had been found to be at the "near genius" level on intelligence tests developed by noted Stanford University professors. The Japanese Exclusion

League's "investigation" undercut the significance of the intelligence test scores by dismissing the Aoki children as "isolated examples" and claiming that "they were not as high as many white children given the same test." Instead, they shaped a public discourse that turned the high scores of multiracial children into headlines that blared out: "White Children Are Superior to Those of Union with Japs" and "Japanese-American Marriages Unwise," as seen in numerous small-town newspapers across the nation.[44]

Richard Aoki would have enjoyed telling the story of how his uncle Gunjiro twice bucked White supremacy. So I was surprised to first encounter this story not from Richard, but in the pages of the *Oakland Tribune* and then in conversation with Chojiro's granddaughter, Brenda Wong Aoki, who originated, wrote, and performed the 1998 play, *Uncle Gunjiro's Girlfriend*.[45] Given the geographic distance between Oakland and Salt Lake City, and the even greater social distance between Jitsuji's and Chojiro's descendants, neither Richard nor Brenda knew they were related until Richard's death brought them together, so to speak.[46] If Richard had known about his uncle Gunjiro, once a social pariah and political resister now turned family hero, I wondered if it would have lessened his sense of isolation based partially on his perception of his extended family's scorn of his father's outlaw activities and his own radical activism. I sensed that throughout his life, Richard saw his own family as the outcasts from the otherwise well-to-do Aoki family. But as I researched more into his life, I discovered that good–bad binaries are constantly disrupted within his family. An ostensibly "good son" of Jitsuji Aoki, who became a successful entrepreneur, church leader, and model of U.S. citizenship, felt emotionally estranged from his father and self-identified as "the *itazura kozo*" ("incorrigible" or naughty brat) of the Sunday school.[47] If Richard had the opportunity to speak regularly with his family, as he began to do later in life, I suspect he might have developed a different, more nuanced vision of his own "deviant" family in relation to the "noble" Aokis, one as complicated as the marriage of Gunjiro and Helen.

2 "Protecting the Japanese"

Experiencing Incarceration

December 7, 1941. I don't recall anything about the immediate effects of Pearl Harbor, such as the radio broadcast or the panic and confusion. I learned later that on December seventh, a few thousand Japanese Americans were locked up, though they committed no crime. They all were loyal citizens—ministers, teachers, community leaders, and businesspeople. The irony of it is that those who championed the hardest for assimilation were often the first ones rounded up. Then on February 19, 1942, President Franklin Delano Roosevelt issued Executive Order 9066, ordering 110,000 West Coast Japanese Americans to be interned in concentration camps.[1] At the time of our evacuation in spring 1942, my parents, my younger brother, and I were living in Berkeley, renting a house a couple of blocks down from my maternal grandparents. My father was working as laundry help and my mother by that time, having two kids, was a stay-at-home mom. I was three years old.[2]

My earliest memory of this period was when we were walking from the bus into the Tanforan Racetrack. You could take only what you could carry, so my father was loaded down, my mother was loaded down, and I had my baby brother. David had just turned two. My first lesson about the responsibilities of being the oldest child was learned in Tanforan. My baby brother and I went running around the track and my brother fell. To the day he died, he had a scar on his forehead, between his eyes. Of course, because a facial vascular wound is much bloodier, it looked worse than it really was. So I'm dragging my brother home. He's got blood streaming down his face and I'm terrified. I thought he was going to die. After they cleaned him up, I got a lesson in responsibility from my father: "You are responsible for your younger brother. Even if he does wrong, you are the oldest. Therefore you are responsible." My protests fell on deaf ears: "He ran, he fell. What am I getting the lecture for?" That first lesson I learned in life: I was responsible for my baby brother. Come hell or high water. I've carried this lesson with me throughout my life.

After about six months of living in the horse stables at the Tanforan Race-track just south of San Francisco, all of us internees were moved to long-term housing. Most of us, including my extended family, were sent to the Topaz, Utah, concentration camp. My first memory of Topaz was of pulling into the camp. The topography was flat, just a vast wasteland. The conditions of the camp weren't that hot—I'm being punny here, because of the weather. In the desert, during the day it got really hot, but at night, it got cold. In the summertime, it was like 110 degrees and we didn't have air-conditioning, unless you called opening up all the doors and the windows of the barracks air-conditioning. In the wintertime, it got cold, like 30 degrees below. But being that young, I probably rolled with the punches. My parents were with me and they were probably reassuring me that everything's going to be okay.[3]

Topaz was a desolate place situated on the edge of the desert, 140 miles south of Salt Lake City. The nearest town is Delta. There was another town called Provo, which was the site of the state mental institution. My father thought it was funny that they put the concentration camp near the mental hospital.[4] I'm looking at a calendar featuring Mine Okubo's artwork produced for a Topaz reunion by activists. It reads: "The maximum population was 8,778 inmates, which made Topaz the fifth largest community in Utah. Five-eighths of the internees were American citizens. Each family was assigned to an empty room, complete with one ceiling."[5] This scene here in the calendar is what I remember the most about the camps—snow everywhere. Snowdrifts were taller than me. And we had no indoor plumbing and the communal bathrooms were situated a ways away. Chamber pots were the solution to that.

One of my few memories of Topaz was when I was at home alone. I was so cold that I put coals into the black potbelly stove until it turned cherry red. As I was standing there warming myself, the teenage next-door neighbor started banging on the door. He felt the heat and wanted to find out what was happening. When he opened the door, he got a blast of hot air. That thing was ready to explode. He looked at the stove, it was cherry red. I'll never forget that. I'm there happy because I'm warm. But he was quick. He opened all the windows and doors. Had he not come, I probably would have set the barracks on fire.[6]

One of my most vivid memories of camp occurred when I first got to Topaz. The camp was half constructed. In the middle of the night I heard a big commotion, so I peeked out of the window and saw these dudes fighting. Now when we were put in those camps, weapons were taken away—small arms, hunting rifles, swords. So people were reduced to fighting with construction materials. That's when I saw somebody get hit by a two-by-four and his head got split open. I said: "Oh, my goodness gracious. Daddy, Daddy, something's happening out there." It was the first act of violence that I ever saw in my life and it really affected me. Later on, my father told me that it was a difference of opinion between those who supported the U.S. government and those against it. He didn't say that they were Kibei versus Nisei, but he did at some point tell me about the Black Dragon Society and their pro-Japanese national-ist views. I thought that he might have been passing on a camp legend, just like urban legends. However, I was doing some research one time when I was at Berkeley, and I ran across some obscure article in a periodical that dealt with the Far East and it mentioned an article on the Black Dragon Society. And I said, damn, they actually did exist. I like to think that those who became anti-U.S. did so because of racism and discrimination in the United States and not because of a love for Japanese imperialism. Some people might argue that from the very first of my being, I was a violent person. But then how could I not be when immersed in that type of a situation? It's not the best thing for a young kid to see someone's head split open like I did. I was shocked. It was one of those things you see and you never forget. Then having my father say later, "This doesn't happen every day, kid. Just so happens that we're in this fucked-up situation."[7]

It's strange to admit this, but in retrospect, the most searing memories I have of the camp—outside of the physical deprivation and the extreme weather—usually involved conflict. I remember my first fistfight. I must have been about six years old at the time. There was a bully on the block. I tried to stay away from him. He was a couple of years older than I was. But one day, he picked on my brother. He was bigger than me and I probably didn't want to fight him. I probably wanted to run like hell. But when he made my brother cry, I knew the gauntlet had been thrown down. I had to fight him because I had learned in Tanforan that I was responsible for my younger brother. I remember rolling in the dirt with him fighting for my very life and I got lucky. I got a good blow into his nose. He bled. There was blood all over him and he went screaming home to mama. I was standing up proud and all the other kids were saying, "Ohh, you whipped the bully." Then my father came into the picture. I thought he'd jump all over me for fighting. But I told him what happened. My father was proud of me. I'll never forget that. The lesson from that: If you know you're right, you might win if you're willing to get hurt. My mother remembers that fight too because his mother was irate about the whole issue and my mother didn't like me fighting. Then my father stepped in and it became a moot issue because the bully's father was no match for my father. They didn't fight but it was enough that my father said, "Wait a minute. Let's get this thing straight. Your kid is a bully and picked on my kid. He deserved to get his nose punched." Tell him, Dad!

If we look at the violence within the group of internees, most of the violence probably occurred within the first six months to a year. I don't recall arguments as I was growing older and getting more attuned to things. It appeared as if a routine had settled in. Adults went to work. Kids went to school. Topaz had three preschool nurseries and two elementary schools. They had a high school and an adult education program.[8] My formal education was the thing that started to bring up contradictions between home and school. One day, it must have been in February, I'd been chosen to play George Washington in the school pageant, probably because of my precocious nature. They said, we'll make Richard, the chatterbox, play the father of our country. I got real excited and ran home and told my father. I thought my father would be proud to know that I had been given this big honor, to portray the father of our country. My father went off. I was surprised at how angry he got. Needless to say, I was in no physical shape to participate in the school pageant. I didn't end up playing George Washington. I didn't even go to school on the day of the pageant. I'll never forget that lesson: I should not think in terms of George Washington, this was not my country. In fact, "my country" put me in this camp.[9]

You asked if my father was ever abusive. He did have a violent streak. He would display his anger and back it up physically. If we ever got into fights, he expected us to fight back. But he was not physically abusive. In fact, he rarely even yelled at us—well, not at me, but maybe at my mother. Now, he didn't have to yell at us to get us to listen to him. You have to understand the strength of my father's personality. Plus, he really thought I was a bright kid; all I needed was to be informed about the rules and I'd pick it up from there. My mother is a bit jealous in a way. She says my father adored me when I was young. That was the time when I was materially comfortable and had adoring relatives. I don't remember any of this, except I have one memory of my maternal grandfather taking me to the canteen in the camps. I'd come back with some candy and be all smiles. My mother always said that both of my grandfathers just spoiled me. You may wonder why my grandfathers more than my grandmothers were the ones who doted on me. But my maternal grandmother wasn't that emotional and both grandmothers didn't speak much English.[10]

Now, guess what the first job my father had when he got to the camp? He joined the camp police security force. All the adults in camp had to work. They had the inmates doing the work of running the camp and regardless of the job, they got paid a measly sixteen dollars a month or so. I had thought that was calculated on the pay of a private in the U.S. Army at the time. That's been burning me for years, so I finally looked up military pay rates and was stunned to find that the inmates made even less than an army private.[11] The sixteen dollars a month comes down to ten cents an hour—kind of like slave labor if you ask me. So the question is: Why did they pick sixteen dollars a month? Nobody has been able to answer that question. So my father's first job was working with the camp security force to establish law and order in the camp. The establishment of law and order is, of course, basic to any community of people. You have to have some authority to handle things like theft, fights, domestic disputes. But he gave up that job after that person's head got split open with the two-by-four. He told me that he was tired of getting in between the warring factions; it was too dangerous. So then my father picked up teaching history in junior high school.[12] That I knew was a natural because he had been to UC Berkeley. But my father ended up resigning and he told me the reason why. When he got to the section on American democracy, he looked at the kids while speaking about freedom, justice, and equality. All the kids had to do was look out the window and see the barbed wire fences, the watchtowers with searchlights, the half-track with fifty-caliber machine guns. It didn't compute. The kids weren't getting the message, and righteously so. It was too tough on him to play that game, so he quit that job.[13]

I do know one of the main arguments for putting the Japanese into the camps was to protect the Japanese. But if you look at the top of barbed wire fences, they're designed to keep the people in. The watchtowers had searchlights that focused into the camps. We weren't free to leave the camps without permission, and one Topaz internee was even shot and killed by a military sentry, supposedly for trying to escape.[14] In other words, it's a damn lie that we were put in the camps to protect us. In fact, the best way that they could have protected us, in my opinion, was to give each and every one of us a gun. You're wondering why I insert this at this moment, but if we go forward to Robert F. Williams, Malcolm X, and the Black Panther Party, that type of logic makes sense to me. I realize that many don't share this view, but at least I'm going to stand up and say this is what I believe.

I remember my father telling me that he was opposed to the war and that he would not serve in the military. He thought, I'm in this camp, my wife's in this camp, my two kids are in this camp, my parents, my whole community is in this camp and you want me to put on that uniform and go fight? You must be out of your mind. So when the U.S. government got a little desperate for manpower and came into the camps to recruit, my father was among those who refused to go. But others in the family joined the military. My mother's sister Yoshiko, her husband joined the army and was very proud. My mother's other sister Decky, her husband was a doctor and became an officer in the army.[15]

The different views toward the military that existed in my family were a microcosm of the larger Japanese American community. The wartime Japanese American Citizens League was hated for encouraging the Japanese American community to cooperate with the government in their own incarceration. The JACL was formed as a civic organization utilizing traditional methods such as the judicial and legislative processes to help the Japanese assimilate. The organization was dominated by young Nisei professionals who were trying to make it into American society. Frantz Fanon, in his book *Black Skin, White Mask,* labels this phenomenon of identifying with the oppressor as being psychologically abnormal. The official line of the JACL during this period was to accept the relocation under the guise of being loyal Americans. True to their own position, they actively encouraged the U.S. government to accept Japanese Americans into the military.[16]

The American Communist Party also failed Japanese America. I'm hot about this one. In 1939, the Soviet Union signed a Non-Aggression Pact with Nazi Germany. But it didn't stop Germany from invading the Soviet Union.[17] This forced the Communist Party of the Soviet Union to change its line, which in turn, changed the line of the American Communist Party to support Allied war policies. So when President Roosevelt signed Executive Order 9066 to lock up Japanese Americans, the American Communist Party not only went along with it, they even suspended their Japanese American members! The Communist Party, as radicals, should have opposed the evacuation of the Japanese Americans. But they didn't.[18]

Now there were some organizations and individuals who opposed the evacuation of the Japanese. First, the Northern California chapter of the ACLU broke with the national ACLU, not organizationally but politically, and opposed the treatment of the Japanese here. The second organization that opposed the evacuation was the American Friends Service Committee, the Quakers. I even voted for Richard Nixon for president in 1960 because of his Quaker connections. There was also an individual here in Berkeley, named Lyckberg, who not only opposed the internment but actually aided the evacuees from Berkeley. From inside Topaz, my uncle Hideo was in communication with Lyckberg. He told me that Lyckberg , who was a pharmacist, used to send medical supplies to the camp. During a wartime situation, civilian consumption went down and military consumption went up. Therefore, if you were in a prison camp, you got virtually nothing at the end of the pharmaceutical food chain. My father was hospitalized in Topaz with appendicitis, so it may have been the antibiotics from Lyckberg that saved his life. When we were up against the wall or inside the wall, you remember those humanitarian acts. I didn't find this out until the 1960s, but when I did I went to his pharmacy and personally thanked Lyckberg and his son. I could see the dialectics in humanity—man is evil, man is good. Unfortunately, those acts of kindness and resistance were few and far between. The general tenor was that of prejudice and hostility against people of Japanese ancestry.[19]

The barracks that we lived in, the ones designed for families, was one long building cut into six consecutive compartments. Each unit was about twenty feet by twenty feet. They were connected in pairs at the entrance, with the two front doorways opened into a little alcove. These barracks were army-style barracks. My parents put up a rope with a cloth to create a partition for some privacy. My brother and I slept on one side of the partition and my parents on the other. All throughout camp, my mother worked as a waitress in the mess halls. She got paid about sixteen dollars a month for that. I recall the food being mediocre and I developed an aversion to canned foods, notably custard. For years after camp, I couldn't eat custard. I couldn't even look at custard. What I remember was chaos in that everybody was struggling to get their fair share of the rations.

What did we do for play? There weren't any parks. I don't remember any playgrounds. There was a sporting field. I remember baseball games being played on the sporting field. There was a big theater, like an amphitheater, in the center of the camp where they would show movies. There's also a picture of me on a horse inside camp. One of my father's friends, Mac Komatsu, somehow got a horse into the camp.[20] I kept thinking over the years, where in hell would Mac get a horse? I just remembered. A rodeo came through the camp one year. These were White rodeo performers going to the camps to entertain "the enemy." So Komatsu probably conned one of the rodeo people. I ate my first baloney sandwich because of the rodeo. There was a table with their lunches for the rodeo troupe and they had these sandwiches in waxed paper.

The mess hall food wasn't very appealing and I managed to get myself one of those sandwiches. Oh boy, that was good. That's probably when Mac scored on the use of a horse. They got me up on the horse and I have a picture of that. That was exciting because there wasn't much for kids to do in the camp. I remember spending a lot of time with my brother just wandering around.

Cameras were forbidden in camps, considered contraband.[21] But later on, there was the liberalization of many policies. An enterprising photographer in Topaz got hold of a camera and went around taking family portraits.[22] There's the one of my brother and myself that everyone seems to love so much. I like to show it to demonstrate that a kid's got a stupid grin on his face, but if you look in the background, you see the barracks. My brother and I were different as night and day. I was the extroverted one; he was more introverted. I was the more aggressive one; he was more passive. I was more intellectually oriented and he was more physically oriented, the better athlete. My father once commented it's a good thing we have opposite personalities and more importantly, opposite tastes in women because that way, we didn't get into fights over girls since we were so close in age. My brother does not remember anything that happened in camp. For years, every now and then, I'd pump him to see if I'd be able to catch him. I'm convinced that he might have been more traumatized than I was because at least I had a happy childhood. If you look at research, the better the foundation in childhood, the fewer problems there are later in life. But my brother, who was only two years old when we went into the camps, didn't have that unconscious happiness to form a solid foundation.

Clash of Empire

I'd like to go back about a half century prior to Pearl Harbor, primarily because there's this myth about Pearl Harbor being a sneak attack. To understand Pearl Harbor, we have to examine how Japan became an imperialist power. When the Meiji government came to rule in 1868, Japan started to rapidly modernize and industrialize, turning a feudal society into a capitalist power. They wanted to develop into an empire, so they expanded their territories, they expanded their markets, and they expanded their global influence, and what quicker way than militarily?

Now people who've studied Lenin's *Imperialism* may question whether Japanese capital was advanced enough to move to the imperialist stage of capitalism. Japan was able to industrialize in two-thirds, maybe half, the time it took most European countries and the United States. Look at how the *zaibatsu* got together to plot out their futures. The *zaibatsu* refers to a conglomeration of the large corporations, the monopolies—the salt monopolies, the steel monopolies. The two biggest *zaibatsu* were Mitsubishi and Mitsui. Now, according to Lenin, the *zaibatsu* needed four things. First, they needed raw resources. Japan doesn't have oil; Japan doesn't have many raw resources. Even their steel industry, in the initial industrial period, was limited because of their lack of raw resources. By the turn of the century, it was quite apparent that for Japan to advance industrially, they had to have resources. Rubber, for example, was a big commodity. Japan—the whole world actually—needed that because before the introduction of synthetic rubber, it was an important industrial commodity used to produce automobiles, clothing, raincoats, and so forth. The second item for the imperialist development is markets. For capitalism to expand, it has to have foreign markets where they can export the goods that they produce. That's why many of the countries all over the world had tariff regulations to protect domestic markets, but they could be opened up militarily. The third area is finance capital. The banking system developed quite rapidly in Japan. The *zaibatsu* all fed into one another, which made their advancement much more rapid than occurred in Europe and the U.S. The fourth area is labor. The capitalist class relies on cheap labor to increase their profits, which explains why Japanese immigrants were recruited to work the sugar cane plantations in Hawaii and do menial labor on the West Coast.[23]

At the turn of the twentieth century, two major centers of imperialism were starting to expand: the United States and Japan. By the late 1800s, westward expansion across the continental U.S. was over. The United States had exhausted North America territorially and began to look outward. In the late 1800s, the U.S. captured Hawaii and then won the Spanish–American War and took over Spain's colonies—Cuba, Puerto Rico, and what's more, the Philippines and Guam. As they looked to the Far East, they see a new kid on the block and he's taking care of business—defeating China in 1894, Russia in 1904, and Korea in 1910. Looking at it from a Marxist perspective, conflict was inevitable between the empire of the United States and the empire of Japan, even though they were allies during World War I. Meanwhile, the U.S. couldn't go any farther west and Japan was securing a foothold in Asia. We're up to the 1930s and Japan invades China and does some of the most horrendous stuff I have ever run across. I heard about the Rape of Nanking from my father when he was home-schooling us. My father was appalled. The Rape of Nanking illustrates how brutal that imperialist expansion was.[24]

I've harbored these insights into the clash of empires and shared them with some, but mostly I've been reluctant to because the idea of U.S. imperialism is repugnant to most Americans. But the U.S. has a long history of imperialist expansion and intervention.[25] By the early 1940s, even before Japan bombed Pearl Harbor, the U.S. froze Japanese financial assets in the U.S., refused to ship metals to Japan, and started an oil embargo—all escalating the conflict. You don't do anything like that unless you're getting ready. That's like playing the dozens, like disrespecting mama: you know that fists are going to start flying. So this brings us up to December 7, 1941—"the day that shall live in infamy," as uttered by Franklin Delano Roosevelt, who in my childhood household, was the devil incarnate. Years later when I ran with the progressives, the liberals, the radicals on the Left, Roosevelt seemed to be revered as a god. In the African American community, they loved Roosevelt. Now, in my opinion, if it hadn't been for Roosevelt, we might have had a revolution here in this country. The labor movement was strong. People were upset because of the depression of the 1930s. Had the Communist Party been on their Jay, we might have had a revolution instead of the New Deal reforms, which saved capitalism as it went through one of its major and periodic crises. I want to be objective and materialist about this notion of a sneak attack on Pearl Harbor. Sure, Admiral Kimmel, head of command of the U.S. Pacific Fleet at Pearl Harbor, probably didn't know that the attack was coming, but they sure as hell knew in Washington.[26] The irony is that Kimmel was demoted and scapegoated for Pearl Harbor, but his supporters are digging up evidence proving that Washington knew the attack was coming and Wall Street helped set everything up by the embargo and freezing of Japanese assets.[27] Then to add insult to injury, Roosevelt put Japanese Americans in the concentration camps.

Internment Camps and Family Stress

Sometime around the last year in camp, I don't remember too much except my mother ceased living with us. She either moved into the barracks for single women or she might have moved in with one of her relatives. I didn't question anything at that time. I don't remember my parents having any fights or discussions before they split up. All I knew was my responsibility had multiplied. I think the reason why I got in the fight with that bully was the realization that I had to take care of my brother because nobody else was around. My brother and I never discussed that issue. I didn't share my innermost thoughts with him even though he and I were close. It was more that, since we were that close in age, our experiences were concomitant. I assume he was drinking in the same data that I was and came to his own conclusions. He never asked me questions. Plus I didn't have any answers for him and he probably knew that too. Richard doesn't seem to know what's going on, but okay, I'll go with the program.

I'm beginning to get a little pissed regarding my early childhood, meaning that period from 1938 to 1942 when my family was intact, my community was intact, and I was growing up a happy little child, with the nickname of Chatterbox and doting grandparents. Then about a week after we left the camps, my mother's father died of a heart attack. He's the one who took me to the canteen and bought me little treats. I guess it all came down on him and he died.[28]

THE UNGRIEVED TRAUMA OF INTERNMENT

The Hurts of History

"My country abandoned me" and "I want to know why I was thrown away," relayed one man, who had entered camp at age two. The stirring documentary *Children of the Camps* explores the anguish expressed by this man and other former child internees. Countering conventional notions that there was little adverse impact on the children, psychologist Satsuka Ina views incarceration as a psychological trauma and scholar Donna Nagata studies how the injury of incarceration had lasting effects, even into the next generation.[29] It was these multiple traumas and abandonments, mostly ungrieved, that bubbled up in the pent-up rage Richard Aoki felt, to his dying day, about the forced removal and detention of "my people" during World War II.

Aoki frequently expressed outrage about the politics of incarceration—the racism, the bypassing of constitutional protections, and the monumental economic losses.[30] The trauma was also very personal—injuries that struck at the very core of his personhood. There were financial losses resulting from the forced relinquishing of his paternal grandfather's successful noodle factory.[31] There was the deprivation of good health for several family members. His maternal grandmother developed tuberculosis and remained in a sanatorium throughout the war. His maternal grandfather died of "coronary arteriosclerosis" one week after returning to Berkeley in July 1945. An aunt on his father's side "became very ill"—from "dehydration, worry, fatigue, and cold," the doctors said—shortly after her arrival at Topaz.[32] An Aoki cousin, a high school senior at the time, suffered third-degree burns on his calf, inflicted while working in Topaz. He endured infection, a skin graft, and ten months confined to his bed. His mother said, "I blamed everything on this accursed evacuation then, thinking if only it had not taken place, my son would not have received his burns."[33] It is unclear what Richard, then aged four, knew about his family's health problems. But he was aware of a pervasive sense of danger and a lack of physical safety inside the camp, as relayed in his narrative filled with fights, violence, and fear.

Significant as the material deprivation was, other kinds of abandonments inflicted deeper psychological and political injuries on Richard. At a tender age, his faith in his parents' ability to protect him was shaken. He would have become aware of the unfairness in the world, of being different, and of being a member of a targeted people. Like the man in *Children of the Camps*, Richard lost faith in America and in the U.S. government's professed commitments to justice and equality. In short, he was deprived of even the illusion of the innocence of childhood.

Compounding these more existential injuries, Aoki suffered tremendous personal and social trauma. The most painful was the loss of his nuclear family. His parents separated inside Topaz. On the one hand, marital discord in the stressful environment of the concentration camps was virtually inescapable. The crowded living conditions, the rudimentary facilities, and the omnipresent sense of injustice and powerlessness compounded the stress, and the lack of privacy made it difficult to resolve problems.[34] There was almost no place to go to get away to think and to discuss intimate issues. In some ways, it is surprising there were so few marital separations. Then too, the strong taboo against divorce in the Japanese American community and the fishbowl atmosphere of the camps would have created additional incentives to stay together.[35] One report on the atmosphere in Topaz noted that "center life is boring," with "nothing doing" and "plenty of gossip."[36] Richard's parents would have given the camp grapevine plenty of fuel, not only because they split up but also because Richard's mother moved out, while the young children stayed with their father.[37] Their marital problems must have been quite severe to endure the gossip and stigma attached to their situation. Richard's father, it seems, became a social pariah not only within the Japanese American community but within his own family, stemming from this moment and worsening in the postwar years.

Akemi Kikumura expressed a feeling common to the children of Japanese immigrants: "I cried for self-pity—pity that we were deprived all our lives of the warmth and protection of a grandfather and grandmother, of uncles and aunts."[38] Though Richard grew up in close proximity to many relatives, he too experienced the emotional deprivation that Kikumura describes. In the prewar period, the Aoki family lived near one another in Oakland and saw each other often. Along with virtually every Japanese American in the San Francisco Bay Area, they all moved to the Topaz concentration camp. But for some inexplicable reason, Richard did not see his aunts, uncles, and cousins inside Topaz.[39] Admittedly, Topaz was a city unto itself—the fifth-largest city in Utah, housing some 8,200 people. Its one-square-mile area was large, but hardly accounted for the impermeable geographic barrier the Aokis experienced. At the very least, on important holidays like New Year's, internees would have traveled a little distance to get together.[40] Something else changed for Richard's family.

Perhaps it was the shame that his father Shozo Aoki's brazen behaviors brought on the family. Or perhaps it was Shozo's growing disillusionment. Before the war, Shozo had been on the path to fulfilling the Aoki family's expectations for respectability through service and accomplishment. Their commitments were fueled by the belief in achievement through assimilation and their view of the United States as a model of modernity and success.[41] As early as 1915, Shozo's older brother Riuzo joined a Boy Scout troop and YMCA group in Oakland. K. Hata founded these organizations for children to learn Japanese language and culture, but more so, to learn "American ways and customs" in order to "become useful citizens in modern ways."[42] His project apparently had the approval of the Japanese consul, in a period when Japan as a nation was modernizing and building itself into a military and political world power. Although these began as all-Japanese organizations, Hata's goal was to have Japanese American children become "purely American" by interacting with (White) American children and hoped that "American institutions [would] cooperate with us in promoting and helping Japanese American boys and girls to assimilate American customs."[43] As an adult, Riuzo led the Japanese American Boy Scout troop in Oakland and taught lifesaving classes with the American Red Cross at the Oakland YWCA pool.[44] In addition, Richard's grandfather—and later his uncle Shigeo—was a pillar of the Japanese Methodist Episcopal church in Oakland.[45] In 1954, after Japanese immigrants were granted the right to naturalization, Richard's uncle Shigeo gave the keynote address at Citizenship Day in Oakland promoting assimilation in an America that "stands for freedom, democracy, and love of fellow man."[46] Richard's father too had generally embraced the family's desires for assimilation through achievement and service. He participated in the Boy Scouts, junior high school basketball, and high school ROTC, and was one of two Aoki siblings to attend the prestigious University of California, Berkeley.[47]

Richard's narrative places culpability on the concentration camp experience for his father's turn from being a patriotic ROTC enthusiast to a disenchanted, demoralized, and angry internee. The incarceration, it is reasonable to assume, played a critical role in changing his father's sense of fairness and justice and thus his assimilationist strivings.[48] This had far-reaching effects on Richard's family life and on his father's postwar activities. But there were also signs of discontent before the war. There were, of course, the out-of-wedlock pregnancy and rushed marriage. But Shozo did not leave UC Berkeley solely because of the responsibilities of fatherhood, as Richard understood. Shozo's grades were, in fact, rather poor from the time he entered the university in August 1934 until he was "dismissed" in May 1938, after having been placed on "probation for unsatisfactory scholarship."[49]

When single parenthood became his life, Shozo's family worried about his ability and motivation to care for his young boys. Shozo's father apparently wanted one of his married daughters to take care of Richard and David. Shozo's sister Minoru wrote to her brother Shigeo: "Before I left camp, Papa asked me to ask [our sister] Haruko and [her husband] Chikayuki to take over the children of Sho, or one of them, so that Sho may be left free to work. I told him I thought that that was an awful poor idea, but since I was only to ask it of them and they were to answer *ojisan* themselves, I consented to do so. I did. I don't think they will."[50] Shigeo wrote back, explaining his offer of financial assistance to motivate Shozo to work: "After Shozo came to Oakland with his 2 kids, I saw that he should work, instead of living off Papa and Mama. So I got him an opportunity to do business for himself, run his own vegetable and fish stand in the thriving grocery store of a friend of mine in San Francisco's Japanese town. I went as far as to offer to back him up to $500 to get him started. (As you know, vegetable and fish markets don't need all that dough, but I offered it just the same). He turned it down, saying politely that he 'didn't feel like working right now.'"[51] We see in this exchange of letters between sister and brother the promotion of hard work and self-sufficiency in the Aoki family's strivings for success. We also see a reproduction of conventional gendered ideas linking masculinity to the role of economic provider and femininity to domesticity and nurturance. It worried and exasperated the Aokis to see Shozo's disregard for their norms of responsibility. Shigeo vented: "I hated to see [Shozo] loaf every day."[52]

Whether it was Shozo's behaviors, the effects of incarceration, or other family dynamics, a distance emerged between Shozo and his siblings. This left Richard and David with some extended family support, but also a lack of the "warmth and protection" of cousins, aunts, and uncles. There is a longing in Richard's narrative for the imagined closeness, support, and sense of belonging created through extended family relations. Would he have developed more trust in close relationships had he been surrounded by a stable and intimate family life? Would he have developed more productive coping skills? These questions raise speculative responses, but it is hardly a stretch to claim that the trauma of incarceration significantly shaped his life.

The Effects of History: "Absent Cause" and Ungrieved Trauma

Fredric Jameson discusses history as an "absent cause": we come to know history not as a thing itself but rather "through its effects."[53] The story can never fully capture the lived experience, however. As trauma studies reveal, the suffering of the Holocaust was so monstrous that it cannot be represented. At the same time, the attempt to do so must be made, for it is through the effort to articulate and symbolize the trauma that meaning is constructed.[54] The son came to see the concentration camps through the narration of the father. To this child, Camp Topaz was seen as an alienating, oppressive, and racist place that erupted in violence and danger. Now a grown man, Richard's framing of incarceration, as he relayed to me in 2003, was also filtered through the lens of the Asian American Movement and the redress movement. Significantly, the redress victory symbolized by the passage of the 1988 Civil Liberties Act, which granted reparations to internees and acknowledged the racism underlying the incarceration of Japanese Americans, changed the national narrative of the camps. By transferring the blame and shame of incarceration from the internees to the U.S. government, the redress movement brought a partial healing to Richard and the larger Japanese American community.

Despite the 1988 act, the Japanese American incarceration remains an "absent presence" in American history. Marita Sturken uses this term to refer to the ways "a historic event [is] marked by silences and strategic forgetting," whose presence is spoken about "through its absent representation."[55] The fiftieth-anniversary events commemorating the end of World War II sparked a wave of remembrance for the nation, but outside of Japanese American communities and Asian American Studies, the representation of Japanese American internment was missing from the national consciousness. Sturken contends that the incarceration created an image "both too disruptive and too domestic to conform to the war's narratives."[56] The deeply moving photographs of Japanese American evacuation by Dorothea Lange depict not the image of hyperaggressive and hypermasculine kamikaze pilots but ordinary women, men, and children enduring great suffering with dignity and anguish.[57] Ansel Adams's photographs taken inside the Manzanar concentration camp show all-American scenes of card playing, churchgoing, people working, men and women in U.S. military uniforms, and many smiling faces. A caption below one cheerful face reads, "Americanism is a matter of the mind and heart," echoing President Roosevelt's famous statement.[58] To that phrase, Roosevelt had added, "Americanism is not, and never was, a matter of race or ancestry."[59] This statement, made in early 1943 at a time when Japanese Americans were already behind barbed wire and being called to serve in the U.S. army, assumed a healthy tolerance for duplicity and a hunger for inclusion in the "great nation." Lange's and Adams's photographs, though signaling different meanings of incarceration, were indeed "too domestic" in making Japanese Americans look like other ordinary Americans and "too disruptive" in showing contradictions just under the surface of American democracy.[60] For Richard, in addition to the history of incarceration, his own mother and, later, his father were, at different times, "absent presences" in his life.

It is not only the physical separations but also the unarticulated absences that shape our histories. Certainly, the representation of history never fully captures the lived experience: "Life is lived, history is recounted."[61] There is always something that escapes representation, and as Sean Homer states, "this excess or leftover . . . [is] the 'non-historical kernel of history,' of the real."[62] Homer later writes, "History is the leftover, the hard impenetrable kernel resisting symbolization, but at the same time only knowable through its effects on the symbolic."[63] For Richard there is more to his incarceration experiences than has been articulated through Japanese American history or the redress movement. It is the trauma contained in the "non-historical kernel of history" that haunted him throughout his life, the injuries that no one could fully articulate or mourn that tore at him. It is this history as an "absent cause" that Jameson refers to when he writes, "History is what hurts, it is what refuses desire and sets inexorable limits to individual as well as collective praxis, which its 'ruses' turn into grisly and ironic reversals of their overt intention. But this History can be apprehended only through its effects."[64] It is this effort to articulate the unarticulated and unconscious injuries of incarceration that motivated psychologist Satsuka Ina to hold workshops for former child internees precisely to uncover the deep kernels resisting representation and to allow for the mourning of these painful losses and abandonments. In Richard's view, these multiple hurts of history—incarceration, parental and national abandonment, racial subjugation—originated at the moment of his incarceration.

How can we understand history through its effects on Richard Aoki? On one hand, Richard was never able to adequately grieve the major traumas in his life. Accumulating, too, were the little hurts barely visible by themselves but collectively creating a rushing torrent.[65] Richard recalled Japanese American parents telling their daughters to stay away from the sons of Shozo Aoki. He recalled being mortified that his own uncle fought his father in front of the family home, showcasing for the whole neighborhood their family's problems and his father's shameful actions. There were also the many relationships that ended. Partially as a result of remaining unmourned, his personal–political wounds bubbled up, at times, in unpredictable and excessive ways. Like the protagonist in Chester Himes's novel *If He Hollers Let Him Go,* Richard, and his father before him, responded to the daily and historical stressors of racial, economic, and gendered oppression in ways both magnanimous and injurious. Still, as George Lipsitz has observed, Himes's protagonist needed every gracious and ungracious thing he had ever done; that's how he recognized himself. This partial self-destructiveness is the cost of oppression.[66]

On the other hand, Richard achieved a place in history precisely because he channeled his anger at incarceration and other injustices into the collective struggles for freedom, justice, and equality—the topics of subsequent chapters. Jameson reminds us that history "will not forget us, however much we might prefer to ignore [it],"[67] but Richard Aoki's life is a testament to those very efforts to create dignity, equality, and a life worth living as he wrestled with his own deep hurts of history.

3 "Learning to Do the West Oakland Dip"

Returning Home

My tour of duty in the concentration camps ended in late 1945. I vividly recall the trip back to the Bay Area because my father somehow managed to score a deal. My father and his friend were to drive two military vehicles—an ambulance and a covered pickup truck—from Topaz to the Bay Area. This other family and their two children were in one vehicle and my father, my brother, and myself were in the other vehicle. We were going to Oakland to move in with my grandparents and my uncle Riuzo in the Aoki family house that still existed. The other family temporarily stayed at Hunters Point housing projects in San Francisco.[1]

One of the reasons why I remember the trip is that there was a stark contrast in the landscape. From the harshness of the Topaz climate, we traveled over some of the most scenic parts of America—talk about breathtaking views. Along the way home, we slept in the two trucks. The other thing is we stopped at gas stations to get food to eat. I remember having my first soda pop—the Nehi brand. I also drank a lot of Bireley's soda, which was unusual because it had a wide opening at the top, instead of the narrow opening like Coca-Cola, 7Up, or Nehi. I remember going to this gas station and they had one of these old-time vending machines where there were rows of these pop bottles and you moved the bottle up to the point where you wanted it, put your coin in, and it had the freezer where you opened it up at the top. I remember my father would show me. I'd ask, "Where's the magic here, Daddy?" The magic trick was to put your nickel in and you got your pop. Oh boy, this is good, it's sweet and bubbly. So this was an adventure for me. I not only had my brother as a companion, but also these two other kids. We had great fun. Maybe because it was a happy time, this trip home is the first thing my brother remembers about the camps.

Postwar West Oakland

In order to understand how I formed my identity and my personal development, one has to understand the economic, political, and social environments
that fundamentally shaped the foundations of my adulthood. West Oakland
had a tremendous impact on my life. I'd like to give a brief overview of Oakland and West Oakland from a historical perspective. First of all, the city of
Oakland is a hard city. It was the western terminus of the transcontinental railroad, which didn't end in San Francisco; it ended in Oakland because they had
no bridges to cross the bay. As a result, Oakland developed into an industrial
town. At its height, Oakland had fifteen hundred factories and was considered
the third-largest industrial city in California. The population of Oakland remained rather stable until the 1906 earthquake. After that, many residential
areas in Oakland were built for and inhabited by commuters from San Francisco. That explains the large numbers of Victorian mansions in West Oakland.
With the 1906 earthquake, the population of Oakland jumped dramatically.
Those settling in West Oakland were primarily immigrants, many Italian and
Scandinavian. East Oakland was settled by Portuguese. So Oakland became a
magnet for immigrants who saw opportunities working on the railroads. A stable African American community began to develop centered primarily around
the economic activity of the railroad. Mr. C. L. Dellums, one of the leaders of
the Brotherhood of Sleeping Car Porters, raised his family in West Oakland. His
nephew Ron Dellums and I ran across one another in the streets in our youth.
The Dellums family was well known in West Oakland. They represented stability; they represented hard work; and through C. L. Dellums, they represented
a striving for freedom. The Brotherhood of Sleeping Car Porters was the first
national African American union to be formed, led by A. Philip Randolph and
C. L. Dellums. People may forget that at one time the railroad companies were
one of the most dominant economic industries in this country. It was a powerful capitalist business group, and for the African American workers to form
the union, get recognized, and improve their wages and working conditions
was significant.[2]

Oakland in general, up to World War II, was not too receptive to the idea of
widespread African American immigration. In fact, in the 1920s, there was an
active KKK movement in Oakland. It wasn't restricted to the semieducated
Euro-American workers. Businessmen, professionals, even law enforcement
were members of the KKK. In 1924–25, they tried to march down through
the center of Oakland. However, that was probably considered too bold a
move and they marched down through Richmond instead. But in 1926 or

1928, a KKK member ran for sheriff of Alameda County and won. He would later be accused and, I believe, convicted of corruption. But the very idea that the KKK was in Oakland is mind boggling to a lot of people today. We also have to remember that the 1920s were the height of the KKK movement in this country. Millions belonged to the KKK. Millions. It wasn't just a Southern thing.[3]

Oakland is generally divided by race and class along geographic boundaries. The flatlands area, close to the bay, is mostly ethnic, and the properties in the hills are owned mostly by Euro-Americans. This is not by chance because in those days, there were racially restricted housing covenants that governed Oakland and Berkeley. Those residents in the Oakland hills and foothills had signed agreements to not sell to people of African, Mongolian, and any other non-White ancestry. In Berkeley, residential segregation was buttressed by a citywide ordinance whereby people of color couldn't purchase property north of University Avenue.[4]

There was a dramatic demographic transformation in the early 1940s. Prior to the war, there were a number of Japanese Americans in West Oakland. When we were evacuated, West Oakland was predominantly Euro-American, Asian American, and African American—in that order. When we returned, the racial order had reversed. In 1941, the majority in West Oakland were recent immigrants from Italy and Scandinavia. By the time I graduated from junior high school in 1954, maybe less then 10 percent of families living in West Oakland were Euro-American and mostly elderly. They were the immigrants who had purchased property around the turn of century and raised families in those houses. As their children moved out to the suburbs, they stayed in West Oakland. Concomitantly, there was a huge influx of African Americans, mostly from the South, who came because jobs opened up in the wartime defense industry. So when the Japanese were evacuated, African Americans moved into those areas. In addition to that, the government created housing projects such as Cypress and Campbell villages. Robert Weaver, the first African American to hold a cabinet position and the first secretary of housing and urban development, was working on housing during the war. I read his book *The Negro Ghetto* and I came across a reference to Campbell Village. Campbell Village was constructed during World War II to meet the housing needs of defense workers. It was considered by the government as the best "integrated" housing development project in the whole country. That was during the war. When my family came back to California, those villages, especially Campbell, had tipped over in racial composition to where the vast majority of residents were African American.[5]

So when my family returned to Oakland, West Oakland had become a thriving, self-contained Black community. Now you have to remember that in 1945, residential housing discrimination was still the law of the land.[6] The forced segregation put the African American community in West Oakland where it was like a separate society in itself, with all classes contained in the community. Neighborhoods began to develop with nicknames like the Lower Bottom, which was the older section of West Oakland with the most deteriorating housing, some of the worst schools, and was the site of the major housing projects constructed during World War II, mainly Campbell Village and Cypress Village. The reputation of the Lower Bottom was that it was a tough neighborhood, and kids from the projects generally had a bad reputation. Another neighborhood, the one I lived in, was called Dog Town because of the large number of junkyards that existed there. A third neighborhood further up the economic scale is now known as Ghost Town because so many people have been killed in that neighborhood. As things really deteriorated in West Oakland in general in the 1960s, the neighborhood suddenly became a killing zone for that community probably because there are more residential units there and higher population density. In the Lower Bottom and Dog Town neighborhoods, there were a lot of factories, junkyards, other light-industrial-related commercial enterprises. The Newton family and the Hilliard family both lived in the Ghost Town neighborhood when I was growing up.[7]

Here I was, about seven years old, in a new neighborhood where the complexion had changed quite a bit. I was amazed at all the African American people everywhere, but that's the neighborhood. Now the first year I recall was a difficult year for me. Being the new kid on the block and partially as a result of the prejudices engendered by the war, I won't say I encountered racism, but the neighborhood kids didn't seem to like me. I took it a little personally at first. Every time I went out, it seemed like I was getting into trouble. Some of them used the word "Jap," but they weren't using it with hatred. They were using it as more of a goading thing. It's hard to explain but there are ways of saying the N-word—good and bad and maybe neutral. These kids were just picking up what they had heard. But the word "Jap" was an automatic fighting word. I complained to my father about how rough life was out there. My father, in an effort to encourage me to face up to reality, made it clear that it was better I went out there and faced what I had to face than to stay home. He didn't want to think of his son being a wuss. They didn't use that term in those days, but I got the message: If I stayed at home, I'd get my butt whipped. But if I went out there, I might win the fight. Contrary to popular opinion, I did not inherit that magical

Asian gene that deals with mathematics, but I did realize at that early age that I had a better chance going outside. So I went out there, battling in the streets.[8]

Meanwhile, my father was starting to become an accomplished barroom brawler and promoter of boxing matches. Boxing was one of the big sports in Oakland at the time, and he was using the entrepreneurial segment of his occupational skills to get involved with that. Also my uncle Riuzo had a black belt in jujitsu and very patiently taught me and my brother the fundamentals. In jujitsu, it's not the size of your opponent that's important; you're almost expecting to take on someone bigger than you. So a combination of my experience fighting that bully in the camps, along with tips from my father and uncle, I got to be real good fighting on the streets. It has been said—and I'm not one to say it—that I was the toughest Oriental to come out of West Oakland, pound for pound. I quickly learned how to do the West Oakland Dip. Let's say you have your little argument, usually you're playing the dozens, a series of insults, ending in a fight. Then you use the West Oakland Dip technique whereby you make a backward quarter turn as if you're stepping away, then you reverse yourself with a right cross, because by stepping back, you've set up to bring the weight of your full body to the point of impact. It took me a few bouts of having it pulled on me to learn that trick. Then if you're good enough, you follow it up with what we call the East Oakland Two-Step, where you put the foot to the person you just knocked down with your West Oakland Dip. I got very good at that.

There were a few occasions where I was able to use jujitsu. These were times when my opponent was big and I figured the Dip ain't going to cut it. I got trouble. So I'll wait till he tries the Dip on me, that sets him up for either a *tomoenage* or a *koshinage*. The *tomoenage* is when they come at you and you go backward, fall on your back, put your foot up at the same time, and put them up over your shoulders. The *koshinage* is when you do a turn into, grab their arm, and give them a hip thing. You use those two jujitsu moves in a desperation situation because if your timing isn't good, it's all over but for the shouting. I lucked out because I can't think of a single instance where I used jujitsu—and I didn't do it that often—that I lost a fight. In fact, when I was in the army, I took on another soldier who was bigger than I was and did a *tomoenage* on him in a barrack fight and became squad leader. The guy was twice as big as me, and I'm exaggerating a bit, but damn. No way I'm gonna whip him with street fighting moves. So I'll let him make the move and do what I need to do and hope it works. Again, I owe my uncle Riuzo. He could see I needed some help in learning the manual art of self-defense.[9]

Now this is where my brother comes in the picture. One time, he and I took on six other kids. Every time he hit them, they went down. I was stunned. I found out that my brother was a natural street brawler, a natural boxer. Even though he was slightly shorter than me, he was stockier. Since I was smaller, I had to rely on being faster. I could deliver maybe three blows to every one of theirs. I kept the knowledge that I was going to get hurt as part of the price one had to pay. But I knew I was faster. I had proved that time and time again. I have to admit there was one time in my life I played bully. I deliberately picked on a kid that was smaller than me. Why I did, I don't know. But I learned a lesson—bullyism doesn't pay. I got my ass kicked. That's the only time some-body smaller than me ever whipped my ass. I'm embarrassed to say that, but I deserved it because I played the bully—and he played me.

The good news is, after about a year or so, things got better in the sense that a little bit of respect had developed for me and my brother. Then another kid on the block moved in. Frank was a couple of years older than I was and he took me under his wing. He had seen me in operation and figured I was good enough to join the club, so I got myself and my brother into the gang. Frank was so nice. He taught me to be cool, taught me how to turn my collar up. Now we're poor, we know that, so we had to get pants a little big, to last longer. But when you roll your pants cuff up, you don't roll it up thick. You take your time and you roll a narrow band, so you looking cool. The girls will love you for that. In fact, he had heard that the girls on the block adored me. I said, "Why?" "Well, you ain't dark." Then he shocked me when he said, "They love your hair. Come here, run your fingers through your hair." I said, "Why?" "Because it's straight. Black and straight!" Frank taught me how to walk the walk. He polished me like a rough stone.

One time, Frank averted a gang fight by cutting a deal with another gang leader. I must have been about ten, twelve; just feeling my oats. Frank claimed that he had the smartest kid around in his gang and pushed me forward. So we had a spelling bee on the street. I shocked everybody by being able to spell the word *encyclopedia*. They had a book there and they kind of randomly went through it. "Can your boy spell that?" "OK, what about your boy?" So I spelled *encyclopedia*, then I said, "There's an old-fashioned way of spelling that word too, like how they spelled in the old days." And they looked at me like say what? So I spelled it the archaic way too. It was like the parting of the Red Sea. Our side won. I liked the way Frank set everything up.

I was saving the worst for last. There was a Johnson family that came from the South and moved in right next door to us. Mrs. Johnson, a single parent, had a daughter Mary, about sixteen; a son, James, fourteen, my age; and her youngest daughter, Ruby, was about my brother's age.[10] Mrs. Johnson had had a hard life in the South and had brought her family to West Oakland because she'd been told there were jobs there. She ended up being a domestic for a family in the Oakland Hills. Every morning early, she would take the bus to the Hills. At night, she would come home after dark with her bag. I volunteered to acculturate James into the lifestyle of the 'hood because he was the new kid on the block. We used to meet his mother at the bus stop because it was dark by the time she got home and she had these packages, leftovers from the employers, maybe casserole for the family, stuff like that. It usually helps to have two teenage males to carry the bags. So I got to know the family quite well. In fact, I got to know Mary quite well. Then along comes a villain, a pimp, who was about eighteen or nineteen, started trying to get Mary to go trick for him. Since Mary was my girlfriend, I couldn't let that one fly. I think Frank was in the reformatory at the time so I couldn't get his help. It ended up being James, my brother, and myself, triple-teaming the pimp one night in an alley. We beat him half to death. He never came back to the 'hood again. This may sound a little cowardly, triple-teaming. But this guy was about eighteen or nineteen, James and I were fourteen, I might have turned fifteen, my brother was thirteen or so. Even two of us may not have been enough. But three of us blindsiding the guy, we could take him down and then do the East Oakland Two-Step so it'll register in his memory bank. Meanwhile, I had introduced James to Frank. So James was developing his needed urban survival skills. Then, the youngest sister got pregnant. That's when the mother broke down and went back to the South and I haven't had contact with them since. When I recall that family, it's with a bit of sadness because of what that woman went through. Lead a hard life in the South to come to West Oakland trying to better conditions for her children. The oldest daughter is pimp material. I mean, she was beautiful, involved with that little Oriental boy next door. I don't know what she thought of me; I think she liked me. Then to have her son running in a gang. Then the youngest daughter got pregnant. It broke her spirit.

The Aoki House

My grandparents had a three-story house that they were somehow able to retain throughout the war. It was on a corner lot at 2603 Union Street, at Twenty-Sixth and Union. My grandfather purchased the house in Riuzo's name because the Alien Land Laws prohibited Japanese immigrants from buying property. Riuzo was the first son born in the U.S. and therefore a U.S. citizen, so the property was put in his name, which was a common custom at that time.[11] We lived in the main house, but at one time my grandfather also owned the house next door on Union Street as well as the noodle factory across the street. The main house had a four-car detached garage, indicating some of our affluence. When I was living there, I recall it was in somewhat of a run-down condition through lack of adequate maintenance. Paint flaking off the exterior walls, doors not exactly right, stairs that were a little rickety. We never used the second-story deck. I remember the doorway to the deck was permanently sealed off to keep us from wandering out and falling through the floor. So I wasn't aware then how prominent the Aoki family was prior to the war. My grandfather had gone into business for himself and started making noodles. His factory was the Oakland Food Products. When I heard about the noodle factory, I thought it was a hole-in-the-wall operation. But if you look at the building that housed the manufacturing plant today, it must have been a very successful business.[12]

The entrance to the main house was on the second floor. You go up a set of stairs and there was a porch that extended the whole length of the front of the house. It wasn't quite Victorian but it was constructed probably around the turn of the century or a little thereafter. When you went through the front door, to the left was a room called the parlor. If you went further in, you entered the living room, a large dining room, and good-size kitchen. I remember the pantry, adjacent to the dining room, because inside it was a galvanized garbage can, cleaned out, that held our rice. Though we weren't rich, we always had that rice bin full. There was also a room called the library with built-in bookcases with glass doors. The first floor, on the street level, may have been occupied at one time. However, after the war, it was used to store crates of household items that were probably packed before the war and they just didn't bother to open them or take them upstairs. On the first floor, there was a washroom, with a *furo*. They galvanized a square bathtub to make the Japanese-style bath. There were also deep concrete sinks for washing the laundry and one of the old-fashioned wringers. I remember because I washed a lot of laundry down there. On the outside was a shed, attached to the back of the building, used to store coal for the living room fireplace. When you go up to the third floor, you run into four bedrooms. My grandfather and my grandmother occupied one bedroom. My father, my brother, and I occupied another bedroom. My uncle occupied the third bedroom. The fourth bedroom had weather damage to it, maybe a leak in the roof, and was not viable. The bathroom on the third floor had a toilet that had a tank, the old-fashioned kind that hung up on the wall, a bathtub, and a sink.[13]

The house next door had a similar type of layout, but was not as large. I don't know if my grandfather sold that house before or after Pearl Harbor. What happened is this family, an African American married couple, professionals of some sort, bought the house. They lived on the upper floor and carved up the bottom floor into two apartments. The Johnson family who came from the South lived in one of those small, dinky apartments.

Libraries, Schooling, and Reading

My grandfather had a library that easily contained a thousand books. Half were in Japanese. I remember one of the publications attempted to justify the Japanese occupation of Shanghai as the Japanese coming to the rescue of their Chinese brethren. Though I couldn't read Japanese, one of the things that impressed me were the illustrations—watercolor sketches with a tissue paper covering. The English-language collection included a complete set of *The Book of Knowledge,* an encyclopedia set designed for young people published around the time of the First World War. Then there was another set of some twenty volumes on the history of countries of the world. I've kept one volume all these years: *The Book of History,* volume two, which chronicles the history of Japan, Korea, and China. My grandfather's collection was like a time warp in that there was nothing in it published after 1940–1941.[14]

My father and uncle also had their own library collections. I recall my father's collection consisted mostly of paperback books, in English of course. They were far different from the books in my grandfather's library. My father's books had a very low reputation because they were more on the lurid side. The first time I read a romance novel was *The Foxes of Harrow* by Frank Yerby. I didn't know until later that he was African American. This was one of the hottest romance novels of that particular period. My father also had another genre, detective novels, which included Dashiell Hammett's Sam Spade character and Mickey Spillane's famous Mike Hammer series. He also had James T. Farrell's trilogy *Studs Lonigan,* about an Irish American boy growing up hard on the streets. Then my father had some African American books too. The one I remember most was Richard Wright's *Uncle Tom's Children,* which consisted of a series of short stories about Blacks in the South and their trials and tribulations. He also had *Strange Fruit,* the novel that ostensibly inspired Billie Holiday's famous song. Now my uncle Riuzo's library was not as extensive as my grandfather's or my father's. He had art books because he was an accomplished artist. His specialty was watercolors. There may have been some martial arts books too because he had a black belt in jujitsu. These books were also augmented by periodicals such as *Life, Saturday Evening Post, Collier's,* and *Reader's Digest.* In addition, my father would occasionally show up with a copy of the *Keyhole,* which was a lurid, X-rated tabloid. Occasionally he would share it with me. I appreciated that.

So here I am in 1945 surrounded by all this literature. Rather than enroll my brother and myself in school, my father decided to homeschool us. I've never been able to get a satisfactory explanation for his decision, but it wasn't hard to justify, with his having studied at the university and my family being literary and having this large library collection. So my father scored two school desks, the kind that opens at the top for pencils and stuff, one for my brother and one for myself. He put them in the library and conducted lessons on reading, writing, and arithmetic. He would try to figure out the grade level, and in retrospect we were academically more advanced than our peer group. My brother, of course, was receiving equal treatment simply because it was too much trouble to design two separate lessons. Then too we could do our home-work together. There wasn't a regular routine every day because of my father's schedule. Some days he'd be there and some days he wouldn't.[15]

To supplement our academics, my uncle Riuzo taught us physical educa-tion, the learning of jujitsu. For the first couple months, all I did was learn how to fall—which came in handy because for the next couple of months, I fell! He was a harsh taskmaster, but there is a motto in the martial arts: Train hard, fight easy. I was more than hungry because I was fighting in the streets every day; I needed all the advantage I could get. My uncle also taught me how to draw. My brother was never interested, but I was, so he would let me into his room and I spent hours hunched over watching him do his thing. Then he would teach me the basics of composition, how to draw a face, a horse, stuff like that. I have this set of fighter planes that I drew in 1952, when I was about thirteen. These pictures show two things. One was whatever art skills I had developed and, two, my interest in military aviation. In fact, this was the one and only ambition I ever had. I didn't thirst to be a social worker, I didn't thirst to be a professor, I didn't thirst to be a Black Panther, but I did thirst to be a fighter pilot. I really owe my uncle a lot for giving me the opportunity to be able to express myself creatively.[16]

My grandfather had the responsibility of contributing to my education by teaching me Japanese. That must be why I didn't attend Japanese language school like so many of the kids did. I learned how to read and write *kanji,* hiragana, and katakana [the Japanese alphabet systems] from my grandfather. When I went to UC Berkeley, I took Japanese language, figuring I was going to increase my GPA so easily it would make their heads swim. The first day, I wanted to show off to everybody that I knew how to speak Japanese because I had learned it when I was a kid. But the TA had to correct me: "We don't use that type of colloquialism in this class." It was then that I learned the Japanese immigrants used a rural dialect from the Meiji period—considered old-fashioned and rather crude. That quickly humbled me. However, my Japanese was good enough for me to get by. In fact, when I was in the army, I took the Japanese language test, an oral test, and passed it.

My grandparents on both sides were Christian and regular churchgoers.[17] I found out that prior to the war, the Aoki family had been quite prominent in the local church. My father, however, had a view of the church that was very negative, that they were a bunch of hypocrites. Though all my grandparents went to church, they never proselytized or encouraged us. Occasionally I did go to the Japanese American Tenth Street Methodist Episcopal Church.[18] But I didn't seem to get along too well with the other students primarily because of my father's estrangement from the Japanese American community. Some of the Japanese American girls had been told by their parents not to have anything to do with me: Don't go out with that Richard boy because his father is a dorobo.[19] Some of the girls were nice enough to tell me, and others just got cold on me. Maybe that accounts for the reason why my first girlfriend was African American.[20]

So my father was teaching us at home, probably using the same style that he'd been accustomed to in his formal education. However, a problem started emerging. I had read all the books in the household by the time I was about ten. That's when I discovered the West Oakland Public Library. There were two librarians, one African American and the other Caucasian, who opened the gates to literacy. It was like finding freedom. Once I got a library card, I could check out any book I wanted, and they had thousands of books. These two librarians, once they realized how serious I was, taught me how to use the card catalog. So I read something like six hundred books in one year. Here I am, ten or eleven now, living in the 'hood, walking back and forth from my place to the library, carrying books, maybe looking like a nerd. But do you know, not once did I get jumped for that. By that time, my reputation was such that I'm a shove this book up your ass. If I can't do it, I got my boys back home. Those six hundred books ranged from Mickey Mouse teenage books to classic literature like Charles Dickens that the librarians guided me toward. When I discovered

Edgar Allan Poe, he mesmerized me for two reasons. Number one was the macabre content of his prose and poetry. It wasn't until later that I discovered he had some serious mental problems. Number two was his mastery of the English language; he was so good at taking the basic English word, building it up to these stories of such a downing nature. I was only about ten or eleven, but felt a kindred spirit.

Then my interests started getting more focused. The first group of books was science fiction books, which still interests me to this day. I read the classics of science fiction—Robert Heinlein, Ray Bradbury, Isaac Asimov. I have wondered why I got into science fiction because I'm not fantasy oriented. I realized it had to do with the plots. These science fiction writers were really writing about contemporary society; it was social criticism in the guise of fiction.

My next set of interests was military history. *Bombardier* by Henry Lent. It was designed for teenagers. How does one become a bombardier, to drop a bomb from the air? One goes to school. One studies mathematics. I think they slightly mentioned the danger, but if they did, I ignored it. I was off once I discovered military and history books—and if you look at history, it's all about the military. In my grandfather's library, *The Book of Knowledge* had sections on the military. I remember one page in *The Book of Knowledge* that had a poem and illustrations that taught a lesson. It showed a soldier riding a horse and it said: "For the want of a nail, a horseshoe was lost." It showed the horseshoe flipping out in the next panel. "For the want of a horseshoe, a horse was lost." So the rider had to get off the horse. "For the want of a horse, the rider was lost." "For the want of a rider, the battle was lost." Then, "for the want of a battle, the war was lost." The lesson to me was one little detail like a horseshoe nail can affect history in such a fashion that it can cost a war. My brother didn't read as much and may have resented having to tag along with me to the library and carry some of my books home. But I just ate them up.

Work and Other Occupations

Getting to my father's occupation, when he comes out of the camps, what's he going to do? In general, hiring Japanese Americans immediately after the war was not a top priority among personnel managers. Even before the war, there was widespread job discrimination, even against well-educated Japanese Americans. There was, of course, general unemployment in the thirties, but it was worse for Japanese Americans. There are stories of engineers working as meter readers or MBAs working as counter clerks. After the war, things weren't better.[21] So my father did not seek employment through traditional legitimate ways. One of the first things he did was to get involved in illegal gambling opportunities in the Japanese and Chinese communities. Then he became a boxing promoter. When I was growing up, baseball was very popular. During the World Series, every apartment, every house, every project would have the game on and they'd be rooting. But I wasn't into baseball. It was slow. Baseball represents nineteenth-century agrarian rural America. Football is industrial twentieth-century America—violent and hard hitting! But for me, boxing was the big-time sport. It was very popular among African Americans in Oakland because many of the world boxing champions at the time were African American. If we look at professional boxing, we can see how immigrant groups have had to resort to that economic lifestyle in order to survive. When you look at the history of boxing, you'll see that there were Jewish boxers at the turn of the century. Irish and Italian boxers in the fifties. In the forties and fifties, African Americans began to gain prominence in the sport of boxing. Joe Louis was considered the champ. But I admired Sugar Ray Robinson more. Joe Louis was a destructive machine; his style was to just stand there and box. My brother was more like Joe Louis. Sugar Ray Robinson was my style. He was fast and prided himself on not getting hurt in the face. In all the hundreds of fights I've been in, I have prided myself on not having any facial scars for sixty-four years. Now, after just a little fall, I have this scar under my eye.

Now I have to throw in Jack Johnson, the first Black heavyweight champion of the world, from back in 1908 when he beat a White man. He was way ahead of his time. He probably would have been even greater if it hadn't been for the racism in this country. He was accused of violating the Mann Act, also known as the White Slave Act, for taking a White woman across state lines for immoral purposes. He had at different times various White wives or girlfriends. That was his real "crime"—consorting with White women. That's how the Feds got him. He left the country as the champion. In order to get back in, he had to fight a White boy and throw the fight. There's a world-famous picture of him in the boxing ring in Havana where he's deliberately lying down on the canvas, shielding his eyes from the sun as his opponent was waiting for him to get up.[22] If we look at boxing today, they're mostly Latinos now. Again this is a means of economic opportunity and advancement for working-class immigrant groups. It's a brutal, brutal profession.

Since my father was a boxing promoter, I got to go to local fights. I'd go to the gym and see the people working out there. There was a boxer, a welterweight, who was raised in Richmond but was training in Oakland gyms because that's where the champions were coming from. He was a promising young man, in good shape, a nice person. He taught me a few things. Close to twenty years later, I was working in an industrial factory and I ran into him again; he was a janitor there. However, there was a marked difference. His face was messed up. His ears were misshapen; they call it cauliflower ears from getting battered so many times upside the head. His speech was slurred, which indicated brain damage. The thing that struck me was how much permanent physical damage he had suffered as a result of his boxing.

One of the benefits of my father's wheeling and dealing was his LaSalle Cadillac convertible. He was getting to be the talk of the 'hood with his big, fancy car. One day, my brother was in the Cadillac with my father when they were going across the Bay Bridge and my father was hitting eighty or ninety. The Highway Patrol stops him and asks, "Do you know how fast you were going?" My brother piped up, "You were doing at least ninety!" I said, "You said what!" If I were there, I wouldn't have said nothing. I was a little disappointed in my brother.

After boxing-promoting days, my father went into business with a couple of buddies from camp and they bought a Texaco gas station in Berkeley. Still, my father continued to supplement his income with extracurricular activities. I remember one day—this was in the early 1950s—my father and I were going to the grocery store on the block, one of the mom-and-pop stores in West Oakland because they didn't have any supermarkets in those days. A customer in the grocery store starts talking about he was a veteran from the Second World War. He done fought in the South Pacific against "them Japs." When he heard that, my father said to me, "Go on home now, boy." I step out the door, run around the side of the store, and peek inside. There was Blue, one of our neighbors, making these statements. My father said something to him. Blue jumps back, pulls a straight-edge razor out of his pocket. Now you have to be of a certain age to understand the significance of straight-edge razors. Up until the invention of safety razors and their widespread use, a lot of African Americans carried straight-edge razors for legitimate purposes. I could see the facial scars on Blue's face from being slashed with a razor. So Blue takes out a straight edge. My father whips out his snub-nose .38 Special. Blue drops his razor on the floor, with a profuse set of apologies. In those days, very few people carried guns in the ghettos. But my father was running around with some nasty circles. He needed a gun.

A couple of months later, my father and Blue are partners. By then, my father was the apartment manager of a big set of apartment houses, maybe a hundred units, in West Oakland. One day, the tenants came home and found that their valuables had been burglarized. Upon investigation, the police were told that my father and Blue had rented a truck, backed it up to the rear of the apartment house, and were observed loading radios and other things into this truck and driving off.[23]

With my father getting into so much trouble, my brother and I went to live with my mother around 1953. Just before we moved out, I remember coming home to find four White detectives arresting my father on a narcotics charge. I underscore narcotics because in those days, illegal drug activity in West Oakland was practically nonexistent. I don't recall seeing much use of marijuana. Heroin, which was the hard drug of the day, was more restricted to the musicians. The reason why I remember the narcotics thing is that it was so scandalous. I'll give you an example of normal police activity in West Oakland. On a Sunday morning, a couple of doors down from us, there were a bunch of police cars and uniformed police were taking the father of one of my gang friends off to jail. His wife is out there with one of these old-fashioned irons, the kind you put on a stove to heat up, and she's getting ready to do him in. Meanwhile, he's bleeding and she's being restrained by these White cops. I thought, she's beaten him half to death, how come they're arresting him? That's when I learned about statutory rape laws. She was supposed to be out of town that weekend and he brought some sixteen-year-old girl into the apartment. She came home unexpectedly and went upside his head with that iron. Now, that was normal. Nobody talked too much about something like that. But in my father's case, four White detectives in plainclothes, in the middle of the night—Wow! I went down to the police station to see what was going on. That's when I found out about the narcotics charge because they wouldn't let me visit him. The next day, though, I suddenly found myself the big kid on the block because my father was so bad!

It was around this time that one of the most humiliating experiences happened. My father and my uncle Riuzo had gotten into a fight. I don't mean an argument. It was a knock-down, drag-out, teeth-losing, black-eye kind of fight. They fought right outside our home where everyone could see them. I know the reason behind their fight and it wasn't because of the war, but I have a feeling that their animosities about the war also motivated the fight. But the main reason had to do with my father's activities. My uncle had had enough of my father bringing shame upon the Aoki name. I was out and about when someone told me about it. It was over by the time I got home, but I could see the blood on the street and sidewalk. I go into the house and they're in their separate rooms, nursing their wounds. Meanwhile, I can't explain it to my brother. He's as shocked as I am and looking at me like, "What's happening?" I'm looking at him like, I don't know, man. But I knew that their relationship had deteriorated and was not entirely surprised by the fight, but to have it out in the street was the shocking part. For days afterward, I walked around with the hood of my jacket down over my head, figuring all the kids were saying, "Yeah, man, you should've seen that one. Two brothers fighting. And Japanese at that." I can laugh at it now, but at the time it was probably one of the most horrible traumas, emotionally, I had experienced because it was so crazy.

Working and Hustling

When I was growing up, my brother and I never received a regular allowance from our father. That's not because my father was neglectful; his source of income was uncertain and the amounts were sporadic. Sometimes he hit the horses and he spent it. When he didn't have it, we went without. But I started to learn that if you work, you get money. So, when I was about nine or ten, I started collecting soda pop bottles. For Coca-Cola and 7Up bottles, I think you got one penny each. For the big bottles, you got a little more. My father made a wagon out of wooden crates and took apart skates to get wheels for the wagon. I had a rope attached to it and would trundle it along. My brother would sit in the back of the wagon and I would pull him along because he was going to be my backup. Even though I was the one running the streets, it was always handy to have backup. Plus, with the absence of my father and less supervision from my grandparents and my uncle, I had my little brother along with me most of the time. So I collected these soda pop bottles, putting them in my little wagon. Since there were a lot of factories around, the workers would come out at break time drinking soda pop. "Hey, can I have your soda pop bottle?" "Sure, kid. Here you go." I never once had the bottles ripped off from me. I'd go to the corner grocery store to redeem them and I'd have my spending money. It was about this time I developed my habit of drinking soda pop. I was happy, happy, happy.[24]

I did other odd jobs in the neighborhood. I ran errands for senior citizens occasionally. As I got known in the neighborhood, a senior citizen might say, "Why don't you go down to the corner store and get me a loaf of bread." One time there was a small factory that did industrial finishing work. They had a contract with the telephone company to electroplate the telephone boxes, the metal boxes on the outside of the house. Guess who they hired for a small amount, twenty-five cents an hour or so? This was a gross violation of child labor laws because that was the most dangerous job I ever had but didn't realize it. I remember getting close to the vats with the chemicals and an older worker drained it. "We drain it and all you have to do is pick this up—don't touch it with your hands—and put it over here. Let it dry. Give it twenty minutes and then move it over here." That was simple and they paid me what I thought was good money.[25]

Then I became a newspaper boy. I was about eleven, so I lied about my age. At that time there were two daily newspapers in Oakland. The *Oakland Tribune* had the largest circulation. It was owned by the Knowland family, who were quite conservative, Republicans all their lives. The other paper was the *Oakland Post-Enquirer,* owned by the Hearst family. I didn't know anything about the Hearst family, but I did know they would hire me as a delivery boy. As I recall there were only a few African American newspaper boys. Most of the ones I dealt with in West Oakland were either Latino or White. I've never been able to figure that out. I do know I had to get my butt up early in the morning, rain or shine, to go down to the newspaper shack. In those days every couple of blocks there would be a converted garage or shed where the newspapers would be dropped off and the kids like myself would fold up the newspapers. I learned how to do the rounds. By this time I had a bicycle and had gotten good at throwing those newspapers right on the porch. Being homeschooled allowed me greater flexibility; after getting up so early, I could take a nap in the afternoon. But I had an asthmatic condition and it was hard work. Like the postman, neither rain nor sleet nor snow, you've got to deliver. Having people call, "Where's my paper, boy?" was not my style. If I'm going to be a news-paper boy, you will get your newspaper and get it on your front porch. If it's raining, I put some wax paper around it and you get it dry. Then when I started junior high school, bright as I was I couldn't hold the newspaper boy job, look after my brother, and do schoolwork. So I did that for a couple of years and I never got ripped off by anybody, not by a customer and nobody jumped me for my paper money.[26]

I want to comment a bit on the literature in the homes of African Americans. As I wandered through the community I was invited into many of the homes mostly for a glass of Kool-Aid. That's when I discovered *Ebony* and *Jet* maga-zines. I loved *Jet* magazine because it was small, you could carry it around with you, and it always had that centerfold. Johnson Publications also came out with *Negro Digest,* which was very different from the content of *Ebony* and *Jet.* It was more political. In this issue that I saved, the first article is on Frantz Fanon. I didn't see very many copies of the *Digest* in the houses; all I remember was *Ebony* and *Jet* and of course newspapers. So delivering newspapers gave me an idea of what was happening in the African American community not only in West Oakland but throughout the rest of the country.[27]

When I was growing up in West Oakland, most of the African Americans I met were recent migrants to Oakland; many of them arrived during the war to work in the shipyards, military bases, and factories. I began to hear tales. I'd already read *Uncle Tom's Children* and *Strange Fruit*. So occasionally I would bring up questions like, "What was it like?" Most of the children I grew up with didn't have a political assessment of the South because they were kids like myself. On rare occasions adults would humor me by sharing their experiences of the South: Why they came here, the grinding poverty of the South, especially the rural areas, the term "chopping cotton," the coming to Oakland for jobs. When I was about twelve, one of my best friends was going to the South to visit his family. I was sitting in his living room, with his grandmother lecturing him on Southern etiquette before she put him on the train. I remember her saying, "When you get to the city now, you hook up with cousin Virgil. You stick with cousin Virgil. Do what he says because they do things differently down there." Here I am, oblivious to how they did things differently. A couple of weeks later, I go down to the train station and my friend gets off. He didn't look too good. He'd been beaten up. So I said, "Man, what happened?" He said, "I'm at the movie theater. These white people told me where I should sit. I say, 'I ain't sitting there. I can't see nothing from there.'" He said they beat his ass, threw him down a flight of stairs. I said, "Where was cousin Virgil, because he's supposed to be backing you up?" Cousin Virgil was of no help. Told me later that's the way they did things down there. I said, "That's a strange-ass place to live. Remind me not to go to the South because I don't understand that." A few years later, the brutal murder of Emmett Till in Mississippi busted up the Black community in Oakland.[28]

Getting back to West Oakland and continuing my upward economic climb: I began to intersperse my legitimate activities with another set of activities which included "five finger shopping," mostly at the five-and-dime stores in downtown Oakland where I used to pick up the toys that I wanted and couldn't afford. I stayed away from the Japanese-made toys because they were cheap and didn't last long. That was the period after the Second World War where the Japanese were taking scrap metal and making toys and shipping them to the United States, but the quality of the work was really poor and even children understood if you had a Japanese-made toy at that time you had a piece of junk. What I loved at the time were cap pistols. Later on I went after jewelry because I could fence it in the neighborhood.

I also participated in "second story" work. But I only hit commercial establishments, not residential properties. One night when I was about twelve or thirteen, I got caught on the roof of a beer warehouse exiting with a case of beer that I felt would make me very popular on the block the next day. Unfortunately, a cop was there too. All I remember is a "Halt or I'll shoot." I almost had a heart attack because police shooting of teenagers in our neighborhood was quite common. Needless to say, I froze. To this day I'm sure had I been African American, he would have shot me. Guess who was the lookout? My brother! I jammed him later: "How was it that the cop got the jump on me if you were supposed to be looking?" Turns out my brother was on his Jay, looking one way. But someone had called the cops and they came in the back way and climbed up the side through the fire escape. So the police took David and me down to the police station. I begged the police not to tell my father, but they did. As usual, whenever my brother got in trouble, I got the blame for it. David knew it was his fault that we got nabbed. I asked him, "Didn't you see them? Couldn't you whistle so I could run? You were the lookout, I trusted you on that." So my father comes down to the station to get us out. He was rather blasé about the whole thing. It surprised me. I suspect that he was more ashamed that we got caught than about the actual breaking of the law. I got reprimanded again because I was the oldest son. David got away scot clean! I don't know if my mother ever found out about this. I imagine my grandparents suspected something because we got home around five or six in the morning. That cop shouting "Halt or I'll shoot" was one of few times when I really felt fear through my bones. It didn't end my activities, but it was a frightening experience.[29]

The "midnight auto supply" work was interesting. As the evening came I would go down to the local auto junkyard and talk to the proprietor and he would give me a list of things that he wanted for the next morning. It might have been hubcaps from a 1930 or 1947 Cadillac, a hood ornament from a Packard model, or a battery from a Buick. Real specific items that he probably told his customers he would have in the shop the next morning. For most of the jobs I pulled, I didn't take my brother. That second-story job was one of the few times I got my brother involved and look how it turned out.

A fourth area was like robbing Paul to pay Peter. The Korean War was in full swing around 1951, '52, and the prices of scrap metal went up sharply—brass, lead, copper, aluminum. There were so many junkyards in West Oakland, maybe two dozen junkyards in the neighborhood. By this time, Frank had left the area and I was, I can't say warlord, that sounds too militaristic; I can't say leader, I wasn't the toughest in the group; but I was usually the one who came up with the idea and the plan. So what's the plan? First, look for junkyards that ain't got no dogs 'cause we ain't dealing with no dogs. Then, hit the junkyard at night, look for the most valuable scraps of metal to throw over the fence. Get our little carts and go scooting down the way. In the morning we go to another junkyard four blocks away and sell them the metal scraps. After a while that enterprise came to a screeching halt as the junkyards' owners began to realize that there was something shifty going on. So there was a diminishing of activities but it was profitable. In fact I came up with a brilliant idea of getting this specialty brass. Brass ingot was going for umpteenth cents a pound— like gold bars! My idea was to get a car, back it up to this factory whose specialty was making brass product, and load up. Some other things came up and it never saw fruition, but I was sure that that was going to be our big score. We could've ended up in the penitentiary for that one. This was not junkyard metal; this was big business and they would not have let us off lightly, especially since African Americans were also involved.

Now, I'm revealing this because very few people are aware that I was involved in these types of activities. I'm showing how I survived economically. I was poor, so to get the things I felt I wanted and needed, this is what I had to do. I realize that people may look down on this type of activity. But even for this, there was a code of ethics. When it came to second-story work, I never hit residential places, only business or commercial enterprises. My five-finger shopping sprees were confined to big department stores and not mom-and-pop stores. Midnight auto supply—well, you got to protect your car and you may have insurance. Illegitimate economic activity has historically been the way that poor people have existed. Take, for example, nineteenth-century England and the poverty engendered by the industrial age, where people were packed into small quarters, driven off the land by the land enclosure laws and other moves by the ruling class to uproot the peasantry and create the industrial proletariat. When many of the industrial proletariat could not find jobs, prostitution and robbery flourished. Frederick Engels's *Condition of the English Working Class* expands on the high crime rate and the reasons for it in nineteenth-century Manchester and Liverpool. Charles Dickens's writings are chock-full of goodies about the life of the poor and their struggles to survive. Another good example is Victor Hugo's *Les Misérables,* where Jean Valjean steals a loaf of bread to feed his starving family and ends up on the galleys.[30]

When we talk about poverty, we can't forget the racial disparities. Growing up, there were very few recreational facilities in Oakland. I remember playing pool, Ping-Pong, and other activities at DeFremery Park, the only recreational center in all of West Oakland. We also made our own fun, playing in the railroad yards. One time my brother and I were walking across an elevated railroad trestle when a train came along, forcing us to hang on underneath to the railroad tie as the train passed over us. I didn't tell my father that we had that close a call because he would have wondered why I was taking my younger brother there in the first place. Another time, a half dozen of us went to the railroad yard but ended up one short. We didn't say anything until his mother started asking us where her son was and we 'fessed up. They found his body that night. The railroad yard was dangerous for a number of reasons. Car bumping was one of them. That's when you bump a boxcar and it glides along and doesn't make a sound so if your back is to it you don't even hear the sucker coming. That's apparently what happened to him. After that I decided my brother and I weren't going to be playing in the railroad yard anymore. This is an example of how poor communities suffer doubly—from having few recreational outlets and from the poor placement of residences next to industrial facilities.[31]

Believe it or not, when I was growing up, I thought life was kind of normal as far as law enforcement was concerned. They made the law, we kept the order. They made that abundantly clear. There was this guy, a wino who we called Brown Bagger, drunk all the time, morning, noon, and night, and homeless. Everybody knew he was a flop drunk, sitting in front of the store just drinking his wine. My father said, "Don't pay no attention to him. You say hi to him, he says hi to you, just leave him be." One night, the cops came and hassled him. He got upset and threw up on the pants of the cop. The cop went ballistic, whopping him upside the head and beating him half to death. I was about eight or nine, and the overreaction just stunned me. I was standing there thinking, Man, that ain't right. It's obvious the man's drunk. That was the first time I ever witnessed police abuse. I told my father about it that night: "I saw something nasty happen today . . ." He just sloughed it off: "That's the way it is." But that made a mark on my mind.

One night I was hanging out on a street corner with my homies, just killing time, talking about what be happening, probably talking about how Sugar Ray and Joe Louis cleaned the clocks of all those contenders, when a police car drives up and two Negro officers get out of the car. Immediately the homies broke and ran. We hadn't been doing anything wrong, so I didn't understand why we fled. But when they ran, I ran. A couple of blocks away when we congregated again, I asked, "What's happening? Those were two of our people in uniform. They haven't even said nothing to us. Why we running?" One of my homies said, "Man, you don't want to talk to those two. They will beat you worse than the White cops!" I was stunned because I initially thought this is a good deal, get to see some people of color here in uniform and I can go and introduce myself. But being the new kid on the block—I was eight, nine, ten at the time—I was unaware of the record of these Negro police officers who had just been hired to keep the community under control. This was a revealing experience for me. I can go on and on about the litany of police abuse practices in West Oakland, but even a cursory overview will lead to no other conclusion than that they are bad for the health of the community. I have to agree with Bobby Seale, who called the police an occupying army.

Formal Schooling

When I was about fourteen and my parents were getting a divorce, we got a visit from the truant officer, who wanted to know why my brother and I weren't in school. I'm sure one of the relatives blew the whistle, though to this day I don't know who. Since my brother and I were thirteen and fourteen, respectively, we were sent to Herbert Hoover Junior High School in Oakland. My brother and I show up at school and we don't know what the hell is going to happen to us. One of the English teachers happened to be the school psychologist. The first thing she did was test us to assess our reading, writing, and arithmetic skills. We aced them all, thanks to my father's homeschooling. Then since she was the psychometrist, she administered the Stanford-Binet IQ test on both of us. When she got the results, she was stunned. So she administered a second IQ test in order to validate the first test because on the Stanford-Binet, I scored in the genius range. Not that I'm going to be that boastful because my brother scored the third highest that she had ever tested at that junior high school. Now comes a problem. What are they going to do with us? We passed the grade-level tests. We passed the IQ tests. The cultural bias of those tests has now been called into question, but in those days, that's what was used. So the principal and the faculty discussed it. It was obvious that we could both pass the GED. However, the psychometrist was sharp. She said, suppose they pass the GED and they're gone. Suppose they want to go to the University of California at Berkeley. They have to start in the ninth grade and complete the A through F requirements. So we'll put Richard in the ninth grade and David in the eighth grade.[32]

When I got to junior high, I had no problems with my fellow students because I grew up in the 'hood and half the kids I already knew. "Richard, what you doing here?" "Oh, the truant officer got you." "We thought you had a cushy deal there." So I got along all right, but there was an incident where I ran into a little trouble. I had joined the traffic patrol. Figured I was going to help the school. I liked the uniform and the sign. The job was to go to stand at the intersection and help your fellow students cross the street. One day three dudes sashayed across the street disregarding my directions. There were crossing against the sign and laughing. Then they called me a clown. I couldn't do anything because I was on duty. If I got into a fight with them, what would happen to the younger kids crossing the street? But I was pissed. Back at school shortly afterward I'm in the hallway wrapping up my sign when these same three dudes come walking by and they're still laughing and still calling me a clown. I'll never forget that, "clown." I went upside their heads with that traffic sign. I broke the sign over one dude's head. Others came and broke it up, and I had to go to the principal's office. It wasn't a visit that I was looking forward to because the principal was known to be tough, fair but tough. I went in there and he asked me what happened. After I told him, he said, "You might be happier not on the traffic squad and we'll forget about this." I was getting off easy on that issue. But pranks were a common occurrence. Had it happened in a middle-class school there might have been more serious consequences, but Doc Hess was a real decent human being and he understood where I was coming from.[33]

I don't know if Huey Newton or David Hilliard has ever mentioned it because I think they're both Herbert Hoover graduates. The school mascot was a black panther. And there was this ditty that we sang that went to the tune of that jazz song, "Did He Ramble": "Hoover had a panther, sat him in the hall, when he saw the panthers you knew you were on the ball. Did he ramble, Did he ramble, Did he ramble all around. Hey in or out of town. Did he ramble, Did he ramble, he rambled till they all cut 'em down." Junior high school kids ate that thing up. You had to have rhythm.[34]

Let me get back to the curriculum. I took English Composition, Elementary Algebra, Spanish One, and General Science One. As my elective, I took woodshop. I have always been a believer that vocational education has its place in everybody's education, to gain the more practical hands-on type of educational experience. For years I have thought of myself as being more of an applied scientist as opposed to a theoretical scientist. One of the P.E. classes that I took had a ballroom dancing component. Now Frank had already taught me how to do the bop, and that's good for the girls on the block and for looking flashy. But ballroom dancing was another social skill that comes in handy in a lot of situations. It made me get closer to the girls, and in my professional life it breaks the ice. By the time I was fourteen I was paying more interest now to the young ladies. I aced out my classes—all As. Maybe I got one B, but that was because I wasn't paying attention. I was always completing my homework before I left school. If there was ten minutes at the end of class, I'd do my homework and be done. So, I graduated midyear from Herbert Hoover in January 1954 because the way the truant office nailed us, I started in school in January 1953.[35]

Comes graduation time and I'm covaledictorian. The deal is the valedictorian is the student that has the highest grade point average for seventh, eighth, and ninth grades. But I had only been there one year. Though I consider the other student the main valedictorian, they made me covaledictorian, saying, "This year we have a surprise, a student who has accomplished a great deal." So the night of the graduation I'm up there before several hundred of my fellow students, their parents, and my parents. I get up to the microphone, I open my mouth, and nothing comes out. I developed stage fright and I forgot my speech, which I titled "What Herbert Hoover Has Done for Me." However, in the wings was the English teacher–psychologist who had helped me rehearse. She just uttered the first couple of words and, man, chatterbox rolled again but at a much higher level. This time he was making his first public speech![36]

As a graduate of Herbert Hoover, I was expecting to go to McClymonds High School in West Oakland, the school my father graduated from. I went there for one day. Unfortunately I went there on a very bad day because the white principal of McClymonds was apparently very unpopular, primarily because he had said something to the effect that "when the Herbert Hoover kids get here, I'm going to put those animals in their cages." We heard about that, so on the first day of school the next semester there was a big riot on campus. Guess who got stomped! This was the first time in the history of the Oakland school system that a principal and vice principal got attacked physically. There was this little Oriental boy who was observing the crowd taking part in the action. Next thing I know I end up going to Berkeley High.[37]

It was a cultural shock to me when I hit Berkeley High School. Herbert Hoover was considered the second-toughest junior high school in all of Oakland, second only to Lowell in West Oakland, primarily because its student population came from the projects. McClymonds was considered the toughest high school. On the opposite end of the spectrum, Berkeley High was considered one of the top high schools in the nation. At least a quarter of their students went directly to UC Berkeley, maybe another quarter went to a private college or university.[38] The reason for this was that during that period a lot of UC Berkeley professors sent their kids to Berkeley High School. So I go from one of the worst junior high schools in Oakland to one of the intellectual heavyweight schools. Remember I had grown up in an African American community. But I did hit Berkeley at a time when the African American student population was increasing, primarily coming from South Berkeley. Still, I wasn't too happy about going to Berkeley because I wanted to be with my homies in West Oakland attending McClymonds. But now I'm living with my mother.

From an academic standpoint, I was very capable. I was covaledictorian of my junior high class. Students were tracked during that time and because I was an Oriental, they put me on the college prep track. They had seen that I was intellectually endowed, scientifically inclined, so I had to take the heavy-duty stuff, which meant more homework. I wanted to take the vocational education classes that I enjoyed. The college prep classes consisted of Euro-Americans or Asian Americans, Japanese and Chinese. I can't think of an African American in my classes, even though African Americans, especially the more affluent ones, were moving from West Oakland to South Berkeley. Don't forget about the racial segregation in Berkeley. So South Berkeley became home to the less troublesome African American population. Still, the Berkeley officials were a little nervous about the increase of African Americans at that school. Along comes Richard who looks Oriental but he acts Black, the way he walks, the way he talks, the way he behaves. I was respectful but I carried myself with an attitude, not a fighting attitude but a self-assured attitude.

One semester I almost broke my mother's bank account. She noticed my grades were slipping and she sweetened up the pot. She offered to pay me five dollars for each A I got. She threw a challenge in my face, so I busted my ass in that semester. It was hard. I had to lighten up on my homies. I had to lighten up on the young ladies. I had to stay up late some nights and because we shared a bedroom, my brother was saying, "What the hell you doing? Turn off the lights!" "Man, I gotta finish this chapter." "Oh yeah, you and Mama and the grade thing." I came home with five As and got $25, though she was only making $1.25 an hour at the time.[39] Here's the other thing. Remember I said my brother had the third-highest IQ that this one psychometrist had ever tested in her career. While his IQ was much higher than mine, my GPA was higher than his. Had he tried, he easily could have gotten straight As. In defense of my brother, in college, he was married and had a kid and a job! I'm surprised he even made it through UC Berkeley. I'm recalling now why my mother made me that offer but not my brother because his grades were worse than mine. We would describe David's demeanor as *nonki* or laid back. I was determined, uptight, questioning.[40] Still, I had other distractions, which included the discovery of a dead-end hallway on the third floor of a building on campus, which was ideal for encounters of the fifth kind. It became a favorite spot for me. I even turned my brother on to it, which got him into good trouble. The Hoover teachers had treated me with respect, but the teachers at Berkeley were more hoity-toity. So I didn't like most of the teachers at Berkeley High School, except my trigonometry teacher, who roused my interest when he said that to be a fighter pilot I'd have to do my own navigation and that required knowing trigonometry.

Socializing

By the time I got to high school, I was bored and not reading as much. Plus, I had two other activities that were taking up a lot of my time: gangs and girls. First, I was in a gang called the Saints. We weren't organized to create trouble. We were organized more along self-defense lines. In other words, the chances of getting hassled were less if you belonged to a gang. Many of the gang members came from families like mine, single-parent homes or both parents in working-class jobs. I'm proud to say that we had members from both West Oakland and South Berkeley. Remember that gangs were based on neighborhoods, so there were East Oakland gangs, West Oakland gangs, North Richmond gangs, and South Berkeley gangs. African Americans from Richmond have fought with African Americans from West Oakland; Whites from Richmond have fought with Whites from Oakland. Recently, the Mien community [from Laos], which is small to begin with, has a gang in Richmond fighting a Mien gang in East Oakland. The only time that there was a suspension of this regional mind-set was when the Black Panther Party was formed and active. It didn't matter whether you came from West Oakland, East Oakland, North Richmond, South Berkeley, San Francisco, Hunter's Point, Fillmore, you were a Panther. So it made me proud that the Saints were able to transcend geographic boundaries.

You asked when I start running with the Saints. You be talking to the dude who brought the name up! Out of sheer perversity, I said, "Let's call us ourselves the Saints because we ain't." Now there are some who might disagree, but I stand by that. There were about thirty of us, about 90 percent African American and the remainder Asian Americans. We had Chinese, Filipino, and of course my younger brother was a member too. We were organized to the point where you got jackets, gray coats with gold piping.[41] I was in high school when we organized the Saints, though the underpinnings had been laid a couple of years before through friendships. After we became the Saints, we were much prouder of ourselves. We carried ourselves much better. We had self-confidence because now we were a force to be contended with. You mess with one Saint, you mess with all the Saints. At Berkeley High School, they had treated me like a shadow. One time, I got into a fight on the campus, which was a no-no. But this guy had been bad-mouthing me and he would not show up across the street at the park where it would normally be settled. So I caught him in the hallway and started kicking the shit out of him. I ended up in the principal's office with the truant officer, who was an ex-cop. The principal said, "Do you know we have the authority to apply corporal punishment?" I looked at him and said, "You and who else?" Ain't nobody gonna lay a hand on me. If you whup my ass here, I'm a come back with my little brother. If you whup us, I'm coming back with my boys. If you whup us, I'm coming back with my father and he will shoot you.[42]

My brother didn't get into much trouble. But one time, he was dating a White girl and some of the White boys in school didn't like it. So they threatened him. This was during the summer session. So I got all the kids together that were still around and we went to Berkeley High School. That was the end of that particular thing. That's one of the advantages of being an organized group. You can do your thing. Not that we won all our battles. There was one night when three gangs got together and ambushed us. We got hurt badly. But it wasn't all about fighting. There was this camaraderie that comes about. As I said, most of the people were from broken homes and the group was a good substitute. A lot of people associate gangs with violence, but they can provide a useful social function. It can give them a place where they're accepted for themselves, where they can get advice, and where they can give support and advice. So I'm not as harsh on so-called gang activity as the average person would be.

I was also getting interested in the young ladies around this time. At one point, I had an Asian American girlfriend in Oakland, an African American girlfriend in South Berkeley, and a White girlfriend from the Hills. I thought I was good, but I found out that type of thing is not appreciated. As I went out of my way to get better acquainted with the ladies, I had a nagging fear that I would get one of them pregnant. But thanks to my father and some of the things he incorporated in the homeschooling, I knew about condoms. I wouldn't say my father taught us sex education, more like Pregnancy Prevention 101. Plus, I remember being a kid when a bunch of us discovered a dead body a block away. She was propped up upside down, under a billboard sign. It was a botched abortion. That's when I asked my father, "What the hell happened?" That's when I learned about abortions, which were illegal at the time.[43] But even before that, I had first learned about sex from the couple in the apartment next to us. I went over there one day and witnessed a few things. Next thing I know, I am lured into one of the rooms and it scared the hell out of me!

Separations and Reunions

When we returned after the camps, my mother went separately to Berkeley and rented a one-bedroom apartment, a block away from her parents' home, which was then occupied by her mother after her father died.[44] I don't know how both my parents' families were able to keep their homes because I know a lot of people who lost their houses. During the period that I lived with my father and his family (1945–53), I saw my mom about a dozen times. I realize that Berkeley may seem close to Oakland, but it was far away to a little kid. We were living in different worlds.[45] She was working for a local laundry and cleaners owned by a Japanese American family. The husband, William Tsuchida, had gone into the army in World War II, not in the 442nd or 100th but in an integrated, meaning White, outfit. He wrote a series of letters to his siblings in Berkeley and they got published. I remember my mom giving us a copy of the book, *Wear It Proudly*.[46]

Generally one of my mother's sisters would pick us up and take us to our mom's home in Berkeley because my mother didn't have a car. It was likely Yoshiko because she and her husband were one of the few Japanese Americans to buy property north of University Avenue, I think on Hearst. Her husband was drafted when he was thirty-two, so the army was taking them old. I was stunned when I saw his photograph in the Army uniform and asked him about his war experiences. Maybe one or two times, I rode my bicycle from West Oakland to my mother's South Berkeley apartment. At times, she came to my father's house. They must have made arrangements in advance because he wasn't around. I don't remember too much about the visits. She would always bring some presents for my brother and myself, some little knickknack.

From an early age, I learned not to ask any questions about my parents' situation. There are some topics in a family that you don't visit. That's true in every family, whether it's articulated or not. One example in my family was the dead silence whenever the war issue came up and what my father and my uncle Riuzo did during the war. I knew better than to bring that topic up at the dinner table or to either one of them separately because they wouldn't say anything. My brother was the only one that I could talk with about our parents. He had some private thoughts. At the time, I thought they were outlandish but now that I'm rethinking that particular issue, it may not have been that far off base. It was some heavy stuff. But we have no direct evidence, only speculation. Only my mother and father could tell you about the decision they made between themselves. I did find it a bit unusual to be living with my father. When I looked around the 'hood, single parenting was not uncommon. But it was usually the mother who raised the children.

My brother and I went to live with my mother when I was about fourteen. I recall being in junior high school. She was pissed when she found out that my father was living with an African American woman. We were still living with my father on Union Street. But when he got this girlfriend, he moved into the warehouse across the street, my grandfather's old noodle factory, and set up housekeeping with her.[47] I suspect the family would not go for her moving in. I'll never forget that evening when my mother and I were Christmas shopping in downtown Oakland. I was already living with my mother and she wanted me to help pick out my brother's present. I wish I didn't see them coming, but I saw them. Here comes my father and his girlfriend. I'm waiting for something to explode. I could tell my mother was upset. His girlfriend was upset. I knew her. She was a nice lady. I was scared 'cause I knew it could have been homicidal. But my father was so slick. He did some fast song-and-dance routine and we kept on going.

After that, my mom filed for divorce. I remember the judge asked for my opinion about where we should live. I had to be honest and stick up for my mother. I said my dad's not a bad father when he's around. The judge awarded custody of us to my mother. When my mother gets to ranting about my father, she tells the same stories over and over again: that their marriage was not a happy marriage; that he seemed to go out and play the town all the time. Then after the divorce, he paid no child support. Whether the first statements of hers are true or not, I'm not a judge on. But when it comes to the financial support after she gained custody of my brother and myself, I can attest to that. That's why I'm amazed that she was able to house, feed, and clothe my brother and myself while we were in high school. We both worked, my brother and myself. But the bulk of the economic contribution to the household was based on her $1.25-an-hour job. She made those dollars stretch. She cooked meals that were hearty enough, and you have to remember we're two young male teenagers who were quite physically active. I think about the mothers of friends of mine, and I get even more amazed by how single mothers are able to survive.[48]

Having a single-parent situation and moving around didn't bother me much. It was commonplace in West Oakland. In fact, one of my friends on the block was living with his grandmother. His mother lived about five blocks down. He said, "She doesn't live with me. But we can go and visit her because it's daytime." We go bippity-bopping down to her place. The front door opens and there are four or five scantily dressed females in there. His mother comes over and hugs him and he introduces me to his mother. She's hospitable and offers milk and cookies. We had a nice visit. That night, I told my father, I went to a place today and I met Roy's mother. He started laughing, "Let me tell you something son . . ." Lesson learned in the ghetto. Bordellos and brothels existed all over West Oakland. Life is hard. So when people asked me about my living arrangements, as strange as it may sound, bouncing around with my relatives didn't boggle my mind.

My mother had a one-bedroom apartment attached to the main house at 1519 Stuart Street in South Berkeley. Before we moved in, she had the bedroom. But after we moved in, my brother and I got the bedroom. I wish I could say that she moved to the couch in the living room. It was more like a big kitchen, with a stove, a refrigerator, and her bed. Still, my mother has stated time and time again that those three or four years when my brother and I lived with her were the happiest period of her life. I have to shake my head because if you look at objective reality, there wasn't too much for her to be happy about. She had two teenagers on her hands. We ate her out of house and home. She worried about paying the rent. But I do know that she was proud that my brother and I both graduated from UC Berkeley and financed our own way.[49]

But I felt cramped. I had moved from this spacious three-story house, where I had my own room, the parlor, but still my own. Plus, I wasn't happy about being away from my homies. That's why I was rarely home. First I took the bus to Herbert Hoover Junior High School. The Eighty-Eight or Market Street line was a direct connection, so why not let me finish there?[50] I had wanted to go to McClymonds High School, but after that riot there, my mama had me going to Berkeley High School. Then, it was walking to school every day. Nobody from Herbert Hoover came along with me to Berkeley, and my brother wouldn't be coming for another year. The dynamics of being the new kid on the block are pretty universal. But I ran into a guy in a similar situation. We were both looking for a friend, so we buddied up. Years later, we found out that our mothers had been in the same grade at Longfellow Grammar School and went to Berkeley High School. Earl Arnett Napper, who's African American, was the closest person to me next to my brother. Earl and I fought side by side, back to back. In addition, he had a slightly older sister, a champion ballroom dancer. We dated steadily in high school and again, years later, after she returned to the Bay Area.[51]

Cultural Excursions

I wasn't engaged much in extracurricular school activities in high school. The yearbook shows that I was the president of the Stamp and Coin Club. I considered myself a philatelist, a stamp collector. Now the difference between my brother and I was that I concentrated on stamps and he concentrated on coins.[52] I ended up in academia, he ended up in real estate. My brother, who was more physically attuned than me, also ran track. But I wasn't that interested in school activities. So after heading home to touch base with my brother, make sure he was cool and doing his homework, I'd hit the streets. Most of the time, I'd go run the streets of West Oakland, a half-hour bus ride away. Sometimes, I'd stay in Berkeley and go to the YMCA youth recreational program. Most of the Saints were members of the Y because some adult sponsored us as a club. Then home for dinner. My mother worked till six, so I'd meet her by the bus stop about six thirty and we'd walk home together. She'd cook and I'd finish up homework if I had any left or I'd do some chores around the house. Then I was out again. We didn't have TVs then, so I would go to the library or some other thing. My mother was quite liberal about my comings and goings, as long as she knew where I was going. My mother thinks Earl is salt of the earth and his mother thinks the same of me. So as long as I was out with Earl, my mother would say, "Go have fun."[53] Once there was this White dude named Bob. He was a legend of this area. He was the toughest street fighter in the history of the East Bay. Bob was married to Earl's cousin, that's how I got in tight with him. One day Earl brings Bob over to visit at my mother's home. It was Earl's perverted way of seeing some action because I almost dropped my jaw when I saw Bob at my door. My mother was at home. Bob steps into that small apartment, sits down, takes off his little porkpie hat, puts it on his knee, and is even carrying on an intelligent conversation with everybody in the room. After they leave, my mother says, "That's such a nice young man that Earl brought over!" My brother and I looked at each other and it was everything we could do not to burst out laughing. Here was the baddest White boy in the whole East Bay and my mother just thought he was such a gentleman.

One of the things I was doing when I was running the streets was getting a cultural education. Oakland was renowned for its cultural life and was part of the Chitlin' Circuit, which were clubs and theaters where Black musicians and entertainers could play. You have to remember the blatant racism against Black entertainers at that time. Maybe you could play at this club, but you couldn't enter through the front door. You couldn't stay at the same hotel as the White musicians in your band. You could be Duke Ellington, but there ain't gonna be no accommodations for you. So Black musicians would go on the Chitlin' Circuit hopping from major city to major city with sizeable black populations.[54]

Seventh Street was the mecca for Black clubs and theaters in Oakland. I'd go to places like Slim Jenkins's club, a legendary club like the Cotton Club in Harlem. Being young, I couldn't walk in the front door. I had to go in the kitchen. "Let the boy sit over here. He ain't bothering nobody." Ooh boy, yippee. I heard all the greats—Ivory Joe Hunter, Jimmy McCracklin, Big Joe Turner, and John Lee Hooker, the mogul. People don't know as much about Jesse Fuller, but he's from Oakland. Jesse Fuller worked on the railroad and was one of the most accomplished blues musicians on the West Coast. I drank it all in. But some aspects of their lifestyle that I saw made me nervous. Lots of drinking and the only time that I ever saw hard drugs in West Oakland, actually saw it, was heroin use among the musicians.[55]

Among the musicians on the Chitlin' Circuit was jazz vocalist and piano player Charles Brown, who recorded the hit song "Merry Christmas Baby." It's become a classic and is still heard around Christmastime. The reason why I'm bringing up Charles Brown, even though his base at the time was Los Angeles, is because his story exemplifies the saga of the African American coming from the South to the West Coast during World War II. This is what he told me personally as I got to know him well during the last years of his life. He was living then in a retirement home right here in Berkeley, and I would see him at a mutual friend's home. Charles Brown was from Texas and graduated from Prairie View College, with a bachelor's degree in chemistry prior to World War II. Because he's African American, he couldn't get employment appropriate to his education. The federal government announced an opening in the Bay Area for a chemist, so he applies. He gets the job and comes out. Then he walks in the front door, they see his brown skin, and all of a sudden, he ain't got no job. So what's he gonna do? That's when he cashed in on those piano lessons his mama made him take. In the late 1940s, he gets his big break with "Merry Christmas Baby." But because of the foibles of the musician's life, along with the great rip-off of Black musicians by the record companies and a slight change in the shifting of musical taste, his career goes down. By the late eighties, he's down to doing one-night stands and small nightclubs. It wasn't until

Bonnie Raitt struck up a relationship with him in the late eighties that the two of them made one of the biggest comebacks in the music world, with him featured as her opening act. She was known for her rock and roll, but crossed over into blues and credits Charles Brown with influencing her blues style. I became a fan of Bonnie Raitt when she was in the depths of her decline. I heard one cut she recorded and it had some pathos in it that I could feel, made me go out and buy that album. Of course, I also admire her politics. In fact, I met her recently at a demonstration where she spoke against the war. By the end of his life, Charles Brown received a presidential citation from Clinton for his contributions to rock and roll and gained the recognition that he so long deserved.[56]

Sweets Ballroom was a Black dance hall—actually more than a dance hall, it was a ballroom. In the 1920s or so, when dancing became popular, a number of ballrooms sprung up in Oakland. One was the Ali Baba Club, but it was for Whites only. Sweets Ballroom was the most-well-known ballroom in Oakland on the Chitlin' Circuit. As the fifties rolled in, their format changed from the big band to rock and roll and that's where I saw Little Richard and a lot of Chuck Berry.

I should also mention the burlesque houses. There are two Black burlesque houses in all of Oakland and both of them in West Oakland. There was the Moulin Rouge and the El Rey. Being curious about burlesque, I was able to unobtrusively take a peek. But my curiosity got the better of me when Tempest Storm married Herb Jeffries. A Black man marrying a White woman was scandalous—the talk of both the Black and the White communities. Here's one of the top strippers in the country, a White woman, Tempest Storm. I mean she was above Blaze Starr, above Sally Rand, she was the queen of burlesque. She married Herb Jeffries, the Bronze Buckaroo. At the time, cowboy movies were popular but because of race segregation, Blacks couldn't be stars in the White cowboy movies. So Herb Jeffries wrote, directed, produced, and acted in a series of westerns, earning him the nickname the Bronze Buckaroo. He later became an accomplished jazz singer. Next thing I know, people in the 'hood be talking about Herb Jeffries marrying Tempest Storm. Around this time, Tempest Storm was on the billboard at the El Rey. The night she performed, I tried to get a peek, but I never could weasel my way through the large crowd. I was curious what all the fuss was about. I knew she was all woman, otherwise she wouldn't be in burlesque. But the thing that boggled my mind was why everybody was upset about their marriage. I did realize that interracial marriages weren't common in those days. Now that I think about it, my father was in the only interracial relationship that I knew of.[57]

Then there was my uncle Hide, my mother's brother, who like Uncle Riuzo stayed a bachelor his whole life. When I was a teenager, he was dating one of the biggest stars performing onstage in North Beach, a White woman. One time he took me over to where she was performing, introduced me to her, and I got to watch her perform. I was underage but because he was going with her, I was able to go in and out of the bars over there. He had already taken me to the jazz clubs and showed me the movie theater on Market Street in San Francisco that showed cartoons twenty-four hours a day. I loved that one. So since I had already seen bits and pieces by that time, I wasn't that shocked. What shocked me was that he purchased a Jaguar sports car for her—and there was a foreclosure on the family home. I discover the car when I was going to visit my grandmother one day. I go hippity-hopping down the street and I see this brand-new Jaguar parked in front of the house. Well, I thought I'd died and gone to hog heaven. My uncle picked up a Jaguar! I had my driver's license by then, I'm going places! If you thought I was dangerous with the young ladies without the car, think of what I would be with the Jaguar! So I went running up the front stairs, I'm banging on the door. He won't let me in because she's upstairs in the bedroom. He did purchase a car for himself—a used car. He let me drive that around. But I was real disappointed because I never got to drive that Jaguar. Then there was a foreclosure on the family home. My brother was a real estate broker and I was able to get that information. And I said, "You're kidding?" But he went into the records.[58]

"Why Did My Father Leave?"

When I lived with my mom, I still saw my father's family from time to time. My grandfather had died in 1950, but I'd visit my grandmother, my *obaasan*, and Uncle Riuzo, riding my bike or taking the bus every couple of months or so. I always made sure to take them *omiage*.[59] If I said, I'm going to visit *Obaasan* and Uncle Riuzo, my mother might help me figure out what to bring. Maybe some food, or flowers from the backyard, or a judo magazine. I could go through the 'hood with impunity because I was still pretty well known.

The reason why I didn't see my father during this period is that he was moving all over West Oakland to avoid his legal problems and then during my first year at high school, he disappeared altogether. That was a shock to me because that was not something I foresaw. He left town and never came back. Nobody would tell me anything. Don't forget, fathers disappearing was not a new phenomenon in the 'hood. But I sat on my curiosity throughout my high school years. Shortly after I joined the military, I requested a weekend pass. I took a .45 with me and came back to Oakland, looked up one of my father's best buddies. I figured if anybody knew why he left, this guy would know. If he was reluctant to tell me, I was prepared to go to the max. I wasn't playing no games. So I went to this guy's place of business, turned the sign from open to closed, and we had a discussion in the back room. I asked him, "Why did my father leave?" and "Where was he?" He gave me answers to both questions. My father had left under adverse circumstances regarding this misunderstanding over the disappearance of the rent money, rent deposits, the items in the apartment house he was managing and it was thought that he and his partner, Blue, had something to do with it. He enlisted in the merchant marines and was waiting for the statute of limitations to run out. I talked to this guy around 1958. So my father had been gone for about four years and figured he needed to wait it out another three years. However, there were some other problems. Even if the statute of limitations ran out, he had left a lot of debts and unhappy people behind, not just my mother, but he owed the family physician money, he owed his attorney money, and I don't know who else he owed money to. So, when his seven years passed and he was able to return to California, he went to Southern California, settled in Little Tokyo, and spent the rest of his life down there.[60] I found out later that my father was also in the newspaper. He was accused of shooting his African American girlfriend. My mother has the clipping. It all caught up with him and he had to leave town in a hurry.[61]

While it was obvious to the whole family that I wouldn't have anything to do with my father, my brother connected with him. David wanted his son to meet his grandfather. My brother touched bases with me because he knew how sensitive a subject it was. I said, "Yeah, go ahead. I'm not going to get that upset because it's your life. You're an adult. It's your decision. What can I say?" So he went down to Los Angeles maybe once every couple of years to visit him. One of my cousins up in Sacramento, my father's favorite niece, also remained in contact with my father by phone and letters. The ironic thing is that of all the relatives, the sibling that had the harshest feelings about my father was this cousin's mother. It must have been twenty years ago, maybe a bit longer, when I was up in Sacramento, and this aunt cornered me at her house and urged me to make peace with my father. I almost had a heart attack. That meant I was the last one in the family that wasn't receptive to that type of a discussion.[62]

The only time I had any contact with my father since he left town was when my brother was dying. I knew I had to give my father a phone call to let him know. I had to drink a pint of vodka, trying to muster the courage. It was one of the hardest things I ever had to do in my life. But I don't know how I could have lived with myself if I didn't. A pint of vodka! I just told him the news and that if he needed to talk to David or visit, he only had a short time to do it. That was about it. The ball was in his court. I had delivered the message; I had done my duty. So he flew to Oakland, visited David at the hospital, and David passed away a couple of days later. Earl was there when my father showed up. I never saw him. He didn't tell me what time he was coming. He also didn't attend my brother's funeral. But then he didn't attend his mother's funeral. He didn't even attend his father's funeral and he was still in town then. I never talked to my brother about seeing our father, but by then, he was so far gone with that morphine sulfate. But I'm sure there was recognition. So you could say I never made peace with my dad. In a way, there was nothing left to resolve. Now it's ironic that I'm the one having to deal with my father's affairs after his death. Over the years I built this reservoir of strength, knowing that the time would come when I would have to tend to his matters. That was the other thing. Of all of my relatives, my brother has been the closest to me in spirit. I didn't have that connection with my parents at all. But I felt a close bond with my brother. It's pretty sad that he passed away, and the alcoholism was more of a symptom than the disease itself.[63]

MASCULINITY, RACE, AND CITIZENSHIP IN POSTWAR OAKLAND

The physical fight between his father and uncle was a pivotal moment in the development of Richard's masculinity. "For days afterward," Richard recounts, "I walked around with the hood of my jacket down over my head." It was "one of the most horrible traumas, emotionally, I had experienced." This altercation signaled a clash between the two primary masculine role models in his life. Uncle Riuzo, who lived with Richard, David, and their father in their grandparents' home, represented the embodiment of "good manhood." One of Riuzo's childhood mentors, K. Hata, was an advocate of Japanese assimilation into American society. Hata worked with the Japanese consul and respectable U.S. institutions, namely the Boy Scouts, YMCA, and YWCA, to promote the membership of Japanese American youth into racially integrated organizations. His purpose was to "assist the Japanese to assimilate [into] American ways and customs . . . to become useful citizens in modern ways."[64] In choosing the newly created Boy Scouts of America, Hata was promoting a normative American masculinity for Japanese boys. Those who founded the Boy Scouts in 1910 feared that an increasingly urban, industrial society and the feminizing influence of mothers and teachers were creating "soft" and "overcivilized" boys. To create physically and mentally rugged men (and responsible workers upon which to build the expansionist nation into a formidable world force), the Boy Scouts promoted physical activity, outdoor wilderness activities, and fatherly influence through the re-creation of the western frontier.[65] Riuzo apparently learned these lessons well. After his own scouting experience, as a young adult, Riuzo spent his Friday and Saturday nights in Oakland as Scoutmaster for a Japanese American troop and teaching a Red Cross junior lifesaving class.[66]

Richard's father, Shozo, also joined the Boy Scouts as well as junior high basketball and high school ROTC, but later in life he diverged from the pathway of normative masculinity and the respectable ways of the Aoki family.[67] Richard traces his father's descent into an outlaw lifestyle to his World War II incarceration. Although a young child at the time, Richard recalls his father's forceful views inside the camps, rejecting—or perhaps more accurately feeling rejected by—the model of American assimilationism. Even earlier, in the late 1930s, poor academic performance and a pregnancy forced Shozo out of the university. The loss of a college education and potential middle-class income and lifestyle, in conjunction with the ways the incarceration emasculated Japanese Americans, demonstrated to Shozo that he fell outside the bounds of what R. W. Connell calls "hegemonic masculinity," or the cultural ideal of (White) manhood.[68]

Shozo represented a complex masculinity. By the turn of the twentieth century, when industrialization had turned independent artisans into waged workers and the western frontier no longer existed for men to demonstrate their manly courage, part of how men "manufactured manhood" was to "rescue their sons from the feminizing clutches of mothers and teachers."[69] On one hand, as a single parent and homeschool teacher, Shozo exerted a strong masculinizing influence on his two sons. On the other hand, Shozo provided an increasingly erratic and unstable family life. Richard recounted: "There wasn't a regular routine every day because of my father's schedule. Some days he'd be there and some days he wouldn't." When absent, Shozo, it seems, was engaged in extralegal activities. Through the lens of an ethnic community with low rates of "social deviancy," such behaviors were condemned as personal failings that brought shame on the larger group.[70] When Richard witnessed his father's arrest on narcotics charges, he was mortified that "four White detectives in plainclothes, in the middle of the night," came to remove his father. As much as the arrest of his most significant masculine anchor destabilized his own sense of security, the arrest also increased his virility, at least through his peers' "male gaze."[71] Richard commented, "I suddenly found myself the big kid on the block because my father was so bad!"

There was no such perk when his father and uncle fought. Instead, seeing his father through the eyes of another respected male figure, it became increasingly hard for Richard to reconcile his admiration of his father with his father's declining parental presence and increasingly unstable behavior. In 1954, shortly before Richard's father vanished from his life, two events symbolized the divergent masculinities embodied by Shozo and his older brother, Shigeo.

After the 1952 Immigration and Nationality Act (also known as the McCarren–Walter Act) extended naturalized U.S. citizenship rights to Japanese Americans, Shigeo Aoki was selected to speak on behalf of recently naturalized citizens at a special Citizens Day in Oakland. Shigeo represented the responsible and patriotic manhood required of U.S. citizenship and fueled the model minority image of Japanese Americans. As an immigrant and former internee, Shigeo worked hard to become a successful businessman and raised three children, all of them honor students.[72] The Citizens Day celebration was presided over by no less than U.S. Senate majority leader William F. Knowland, longtime Republican Party leader and son of the editor and publisher of the influential *Oakland Tribune*. Shigeo's speech reflected the patriotic and assimilationist tones of the Japanese American Citizens League: "We are U.S. citizens because, to us, America stands for freedom, democracy and love of fellow man. . . . I chose to become a citizen of the United States because I love this flag and the republic for which it stands; because I believe in the guiding principles of our Constitution, because I want to be proud of my children and my children to be proud of me. And I believe that here in this wonderful country is the best opportunity in the world to accomplish these dreams."[73]

Shigeo's speech reinforces the notion of the United States as a pluralistic society, with opportunities for all who exhibit hard work, diligence, and frugality. These ideas build on the virtues of individual advancement through perseverance, promoted by Samuel Smiles in his influential *Self-Help* book (1859). The Japanese translation of *Self-Help* was an immediate and smashing hit after its 1871 release. Its translator linked individual achievement with national advancement, as the new Meiji government embarked on a program of rapid modernization and industrialization. These ideas may well have influenced Shigeo's father, a successful entrepreneur and family patriarch. The ideas in Shigeo's speech also anticipated the popularization in the 1960s of the model minority image, which served as a foil to Richard's choice of political protest through Black militancy. According to the logic of Shigeo's speech, the ability or inability to achieve success in such an open system resided primarily in an individual's personal attributes, rather than institutionalized racism or other structural barriers. Richard's father's apparent failure to display the values promoted in *Self-Help* resulted in the development of a "marginalized masculinity," R. W. Connell's terminology for a manhood developed at the margins of "hegemonic masculinity."[74]

A month after Shigeo was lauded in the pages of the *Oakland Tribune* for his outstanding citizenship and respectable manhood, Shozo also made the newspaper, but under very different circumstances. Shozo's alleged shooting of his girlfriend while living in an abandoned warehouse is perhaps the ultimate symbol of botched manhood. He failed in his masculine roles as economic provider and protector. He further abdicated his masculinizing influence and fatherly involvement in the lives of his sons, first when he relinquished custody of his children to his estranged wife and even more vividly when he abruptly split town.[75]

The divergent models of masculinities exhibited by his father, uncles, and grandfather provide a backdrop against which Richard developed his own brand of manhood, as he eagerly joined the army "to be a warrior," a pilot, and possibly "the first Japanese American general in the United States Army." He was going off to war to become a man.

4 "I Was a Man by the Standards of the 'Hood"

Joining the Army

So we leave West Oakland and fast-forward to Berkeley High School, where I was a conscientious student from 1954 to 1957. When I became a senior in high school, I began to think of what I would do after graduation. I hadn't been too happy at Berkeley High School. In looking at my options upon graduating, number one, I could get a job. During high school, I did decrease my activity in "extramural fund-raising" at night, primarily so that my mother wouldn't worry as much. I then worked as a gardener's helper, a parking lot attendant, a department store stock boy; those jobs gave me some idea of the job market, which looked pretty bleak. The second option was to follow in my father's footsteps and go back to West Oakland and start some "business" of my own. That would also worry my mother. By that time, I began to realize that in the long run, it was not a winning proposition. I was getting more civilized at that point.

The third option was to continue my formal education at UC Berkeley. I qualified for admission, but there were some things that held me back.[1] Number one, I don't recall any teachers actively encouraging me to continue my formal education. I got the feeling all they wanted was to get me out of there, period. Number two, though I was academically qualified, would I even be able to get into Berkeley? You have to remember that World War II was still fresh in the minds of a lot of people, and some Japanese Americans felt that Harvard might have been a better choice for me, that prejudice and discrimination would be less severe on the East Coast. Number three, it cost money. They didn't have financial aid programs then and scholarships alone don't do it. It's unfortunate that I didn't notice until I recently reread my yearbook how much encouragement I was getting from my female classmates to join them at Berkeley. But at that time, I had already decided to go to the military—my fourth option.

Here's the way I went into the military. I sat back and said, "I'm seventeen now, I can enlist." At the time, Ted Williams was considered one of the top baseball hitters in the country, hitting home runs.[?] He had this natural ability to see an object in motion and connect with it. This is really important if you're a fighter pilot. I passed that with flying colors. I was so happy. Then came the disappointment. They had too many fighter pilots in the air force at the time. The Korean War had ended, so they had a surplus of fighter pilots. If I waited a couple more years, they'd probably take me. They said I could sign on as an enlisted man in the army for four years and hope that openings would occur. The idea of waiting four years on a hope didn't strike me as reasonable.

I decided, if I'm going into the army, I'm going into the infantry. I'm going to war. I'm going to be a warrior. I'm not going to be stationed on no ship; I mean not in no Coast Guard. I ain't servicing aircrafts; I want to fly them. I figured it out. In twenty years, I could probably be the first Japanese American general in the United States Army. Some pathway had been opened up because of the 442nd. I knew of Japanese Americans who served in the U.S. Army—an uncle, a cousin, and one of my mother's bosses. I'd heard of Ben Kuroki in the U.S. Army Air Force. During World War II, they didn't have a single Japanese American pilot in the army air force. But Ben was a tail turret gunner. He was one of the survivors of the notorious Ploiesti oil field strike in Romania, where a hundred and fifty bombers went over there and fifty of them were shot down. I mean that's hard to take. He got a medal for it. So Sergeant Ben Kuroki's deeds were imprinted on my mind. Army sounded like a good place.[3]

So I'm seventeen years old, going to make my first career decision, independently and responsibly. Influencing me was my unhappiness at Berkeley High School and my desire to leave the 'hood. I might add, the boy can leave the 'hood, but the 'hood doesn't leave the boy, as a preview of things to come. Then too, economically I had to support myself. My mother had been patiently raising my brother and myself on minimum wage and needed some relief. Plus, there was universal military training, which meant everybody had to register for the draft at the age of eighteen and the chances of being called up were quite high. In other words, it was assumed that every young man would serve in the U.S. military at one time or another, whether they volunteered or were drafted.[4] I thought, since I'm going to have to serve anyway, I might as well go in now and get it over it with. So there was this push-and-pull effect, where I was getting pushed by my circumstances and being pulled by my desires. So I went down to the army recruiting office and said, "Here I am! Take me!" They were overjoyed. Here I was, a bright young one, volunteering for the military.

Next, I went to tell my mama. I'm going off to the war, Mama. I'm going to join the United States Army and I'm going to be an infantryman. Mama looked at me like, You what! Drug use was not as prevalent among the youth in those days, but I'm sure that might have entered her mind. What has this boy been smokin'? So I had the recruiting sergeant visit my mother. He came to our small apartment on Stuart Street where my mother, my brother, and I were living and went over his spiel. Because I was seventeen and hadn't graduated from high school, she had to sign off. This was October of 1956 and I was scheduled to graduate in January '57. That was around when the Soviet Union put down the Hungarian uprising. I thought there was going to be a war.[5] I knew that in time of war, promotional opportunities would come very fast. In fact, I even had the fantasy of a battlefield commission—that's when everybody else is wiped out and you're highest-ranking enlisted man left and they put you in charge, making you an officer right there on the spot.

All I wanted to do was get in as a grunt. Learn that stuff from working, start moving up the career ladder. My mother objected. I said, "Mama, this is the one decision in my life that I came to independently. I want to go. Plus, my country needs me now." She said, "I've been talking with some of my friends, especially Bill Tsuchida, who was a medic, and I think you should go into the medical corps."[6] I looked at her like, What?! He was a noncombatant; he didn't carry a gun. I don't like that. He was running around, fixing people up. In the army, I want to put the other people down. I'm from West Oakland. So a tug-of-war started. I wanted to get in the military, my mama wouldn't sign the papers because she wanted me to go into the medical corps because she had this impression that my survival would be enhanced if I were a medic. This flies against statistics. In Vietnam, outside of second lieutenants, medical corps caught the most hell in combat. Meanwhile, the sergeant called me aside and said, "Look, boy, I know what to do—a compromise. Sign up for the army, go in the medical corps, get your training, then request to transfer to the infantry." I said, "Can you do that?" So I said to Mama, "Okay, I'm a medic." She still didn't sign off because I hadn't graduated from high school. But the recruiting sergeant said, "Look, he's only four months from graduating. We're taking him right now. Tomorrow, we'll put him in a reserve outfit, and when he receives his high school diploma, we'll call him up for active duty."[7]

By that time I had read the autobiography of Audie Murphy, *To Hell and Back*. I'll never forget that title. Here was an enlisted man who was the most individually decorated hero of World War II. After he returned home, they made a Hollywood star out of him. Audie Murphy was like a role model to me. Man, he took a machine gun and took out twenty Germans! Whoa, he bad! He got his back shot up and he still has shrapnel in his abdomen from that other thing, accounts for that little limp there. I overlooked the fact that he got shot up quite a bit. He's young, he'll get over it. I figured I could take the hurt. I mean, I grew up in West Oakland, throw your best punch at me. So, there I was, I must have been on a cloud throughout the last four months of high school. I was leaving that funky-ass school. I was going off to the war.[8]

Military Misadventures

So three days after graduation, I report for basic training down to Fort Ord, California, a major training center for the U.S. Army on the West Coast.[9] I was feeling good! Before I go, I made my mother happier, I think, because I made her the beneficiary in the event that I didn't come back. Now you have to remember, ten thousand dollars in 1957 was a big chunk of change, considering my mother was only making a dollar and a quarter an hour.[10] I had done all I could to keep peace on the home front. Well, this has been repeated in millions of households, the boys at the Greyhound bus station and the families there, waving them off. I was eighteen. I'd been sworn into the United States Army. Even though I couldn't vote and I couldn't drink legally, I was a man by the standards of the 'hood!

My first night there, I get down the corridor. It's dark, it's cold, but it's cool. Then, I heard in the barracks, pass the word down, tomorrow night we're going to have a GI party. I thought, "Oh boy! I no sooner get in and we're going to have a party! Blessed me, I've died and gone to hog heaven." Well, the GI party was when they have enough men for a company—there were 250—we'd have to clean our barracks, which we were going to live in for the next couple of months. I remember being on my hands and knees with a toothbrush, cleaning the floors of the barracks. That was the GI party I had been excitedly awaiting all day.

Then it got a little bit stranger. The first couple of weeks, I had to take a series of tests. I took the Japanese language test to determine my fluency and I passed that one. I took the Officer Candidate School test, and ranked the third highest out of 250. By the second or third week, I was feeling pretty good. I mean they were working me to death, getting up early in the morning, running around doing various things, but then, they were starting to show me some respect. They gave me my first rifle. I said, "Oh boy, the M1 Garand!" Yeah! I knew about the M1 Garand. Due to my interests, I dug up manuals for it and everything else while I was still in high school. Then one day, a White southern officer, a second lieutenant out of West Point, misspelled the word "comman-der" on the black board. I wasn't the only one of the 250 recruits that noticed, but I was the only one who raised my hand. I used to do it all the time in high school. "Sir!" "What's the problem?" "I believe you misspelled the word com-mander, sir!" He looked at the black board and said, "What is your name again?" "Private Aoki, sir! 19572630!" That was my number, 19572630.[11] I sat down and I felt proud, not noticing this quietness around me. You can't cut a boy from West Oakland. For the next week, I was assigned a whole bunch of extra detail. They call them dirty detail because they're dirty. One of my buddies in another barrack in the same unit told me, his sergeant climbed all over that barrack that night and told them he never wanted to hear anybody in his bar-rack correct an officer like that stupid Oriental did. He would personally take him out. I was in for a week of dirty detail trouble.

When life gives you a lemon, you make lemonade. The first couple of days I had to do KP duty, kitchen police. That meant getting up early in the morning and working in the mess hall to prepare the meals for breakfast, lunch, and dinner. You don't get to go to bed until late, after the mess hall is all cleaned up. Presiding over was the mess sergeant, who is generally a grumpy old man. Here's the good news. During the downtime, this mess sergeant and I would have coffee and we'd talk. He was a White sergeant from the Midwest. He was a nice guy, what we called a lifer, a twenty-year man. I think he asked me why I came into the military and I said I came from a broken home. That was kind of an unusual thing in those days. Then he found out I was eligible to go to Berkeley and he kind of looked at me like, why didn't you go, boy? He shared with me that he also came from a dysfunctional family, that he beat his father up before he enlisted. He encouraged me to get out of the army and go to college. He was a high school dropout and that's why he was in the army. He said, "You have a mother and a younger brother." For a lot of people in the military that I ran into, that was their life. They had nothing else.

So after a couple days, I got new dirty duty orders. Cleaning heavy weapons. It's environmentally hazardous to your health because you're using caustic toxic chemicals to clean Browning Automatic Rifles, .30-caliber light machine guns, .50-caliber machine guns, and small mortars. But you make lemonade. I had the opportunity to fire a Quad .50, which is four .50-caliber machine guns mounted on the back of a half-track. You get into the seat and you aim that little sucker and you cut through a button and four .50-caliber machine guns go off at the same time. That's about the closest I've come to an orgasm with-out having sex in my whole life. I was stunned by the firepower of it all. So I was a little bit happy with that part because even though I had this thankless job of cleaning all these dirty weapons, I also was given the opportunity to play with all the toys I had read about and got hands-on experience. Most of the noncommissioned officers that I served under, once they realized how committed I was, would allow me more leeway than they would normal soldiers. Maybe it's also because I appeared to be a nice guy. When I said, "Can I fire this thing?" "Oh yeah, we got to test it anyway, boy! Better get up there in the seat now! Now point it over there, see where that thing is? Okay now! You ready?" "I'm ready." "Everything's in operating order?" Yeah, yeah, I checked all safeties off. "Push the button!" *Tttttt!* I said, "Whoa!"

Then after a couple more days, I got my third dirty detail and that was cleaning out the regimental headquarters. You wanted to make sure that thing was clean, clean, clean! I remember everybody was laughing as they were staring at me across the room, but I did the job. And it gave me access to the files. So I started going through the personnel files at another down period. I'm having my coffee and wondering what's in this thing. I started looking and I discovered a few things. Number one is the average educational level of a noncommissioned officer who was training us was eighth grade. That stunned me, in a way. But it also made sense. College education was not as widespread as it is today. Also, the pool of the noncommissioned officers—and they included poor whites, African Americans, and Filipinos—were what we called retreads. Let's say you were drafted in World War II and you served your time and you got out and you had trouble finding a job because you aren't a high school graduate. Another war comes along, they call you back. Why not serve twenty years because you ain't going nowhere on the outside. Number two is you don't have to be that bright to be a soldier. I'm not putting the soldiers down, but you don't need that much education to learn to blow somebody away. It's pretty well known that military weapons are the simplest weapons to handle and strip down and reassemble because they're designed for the industrial proletariat or peasantry whose literacy levels didn't have to be that high. So it makes sense why my buddy's sergeant climbed all over his group about my correcting that officer's spelling. On the other hand, I had respect for the noncommissioned officers because they've been through the war. In other words, all those training officers were veterans and not just fresh out of West Point.[12]

There was one time when I did challenge a noncommissioned officer. Somebody had told me if I could beat up the first sergeant, they'd make me a first sergeant. I think somebody had a joke in mind. What happened was I got KP on two consecutive days and I thought that was unfair. See, my name began with A, so I got the Friday weekday duty and then I got Saturday weekend duty. I was told the first sergeant was responsible and that if I can whip his ass, he'll promote me real fast. So I went to his office and I said, "Look, you did me wrong." He invited me to go out behind the orderly room after duty that night. I went back to the barracks and proudly announced that my buddies were going to see the whoppin' of their lives. This boy from West Oakland was going to be kicking some first sergeant's ass. That evening, the first sergeant and I meet behind the orderly room and half of dozen of my buddies are there, and I proceeded to get to work. I got knocked down three times. I wouldn't have gotten up after the first time down except my buddies were saying things like: "Man, I wouldn't take that shit from him! Come on, get up, boy! You can do better than that!" I didn't lay a hand on him and I was fast. He was bad! Every time he hit me, I went down and I don't even know where those blows came from. He did help me up after the third time and whispered, "You got guts, boy." I wasn't hearing too well because my head was spinning. He didn't permanently mark me, but I could feel my eyes swelling up. It was one of the most humiliating fights in my whole life.

To make me feel better, though, the next week, we all had to show up at this parade for the general or something. So I'm wearing my regular Class A uniform with my Mickey Mouse little sharpshooter medal on—that's what I'd earned that far. The dude comes out and I took one look. He's a master sergeant. That means he's got three stripes up and three stripes down. Then I looked at how many years he's been in the service—close to twenty years. Then I looked to see how many of those years he had been in a combat zone. He must have spent the entire World War II and the Korean War in the combat zone because he had six years of what we call hash marks. Then I looked at his ranger patch, and I said, "Oh, shit! He was a Darby's Ranger!" Darby's Rangers were the first American troops to hit Normandy, before the regular troops. They even made a movie called *Darby's Rangers* that I saw before I went off to the war.[13] He had a Combat Infantryman Badge, another one of those that you don't get out of a Crackerjack box. He had two Silver Stars. The way you can tell duplicate medals is they put an oak leaf cluster on your regular medal for each additional time you get the same medal. I said, "Two Silver Stars, a Bronze Star, a Purple Heart with three oak leaf clusters, and all those service medals. He was in Europe. He was in Korea. What didn't he do?" That fight was humbling. I didn't hold any ill will toward him. I just thought I had made an error in judgment; I should at least know who I'm going to fight before I challenge them. Had I known he had all that, I would have said, "How many more days of KP do you want me to do?" I think the worst part was when I told my buddies, "I'm going to whop his ass. You boys don't know it, but I'm from West Oakland." I got my butt whopped after bragging about the merits of being a West Oakland thug! How they laughed! I did berate myself for being really stupid because somebody tried to explain to me: "No, Richard, the guy ain't messing with you. It just so happens because your last name's at the beginning of the alphabet, you got the weekday duty and then you got the weekend duty and it happened to be back to back." But I think I overlooked this explanation because I was so anxious to kick his butt so I'd move up fast. Once I realized who I had messed with, I was careful after that regarding who I fought.

I did fight with a squad leader another time before that and I kicked his butt. Some White boy tried to run all over me, so I went up in his face and we started fighting in the barracks. You know sometimes you give somebody a little bit of power, they take advantage of it. He was an asshole, bossing everybody around, including me. So everyone in the barracks rooted for me to kick his ass. I realized I couldn't whip him with street fighting, or boxing, so I did a jujitsu move, the *tomoenage,* on him. I grabbed his field jacket, went backward over a bunk, flipped him over, he went into two bunks, the bunk broke off at one of the stands, and I was getting ready to go upside his head when somebody stopped the fight. So I learned you pick your fights. You first hope that you don't have to fight. When you do, you have to go all the way. With the first sergeant, I made an error of judgment. With the squad leader, I didn't.

About that sharpshooting medal I got, at one point, I was so good with the rifle that I was able to hit, with an M1 Garand with open sights—no telescopic sight—a twenty-four-inch bull's-eye at six hundred yards. That was phenomenal. Now, because they knew how good a shot I was, I was asked to help qualify other soldiers. Let's look at it this way: as an instructor, if your students don't cut it, you think they're going to keep you on? They'd see the cluster patterns of the bullets and know if a trainee wouldn't make the minimum score. So they'd say, "Come here, Richard. Go to point twenty-seven because they won't know who fired." I'd say, "How many points does he need?" "Twelve points." "So if I hit one bull's-eye and a shot in the six range, that would get him in the qualifications, right?" "Yeah. Can you do that, Richard?" Give me a break. That's only three hundred yards. Now, the reason why I was excited about being called upon was because I got extra practice—and respect because they'd say, "Aoki here is the best we got."

One time, while out on night maneuvers, I was the medic assigned to a unit of trainees. Rather than go to Fort Sam in Houston for my medical, surgical, and X-ray training, they held me back at Fort Ord for on-the-job training. This was a rare occurrence. There were several reasons for it. Number one, I was really good in all my classes. Number two, there was a flu epidemic at Fort Ord in 1957. The general hospital at Fort Ord got hit hard by the flu, and they needed medics fast. The third reason was they were aware that I was temporary. I had made clear to almost every commanding officer I reported to that I'm only staying in the medics until I could go to the infantry. They all looked at me as if I was crazy because most wanted to get out of the infantry and into the medical corps. So I'm retained at Fort Ord by fortune or fate and performing my on-the-job training at the general hospital. Whenever basic training units were conducting exercises, I'd be one of the people sent out to sit in the ambulance on standby in case there was an accident, and there were lots of accidents.[14]

So there I was one night during this training and somebody yells, "I'm hit! Medic, medic!" So I grab my little case, wait for the cease-fire signal to be sounded, and run up to avoid being hit by bullets. They said, "Cease fire," the floodlights went on, and I start running toward the guy that said, "Medic, medic, I'm hit!" Then an explosive charge goes off. The machine gun has stopped firing, but whoever was in charge of explosives was a couple of seconds off. I jumped up just as this explosive charge goes off and boom, I get knocked off my feet and hit the ground. Now there are two of us hurt. The other medics—there are a couple more out there—call the hospital: "You better get a couple of ambulances out here because we got some multiples now, including the corpsman you sent out." So we get back to the hospital. I'm conscious and I'm shaking my head and I'm trying to figure out what the shit happened. I couldn't understand how somebody got shot because the machine-gun barrels have four-by-fours underneath them so they would be eighteen inches off the ground for the people crawling underneath the barbed wire. What happened was they were using outdated ammunition. In other words, the military saved their brand-new ammunition for the front lines but used surplus ammunition for the training. A short round means that the powder in the bullet has deteriorated. Some of that ammunition I saw was twenty years old, maybe older. So instead of a flat trajectory, the bullet dropped and the guy happened to be where the bullet dropped. His wound was superficial. My case with the mistiming of the explosive was not serious either. I got a piece of shrapnel in my shoulder and I think I had a concussion. It was just one of those one-second, two-second things: had I stayed a second longer I'd have been okay. But I figured when the cease-fire hit and the floodlights went on, my job was to get to that guy as fast as I could. I was hippity-hop running and I hopped my way into a hospital bed.

The commanding officer wrote me a brief letter, dated March 14, 1957: "Dear Private Aoki, On behalf of the officers and men of the RFA Regiment I wish to convey our wishes for a speedy recovery. If there's anything we can do to assist in making your stay in the hospital more comfortable please do not hesitate to call."[15] He hand-delivered the letter to me during my weeklong stay in the hospital. If you'll notice, there is no mention of why I was in the hospital. What's he going to say? We're sorry that we fucked up? I didn't even tell my mother about this. To this day she doesn't know that I was a casualty. I'm just bringing this up to say that friendly fire was real commonplace. But they didn't call them friendly fire; they called them accidents. It wasn't until during and after Vietnam that they realized that a large number of casualties were the result of friendly fire.

A little further into my military service, I happened to go through the NCO Academy at Fort Ord. It's like the community college of the army. You can go for two reasons: to become a terminal noncommissioned officer or to transfer later into OCS, Officer Candidate School, at Fort Benning, Georgia. I was taking this class in sniping at the NCO Academy and was talking with a guy, not in the class but somebody I met in the army who had an MOS, Military Occupational Specialty, as a sniper. That's when he told me about what to do if you only have one shot left. Oh, this guy was good. In fact, to this day, I pass on his tips to others. You take out anybody carrying binoculars because they're either an officer or a forward field observer. You take out anybody carrying a handgun sidearm because that's probably an officer or at least an enlisted man with heavy responsibilities. You take out anybody carrying a radio because that takes out the communications part. Then he said you take out anybody carrying a Red Cross bag. I looked at him and I said, "Say what? Wait a minute man, the Geneva Convention said we're not supposed to shoot a medic because they're noncombatant." He said, "Look at it this way, Richard. What does a medic do? Patches up the wounded. What happens to the walking wounded? Well, if they're still walking, they send them right back to the front lines again. We can't be sparing nobody!" That's what war is all about. Now, from the moral point of view, it doesn't sound too cool. But when you're out there, you got to do what you got to do.

After that, every time I got into a simulated combat situation, first thing I did was take off my helmet with the Red Cross on it and put on a regular steel pot. By that time I had sergeant ratings. I took a razor blade and took off my chevrons. At the PX, I would buy these small metal insignias and put them underneath my collar so that you and I are the only ones that could see my rank. You've noticed my habit of putting my political buttons underneath my collar? The only person that needs to see my political button is whoever I'm talking to. But if you're looking from far away, you can't tell. You got a Red Cross on it, you take that sucka off! You use it for a rag. My medical kit? I used to find an empty ammo can and dump my medical kit because it's got that Red Cross on the side of it, which easily identifies you as being a medic. Then I would say, "I'm ready." I've had people look at me kind of strange, but nobody said a word.

After I had been in the service a few years, I volunteered to further my training and became an X-ray technician. I was number one in my class and it was decided to offer me a chance to teach the next cycle of technicians coming through. My assignment was to teach the X-ray physics part of the curriculum. Because I had one year of physics at Berkeley High School, it made me ace the final test for the class.[16] The reason why I bring it up is that that was the first formal teaching experience I had. I'm told I did a good job. Reason number one is I'd already been through the course and I knew it backward and forward. Number two is that by that time I was a junior NCO and I'd become accustomed to giving orders and I hoped I did it judiciously. Number three is the way they teach in the military is pretty straightforward. They give you a military manual and you just go by the books and make sure that the students get enough knowledge to pass the tests, which are standardized, fill-ins, multiple-choice tests. So that was my first experience in formal teaching, if I can call it that. By the time I started doing the political education classes for the Black Panther Party and later on as a teaching assistant at UC Berkeley, I had enough exposure that I was able to carry it off pretty well. I hadn't thought about that until recently, but the military is where I first realized that I could teach.

At some point, I was made barracks sergeant, in charge of a whole barrack. I was a corporal at that time and I'm sure there were others who had been corporals longer than me. But being barracks sergeant was not something people would scream and holler about, so when the volunteering part came in, I became the barracks sergeant. Everybody agreed I was a nice guy. I wouldn't be nasty to anybody. First thing I had to do was settle a dispute. The White southern soldiers wanted country and western. The African American soldiers wanted rhythm and blues. And my best buddy wanted opera. Maybe I wanted to say to the captain, "I don't want to be barracks sergeant," but I can't bring this Mickey Mouse thing to the captain. And these dudes are getting ready to fight. Okay, I got a solution, gang. Here's what we're going to do. We're going to have a couple of hours of radio listening time (we didn't have TVs in those days). White soldiers play country and western upstairs, the Negro soldiers play rhythm and blues downstairs, and my buddy who liked opera music, well, he's got to go to the latrine. This decision reflected my judgment as a leader in that I prevented a race riot from breaking out and everybody got what they wanted to a certain extent. I was very proud of myself for that one because can you imagine, two groups of people that had access to guns, having a little dispute about music?

On Patriotism, Racism, and Homophobia

You're wondering about my gung-ho patriotism during this time. After all, my father had gotten a little jaundiced to the government during World War II, but he wasn't around at that time. He had split town during my first or second year in high school. At Berkeley High School, where I went, red, white, and blue was the thing to do. They had me long enough to inculcate in me my duties as a citizen, and it made sense to me. Had I gone to McClymonds High School in Oakland, I might have gotten a more critical view of American history and society. I was also living with my mother at the time and she was more patriotic than my father.

In the 1950s, one could see the height of the public's respect for the U.S. military. I never had to wait more than fifteen minutes when I was hitchhiking if I was wearing my Class A uniform. I went up and down California. There was only one time that I got into a hassle when hitchhiking. At the time, I also believed in promotion based on merit. I thought it was great because I was accelerated in a number of positions that I held. To me, the military was different from the police. The police, they're killing us. But the soldier was there to kill for the country. So back then, I never thought of them as being one and the same. I remember that during my training, I went to this one Protestant church service on Sunday. You had a choice on Sunday morning of either staying in the barracks until noon when we could leave, or they would release us in the morning if we promised to go to church service. I figured I'm a Free Methodist, so I went to the Protestant service this one day. It might have been because I was tired from my arduous duty but I swear, that chaplain was up there pounding on the pulpit about "killing commies for Christ!" This was the Cold War period and it was fiercely anticommunist.

The only overt racism I can recall was when eight of us, a Chinese American, myself, and six African Americans, were being promoted at the same time, and the first sergeant, who was White, came back and said the colonel was not approving the promotion. I said, "Say what?" The colonel felt that he didn't want the majority of his noncommissioned officers to be minority. I'm thinking, the next time we go out on maneuvers, we going to have one less colonel in this division. Now here's what happened. The deal was if eight White enlisted men can be promoted at the same time, the colonel would go for it. So they went on a crash program to train and test and qualify eight White soldiers to be promoted with us. I was pissed at the unfairness of that! We had worked real hard, done everything we were supposed to do. I knew these other soldiers weren't qualified. I wouldn't have gone out on combat with them. We're out there in the boondocks and we're under fire, how am I supposed to count on him to work a .50-caliber water-cooled machine gun? And my life depends on it. That's the only overt case of racism I ever ran into. But again, it was the period of time. Had I stayed in maybe two years more, I'd have been out on those aircraft carriers, battling like the sailors did in Vietnam. Or maybe involved in one of the two thousand fragging incidents that occurred there.[17] Now remember, I believed in meritocracy at the time. I wouldn't have cared if they were all White officers, but they needed to be qualified. Some of the best sergeants I had were White sergeants; they were just brothers.

There are a couple of things I'd like to mention before we leave my illustrious military history behind. One time I got an overnight pass. When I got to town, I spotted a cocktail lounge to get a drink with my false ID. I walked in and I'm a little amazed at the plush carpeting, velvet drapes, Steinway piano. I sat down in this dimly lit bar and ordered a drink. It was something like a whiskey sour. I wanted to show the bartender that I wasn't just a beer and whiskey type, that I had some couth. A couple minutes later, a second drink was placed in front of me and the bartender points to a middle-aged gentleman seated way across the bar. By this time I knew something about barroom ethics and I told the bartender to reciprocate. Next thing I know the guy is sitting right next to me, telling me how he loves soldiers. I thought, "This is a little weird for my tastes." Then one of his hands went where it shouldn't have gone. He was sitting on my best side, on my left-hand side, so I was able to spin around, knock him off the barstool, and send him a few feet away. I was ready to use the barstool to hit him when I realized I couldn't stick around because I had false ID. Whether the civilian police or the military police came, I'd be in trouble. So I scooted out of the lounge, scooted back to the fort. The sergeant who just issued me my pass wondered what the hell I was doing back so soon, so I had to confess to him that I got into a little trouble and the police might be looking for me. I told him what happened. He started breaking out in laughter. He said, "What was the name of that lounge?" I said, "The Gilded Cage." He laughed even more. He said, "That's a faggot hangout. Every soldier on this base knows you don't go there, man." He was cool. He deleted the records to show that I had been issued the pass. The cops never did come around.

I've often felt a little guilt about that one. Then again, that was a natural thing to do in those days. When I was growing up, there were always whispers in the Japanese American community. In the African American community, the same taboo. Stonewall began the movement for the respectability of gays. San Francisco has always been known as a gay hotspot, but it wasn't until the gays started fighting back, after Milk and Moscone were killed, that their respectability started to come more to the fore. What I'm trying to underscore is that a group that is oppressed and discriminated against usually doesn't get attention unless they fight back. My personal thing is I don't care about a person's sexual orientation. It's their own business. If gays, lesbians, bisexuals, transgenders have legitimate grievances that need to be dealt with, they shouldn't be discriminated against because of their orientation. On the other hand, that man made a mistake when he put his hand on me. My reflexes were sharp in those days. I've had people comment, "I ain't never seen anybody move that fast." But that's partially because I was in good shape and I had good training, so I wasn't surprised I knocked him off the stool. In fact, my feelings came about after the physical encounter because I didn't even think about the whole thing until I dropped the guy.[18]

On Reserve

I was in the military a total of eight years—a combination of active duty, Ready Reserve, and Standby Reserve. I was in active service for almost a year. Then I went into Ready Reserve. When you hear about the reserves today, they're not really ready to go. They give them a month leave time for their employment, then three months of training before they send them over to Iraq. They called us "weekend warriors" because we had to attend one meeting a week and two weeks of summer camp at Camp Roberts in Southern California. Now the reason why my active duty time was more than most—about ten months compared to the usual six months—was that I volunteered for active duty on several occasions. If I saw something interesting, like they called for volunteers to do training with the Green Berets or something, then I'd talk to my company commander, who said, "Day one take Aoki." I got called up for the Berlin

Wall crisis in 1961 and the Cuban Missile Crisis in 1962. The last couple of years I was in Standby Reserves. That was all part of new program, the Reserve Forces Act, to encourage more people to volunteer as opposed to waiting for the draft.[19]

Proletarian Jobs

I separated from active duty in 1957. I got three hundred dollars in bustin'-out pay. Oh, whoopee! I went up to San Francisco and I blew all three hundred dollars in one weekend—checked in at the best hotel, nightclubs. Although I was still slightly underage, I had my military ID, which was enough for me to get into the nightclubs, bars, and strip joints. I returned to Berkeley that Monday, broke as ever.

Thus began my formal working-class history. I went to the California Department of Employment and they matched you with a job opening. I was informed that there was an opening for orderly at a local hospital. So I zippidied to the local hospital and went to the personnel department to apply for a job. The person in charge was stunned because of my background. In those days male hospital orderlies were quite common. Unfortunately, the wages were rather low, the minimum wage of $1.25 an hour.[20] As a result, the pool of hospital medical orderlies was a real mixed bag; I even ran across a number of alcoholics. They were mostly Whites and African Americans. Their educational backgrounds were probably at the high school level; no college. Because of my military training, I was hired right on the spot. "Can you come to work tonight?" "Yes sir, I'll be here. I have to go running to the department store to get myself my little white duckies, white shirt, short sleeved, white pants, white shoes, and stuff. But I'll be here tonight!" I was hired as a medical surgical and emergency room worker. I had to start on the night shift, but I didn't mind being low man on the totem pole. When I worked at the Fort Ord general hospital, I had been entrusted with a great deal of responsibility, which included giving injections and blood transfusions. I must have given thousands of immunization injections to troops leaving for overseas. So it surprised me a bit that I didn't have much latitude in the decision-making sense at the regular hospital. As an orderly, you can't do hardly nothin'. I did get called into the office one time for commenting about a nurse who I thought did the wrong procedure on a patient and was told that I was correct in my observation but I should confine my thoughts to myself. I said, "Okay, I understand." But I had a job. Got my own apartment. Yippee! Didn't realize I was doing some block busting too.

My apartment was off San Pablo here in Berkeley, a Whites-only area. I was one of the first Japanese Americans to move north of University Avenue. When I went in to rent the place, I was wearing my army uniform. I was still proud. I even went to my former high school and paraded around a bit. I was back. I had done good! There were comments from some of my fellow students about how surprised they were that I had turned legit. In other words, usually when kids disappear from the 'hood, they go to serve time. I think the manager was probably a veteran himself and that's why he rented to me. He looked at me like, "Ay boy, you ain't Black so I guess it's okay." About a year after I moved in, he showed me the restricted housing covenant.

So there I was beginning my civilian employment history at the bottom of the occupational rung, but with an honest job, at minimum wage. And I was minimally satisfied, except things began happening. About a year later, I set up housekeeping with a nurse. She got a job at a hospital in ritzy Marin County. She told me that there was an opening for a hospital orderly there, and wouldn't it be nice if we could be in the same place? So I went over there with my short résumé. Although I was the most qualified of all of the applicants, they couldn't hire me. I said, "Say what? This doesn't compute. Why?" I was told the patients wouldn't understand. We have to remember this is a hospital in Marin County, a bastion of upper-class White society. I still had my job here so what's the big deal? But racism had reared its ugly head, interfered with my ambitions for working-class upward mobility. I don't care about sitting in at an old lunch counter, but when you're talking about jobs, you're talking about something serious there.

I'm setting up housekeeping, I got my car, but I'm working a minimum wage job. I figure out that I can make more money as an agricultural worker because in the fields, I was told, you're paid by the amount of work that you do. Now, I was under the impression that the more you picked, the more you got paid. My two talents would be realized because I am a hard worker and a quick learner. I'll do anything if I can earn a decent living. What's the big deal about picking fruit? So I went down to the lower part of downtown Oakland, where the labor contractors gathered early in the morning—five, six o'clock—to put together crews to work in the agricultural fields in San José. In those days San José was an underdeveloped city and there were beaucoup farms there. I signed on to pick strawberries and got on an old beat-up chartered bus with the rest of the workers who gathered that morning. Most of them were winos who did that type of work just so that they could get enough for their room and a bottle. But I had a different plan. I was going to work hard and come home rich. So I got out in the field and it started getting warm. I didn't think too much about that. Then I started picking strawberries and I said, this isn't that bad a job because there's nothing like fresh strawberries. I was picking a strawberry and putting it in the basket bag; picking a strawberry and eating one. They tasted delicious in the hot sun.

I worked my ass off, but I began to notice that there were other workers there beside the winos. The first group of workers that impressed me was the Filipino workers, the *manongs*. These were older Filipino immigrants who had worked all their lives in the fields, and looked that way. I said, "Damn, these dudes work hard. They don't complain, they just do their business. Salt of the earth." Then I observed the Mexicans. There were not only men out there, but there were women—wives and sisters. That wasn't half as startling as see-ing their kids there. I said, "Wait a minute now, what are these kids doing out here? Shouldn't they be in school?" I was a bit naive there. I felt like there was something wrong. So I'm talking to one of the Mexican guys and I asked him, "I ain't jamming you, but why aren't your kids in school?" Then he told me that, number one, because they follow the crops, this disrupted their children's education. Number two, because of immigration laws their kids were like invis-ible. That's when I began to see that there's a bigger problem that I'm not quite aware of. Then, at the end of the day when they tallied up my earnings, minus the transportation costs, the water, the baloney sandwiches for lunch, I made eight cents an hour. Not only that but I had a stomachache too because of eating all those strawberries.

So that ended my career as an agricultural worker and I went back to the orderly business. But I still wasn't making much money. So I picked up driving trucks, a nonunion job. As I started to learn more about working-class condi-tions, I began to realize that I would be better off in a union. I was trying to get into the Teamsters union because their drivers were making good money. I will admit that I was anti-union when I graduated from high school. It's no acci-dent that labor history is seldom taught in school. For one, the class monopoly of the educational system would prevent the widespread dissemination of working-class struggles. This is similar to the neglect of ethnic history—African American, Asian American, Latino American, Native American. For another, the labor movement has a violent history. I'm not just talking about the physical brutality between the police and the workers, but also the corruption at the top of the unions. It disturbed me that James Hoffa, the head of the Teamsters nationally at that time, was so obviously corrupt. I asked some of my fellow truck drivers who were Teamsters, "I don't understand why you tolerate such a crook"—and I whispered it because I understood he's a powerful person. One driver told me in essence, "He may be a crook but he's our crook." Until Jimmy took over the union, they were working under harsh conditions for low wages. Jimmy gave them respect. Jimmy gave them their living wages. As long as Jimmy delivered the bacon, they were going to vote for him.

While I worked as a truck driver, I got a proletarian experience and I started meeting people who were former members of the Communist Party, the Socialist Workers Party, the IWW. I often repeat the story that Malcolm X told. When the house is burning, the house slave runs around trying to put out the fire and save his master. But the field slave hopes the flames blow harder and burn down everything.[21] Because of my work experience and my political discussions and readings, I became aware that I was a worker, a field slave. I started reading a lot when I entered the civilian workforce, but this time I was searching. In the past I was scanning and then I'd devote time to certain areas that piqued my interest—science fiction, military history, maybe some novels that related to social issues, like James T. Farrell's trilogy on the hardships of life as an Irish American working-class person. But now I was reading material about the pressing social issues of the day. As I read, I noticed that the people who were the most articulate in defending the rights of the workers were these ex-Communists.

I ran across several works that explained the whole agribusiness to me. The first thing I read was *The Grapes of Wrath* by John Steinbeck. In that novel he recounts the saga of a poor midwestern farming family who was dispossessed by the Depression and came to California in search of employment and a better life. Though they were White I could understand the pathos of that. Then I saw the movie with Henry Fonda. I'll never forget what Fonda said as he was leaving his mother about how he would be wherever there was oppression. So, I said, "Wow. That's heavy." Here he is, he gets in all this trouble, a decent person, trying to do right, his best friend's killed, the law's after him, he's got to leave his family, he's got to leave his mother. She said, "Where are you going? What are you going to do?" That's when he replies, "Wherever there's oppression, I'll be there."[22]

Though I had been so patriotic, this felt like no big change for me. I was saying, "Wow! This hit the mark here. Maybe the people that were badmouthing John Steinbeck were off base. Let me read some more." Being a fast reader and having the time, I went to the library and read practically everything Steinbeck wrote. The work that he's never been given adequate credit for was a book entitled *In Dubious Battle,* about the exploits of a communist union organizer.

I'd learned by that time that Steinbeck was a local boy, born and raised in the Salinas Valley. So he wasn't just writing off the top of his head, like a lot of writers. He was writing about something he knew about. Not only that, but he was putting a spin on it that was contrary to the American myth of free enterprise—a decent day's wages for a decent day's work. I might say I was mildly disappointed in one of his last books, *Travels with Charley,* which he wrote based on a cross-country trip he took with his dog to discover the heart of America. I thought that was a bit mawkish, but that kind of revealed a biased side of me regarding his writing. It was written in 1962 and by that time I had a strong political position regarding the United States, so naturally I was a little taken aback. But this is not unusual, where early in a person's life they're a firebrand but mellow out through the years. I like to think of myself as not being in that category but history will only be able to set that straight.

Then I ran across an author by the name of Carey McWilliams. Now, I was already familiar with McWilliams because he had written a book about prejudice against Japanese Americans. It was one of the first books I ever read on the internment of the Japanese in the United States. Then I ran across *Factories in the Field,* written about the same time as *The Grapes of Wrath,* but *Grapes of Wrath* was more popular because it focused on the White agricultural working class, whereas McWilliams focused on Mexican Americans. Then I ran across another book of his, *Brothers Under the Skin,* which was devoted to people of color. I said, "Lord have mercy."[23]

It was about this time the presidential election of 1960 occurred. It was my first time being eligible to vote.[24] The two candidates were Richard M. Nixon and John F. Kennedy. You'd be surprised that I voted for Nixon. Here's why. I had had very little political education up to that point. But I did know that Franklin Delano Roosevelt signed Executive Order 9066 [which led to the incarceration of Japanese Americans in 1942] and was a Democrat. So I was critical of the Democratic Party. Then, because of my association with the African American community, Abraham Lincoln of the Republican Party stood out as a person of integrity who was known for winning the Civil War and ending slavery. So I was anti-Democrat and pro-Republican. Plus, I still held the belief that hard work will get you rich. The issues were obviously clear to me. Richard M. Nixon was a relatively poor White boy from California, had a down-to-earth wife, was anticommunist, and was raised as a Quaker. We know that the Quakers opposed the internment of Japanese Americans. We go over to the other side and we see John F. Kennedy, a rich White boy, whose wife appeared to be a dilettante socialite. It was rumored that not only was he pro-Communist, but he was also pro-papist, that if he was elected president, the pope in Rome would run the United States.[25] With that knowledge in hand I marched off to the polling place in 1960 and cast my first presidential vote for Richard M. Nixon.[26] At the time, the internal logic of my reasoning was compelling. But the truth of the matter is that in 1960 the extent of my false consciousness was pitiful, and I didn't even know it. I had agonized over that decision because it was my first presidential election. I already had classified myself as an adult when I signed those army papers at age seventeen. I figured if I was old enough to be killed, I was a man. So voting was one more sign of reaching manhood.

Friedrich Nietzsche was the first philosopher who attracted me, especially his book *Beyond Good and Evil*. I'm well aware of its misuse by the Nazis. However, I was attracted by his philosophy, which appeared to have some answers to basic questions involving societal issues and possible solutions. I was intrigued by his theory about the *Übermensch*—it's a German word meaning overman, but not in the same vein as the Nazis, who felt that the superman was racially superior. I thought about it more in the sense that in every society there's a small minority who sees more, understands more, and can do more to improve society. This is similar to W. E. B. Du Bois's notion of the "talented tenth," though I didn't read Du Bois until maybe ten years after discovering Nietzsche. In addition, Philip Wylie wrote a book in 1942 called *Generation of Vipers*, which was a harsh critique of American culture and American institutions. He was an iconoclast of the first order and lambasted American cultural mind-sets. He got into a lot of trouble because of his attack on "momism," where he blasted the image of the modern American homemaker of that period. Years later, he wrote science fiction. This was a way to get around the Red Scare because these science fiction writers were really writing about contemporary society. It was social criticism disguised as fiction. The genre also provided a great deal of opportunity to explore alternative societies. Philip Wylie's also the author of the best seller *When Worlds Collide*, which also became a blockbuster movie. Nietzsche and Wylie were two philosophers I felt most comfortable with during the early sixties.[27]

Then I picked up a rare copy of the *Writing and Speeches of Eugene Victor Debs*. I was told that he was influential in labor organizing and that he was a socialist. That didn't scare me that much—at least he wasn't a Communist. Being a socialist was a little more acceptable. I read his book and was inspired. He wrote, "I do not want to rise above the masses, I want to rise with the masses."[28] That's a *Grapes of Wrath* philosophy. Powerful! Eugene Debs was also for universal union membership regardless of ethnic group. This was a contrast to Samuel Gompers, who founded the American Federation of Labor, which really was an association of craft unions that was anti-ethnic to the core. When U.S. labor history is taught Gompers's name comes up as one of the giants who helped better conditions. But he didn't allow in Asian workers or any unskilled workers—only the White labor aristocracy. These sentiments continue to this day in a way. I remember when Watts busted loose in 1965, I was working in this one factory where 90 percent of the three hundred people working the line were White southerners. Half of them didn't show up for work the day after the Watts riots. I asked the foreman, "We got to get the show on the road. Where the hell is everybody?" He said, "Man, they're at home in Rich- mond or wherever in their tract homes, and they got their front doors barri- caded and their guns out for that invasion coming in from Watts." I said, "There ain't going to be no invasion coming from Watts." So on one hand, these coworkers of mine were strong union people, you know proletarian-oriented, class-conscious workers. But when it came to race, half the workers, being White southerners, were freaked out over Watts. I was stunned.

Then, I was given a book called *Labor's Giant Step,* by Art Preis, who was a Trotskyist. It dealt with the organization of the CIO, Congress of Industrial Orga- nizations, which was far more progressive than the AFL. Of course, their union- izing heyday was the 1930s. I was amazed at how much I didn't know about even recent labor history. While I knew about the Depression, I didn't realize that there were upsides of the Depression, like the organization of the indus- trial working class. Now, the fact that the AFL-CIO merged is hard for me to venture into because of the different history of the two groups. The Com- munist Party—and it has to be candidly admitted—played an important role, along with the Socialist Workers Party, in the organization of the CIO. Their major contribution included inclusion of ethnics in general, but African Amer- icans in particular, in the industrial unions. I was dating somebody at that time and she later became a leading member of the SWP. She was just joining that group at the time and she's the one who gave me *Labor's Giant Step.*[29]

When I first ran into the Young Socialist Alliance and Socialist Workers Party crowd, they were more than happy to provide me with a list of suggested readings. Later, the Black Panther Party had their reading list as well. So I was just gradually absorbing this stuff. There was a constant process of theory and practice. I wasn't aware of dealing with contradictions adeptly at the beginning, but I learned to read and think more critically. What began as a process of experiencing something led to my reading books that enhanced my understanding of the social phenomenon and economic foundations of it all. It made sense to me. So I was able to learn the theoretical stuff from others who had researched and thought deeply about the issue. Then I was able to test my objective material conditions against that theoretical construct. I didn't think about it at the time, but I did realize that there was harmony between objective reality and theoretical construct, otherwise there's confusion. If there's confusion, there's not going to be a revelation of truth. Not the Almighty Truth, but a better understanding of society and its social problems such as racism and economic inequality. If you notice, I'm going back and forth from the readings to the job and the job to the readings, because that's the way I developed my class consciousness.

I remember the first labor strike I participated in. It was in the early 1960s. I was in the printer's union and we went on strike here in Emeryville.[30] The union's business agent drove up to the strike line in his Cadillac, popped open the trunk, and started distributing materials. First of all he pulled out a couple dozen ax handles he bought at the hardware store. Then he pulled out three-by-five index cards. Then he pulled out a box of thumbtacks. We put "On Strike" and our union local on the index cards and we thumbtacked them to the ax handles. Then we were told not to let any trucks in or out of the plant gate. After the first truck got its headlights and windshield busted, no trucks went in and out of the plant gates. We won that strike. Unfortunately the more conservative international that this union local belonged to considered it a wildcat strike and refused to recognize our strike—declared us outlaws in a way—even though we won. We countermoved that by joining the more radical international. I found out later from the business agent that his claim to fame was that he was the one that welded the gate shut when the workers took over the Ford River Rouge plant in the 1930s or '40s. We were having a drink at a bar afterward and I said, "You're not like the regular business agents I've seen in the union. I mean, you've got your Cadillac, that comes with the territory." In those days, Cadillacs were like status symbols, not only among the aspiring working class but ethnics. My father had a Cadillac LaSalle that made him the big man on the block. So I understood the importance of a Cadillac. What I wasn't prepared for was that this business agent had been a member of the Communist Party too at that time, during the thirties.

The final industrial job I had before going to UC Berkeley was at a paint factory in Berkeley. I started on the assembly line. But they needed paint technologists for the quality control part of the assembly line. So I went through a program at Oakland City College to secure a certificate as a paint technologist and started making seriously good money—six dollars an hour![31] However, there were some minor problems I ran into. At one point I was asked if I would like to be a working foreman, coordinating the activities at both the production line and lab for the swing shift, the evening shift. I would be paid a quarter more an hour, which was a big-time raise back in the mid-1960s. So I was happy about that. If a big production order had been scored by a salesperson, then sometimes we would work twelve-hour days, seven days a week. It was hard, backbreaking work, but the paychecks at the end of those periods were really great and I started putting money away for college.

During the first couple of nights as working foreman I sat down and analyzed the flow of the production line. I'd been at that paint factory more than a year now and I'd worked all the shifts—day, swing, and grave. So I came up with a plan to increase production by some 20 percent, with a minimal amount of input by workers. It was just a matter of scheduling certain things at certain times and letting the machines do the work. The only extra work was relaying the setup times that would be required when we ran a bit over. In actual numbers the production capacity went from 100 to about 120 percent. I said, "Wow, they picked a good man for the job." I can sit here in my little office and occasionally go out to the production line and see that everybody's doing what they're supposed to be doing. Go down to the lab, see that everybody's doing what they're doing. Then go back to my office. However, the union representative came up to me a couple of nights later and said that he had a little problem with me. He said, "Congratulations on being made foreman. You're all right. On the other hand, you are getting a reputation." I said, "Oh, a reputation." "As a rate buster." A rate buster is somebody that's pushing the production line a little bit too hard. Not only that, in the union contract, the workers had agreed to X amount of production per night. By my making it more efficient, and increasing it by some 20 percent, I was not a team player here. In addition, if I did not cease and desist, an accident could possibly befall me, like a wrench dropping from the third floor. I got the message real quickly, and I said, "Maybe I'll go back to production or quality control. I don't think this working foreman thing is a good idea on my part because I got too much pressure on me. I got the boss giving me more money and pushing me forward and I got my fellow workers saying, 'We don't begrudge you or your quarter more an hour, but you're making us look bad. Plus, we signed this contract three years ago. You were there.'"

Some might say unions are inefficient; they're slowing down production. But I started to have a better understanding of capitalism by that time. I didn't like being a pawn in the struggle between capital and labor. I have to admit that in 1960, when I voted for Richard Nixon, I was antiunion. But when I became a worker and saw the advantages of being in a union and then began reading labor history, I became a big supporter.

So I'm still working at the factory and I'm back on the line again. No sense in getting hurt over this one. Then one day I made a bad mistake. I misplaced a decimal point on my sample brought over from the lab and ruined ten thousand dollars' worth of paint. Instead of 1.6 pounds of royal blue, I told the production manager to put in sixteen pounds. I'll never forget when the guy said, "Are you sure?" "Aw, man, I've done this hundreds of times, I'm sure." "Doesn't look right to me, but if you say so, I'll do it." That threw that product way out of standard, way out. The color was off, the viscosity was off, the pH was off. Being workers, we got industrious. The foreman said, "We might be able to fix it." So they took the time and put it through another mill to see if they could mill out the impurities. It didn't work. Then they put it into another mill to improve it and that didn't work. By this time the plant manager and the people upstairs had caught wind that there was something wrong. Being capitalists, they quickly decided that the line was taking up too much time trying to correct the mistake I made, they took the tank and they put it in the discard yard. I could see ten thousand dollars flying away from the company. Then I thought about retribution. It was my mistake. I owned up to it. Everybody knew it, even if I didn't own up to it. I sweated about that. If they take it out of my salary, that's going to be a long time to pay off ten grand. I don't need this debt on my shoulders right now. Or, even worse, they could say, bye.

For a couple of weeks I kept my mouth shut about that issue, hoping people would forget about it. Then I talked to the plant manager. I had to. I said, "You remember that tank of stuff that came through a couple of weeks ago that had a little problem with it. What did the bosses upstairs finally decide to do to resolve that issue?" What he told me shocked me. He said they had a meeting about it. I said, "You had a meeting about it?" Probably was the only thing on the agenda. Not only was it ten grand worth of paint, but it was one of the highest-priced products they had, under their normal labeling. He said, "They made a decision to can the product." "They did?" "They sent it to canning. Put it into one-gallon containers. Put another label on it, not the company label." Oh, before they sent it to canning, they thought maybe they could use it to paint the interior of the factory. But it was so defective that the plant manager said, "You ain't painting my factory with that messed-up stuff. That'd be chipping and cracking and peeling in a week!" So they canned the stuff. Put another label on it. Then called the sales staff in and said, "Look, tell the people when they get out on their rounds that we got a deal for them. We got a sale on it this week, half price." They knew how defective that product was, and they still have the nerve to can it and ship it out to be sold. And they sold it, as is. I didn't say anything because I wanted to keep my job. But I did learn a big lesson about the functioning of capitalism.

On Leaving the Military

So I'm working, setting up housekeeping with my girlfriend, and trying to save money to go to college full-time. My eight years in the Army Reserve was up and I got my honorable discharge in late 1964.[32] The army called me in and asked me to reenlist. They figured since I had already served eight years, signing up for another eight and then four more would give me twenty years and a pension. As an inducement to reupping, as they call it, I was promised three things. Number one, direct admission to Officer Candidate School because everybody knew I was qualified. I had taken the OCS test and scored third highest out of 250. Number two was assignment to the 101st Airborne Division, which I had requested several times but was denied because I was not as qualified as others. There were two airborne divisions in the United States Army: the 82nd and the 101st. I've always liked the 101st because of their screaming eagle patch. Number three was a reenlistment bonus of thirty-five hundred dollars. Well, I didn't break stride in my haste to leave. I politely declined their generous offer because by that time I had acquired a moral opposition to the war in Vietnam. I explained it to the colonel in charge that I was ambivalent about the U.S. government's policy on Vietnam. As a noncommissioned officer, it would be difficult for me and dangerous for my men to be in combat because if one has doubts, that could slow down the decision-making process and in the military that could be fatal. So I said, in deference to my safety and above that, the safety for those who served under me, it was best that I left.

In retrospect, the decision to go into the military was a good move and the decision to leave the military was a good move. I went into the military enthusiastically. It didn't disappoint me in a lot of areas. There were a few bumps in the road, some of the racist incidents that I saw and some of the incompetence, but by and large, it was a good experience. If it hadn't been for the war in Vietnam, I probably would have been serving twenty years and retired by now. I'd be the first Japanese American general of the United States Army! But I had become much more aware of political things and after I left the army, I was freed up to work in the radical movement for justice.

MILITARY MISADVENTURES AND
COLD WAR MASCULINITY

Two photographs of Richard and his brother, David, are revealing of the ways Cold War militarism impacted their lives. The first photograph shows two boys, aged six and seven, dressed identically in striped shirts and overalls, using their left arms to steady their right shooting hands, with eyes peering down the top of their toy guns. Their guns look like crude replicas of semiautomatics or Colt .45s developed after the western era and used in the postwar period. With looks of determination, especially in Richard, they aim at an unknown enemy. If this had been the nineteenth century, they might have been shooting at Native Americans, played out in countless fantasies of cowboys and Indians. If this had been World War II, they might have been shooting at "Japs." But the photograph is dated May 1946, at the beginning of the Cold War, suggesting that the enemy targeted by these boys were "commies" or other alleged subversives.

The second photograph, dated July 1948, shows the same boys, but now with revolver-style toy cap guns and holsters so large they cover their bodies from waist to knee. The big guns these boys carry symbolize the growing strength of the United States as a military, political, and economic world power. Their holsters, cowboy hat (on David), and six-shooters signify their play as a western fantasy. Scholar Michael Kimmel discusses how the explosion of western novels and films in the twentieth century enabled American men, struggling with a crisis in masculinity, to feel manly. By the late nineteenth century, increasing industrialization and urbanization alienated men from control over their labor and bodies and created a need for proof of manhood. Prior to that, writes Kimmel, the independent artisan, small farmer, or shopkeeper achieved a secure manhood through ownership of his work, craft, or body, and the landed gentry exerted power through landownership. Those who could not secure work or property could "go West, young man" to tame the wild frontier. But with the closing of the frontier in the late nineteenth century, manhood no longer achievable through physical expansion could still come through escape to a fictionalized frontier. The heroic cowboy of the western novel served to re-create a rugged manhood for Americans facing a "crisis of masculinity."[33] Although western heroes were notoriously White (another way for fragile manhood to control the encroachments of Reconstruction-era Black rights, women's rights, and later the Civil Rights Movement), Japanese American boys could identify sufficiently with

America, in reality or as aspiration, for them to play out frontier fantasies of masculine power.[34]

Richard and David were merely boys playing, one might argue. The themes of their play, however, were not arbitrary, but created in a particular historical and gendered context. The Cold War and the masculine ideal produced in that era loom large in Aoki's narrative, shaping his ideas about nation, work, masculinity, and family. Aoki begins this chapter as an enthusiastic soldier and ends as an increasingly class-conscious worker. Both experiences were shaped by Cold War imperatives. The events of World War II—territorial invasion, colossal killings, and nuclear destruction—created widespread fears, in the United States, Soviet Union, and throughout the world, of nuclear attacks and threats to national security. The Cold War was also an ideological struggle between capitalism and communism, fueled by national desires for global dominance. The United States responded with massive militarization and intense state repression of subversive activities, real or imagined.[35]

The unprecedented material prosperity in the postwar period could have inspired in the United States a sense of economic and political confidence. Instead, the paradox of the Cold War was that there was anxiety amid abundance. In the midst of plenty, the nation suffered a foreboding anxiety about external and internal threats to its still fragile and recently acquired world power. Recent events spurred this anxiety. The Great Depression hung over the nation as a reminder of how quickly prosperity could turn into despair. Japan's bombs dropped on Pearl Harbor shattered America's sense of invincibility. So despite its Allied victory and its growing world hegemony, the United States had a foreboding fear that Soviet threats from abroad and subversive threats from within would weaken the nation. Ongoing Soviet threats of nuclear annihilation, exacerbated by the USSR's launching of the world's first intercontinental ballistic missile and first human-made satellite, *Sputnik,* both in 1957, inflamed U.S. fears. Then too, dangers seemed omnipresent as multiple Third World anticolonial movements threatened the capitalist world order.[36] Preserving U.S. strength and security required heightened vigilance, weaponry, and defense preparedness and training. To ensure a ready reserve of military personnel, Congress passed the Universal Military Training and Service Act in 1951, requiring all men, ages eighteen to twenty-eight, to serve in active duty for six months in a branch of the U.S. Armed Forces, followed by seven-and-a-half years of reserve service. Compulsory military service, or the draft, was also in effect for much of the Cold War (1940–72).[37] In this expanded Cold War military buildup, it's not surprising that boys like Richard and David developed a keen interest in guns and dreamed of becoming warriors. Universal military training provided the opportunity for the fulfillment of those dreams, and Richard jumped to join the army while still in high school.

Still, Aoki's story is not one of a typical (White) American. His family was released from the Topaz, Utah, concentration camp a mere dozen years before he joined the army. Such blatant mistreatment could have spurred—and did spur—an oppositional consciousness. But in a community marked as different and inferior and in a period of overwhelming pressure to conform, most Japanese Americans sought acceptance through accommodationism. The significance of Japan to U.S. Cold War interests—to repel communism and to develop a U.S.-led capitalist world system in the Asian region—fueled the start of honorary Whiteness for postwar Japanese Americans. With unexpected swiftness their images transformed from yellow peril threats to model citizens, and Japanese Americans gained unprecedented opportunities for assimilation into suburbia, upward mobility into mainstream professional jobs, and expanded political rights.[38] Aoki's family, for the most part, followed the conventions of the 1950s. Their patriotic values and the larger Cold War enthusiasm for American militarism, as well as Aoki's own masculine interest in guns and war, shaped his pro-military views at the time. By 1956, when Aoki made the decision to join the army, his father's anger over the incarceration was diminishing and, more important, his father was out of his life. Moreover, as the older son in a working-class, single-mother family, by joining the army, Aoki demonstrated masculine responsibility and economic self-sufficiency. In his own words: "I'd been sworn into the United States Army. . . . I was a man."

Another source of Cold War anxiety centered on "the crisis of American masculinity," borrowing from the title of a 1958 essay by Arthur M. Schlesinger Jr., Pulitzer Prize–winning historian and soon-to-be special assistant to President Kennedy. Cold War masculinity was a fragile identity. In contrast with the "utterly confident" manhood that had previously existed in U.S. society, men in the 1950s were "afraid that they [would] not be men enough."[39] What caused this anxiety? According to Schlesinger, the increasingly blurry boundary between men's and women's roles. In the home, "the American man is found as never before as a substitute for wife and mother—changing diapers, washing dishes, cooking meals," while "the American woman meanwhile takes over more and more of the big decisions, controlling them indirectly when she cannot do so directly." Outside the home, "men design dresses" and "women become doctors, lawyers, bank cashiers, and executives."[40] In this particularly White, middle-class version of gender relations (after all, women of color and working-class women had been employed outside the home for decades), Schlesinger articulated the fears of the day—increasing gender (and sexual) ambiguity. A decade earlier, Philip Wylie, in his 1942 best-selling book, *Generation of Vipers*, had blamed sexually frustrated women for creating weak and passive sons through their overprotective and overindulgent parenting, coining the term "momism" to refer to the phenomenon. Momism and the modern woman were thus held liable for emasculating boys and men.

In Cold War discourse, the physical body was linked to the American body politic. Robert D. Dean argues that John F. Kennedy's presidency was premised on the projection of a powerful manhood to counter the "soft" masculinity that rendered the nation vulnerable to enemy takeover. Kennedy himself wrote an article published in *Sports Illustrated* that voiced alarm about the decline in physical strength and stamina of many Americans, and identified the trappings of postwar prosperity—an overindulged, privileged suburban lifestyle, consumer culture, and television—as the main culprits producing "soft Americans," as his article's title underscored.[41] Jack LaLanne's hard, strong body now became a symbol of Cold War manly fitness and national vigor. That Philip Wylie was one of the two "philosophers" with whom Aoki most closely identified is suggestive of his adoption of conventional gendered identities and anxieties. It was important for him, a short, thin, and youthful-looking Japanese American, to assert masculine prowess through defense of the nation. He expressed a desire to join the Green Berets, the elite volunteers, the "supermen possessed of hard bodies."[42] He wanted to join the infantry to fight on the front lines like a real man. His story about being hit by shrapnel during military training is an assertion of courage and bravery, and an important marker of manliness for one who did not actually see combat duty. His account of fighting and beating a higher-ranking and larger soldier shows that size is not necessarily equated with strength. Moreover, his use of jujitsu skills links masculine strength to Japanese culture, at a time when Japanese American men were increasingly seen as effeminate and passive (in sharp contrast with the World War II images of dangerous, hypermasculine kamikaze pilots and invading soldiers). As Viet Nguyen argues, violence was a tool for the remasculinization of Asian American men.[43]

Aoki's series of working-class jobs in the late 1950s and early 1960s further shaped his masculine identity. Aoki had internalized the ideal of the man as breadwinner, so pervasive in the 1950s ideology of the nuclear family.[44] His ambivalence toward his father provided additional incentive to prove his manhood. His father represented a complex masculinity—a flexible or ambiguous gendered identity (in his role as primary parent and homeschool teacher), a hypermasculinity (as a ladies' man, tough fighter, and outlaw), and a failed manhood (as a marginal economic provider and ultimately an entirely absent father). Richard sought a more consistent manhood, working hard and developing innovative ways to increase productivity at the factory and in his pocketbook, while growing his savings to support his return to college and future plans for a family. But experiences in the workplace challenged Aoki to rethink the benefits of the workaday world.

Around this time, Aoki picked up a copy of Eugene V. Debs's *Writings and Speeches*. Speaking in 1905, the year of the founding of the International Workers of the World (IWW), Debs articulated the historic changes in modes of labor from artisans, whose ownership of simple tools enabled their livelihood, to the factory, where "the most intricate and costly machinery" was used by workers to produce profits but was owned by the capitalists.[45] "In a capitalist society," stated Debs, "the working man is not, in fact, a man at all: as a wage worker, he is simply a merchandise."[46] Under capitalism, it became increasingly hard to display the rugged, self-reliant, and confident manhood of the western frontier. More than fifty years later, Debs's words resonated with Aoki's experiences. He articulated a need for industrial unionism, which organizes all workers in a single industry, rather than promoting hierarchy through craft- or skill-based organizing. Instead of "harmonizing" relations between capitalists and workers, as craft unionism does, Debs argued for the dismantling of capitalism through class struggle. For Aoki, as a young working-class man gaining labor consciousness in the late 1950s, Debs's IWW model of industrial unionism and class struggle would have meant greater ownership not only of his labor and his body but also of his manhood.

Inherent in the nation's anxieties about weakened masculinity was a fear of, as Schlesinger put it, "sexual ambiguity."[47] The nation was rife with threats to the gendered and sexual order. In 1948, Alfred Kinsey published his shocking research claiming widespread male homosexual behavior and premarital sexual activity.[48] Then in the early 1950s, the media became fascinated with Christine Jorgensen, the first widely publicized case of sex change surgery. To many, men's and women's sexuality needed to be contained. After all, "sexual depravity," like communism, had already invaded the nation. So while containment is usually thought of as a political strategy to prevent the spread of communism, historian Elaine Tyler May argues that it was also a prescription for upholding the nuclear family and its conventional gender relations.[49] Homosexuality, it was feared, not only distorted an idealized heterosexual masculinity and destabilized the nuclear family but, in a time of foreboding national anxieties and fears of nuclear annihilation, it further made the physical body and the national body vulnerable to internal and external penetration. In the halls of Congress, senators and representatives were alarmed that homosexuals, through threats of exposure, were vulnerable to blackmail. Not only that, but the very act of transgressing boundaries might enable one to transgress other boundaries, such as working as a spy or traitor—or so it was feared. Republican Party chair, Guy Gabrielson, circulated a letter to thousands of party members stating that "sexual perverts . . . have infiltrated our government" and were "perhaps as dangerous as the actual Communists."[50] And in 1950, the State Department fired 91 employees suspected of being homosexual and another 119 the following year. As K. A. Cuordileone observed, "When viewed from the vantage point of sexuality, anticommunism was more than a defense against Communism; in its broadest cultural manifestation and most feverish imaginings, it was a defense against America itself—its self-indulgence, its godlessness, its laxity and apathy, its lack of boundaries, its creeping sexual modernism—which is why it could be so readily wedded to family values and sexual containment."[51]

In this context, it is not surprising that Aoki internalized the widespread fears of both homosexuality and communism. In telling the story about how he knocked a man off his stool at what turned out to be a gay bar, Aoki admitted the antigay beliefs he held in a period of rabid homophobia. Tempered through today's more sexually tolerant climate and Aoki's own changed views on gay rights, he winced in half-apology as he told this story. Still, his narrative was simultaneously an assertion of his own masculine vigor and heterosexuality. While Aoki has taken baby steps over the years toward supporting gay liberation, his politics changed dramatically from general support for the chaplain's "kill commies for Christ!" sentiment, the glorification of "going off to war," and a hustler–overseer's desire to increase production while doing little actual work himself to embracing revolutionary socialism.

5 "My Identification Went with the Aspirations of the Masses"

The year 1964 was big for me, though I didn't realize it at the time. I was twenty-five years old and starting to settle down. My younger brother had gotten married, had a child, and decided to go to UC Berkeley, and I'm still tiptoeing through the tulips.[1] I got to get serious. By '64, I had set up housekeeping, so my domestic life was getting fairly well settled. Although I had a good-paying union job, I didn't see myself working in the paint factory for the next forty years. This one African American supervisor bugged me all the time, in a positive way, to take advantage of the educational opportunity I had. So I thought about it and came up with a plan to attend community college full-time for two years and then transfer to UC Berkeley. I was eligible to go straight to UC Berkeley, but for financial reasons, I stayed at Merritt, which was free back then. I worked part-time, either the graveyard or night shift, so that I could attend school during the day. My girlfriend and I had started a bank account and we were putting money in there like you wouldn't believe.

My girlfriend was working full-time as a clerk in one of the science departments at UC Berkeley. She had been born and raised in Southern California and went to UCLA for a semester, decided it wasn't for her, and moved up to Berkeley to get away from home. She came from a broken home—her parents were divorced. We met in a night class that we had together in about 1963 and hit it off. We started making plans for the future, so it was even more important that I complete my formal education. Her father was English; her mother was half White, half Basque. So she had an exotic cut to her, darker hair, darker features, and a body like you wouldn't believe. Probably the closest thing I had to happiness was about that period of time.

Now the classes I took really didn't shape my politics because I had already read so much on my own. Around 1962 or '63, I was struck by John Kenneth Galbraith's book, *The Affluent Society*. The book is a paean to modern industrial

97

America, where there was a chicken in every pot and a car in every garage. By the early sixties, the United States had been riding on a wave of economic prosperity that resulted from its involvement in the Second World War, post-war industrial production, and the switch from military to consumer goods. The standard of living for most Americans began to rise. This gave the illusion that permanent progress was being made, that the working class as such would probably disappear as middle classization occurred, resulting from and being part of this affluent society. Galbraith is associated strongly with John F. Kennedy and that liberal tradition. The book was popular reading even among nonuniversity populations, as an example of how far the United States had progressed. Be that well and good, one also has to take into account, at what cost—which groups were not included?

About the same time I read another book, *The Other America,* which just knocked me off my feet because Michael Harrington "discovered" the poor White, especially of Appalachia, that this affluent society did not reach at all. I also started to read about African American or Negro economic progress, which apparently did not exist at all—except in isolated instances like the long-shoremen's union on the West Coast, under the leadership of Harry Bridges. That union provided opportunities for people of color, especially African Americans as well as Asian Americans on the Pacific Coast and Hawai'i. Now, West Oakland benefited from the struggles of the longshoremen's union, and there was a prominent Japanese American who was a well-known member of the union.[2] By and large, the conditions of people of color had not improved significantly by the early sixties.

Concomitantly, two political issues began to emerge as potentially explosive. One was the war in Vietnam. Contrary to popular opinion, John F. Kennedy was a hawk. I was in the army when he was elected president and I recall his ordering the activation of the Fifth and Tenth Green Berets at Fort Bragg, North Carolina. I remember because I volunteered to work with the Green Berets. I applied and was turned down, primarily because I didn't have enough time and grade. The second issue was the Civil Rights Movement and the Black liberation struggle. In 1954, the landmark Supreme Court decision of *Brown v. Board of Education* overturned the *Plessy v. Ferguson* decision of 1896 and thereby eliminated the separate-but-equal doctrine. But it took protest by those most affected by the ruling to get this enforced. In 1960, young people, especially students, started going into motion with the Greensboro, North Carolina, sit-ins. During the sixties social issues, not only here but across the world, were advanced forcefully by students.[3] At one point, there was discussion in

Old Left circles about whether there was a student class, because students were influencing history when they began to organize, to protest, and to obtain meaningful political and social gains. I recall a statement about the students being a separate class. But I never bought into the student class theory. If you examined the student climate of the sixties, they weren't student causes per se; rather, they were students going out for various causes. At that time, these ideas came up real fast. If you didn't have a good grounding you could have easily gotten diverted.

So I'm looking at this nonviolence stuff. My heart is with the struggle. I knew that racism was wrong. I knew that the struggle of Black people in the South for basic economic, social, and political rights was very important. Having grown up in West Oakland, I had some idea of what they were up against down there. That's when I thought, let me look around and see what I can do to help. At one point during this period I participated in a picket line sponsored by the Congress on Racial Equality against a local Japanese American real estate broker because of his policies. As I got to know the CORE people better, they asked me if I would like to join them on the Freedom Rides to the South. I said, "Yes, but I'm taking a .45 with me." At that point they dropped their invitation and suggested I could help more by staying home.

For some strange reason, I became enamored with the Student Nonviolent Coordinating Committee. For years I've wondered why I would gravitate toward SNCC because the very inclusion of nonviolence was a no-no personally. But to me, SNCC's voter registration was one of the few successful civil rights actions because it got to the issue of power. Now I couldn't care less, like Malcolm said, about sitting at some lunch counter. Show me the beef. I saw some bulletin that said James Forman was sick with a bleeding ulcer and I wrote and made a donation.[4] I devised a policy I've held lifelong of giving 10 percent of my earnings to individuals and organizations that I felt were worthy of my hard-earned money. Unfortunately 90 percent of those contributions were not tax deductible, but that hasn't bothered me at all. Later my decision was affirmed when Forman, Ruby Doris Smith, John Lewis, and a few others recognized that the Black nationalist ideology of H. Rap Brown and Stokely Carmichael was the wave of the future and rather than fight them, they moved aside and turned the organization over to them. Usually when there is a power struggle, the old guard destroys the organization rather than give up power. I wished I had kept the copy of that SNCC newspaper announcing the elevation of H. Rap Brown and Stokely Carmichael to leadership positions. When I saw their picture, I almost had a heart attack. They appeared to be the most nerdish-looking African American students I had ever run across and I cried, "Jim Forman turned the group over to this bunch of kids who look like nerds?" But six months to a year later, Burn Baby Burn, and I'm saying, "I died and gone to hog heaven." SNCC, in their Black Power phase, was directly confronting the issue of power.

Now SNCC is my only connection with the Civil Rights Movement because I went to Black nationalism so fast. The other civil rights groups in the South and North did not appeal to me. My identification went with the aspirations of the masses more than with the integrationism of the incipient middle class or the Black bourgeoisie, as delineated by E. Franklin Frazier.[5] As Malcolm X says, who wants to integrate in the United States?[6] Later on, my academic experiences strengthened my opposition to assimilationism. If you read sociological works, you'll run across Robert Park and his theory of the marginal man. He said that when people were straddling two cultures, the marginal man is positive in that he sees both halves of the deal.[7] As a sociology undergrad at Berkeley, I argued that Robert Park was too optimistic about the outcomes because where I come from, being marginalized had always been the downside. When Marx talked about alienation, I said, "This is it!" Not only am I alienated from production but I'm alienated culturally. Why? Because of the very nature of capitalism. The foundations that produce this alienation appear in the social structure. It's inevitable. It's a dialectic—what affects the base is also going to affect the superstructure. I hadn't thought about it that way until right now when you asked. It ties some things in my own mind about why even from my childhood, I felt alienated, in Marxian terms, from American society. Due to the concentration camps, with my parents divorced and separated, and growing up in West Oakland, I had no real assimilationist feelings nor was I a great supporter of integration. I found out later that Malcolm X seemed to have the same mind-set and maybe that's why it was easy for me to accept Malcolm. I do believe that all separatists are nationalists but not all nationalists are separatists. Instead of going inward into "the great society," why not go outward to the rest of the world, to the rest of where your people are? So that answers the question I've thought about all my life. I always felt that I was outside looking in. And that's an advantage because you can see a lot more.

You're going to laugh at this. In the Peanuts cartoons, guess who I considered my alter ego? Snoopy. I'm not fooling. I got a lot of little ones running around saying, "Lead us to freedom 'cause you're the great leader. You will take on the Red Baron." In the TV series *Alf*, I identified with Alf, the alien from outer space. And in *Mork and Mindy*, with Mork, another outsider. So from the psychological point of view, I became convinced that I've been alienated from society most of my life. I'm glad in a way that I felt alienated because it kept me open to these radical ideas. I mean, like integration ain't gonna bring us liberation. It's only going to happen to a small group that can economically afford this. I felt this way even before I became a communist because I had grown up in segregated communities.

Radical Readings

After I finished reading works by Steinbeck, Harrington, and others, I was forced toward Marxism because there was no other way to go. It's one thing to outline the problem, it's another thing to come up with a solution. So I'm going along and reading one political book after another, trying to understand what's happening politically. I also read the [UC Berkeley] *Daily Cal* and would go up to "the Ave" [Telegraph Avenue] to see the notices on the board. I was fortunate to be in Berkeley because at that time, around 1961, '62, '63, just about every Old Left organization in the country had a branch in Berkeley and I made a point to attend as many public gatherings as I could. The anarchists, the IWW, the Communist Workers Party, and the Socialist Party were all here. As I attended these functions, I began asking cogent questions and listened very carefully to their answers. My being a member of the working-class proletariat also enhanced my understanding because I didn't have to make the class shift. What they were saying pretty much resonated with me. The international perspectives of these groups were also attractive to me because, unlike a lot of activists who acted as if Berkeley was the center of the universe, I generally took a world view. I think that had to do with my upbringing and my military experiences. I realized there was a bigger world out there, beyond the borders of the United States.

In my survey of these Left groups, I figured out I'm not an anarchist. The Socialist Party was too mild for me. They're essentially social democrats—in other words, the left wing of the Democratic Party, still siding with the capitalists despite their name. It came down to the CPUSA and the SWP.[8] I went to some meetings of the CPUSA's youth group, the Du Bois Club. Even though W. E. B. Du Bois joined the CP—very late in life I might add—I thought using his name was somewhat opportunistic because, in my opinion, the CPUSA did very little to advance the struggle for freedom, justice, and equality among African Americans. This is when I discovered that, to my horror, the CPUSA advocated the internment of the Japanese in concentration camps in the United States.[9] A leading Japanese American CPUSA member pushed the party line and its endorsement of the internment to the extent that he was almost killed in Manzanar.[10]

Then there were the SWP, a Trotskyist group. To the credit of the SWP, they did oppose the internment of Japanese Americans.[11] There seemed to be two groupings, a generation gap, within the SWP. Virtually all of the older SWP members that I met had been involved in the massive labor movement of the thirties. They had tales to tell about their struggles during the thirties and their trials and tribulations during the forties and fifties under McCarthyism. The younger grouping was coming off the college campuses, many from UC Berkeley. They pushed the Young Socialist Alliance up front more because they were considered less subversive than the parent organization and could serve as a recruiting ground for the party. The YSA was very friendly and I gravitated very slowly to them. They were all White in the SWP/YSA; however, they struck me as being decent White folk who would give serious answers to my serious—and sometimes not too serious—questions. As I moved a little closer in their direction, they threw something on me that helped me make my decision. They told me to "go to the classics." So I delved into radical intellectual history. They told me that even before the *Communist Manifesto*, read Hegel's *Phenomenology of Mind*. I couldn't make heads or tails of it. I thought maybe the English version was a poor translation, so with my little bit of German language and my German–English dictionary, I read the work in its original language. It was still kind of ephemeral. Now I know why, but at that time I was kind of mystified. But I knew that Marx gave a lot of credit to Hegel for helping him set up dialectical materialism, or rather the dialectics part of it because Hegel was no materialist. Hegel actually believed in the mystical. How he can use spirit and mind as the basis for reality is beyond me. Marx was a materialist and that made sense to me.[12]

Then I read the *Manifesto*. It was a short work, but it was chock-full of goodies and it made me understand war in a new light. I had read a dozen books about war but had never thought about why war was so prevalent in world history. But after reading the *Manifesto* it became obvious. If there is class struggle and war is the result, you will have continuing warfare. I started thinking about the economic and political basis of war. I thought about slave revolts in Rome. The peasant revolts appeared to be a move toward a redistribution of private property in feudal times. Then we look at wars under the imperialist system. The First World War was just a war of family dynasties in Europe. Having divided up Asia, Africa, and Latin America, they now wanted to redivide it up amongst themselves and that war led to the Second World War. Things started dropping into place so fast it made my head spin. The war between England and Germany in World War I should not have been fought by the working classes of the two countries. One of the key questions in that period was, should the workers go along with the imperialist wars? Rosa Luxemburg said, "Workers shouldn't pick up guns against one another."[13] I say, "Let the capitalists kill each other over rights in Asia, Africa, and Latin America."

These readings helped me understand the whole notion of the history of struggle. Marx's *Das Kapital* was an eye-opener because it explained the basis of capitalist ownership and production. Where does profit come in? Labor. Labor is everything. I was stunned by Engels's *The Origin of the Family, Private Property, and the State* because it provided me with an understanding of evolution and revolution. Then I discovered Lenin's *Imperialism: The Highest Stage of Capitalism*.[14] That's a bold statement and its theoretical foundation is rock solid. Lenin, who lived during that high point of imperialism at the turn of the twentieth century, could see events unfolding and analyzed them very well. Marx couldn't explain imperialism because society hadn't reached that stage of economic development. But by the late 1800s, capitalism developed into its imperialist stage.

You commented that this is heavy reading to do on my own. I've prided myself on being an eager beaver when it came to reading and on being able to comprehend heavy theoretical material. Huey also had that ability—of being able to take these complex ideas and understand them. He was even quicker on the uptake than I was. It wasn't like I could take a class on Marxism at school. Well, I did take one Marxist philosophy class at Berkeley.[15] The professor matched his activism in the classroom with activism in the plaza and then they refused to tenure him. That was the only formal Marxist class I took in college or in a political education study group.[16]

I also read all the books by Trotsky as well as the works of American Trotskyists such as James P. Cannon.[17] Around that time George Breitman of the SWP started pushing the speeches and writings of Malcolm X.[18] That was an eye-opener to me. I naturally gravitated in that direction because of my association with the Black Muslims. At one point I had seriously contemplated joining the Nation of Islam. Now this may surprise you given my views on religion. But at that time, there were few organizations that I saw doing things to help the African American community. I got to hear Minister Malcolm X speak on several occasions when he visited the Bay Area. I was impressed! Number one, he spoke out against integration. Why is everybody so hot to integrate? Malcolm X said that the United States would sink like the *Titanic*. Another thing that impressed me was their positive stance on racial identity. Again, Malcolm X was an excellent vehicle for articulating pride in being Black. The Nation of Islam was transforming Negroes into African Americans. I grew up on the same block with this one dude who was a musician. The life of a musician is hard and he was strung out on heroin. Then one day I ran into him wearing a suit and a little bow tie and selling *Muhammad Speaks* [the Nation of Islam's newspaper]. I said, "Is that you, my brother?" Physically he looked so different. He had been transformed into a Black man. To verify this I looked deeply into his eyes and they were crystal clear. I was stunned that he went from being a living zombie to a human being. It was like a miracle—and I don't believe in miracles—but to see him transformed like that was inspirational. I wondered, how did this happen? It was his conversion to the Nation of Islam.[19]

Meanwhile I'm getting in debates with White radicals and bourgeois Blacks, defending the Black Muslims, which is a weird type of situation to be in, but my position was, show me the beef. What other organization has done this good a job in taking the wretched of the earth and transforming them into decent human beings? True, the mythology and the religious overtones made me a bit nervous. As I was attending Muslim services at the temple on Seventh Street in West Oakland, the minister became very interested in recruiting me to the Nation of Islam. Because of my Oriental background, I think he felt I might have been a reincarnation of their founder, a mysterious Oriental misfit, Mr. Fard. I was interested in becoming a member of the Fruit of Islam, an elite group of young men entrusted with defending the faith.

Socialist Workers Party/Young Socialist Alliance

After doing all this reading, attending meetings, talking with people in coffeehouses, that kind of stuff, I became convinced that the YSA/SWP had the correct political line for what I needed. I embraced Trotskyism at that time, or I wouldn't have joined. I thought Trotskyism was a logical extension of the tradition of Marx, Engels, Lenin, and other revolutionaries. I know there had been a split between Stalin and Trotsky. But I felt Trotsky had made important contributions to the Russian Revolution. Don't forget, he was head of the Red Army during the Russian Revolution. Trotsky's internationalism was part of the worldwide socialist movement, whereas Stalin's "socialism in one country" idea led to what Trotsky called "the degenerate workers state." Now China was interesting because the Trotskyites had labeled China a degenerate workers state. But I supported the Chinese more than the Soviet Union because I admired the way Mao Tse-tung pulled that revolution off despite lack of support

from the Soviet Union. China was playing a much more significant revolutionary role in the Third World. In fact, I knew there was virtually no liberation front
in the entire Third World that followed the Moscow line.

A little before I joined, I was approached to write my first political leaflet.
This was around 1963. It was in defense of the Black Muslims in general and
Ronald Stokes in particular. They had maybe one Black member in the entire
YSA/SWP in the whole Bay Area at the time out of a membership of maybe
fifty, sixty in Berkeley, Oakland, San Francisco. Someone had to write about the
police killing of Ronald Stokes, and I volunteered because I knew Muslims in
the area and it was a bad deal. On the flyer, it has "Berkeley Young Socialist
Alliance" and "labor donated"—we got to do that.[20] But I didn't sign my name
to it. I knew better than that. I hadn't yet joined the YSA or SWP when I wrote
that article, primarily because I was still in the army. I didn't feel free to join
anything until October '64 when I got my honorable discharge.[21] This way I
couldn't be accused of doing anything.

Merritt College

I had already been taking vocational classes at Merritt [then Oakland City Col-
lege] since 1960, but enrolled only sporadically. Then in 1964, I became a full-
time student, with the goal of transferring to Berkeley. I knew before I started
that Merritt was considered a little Harvard of the East Bay among the community colleges. At that time, Merritt sent more transfer students to Berkeley
than any other community college campus in the Bay Area. Now here's another
thing. When Laney Vocational School in downtown Oakland and Merritt Business College in North Oakland came together to create Merritt College and
Laney College, they asked for volunteers from the Oakland Unified School District to teach there. They drew their faculty from the University of California. At
one point, Merritt would only hire University of California graduates to teach
English 1A. So the Merritt faculty were the cream of the crop.[22]

Unlike many students who were taking hobby lobby classes, I was older
and serious. My first semester, taking into consideration UC transfer, GE and
the major requirements, I took English 1A, Political Science 1, German 1, and
Chemistry 1. Chemistry was an interesting class to me when I took it in high
school. It did help to advance my occupational career because it qualified me
to take the paint technology program offered by Merritt College. Political Science 1 and English 1A fulfilled GE requirements and were transferable. I took
German because four semesters of German was required for the chemistry
major at Berkeley.[23]

After I joined SWP, one of my "assignments" was to set up a student club at Merritt. YSA/SWP had nothing at Merritt College; I mean they could barely get a foothold at UC Berkeley. So three others YSAers were sent with me to set up the Socialist Discussion Club with the goal of, first, setting up an organizational body to attract those interested in radical ideas and, second, sponsoring public forums where I could invite speakers to talk about issues related to socialism and, hopefully, revolutionary socialism. I had in mind bringing in SWP speakers because that was the organization I was a member of and they had a wealth of talent. We decided to form an independent group rather than a chapter of the Young Socialist Alliance. Don't forget the old guard leadership of the SWP had just come out of the McCarthy period and were a bit nervous about being too up front. UC Berkeley could start a YSA, but we're talking about community college, which tends to be more conservative. So we thought a Socialist Discussion Club would be more palatable to the administration, to the community, and to the students, especially with the notion of *discussing* ideas. But we also wanted to be clear about our politics from the start. We wanted to distinguish ourselves from the regular student government as well as the mainstream political groupings like the Young Democrats and Young Republicans.[24]

I approached my professor of East Asian history, Dr. Yale Maxon, to be the faculty sponsor of our group. He was about the most political person I could think of on campus. He had attended Stanford University, got his doctorate at UC Berkeley, and was a specialist in East Asian history. He was a Caucasian who spoke Japanese and Chinese fluently. He was a naval officer during World War II and became the official interpreter between the war tribunal and Tojo [Japan's prime minister].[25] Here he is, a graduate of Stanford, a Naval Intelligence officer, and politically liberal—I was impressed. He was there when I needed the man, busting all his East Asian history and culture on me! I thought I died and gone to hog heaven.

I took Asian History 19A and 19B from Dr. Maxon because I wanted to learn more about the history of the peoples of Japan, China, and India—the three areas he concentrated on. It was a two-semester sequence and by the end of the second semester, he took a liking to me and I enjoyed his teaching. He was a heavy dude. He was asked to find people who knew about social problems because the Ford Foundation was funding projects. He came to me and laid it out. I wanted to address the problems of gifted students from the lower social-economic structures. So I went out and interviewed people. My thing was that given enough support, the gifted students from the lower social-economic structures could survive in the system. About that time, I began to realize that in the gang I used to belong to, there were a lot of bright kids in there with me—my equal and better—but because of circumstances, their potential was not being fully realized. This is probably the only document that I've ever written that had a liberal reformist philosophy behind it—we've got this problem, we can solve it by throwing in resources. Had I known then what I know now, I would have had a much different bent on this. But when I reread this, it struck me that, from earlier than I remembered, I was concerned about the people and I was willing to come up with solutions.[26]

So Dr. Maxon kindly accepted the offer to become the faculty sponsor of the Socialist Discussion Club, which blew up in his face in a way. See, we put an announcement in the student newspaper about our meetings. We printed out flyers on a mimeograph machine and stood in front of the school and said, next week there's going to be an organizational meeting for progressive-minded students interested in a discussion of socialism of all varieties. To ensure that the radical variety got discussed, we chaired the meeting. A school reporter came to that first meeting and reported that the chair of a new club calls himself a "revolutionary socialist." In that same newspaper article, Dr. Maxon said he believes in "democratic socialism," which he defined as working through information rather than violence.[27] I was glad those differences got out because to me, "evolutionary socialists" do a lot of talking, but "revolutionary socialists" get things done. The YSA and SWP were impressed—front-page news! But I also felt a little guilty that maybe I had set Dr. Maxon up in his career. What if they ask him to leave Merritt, where the hell else can he go? I had no bone to pick about the way he distanced himself from revolutionary politics. He didn't need his protégé getting off on the front page of the Merritt College newspaper. He was a liberal and this showed his political limitations. But he didn't drop being our sponsor. I was also sweating my own stuff. This was February 1964 and I didn't get my honorable discharge until October. I didn't know there was a reporter at our meeting. Still, my primary objective was to keep the club going and it was still around when I left Merritt two years later.

There was a hard core of four of us who started the Socialist Discussion Club. Two of us were from YSA/SWP, including a White woman from YSA who was also a student at Merritt. The other two were White men. Before that first organizational meeting, we met and they said, "I think Richard would make a good chair." "Yeah, I'll do it." I had to. It was my home turf in a sense; I was from Oakland. I was there as a serious student; the others were just signing up, taking a class here and there. I already knew most of the people attending the meeting. I don't think we ever had more than a dozen members and most of them were White. Most of them were male. I don't think we had a single African American as a regular member because the African Americans went into the Soul Students Advisory Council. I was one of the few non–African Americans allowed to attend the meetings of the Soul Students Advisory Council. I said, "You guys can go to our meetings anytime." Then Bobby [Seale] reciprocated: "Brother, why don't you come to our meeting." So our two groups starting linking, not formally but in a collegial way, thanks mainly to Bobby's leadership of the Soul Students Advisory Council and my leadership of the Socialist Discussion Club.[28]

Meanwhile, I'm devouring Black literature, mostly protest literature, because of the strong Black nationalist influence at Merritt. I'm saying, "Wow, this is heavy. This is where it's at." I gravitated toward the politically loaded Black writers. James Baldwin, *The Fire Next Time*. Richard Wright—I had read *Uncle Tom's Children* when I was a child, but I didn't read his major work, *Native Son,* until I got to Merritt. As I was exploring ideas about nationalism, I'd ask Bobby and Huey, "What do you think about this?" We'd trade off. I was reading Malcolm X because of the YSA/SWP. Their reaction was, "A White group pushing Malcolm?!" I said, "This dude named George Breitman was a personal friend of Malcolm and a member of SWP and put together some of Malcolm's speeches." SWP had a bookstore at that time in Berkeley, so I had access to all that radical literature and carried some of it over to Merritt College. Howard Zinn's book *SNCC: The New Abolitionists,* made me feel good about the ascension of H. Rap Brown and Stokely Carmichael into leadership positions in SNCC. Bobby and I just chortled over Melville J. Herskovits's *Myth of the Negro Past.* This is a classic because it dispelled the notion that Black people had no culturally transmitted characteristics from Africa, and Herskovits actually did a scientific study to prove that the mannerisms, the music, call-and-response originated in Africa. I read Herbert Aptheker's works on slavery and the issue of resistance, that there were slave revolts during that period of time.[29]

The Vietnam Day Committee, International Protests, and Robert Williams

Through my work in the SWP/YSA, I got more involved with the antiwar struggle as the war in Vietnam started picking up. I remember there was an antiwar rally in San Francisco with about two thousand protesters. This was around 1963.[30] That may seem early, but the Bay Area was ahead of the nation when it came to protesting the war in Vietnam. That's when the Vietnam Day Committee popped into the picture. I remember joining the VDC in the middle of '64.[31] At that time, I had a couple more months in the Standby Reserves until my honorable discharge in October 1964. Plus, they weren't going to call up the Standby Reserves to active duty until the Ready Reserves were called up. So for all intents and purposes, I was on my way out. The reason why I remember '64 is that Lyndon B. Johnson was running for president of the United States and the Gulf of Tonkin had just happened.[32] I was stunned to hear about the Tonkin incident. It served Johnson well. He issues the Gulf of Tonkin Resolution and Congress pushes through for war. But I knew somebody that had a shortwave radio. So we were listening to broadcasts from all over the world. What was Moscow saying about this? The version was different as night and day. So I'm thinking this is kind of shaky. Plus, by this time I had come to the decision that if we're sending troops seven thousand miles away to fight for freedom, justice, and equality, we should be sending troops to Alabama, Georgia, and Mississippi to enforce civil rights.

In the Bay Area, the VDC spontaneously emerged out of the energy of students at Berkeley and other progressive-minded people in the community. It developed and grew so fast that all the Old Left groups sent their cadres into the VDC, not the other way around. Usually, when a group started in those days, they were front groups. But the VDC was the opposite. The VDC just sprung up! I recall being in the YSA/SWP and trying to decide, should we go in? Of course, it was obvious that the antiwar movement was the only game in town outside of the Civil Rights Movement, which was just toddling along. So the Old Left had an opportunity to work a mass movement that they hadn't had in thirty years. Their membership exploded because all of a sudden, young people were thirsting for direction. The VDC was a broad-based organization. In fact, every major Old Left organization, with all their different political tendencies, was in the VDC. It was incredible in a way that all these different groups could get along in the VDC. We even printed the perspectives of the various Left organizations in a pamphlet, *Did You Vote for War?*[33]

So I'm in the VDC looking for a way to make myself a valuable contributor. But I didn't want to be too public because I'm still in the army. One faction of the VDC was talking about stopping the troop trains. I said, "Whoa! If that's what you want to do, okay. But that's a little shaky there for me." I mean, they could have gotten killed.[34] Then I accidentally bumped into an international group that was part of the VDC. What happened was that my fiancée at the time was in the YSA and VDC. Her best friend was Native American, Cherokee,

and also active in the VDC. They had met working together in the same department at UC Berkeley. So through her job, her friend was mentoring all these
graduate students and helped get foreign students into the VDC. They were
invaluable sources of information because they had direct connections to Third
World countries. I was most interested in Third World peoples and politics,
so we set up the International Secretariat of the VDC, which was a clearing-
house for overseas correspondents.[35] I was stunned to discover the pockets
of resistance all over the world and the kinds of anti-American, anti–Vietnam
War sentiments emanating from those countries.

The VDC wanted to expand further overseas. The international students
started corresponding, mostly by letters. For example, a group in Japan would
send a letter about their antiwar activities to the VDC Berkeley. We'd type their
response and encourage them to participate in the International Days of
Protest.[36] The International Committee put together a booklet to circulate
information on the general antiwar movements and the International Days of
Protest activities going on around the world.[37] Most of the articles were gathered and written by Third World graduate students, non–U.S. citizens, so it
was best not to publicize their names. Suzanne Pollard and I were the only
ones who used our real names in that publication. Suzanne was the director of
the publication and a grad student at Berkeley. I had guts enough to put my
name on it because everyone already knew I was an activist. We had gotten so
much correspondence that we divided the report in sections—Latin America,
Europe, Asia, Africa, and the Middle East. The section on Asia was quite extensive. I had corresponded with people in Japan the most, so this was the length-
iest section. We had excerpts of statements against the war from university
professors, students, socialist organizations, and labor unions in Japan.[38]

The antiwar movement really started to heat up after the VDC formed. I
remember going to Washington, D.C., for a large rally against the Vietnam War.
I went on behalf of the International Secretariat of the VDC because it was too
dangerous for most foreign students to attend. That's when Fanon was starting to get to me. Yeah, I'd do it for the cause! SWP also sent a large delegation.
I think one whole floor in a hotel had SWP and YSA members representing
every chapter across the nation. So I was wearing two hats when I went to
Washington in support of the people. I was representing the International
Secretariat of the VDC and I was voting in the SWP/YSA bloc.[39]

Now here's the corker. The VDC was considered so dangerous that the headquarters in Berkeley was dynamited. The scariest part is that the night it was
dynamited, I was in there earlier that evening, working the mimeograph

machine in the back room. And it was that back room that got blown to bits. If you look at the newspapers at the time, there were photographs showing that and I said, "Boy, oh boy, they're taking us seriously." It wasn't like I thought the Feds did it. I mean, it was pretty much common knowledge that local right-wing nuts had decided to make their move because they saw us as a Communist-front organization.[40]

I forgot to mention that I contacted Robert F. Williams, who was living in exile in Cuba, to try to enlist his support for the International Days of Protest. The SWP was the backbone of the Fair Play for Cuba Committee. So it was through the SWP that I got connected with Rob and got acquainted with the Cuban Revolution. I wrote him a short note in September 1965 and sent the letter through Vernel Olson of the FPCC in Ontario, Canada. I told Rob Williams that because of "your stature as a leader and spokesman for the vanguard elements of the Black people of America, along with your close affiliation with the leaders of forces of national liberation struggles," I was contacting him on behalf of the International Committee of the VDC. We wanted his help in getting the word out that a "segment of the American people is actively opposing the war in Vietnam. We would like to spread this information to the entire world since the basic questions involved, opposition to American Imperialism, self-determination of colonial people, racism, genocide, etc., are of an international nature."[41] The next thing I know I got a reply from Rob himself in Cuba. I almost had a heart attack. It boggles my mind that he even wrote back to me. By that time, I'd read Rob Williams's book, *Negroes with Guns* and also Truman Nelson's book, *People with Strength*. Nelson was a radical journalist and his book, also on Rob Williams and the incident in Monroe, was much more political. Today, not too many people are aware of who Robert Williams is and what he did. But he was one of our heroes. In the 1950s, he was an NAACP chapter president from Monroe, North Carolina, somebody you wouldn't think would be too radical. He did something different—he armed his branch of the NAACP against Klan activities. He had troubles with the national headquarters of the NAACP because this was not their line. In the process of struggle, he was framed on a kidnapping charge and had to leave the country. He next appeared in Havana, as a guest of Fidel Castro. After reading those two books and newscasts and newspaper accounts, I began to develop a healthy respect for Rob Williams.[42]

I thus began my correspondence with Robert F. Williams. About six months later, all of a sudden his letters started coming from China; he had left Cuba to live in China.[43] I agreed to become a distributor for his political newsletter, the

Crusader. As I was getting more active, I began asking around to see if there were any more Asian American radicals. I found out that a Japanese American woman in Harlem was also corresponding with Rob and distributing the *Crusader*. That's how I first heard of Yuri Kochiyama. I didn't discover until later that Yuri was there when Malcolm X was assassinated. At that time, there were only a handful of radical Asian Americans that I knew of. There was Grace Lee Boggs in Detroit, Shoshana Arai was in Chicago working with SNCC, and Yuri Kochiyama in the Organization of Afro–American Unity in Harlem. I knew about the Japanese American members in the Communist Party (CP), but I didn't want to have anything to do with them. Getting back to Yuri and myself, I've always maintained that if I had been in New York, I probably would have joined the Republic of New Africa and if Yuri'd been in California, she would probably join the Black Panthers.[44]

I was surprised by Rob Williams's move to China, but I politically understood that the Sino–Soviet split was behind it. I was turned off by how rhetorical the debate was until I began to understand the reality of the politics. The Soviet Union was supporting Cuba, buying its sugar at a good price, so Cuba had to side with the USSR. But in general, the revolutionary struggles of the Third World in the late fifties and early sixties did not embrace the Moscow variety of communism. I sided with China because they seemed to be more Third World oriented and the stronger supporter of the African American liberation way back when the Civil Rights Movement was chugging along. If you look at history, there's that photograph of Mao-tse Tung welcoming Robert F. Williams, and it wasn't too many years later that Huey P. Newton and other Panthers were warmly greeted by Mao. As a Japanese American, I sure didn't appreciate that the CP didn't step forward to defend my people when we went to the camps, and the CP created a nonaggression pact with Nazi Germany! Give me a break.[45]

Even after Rob Williams left Cuba, I remained a strong supporter of the Cuban Revolution. So it may surprise you that in the early 1960s, I was reticent to support the Cuban Revolution. During the Cuban Missile Crisis, I was still in the military and packing a M1 Garand, ready to defend our country against this invasion ninety miles from home and coming our way. I was only beginning to understand about Third World politics. Still, even I understood that the Cuban Revolution was creating fundamental change; it wiped out the organized gambling and criminal interests in Cuba, stopped prostitution, and improved race relations. I admired Fidel for his Moncada fortress attempt, even though it was a fiasco. That attack on the Moncada fortress was like John Brown's attempt to take Harpers Ferry, where a group of people armed themselves hoping to seize

This banner, created for Richard Aoki's memorial service by Pete Bellencourt and commissioned by It's About Time/BPP Alumni, shows his most famous ties: with the Black Panther Party and Third World Liberation Front. He also was an important leader of the Asian American movement, represented by the small AAPA (Asian American Political Alliance) button on his beret.

Richard's maternal grandparents, Tatsumi Nakazawa *(left)* and Shizuka Nakazawa. Collection of Richard Aoki.

Richard's paternal grandparents, Fusa (Sone) Aoki *(left)* and Jitsuji Aoki.
Collection of Richard Aoki.

Richard's paternal grandfather, Jitsuji Aoki, a successful immigrant entrepreneur, in front of the family's large house in West Oakland, 1937. Collection of Richard Aoki.

Oakland Noodle Factory, 1931. Jitsuji Aoki established his factory in Oakland, California, as early as 1903. He publicized his trademark "Chop Suey" Chinese-style noodles as providing modern conveniences and good nutrition. By 1930, the factory produced more than a ton of noodles daily and distributed them from coast to coast. Collection of Richard Aoki.

Shozo Aoki, Richard's father, in ROTC (Reserve Officers' Training Corps) uniform, 1931. Before World War II, Shozo participated in Boy Scouts, junior high school basketball, and high school ROTC, and he appeared to be fulfilling the Aoki family's expectations for respectability through achievement and service. But the wartime incarceration challenged his sense of fairness and justice, resulting in a disillusioned, demoralized, and angry internee. Collection of Richard Aoki.

In 1909, Richard's great-uncle Gunjiro Aoki, a servant in the Emery household, made national headline news when he boldly crossed racial and class boundaries by marrying Helen Gladys Emery, daughter of the archdeacon of the Episcopal Church in San Francisco. John Oakie Collection.

Richard *(left),* age 6, with his brother, David, mother, Toshiko Aoki, and maternal grandfather, Tatsumi Nakazawa, December 1944. The barracks of the concentration camp in Topaz, Utah, are in the background. Half a year after this picture was taken, his grandfather died of a heart attack within days of returning to Berkeley. Richard's mother was still in Topaz at the time of his death. Collection of Richard Aoki.

Richard *(right),* with brother, David, and father, Shozo Aoki, at the Aoki family home in West Oakland, California, shortly after returning from the concentration camp, ca. 1946. In two unusual moves, Richard's parents separated inside Topaz, and after leaving the camp Richard and David lived with their father in their grandparents' prewar home. Collection of Richard Aoki.

After the war, Richard *(center)* and David *(back right)* joined a multiracial gang, the Saints, ca. 1956. Collection of Richard Aoki.

With dreams of becoming the first Japanese American general, Richard joined the army straight out of high school, 1957. Collection of Richard Aoki.

David and Richard *(right)* shoot at an unknown enemy with crude replicas of semiautomatics or Colt .45s, 1946. The photograph reflects themes of Cold War militarism. Collection of Richard Aoki.

David and Richard *(right)* with revolver-style cap guns and oversized holsters, 1948. The big guns symbolize the growing strength of the United States as a military, political, and economic world power. Collection of Richard Aoki.

military control, especially the arsenal, to arm the people so that they could struggle against slavery militarily. In the Moncada attack, Fidel was imprisoned and most of the Cuban group was killed. John Brown too was killed. But John Brown's actions sparked the American Civil War and Fidel's, the Cuban Revolution. When I found out about Fidel's speech "History Will Absolve Me," delivered at his trial for the Moncada incident, I was impressed. Fidel outlined why he did what he did, that this was not an adventuristic, anarchistic, terroristic move, but it was something that had to be done. I liked the way he integrated the United States Constitution as justification for his self-defense actions. That floored me, to see somebody able to take United States political philosophy and turn it 180 degrees, when he said, "You know, when you're oppressed, you got a right to throw the shackles off and rebel." To this day I have a copy of Fidel's speech before the court. Pardon me for getting excited about that, but the Cuban Revolution kind of slipped up on me.[46]

Third Worldism and the Tricontinental Movement

The concept of the Third World became quite popular among radical intellectuals. Initially the term was "tricontinental," meaning those places in Asia, Africa, and Latin America where revolutions against Western colonialism and imperialism were occurring. One famous publication was *Tricontinental*, put out by the Organization of Solidarity of the People of Asia, Africa and Latin America. About the same time, the radical intellectuals, primarily in France, began to refer to Asia, Africa, and Latin America as the "Third World."[47] This referred to the countries in Asia, Africa, and Latin America that were struggling for independence as part of the Non-Aligned Movement. That is, they tried to keep separate from the Cold War conflict between the U.S. and Soviet Union. The First World was the U.S., Europe, and probably Japan, and the Second World was the Soviet Union. One question that came up was about Japan—was it a First or Third World country? To me, the criterion was imperialism. If a country was imperialist—and Japan clearly was—they could in no way qualify as being a Third World country. China was always kind of a big question mark as to whether they were a Second or Third World country. But the Chinese Communist Party, under Mao Tse-tung, gave more political support and probably military support to Third World liberation struggles than did the Soviet Union. As I read more about revolutions and looked at the world, I could see the Soviet Union wasn't playing a progressive role in any of the Third World countries. I already mentioned my views on the Sino–Soviet split. Plus, I was turned off by the Communist Party and its failure to oppose the internment of Japanese

Americans. So I was eager to learn about Marxists like the Chinese Communist Party. By the time I discovered Che Guevara and Frantz Fanon, I was a huge supporter of Third World Marxism.[48]

When I got to Berkeley in October 1966, the first thing I did was join the Tri-Continental Students Committee. By then, I was doing very minimal organizing with the SWP. I had met many of Tri-Con members, these radical foreign students, because of my connections through the International Secretariat of the VDC. Since I was now a student at Berkeley, they invited me to join them. There were only two of us nonforeign students, myself and my fiancée's best friend, who was Native American. I thought it was an honor that they included me. So here I am, a full-time student at Berkeley, majoring in sociology, fulfilling my American Dream, but also working with the most radical political organizations around.[49]

In April 1968, Tri-Con organized an event in support of the National Liberation Front of Vietnam that got me accused of treason and sedition. This was big time. I mean, I looked around and there was nobody that I had even heard of in the movement getting those charges. Up to that point, I was taking my lumps, but this was big time—treason and sedition! I was traumatized. So here's what happened. Tri-Con organized this event to raise funds for the National Liberation Front. We had as our featured speakers Bobby Seale and Eldridge Cleaver of the Black Panther Party; John Gerassi, who was recently fired from San Francisco State for his politics; Nguyen Van Luy, who was from North Vietnam; Don Duncan, an ex–Green Beret; and Pete Camejo, a YSA/SWP leader. Young people today may know of Peter Camejo as the Green Party candidate for California governor and for vice president running with Ralph Nader for president.[50] On the flyer was a logo of the world resting on an outstretched arm and a hand gripping a gun. It was an AK47–M68 hybrid.[51] Guess who designed that logo? I wanted to show Asia, Africa, and Latin America on the globe. I could have put a book there, but I don't know of anybody winning freedom by throwing books at the enemy. Yes, the book is important, but there is a time when other tools are necessary for liberation. Our program may have been a bit more radical than most, but it wasn't out of step with the times. The antiwar movement had been gaining strength, and about the same time there were people here in the medical and health community who were putting together a shipload of medical supplies, equipment, stuff like that, to be sent to North Vietnam in the form of humanitarian aid.

Before the event, one of our more zealous members went to the newspaper to help publicize the event. It made the front page of the *Berkeley Daily Gazette*, the only daily in town.[52] This one professor, the resident anticommunist faculty on campus, complained to the administration that our program was "treasonous" and a "flagrant misuse of campus facilities."[53] Guess who had gotten the permit to use Pauley Ballroom? The newspaper article identified me by name and listed my political credentials: "Richard M. Aoki, a UC sociology senior . . . is a captain of the Berkeley branch of the Black Panther Party and former international chairman of the Vietnam Day Committee."[54] I was stunned. One of my cover's blown now. The vice-chancellor wrote to this humble student that had unfortunately signed for the use of Pauley Ballroom, the biggest, most prestigious ballroom on campus, for the event, which was going to draw in thousands. The letter was handwritten on University of California stationery and stated, "The legality of your April 1 meeting, having been questioned by a member of the faculty, I sought an opinion from the Office of the General Counsel. That opinion indicates a distinct possibility that the meeting would involve unlawful treasonous and seditious acts."[55] They were throwing the law on me! Trying to scare this boy. I went to the law school in Boalt Hall and asked the librarian for the federal codes that were identified in the letter. I think the penalty provisions were a minimum of twenty years to a firing squad. I choked a little bit and said, "Oh, my goodness gracious, what am I gonna do now?" I got two options. I could run like hell, or I could go meet with the dean as the letter said to do. Being an organizational man, I took the responsibility. So I met with the dean and as it ended up, we held the event but were unable to collect donations at the door for the NLF. We did collect money for Huey Newton's defense fund, but not for the NLF. [56]

The next day, we got a meeting in this apartment, and it was a warm day, but some people in Berkeley must have wondered why the fireplace was going full blast. We burned our membership list, our mailing list, our correspondence, literature we had left over from events—anything that could be traced back to the group—and we dissolved. It was too close a call. The Asian American Political Alliance came along at the right time. Many of the Asians in Tri-Con went into AAPA when it formed a month after Tri-Con dissolved. And AAPA's politics were quite similar to Tri-Con's.

Radical Sociology at UC Berkeley

After getting a fine education at Merritt, I transferred to the University of California at Berkeley in fall 1966. At Merritt, I took two sociology classes that piqued my interest: Introductory Sociology, with the textbook written by UC professors, and Social Problems. I also understood that sociology was the most radical department at Berkeley. So I immediately declared sociology as a major and was fortunate enough to take classes from giants in the academic field of sociology. These professors included Leo Lowenthal, who taught social theory. When he gave his lectures it was like he had a photographic memory. He could quote things without the use of notes. His intellectual capacity just stunned me. In his class, I elected to write a term paper doing a Marxist critique of Michels's "iron law of oligarchy." The key to my term paper was a book by Vilfredo Pareto. I searched and searched, but couldn't find a copy of the book in Berkeley. Based on all the other readings I had done, I knew that I needed to obtain that book in order to round out my paper. So I went to Professor Lowenthal's office. This is a social theory class required for the major, six hundred students in there, he doesn't know me from Adam. As I get to know him a little bit better, I found out he was a refugee, a Jewish German who came to the United States during the thirties when the Nazis were coming down hard on the Jewish people. So I told him about my problem finding this one book. He said, "Come back tomorrow." So I returned the next day and he had his personal copy of Pareto's work. I said, "Oh my goodness. Thank you for loaning it to me." I got home, opened up the book and it was the first edition with an inscription, "To my good friend, Leo Lowenthal," from Pareto. Apparently, Dr. Lowenthal was able to cart that out with him when he left Germany in a hurry, but with that book, I was able to complete my term paper. The grade wasn't as good as I had anticipated, but at least I was able to turn in a decent paper and I made sure he got his book back. In some of the subsequent discussions I had with him regarding his view of the United States and where it was going in the 1960s, I felt that he was seeing some of the same social phenomena occurring in this county that he had seen emerge in Germany. He was one of the finest intellectuals in his mind, the clarity of his presentations, and his compassion for an undergraduate student.

I never took a class with Professor Robert Blauner, who was new to the Sociology Department, but I knew him through Professor Paul Takagi. Professor Blauner's specialty was race relations—that's what they called it in those days. But he was way ahead of the other academicians because he formally proposed the theory of the internal colony, that colonialism, not just racism, described the oppression of Blacks in the United States.[57] This was the philosophy of many Black nationalist groups that I had been associated with for years. Another new faculty, an African American sociologist, was Professor Troy Duster, who, along with Blauner, advanced an understanding of race within sociology. I took a class with Professor Herbert Blumer, who was an expert in the field of collective behavior and a disciple of George Herbert Mead. Now collective behavior may not sound that interesting, but it did include mass movements, so that piqued my interest. If you understand a group's behavior under certain conditions, it can help you out organizationally, so I felt that was a worthwhile class. At the same time, I took a social psychology class in the Psychology Department. Here I was, taking two social psychology classes, one in the Sociology Department and one in the Psychology Department, and they were as different as night and day because of the political orientations of the two fields. The psychology course, taught by a clinically oriented professor, discussed a lot of case studies and I said, "I don't need this."

I didn't enroll, but I audited Professor Richard Lichtman's class. Guess what he specialized in? Marxist philosophy. I audited his class because I saw him out on the picket lines for various political causes. I said, "Well, this makes sense. If you're teaching Marxist philosophy, you've got to do what Marx said, akin to, 'Up to now, philosophers had written about history, now is the time to make history.'"[58]

I found my formal education to be very helpful because I was able to constantly test the activity on the streets against the theories I was learning in the classroom—testing the theories against what I saw in my day-to-day political activity and sharpening my decisions as my mind was becoming sharper and more critical. You could find me sitting in the front row in the classes of the professors I respected because I wanted to gather in as much knowledge as I could.

During all this intense political activity, I was able to stick to my academic plans as a full-time student. I progressed through my two years at Merritt, two years as an undergrad at Berkeley, and two years as a grad student at Berkeley—all concurrent with my political activism. I made normal academic progress! I was on a mission and there were a lot of fortunate things that enabled me to survive. First, I was young and I was hard and I was driven. I was in my late twenties and in good physical shape. So I was able to withstand the rigors of that type of pace with a minimum amount of discomfort. Second, to say I was bright doesn't hold water. I hate to say it, but graduate school was a cakewalk after my undergraduate studies. That was because I went to a professional rather than an academic graduate program. I was doing so much in that set of time that I had to chart out what I was doing. If I wasn't young, if I wasn't politically grounded, I'd have gotten lost somewhere in the shuffle.

THE OLD LEFT, THIRD WORLD RADICALISM, AND VIETNAM

The Socialist Workers Party and Black Liberation

Aoki is best known for his work in the Black Panther Party and Third World Liberation Front. Yet, I contend that his participation in the predominantly White Old Left, through the SWP/YSA, was pivotal not only to his radicalization but paradoxically in moving him toward Black nationalism as well. In the early 1960s, at a time when Aoki was deciding whether to join the YSA and SWP, the *Militant,* the SWP's weekly newspaper, was filled with articles on Black radicals as leaders of the SWP, YSA, and the Cuba solidarity movement; on the all-Black Freedom Now Party; and on the radicalization of the "Negro struggle," as it was then called. By contrast to the mainstream press's vilification of the Nation of Islam as an "anti-white, anti-integration, anti-Christian cult,"[59] the SWP strongly denounced the racist treatment of the Black Muslims. After Malcolm X left the Nation of Islam, the *Militant* gave extensive coverage to his evolving political ideas. The *Militant* also gave strong support to Robert F. Williams as he fled to Cuba to escape the Monroe kidnapping charge. Aoki, listening to a tape-recorded speech by Robert Williams at a Berkeley YSA meeting in November 1961, would have been impressed with Williams's message that "the Cuban revolution meant a new life for the Negro people as under Castro all discrimination had been eliminated."[60]

Most historiographies date the emergence of Black Power to the assassination of Malcolm X in February 1965, Stokely Carmichael's popularization of the Black Power slogan in June 1966, and/or the formation of the BPP in October 1966.[61] But in the *early* 1960s, the *Militant* recorded a "new mood" in the Black community that was bubbling up, becoming impatient with the gradualism and integrationism of the Civil Rights Movement. This historic political climate was crucial to the development of Aoki's radical ideology, as he read the pages of the *Militant.* SWP leader George Breitman exclaimed that "the best article of 1961" was Julian Mayfield's essay "The Challenge to Negro Leadership: The Case of Robert Williams," which told the story of Black self-defense against Klan violence in Monroe, North Carolina.[62] To Breitman, Mayfield's article was important because it captured the "current moods and trends in the Negro movement," showing how "the emergence of a new young leadership offer[ed] a serious challenge to the middle-class legalistic and pacific spokesmen in the struggle for Negro equality."[63]

The new Negro struggle was critical of the Kennedy administration's "fail-ure to take a firm civil rights stand" as well as being "sorely disappointed" with the top civil rights leadership.[64] In contrast with the popular appeal of King's "I Have a Dream" speech at the 1963 March on Washington for Jobs and Freedom, the *Militant* claimed that "the best speech . . . was never heard."[65] The *New York Times* reported that after a religious leader threat-ened to withdraw, march organizers asked John Lewis, chair of SNCC, to revise his speech because it was "not consistent with the tenor" of the pro-gram.[66] The *Militant* was more to the point: Lewis's speech was censored because of his "blunt criticism of Kennedy and the Democratic Party."[67] The *Militant*, as well as Malcolm X, asserted that the Kennedy administration, in order to control the march, gave power to the so-called Big Six civil rights leaders by providing money and media outlets, and by projecting them as the key march organizers.[68] In his original speech, published in the *Militant*, Lewis criticized the federal government in unambiguous terms: "We march today for jobs and freedom, but we have nothing to be proud of. . . . In good conscience, we cannot support the [Kennedy] administration's civil rights bill, for it is too little and too late. There's not one thing in the bill that will protect our people from police brutality. . . . The nonviolent revolution is saying, 'We will not wait for the courts to act, for we have been waiting for hundreds of years. We will not wait for the President, the Justice Depart-ment, nor Congress, but we will take matters into our own hands and create a source of power, outside of any national structure that could and would assure us a victory.'"[69] Lewis also voiced the "new mood" of the Negro strug-gle: "We cannot be patient, we do not want to be free gradually. We want our freedom, and we want it *now*. We cannot depend on any political party, for both the Democrats and the Republicans have betrayed the principles of the Declaration of Independence."[70]

Young people like Lewis were increasingly demanding "freedom now," and for some this required a new method of contestation. An anonymous "freedom rider" wrote in the *Militant* that while "at present there is no bet-ter form of direct action open to minority groups than non-violent tactics, the policy of absolute passive resistance to violent, savage attack is suicidal."[71] Half a year before this statement was printed, Robert Williams was forced to flee the country because his armed self-defense engendered the wrath of the Ku Klux Klan and the local police. Williams had earlier expressed, "Nonvio-lence is a very potent weapon when the opponent is civilized, but nonviolence is no repellent for a sadist."[72] To emphasize the urgency of the situation,

Williams said elsewhere, "The majority of white people in the United States have literally no idea of the violence with which Negroes in the South are treated daily—nay, hourly. This violence is deliberate, conscious, and condoned by the authorities. . . . It is our way of life."[73]

As reported in the *Militant,* prominent Negro leaders, professionals, and artists were also voicing critiques of White liberalism and mainstream politics. On integration, famed author James Baldwin boldly stated, "It is not simply a question of equality. It is impossible for any Negro in this country to be fitted into the social structure as it is. The structure must be changed, made more human, more humane."[74] On the hypocrisy of demands for nonviolence, playwright Lorraine Hansberry, author of *A Raisin in the Sun,* observed in 1964 that the late president Kennedy was "willing to blow up the world when he couldn't have his way." She added, "I think the whole idea of discussing whether or not Negroes have the right to defend themselves is an insult."[75] Journalist William Worthy stated, "More and more you hear people saying that the lessons of Africa is that people don't get their freedom until they start shooting. . . . [This] has become a part of the thinking of a significant section of the colored community."[76] On White liberalism, Paule Marshall, author of *Brown Girl, Brownstones,* asserted, "White has come to suggest more and more to me a sluggish callousness, a force opposed to change, even when that change is necessary to survival." She called for a new "nation-wide civil-rights organization . . . far more militant than any existing today . . . totally committed to the liberation of the black man by whatever means necessary."[77]

Beginning in March 1964, after Malcolm X left the Nation of Islam and started his own organizations, the *Militant* gave extensive coverage to Malcolm's travels, activities, and developing ideas and published the full text of many of his speeches, including the three talks he gave at Militant Labor Forum programs, sponsored by the SWP. In these speeches, while acknowledging his still-developing political ideas, Malcolm showed an increasing radicalization: "While I was traveling I noticed that most of the countries that had recently emerged into independence have turned away from the so-called capitalist system in the direction of socialism."[78] He also added, "You can't have capitalism without racism."[79] Aoki eagerly read Malcolm's speeches in the *Militant* and in *Malcolm X Speaks,* which Breitman edited.[80]

In "Lessons for Whites on the Negro Struggle," Breitman warned that White progressives must come to understand why the majority of Negroes see "the average White person as their oppressor . . . if they hope to play a serious part in the struggle for equality," even as there are "whites who oppose racism" and "not all whites are responsible for racial oppression."[81] Similarly, the SWP candidate for governor in Michigan, Frank Lovell, opposed the notion that Negroes were "asking too much too fast," asking White workers if they would be patient when "patience means a continuation of second-class citizenship," being "the last hired and first fired," or being denied housing and educational opportunities. He offered a Marxist analysis: "Anti-Negro discrimination was originated by the employers, the capitalists . . . [to be] economically profitable . . . [and to] divide and conquer" racial groups who otherwise hold similar class interests.[82] That White Leftists like Breitman and Lovell held Whites, rather than Blacks, culpable for self-reflection and change would have captured Aoki's attention and strengthened his faith in working with White radicals in the struggle for racial equality.

It wasn't just Breitman but SWP as an organization that offered strong support for Negro liberation. In 1963 the SWP reaffirmed its commitment to Negro autonomy and self-determination. In titling their convention resolution "Freedom Now," the SWP echoed Breitman's view that "the new militants don't want *progress;* they demand *Freedom.*"[83] This "new stage" of the Negro struggle provided an opportunity for "Negro nationalism and revolutionary socialism . . . [to] be welded closer together in thought and action" on the basis of "their common sympathy and support for the colonial revolution and hostility to imperialist domination" and because "the working class cannot achieve its aims without the Negro people achieving theirs."[84] The SWP stated emphatically, "We, as supporters of the right of self-determination, would support the Negro demand for a separate nation and do everything in our power to help them obtain it."[85] Toward this end, the SWP pledged to "better educate the entire membership; [to] give ourselves a deeper and more sensitive understanding of the Negro people"; and "to encourage and expand our work in the Negro struggle."[86] The SWP further recognized that "while our white members cannot aspire to leadership of the Negro organizations, they can play important auxiliary roles" and that "just as most workers in the party are expected to work in their unions. . . most of our Negro members will belong to Negro organizations, which seek to build along militant lines."[87]

There were those in the SWP who opposed the position of "Freedom Now" and to its credit, the *Militant* printed their views. A minority tended to believe that "the present struggle, North and South, is decisively integrationist in character" and opposed nationalism for "diverting the struggle from the revolutionary road."[88] As he contemplated joining the SWP, what would have been important to Aoki was that the majority of the organization offered strong support for Black liberation and self-determination. The SWP's views on the Black struggle as well as on the Cuban Revolution were important influences on Aoki's turn to Third World Marxism.

Cuba Libre

While historiographies of the U.S. New Left have generally ignored the influence of the Cuban Revolution, historian Van Gosse cogently argues that *Fidelismo* was critical to the New Left's development.[89] In contrast with the conventional vision of the New Left as a White college student movement, beginning and ending with Students for a Democratic Society, inserting the Cuban Revolution into the "long '60s" highlights the anti-imperialism and international solidarity of the Left movement. The Cuban Revolution, in part because it made visible the contradictions in U.S. society, was undeniably instrumental to the development of a broadly defined U.S. New Left, U.S. Third World radicalism, and national liberation struggles worldwide.[90]

The Fair Play for Cuba Committee, formed in 1960, was unique as an independent radical project created during the Cold War.[91] Indeed, the Cuban solidarity movement was not a struggle for inclusion in the American Dream but rather intended to provide support for a socialist country, led by an avowed Marxist–Leninist with Soviet connections during the Cold War, only ninety miles off the coast of the southern United States. Formed almost accidentally by liberals, CBS reporter Robert Taber and wealthy contractor and Democratic leader Alan Sagner, the FPCC moved rapidly to the Left. Despite concerns about red-baiting and the FPCC's public image, Taber agreed to a marriage of convenience with the SWP. The FPCC gained the SWP's organizational resources and the small SWP (with only four hundred members) entered the national political scene, even if in a "covert and unacknowledged fashion, as required by the Cubans."[92] Although the FPCC no doubt would have expanded on its own, Gosse writes that "it grew that much more because of the distinct organizational impetus it received from the Trotskyists."[93] Primarily through the leadership of SWP cadre Berta Green, SWP members founded or helped to create FPCC chapters nationwide. In about six months, "this combination of SWP activism, black nationalist revival, and the first stirrings of the New Left"[94] grew the FPCC "from three local chapters plus a claimed 2,000 members receiving the *Fair Play* bulletin, with no systematic program, to an organization claiming 7,000 members in twenty-seven 'adult chapters' and forty Student Councils."[95] Given the SWP's instrumental role in the FPCC, it is not surprising that the *Militant* gave extensive coverage to the many gains of the Cuban Revolution, including a successful literacy campaign, an increase in farm ownership by common people, and a reduction of color and class inequality.[96]

The FPCC was also unique in its ability to bring together Black and White activists as well as radicals and liberals—groups typically historicized in separate social movements—into an international solidarity movement for a project no longer popular with the American mainstream. From its start, with a full-page advertisement placed in the *New York Times* on April 6, 1960, its original thirty signatories included the renowned French intellectuals Jean-Paul Sartre and Simone de Beauvoir, novelists Norman Mailer and James Baldwin, activist Robert F. Williams, historian John Henrik Clarke, and CBS reporters Robert Taber and Richard Gibson. That eight of the thirty were African Americans, including Baldwin, Williams, Clarke, Gibson, and novelists John O. Killens and Julian Mayfield, suggests the importance of Black–Cuban solidarity to a country that is one-third Afro–Cuban.[97] The *Militant* recognized this unity, giving front-page coverage to Robert Williams, William Worthy, and other Black leaders of the Cuban solidarity movement. The SWP newspaper reported on the trial of Worthy, a foreign correspondent for the *Baltimore Afro-American,* who was charged with entering the United States from Cuba without a valid U.S. passport in October 1961, despite being a U.S. citizen by birth. His passport had been confiscated for unauthorized travel to China in 1957.[98] Worthy was among the numerous Black members of the FPCC and a signatory on "Cuba: A Declaration of Conscience by Afro-Americans," published in the *Baltimore Afro-American.*[99] Among the twenty-seven distinguished endorsers of the Cuba document, including W. E. B. Du Bois, LeRoi Jones (later Amiri Baraka), Harold Cruse, Shirley Graham, John Henrik Clark, and Richard Gibson, "the most important . . . was Robert Williams, who has personally been in touch with Castro."[100] Williams was so important to Afro–Cuban solidarity that when Castro decided to prioritize the recruitment of Black Americans, he sought out Williams as his personal guest and key leader, and Taber himself traveled to Monroe, North Carolina, to invite Williams to be the FPCC's national spokesperson.[101] It was through his SWP contacts that Aoki connected with Robert Williams to enlist his endorsement of the Vietnam Day Committee's International Days of Protest in 1965. In short, the SWP's support of the Cuban Revolution and its coverage of Afro–Cuban solidarity further signaled to Aoki the party's commitments to internationalism and Third World radicalism.

It is not surprising, then, that an SWP comrade of Aoki's stated that the Cuban Revolution and the Civil Rights Movement were the two primary forces sparking political action among her generation.[102] If Aoki's memories are correct, it is indeed surprising how late he came to Cuban solidarity. That he was "packing a M1 Garand, ready to defend our country" during the Cuban Missile Crisis in October 1962 after the SWP strongly defended Cuba's right to self-defense is revealing of the uneven and contradictory nature of political development.[103] But if the FBI reports are correct, then Aoki came to support the Cuban Revolution much earlier. According to the FBI, at a Berkeley YSA meeting on November 26, 1961, Aoki was among those defending the Cuban Revolution and Fidel Castro against charges by some YSA members that by accepting Soviet aid, Castro was a "traitor to socialism"; the latter was upholding the Trotskyite line against Stalin.[104] Perhaps Aoki's remark on being "ready to defend our country" was in reference to the Bay of Pigs invasion in April 1961.

The Paradox of the SWP and Black Nationalism

The long-standing debate between Marxism and Black nationalism revealed a paradox in SWP's program on the Black struggle. As revolutionary as its program was on Black liberation, the SWP failed to attract large numbers of Black members. The SWP was in a nearly impossible bind as a predominantly White organization working to support Black self-determination, while seeking to move the Black movement toward socialism, without trying to exert White domination over the Black struggle, as Black critics charged.[105] The SWP's revolutionary commitments to Black radicalism drew Aoki into the party, but the very tensions represented in this paradox also fueled his departure around 1967.

These tensions are further revealed in a debate in 1964 between Harold Cruse, Black social critic, and George Breitman, SWP's foremost theoretician on the Negro question. Cruse's article "Marxism and the Negro," published in the *Liberator,* began with his criticism of the SWP running a Negro, Clifton DeBerry, as its candidate for U.S. president; Cruse denounced it as "crass and opportunistic" for the SWP to compete with the all-Negro Freedom Now Party.[106] This, of course, provoked Breitman's response, which appeared in a four-part series in the *Militant* titled "Marxism and the Negro Struggle." In their articles, Cruse and Breitman charged each other with using a nondialectical analysis and seeing a particular group frozen in time. Cruse critiqued the Marxist concept that the working class in industrialized nations is the most revolutionary sector when in the United States, as Cruse opined, "White labor . . . went conservative, pro-capitalist and strongly anti-Negro" and "abandoned the Marxian historic role assigned to it."[107] Breitman responded that White workers have the potential to *become* radical, opposing Cruse's contention that for Marxism to be viable, White labor "*must be* a radical, anti-capitalist force in America and must form an alliance with Negroes for the liberation of both labor and the Negroes from capitalist exploitation."[108] While acknowledging that "the overwhelming majority of workers in this country today are not radical, thanks to capitalist brainwashing," Breitman asserted that "[Cruse] lives in a world that is changing with dizzying speed, but he thinks everything is going to change except the workers."[109] Breitman posited that White workers will inevitably be changed by the social conditions around them, particularly the independent Negro movement and the automation of industry resulting in greater unemployment and increased insecurity for all workers.[110] Therefore, Marxist theory does not require that White workers "must be" radical but that they "must *become* radical if they are to solve their own problems."[111]

By applying a dialectical method to adapt Marxism to existing conditions, Cruse argued that in the early 1960s the people in the colonial world were the main revolutionary forces in the world. He extended this revolutionary role to U.S. Negroes, whose conditions were akin to "domestic colonialism."[112] But the U.S. Marxists, he insisted, rigidly adhered to the "working class–socialist myth," blindly promoting the working class as the most revolutionary force.[113] Breitman countered that, as stated in their 1963 "Freedom Now" convention resolution, the SWP believed that "the colonial struggle is the center of the world revolution today" and has been since the 1949 Chinese Revolution.[114] As early as 1932, "far from believing that workers in capitalist countries are the only revolutionary forces, Trotsky insisted many times that 'the decisive word in the development of humanity' belongs to 'the oppressed colored races.'"[115] Rather than putting this as a dichotomy, Breitman's position was that anticolonial movements both in the imperialist centers and in the Third World can work toward dismantling global capitalism and imperialism, and thus have the potential to be mutually reinforcing.

In 1964, as Aoki was developing his own ideas on socialism and Black freedom, this debate between Breitman and Cruse provided Aoki with the analytic tools to develop his own views on the relationship between Marxism and the Black struggle. He could see in many ways the SWP's earnest commitment to Black liberation. But the debate also revealed tensions under the surface of SWP's theoretical position on the "Negro question," strains that would propel Aoki's exit from the SWP a few years later. Still, even after Aoki left, he considered it "generally a plus for me to be in the SWP." The experiences and political analysis gained by working in the SWP and YSA played a significant role in the development of Aoki's nationalist–internationalist socialist politics and, as I contend, enabled him to cultivate Marxist–Leninist ideas in the BPP, the Asian American Movement, and the U.S. Third World Left.

6 "The Greatest Political Opportunity of My Life"

Pre-Panther Days: Meeting Bobby and Huey

My joining the Black Panther Party was about being in the right place at the right time—or the wrong place at the wrong time, depending on how you look at it.[1] Had I gone directly to [UC] Berkeley, I would have missed out on the greatest political opportunity of my career because Merritt College was a hotbed of Black nationalism.[2] That time was the beginning of racial polarization nationally, and at Merritt it started to be really extreme. Donald Warden's Afro–American Association was perhaps the first Black cultural nationalist organization in the Bay Area, and it drew some of the mightiest, young African American intellectual revolutionary nationalists—from Merritt College, UC Berkeley, and San Francisco State. But many of them left to join more politically oriented groups.[3]

It was through another Merritt College student group, the Soul Students Advisory Council, that I got to know Huey Newton and Bobby Seale. They went on to start the BPP because of the limitations of these Black cultural nationalist groups. I was really impressed when I first met Bobby because Bobby, to me, was a poster child for Booker T. Washington's model of a man, being vocationally skilled and having all the talents. He was a carpenter, a sheet metal worker, he could read blueprints. Plus, he'd been in the military, gotten married, and was a student at Merritt to uplift himself. But there was a difference in Bobby's case. He was not just satisfied with the Booker T. Washington model of uplifting. He was thinking politically. At one point he joined RAM, the Revolutionary Action Movement. RAM was founded in the early 1960s by Max Stanford and their base of strength was Detroit, Cleveland, and Cincinnati. The word on the street was they were a clandestine, underground organization. Bobby's alliance with RAM was brief due to the fact that he opposed the clandestine political thing.[4] Now Bobby was easy to get to know because he's basically a friendly guy.

About the same time I met Huey Newton. Huey initially came across as a young thug, running the street. I think Bobby was far ahead of him at that time theoretically.[5] But Huey had this thirst, even though he was barely literate upon graduating from high school.[6] Then Bobby told me about the donnybrook Huey had with a local thug, who I had grown up with and gone to Berkeley High School with. This thug belonged to the baddest gang in the East Bay, a gang I wouldn't even take the Saints against in my wildest dreams. They were smaller than the Saints, but as a group they could clean the Saints out. I wouldn't even dream about taking on their warlord. The lieutenant of this warlord was the guy that Huey took on. I was stunned.[7]

So one day Huey and I are drinking wine and we decide to go to Stubby's Pool Hall, which we considered the local Colosseum. Some of the most legendary battles among thugs occurred at Stubby's. So Huey and I walk into Stubby's and there's a half dozen dudes in there, a little younger than we are, and Huey starts playing the dozens with one of them. I'm saying, "I'm going to see some action now!" Huey, being quick of mind, swiftly gets the better of the guy. I see the guy getting ready to do his number. He's halfway through the West Oakland bit when Huey hits him with a blow that I didn't see coming. Bam! Took him down. Now that surprised me a little bit. I've always prided myself on being fast, but that was one of the few times I've seen somebody faster than me. Unfortunately, this guy's friends started getting nasty and jumped Huey. What am I going to do? So I jump into the picture. Huey and I end up battling half a dozen dudes. We know we got to get away. We fight our way out to the sidewalk, back to back, side by side. We're trying to get to my car across the street. We're doing a good job, we're not going down, but we got six dudes on top of the two of us. This is getting a little bit tiresome. One of Huey's relatives happened to be driving by, jammed on the brakes, reached in his glove compartment, pulled out a .32 pistol, and shot a round in the air—or as we say on the block, popped a cap—shook up the dudes we were fighting, and Huey and I were able to get away in my car. That was one of the few times I'd seen Huey in action.

The pool hall thing was to me the street standard I used in gauging pugilistic ability. I'd seen Bobby fight a couple of times, and he ain't no slouch either. But Huey impressed me because he's fast. Huey had my style of, if you're a little smaller, you got to get more blows in there than the other guy. He was quick.

But Huey was also getting into serious trouble. There was one time multiple felony counts were dropped on his head. So Huey went to a lawyer, an African American community lawyer, whose heart was in the right place, but he had the skills of Algonquin J. Calhoun. Algonquin J. Calhoun is a character in the *Amos 'n Andy Show,* an attorney who, if you spit on the sidewalk and you're his client, by the time he gets through with you in the courtroom, you'll get the death penalty. His heart was in the right place, but his legal skills were lousy. This attorney told Huey, "Look, we can take these multiple counts and reduce them to a handful. But you got to cop." I said, "Huey, you're caught between a rock and a hard place." This is where Huey impressed me. He goes to the Merritt College library, checks out the books, and starts reading the California penal code, about three inches thick. I think, "Oh no, Huey, you're going to defend yourself?" I didn't go with him to court because I didn't want to see a repetition of somebody being sentenced to jail. But Huey beat the charges.[8] I was amazed. This is before the Black Panthers started when I was running the street with Huey.

Then there was a plan that Huey and I had for economic upward mobility. We had the idea of emulating one of his friends, who was the number one pimp in North Oakland. We saw this guy's fancy clothes and the two .45s he carried around. I remember going over to this guy's apartment one time and looking over his stable. When we got inside the apartment, he took off his jacket and had shoulder holsters on both sides with .45s. That was before I started packing regularly. I mean, I packed occasionally but damn. We didn't want to compete with him, so we went to West Oakland and looked over the possibilities there and in the process got to talk to a lot of prostitutes. We talked to the women and they were in bad shape. I mean, they were out there because they were mothers trying to make ends meet. Pimping was lucrative, but Huey and I could just not become pimps.[9]

What I'm tying to get to is that prior to the Panthers there's a contrast in my relationship with Bobby and Huey. With Bobby, it was more political. As I got to know him better, my respect for him grew and he began to treat me really well. But with Huey, it was more for the street quality. You have to remember that Bobby just got married, whereas Huey was single, younger, living the life. Still, the thing that united the three of us was politics.

Black Nationalism Conference

In September of 1966, the biggest Black nationalist conference ever held on the West Coast was in San Francisco, at the Fillmore Street YMCA.[10] It was sponsored by practically every major Black nationalist group. There were about three hundred African Americans there from a broad spectrum of the Black community, including intellectuals, writers, artists, musicians, poets, prostitutes, students, hoods, winos—and several Black undercover cops. It was about half men, half women, and mostly young. Meanwhile, Whites who were coming up to the auditorium door were denied admittance. There were almost some fights over that because up to this time, Whites always attended. Initially I felt a little uneasy about excluding Whites, primarily because if your politics are true blue, it stands up to the glare. But you also have to understand that Stokely [Carmichael] had just come out with the Black Power slogan and this was the beginning of the exclusion of Whites from the civil rights groups. And rightly so, because many of the groups felt that the Whites were retarding further progress. So I show up and I get in. Two reasons. Number one is Bobby invited me and told them that I had a contribution to make. Who is going to argue with Bobby? Number two is I ain't White. I was there because I was one of the brothers! But if they had asked me to leave, I would have left.[11]

Those people who are fighting for their rights are the ones that should call the shots, and this is what I told the Socialist Workers Party. The SWP may be in the forefront of the struggle in a way. But they are not able to liberate the Negro. The Negroes have got to liberate themselves. I don't know how—maybe through an international socialist organization because at that time "revolutionary nationalism" was still not part of the regular political vocabulary and that limited my argument base, but I was beginning to get a little fired up about nationalism and I was going back to the books. I was reading everything anybody in a Marxist, Leninist, or Maoist tradition had written about nationalism and came to the conclusion there's cultural nationalism and revolutionary nationalism. So the dual purpose of the exclusion was number one, psychological in nature—Blacks determining their own destiny—and number two, freedom of expression.

The keynote address was given by Kenneth Freeman, and don't forget, Kenny came out of the Afro–American Association and the Soul Students Advisory Council, and was the editor of *Black Dialogue,* one of the most influential Black nationalist publications in the Bay Area. Kenny talked about colonial revolutions and how we have to learn from them. He urged everybody to read Fanon. He urged everybody to read Malcolm X. He praised the Chinese Communist revolution, but said Black people can expect no material aid, no one's going to be shipping guns to us. Blacks got to do it on their own, to struggle independently.

There were multiple sessions over the three days of the conference. One panel was on paramilitary groups, which was "essentially a presentation and exposition of right-wing groups and their relationship to the Black liberation movement."[12] The conclusion was, "Blacks should prepare to defend themselves, their families, their communities, and their nation, through the formation of groups such as Deacons for Defense and Justice and Robert F. Williams."[13] In the final plenary session, the most important thing was for a united front organization to carry out the tasks of the conference and the name "Black Panther" came up at that conference. I even wrote it down in my report.[14]

Another panel was on Black youth and the draft. Several minutes before the panel began, I was asked to speak. I'm sitting there minding my own business, probably chewing the fat with Bobby or something, when I'm approached and somebody says, "Would you like to speak on . . ." Somebody must have said I was with the Vietnam Day Committee and resisting the draft, fighting the cops at the induction center, fighting off the Hell's Angels. They also knew I was a veteran. So what line am I going to use? I'm thinking, I got to be careful. So I got up there and said, "We got to be against the war in Vietnam." Safe so far. So I decided, I'm on a roll here, what do I talk about next? I remember I said the war in Vietnam is a trick bag when it comes to African American people and their survival. I said there's "double genocide" being committed where young Black people are being drafted against their will. Look at it from Mr. Whitey's point of view, if the Black soldier kills an Oriental Viet Cong, that's one less Oriental running loose. If the Oriental Viet Cong kills the Black soldier, one Black soldier ain't coming back. This must have hit some chord because we know now that African Americans and Latinos were disproportionately called up by the draft and hit by casualty rates, and I remember a lot of applause. Yay! I'm on a roll. I got the war. I got the double genocide.

Then I went a little bit further. I'm pushing the envelope. I said, "Black men shouldn't fight in the war; they should resist the draft because it's a freedom-of-life thing. If it's so important that you're going to die, you better have a vote in where you want to die." People in the audience probably looked at me like, "Well, you were in the military. What was the secret of your success, boy?" I said, "I volunteered. People right now ain't got no choice. You don't go, they're sending you to the penitentiary." I think by that time Muhammad Ali had made his stand and I think I used the phrase he used about the reasons he wasn't going to fight. He said, "No Vietnamese ever called me the N-word."[15] I remember also saying, "I was in a concentration camp as a loyal American.

Those concentration camps still exist today. And who do you think they're planning to put in there next as far as I can see? Black people."[16] I got a good applause on that one. I was starting to get good at my public presentation.

In my report, I summarized the positive aspects of this conference, which included: attack on mere rhetoric; creation of an organization that was anti-capitalist and rejected the Democratic Party; recognition that the masses must be organized and that the leadership should come from Blacks themselves. The weaknesses, and this is my personal political analysis, was that there was a lack of a comprehensive and revolutionary program. Of course, you can't expect a miracle overnight, and maybe I was a little too idealistic in that sense. And there was a lack of political action. However, I also pointed out that "the Black nationalist movement is in an embryonic stage of development and is constantly undergoing transformations. This makes it rather difficult to delineate specific currents in the movement, but at least attempts are being made and mistakes of the past are being learned from."[17]

I presented my report to the entire general membership of the San Francisco, Berkeley, and Oakland SWP. We're talking maybe a hundred people, maybe more. They got everybody together to listen to my report because they couldn't go [to the conference]. This is when my relationship with the SWP started to get a little strained. I wrote in my report:

> Black nationalism is a major current within the Black liberation struggle in the US, which in turn is intricately woven into the international class struggle. The origin and development of Black nationalism is the direct result of the American capitalist system, which has placed the Black people into a position analogous to the colonial peoples. . . . Revolutionary socialists must be ready, willing and able to learn from militant Black tendencies and to absorb everything progressive in their spirit and ideas. At the same time, it must never be forgotten that we [meaning the SWP] have things to contribute as well as learn. The fundamental purpose of this education is to provide consciousness concerning one important, possibly the most important, tendency within the Black liberation movement. According to a resolution adopted by the 1939 SWP convention, "The SWP must recognize that its attitude on the Negro question is crucial for its future development. Hitherto, the Party has been based on privileged workers and groups of isolated intellectuals. Unless it can find its way to the great masses of the underprivileged, of whom the Negroes constitute so important a section, the broad perspectives of the permanent revolution will remain only a fiction and the Party is bound to disintegrate."[18] . . .

The *role* of the SWP is to assemble and programmatically equip the forces that will lead the coming American revolution. The SWP agrees that the first task of Blacks is to organize themselves independently. But the Black liberation struggle does not exist in isolation from other forces and conflicts at home and abroad. The *tasks* of the SWP is to educate its own cadres on every important aspect of the Black liberation struggle, to provide aid to the most advanced elements of the Black liberation movement. Finally, the SWP must begin to lay down the foundations that will lead to a principled alliance between the Black people and the white workers, so that they can together destroy American capitalism, which stands for slavery, suffering and death, and can create an international socialist society based on freedom, justice and equality.[19]

Birth of the Black Panther Party

Comes October of '66, a month after the conference, Bobby and Huey come up with the idea of forming a political group.[20] Of course, the mandate of that conference was "Go forth and multiply. Organize." Bobby from the very beginning understood the importance of organizing and often said, "We're not outgunned, we're outorganized." So they start writing the Ten-Point Program. I don't think it's ever been mentioned, but if you look at a copy of [the Nation of Islam's newspaper] *Muhammad Speaks* in those days, and probably to this day, you'll see that they have a Ten-Point Program that tells exactly what they're all about, what they believe, what they want.[21] I can't underscore enough the importance of a program for a political organization so there's no misunderstanding of where the organization belongs. I get leery of political groups that are vague in their background, vague in their ideology, vague in their organization.[22]

The Ten-Point Program wasn't something that they just hashed out, that we just slapped together, because I was involved in that. They did most of the work in the poverty center where Bobby was working, mostly in the evenings and on the weekends. I recall Bobby's wife and Huey's girlfriend helping to put it together, along with Melvin Newton. You have to understand in that period of time, the production of the whole thing was a lot more complicated than it is today. First of all, it had to be written and then typed. Bobby relates how Huey came with the grand ideas and Bobby massaged it a bit.[23] Then they'd get it typed up. Then you got to cut a stencil and if you make a mistake, you'd have to do the whole stencil again. Then, if you have a hand-cranked mimeograph machine, this slows down the operation. Of course there were power mimeograph machines, but they were more expensive. Richard might come in when it comes to putting the stencil on the machine. It took several days to do that. So I was part of that process that cranked out the program.[24]

Once the program was put together, we started talking about organization. It was agreed that Bobby would be chairman, that he would be the public face of the organization, because every organization needs a spokesperson and usually it's the chairman or a designated spokesperson. That may have come from the dictum "From each according to his abilities." Bobby was a pretty polished public speaker and he had presided over the meetings of the Soul Students Advisory Council, so it seemed natural that he would be chairman. There was no question when it came to the warlord, the minister of defense. That was Huey! Huey had a good reputation in the 'hood. This all seemed very logical based on their abilities.[25]

So I'm excited that Bobby and Huey have launched this thing. About a month later Bobby and Huey come over to my place in Berkeley, where I joined the organization. This is that meeting where Bobby and Huey come to me, ostensibly for the guns. When I was in the military, I learned "always be pre-pared," which I interpreted as meaning you should have your own small col-lection of self-defense weapons because they may not be readily available in the event of a major hostility. So I, as a hobby, began to read about small arms and began to pick up a few. I wasn't the only one in the movement doing that, I discovered. And it is a basic right under the Second Amendment of the United States Constitution. So I shared my concerns with Bobby and Huey regard-ing how we were going to enforce all this and that I'm willing to contribute to the pot in any way I can, besides talk.[26] I don't know whether I joined the Black Panther Party at this meeting or when I was helping with the Ten-Point Plat-form. All I know is I'm not giving my guns if I'm not a member. You find the guns come with me and I come with the guns. On his website, Bobby Seale states, "Within two weeks, the first six members of the Party were: Bobby Seale, Huey P. Newton, 'Little' Bobby Hutton, 'Big Man' Elbert Howard, and two broth-ers, Reggie and Sherwin Forte. Within two months additional members were: Richard Aoki, Orlando Harrison, Warren Tucker, Big Willie, John Salon, and six other young black males . . . and two females."[27]

Shortly after the party was formed, the party developed a membership process. I'm sure the application form was Bobby's contribution because of his poverty program work, he'd be familiar with some of the bureaucratic processes to start an organization. Besides name, address, and whatever, the form asked about vocational skills. But Bobby went a bit further and had an item on the application form regarding whether the applicant was a graduate of a certain state institution and what they were in for. I thought that was a little bold. I mean, "Bobby, you can put employment on it, but you don't ask this type of stuff." He said, "Yeah, but the skill." "Yeaaaah! You smart, Bobby."[28]

We're feeling good now. We're getting the show on the road! In a couple of weeks, I guess November, December, we did a survey in the community. We mimeographed copies of the program and passed them out all over town, at the barbershops, pool halls, bars, wherever people would congregate, we would hand out the program. The newspaper hadn't started yet. We wanted feedback from the people that we handed literature out to. The one thing that came up time and time again was item number seven, about ending police brutality. Bobby had referred to the police as an occupying army and we had internalized that in the program. Now, how were we going to stop the police? Well, there was a community-based organization in Los Angeles called the Community Action Patrol or CAP. In response to complaints of police brutality, they would follow police cars in their neighborhood and take along tape recorders and cameras to observe the activities of the police. Now, the CAPs people had a rough time 'cause the police did not like what they were doing. Huey went to the penal codes and found that a person has the right to have weapons as long as they were visible. Voilà! Bobby and Huey figured out the way to avoid the cameras and tape recorders from being busted up was we would back it up by armed self-defense. That's when the first shotgun patrol started.[29]

A couple of nights later we began the patrols and made quite a sensation in the community. We would cruise around and whenever we saw somebody being arrested in the ghetto—and you see a lot of people being arrested at night, especially the weekend—we'd stop the car, get out, and we would all stand there observing what the police was doing. Needless to say the police reacted with a bit of alarm and some fear. I remember several times, some person was being arrested, might have been a traffic stop, couple of cops busting him. We roll up, surround the cops. They'd radio out and they surround us. And the next thing you know the community is surrounding them. That was awesome.[30]

Even More Important . . . Political Education

I think even more important was setting up the political education classes. These classes included classes on Malcolm X, African civilization, Afro–American history, Afro–American culture, and Mao. The Mao thing caught me a bit off guard because that was not my idea.[31] I wasn't that well versed in Maoism.

I had read his selected works, or scanned through them. The only thing that impressed me about the revolution in China was the Long March. I always read that as a military victory, which it was, but for a long time, they neglected to understand that this was the political glue that held that group together. I think Huey asked me if I would contribute to the Maoist study because, wasn't I a Marxist? In other words, to him at the time, a communist was a communist.

So we'd be sitting around and I'm going with the flow. I said, "Well, you know that in the struggle for the curriculum, they had to offer the history. Now what books are we going to have?" My suggestion was, let's start with the basics and move upward gradually. Everybody can relate to Malcolm X; let's start with Malcolm X's *Autobiography*. Then have a second level, with Frantz Fanon, or maybe politically oriented African American writers like Ralph Ellison, Richard Wright, even James Baldwin. I say "even Baldwin" because although I try to be objective I was stunned by the fact that he wasn't solely writing for the political end of the movement, that he had another subject matter as a writer that he wanted to advance. When it was announced that he was going to be at Berkeley I made sure I was there. I had read his book *Fire Next Time,* and whoosh!—that's a powerful document. I recall the statement about being a conscious Black man in America is to live in a state of perpetual rage. So when I found out he was coming to town, got to see this brother is heavy. I hadn't read *Giovanni's Room*. When he began speaking, along with the mannerisms, I began to realize that possibly he was gay. I do recall this reaction on my part as I began to suspect. I prided myself on providing people with a wide latitude of personal idiosyncrasies. Hopefully they'll do it for my case as well. But it was a personal disappointment on my part; it had nothing to do with him. I don't think it was the politics then so much as it became a more personal thing, and that's what I try to avoid. When it comes to personal/political types of things, I try to separate the two. It's the political that's important—you focus on the political, then the personal is dealt with, and not backward. I think I was able to transcend the personal with Baldwin because I went on recommending that people read *Fire Next Time* and the brother is heavy.[32]

Third level, to me the highest level, would have been the more basic Marxist and Maoist works. I should add that part of the PE [political education] classes was teaching the code of conduct, which was virtually lifted from Mao.[33] What I felt in the education area was a sense of discovery that these young African American males are coming in out of the public school system fucked up in their academic skill level. Not because they were fuckups; because the system was fucked up. However, the thing that amazed me was how quickly they could absorb the political stuff, and the technical stuff. Once they were motivated, once they were brought into the party, I was amazed. I'd seen Huey move that way. But to see a whole group coming in and in a couple of weeks, I saw some students go from almost illiterate to finishing off Malcolm X, jumping to Fanon, and then dialectical materialism.

I was made minister of education for about six months. I have to admit I was not a full-blown minister of education.[34] My job was to help set up the first PE classes for party members. I had just started UC Berkeley in October 1966 and was then made branch captain of the Berkeley chapter.[35] Around the same time, I was given the title of minister of education. How that title came about was that a student group wanted a representative from the BPP to speak on campus. So I touched bases with Bobby and Huey. They said, "Since you help with the internal education, and you're at Berkeley too, you might as well." "Who do I say I am?" "Branch captain" may sound too militant with UC Berkeley. But "minister of education"—hey, that's cool. So I was allowed to pass myself off as minister of education for that event.[36]

George Murray was the first full-fledged minister of education. When it was announced that he was selected, I said, "Yeah!" because his rep was good. He was teaching over at San Francisco State and was instrumental in the TWLF strike there. In my mind, you had to be a teacher to be the minister of education. Plus, my thought is it should be a Black person. Later, Raymond "Masai" Hewitt was minister of education. I also think that Ericka Huggins may have been minister of education at one time, when she was the director of the East Oakland Educational Institution, the BPP school.[37]

Now, I'm not altogether sure I'm the one that introduced the Red Book of Mao's quotations to the party. It sounds logical since I was the closest to Berkeley. So in Legacy to Liberation, I said if I wasn't the one who introduced it, sooner or later Bobby and Huey would have discovered it.[38] It's one of those deals of what is the difference who introduced it? What stunned me was, of all the Marxists, Mao would be the one. Don't forget also that Robert F. Williams was in China by that time. So, Maoism is being taught by the Panthers. I don't recall myself ever doing any formal lectures. But then who else was there in the organization at that time that could speak more knowledgeably about Mao than myself? But Huey could have picked that up real quick. Now it's well known that we sold the Red Book up at UC Berkeley. Bobby discovered those Red Books would go like hotcakes, and that money was to be made in great sums for the purchase of our "equipment." But I didn't see it as just a moneymaking proposition. I thought that it was a valuable political tool on the part of the party because it did an excellent job of distilling Marxist–Leninist–Maoist ideology. So the Red Book served two functions—economic and political consciousness-raising.[39]

Little Bobby Hutton: "The Best of the Youth"

This brings me to how Little Bobby Hutton became treasurer of the BPP. As the organization began to pull in the big ducats, it became apparent that somebody had to be responsible for the revenues; maybe only a couple of hundred dollars, but that was big-time money. Both Huey and Bobby at that time were scrupulous about party funds, that party money was to be spent for party business. So this issue came up before the membership, that we needed to have a treasurer, somebody the group trusted the most to handle party money. This was an important job—if the money gets funny, you lose credibility, and of course, you lose the money. Now by that time the group had about twenty members, almost all of whom were thugs or ex-thugs. They voted Little Bobby Hutton, who joined the party when he was only fifteen years old, to be the treasurer. What impressed me was everybody trusted him with all the money.[40]

For years I wondered who authorized Little Bobby Hutton to carry a shotgun. When I found out the shotgun was loaded, I said "Shit!" I am not about giving a 15-year-old a loaded shotgun. I had this thing fixated in my mind, seventeen is the youngest because when I was in the military that was the cutoff. But when a senior member of the party says, "Yeah, I did it," oh, that answered that question. That was Big Man, whose judgment I trusted. Big Man had confidence in Bobby's maturity, self-control, self-discipline, general all-around good sense. In my mind, Bobby was a very intelligent, very mature, and an easygoing guy. In fact, there were a few occasions where I wondered why he was in the party because he smiled a lot and didn't seem to be as hard outwardly, but he was serious when he needed to be. Any responsibility that he undertook, he did it, and he did it well. He was one of the most mature teenagers I had ever met in my life.[41]

It's well known how the cops gunned down Little Bobby in 1968. He was one of the first to be killed in the line of duty. "You can kill the revolutionary, but you can't kill the revolution" is a truism. Currently, Big Goree, a nephew of Little Bobby, is keeping Little Bobby's memory alive as well as being a contributing editor to the *Commemorator,* a newspaper created by veterans of the BPP. In addition, we are all still pushing for the creation of Little Bobby Hutton Memorial Park, where DeFremery Park now stands. To me, Little Bobby represented the best of the youth that came out of that time.[42]

Self-Defense to Stop the Violence

In the early years, Elbert "Big Man" Howard and I were the main people teaching the weapons training.[43] Huey would take care of teaching the law: "These are your rights, now this is what you need to back up your rights. Richard will conduct the session here." About this time my apartment starts to be used for the self-defense weapons training classes. All this is legal. One day, as we're leaving the place with our pistols strapped on us, shotguns and rifles—I was taking a half dozen of the new recruits up to the target range—my landlady says "hello." She just kind of shook her head. There was another time that I took another group, three carloads, up to the range. As we were rounding the corner at the top of the curve, we can see downhill and adjacent to the semi-public range that we planned to use, we saw twenty police cars parked in the lot; there were twice as many cops on the adjacent range. We parked above the range. I walked down to the range master's office to see what's going on and it just so happened that this police department was doing its monthly training exercises up there. So I aborted the training session and we quietly coasted down the hill, back into Oakland, and I thought, "Boy, that was close, because we had just started the shotgun patrol."

When I talk about self-defense, it's not just about the weapons training. Although Mao said, "Politics comes out of the barrel of a gun," it has to be understood that the politics guide the gun. I transplanted martial arts philosophy to it—that it's a skill, it's a way of being, you can't have impure thoughts there. Commandism, which is a Maoist term, in my classes was condemned. Commandism is an overly militaristic approach that affects personality to the extent that politics becomes secondary to the military side. In other words, I pushed the spirit of self-defense, that aggressive action and negativity come from the oppressor, who instigates all the violence. We're trying to stop the violence. This is a tool to help stop the violence. I personally never had any problems with commandism with those I trained, though I do acknowledge the stories of people coming to the party because of the guns, and not for the whole political thing. You get a mass movement, you're going to get a broad spectrum of people who are interested for a variety of reasons.

The Lumpen

Under traditional Marxist delineation of classes, the lumpen proletariat is the bottom stratum of society that consisted of prostitutes, pimps, gangsters; in other words, people who are career criminals. Number one, Marx says they should be recognized as such, that from a sociological position, they are a separate grouping from the so-called honest working poor. But the Panthers expanded the definition of the lumpen to include the honest working poor. When we talk about career crime, we're talking about crime in poverty-stricken neighborhoods in a racially oppressed community. So there's a blurring of the line between the honest working poor and the criminal element with frequent crossover. I'm stunned at the number of God-fearing, hardworking African American families with at least one child with a career criminal record, and it busted up the family. When I was growing up in West Oakland, I did both. I worked hard when I could find a job, but when there were occasions and opportunities I did what a poor person might do. So when the Panthers came up with their concept of lumpen, I helped recruit from pool halls—O'Reilly on Fifty-Fourth, Stubby's on Sacramento Avenue, a couple of pool halls on Seventh Street. If you're young and you want to get the word out, you go to places where your people are and where you're comfortable.

Some people say the lumpen element contributed to the downfall of the Panthers because they were quick to use intimidation and violence and they lacked discipline.[44] There is a basis for that argument. On the other hand, I was trying to link up one of the brothers off the block—out of the pool hall, high school dropout—with a college student or college graduate. I thought that there would be this interchange where the toughness of the street would go in this direction and the academic acumen would go in that direction. I've been amazed, and yet not amazed, at the high percentage of the former lumpen who went off to college and became professionals. I say this is partly due to their experience in the BPP. Now people might say I'm giving the BPP [too much] credit, but the BPP was a consciousness-opening organization.

I have Harvey [Dong] to thank for looking at the phenomenon of political consciousness as being very important. I've always pooh-poohed the intangible. But then that's only one half of the dialectic. In the sixties there was a big intellectual debate about the humanism of Marx, that he concentrated too much on the political economy of changing the society and the flow of history. But when Marx had to make a decision whether to focus on the political economy or on the more humanistic aspect of his philosophy, he chose to go toward the political economy and the result is his magnum opus, *Das Kapital.*

"The Greatest Personal Mistake I Ever Made"

One night after a shotgun patrol—it was in December 1966—I tell my fiancée what I've been doing at night, and maybe she's already heard some things from our landlady, who'd seen us leaving with our weapons. Not only that, but our apartment is turning into a classroom for self-defense classes. Here I was, just started at Berkeley, on my way to the American Dream, set up housekeeping, domestic tranquillity prevailed. In my enthusiasm for being a member of a truly revolutionary group, one that would require my commitment to the cause, I didn't notice how very upset she had become. The Black Panther Party for Self-Defense appeared in her mind to be almost suicidally crazy. She was most concerned about her safety: What if the cops started busting out the door? I, on the other hand, being self-righteous, wouldn't give an inch. So here I was, had to make a decision between my fiancée and the party, which is only a couple of months old. How could she understand where I was coming from? I could barely articulate it in my own mind; I'm standing in the doorway like I don't know if the moment you step in that door, you gone, you history. Here's the other part of compartmentalizing my life. She didn't know the full extent of things but as she found out, and she found out quickly, it went downhill rapidly, much more than if there had been a gradual buildup. Now I can't speak for how she arrived at her conclusion. My thing was, I got to make a decision. I mean, this is a hard one to make. But a man's got to do what a man's got to do. Now I could feel comfortable with my little American Dream thing. On the other hand, the Black Panther Party for Self-Defense was a revolutionary nationalist organization, ready to take care of the business. To me, this was the first group that not only talked the talk but walked the walk. Don't forget, we've had a few victories in the streets by that time and let me tell you I was pumping my chest. She said I better make the decision there and now. I said, "Okay." She said, "I'm packing." I said, "I'll help you." And she left. I remember sitting in a bar around Christmastime of '66, in downtown Oakland, with all the Christmas decorations and the Christmas music. Charles Dickens himself could not have created a bleaker scene. She left me. But I didn't break stride.[45]

Now that I'm doing this biography, this issue has reemerged. It may have been among the greatest personal mistakes that I ever made in my whole life. You asked, "Do I think that there was a way I could have reconciled it at the time?" That's one of the things about the flow of history. If I gave it a great deal of thought, maybe in the far recesses of my mind, I could have come up with a positive resolution. But this was a dialectical process that reached a point of the opposite turning into the unity of the opposites, appearance wise. But in reality, what could I have done? Because there was no way of integrating the two processes as they were moving along. No way for it. Now the question is which one would have been better for me personally? However, there's another way of looking at that. Which one was the best path of living? I would have been a different person today had I gone with the other way. But what you see today, politically and personally, is what you get, with all the positive parts and I'm hoping very few of the negative parts. When I refer to that as a significant crossroad, that is true. That was one of the heaviest scenes I know, and because of circumstances, I didn't have much time to adjust. What is important is the flow of the masses to bigger and better things. I stand by Eugene Debs's statement, "I don't want to rise above the masses. I want to rise with the masses." So if you have to lose your personal identity, if you have to sacrifice yourself, it's worth it. On the other hand, that voice way back says, "Richard, that was a fucked-up decision you made."[46]

"Stop for Little Kids"

The next thing that happened after the shotgun patrol was when the community in North Oakland came to the party and asked us for help in the educational field. Namely, Santa Fe Elementary School on Market Street was experiencing a series of accidents, primarily because Market Street was a major boulevard for commuters in and out of Oakland. The parents had petitioned the city to put a stop sign on the corner, but the city had not responded. The Panthers said, "Let's look at the vehicle law. They can't be traveling more than X miles an hour in a school zone. That means we got to enforce the traffic thing because there ain't no traffic cops around." So we became traffic cops. I'll never forget the looks on the commuters' faces as they were streaking down the streets and came to a screeching halt as we stood up and said, "Stop for little kids." We had shotguns out there—I was standing there with a shotgun myself—as if to say, "I think you better stop." Along comes John Law, wondering what we're doing. We tell them: "You should be thankful. We're doing your job. We're directing traffic to protect the little kids." Needless to say, the cops weren't happy with our appearance. They'd already been bugged by our shotgun patrols and now we're starting to take their jobs away from them. A week later, that traffic sign went up and the community said, "Yeah, team."[47]

The Party Grows

About a month after the party started, I was made branch captain of the Berkeley chapter—a chapter with only one member—myself.[48] Alex Papillion, who was in the Soul Student Advisory Council at Merritt College, lived in Berkeley. So he was asked to help to beef up the Berkeley branch. My man Alex was a gutsy son of a bitch. He and I stood off the Berkeley Police Department by ourselves one day by having a rally at Berkeley High School at noontime to reach out to the students. So here's Berkeley High. There's a park across the street and across this street is the Berkeley Police Department. So we had the kids come out to the park for lunch, set up our little chair, got our literature. We were packing—you know we got their attention. Then the cops started looking out the windows wondering, "What the hell's happening at the park across the street? Oh, shit! Black Panthers. Those Oakland Black Panthers! They're in Berkeley now!" I remember Alex waving his gun around that day. He was making a point in his presentation, that we had a right to self-defense. I thought that was bold. I kept my hand on my gun in my holster when I spoke. I don't recall if anyone joined that day, but I know a lot of teenagers from Berkeley High School will never forget that day when these crazies rolled up.

So we're working to build the party in the Bay Area.[49] West Oakland's organized. North Oakland's organized. We got Berkeley down. What about East Oakland? In East Oakland there was an organization called ODAC, Oakland Direct Action Committee, led by Mark Comfort, a giant of a man. Mark Comfort was, I believe, a military veteran. I would classify Mark as one of the few revolutionary integrationists, somewhat in the same category as Robert F. Williams. He really was a down-home boy, typical of the transplants from the rural South, moves to the big city, to the urban North, and was married to a White woman. When the Civil Rights Movement hits Berkeley and CORE [Congress of Racial Equality] and other nonviolent groups begin their protests, Mark got involved. So Mark and I meet on this picket line probably in '62, about the same time I made the SNCC connections. I'm talking with him, a big dude, he's got a couple dozen people with him, young bloods from the 'hood. He says, "Come over to my place anytime." So I walk to East Oakland, had dinner with him. Then I discovered he was not nonviolent.[50]

One time, he made front-page news because there was a hamburger joint, with carhops and all, that primarily working-class Whites went to, and his cousin was beaten up by a group of White bullies. I was stunned when I read about it in the papers. Mark, according to the papers, cleaned out the counter from one end to the other. I said, "Whoa!" So I called him, said, "Man, why didn't you call me? I was just coming down the street from the place. I'd have been there helping you." So here is Mark, he's doing the civil rights thing but he hadn't fully adopted this nonviolence principle.[51]

There were about a hundred members in ODAC, mostly young bloods from the streets. So as the party established itself in West and North Oakland, somebody came up with the bright idea, "Let's go see Mark Comfort." We go touring over to East Oakland, talk to Mark Comfort, and he brings ODAC into the BPP. If we look at this militarily, this is a big plus because ODAC had probably as many people, maybe more than the party had at that particular time. We got all of Oakland locked up, and a little part of Berkeley. That was big, especially given the turf wars going on.[52]

So we're talking about consolidating the Bay Area. North Richmond came on board after the Panthers got involved with Denzil Dowell, the young man who had been blown away by the cops.[53] His mother wanted to voice her concern publicly, but she had been denied permission to have a rally there. Don't forget, by this time the police patrols had occurred, and word traveled real fast to North Richmond that there are some crazy dudes out there that might secure two square blocks for a rally. Now here's the corker: historically, young gangs, African American, Latino, and now even Southeast Asians, have been battling for Richmond and Oakland. When I was growing up, the vestiges of the White working class was leaving and African American gangs in both cities were blowing each other away. To my gang, North Richmond was enemy territory. I remember one time we thought we were going to do something slick. A couple of carloads of us went out there. But we beat a hasty retreat, with even the women and children throwing rocks at our cars as we were conducting a strategic withdrawal. At the time, I was led to believe that the North Richmond people were a little bit below the civilized society. They still had pigs and chickens running around in their backyards. But they were tough, project tough. So when the request came in for the Dowell rally, my response was, "Oh, shit." But duty calls.

So we go scooting out there, we hold down the park, about thirty of us against about a hundred, a hundred and fifty Contra Costa sheriff's department officers, including one helicopter, as I recall. I have to admit, I was scared because if something went down, all of us were going to get killed. I'm responsible for one part of the perimeter. Bobby and Huey took another part and Mark Comfort another. It took the four of us so that Denzil Dowell's mother could address the community about the murder of her son. I don't know if I was in charge of security that day, but I did play a leading role. It was my job to make sure that everybody knew where they were supposed to be, and I did tell the rifleman that if shooting started, hit the helicopter first.[54]

I will underscore, that was one time that I admit I was scared. I wasn't scared of dying. I was just scared. That transcended even dying. But the irony is, if we got wiped out, that may not have stopped the movement. When they saw us, I think the enemy shitted green apples because they had never, the whole country had never, seen anything like this. Disciplined, bold—we were some bad motherfuckers. The next weekend, the community embraced us. Oh, I ate good. I had a young lady come up to me, feel my uniform, my beret was on tight enough, I'll tell you, it was something else. It was something else because some justice had been served regarding Mrs. Dowell's loss. An example had been set. We demonstrated that we could stand up to fight, providing some inspiration and some hope.

The North Richmond event started to put the party on the map in the Bay Area. Every time we turn around, they got little groups of these Panthers. Those crazos out of West Oakland are branching out all over the place.

What happened next is that the state legislature decided to strike down the various laws regarding the bearing of arms. Up to that point, sections of the penal code allowed people to bear arms in public—could be at rallies and demonstrations, on the shotgun patrols. The California state legislature decided to negate those laws, specifically targeting the Panthers. When we read the newspapers, we decided that the party would attend a state legislature meeting to register our concern. It was decided to split leadership up based on the British military command system, where two officers are in charge of a group. So Bobby and Huey split up. Bobby was to lead the delegation, which included Eldridge Cleaver, Emory Douglas, Mark Comfort, and Bobby Hutton. Huey stayed behind. I personally didn't expect any big deal. I thought they'd go up there, deliver the message, and come back. That's one of the reasons why I wasn't so hot on going because I didn't think there was going to be any action. Maybe I had a midterm that day too, I don't know. Next thing we know, they all got busted. Huey and I spent a great deal of time getting the brothers out. This was an emergency. Huey made the legal connections. I helped him raise some of the money. A lot of money had to be raised in a short period of time. Many were sympathetic and decided to get involved.[55]

The *New York Times* had now brought the Black Panthers on the national radar scope. Almost every historian will agree that the Sacramento incident brought the Panthers to national prominence. So this naturally enhanced the visibility of the party, and chapters began to spring up throughout California and later across the nation.[56]

On Leaving the SWP

So I'm a busy little bee. I'm in the BPP and still a member of the Socialist Workers Party and the Young Socialist Alliance, though my activities with them were minimal. My relationship with the YSA/SWP had gotten strained ever since I delivered that report on the Black nationalist conference. Right after that, the BPP began and I'm working to build the party. Around February 1967, I met with the executive committee of the YSA/SWP to deliver one more report on what the Left called "the Negro Question." They were stunned by what I was doing as a member of the BPP. They went into executive session, came back, and said that I would be asked to be placed out of my assignment as the resident expert on the Negro Question. They wanted me to work on something else. I innocently asked why and forced them to admit that they were apprehensive about my work with the BPP because it could lead to some heavy-duty stuff and then if my SWP membership is revealed, it might not reflect well on the SWP.[57] I said something about, "I thought the SWP was in the forefront of the struggle, the most advanced among the White groups out there. The SWP has a golden opportunity to rank up with the cutting edge of the national liberation movement here. It's reaching the point to either fish or cut bait." Around this time, I was told that the senior leadership thought that I was a member of the Johnson–Forest Tendency. This was the tendency comprised of C. L. R. James, Grace Lee Boggs, and Raya Dunayevskaya. I'd never met them and I didn't read their position paper until years later. By the time I discovered them, things were moving too damn fast and I didn't have time to link up with them.

The SWP leadership replied to the effect that "well, you can't be a member of both groups. You've got to choose." I was pissed. I went to Huey, "I got a little curve ball thrown at me." I told them what it boiled down to and asked how he felt about my membership and what I was doing. Huey said in a sense, "You're a Black Panther. I don't care what other organizations you're involved in." The BPP did have a prohibition about members belonging to other Black liberation groups, which was probably the result of the struggle with the Republic of New Africa and Karenga's US Organization. But my being in the SWP was no problem to Huey. Basically, he said, "It's up to you, Richard." I thought, "Oh shit, I got to make a decision again." So I wrote my letter of resignation and hand-delivered it to the SWP leadership.[58]

When I cut through all the pluses or minuses, it was generally a plus for me to be in the SWP. I had invested my time with the main Trotskyite political tendency in this country for a number of years. There were a lot of decent people in that organization. I have respect for the senior leadership that struggled for proletarian gains during the thirties and forties, and who went through the political repression of that particular group. I developed some personal friendships there that go on to this day. But in the sixties, there was a difference between the older and younger generation. When I say my report on the Black nationalist conference was not well received, let me put it this way. As I gauged the audience—there were about a hundred members there, almost all White— I noticed that the older leadership didn't seem to appreciate some of the things I had said. This was possibly due to the fact that they had been excluded from attending the conference, or partially from the fact that maybe they didn't understand the full significance of Black nationalism, or maybe they did. The younger members, who were mostly students from Berkeley, my generation, seemed to be more enthusiastic. Those that wanted to come with me but couldn't because of their race became quiet supporters of the Panthers. To this day, I don't regret the decision to leave, and I was able to step to a higher level as a result of that break.

Free Huey

In October 1967, it was alleged that Huey killed one cop and wounded another. I was stunned by the enormity of the situation, shocked about how symbolic it was that the Ministry of Defense would be the first one to go down. One of the great things of the BPP was that they couldn't call their leadership a cheap trick. When the struggle was the hardest, the leadership was there. But the reality of the situation is they got Huey. Top it all off, Bobby's in jail! This is where Eldridge and Kathleen Cleaver jumped on there something fierce. Decisions had to be made hard and fast. Eldridge and Kathleen did a superb job in organizing Huey's defense, locally, regionally, nationally, internationally. They were able to hold the party together. Demonstrations had been taking place in front of the courthouse on a daily basis, as the hearings and trials moved along. At one point during that period, the Asian American Political Alliance was there with a sign stating, "Yellow Peril Supports Black Power," held by two Asians, who were among the founders of AAPA. By then, I had begun running with the Asians.[59]

In February 1968, an event took place at the Oakland Auditorium in honor of Huey's birthday under the theme of "Free Huey." That was one of the few times I got pulled back fast because the party needed everybody. I was put on security. So I'm standing up there watching, looking down, and the announcements come forth. Stokely Carmichael of SNCC is here and he will be our honorary prime minister. I said, great god, we got Eldridge Cleaver up there, Bobby Seale, I can't remember if David Hilliard was in jail at the time or onstage. All the leadership was there, except Huey. That's why we were having the party, for Brother Huey's release. From SNCC, Stokely Carmichael, BPP prime minister; James Forman, BPP minister of foreign affairs; and H. Rap Brown, BPP minister of justice. I felt so good when they made those announcements because to me, bringing SNCC into the BPP represented the quintessential part of the consolidation. I didn't realize it at the time, but this was merely symbolic. It was my understanding that thousands more would be joining the party. The party ain't more than a year and a half old and now we see the merger of these two great organizations with two sets of leadership that you can't find nowhere else in the whole country, which validates why I hung with the Black Panthers.[60]

Field Marshal

Meanwhile, I had been quietly made field marshal.[61] This happened around April '68 when the Tri-Con incident exploded in my face. It was Huey that made the decision to make me a field marshal without portfolio, so I was above branch captain. I think Bobby and I also discussed my role. This probably came about at my request because I was getting actively involved at Berkeley with Third World organizing, the Asian American Movement, and Ethnic Studies. Plus, by that time, the BPP got so large and with Forman, Brown, and Carmichael joining the group, the party was in good hands as far as leadership, with people much better qualified than me to head the Berkeley branch.[62]

My mission as field marshal was to be fruitful and multiply because of the internalization of Che Guevara's exhortation of many more Vietnams. If there is a BPP in the Black community giving them holy hell, why can't that happen in the Latino community? We saw that begin to develop with the Brown Berets in Southern California and the Young Lords in Chicago. So I brought up the prospect to Bobby and Huey about what about an Asian American BPP? The idea of "Yellow Panthers" never crossed my mind, but Alex Hing did a good job in justifying the title. The principal thing about a field marshal was their rank enabled them to cut across branches. In other words, at the local level, the highest rank when I joined was branch captain. Who do you have after branch captain? You have the minister of defense. However, the minister of defense can't be everywhere, he can maybe have a couple of deputy ministers of defense. But it's more reasonable to have a field marshal. There were two qualifications that were always very important. Number one, you had to know the political program, upside down, backward and forward, because you might be called upon to create a branch or to inspect a branch that springs up anywhere. Number two, being a field marshal, you had to be a veteran. That's why field marshals were all men, but I remember hearing that there was one female field marshal. Don Cox was the quintessential field marshal.

Asian Americans and the Black Panther Party

In the late 1960s, a radical Asian American group started to form in San Francisco Chinatown. The Red Guards went to Bobby and David and asked to join the party; Huey was in prison. By then, membership was closed to non-Africans. So word got to Richard, we got a set in San Francisco Chinatown: "You appreciate the environment there, brother. A pool hall, the bars, and the lumpen." In fact, I refer to Alex Hing as an original lumpen. Meanwhile, since I was knee deep with AAPA in Berkeley and the Red Guards were over in San Francisco, there was no way logistically that I could do both. I've been up to almost every assignment, every mission, but there are some things that I knew were impossible to do. So Bobby and David and later Don Cox in the San Francisco BPP worked with Alex and the rest and encouraged them to form their own Asian American group modeled on the BPP Ten-Point Program. I have to say, forming Red Guards was a stroke of genius. It also validated what I was doing in Berkeley, exploring the possibilities of a Panther-like group. I don't mean with all the bells and whistles, we didn't wear all these uniforms and stuff, but I'm talking about political program. You'll see this when I get to AAPA and I go over the political program.[63]

But there were also Asian Americans who joined the party—six that I know of, including two women.[64] Five were Japanese Americans, all Sanseis [third generation], including one who was half Japanese and half White. Why the predominance of Japanese Americans in the party? Off the top of my head, I'd say this was probably due to their greater assimilation and, second, to the experience of the concentration camps. The third variable was, for the males at least, I'm pretty sure all of us grew up in multicultural neighborhoods.[65]

Three of us were featured in *Giant Robot,* so I can talk about them. But the others I won't name. Guy Kurose was in the Seattle chapter. He passed away at an early age and *It's About Time,* a newspaper by Black Panther veterans, paid a nice tribute to him. Guy continued to carry the banner of freedom, justice, and equality, even after the demise of the party. Yeah, Panthers! Guy and another Sansei brother were active with the party in Seattle. At the time— this would be the late sixties—I heard about them and I said, "Right on." But I couldn't go up there and talk to them because I was busted and couldn't leave California.[66] Lee Lew-Lee, a Chinese Black from Jamaica, was with the New York chapter, where he also joined Asian Americans for Action. I didn't know him at the time. However, I want to point out that Lee Lew-Lee has made an important contribution by producing the documentary *All Power to the People.* To me, it's the finest documentary on the history and influence of the BPP I have ever seen.[67] Then there were two Asian American women, both in the Berkeley chapter. How they came to join the party was that they had both gone down to the Oakland headquarters. But since they were from Berkeley, they put them in my branch. One was from a prominent family in Berkeley, and I promised her that I would never reveal her identity. She played a minimal role. The other woman was also middle class, whereas the men were working class. If I mention the contributions of this other woman, she would be identifiable. But in my opinion, her contributions were significant. That's all I can say on that. So at one time, half of my branch was Asian American.[68]

All six Asians joined the party in about the first year and a half before the party started limiting membership. By the time Alex Hing and the Red Guards wanted to join, they were told to form their own group. I don't know why the party began to limit membership to Blacks only, but it makes sense. When a group is starting to form they look at anybody. There's Richard, let's bring him in. He ain't Black; well, we'll consider him half-Black. In fact, one of my closest friends, upon learning about my current medical problems, said, "See, I told you you Black. You got the hypertension, you got the diabetes, you got . . ." There were also Latinos in the party in the beginning. In Oakland alone, there were about three or four. But when the Brown Berets started gaining influence in Southern California there were enough to form a Brown Beret group up here.[69]

Why would an Asian American join an African American group? Because the struggle for freedom, justice, and equality transcends racial and national boundaries. It's like that famous theologian said:

First they came for the Communists, but I didn't speak up because I wasn't a Communist.
    Then they came for the trade unionists, but I didn't speak up because I wasn't a trade unionist.
    Then they came for the Jews, but I didn't speak up because I wasn't a Jew.
    Then they came for me, and there was nobody left to speak up.[70]

Blacks were in the forefront of the struggle for national liberation, not just for Black people, for all people of color and some White people too. So it would seem natural that I would want to join an organization that's purely revolutionary. Plus, there was nothing else out there and the party said, "Come on in."

You're wondering how my being Asian affected my role in the party. Let's look at values. Here you have a group that's priding itself on defense. Talk is one thing, but it boils down to practice. I could put self-defense into practice— supplying guns and carrying, and even more so, I could teach self-defense. That sort of takes away from the racial thing. The badness cuts across a lot of things. Also, it was openly known that Huey, Bobby, and I were tight. Hey, man, you with Huey and Bobby, you cool. Plus, I was never pushy. It's just a part of my personality. I'm not one that gets my rocks off on being egocentric. So I never had any confrontations regarding that issue.

On Women and the BPP

Why is it that the Panthers always get jammed about sexist attitudes in their group? Think about it: of all the literature you've read on movements of the sixties, no group has been lambasted more in this area. Yet it's the only group I know of, coming out of the sixties, that had women in prominent places of leadership and made significant contributions. I'm a little annoyed too because they're so highly critical! There's another dimension people don't understand. We were a combat party. We weren't a discussion club. We took to the streets and fought hard. That first year or two the male leadership was decimated down to the third level! I can remember at one point I was the only one out. Everybody else was in prison. I felt lonely . . . damn! I respect the women who joined the party. I didn't oppose Huey's decision to allow in Tarika Joan Lewis. But I was surprised that a woman was asking to join and I was critical. What happened was Tarika's older brother, John, had joined the party and she got all fired up. How would you like to be sitting at the table carrying this big .357 and this girl comes up to me, "I want to join." I thought we're in a combat party, that was my self-image in the first month or so, and women don't normally serve in a combat party. We just dealt with a youngster over here, I'm talking about Little Bobby Hutton, but a girl now, c'mon. But I wasn't in charge of membership qualifications, and I went with whatever Huey had to say and it was impressed on me that we were going to build a People's Party.[71]

I don't think Tarika was the first woman to join, but the others didn't stay around too long. That's why Tarika is given that honor of being called the first woman to join the party. To this day, she is holding up high the banner of free-dom, justice, and equality. Of all the presentations I've ever heard regarding the origins of the West Oakland community, Tarika's grasp—social, economic, and political, because she grew up in the 'hood—is amazing. She has a mas-ter's degree in performing arts and she plays a mean violin. Later, it was easier to accept the women because the women did their jobs. So later, I didn't blink an eye when I was told, "This sister's on the security squad with you." Of course if I didn't know the senior officer whose judgment I respected I might have said, "I don't know," but she was serious as a major heart attack. And of course, people like Kathleen [Cleaver] and Assata [Shakur] exemplified the finest of the women in the BPP.[72]

Black Politics

An idea came up for a publication of a monthly magazine, along the same lines as previous Black nationalist publications, such as *Soul Book,* with Bobby Seale as editor, or *Black Dialogue,* with Kenny Freeman as editor. The newspaper of the party was going by then and most radical organizations in that day had two publications: a newspaper and a magazine.[73] The magazine idea came up, and I convinced the party that this would be a worthwhile venture. However, it would have to be along alliance lines because the BPP newspaper was already taking up a lot of the resources. The talent of the Panther newspaper was extraordinary, including Sam Napier and artist Emory Douglas. I'm talking heavy-duty stuff. But with the magazine, we could offer articles of lasting interest. Now what would make this publication different from other previous Black nationalist publications? The answer was the portion of articles that would be technical in nature, short theories of self-defense with long, detailed, well-written, well-illustrated articles on the usage of self-defense equipment.

From January '68 to around spring/summer of '69, *Black Politics,* a journal of liberation, came out every month. I believe I wrote the first article in the first issue. There were articles on African civilizations, critiques of Fanon, a special Bobby Hutton issue. You would be amazed at the breadth of those articles. We published maybe seven articles each issue, some were illustrated, some not. Everybody on the editorial board wrote something. We had a lot of talent. We also reprinted seminal articles written by Che, Fanon, and Lenin. We put out positions on Vietnam. The decision regarding the inclusion of articles was generally a collective effort. We didn't have a regular business meeting for the editorial board, but before every issue could be printed, we had to agree on which manuscripts to include. It would take three days and four nights to do something like that. It was hard work and a handful of us were able to put it out. I was a student at the time, which helped me because my skills were being developed in the classroom. I don't have a complete list of the articles I personally wrote and because we used nom de plumes a lot, I can't really identify who wrote what. I donated my complete set to UC Santa Barbara. I believe that's the only complete set in the whole country, with one exception, the dude I called the Reverend Thomas Sanders.[74]

Reverend Thomas Sanders was the business manager of the publication, the only White person working on the journal. He was born and raised in Texas. He joined the Texas Communist Party in the fifties, when it was life threatening to do so. He came out to California, married a Chinese American woman, joined the SWP. When I met him, he was the Bay Area organizer for the Fair Play for Cuba Committee. When I began the discussion regarding the Negro Question in the SWP, he was the only adult member that seemed to understand what I was trying to say. He left shortly after I split, as I recall. But I remained with him. I would characterize him as the John Brown of the 1960s liberation struggles. The Reverend Thomas Sanders.[75]

Around this time, I had made connections with the West Coast consul general of the Republic of New Africa (RNA), who was a student at Berkeley. I'm up at Berkeley recruiting, and I must have met every African American male student on the campus at least once. I ain't running around standing in front hawking the papers. I'm talking to the brothers: "Say, brother! Where you from? Oh yeah, you went to high school at . . ." So I'm talking with this dude and he looks at me, "You a Black Panther?" There was a little gasp. I thought it was because I was Asian, or Oriental as we were called. This is somewhere around late '67 or maybe spring '68. He was married and a vet. We started socializing on campus. Then one night when I was over at his place, he revealed to me that there was an RNA chapter in Berkeley and he was the West Coast consul general. I can't believe it. I said, "Say what?!" Not only do I discover that there is an RNA chapter at Berkeley, but it has at least twice as many members as the BPP chapter in Berkeley. Even though we were in different groups, our political directions were pretty much the same place. He's invited to join the editorial board of *Black Politics*.[76]

The editorial board normally consisted of at least two or three senior Black Panthers, including myself, and at least two RNA representatives. Several independents who were not members of any organization but felt comfortable in working with the BPP and the RNA were also on the board. There was even a woman on the editorial board.[77] You asked if I was on the editorial board the whole time. Considering how I think I might have been the originator of that publication, yes, from beginning to end. Because of the technical articles in the magazine, none of us used our real names. The only person that used his real name was the Reverend Thomas Sanders. Somebody had to be out there for the legal stuff: check the bank account, mailbox drop, and stuff like that. None of us was willing. Based on my experience signing for the Pauley Ballroom for Tri-Con, I wasn't about to sign nothing no more.[78]

The thing that helped it get along was even though the party was unable to allocate financial resources for its publication, we on the editorial board managed to raise funds from amongst ourselves and our connections. Not only that, we found a printing press about the size of a suitcase.[79] We were able to put the printing press, the stencils, the ink, the paper in the trunk of a car. It was never published in the same place twice. We invested a lot of money in that equipment and we weren't about to see it get suppressed. See, at the time, it wasn't just the Black Panthers, but Leway, an Asian American group in San Francisco's Chinatown, had the cops come in and bust up typewriters and grab machines and everything out the file cabinets. I won't take the entire credit for the idea of the mobile printing press, but I think I had a lot to do with that. The press run was usually about five hundred copies, maybe a thousand. We distributed the magazine nationwide and used connections in the cities that agreed to be distributors for the publication. At the local level, they were placed in bookstores, and this is where the Reverend Thomas Sanders comes in. He did all the connecting. A Black Panther in San Francisco might say, bring me ten copies. He did a hell of a job.[80]

You asked if there were any ideological conflicts because of the different groups involved. I can't recall anything serious. It was a smooth-running editorial board. We were all adults. We all pretty much knew what we were doing. Of course, I recognize there was tension between the Black Panthers and the RNA. There was a critical period that was really strained that centered around Maulana Ron Karenga, who headed the US Organization in Los Angeles. Karenga was also a member of the RNA when members of the US Organization killed Black Panther leaders Bunchy Carter and John Huggins at UCLA.[81] The RNA leadership asked Karenga to come forth and give his version of what happened, but since he didn't appear, they expelled him.[82] Locally, while it got a little shaky at some of the editorial board meetings, a lot of the smooth running had to do with the interpersonal relationships among board members and I had overseen the selection of that editorial board.[83]

I personally didn't make a big bone of contention about ideological differences. In fact, I supported RNA's demand for the five states—Mississippi, Georgia, Louisiana, Alabama, and South Carolina—as a land base for the Black Nation.[84] I believed in the Black Nation position primarily because by that time, I had met Reies Tijerina.[85] His organization, the Alianza, put forth the demand requiring the state of New Mexico as a beginning for the Indo-Hispano people.

He was a charismatic speaker and what he had to say made sense because while on the surface, it might look cultural nationalist, I have always held the belief that people of color in this country are nations within the nation. The colonial position of our peoples of color was similar to that of Third World countries. I had questions about the group actually working it out because it is more utopian, in a scientific sense, and there are examples of utopian societies not succeeding, even if they were based on land. The point is we had both Black Panthers and RNA representatives on the editorial board of *Black Politics*. That's never happened anywhere else that I know of.

It was called to our attention some years ago that there was a congressional investigation of our publication. A congressional investigation—you know you've made the big time! The thing is, they were able to identify half of the editorial board and contributors to *Black Politics,* myself included.[86]

Huey's Release from Prison

Good news, Huey is released in August 1970. Part of the celebrations upon his release included a triumphant return to Merritt College. At that time, I'd been appointed to the faculty of the Ethnic Studies Department at UC Berkeley, newly founded as a result of a student strike.[87] I'm sitting in my office, having my coffee, when I got a phone call. The major link between me and Huey all through this period required my return to active duty on the front line. So I called my secretary and said, "I'm taking the day off. I'm going off campus." I went off campus to my Cadillac, where in the trunk, I had a briefcase with my equipment. I went down to Merritt College to connect with the senior party officials who briefed me on what was coming down. Huey was scheduled to appear in the Merritt College Auditorium. Word had reached security of the party that there might be some trouble and they decided to get me into the action too. I was assigned preliminary responsibility for Huey's safety during his presentation. I have a photograph showing Huey speaking and myself, on security, sitting to his left. I have another photograph of me and a sister, who was also on security at that event.[88]

Before we went onstage, the president of the college asked who was in charge of security. I was the one that was shoved in front. I knew him from my Merritt College student days. He was concerned about the possibility of violence. I reassured him that I was going to do my utmost in preserving the peace because that's why I was there. My talents, my expertise were now being called to the front. That made my head swim a little bit because an hour or so before, I'm sitting in a comfortable office at UC Berkeley, sitting at on my desk having my cigar, drinking my coffee, but the word had been given. As Huey was making his presentation, some idiot in the middle of the audience jumped up and started getting off on Huey, claiming among other things, that Huey was Satan, that Allah did not like what Huey was doing. He had a serious beef with Huey to the point of challenging Huey physically. Oh, shit. I was thinking about Malcolm and that distraction from the audience when he got assassinated. I was getting ready to Freddie there; that dude was history in my eyes. I was impressed with how Huey was able to control the situation so that it didn't end up embarrassing the party or the college.

So here it is 1970, and Huey and I are reunited. I put my life in his hands again. I came out alive. I think some people question my personal loyalty to Huey. Well, Huey was one of the few people I've ever trusted with my life. If I trust somebody with my life, at their decision, it's a life-or-death warrant for me. That's got to be somebody whose judgment—not necessarily emotional stability—is clear. Huey was one of those.[89]

Around this time, since I was on the faculty at Berkeley and an administrator too, I was approached about the possibility of getting Huey into graduate school there. J. Herman Blake of UC Berkeley's Sociology Department, who I first met in the Civil Rights Movement, approached me. So I discreetly explored the possibility. I went from department to department, professor to professor, just kind of throwing an idea out there. I wasn't surprised by the reception. Even from the most so-called committed activist professors and administrators, they didn't think it would be appropriate. I, of course, argued with a great deal of fervor. I was unsuccessful and there were others, I think, who were quietly going around doing the same thing. I mean, here's Huey, comes out of the Oakland public school system, semi-illiterate, blazes through Merritt. But they questioned: "He didn't do the four years of undergraduate?" Give me a break. His prison time was doing four years. I was willing to argue life experience. Unfortunately, the climate wasn't right. But J. Herman Blake ended up at UC Santa Cruz. He became provost at Santa Cruz and managed to swing Huey's admission to graduate school there and Huey ultimately got his doctorate.[90]

On the Split in the Party

Huey is out of prison and he's got the helm of the party now. Bobby's starting to see his way clear of his legal difficulties. Eldridge and Kathleen are still out there chugging along. Emory's been hanging in all these years. Big Man, the hard-core, don't give up. Then the next thing I know, I was caught off guard by the Bakuninist/anarchist turn of the party, which was in the party newspaper:

"Catechism of a Revolutionist" by Bakunin.[91] It's like it's the party line. What is going on here?! Then Huey and Eldridge split acrimoniously, in a public setting.[92] Now I'm estranged from Huey and organizationally from the party in that I wasn't directly or even indirectly involved with the party at that time. But I'm still a member. I consider myself a member to the extent that when I get called, I respond quickly. Almost everybody was talking about the split, but based on personal issues—the strong personality of Huey clashed with the strong personality of Cleaver. But I tried to analyze the political differences so I could make an intelligent decision about which way I was going.

My political analysis boiled down to this. Huey was developing his theory of intercommunalism and putting forth "it's the people that change society."[93] That bothered me in a sense that Huey was emphasizing the people, and not the class and class struggle. Though Huey's unlearned but developing, and I'm having a little bit of problem understanding his theory, I thought I saw the germs of his ideas bubbling up, that it was a breakthrough in revolutionary intellectual thought. I was impressed with Huey's efforts to adapt Marxism–Leninism to a Third World situation. The few discussions I had with him led me to believe that Huey could be an African American Marxist. He understood the basics of Marxism and could take it higher than Maoism. Eldridge's position was anarchy. To me, anarchism essentially boils down to a small elite that's going to be the engine of history to change society.[94] History has proven that anarchy doesn't work. In the early 1960s, when I first began my readings of political theory, anarchism popped up as one of the alternatives to the system. If you study the history, Mikhail Bakunin and Peter Kropotkin are considered the founders of the modern anarchist movement. But I always measured the theories against action and programs, and of course anarchy in my readings had no political program outside of this violence thing.[95] That's where I start to separate myself from anarchism. Of course I admire anarchists like the Haymarket martyrs in Chicago, who while on strike for an eight-hour day, got railroaded into a conviction and executed by the state, and Sacco and Vanzetti, anarchists and Italian immigrants executed by the state for their political beliefs. But anarchism has never successfully demonstrated that it works. Had I not talked to Huey about intercommunalism and halfway understood where he was coming from, it would have been a lot harder for me to justify my position on the split.

Not only did the party split but virtually all of the Third World organizations were discussing the differences between Huey and Eldridge. There was one point when two Asian Americans tried to reconcile the conflict between Huey and Eldridge. I was sitting in a classroom up at Berkeley, minding my own business. All of a sudden the side door of the lecture hall opens and there's Alex Hing and a couple of other Third World people, all in their battle gear, ready to go to war! They motioned for me to leave: would I talk with them? Alex said, "Look, this split between Huey and Eldridge is getting out of control. We got to talk." I found out later from my classmates that they thought it was so heavy that the Third World students started evacuating classes because I had left so abruptly. They thought, "Uh-oh, Richard's pissed at the professor and he's going to blow it up." That's how dramatic it was. So we get to my place and Alex and I start talking. It's minister of defense of the Red Guards to minister of defense of AAPA.[96] I'm stunned. This is the situation—as if I didn't know: the split in the party was reflecting itself in a split in all of these organizations like the Red Guard, and AAPA to a certain extent, but AAPA I was able to control. I didn't worry about them. Meanwhile I'm thinking Alex is probably with Eldridge: am I going to have to shoot Alex, or he's going to have to shoot me, or what the hell is going on? But Alex was cool. He wanted to see if we can get Huey and Eldridge together again; he'll represent Eldridge's side and I'll represent Huey's side to begin this rapprochement. I looked at Alex and I said, "You bad, Alex. Maybe this breach can be healed." Of course in retrospect, there was a snowball's chance in hell. But I give it to Alex for analyzing the situation and coming up with a plan; I hadn't even thought about that. Alex and I had known each other, so we had this working relationship. He trusted me enough to approach me, even though I was with Huey's faction, and everybody knew that. So we called Eldridge in Algeria from my apartment. It costs $117. You know why I remember? Because Alex didn't pay. I think possibly the inclusion of this material in the book will remind Alex that he promised to pay half of the bill.[97] Alex had the number and dialed. Let me tell you, we got through faster to Eldridge in Algeria from the phone in my Berkeley apartment than I would have calling my mama in Berkeley. What happened was Eldridge would not speak to either one of us. Don Cox served in Algiers, and Don and Alex talked. End of rapprochement.[98]

Now I didn't talk to Huey directly, but I did have to report what happened. So I went through intermediaries that I trusted who had direct connections with Huey. I got this response of no further exploration of that topic needs to be conducted from now on. Not a reprimand. More of you shot your best shot, Richard, but from the supreme commander's point of view, he ain't going for it either. See, I didn't have time to call Huey to double-check on this because I had Alex breathing down my neck, but I figured that since Alex figured I had enough representational power, at least he could deal with me on that issue.

A lot of people are under the impression that my defense of Huey is based more on a personal relationship. But whenever I made a judgment call regarding Huey, it's personal and political. In the case of the split, I had to really pull myself away because I knew both of them, so my personal feeling might cloud the real political issues. I'm telling you, I was stunned by the charges that went back and forth. When the killings started, it got to a point where no one wanted to talk. I think Alex should get credit for his bright idea, even though it got me into a lot of trouble along the way, and he still owes me for half of that $117.

The Demise of the Panthers

You asked about my thoughts on the party's turn toward electoral politics and community service programs. That's a hard one for me because the party's reformist turn, in my opinion, led to its demise. I'm having difficulty gauging when that turn took place. To me, it could've been averted in '68 when Cleaver ran for president on the Peace and Freedom Party ticket. It was my opinion that he should have run as an independent on the Black Panther Party ticket, with Huey or Bobby as vice president. I understand that the Peace and Freedom Party was a much bigger organization and had more money. But for the Black liberation struggle to succeed, a politically independent party had to come out from the national Black American community. By '68 the BPP was well known, so Eldridge should have run as a Black Panther with the BPP program. Don't dilute it with the war thing, just the program. So I'm in favor of electoral politics when the organization can participate. If the government says you can run candidates, run your candidate. But there are times when they say your organization is outlawed, then don't run it. But you don't go underground until you absolutely have to go underground.[99] Now here's the second part. The foremost reason for running candidates is not to get elected per se but to get the political program out to the people. It doesn't matter how many votes you get because you're still working in the system. It's doubly sticky if you're in an alliance with a group that supports the system and you don't. There's a contradiction there. There's no contradiction if you run the Panther on the Panther platform. They have a claim to be revolutionary.[100]

As for the community service programs, part of my mission was to acquire my master's degree in social work to help develop the Panthers' "survival programs." But there's a difference between doing community service programs within the confines of the system and having community service programs outside the system.[101] More and more party members agree that by 1973–74, the party's over.[102] Bobby had resigned, a number went into exile or were sent to prison. I had already broken political connections with Huey, but I didn't break all personal connections. In my mind, the demise of the party had do to with, number one, not running on a Black Panther platform as early as 1968. Number two, the split in the party in '71. A third factor that's insidious is the entrance into the party of a large number of opportunists—you have reformism, anarchism, opportunism, class collaboration, ultra-Leftism, and just sheer human greed. Number four, massive police and FBI repression. In April 1968, the police gunned down Bobby Hutton in Oakland. In January 1969, Bunchy Carter and John Huggins were assassinated at UCLA and later that year the police killed Fred Hampton and Mark Clark in Chicago. Don't forget, Huey, Bobby, David, Eldridge, are all in and out of prison or in exile. So the primary, secondary, tertiary party leadership all over the country was getting decimated and rank-and-file Party members were getting harassed every day by the police.[103]

Of course, everyone wants to talk about the violence within the party. But it needs to be understood in this context of heavy external repression. I was concerned because too many Panthers were being killed and not just by the police but, after the split, also by other Panthers.[104] Sam Napier was one. Sam had been such a solid soldier, hung in so tight so long and then was done away in a cowardly fashion. I had strong feelings about that. I realized I had to protect myself. I even had bodyguards for a while. Let me put it this way. I talked to individuals personally to find out what they were thinking and why. I was stunned by some of the responses I got. Individuals from branches I thought would go one way had gone the other way. Once I decided that Huey's line was correct and with Sam getting killed, I went into self-defense mode as I'd been accustomed to on and off all my life. It's kind weird from today's perspective. "What's he carrying in his briefcase?" I wasn't about to be caught unaware anywhere.[105]

The Significance of the Black Panther Party:
"The Greatest Thing We Ever Did"

Even with these problems, I stand behind my conviction that the formation of the BPP was one of the greatest things to happen to twentieth-century America as far as the struggle for freedom, justice, and equality is concerned. It may not have been the perfect organization, but I'm amazed at its importance not only in the world but in my personal life. Let's examine briefly the influence of the Black Panther movement in a historical sense. First and foremost, the BPP was a leading organization in the struggle against oppression, influencing far more than people give them credit for. Let me cite some of their concrete influences politically and organizationally. Number one, Latinos like the Brown Berets in Southern California adopted similar strategies and tactics in the struggle for liberation in their community. So did Asian Americans, through the Asian American Political Alliance and the Red Guards. I've got to give the Red Guards credit because they deliberately paralleled the program and organization of the party. I was the Black Panther influence on the Asian American Political Alliance and we'll get to what I might have contributed [in the next chapter]. In the Puerto Rican community, we see that the hitherto unknown Young Lords gang becomes the Young Lords Organization, a political group modeled after the BPP. Then we look at the most oppressed, depressed, suppressed racial/ethnic group in this country, the Native Americans—and we find that the founders of AIM, the American Indian Movement, have publicly credited the BPP for their program and activities.[106] I haven't even mentioned the party's international influence.[107] You had the BPP looking overseas to anticolonial revolutions, and you had Third World struggles looking to U.S. liberation movements. So there was this simultaneous interaction of the national and the international around the Black liberation struggle here.

You asked, "What was it about the Panthers that made people want to emulate them?" That's a hard question to answer because motivations differ from person to person. But I think the common thing, at least for the first group that came in, was struggle. I mean, they were sick and tired of being sick and tired. So when an organization such as the BPP springs up, it got attention. But the party had to do work to convince the people. There were people who never would have been connected with the BPP until the party demonstrated its commitment to serving the community—through its free breakfast programs and police brutality patrols.[108] I want to mention three such people. Father Earl Neil was a local minister who became, you might say, the chaplain of the BPP. It's kind of heavy to have an established minister step forward and offer his church and give support to the party. Dr. Tolbert Small eventually became the party physician as well as a physician to the community. He is now the director of the Harriet Tubman health clinic in East Oakland. Mrs. Ruth Jones Villa, a senior, was instrumental in engendering greater support for the party in the community. In other words there's a dialectical process going on. As the party was defending the community, the community began realizing what the party was doing and they started defending the party. That helped the party no end on that issue because we were suffering casualties of youth, I mean, we were getting cut down.[109]

Another way to gauge the BPP is that J. Edgar Hoover's called the BPP "the greatest enemy" to the continuance of American society as we know it.[110] That shows you that the government, the FBI, felt threatened by the party, that the party could challenge the power structure and its racist and capitalist structure that oppressed the poor and people of color. Now, you asked a question that pushed a few of my buttons. Some have asked, "Who would be afraid of a group that ended up getting many of its members killed, imprisoned, sent underground. How can you really be afraid of a group like that?" That's something that I've pondered at great length, and I think the question itself is wrapped up in a Greco-Roman perspective, limited by Aristotelian logic. What I am saying is that this method of summing up events, looking at pluses and minuses, is too static. You have to be dialectical. The plus and minus thing may be handy for adding up scores, but in summing up a political movement, the best way to get a handle on it is seeing its totality rather than trying to isolate things.

For example, the tragedy of the party in terms of the loss of lives was serious, but it should be viewed dialectically. It's true that at least two dozen party members were killed in the line of duty. It's true that dozens more went to jail. True, several are in exile. There are members of the party who are still serving time in prison, still in exile. This is scandalous. Lives were shattered. It's amazing that the BPP took as much as it took, physically and psychologically. On the other hand, this was the only way a group of oppressed people could effectuate the changes that came about by their resistance. All they had to offer was their bodies and their lives. I've always felt a little guilty about helping to convince David Hilliard to become chief of staff because almost as soon as he did he got in a whole lot of trouble. Not only he, but his whole family 'cause they all joined the party. For years I avoided his wife, Pat. But one day I 'fessed up to her. I blurted out an apology and said, "I'm sorry I had a hand in convincing David because you people went through hell." She looked at me and you know what she told me? She said, "That was the greatest thing we ever did." I said, "Say what?" She said, "If it hadn't been for David joining the party and us getting involved our lives would not have meant a thing."[111]

My delay in responding to your question about the significance of the party is because I don't want to delve into the Black Panther experience, to sum it up. But I could sum up my own experience. At the BPP thirtieth anniversary reunion, I had a talk with Kathleen Cleaver about whether it was worthwhile. She pretty much convinced me that it was.[112] If you look at it on the surface, some would say, "That was the worst thing Richard could have done in his life."

Materially, this probably is true. But that's never been my set anyway. By accident of history, I was in the right place at the right time, where I had to make a decision. I didn't do this for the money. I didn't do this for the fame. I made my decision and it had to do with this vision of a better society because the current one is so messed up. I'd like to think of myself as being one of those in the forefront of the struggle. It goes back to this: the struggle for freedom, justice, and equality transcends racial ethnic barriers and if you have the chance to help, do it.

JOINING THE BLACK PANTHER PARTY

A Japanese American in the Black Panther Party? This comes as a surprise to most, including many Panthers themselves. Richard Aoki was the most prominent non-Black member of the BPP.[113] But there were a few others as well, including Japanese Americans Mike Tagawa and Guy Kurose and a Filipino brother in Seattle, Afro–Chinese Lee Lew-Lee in New York City, and two Japanese American women in Berkeley as well as a handful of Latinos in the Bay Area. This may be less unexpected to those aware of the Panthers' cross-racial work, particularly with the Peace and Freedom Party. Even nationalist groups like the Republic of New Africa (RNA) included a few non-Blacks, most notably Japanese American Yuri Kochiyama. Still, the overwhelming public perception of the BPP is as an all-Black organization. The telling of Aoki's story thus allows us to study the complicated ways that race operated in the nationalist movements. While Aoki chose racial unity, he, like everyone else, could not fully escape the ideological and structural organization of race in the United States. He operated, as I contend, in the nexus of racial solidarity and racial ambiguity.

Aoki is best known for giving the Panthers their first two weapons, enabling their famous police patrols. This single act of solidarity signaled his commitment to the BPP. For Aoki, it was an effortless gesture. Living in West Oakland, he had seen the effects of anti-Black racism, and after developing a political consciousness, he became all the more committed to Black freedom. Knowing this, Seale and Newton had anticipated that Aoki would help them. But others admired Aoki's contribution precisely because he was viewed as an outsider; they did not expect a non-Black to contribute so much toward Black liberation. Still, while Aoki was allowed to informally call himself the minister of education, he was never given the official title despite his advanced theoretical training—the most advanced in Marxism–Leninism in the party's early years, according to Seale.[114] Was he overlooked because his political education at the time was rooted in Marxism–Leninism and not Black revolutionary nationalism? Was his racial identity a barrier to visible Panther leadership? Even as Panther leaders promoted cross-racial unity, would the rank-and-file membership or public perception in a period of heightened nationalist consciousness bind leadership to Blackness?

The duality of solidarity and ambiguity operated within two important racial contexts. First, against popular notions of cross-racial conflict, a vibrant history of Afro–Asian unity exists. Black radicals like W. E. B. Du Bois, Richard Wright, Robert F. Williams, and Malcolm X have long articulated a shared oppression and liberation with Asians and Asian Americans.[115] The Afro–Asian conference in Bandung, Indonesia, launched the global Non-Aligned Movement and the concept of Third Worldism.[116] The global gaze of radical U.S. movements brought into view national liberation struggles in Asia, Africa, and Latin America. The BPP studied Mao's writings, sold the "Red Book," and featured writings by Asian revolutionary leaders in the pages of their newspaper. Several party leaders, including Cleaver and Newton, on separate delegations, traveled to China, North Korea, and North Vietnam in the early 1970s. It was in China that Newton felt a "sensation of freedom," "a psychological liberation I had never experienced before."[117] Although little known, Elbert "Big Man" Howard represented the BPP in Japan around 1970 and felt a kindred spirit with poor Japanese workers who "faced discrimination as severe as black people in the United States."[118] At a Black nationalist conference, Aoki raised the idea of "double genocide," that the elimination of both Vietnamese and U.S. Black soldiers served the interest of U.S. empire building.

That Aoki was invited to speak about Japanese American incarceration at an early BPP meeting is suggestive of the ways Panther leaders saw anti-Asian racial oppression not only globally but domestically as well.[119] When the Panthers went to Sacramento, Huey Newton prepared a statement, read by Bobby Seale on the steps of the state capitol, that connected the "enslavement of Black people" with incarceration of Japanese Americans, the "dropping of atomic bombs on Hiroshima and Nagasaki," "the cowardly massacre in Vietnam," and the "genocide practiced on American Indians."[120] Newton's brief statement was not only a call for Black liberation but an appeal to Afro–Asian and Third World solidarities. These were ideas that drew Aoki to the Panthers and their structural critiques of capitalism, imperialism, and racism.

While the Panthers emerged in the shadow of Bandung, another racial context was emerging in the United States. In the same year that birthed the Black Power slogan and the BPP, articles in the respected and widely read *New York Times Magazine* and *U.S. News and World Report* popularized the image of Asian American assimilationism.[121] In January 1966, William Petersen's article "Success Story, Japanese-American Style" argued that both Japanese Americans and "Negroes" were "objects of color prejudice," but with very different outcomes. He attributed Japanese American exceptionalism to their focus on education and hard work. These were racially coded messages. Petersen, a liberal sociologist influenced by the assimilation theories of the Chicago school of sociology, associated Asian American success with individual efforts, and promoted this over Black demands for power and self-determination.[122] His article reinforced views of the United States as a liberal democracy. The nation's alleged commitments to racial equality and democratic processes negated the kinds of institutional racism claimed by Carmichael and Hamilton in *Black Power* as well as any need for outside-the-establishment methods of contestation.[123] Through perseverance and academic striving, rather than protests on the streets, minorities could gain upward mobility and acceptance into the great nation, or so Petersen implied.

The granting of honorary Whiteness to Asian America, as in Petersen's article, blinded others to the continuing racism against Asian Americans. As Laura Pulido observed, Black Panthers in Los Angeles barely registered Asian Americans on the political radar and felt little solidarity with a group they viewed as politically passive and free from discrimination.[124] This popular image of Asian Americans, internalized by many rank-and-file Panthers, would have limited Aoki's role within the BPP, even as BPP leaders like Newton and Seale saw a shared oppression and solidarity with Japanese Americans. Aoki's awareness of his insider–outsider status is revealed in his remark: "I was there [at the Black nationalist conference] because I was one of the brothers!" But almost in the same breath, he added: "But if they had asked me to leave, I would have left."

Aoki resolved the tension between racial solidarity and racial ambiguity by rejecting Asian American assimilationism and allying with Black oppression and models of liberation. This stance marked him as different and potentially dangerous. He suffered the scorn of mainstream America and mainstream Japanese America. Moreover, the existence of Afro–Asian alliances suggested that Black nationalism as a revolutionary politic had far-reaching appeal beyond the Black community. Perhaps Aoki wasn't off the mark when he stated that he would have been killed if he had made visible his participation as an Asian American leader of the BPP. Even as no one fully subverts his or her own racialization, individuals like Aoki and organizations like the BPP sought to transcend racial boundaries in the struggle to create a liberatory society.

Militancy and Community

In creating *Black Politics,* Aoki drew from his commitment to Third World solidarity to transcend not only racial borders but also organizational boundaries. There was no certainty that different Black nationalist groups could work together, despite an appeal by Newton and others for collaboration. There were, for example, publicly voiced differences between the BPP and the Republic of New Africa.[125] As the main person recruiting Bay Area BPP and RNA leaders to serve on the editorial board of *Black Politics,* and to jointly produce and distribute the political magazine, Aoki offers a model of principled political work. In addition, Aoki's political insights created a more nuanced and complex understanding of Black revolutionary politics. Aoki offers, for example, an original interpretation of the split in the BPP. That split is most commonly attributed to the debate between Newton's serve-the-people programs and Cleaver's militarism.[126] Grounded in dialectical materialism, Newton argued that Cleaver's emphasis on armed action, once useful to promote organized, disciplined self-defense, was by the early 1970s, alienating the party from the majority of the Black community.[127] Others asserted that Newton's shift to community service spelled the demise of the party's revolutionary program.[128] By contrast, Aoki's political analysis, promoting Newton's Marxist-influenced theory of intercommunalism over what he saw as Cleaver's anarchism, complicated the well-trod dichotomy between community service and militaristic strategies.[129]

Throughout his narrative, Aoki offered insights on political strategies that promote community participation, empowerment, and organizing. He tells of how ordinary people surrounded the police, ensuring the success of the Panther police patrols. He reminds us of Seale's statement that "we're not outgunned, we're outorganized." By disclosing his fears when facing off the police in Richmond, Aoki reveals a human side to courageous militant actions. His story further reveals how the significance of an event is not always clear at the moment it is occurring and how activist choices are sometimes shaped by routine aspects of life. Aoki, for example, stated that he didn't participate in the BPP's now famous Sacramento action because "I didn't think there was going to be any action" and "maybe I had a midterm that day too." While Aoki remained committed to self-defense, by connecting military strategies with community organizing, he put into practice the BPP's renowned slogan, "All Power to the People."

Aoki's participation in the BPP dramatically changed his life. Despite the personal sacrifices, joining the BPP was the greatest thing that happened to him personally and politically. Aoki would agree with Pat Hilliard that if it hadn't been for joining the party, our lives "would not have meant a thing."

7 "Support All Oppressed Peoples"

The Birth of the Asian American Political Alliance

Here I am at Berkeley, sitting in the campus dining commons, when a woman approaches me and asks, out of the clear blue sky, if I'm politically inclined. Emma Gee and her husband, Yuji Ichioka, were working with the Peace and Freedom Party on the forthcoming elections and wanted to gather together politically conscious Orientals for a meeting at their place.[1] The first thing I thought was, Yuji Ichioka, that's Japanese; Emma Gee, Chinese. It may sound surprising that the existence of an interethnic couple was unusual in the sixties, but it was. So I went to their apartment to see what's happening. Yuji was presiding over the meeting and Emma's a gracious host.[2] There were a half dozen other Asian Americans at that meeting, mostly students from UC Berkeley. This small group went on to form the Asian American Political Alliance, one of the most important Asian American political groups to come out of the sixties.

Let me enumerate AAPA's contributions. First, the very term "Asian American" was coined in AAPA. Second, they were explicitly political—antiwar, pro–Black Panther Party, and one of the earliest groups of the Asian American Movement. Third, its membership was student and community and that was unusual. Fourth, AAPA represented the Asians during the Third World strike and helped form the Asian American Studies program at UC Berkeley. Now I have a bone to pick. In all the books on Asian American history and the AAM, I have found that AAPA has been neglected, overlooked, or distorted.[3]

Prior to the strike in winter '69, there probably weren't more than two dozen of us in AAPA. We were racially mixed—about 40 percent Chinese American, 40 percent Japanese American, and 20 percent Filipino American. Most were students, including Harvey Dong, Vicci Wong, and Lillian Fabros. Lillian was a firebrand in the struggle for farmworkers' rights and important in linking up with Latinos because of their grape boycott with the University of California. Community people like Emma Gee and Bob Rita joined as well. Bob Rita was Filipino Chinese from Hawaii and had been among the first to organize Filipino farmworkers along with Larry Itliong and Philip Vera Cruz. I met Bob during my first year at Berkeley when he was manning a table for the farmworkers and we struck up a conversation. I got Bob into the meetings. Then Bob brought in Nicky Arai, a movement photographer, and Andy Higashi, a working-class kid from San Pedro who worked as a printer. There were hardly any Koreans in AAPA because the Korean population in Berkeley and in the United States was very small. It wasn't until the strike that Korean Americans appeared, including graduate students Elaine Kim and Jerry Suhr. Both became faculty members of Berkeley's Asian American Studies program.[4]

Before AAPA, I had never interacted on a militant basis with all Asians. In fact, my view was that the Asian Americans were politically backward. At Merritt College, I had checked out an Oriental fraternity, but all they wanted to do was party. I just shook my head and walked away. So I was astounded at that AAPA meeting to see so many political Asians. Don't forget, up to this time, there was no such thing as an AAM and only a few known Asian American radicals, and just about all of them had worked in the Black movement. Yuri Kochiyama was in New York, working with Malcolm X, Robert F. Williams, the Republic of New Africa, and the Asian Americans for Action, when it formed. Shoshana Arai was in Chicago working with SNCC. Grace Lee Boggs was in Detroit working in the Black movement. We were what Miriam Ching Louie called the "bumblebees."[5] Then there were a half dozen Japanese Americans in the Communist Party, but I sure as hell was not going to interact with that group.[6] Was I looking for Asian American camaraderie? I didn't have time to think about it. But I did feel comfortable with AAPA because we were all Asians and political like I couldn't believe.

The initial struggle in AAPA centered on the issue of identity. It was almost déjà vu to me since I had already been through it with African Americans and could see the same issues coming up: Where are we from? What are we doing here? Where are we going? Who are we in relationship to the dominant White culture? In the past I didn't think the identity issue was that important, but I realize that unless you have your identity, you can't go to the political level. So I patiently sat through it to see how that would resolve itself. The discussion went real fast primarily because the group was already at a higher political level than most Orientals at the time. Once the identity issue was settled, then boom!—the group started coalescing behind AAPA's program and getting involved in activities affecting our own communities and connecting with African American issues, like the Free Huey Campaign. If you were more advanced, you also talked about class struggle. But the issue of identity had to be dealt with. Out of this, the term "Asian American" came into being. Yuji Ichioka chaired the meetings where the group struggled with this concept and consensually adopted the term "Asian American"—Asian for our cultural heritage, American because of our nationality or citizenship.[7] It's similar to what African Americans went through as they changed from Negro to Black and rejected the label foisted on them by White dominant culture. Up to that point, we had been called Orientals. Oriental was a rug that everyone steps on, so we ain't no Orientals. We were Asian American. That was so revolutionary I shudder to think of how quickly that process of the consciousness-raising brought the group to another level.

So we came up with the name Asian American Political Alliance. We also created a logo for AAPA. The Black Panthers have their black panther logo. What are we going to have? Crossed chopsticks? That actually came up. Yuji impressed everybody with his scholarly and sage, but cynical, advice. I believe it was Yuji who came up with our logo, the Chinese character for east. In kanji [the Chinese-influenced Japanese language system], it's also east or *higashi*. Now what do we stand for? James Brown said, "Say it loud—I'm Black and I'm Proud." What are we supposed to say, "I'm Yellow and I'm mellow." Hell no! The Black Panthers' had a political program. We had to have a political program. One of the first things was our position on the Vietnam War. That was easy. Everybody was against the war. Then, where do we stand on the BPP? Had I gotten up there at the beginning of the meeting and said, "I'm Richard Aoki. Everybody here knows me. I've been coming to the meetings like everybody else. I'm a member here. I'm also a Black Panther, branch captain, occasionally I could be the minister of education." It wouldn't have washed. So I just kept my mouth shut about my membership and my rank in the BPP. I may have revealed it to a few, but I wasn't about to jump overboard saying this. However, support for the BPP was unanimous. Oh, happy day.

From early on, we figured out which other Asian clubs were on campus. There was the Nisei Student Club for the Japanese Americans, the Chinese Students Club for the American-born Chinese, and the Chinese Student Association for the foreign-born Chinese.[8] But these were essentially social clubs and were not political in nature, nor were they intended to be. We started raiding the other groups, meaning we started attending their meetings, talking to their people, and inviting them to our meetings. Lo and behold, we started attracting not only their rank-and-file members, but also their leaders. Wai-Kit Quon comes in from the Tri-Con and the foreign students group—this is where my connections helped. Bing Wing Thom, another graduate student, also came in. Then the presidents and past presidents of the Nisei Student Club, the Chinese Students Club, and the Chinese Student Association all started attending our meetings. I hadn't seen this many Asians get together, talk politics, and agree on a program that I could live with and that had Huey's blessing because I was making sure Huey was aware of the work I was doing. I said to him, "Man, you're not going to believe this. I'm running into a bunch of Orientals who are political!"

AAPA's Political Program and Activities

After we handed out our political program, we sponsored an event on July 28, 1968, at UC Berkeley. Why we did it during summertime, I don't know. This also created a minor problem because who would give the presentation for AAPA? We had hammered out our four-point program. We got Dwinelle, one of the biggest halls on the campus. We invited all these other people to join us to celebrate the emergence of a new political organization called the Asian American Political Alliance. So we had this meeting. Everybody in the room looked at Yuji, make the speech, Yuji; Yuji declined. Emma, make the speech; Emma declined. Now comes a minor crisis. We got the organization. We got the program. Who's going to step forward and be the official spokesperson for this event coming up? Somebody said Richard. I said, "Say what?" I was a little apprehensive for two reasons. First, I was reluctant to step up and say I'm the spokesperson because we've seen too many spokespersons killed. Second, I'm more in the extreme Left. Richard already in trouble with the Tri-Con thing. I don't need this. All I wanted to do was to complete my studies at Berkeley and keep the party going, but AAPA got in my face and overran me.[9]

In light of the fact that nobody else was willing to do it, I said, "If you want me to do it, I'll do it. But I want to put it to a vote of confidence. If there's a sizable opposition, somebody else can do it." I mean, what does it take to go over a four-point program? So that's how I was elected to be AAPA's spokesperson. Now I've always been good at representing organizations I belong to because I know the program and stick to it. So even though I was in the left wing of AAPA, I wasn't about to give my personal line; I represented the group.[10]

At AAPA's public debut, I presented its four-point political program. Little did we know that we were making history. Here's the gist of my speech:

Number one, we Asian Americans believe that American society has been and still is fundamentally a racist society and that historically we have accommodated ourselves to this society in order to survive. (In other words, we have been and still are victims of white racism.) Point number two, we Asian Americans believe that heretofore we have been relating to white standards of acceptability and affirm the right of self-determination. . . . We're tired of hearing the racist chant, "If you are white, you're all right." This has wreaked havoc upon our cultural identity. We see, for example, in the Japanese American community, the effort to surgically change the shape of the eyes. This is similar to the hair straighter and bleaching cream syndrome in the African American community. Prospective members have been saying, "What are the white people going to say about our group and the Oriental community?" This revealed how brainwashed some people are.

Point number three, we Asian Americans support all non-White liberation movements and believe that all minorities in order to be truly liberated must have complete control over the political, economic, and educational institutions within their respective communities. (Now I was being very neutral in my presentation in a sense I'm not banging it up and down but just explaining the program.) We unconditionally support the struggles of the Afro–American peoples, the Chicanos and the American Indians in their efforts to obtain freedom, justice and equality. Point number four, we Asian Americans oppose the imperialist policies being pursued by the American government. (I mentioned in particular "being unconditionally against the war in Vietnam period.") In conclusion I would like to add that the Asian American Political Alliance is . . . an action-oriented group and we will not just restrict our activities to merely ethnic issues, but to all issues that are of fundamental importance pertaining to the building of a new and better world.[11]

I saw this as our coming out, the introduction of AAPA and our new program. So though AAPA had already done a number of activities, like the Free Huey rallies and the McCarren Act protests, to me, July 28 marked the official debut of AAPA into the arena of realpolitik.

My speech introduced AAPA's program, called "AAPA Perspectives." It begins: "We Asian Americans believe that we must develop an American Society which is just, humane, equal and gives the people the right to control their own lives before we can begin to end the oppression and inequality that exists in this nation."[12] The other four points were the ones I mentioned in my July 28 speech: America is a racist society that oppresses Asian Americans; we denounce racism and affirm the right to self-determination; we supported all oppressed peoples in their struggles for liberation; and we oppose U.S. imperialist policies. I was a little stunned by the advanced nature of AAPA's politics. It dawns on me that Tri-Con was responsible in a way for the AAPA political program primarily due to the influence of Wai-Kit Quon. In keeping with the BPP's Ten-Point Program, we included the program in every issue of AAPA's newspaper.[13] Unlike academic publications, there's no listing of the editorial board or staff in AAPA's newspaper. It was about the collective and very democratically run.

About this time, the term "Asia, Africa, and Latin America" began to transmute itself into the phrase "Third World." AAPA was quick in picking up that concept not only in the international arena but also around domestic Third World issues. One issue of AAPA's newspaper had Bobby Seale on the front cover and an article on Robert F. Williams by Mary [Yuri] Kochiyama.[14] On the cover of another issue was the headline "Third World Power" and another had the article "Third World Roots: Bandung," so that people could understand the origins of Third World consciousness.[15] Number one to me, of course, were the rallies for Huey Newton and the BPP. From early on, AAPA attended the Free Huey rallies. There's that famous picture of two Asians holding the sign, "Yellow Peril Supports Black Power"; they're both AAPA people.[16] That photo is one of the best examples of solidarity between ethnic groups that you could think of and it contained a powerful message. It was in your face.

Then during the Huey Newton trial, there was an Oakland City Council meeting and AAPA decided to put in an appearance to demand justice for Huey. In fact, there were two Orientals on the city council at the time—one Chinese American, one Japanese American. We said, "Wow, two of our people are on the city council. Let's go down and see what we can do." When we got down there to do the protest, all we saw was a solid row of cops. We looked at the city council members up on their little platform, along with the mayor and the police chief, and we demanded speaking time. I believe we were denied. So we caucused briefly to figure out what to do. My position was confrontation. But it was a minority position in our caucus. One look was enough to convince the others in the delegation that it was not going to be a win–win situation. We're going to get hurt. We're going off to jail. We're going to be joining Huey. At the time I didn't feel like retreating, but I'm a team player and if the rest of the team says, "Let's pick up our marbles and go back to Berkeley," I went along. In a way, this reflected the political consciousness of the group—that there are times when you bust them up and there are times when it's better to retreat, even though you've got the moral high ground. You could appeal to the two Orientals to listen, but our group got a lesson in the difference between Orientals and Asian Americans.[17]

Though we agreed on our positions, there were also internal political divisions within AAPA. On one extreme, there was the left wing that was Maoist, Black Panther, Black liberation struggle. On the other end were the moderates—the pacifists, liberals, social democrats, reformists. In the middle was a centrist grouping. They were the largest grouping and left leaning, but as in a lot of organizations, the centrists go whichever way the argument sounded the best. I place myself in the left wing. I've always been clear about where I stand, though I wouldn't jab my politics down anybody's throat. My recruitment method was to logically lay out my position, to struggle with the question. If it's done correctly, then the person will have a heightened sense of awareness and political consciousness.

AAPA didn't have formal political education classes. But we had self-defense classes, which were divided into two categories: martial arts and small arms. I was amazed to discover the hidden talents of our AAPA membership. I've never seen so many black belts in my life. Bob Rita got up and showed us Hawai'ian Kembo. Wow! Bryant Fong was the man with the Tai Chi. Whoa! I think Harvey Dong was studying White Crane at that time. After those internal training sessions, I had no doubts that Asians could hold their own.[18] About the small arms, I'm back at the range again. This time instead of having Black Panthers, I had AAPA people. The Red Guards didn't make any bones about their self-defense activities. But in AAPA, we tried to keep it discreet being UC Berkeley students. I said to myself, I've got to be careful. In the training, I stuck to technique. I found there was no need to teach any philosophy of armed struggle because they wouldn't have gone to the small arms classes if they didn't already believe in it. It went like, "I'm going up to the country next weekend. Anybody that wants to come has to go through this little safety thing first." I was religious about safety. "Okay, gang, at ten o'clock, we'll meet over at Sproul Plaza. Who's got a car?" We would spend the whole day doing what we needed to do. The important thing was gaining confidence. It was a political tool to me too because this would sift out those who were serious from those who weren't. While AAPA didn't profess any pacifist orientation, I was sensitive that there were differences. If you look at attitudes, I would say 90 percent said armed struggle is the way to go.[19] But when you look at those who would train and acquire equipment, the numbers dropped. But still, a significant number of the group went along with the training. I was a little surprised when the women started going, but after my experiences in the BPP, I wasn't about to question anything. Now we didn't organize any formal security within AAPA. It was more like, since I had the most experience and was the only veteran in the group, if we thought there might be trouble, I would usually volunteer to be point person.

Japanese American Struggles

With its large Japanese American membership, AAPA was concerned with issues affecting this community. In 1968, Spiro Agnew, the vice presidential running mate to Richard Nixon, uttered that infamous "fat Jap" remark to a reporter.[20] AAPA was incensed over it and we decided to bust up a "Speak to Nixon–Agnew" meeting being held in town. The deal is that Senator William Knowland, whose family published the *Oakland Tribune,* hosted the Republican event in Berkeley of all places. Who would be the person to represent AAPA and take the lead in such a bold move? Hands don't go up and I'm saying, "Well, if I do this, I could go to jail." But I volunteer. We get inside. I raise my hand and read from AAPA's press release into the whirling tape recorder, presumably for Nixon and Agnew to hear. I stated, in part, "The Asian American Political Alliance vigorously protests the racist epithet, 'fat Jap,' recently uttered by Agnew. We must reluctantly concur with the Kerner Commission's finding that 'white racism' is the fundamental cause of civil disorders, and that 'white racism' seems to have infected a person running for the second highest political office of this country." I politely ended with, "If the Republican Party is victorious in November, we would humbly suggest to Nixon that he would refrain from sending Agnew on goodwill missions to the rest of the world with the exception of either Rhodesia or the Union of South Africa."[21]

What happens next is a bunch of AAPA people bust up the gathering. Internal security jumps up and then AAPA jumps up and all of sudden, they realize they've got something on their hands. The next day, the *Hokubei Mainichi* and the *San Francisco Chronicle* jump up: "Asian American Political Alliance Walks Out of Nixon-Agnew Meeting in Berkeley."[22] Ray Okamura of the JACL also spoke at that meeting. I was stunned that Ray wrote me a note afterward because that wasn't his style. If Ray had been at the AAPA meeting prior to the speak-out, he might have said, "Well, that's being a little too radical to disrupt a meeting like that." But after the meeting, he sent me a note: "That was a great turn-out by the AAPA last night. The dramatic walk-out was effective and you gave an excellent statement."[23]

Though we differed with the JACL politically on many issues, we did work with them to repeal the McCarran Act. This was primarily because of Ray

Okamura, who headed JACL's struggle in that area. Ray's a real nice guy and he and I got along personally. So I avoided any harsh criticism of the JACL when working with Ray because I thought it was more important that we got along and could work on the McCarren Act campaign. AAPA's newspaper featured Yuji Ichioka's article on the McCarran Act, or Title II of the 1950 Internal Security Act: "The most crucial feature . . . [is] its recommendation for the usage of 'detention centers,' in the case of a national emergency, presumably when guerrilla violence has reached uncontrollable proportions." If that wasn't bad enough, the government wouldn't even have to show evidence of any subversive activity. This blatant violation of due process echoed what happened to the Japanese Americans during World War II. But this time, the government was targeting militant activists. So AAPA got involved, along with other Japanese Americans on both coasts, and we won. The McCarran Act was repealed.[24]

Another important issue was the U.S.–Japan Security Treaty, which was an effort on the part of Japan and the United States to shore up their interests in the Far East during the Vietnam War by signing a military agreement.[25]

Then there was "Japan Week" in San Francisco that we protested. It was billed as a festive week of flower arranging, dancing, and martial arts. But we knew that business interests and conservative politicians backed the week, that the Japanese destroyer *Amatsukaze* was to arrive in the San Francisco Bay, and that there would be a banquet to honor Spiro Agnew. So AAPA, with other groups, protested with slogans like "Death to the Security Pact" and "End the Asian War."[26] One of those events was quite lively because we tangled, literally, with another group that was for the signing of the mutual military pact. What happened is that there was a meeting of diplomats from the United States and Japan to discuss the renewal of the treaty. So we picketed the front of the posh hotel where they were meeting. AAPA was still small at the time; maybe only twelve to fifteen people were out there, but we were a determined bunch. Out of the clear blue sky, a group that supported the treaty showed up across the street from us. What was even more surprising was the police allowed our group and their group to converge at one point. It looked like we were being set up. However, in the minor melee that took place, we got the better of the other group and they retreated. I was amazed to see the talent unveil itself as we were pushing and shoving. That was a first time that AAPA saw some street fighting, which was minor, but it demonstrated that AAPA would follow through on their commitment to the cause.

AAPA had a clear international focus. We were against Japanese imperialism. We supported the national liberation front struggles in Asia, Africa, and

Latin America, particularly Vietnam. These ideas were incorporated directly into the AAPA program: "We Asian Americans support all oppressed people and their struggles for Liberation" and "We Asian Americans oppose the imperialist policies being pursued by the American Government."[27] In AAPA's newspaper, we stated our support for the NLF [South Vietnamese National Liberation Front].[28] When there were antiwar demonstrations, AAPA participated. We started receiving communiqués from other organizations who looked to AAPA as the organization that represented the militant segment of the emerging AAM. Having official spokespersons allowed us to link up with the other radical progressive groups and I became bombarded with going out speaking for the group. One example is the Students for a Democratic Society regional conference in the Bay Area. The SDS conference was big time and AAPA was invited to speak. This happened a little before Japan Week, so I blasted U.S. and Japanese imperialism, especially their aggression in Vietnam, their neocolonial expansion into Asia and Africa, and the Mutual Security Pact. I ended with a glimmer of hope, namely, that Asian American activists were organizing protests and that SDS and AAPA could work together.[29]

Bay Area Asian American Radicalism: AAPA and the Red Guards

Unbeknownst to us, a journalist by the name of Tom Wolfe wrote a sensationalist article for *Esquire* magazine. "The New Yellow Peril" mentioned both AAPA and the Red Guards as being dangerous organizations. I don't regularly read *Esquire,* but someone said, "Richard, you got to read this." On one hand, I felt good that AAPA and the Red Guard made national news. On the other hand, what he had written about us, it might have been better if we hadn't. The Red Guards in Chinatown accused AAPA of running gun-training sessions. When I read that article, I almost had a heart attack. I locked all the doors, closed all the windows, took my guns out, and said, "They're coming for me."[30]

So there's a fraternal relationship between AAPA and the Red Guards all the way through. If they got into a fight, we'd back them up and when we got into a fight, they'd back us up. There were differences between AAPA and the Red Guard, but there was no conflict. Red Guard was more Maoist than the average AAPA person, but the left wing of AAPA was also Maoist. There were also class differences. The Berkeley people in AAPA were more middle class and the Red Guard had semi-lumpen elements. There's always personality conflicts that come up, but I try to avoid them because they don't count for anything in the long run. The important thing was the political similarities of the two groups. I had even thought of a merger for the groups, but it would have required a lot of work. Plus, I feared that with a merger, the two groups might be destroyed by internal conflict. I've seen that happen. It was better to have AAPA do its thing at Berkeley and the Red Guards do its thing in San Francisco. AAPA was close to the Oakland Panthers and the Red Guard to the San Francisco Panthers.

Women in the Struggle

You asked about the role of women in AAPA. AAPA underscored the fact that "women hold up half the world." The membership was maybe fifty–fifty, or maybe two to one in favor of males. This was significant because at that time, most of the groups I belonged to politically, including the BPP, had few females as members and women leaders were virtually nonexistent. Not only that but AAPA's newspaper had an article on women's liberation.[31] So AAPA was one of the first ethnic groups and radical groups to bring up this subject.

The thing I recall the most was that the AAPA female was bolder and more assertive than the average Asian American female. The political stances they adopted they held on to and they worked hard to see that the mission was completed. It's hard for me to pinpoint female leadership in AAPA, but when people talked about AAPA they would talk about different females in the group as being committed when it came down to the nuts and the bolts and assuming responsibilities. At that point in AAPA it wasn't that important but when the strike came, that's when it became important and these strong females begin to develop. There are a few women that stand out. Vicci Wong was noted for her political clarity and sharpness. Lillian Fabros was mild mannered, but you could sense there was strength in her and her commitment to the struggle of farmworkers. Emma Gee has been overlooked, but I give her a lot of credit for the initial formations of AAPA, because of her being such a gracious hostess to the group at our meetings, which were held at her and Yuji's apartment.[32]

First Asian American Studies Class: Asian Studies 100X

The Asian American Political Alliance, as part of its protracted program, instituted the first Asian American Studies class at UC Berkeley. This idea came up primarily because of the controversy behind the 139X class taught by Eldridge Cleaver. The logic was that African Americans wanted their classes. The Latinos through the Mexican American Student Confederation wanted their classes. Why not have an introductory class on Asian Americans? Through our initial explorations, we were told that if we raise some money from the community, the university might donate in kind. So I thought that it was worth pursuing.

Around spring or summer of 1968, Yuji Ichioka and I, representing AAPA, and James Hirabayashi, an anthropology professor at San Francisco State University, who is also the brother of Gordon Hirabayashi, drove down to San José to attend the JACL regional conference and make a presentation to the group and request some funding.[33] As I recall we received a nominal amount.[34] I didn't think anything big would come out of a little class, but AAPA was excited by it. We were using a mechanism where students would initiate courses, though a professor would be in charge. We had a few sympathetic professors who were willing to risk their reputations to support our request. The key was the hiring of the teaching assistants. That was the hook: the teaching assistants would have the freedom to develop the content and delivery.[35]

Professor Paul Takagi sponsored the course and gave the first orientation. But after that a series of guest speakers came in. They could only teach one class each because after the Eldridge Cleaver controversy, UC Berkeley set a new policy limiting speakers to a single appearance. The syllabus shows that guest lecturers included UC Berkeley professors like Frederic Wakeman speaking on China and George De Vos on the Nisei personality. We also invited community people to speak, like Yori Wada on the Japanese American community, Karl Yoneda on the Issei labor movement, and George Woo on radicalism. There was also a panel on the concentration camps. But the real teaching took place in the sections run by the four teaching assistants: Alan Fong, Wai-Kit Quon, Ling-chi Wang, and Richard Aoki. We all agreed on that. The AAPA newspaper stated, "The course is structured in such a way that the discussion section will be the pivotal point of the course, aiding both the coordination of the lecture materials and the gathering of other materials for further research and interpretation."[36]

The Third World strike came along that quarter. We weren't going to cross the picket line, so we moved our classes off campus. Besides, classes that were held on campus were getting disrupted by strikers. We did a last-minute scurrying around to find places to meet. Barrington Hall, a cooperative student center, is where we conducted most of the lectures because they had a conference room that was big enough to hold the whole class. It was easier to find places for the smaller sections because we could use apartments and we did.

In my sections, I was going to talk about immigration, settlement patterns of Japanese Americans, and so forth. But now we're in the middle of the strike. The timing was good and bad. Bad in that I don't think any of us did much teaching. We were all focused on the strike. We'll cancel class today because from twelve to one we're going to close down Sather Gate. But it was also good in that we had this captive audience who were generally interested. Also, they knew who the significant Asian figures were—the TAs because the TAs were all AAPA people. That's how we got picked to be TAs. The TAs were also in the leadership of the strike. The only places students could go to for reliable information on the strike was to come to class.

You asked how the students, even those who would take an experimental course, responded to the strike and to classes being canceled. There were those drawn to AAPA because of the strike. Remember at the beginning of the strike, there weren't more than two dozen AAPA members. But AAPA membership increased exponentially when the strike came because if you're Asian and sympathetic to the strike, this was the organization to join. We had a program, a track record of activity, a publication, regular meetings, and there are members you could talk with. Then, there was a group for whom this was all new. At a wedding I recently attended I ran into a guy who had no connections with AAPA, but signed up for the course to take a class with his friend, who was in AAPA. It turns out that this guy's and his buddy's fathers were ex-442nd [the racially segregated Japanese American army combat team during World War II, representing, to Aoki, more conservative politics]. So he signs up for the course fresh from Southern California, bright eyed and bushy tailed. He said he was stunned when he met me. He said, "You blew my mind and then somebody whispered in the class, he's a Black Panther too." The guy said, "Oh my," but he hung in with the program. The good news is that we hadn't seen each other in thirty-odd years since he was in that class and then he helped to build Asian American Studies at UC Berkeley. But when I ran into him at this wedding, I found out that he's quite active in the Los Angeles section of Not In Our Name [an organization opposing the war in Iraq]. Then too there were those that came in and said, "What the hell is this all about." They didn't stay too long. As far as I was concerned, if you don't like it, you can leave.

But I would say that most became politically aware and involved through that class, if they weren't already involved in AAPA. And AAPA went on to provide major leadership for the TWLF strike that developed that quarter.

FOUNDING THE ASIAN AMERICAN POLITICAL ALLIANCE

On AAPA and Aoki's Leadership

Richard Aoki's statement that AAPA was "one of the most important Asian American political groups to come out of the sixties," yet almost entirely ignored by history, was indeed correct. The very introduction of the term

"Asian American," credited to Berkeley's AAPA, transformed the social consciousness of a racialized people and of American society at large. Asian Americans moved from seeing themselves as politically passive Orientals—the opposite of and inferior to Occidentals—to gaining racial pride and the power to contest racism. AAPA was one of the first organizations to promote pan-Asian unity in its program and membership. This signified nothing short of a new racial identity for groups whose previous self-definitions were in "ethnic disidentification" from one another. Yen Le Espiritu referred to disidentification as "the act of distancing one's group from another group so as not to be mistaken and suffer the blame for the presumed misdeed of that group."[37] Relations within the global political economy often shaped the images of Otherness. During World War II, for example, "I'm Chinese," "I am Korean," and "I am Filipino" buttons were worn to create distance from the fierce anti-Japanese hostility and to protest Japan's occupation of their homelands. But as Cold War imperatives marked Chinese Americans as suspect and the demilitarized and emasculated Japan became a U.S. ally, interethnic relations shifted once again. Espiritu correctly contends that social and demographic changes enabled pan-Asian formation to occur in the 1960s, but not earlier. Third- and fourth-generation Chinese, Japanese, and Pilipino Americans shared a common youth culture and language and came together on college campuses.[38] Beyond demographics, war, colonialism, and social movements shaped the development of Asian American pan-ethnicity. Notably, the Asian American Movement emerged in the shadow of Bandung. The Non-Aligned Movement connected Asia, Africa, and Latin America in a common struggle against colonialism and racism. This global movement helps explain why the pan-Asianism that developed in the Asian American Movement was intricately linked to Third Worldism.[39] Thus, AAPA's coining of the term "Asian American" helped launch a new social movement, the Asian American Movement (AAM), and a new identity based on political resistance, racial pride, and alliance building across ethnic (pan-Asian unity) and racial borders (Third World solidarity).

Berkeley's AAPA helped launch the AAM, not only through its pan-Asian formation, but also by creating AAPA groups at numerous college campuses throughout the nation. In an unprecedented gathering, the Asian Experience/Yellow Identity symposium, held at UC Berkeley on January 11–12, 1969, brought together Asian American student organizations from more than a dozen college campuses throughout California and beyond. The participants decided spontaneously to establish themselves as AAPA chapters. At San

Francisco State College, AAPA played an instrumental role in establishing the first School of Ethnic Studies in the nation. At Yale University, AAPA helped create the first journal in Asian American Studies, *Amerasia Journal*. And at Columbia University, AAPA helped found the first national Asian American revolutionary organization, I Wor Kuen. Together, this loosely based alliance of AAPA groups, inspired by Berkeley's AAPA, helped spark the emergence of the nationwide AAM.[40]

Aoki played a significant role in the development of Berkeley's AAPA. An original member, he served as the second chair of AAPA during the TWLF strike as well as AAPA's treasurer and a regular spokesperson for the organization.[41] He further influenced AAPA's ideological development through his socialist politics and political associations with Black radicalism. Aoki did not need to announce his BPP membership—and for the most part, didn't— to be seen as a model of militant manhood. With his army jacket, his sunglasses worn even at night, his cigarette in hand or dangling from his mouth, his Black oratorical style, and the militancy of his words, he was an image of "bad ass" masculinity.[42] At a time when, popularized as model minority success stories, Asian American men were represented as nerdy, academically minded, obedient sons, many Asian American youth, both men and women, gained racial pride and empowerment through Aoki's example.[43] Bryant Fong recalled his first encounter with Aoki at an AAPA event at UC Berkeley in 1968. After experiencing a boyhood in South Berkeley filled with racial teasing and physical fights with both Black and White kids, Fong was shocked when a complete stranger, a Black teen, defended him against the racial taunts of White peers. This Black youth also taught Fong to play football and, in what was previously unprecedented, regularly picked a Chinese American (Fong) as quarterback on his high school intramural team. To Fong, the Black freedom struggles and Third World unity encircling him in the mid-1960s dramatically transformed Afro–Asian relations. So when Fong heard Aoki speaking in his Black street style about Japanese American incarceration, a topic he knew nothing about, Fong was surprised and impressed. Aoki's boldness and militancy inspired a racial pride in Fong, not unlike Malcolm X's impact on Black Americans. Fong went on to become the third and final chair of AAPA.[44]

Aoki's unapologetic audacity and radical critique were also seen in his writings. Identified as R.A., Aoki wrote an article for AAPA's newspaper titled "Running Dogs Meet Their Master." Using Marxist analysis and provocative language, Aoki contended that the real purpose of Japan Week in San

Francisco was "to further cement the relations between U.S. imperialism and Japanese neo-colonialism." He charged the Japanese government with being "a running dog of the U.S. aggression in Vietnam," arguing that Japan "profits from the war in exchange for its political support."[45] Aoki further served AAPA as a steady organizer and as an example of courageous and principled opposition to oppression.

Aoki's age (a decade older than most AAPA members), political experience, radical ideology, and links with Black militancy all contributed to his being sought after for AAPA leadership. But Aoki differed from most AAPA members in one significant way, one that partially limited his leadership. AAPA as an organization consistently stressed the participatory democracy and collective leadership promoted by the Student Nonviolent Coordinating Committee, the New Left, and many in the AAM. An early AAPA internal document maintained that "leadership must be redefined and democracy must be used as often as possible. Leadership, as we understand it, is *effective action;* it is *not* making good speeches, rallying people, or having charisma per se. It is leadership when those qualities lead to effective action."[46] In the first issue of its newspaper, AAPA opposed "rigid, traditional levels of structure in which a few make the decisions, present them to the body, and allow it to vote yes or no."[47] Instead, "non-structure is highly emphasized," with members organized into six-person "US Groups," each to work on a distinct project.[48] AAPA emphasized "task work groups," in this case focusing on "Chinatown, Black Liberation, China Policy, McCarran Act, and Peace and Freedom."[49] A year after AAPA's demise, its third chair reflected on the group's structure. AAPA began, noted Bryant Fong, without any formal structure because such a structure would have felt too confining and would have impeded building trust among its members. Later, through necessity, representatives were elected by the entire body and given decision-making powers, but not without first consulting everyone. Votes on matters would take place in mass meetings.[50] AAPA was following the advice of Ella Baker, renowned for her sharp criticism of the charismatic leader model. Baker asserted that such hero worship reinforced the dominant society's emphasis on individualism and narcissism (usually personified by the male body) and, most significantly, diminished ordinary people's belief in their own power to effect change. Baker insisted, "Strong people don't need strong leaders."[51]

By contrast, Aoki articulated a top–down leadership structure for AAPA, at least during the TWLF strike. In a 1970 graduate student paper, he wrote, "During the TWLF strike at UCB the structure was tightened overnight to meet the crisis, and the chairman ran AAPA like a military organization complete with a ranked chain of command. In fact, he accepted the chairmanship on the condition that he be given unlimited authority for the duration of the strike."[52] Here we see Aoki's belief in leadership models that promote well-defined roles, official titles, and a clearly demarcated chain of command. These were his leadership models in the U.S. Army, the Socialist Workers Party, and the Black Panther Party. To him, official and even hierarchical roles, if not abused, resulted in increased efficiency. He was, in fact, rather impatient with what he viewed as AAPA's ultrademocratic style, including time-consuming meetings and the consensus process. He regularly left AAPA meetings after a couple of hours, rather than stay until the conclusion of process-oriented, four-hour meetings.[53] Still, Aoki firmly supported democratic structures and processes. When speaking as an AAPA spokesperson, he represented AAPA's position, even when his own views differed. He believed in discussion and the participation of many in the creation of change. So his emphasis on top–down leadership was primarily in service to establishing clearly delineated roles and responsibilities and in instances when quick decision making was needed. Rather than viewing collective and hierarchical leadership in oppositional ways, community organizers discuss the need to match organizational structure to goals, constituencies, and contexts.[54] Aoki functioned well as AAPA's chair during the TWLF strike owing to his organizational abilities and respect for the collective leadership of AAPA and the TWLF.

On Women's Liberation

Aoki's views on women in the movement warrant some discussion. In the late 1960s, the AAM and the overall U.S. Third World movement focused primarily on racial, class, and national oppression. There was no statement opposing sexism in the BPP's Ten-Point Platform and Program, nor in the programs of most of the Third World Left groups patterned after the BPP, with the notable exceptions of I Wor Kuen and the Young Lords Party.[55] AAPA was no exception.[56] At the same time, activist struggles created a heightened consciousness that fostered a critical examination of other forms of oppression, and U.S. Third World women developed ideas of double and triple oppression. These efforts expressed themselves in anthologies like *Black Women* edited by Toni Cade (1970) and matured into sophisticated analyses like the "Combahee River Collective Statement" (1977). AAPA, like the Panthers, offered unprecedented opportunities for women to see themselves as capable and effective leaders, to engage in social justice organizing, and to develop a racialized, gendered consciousness.[57]

By summer 1969, AAPA's newspaper included a lengthy article, "Notes on Women's Liberation," which together with drawings of a Vietnamese woman holding an assault rifle juxtaposed to a "Miss Chinatown USA" beauty pageant queen, covered two full pages of the eight-page newspaper.[58] Through these images, AAPA promoted a different role for women, one that opposed the traditional focus on appearance and instead embodied the most militant expressions of resistance. The author revealed contradictions in the popular views promoting linear progress in gender equality: "More women are going to colleges and graduate schools. . . . [But] the percentage of women in college in proportion to men is about 10 percent lower than in the 1920s. . . . [S]he now has the freedom to work. She can get a clerical job with poverty-level pay or a skilled job with 60 percent of man's pay."[59] Still, the article did not identify root causes of women's oppression; later, the Combahee River Collective would promote a feminist, antiracist socialism as an alternative. AAPA's article did not offer any prescriptive solutions other than the nebulous needs to prioritize women's issues and to develop a unity between sisters and brothers: "The realization of women's liberation will require the efforts of both men and women. . . . It is freedom for everybody or freedom for nobody."[60] This idea of struggling against sexism within antiracist movements was common among Asian American and Third World women activists, who felt alienated from the mainstream women's movement by its inattention to racism and class inequality.[61]

Aoki's views on women developed in this contradictory context that fostered both attention and inattention to sexism. He treated women with respect and supported the leadership of AAPA women. But he also embodied a macho masculinity, one that emphasized combat strategies and the physicality of events, and struggled to see how women fit into such actions. In addition, Aoki, like so many others, adopted a leadership model that minimized women's leadership. His main reference to Emma Gee, AAPA's cofounder, was as "a gracious host." Such an assessment ignored her other contributions. Gee taught some of the earliest Asian American Studies classes at UC Berkeley and UCLA and further helped to build the field through her editing and writing. The most important Asian women's anthology in that period, *Asian Women,* developed from a course she taught at UC Berkeley. She also edited an influential anthology, *Counterpoint,* that not only produced knowledge but also sought to critique the methodologies and theories of the nascent field of Asian American Studies.[62] By contrast to Aoki's framing, Karen Sacks uses the term "centerwomen" to argue that work such as hosting dinners and building social networks, often performed by women, are crucial aspects of organizing and ought to be viewed as leadership.[63]

As AAPA and other groups devoted greater attention to gender equality, Aoki's activist work and consciousness were challenged. He was surprised when, early in the BPP's formation, Huey Newton allowed women into the organization. To Aoki, a group like the Panthers that relied so heavily on military strategies, including their famous police patrols, would require men's participation. But he deferred to Newton's leadership. A couple of years later, Aoki noted about AAPA, "a significant number of the group went along with the [weapons] training. I was a little surprised when the women started going, but after my experiences in the BBP, I wasn't about to question anything." The experience of witnessing women's dedication and leadership helped modify Aoki's views. While he emphasized men's leadership, he also opposed gender oppression, readily identified women as AAPA leaders, and, significantly for him, was willing to work with and train women on internal security matters. Indeed, the Third World social movements contained a transformative capacity that moved Aoki and many other activists in the direction of greater gender equality.

8 "It Was about Taking Care of the Collective"

Prelude to a Strike

Students at Berkeley were active for months before the Third World Liberation Front strike began. The African American students had been negotiating for almost a year for a Black Studies program.[1] The Latinos were pushing the university to boycott grapes, in support of the farmworkers' struggles.[2] At the time, there were many Filipino farmworkers working alongside Chicanos in the fields of California. In the Asian American Political Alliance, the Filipino section was all over that issue. AAPA too had been negotiating with the university for its first ever Asian American Studies class. The African Americans set the tone: "We've been negotiating so long and it looks like they'll never deal unless we go on strike." My position was, I support the African American students going on strike. I figured the Latinos will join them. AAPA, as an organization, had to decide whether or not to strike. The majority voted yes, but there was a small minority opposed. There was a range of reasons: the establishment is too powerful; this is not a just cause; don't rock the boat; we're Americans.[3] I didn't agree with these reasons, but when one considers the brainwashing of people of color in this country, it's not surprising that some would oppose this very bold step. But I wasn't interested in a long-drawn-out process. My thought was, we go on strike. Still, I have to admit that, at the time, I didn't see the strike as that politically important. Remember, I had been working on life-and-death issues with the Black Panthers and I was getting tired out by the political stuff by then. Maybe too I was preoccupied with my own academic career. So when the strike came up and we had a meeting, I wasn't paying that much attention.

I do remember that there was a vote on who should represent AAPA during the strike. The African Americans and Latinos wanted somebody with high rank to speak for the Asians. It's an issue of protocol; you got to have a chairman.

Yuji Ichioka had left the area by then and there was a vacuum in the formal leadership. I was AAPA spokesperson and that's why I reluctantly accepted the chairmanship of AAPA for the duration of the strike. I looked around and there was nobody else that could have done what I did. I was older. I was more politically advanced and more radical than most. I was more working class at this predominantly middle-class university. I said, "I wouldn't accept this unless there's substantial support for my becoming chair." I didn't want no 51 percent to 49 percent vote because this was serious business. If I didn't have the support of the membership, I would have gone under. So they voted and I become the chair of AAPA for the duration of the strike.

Getting back to the TWLF, we had to figure out how we were going to share power. It was a big deal. So I had the idea to bring the leaders of the San Francisco State strike over to talk with us. Roger Alvarado, Benny Crutchfield, and Alfred Wong met with a small group of us from Berkeley, which included Charles Brown, Manuel Delgado, LaNada Means, and myself. We had similar aims. We wanted Ethnic Studies classes, a Third World College. We were concerned about our communities. And most of us males were military veterans, which was unique and probably the one single factor that made both strikes result in a victory. So we had this meeting off campus while the State strike was going on. This must have been around December '68 or January '69.

The issue of the organization came up. What do we call ourselves? Third World Liberation Front. Yeah, team! Everybody agreed on that one. How were we going to run the strike? What would be the composition of the group? Were the Blacks going to lead it because they're the largest oppressed national minority? I'm using the term *minority* for lack of a better term, but it is historically appropriate and was used in those days. The Latinos could have countered that the Latino community in California is the largest oppressed racial/ethnic community and should lead the strike. Of course, the Asians could have argued that there are more Asian American students at the University of California than any of the other minority groups. I wasn't about to espouse that, but it was a reasonable argument. Lo and behold, the Native Americans could have claimed leadership as the most oppressed, suppressed, depressed group. So this tenseness started to build up in the meeting. That's when the San Francisco State people slammed their hands on the table and told us, "Do it equally, because no one group has that one monopoly. We learned that you got to learn how to trust each other when you're in a battle like this. If you can't trust one another, don't even go on strike."

Based on that wise input, we created a sixteen-person Central Committee to run the strike, four representatives from each group.[4] The African Americans had a bit of a problem about which student organization would assume leadership. In Berkeley, the Black Panther Party had a chapter, the Republic of New Africa had a chapter, and there were cultural nationalists too. There was a compromise reached that I was deeply involved in. Charlie Brown of the Afro–American Student Union, who was close to the cultural nationalists, became the official spokesperson for the Blacks, but he had backup. Jim Nabors, the West Coast consul general of the Republic of New Africa, was a wise choice because the AASU had about three times as many RNA members as Black Panthers in it.[5] There was also Don Davis and Carl Mack Jr. Among the Latino groups, there was conflict between MASC [Mexican American Student Confederation] and MEChA [the Movimiento Estudiantil Chicano de Aztlán]. MASC was more revolutionary and became the main leaders. Manuel Delgado was key, though Ysidro Macias and Jaime Solis were also considered equals.[6] The Native Americans had a problem in that there were less than a dozen Native American students at Berkeley out of some twenty-seven thousand students. But LaNada Means and others represented Native Americans. I saw them connected nationally to the American Indian Movement. For the Asians, it wasn't that difficult. I was official spokesperson for AAPA, so it was natural for me to become the official spokesperson for the Asian American students. My policy on the other three Asians was let them rotate. In other words, Asians got four slots; Richard would be permanent, the other three would come in on a need basis. My thought was that there was potential there, but a lot of people needed training fast and this was the best way to do it. The group would pick the other three.[7]

The Central Committee met quite frequently during the strike, almost every night, and had very productive meetings. The leadership was reflective of the rank and file. That's why we were successful; we didn't lead from the top down. The words "participatory democracy" would gain favor a couple of years later with the White students. We actually practiced it because we would have mass meetings and critique each day's activities to strengthen things up. Because many of us were veterans, when it came to the idea of combat, we didn't have to discuss much. We knew immediately that we set up our combat units; we set up our communications units; our first aid units; our counterintelligence. Asians were good with the police monitoring equipment.

We had a unique way of deciding the location of our meeting. One night the Latinos would have the responsibility for picking a safe house and at the last minute give the address to the other three groups. Another night the African Americans would pick the site. This was to enhance security. We met at churches whose ministers were sympathetic to the students. We met in hotel rooms. We met in bars. The Asians went as far as renting an apartment for its headquarters a block away from the university. By that time the university had banned us from campus. One time the African Americans picked an unusual place: the basement of a house on the Oakland–Berkeley border. For some reason the city line passed through the middle of the house. We had instructions when we got to the house: if the cops came in from Berkeley we would leave through the Oakland door, and vice versa. Everybody thought that was hilarious.

From the beginning the leadership had a slight dilemma. What is the strike going to be like? We couldn't predict what was going to happen, but we prepared for the worst. Some of us looked at what was happening at State. They started in November and were still fighting in January. The San Francisco State strike was the longest, costliest, bloodiest strike in the history of the state university system. The struggle we were waging was the longest, costliest, bloodiest strike in the history of the UC system. The important thing is we hung in there for months. No other student group before or since has been able to say that. Why were we able to do it? Because of the righteousness of our position, the commitment of our people, and our willingness to fight hard.

My position was that the university is either going to give up in a couple of days or we're in for a long haul. With the preponderance of veterans on the Central Committee, we made concrete plans. Let's go in prepared for the long haul. Everybody agreed. Now we didn't close the campus down on the first day. From an organizing point of view, it was obvious that unless a large segment of the student, faculty, employees, community, and even parts of the administration could be won over, it wouldn't succeed. Every effort was made to get the support of these particular groups. I was assigned to talk to the few Asian American professors on campus. So I'd be knocking on doors during office hours saying, "Hello, Professor. I'm Richard Aoki. Brother, let me tell you . . ." I have to admit, I didn't expect to get much support, but you got to do those things because you never can tell. The irony is that many of the faculty who supported us were junior faculty, people who had a lot to lose because they didn't have tenure. I have a great deal of respect for those who stepped forward in that period of time, risking their professional careers, by supporting the strike.[8]

We also set up informational picket lines, handing out flyers to students, faculty, and other employees to publicize the righteousness of our cause.

Toward the beginning of the strike, it was one of the coldest days in Berkeley in twenty years. That night we had our mass meeting. It was so cold that Mary Ann Takagi, the wife of Professor Paul Takagi, drove their station wagon up to our picket line, with a big urn of coffee, cups, and donuts, and it was a welcomed sight.[9] Even I was freezing my ass off. Somebody came up to me and complained about the cold: "It was cold this morning on the picket line." My response was, "We invited the cold weather just to test out the intestinal fortitude of everybody here. If you're complaining about a little cold weather, I think you should go."

I wanted people to be serious because I knew that if we were in it for the long haul, things would get ugly. After we began solid picket lines that no one crosses, the police started coming down hard. When one talks about violence, I stand firm that we didn't initiate any violence. We did our utmost to prevent it. The violence came because the university was intransigent in their position. They wouldn't give an inch.[10] We stated our position:

> The TWLF has been accused of acts of violence and destruction on the campus. It is true that some people have thrown rocks and bottles and have broken windows of buildings. But the question that must be answered is where the violence originates. Clearly, . . . with the police who . . . provoked the violence by disrupting peaceful, informational picket lines . . . by brutally attacking strikers and bystanders. . . . The violence of the strikers, on the other hand, has been a defensive reaction to the initial violence of the police.[11]

Here's the good news: "The attempted repression of the strike attests to our effectiveness. The power of the people is threatening the authorities' control."[12]

Militancy on the Front Lines

Even before the police came down on us, we had to fight it out with our fellow students. We had our informational picket line and somehow the fraternity boys decided that they weren't going to take a bunch of colored people blocking the entrance to the campus. Now you have to understand, at the beginning of this strike, when we talk about numbers, it didn't look too meaningful. At the time, there were maybe eight hundred African Americans at Berkeley, maybe three hundred to four hundred Latinos, maybe two thousand Asians, and Native Americans, we're talking about half a dozen, possibly.[13] So numberwise you could see that on the picket lines in front of the campus, we didn't look that awesome in the beginning. But we augmented the lines by appealing to the more progressive White students, which included SDS and the Old Left. So what happens is the frat boys hit our picket line, trying to hurt our people. That's when it started getting ugly because we took up the self-defense mode: "We're not taking no shit from you frat boys." We kicked their asses.[14]

It became apparent that a frat group was not enough to contain us, so it escalated a bit more and they sent some plainclothes policemen in. This is kind of funny in a way because they were easily identifiable; they're usually middle-aged Whites with potbellies. Then we had a little scuffle where one of the plainclothes cops got knocked to the ground and his gun fell out of his holster and disappeared into the crowd. That was a coup for us because somebody got their hands on something fast. So what's the next step? University Police, who were virtually all White in those days, give me a break. We defended ourselves righteously.

Another time, an AAPA member and I were on the picket lines at Sather Gate. He was at one end of the line and I was at the other end. I could see that we were going to be hit. I knew that my end of the line was pretty solid. There were a couple of African Americans there who could hold that end. So I went scooting over to help this AAPA brother, thinking he may be in trouble. But he apparently had some martial arts training. He had a short little picket sign and he was just cleaning their clocks every time he turned around. I was stunned. At the beginning of the strike, when Charlie, Manuel, LaNada, and I were talking about the possibility of violence, someone asked, "What about your group, Richard? Your people aren't exactly known for their pugnacious abilities." I have to admit, I was a bit apprehensive at first. You have to remember that back then, the image of the Asian American male was not that of a robust street fighter, especially the middle-class types. I was an anomaly among the Asians in my own mind. The good news is AAPA had had exposure to self-defense during its evolution and a lot of the AAPA people had Black belts in the various martial arts. Well, this brother's demonstration of his expertise and his seriousness amazed me because they were giving tit for tat. I'm not exaggerating because that's exactly what happened.[15]

I remember during a strategic withdrawal, all of us were running across campus, being chased by I think it was the highway patrol that day. I was behind two guys, one was Asian American, the other African American. The Asian American was running so fast, his wallet dropped out of his pocket. The African American, without breaking stride, was able to pick up the guy's wallet and keep on going. I said, "Right on." Later on, two Asian Americans were running across the grass. One slipped on the wet grass, spun, and did a somersault in the air. The guy who was running alongside him on the concrete was able to snatch him as he was hitting the ground—and without breaking stride because we had some motivation coming from behind us. There was another Asian American striker that got into an umbrella duel with a White female professor. We were blocking the entrance to the School of Social Work building and she was determined to get inside. We were determined not to let anybody in or out. It had been raining that day, so both sides had umbrellas and a duel took place. I had mixed feelings about that because I'd taken a class from that professor the year before and she was awesome in the classroom, so I had to jump in and break it up.

It started getting ugly when the UCPD and the Berkeley Police Department started moving in and the brutality escalated. Cordell Abercrombie was one of the first to be beaten by the police. They arrested Cordell because he resembled one of the African American strike leaders and they beat him. When we got him out of jail, his head looked horrible. He had knots all over, eyes swollen shut. We were pissed! I had a chance to talk with Cordell. "What happened, man?" He says, "They beat me." I say, "I can see that. But why?" We were following the protocol that the Black Panthers had laid out. You get busted, you go down. That was based on the fact that you don't do nothing to us after you bust us. But they broke the rules of the game. What they did to Cordell was unprofessional. Cordell said, "They kept asking me the same question: 'Are you going up on the strike lines again tomorrow?'" Every time he said "yeah," they hit him.[16] Well, the next day, about seven in the morning, on the north side, two cops got ambushed. One was beaten with his own club, which was broken over his head. An eyewitness, whose vision was poor, stated that I was observed in that group. I have steadfastly maintained that that person, who wears glasses, needed stronger lenses. After that, nobody else got beaten up while in custody, at least for a while, because the word got out. Look, there are rules here.[17]

From the start, there were signs that this strike was going to involve hard fighting. Just as the strike started, Wheeler Auditorium, the largest lecture hall on campus, burned down. I was at a Central Committee meeting in Oakland of all things. We got a phone call in the middle of our meeting telling us something horrible had happened at Berkeley. We looked out the window and could see the flames going two, three hundred feet high. We knew something big was burning. Of course, we knew they would blame the fire on the student strikers. So we had a hurried meeting about how to respond to this. We excluded LaNada for this one because it was too heavy. We're talking about arson. People were going to be facing time on this one. LaNada was female, the youngest among us, and if the Bureau of Indian Affairs found out that she was mixed up in something like this, they'd withdraw her funding and she'd be kicked out of school. So the morning after the fire, Manuel Delgado, Charles Brown, and I conducted a press conference at eleven in the morning. We did it in the morning to make it on the six o'clock news. We invited everybody, including the reactionary press, because we wanted to get our story out. At the press conference, we denied we had anything to do with it. But then we had a second press conference for those reporters who wrote what I call objective pieces about the strike. There, we were a little more candid, saying, "Well, that's the way it happened," as if to say, maybe we did it. The reporters wanted somebody from the TWLF leadership and I got the brass ring. That was the first official press interview I ever gave about the strike. I told the *Berkeley Barb* that "I personally disavow petty acts of vandalism because they're petty." That's exactly how I felt. I also stated: "Who was responsible for the fire? The university. The university had set up the conditions for the violence to get unleashed."[18]

Now it's obvious that after the fire and after the initial fights on the line, things were going to get out of control. That's when the Alameda County Sheriff's Department was brought in. They were known as the "blue meanies" because they wore blue jumpsuits and they were mean. So we're battling, hand-to-hand combat, we're trying to get our licks in when we can. I've got to say something about the role of the female members of the Third World Liberation struggle. They were no shrinking violets. You put a brick in a handbag, go walking along, get a chance to back up a brother, *whampup,* then you go running. That's the way it was. If we needed something at one end of the campus and it didn't look good for one of us to be carrying it, a sister would be entrusted. One AAPA member was also able to do that. He looked so much like a nerdy Oriental student, he was able to go right through those lines with the treasury of the TWLF in his pocket. I'll never forget how he was able to navigate through one of the worst riots we ever had. I was worried: man, any second now they're gonna pick him up and there goes our treasury. People battling to the right of him, battling to the left of him, and he's just going along from one end of the campus to the other.

During a period of time when about a hundred of us were arraigned, we were sitting in court, waiting for our names to be called. They called a name out and this White girl stands up. Some dude in a five-hundred-dollar suit, a lawyer hired by her rich family, talks to the judge and she gets to walk out of the courtroom. Now I was puzzled about this girl who looks like she's right out of a sorority. I told the person next to me to hold my place so if they call my name, tell them I'm here. I go running down the hall after the girl and her attorney. I thought I knew everybody on the strike line and this White girl didn't compute. So I said, "You got arrested? What happened?" She said that she was leaving one of the buildings and her White hippie boyfriend was out there battling with the cops. They were kicking his ass. So she screamed out the first thing that came to her mind: "Pigs off campus." That was one of the slogans we used. That got her busted. Now this was an educationally enriching experience on police brutality for her. You might say that the university helped her get a well-rounded education.

Another time when I was arrested, I got out of jail real fast. This was strange. I was pretty sure we didn't have any money left in the legal defense bail fund because I had talked to Steve Wong and this African American brother who were working on the TWLF bail fund. So I asked the bailiff, "Who sprung me?" It turns out a classmate of mine was out there when the cops took me down. She jumped into her Mustang, a gift from her parents, and wrote a check out for the bail, and I was out. During one of my trials, another fellow student of mine told the judge that she supported me and so did the rest of the students in the Graduate School of Social Work. It helps when you get character witnesses who look respectable in the eyes of the judge. It was a trip being in the Graduate School of Social Work, meeting all these White females from wealthy families, who had been to the best universities as undergraduates. They were affected by what was going on right in front of them. Not to mention that I was their classmate, they saw me beaten down and dragged off like a common criminal, and they would soon vote for me to be the student body president of the School of Social Work.[19]

I remember one time I got thrown into jail and this bailiff grabbed me by the back of my collar and my trousers and threw me into a holding cell with about thirty other prisoners and said, "Here is an Oriental Communist student from Berkeley." When I got to my feet and brushed myself off I thought, "Everybody's gonna want a taste of me. I'm gonna have to fight every mothafucka in this cell now." So I'm getting ready when I heard, "Say, Richard." I looked around and, believe it or not, there was this guy called Tiny in the cell. If you ever want to meet the baddest dude in jail, ask for Tiny, 'cause they always call him Tiny, even in motion pictures. Turned out to be a dude I knew from West Oakland. I hadn't seen him in years. We started talking and I had to briefly tell him what I was in for, that I'm up at Berkeley doing things. Tiny got up and said, "I want everybody here to meet my homie, Richard. Don't want anybody messing with him. He's not a common criminal like the rest of us. He's a political prisoner." I said, "Right on!" After that everything was cool until mealtime. We got the baloney sandwiches. I started a little ruckus over food. They threw me in solitary, the hole. Now here's the good news. That gave me a chance to do my homework because my classmates would bring me the class notes and assignments. The professors were told I was doing participant research and that's why I was absent from the classroom.

Now we invented a few tricks that added to the authorities' confusion. Normally in a strike you try to hold something down with your line, like close down Sather Gate. When the cops started really attacking us, what we did instead is move the lines and do snake dances all over the campus. The beauty is we knew the territory, so we could go in one building and come out three, four different ways. The cops didn't know that and they sure as hell weren't going to chase us inside the building because we had surprises in store for them. It was my idea to set booby traps but it got vetoed, "That's too dangerous, Richard." But there were things that we did. Somebody in our group came up with this idea. Butyric acid is one of the foulest-smelling substances around and it's readily available in the labs at Berkeley. A drop of that stuff will necessitate closing off this whole place. Well, one of the committees that wasn't on the official list would visit the offices of professors that we were not enamored with. Then at midterm time, we said that if we're not taking midterms, nobody's taking midterms. I announced that nobody should take midterms for their own safety. A group of strikers went in and booby-trapped the seats of the lecture hall with time devices that would set off firecrackers. One of the strikers apparently was hard of hearing. He went to take his midterm and the seat he sat in had a firecracker underneath it and it went off. His sister got all over me that night, "He can't hear! He can't hear, Richard! You're responsible for that." She was half in jest. Her brother claimed that I must have been looking with my field glasses and saw him sitting in that seat and had it explode. But he shouldn't have been taking that midterm. He ended up all right, though, because we were not a bloodthirsty group. These things had to be thought out. I mean, when people were talking about C-4 explosives, that's when I drew the line.[20]

This is what would normally happen. We'd have our line up there and the police would have their line. Sooner or later one of their people would do something nasty and attack our line. Then we'd either run or fight. One day we came up with an ingenious plan. By this time our tactics were pretty good and we had good discipline. The plan was we'd have our main picket line. Then the police would for some reason attack the main picket line. Normally the orders would have been "stand and fight." But this time, the plan was for the main strike line to pull back across the street. Let the police move forward, while another group of strikers would hit them from behind, then run. The main crowd would then counterattack. A beautiful plan, but for it to work, we needed a volunteer to ignite the situation and it involved being able to run real fast for about twenty feet. However, if the person wasn't swift enough, the police would have made the Cordell Abercrombie beating look like kindergarten. So the Central Committee had a meeting. This was not mass meeting time. We talked about the plan. I wasn't about to volunteer. I'm thinking, "I'm better in this position over here. I don't think I want to be out there." But there was a volunteer and this volunteer surprised me. He was an African American student who was not noted for getting into the center of things. Some point before this meeting, he had told me, "When the attacks come, I want to be in the third wave." But during this meeting—he was on the Central Committee at this time—he raised his hand and volunteered. I took him aside and said, "Look, my man, we been drinking this wine, but let me tell you something, I'm not volunteering for this one. I'm sorry, but I'm not that fast. Do you understand what this means? Just one split second off and you could be history." He looked me straight in the eye and said, "I'll do it."

That day we agreed that an Asian would be the person in charge of the field. We didn't always put our strike leaders out there in charge of the field. We tried to spread that one out a little bit because that was a dangerous position. That person was usually anonymous; the police didn't know who they were. So I'm in the background that day. Bryant Fong is with me; he's the radio man. We're waiting for the word about when we're going to attack after the main picket line is attacked and retreats. We're hiding in back of the police. We were to hit them from behind, then run like hell. When they turned around to chase us, that's when the main group would turn forward and we'd break up their ranks. This has to do with field tactics. So I'm waiting and waiting and there's no word. I sent somebody to go all the way around to the main strike line and got the most awful story I ever heard. For some reason the Asian American field commander and the African American who was going to be the key player had assessed the situation out in the field and decided it was too risky. So they called it off, which is okay because you don't give orders from the top down, you've got the people on the front lines making the decision.

If they say, "Man, don't look good to us," you got to respect that. But what they did instead I couldn't believe. Bunch of them went and got watermelon and got fried chicken from those grocery stores on Telegraph Avenue. They took the food back to the front of the campus, laid out tablecloths, and had a watermelon-in. Then they started singing, "Who's making love to your old lady while you are standing guard out there?"[21] That was a popular rock-and-roll/R and B song at that time. The whole thing made the cops pissed. But they couldn't do anything. This was worse than hitting them. They were frustrated just standing there, visually seeing the worst of this stereotype, and the group was partying in front of them. I couldn't believe it! I said, "We're going to talk tonight!"

I understand the need for strategic retreat because there was another situation where I was in charge of the field. Our plan was to storm the main administration building at Berkeley, which was across the street from the campus at the time. We spent three days building up to it. On the day we were gonna storm the building, there were two, three, four thousand students on the campus side, ready to cross the street to take over the building. I was out there doing my recon. I looked through my field glasses and saw the San Francisco Tactical Unit. Now, AAPA had already tangled with the tactical unit because of our community work in San Francisco Chinatown. It's my professional opinion that the San Francisco Tactical Unit is the most bloodthirsty of all the police departments around here. So I'm horrified. So I get on the walkie-talkie and abort the action. I said, "Tell the people do not cross the street. Just stay on the campus side because the tactical unit is guarding the building. Somebody could get killed." I had to answer for that that night when we had the Central Committee meeting. "Richard, we spent three days building up to this." I said, "Look, I'd be the first one there if it wasn't the tactical unit. I was looking forward to taking over that building! But once I saw the relationship of the forces, I had to call it off." The possibility that somebody could get killed was foremost on my mind, especially with these cops. I wouldn't even call them pigs; these were the hogs of the establishment.

To show how serious we were about being prepared to face police attacks and arrests, I found an AAPA document that I was involved in creating. It was approved by AAPA and put out by the committee of cadres, strike committee of AAPA. Since we were part of the TWLF and therefore responsible for operations, we issued this mandate urging everybody to "pay all outstanding traffic tickets immediately." I'm sad to say, among the first people arrested during the strike were ones that didn't clean up their warrants. We also gave instructions on how to dress on the picket lines and to "notify the committee of cadres and/or monitors where you go, so that there are witnesses in case of arrest and also to provide help if necessary." We told people to memorize the number of the West Oakland Legal Switchboard and "have at least two dimes for phone calls." We told people how to smear Vaseline on their face to defend against Mace. We also had our own medics ready to help with the problems we were anticipating. The short of it was, "Do not resist arrest" but "be united, alert, earnest, and lively." The latter was a quote we borrowed from Chairman Mao.[22]

One of the things we advised on that AAPA leaflet was to "leave expensive cameras at home." It turns out that the first Asian arrested in the strike got in trouble over his camera. He was one of the few who voted against the strike in our AAPA meeting. Comes the strike and the picket lines, he gets his expensive camera and goes taking pictures because he's at Berkeley and this is exciting. He seems to have imagined that since he voted against the strike, there's a big sign up above his head exempting him from police brutality. Apparently the police can't read. He's going around, gets close to a cop to take his picture, next thing you know, there goes the camera, and there he goes in the opposite direction, off to jail.[23]

So I'm at the TWLF Central Committee meeting that night, looking over the arrest list. It's exciting. The first Asian got busted. The TWLF Central Committee says, "Better take this back to AAPA to decide what to do." So AAPA has an emergency meeting. First Asian got busted today. That means umpteen hundred dollars in bail money. Somebody says, "What's the person's name?" The name comes up and somebody says, "That's an AAPA person—an AAPA person that voted against going on strike." Dead silence in the room. I remembered him voting; his dilettantish attitude didn't sit with me. So I'm waiting to see what happens here. This guy's brother, who was a leader in AAPA and voted for the strike, stands up and says, "He voted against the strike. We're not getting him out of jail. He can rot there." I felt the same way, but I knew I had to stand on principle. So I got up and said, "Be that as it may, we're fighting about fairness. We're fighting about being more open. We're fighting about doing what's right. I think we should bail him out." Everybody looked at me because they expected Richard to be the hard one. Though we didn't have much money in our bail fund, I proposed we spring for his bail. I even said, "I'll go down and get him out." Afterward, this guy became a born-again AAPA member. For the duration of the strike he took good pictures of what came down.

The thing on arrests that we learned from the San Francisco State strikers was, do not allow the leadership to take too many arrests. By the time we met with Roger, Benny, and Al, they had like forty arrests among them. So they suggested that we rotate who gets busted so that no one gets too many arrests. So we rotated the visibility of our leadership and had people who could take the helm. If LaNada went down, Patty would have picked up the slack. If Charlie went down, there were four or five good people in his group, including Don Davis, Carl Mack Jr., and Jim Nabors. The Latinos had the trio of Delgado, Macias, and Solis. As for the Asians, when it came to public speaking, Jeff Leong was able to step in on several occasions. This was great advice from an organizational standpoint. Out of the 147 of us arrested, charges were pretty much spread out across the board. Nobody really took a huge portion of the arrests. There were, however, several in the rank and file that got arrested and we had to physically restrain from going back the next day.[24]

I got busted three or four times during the strike.[25] The newspaper listed at least one hundred strikers, identified by name, arraigned over a two-day period primarily on two charges: blocking and obstructing public passageways (meaning closing down the university) and assault and battery, which stemmed from police brutality.[26] Most of the charges on me were assault and battery because I'm going to defend myself when attacked. The main charge against me was an alleged assault on six police officers. That happened on the day of the big bust when fifteen or sixteen of us were arrested, including half of the TWLF leadership. So what happened was that Manuel and I were on our way to a meeting with representatives from the university. We didn't take Charlie and LaNada—thought it'd be better to split our ranks. Though normally we weren't permitted on campus, the university administration said they'd meet with us if we were willing to meet with them. University promised us safe passage across campus, but they forgot to tell the Alameda County Sheriff's Department. So Manuel and I go bippity-boppin' along when about twenty of them ambushed us. We fought like hell. I allegedly assaulted six deputies. That was my only case that went to trial.[27]

In addition to the arrest, I got a letter from the university's Committee on Student Conduct saying, "We're going to put you on trial and maybe expel you from school."[28] This is my first year in graduate school, I don't need this. A bunch of recent graduates from Boalt Law School volunteered to defend us. Ken Kawaichi, with the office of Yonemura and Yasaki, got assigned to represent me.[29] So I went before the Committee on Student Conduct consisting of four students and four professors who are to determine my guilt or innocence. I quickly assessed the group. The four students seem more liberal and likely to vote for acquittal. But the four professors seem to be on the conservative side and were probably going for the hanging. It looked like a hung jury. Then the most conservative-appearing professor on the committee got up and read their verdict: not guilty, eight to nothing. I almost fell out of my chair. I couldn't believe it. Afterward, my lawyer asked why they voted the way they did. The professor said that with a grade point average as high as I had—a 3.84, an A average—there was no way I could have time to get involved in that crazy political activity.[30]

So I get acquitted by the UC Student Conduct Committee, but my state criminal trial is still pending. By this time a number of Asians had been arrested. The defense committee was trying to consolidate the cases, making it easier to handle. Ken Kawaichi, who's representing me again, agreed to negotiate all the Asian cases before the Alameda County criminal justice system. In his meeting with the district attorney, he was able to ameliorate all the other cases. Then it came down to my file and the district attorney informed him that the deals they'd cut for the other Asian American defendants didn't extend to me. They were taking me to trial and going for the maximum sentence. According to my attorney, the DA seemed to have some real deep emotional feelings about my general well-being. So my attorney asked me what was happening because this was rather unusual. I had to inform him that over the last couple of years I had joined that group, become a field marshal, been in a lot of trouble in Oakland, and I think its payback time. So we go to trial. I'm charged with assaulting these six police officers. I allegedly took down the field commander of the Alameda County Sheriff's Department, delivering karate-like blows, sending him to his knees. His lieutenant, a sergeant, was also injured to the extent that he required hospital treatment. Another person was hurt and another. I'm saying, "This is obviously a whole bunch of lies!"

So my attorney comes up with, "How tall are you, Richard?" "Five five." "How much do you weigh?" "A hundred and twenty-five pounds." Well, let's get the six deputy sheriffs up here. So he had us do a lineup with me standing against the wall with the six men I allegedly assaulted and none of them are less than six feet two inches, two hundred and umpteen pounds. The jury broke out in laughter when they saw the lineup. Then there were the character witnesses, my fellow students from the School of Social Work, most of them White females from the best colleges, Smith, Swarthmore, and Vassar graduates, attesting to my good character and why they voted me in as their president. While the jury was out deliberating, that's when I discovered that this was my attorney's first criminal case. Say what?! Now the good news is he wasn't a fool. The jury came out and delivered their verdict. Not guilty. I was acquitted.

The district attorney blew his cool and demanded a poll of the jury. Now all throughout the trial, the judge kept assisting the district attorney, saying things like, "I wouldn't use *Dabney v. Missouri, 1932.* I'd use *Cronkite v. Maryland, 1863.* That would be much more appropriate than your argument." I'm saying, "What side is that damn judge on?!" When the last juror said "not guilty," I jumped up. Afterward, my attorney jammed the foreman of the jury: "What did you guys talk about when you were discussing my innocent client's fate?" The foreman of the jury said, "Look, we think he did what he did, but the state was asking for too much as far as sentencing was concerned." In other words, he probably did kick the shit out of some of them, but maybe they had it coming. If it had been the Berkeley police, there may have been a different outcome. But this was the Alameda County Sheriff's Department, the blue meanies, and their reputation was scandalous. It's amazing, in my dealing with the criminal justice system, how twisty the road can be. I don't think there are too many redeeming features about the criminal justice system, but it goes to show that you never know what might influence people, even those who seem the least likely to offer fairness.[31]

Getting back to the day we were arrested walking across campus to meet with the university representatives: Manuel and I were taken to the Berkeley City Jail, so we get out of jail fast. But after our arrests, a second group got busted.[32] They were taken to Santa Rita. They're in the custody of the blue meanies, which means trouble for our people. We don't have any more money in the bail fund. So I approached an African American bail bondsman I know: "Look, man, we got a bunch more that just got busted down in Santa Rita and I'm worried about their general well-being. If the cops know they can keep them for three or four days, they're going to work them over the first night. We got no money right now. But I give you my personal word that you will get your money back, that nobody will skip bail." Now this bail bondsman was known to be a little hard hearted, but because the cause was right and I guess he trusted me to a certain extent, he helped us. We spring everybody out that night. Now this is trust because it showed we don't leave our dead and wounded behind.

A few months after the strike, there's a blurb in the newspaper about my being appointed to the faculty at Berkeley. I'm sitting in my office in Asian American Studies and the administrative assistant says a certain gentleman is here to see me. It was this bail bondsman, who was happy to read that I had a job and was in a position to repay him. I laughed, "Man, you know half of my first paycheck was going to you, brother." I don't even want to go into how much it was. I did have one student ask me, "If you're so smart, why ain't you rich?" But to tell you the truth, I never got fixated on money. It wasn't like I deprived any of my children of food in their bellies or a roof over their heads— not that I had any children. I don't think those in jail even know how they got bailed out. But it wasn't an individual thing. It was about taking care of the col- lective. And I got taken care of too.

Now I've dwelt quite a bit on the militant activities of the strike. That's pri- marily because I was on the front lines most of the time. This was important work because without this series of actions—trying to close down the univer- sity—we wouldn't have had any negotiating power at the bargaining table. In other words, the strike group who risked their liberties and careers by engag- ing in these so-called illegal activities had to do it because there was no other way to get the university to recognize the seriousness of the issue and to act accordingly. As I said, at the beginning of the strike the Academic Senate over- whelmingly ignored us. That changed by the end of the strike because of our militant actions. The administration doesn't want a strike. The students don't want a strike. I mean, we were there for an education. But the intransigence of the university, its refusal to implement our modest proposals, forced us into the strike. This was revolutionary in 1969 because the idea of Ethnic Studies had never come up before.

While I have focused on the more militant aspects of the strike, a lot of other important work was being done by those in the TWLF. A number of commit- tees were established from the beginning, which included the publicity com- mittee, the fund-raising committee, legal defense committee, and a speakers bureau as well as a strike support liaison, community liaison, and a group for administrators, faculty, and employees. We also had a first aid committee because if we were going out there to fight, there were going to be casual- ties.[33] A lot of credit goes to those students that took on responsibility for those activities and did an outstanding job. I would have liked everybody on the front line, and I'm joking in a way because not everybody could be on the front line. Other things had to be done to logistically support the militant actions. You don't want to risk arrests unless your bail and legal defense committees are functioning.

The Strike Comes to an End

All I remember is that AAPA took a vote on whether or not to end the strike. The vote was three to one to end it, which I took as a lack of confidence in the leadership.[34] One of the leaders of AAPA, who had voted with the majority to cool it, told me later that he had made a mistake. He had believed at the time that arbitration and a more civil tone on our part would go further in the university accepting the strike demands. But as he observed as things went on, this wasn't the case. History has borne out that that vote was defeatist in its thrust. Let me put it this way. I had the hard-line vision that this was protracted warfare, not some short Jiffy Pop operation. It may surprise some, but I welcomed the presence of the National Guard, not for the reason they were sent in, but because it demonstrated an elevation in the stakes. I remembered what Che Guevara had said about many more Vietnams. If we tied down National Guard units here, they won't be sending them to Vietnam. It also meant that we were gaining power. The authorities felt threatened and called in the National Guard. I know some can't believe that we could have fought off the six hundred police and one thousand National Guardsmen.[35] But you have to remember, we're veterans. We'd been in the military. The National Guard, in general, has a reputation that might be less than their image conveys. Plus, there was a plan—a good plan that would have worked, had it been implemented, with a counterattack to the National Guards, shutting off electrical power or water, and taking out the computer center. But the issue came down to this: We had been on strike for months and I had to be reminded that the troops were tired. I could sense that as we met for the final vote. There was just a half dozen of us who sat in one corner of the room and were willing to go one more mile with these plans. Those voting to end the strike pointed out that the university was on its hands and knees now. It looked like we were getting our major demands. The shifting of the name and structure from Third World College to Ethnic Studies Department didn't sit well with me, but the people had voted.

When I read about the Academic Senate vote in the newspaper, I was shocked.[36] I remembered how a few short months prior, they had voted the other way. It was a turnaround like I've never seen in all of my decades of experience in higher education. Why did that happen? Was that because the faculty said, "Oh, the students were right, we were wrong." No way. In fact, I don't think many of the faculty wanted to vote for Ethnic Studies. But we put pressure on them and changed the odds. Among the most important factor is the cost. It cost a hell of a lot for them to repress us—from the UCPD to the Alameda County Sheriff's Department and the National Guards, and that wasn't all. Think about the collateral damage of buildings going up. So you had this uncertain, unstable situation and it was costing them money. Now let's look at the image. Every night people turn on the TV set and see turmoil in Berkeley. More and more people were joining in as we built a mass movement based on some righteous principles. All we want is a decent education for our people. Is that too much? Carl Mack Jr., Berkeley High graduate and first Ethnic Studies Department chairman, did an excellent job securing churches where the African American students could meet.[37] This then engendered moral support as well as, I hope, financial backing of many in the Black church. It wasn't just ethnic people supporting us. If you look at that arrest list that was printed in the newspaper, I'll bet you more than half of them are White. I've identified all the Asians and most of the Blacks and Latinos on that list, so the others were righteous White students, male and female, who joined our picket lines.[38]

It was also important that we kept the pressure up on the military front. I hate to keep going back to this, but I'm a little biased because that's where I spent most of my time during the Great War. If they didn't have the specter of the disruption and the destruction of the university, the faculty wouldn't have changed their votes. Sure the other side brought in the National Guard, but we're bringing in more people. We had people power. We'll shut this university down![39]

Then, there was our focus on Third World solidarity. Remember that even before our strike started, the San Francisco State people told us that we had to trust one another before going on strike. If you can't do that, then don't even think about it. They also told us that we need to consciously figure out what our differences and similarities were and to maximize our similarities. We had more than enough to be similar about, the common oppression based upon skin color, the exploitation of our people, our labor historically. We could all agree on the war in Vietnam. It ain't for our people. We may not go as far as to say it's an imperialist war, but we could see that it's wreaking havoc on the Third World communities, especially African Americans and Latinos with their high casualty rates. Then we needed to minimize stuff like the cultural nationalism that existed in these groups. It's a simple principle and one that I stick to to this day: Maximize similarities, minimize differences.

One of the most striking images of Third World solidarity came out of the Berkeley strike. After a TWLF Central Committee meeting, a reporter and a photographer from the Nation of Islam's paper, *Muhammad Speaks,* came up to the campus. They had heard about the strike and wanted to do a story on it. At that time, the Black Panther Party and the Nation of Islam probably produced the two main national newspapers for the African American community. They got the TWLF leaders together for a group picture featuring Manuel "Mad Man" Delgado, Charles "Downtown" Brown, and Richard "The Hit Man" Aoki.[40] Shortly thereafter, the *Sun Reporter,* which is the number one

African American newspaper in the Bay Area, reprinted the same picture, along with an article.[41] I remember getting a note from an instructor I had at Merritt College. He had become a professor at Cornell and told me that the students at Cornell had made this photograph into a poster for their occupation of the main campus building. So that picture became kind of famous and served as a visual symbol of Third World solidarity. The one thing I regret is that LaNada Means was unavailable at that particular time. But she one-upped us because a couple of months later, she was on the cover of *Ramparts* magazine, which was then coedited by Robert Scheer and David Horowitz. At that time, David Horowitz had contributions to make, unlike the hard right turn he's since made.[42]

Of course when different groups get together there's the potential for conflict. I could see many sensitive things that could have gone to violence. But by struggling together we were able to put into operation our principle of maximizing similarities and minimizing differences. When you participate in the struggle together, you get to know and respect each other. I mentioned how this one African American saved an Asian American student's wallet. That same African American loaned me his father's gasoline credit card. I was a poor graduate student, but I had a car and I needed to patrol the area to figure out security for the strike. Credit cards were a novelty in those days. Though he didn't know me before the strike, this brother turned over his father's gasoline credit card to me for the duration of the strike. Another example is that time I got accused of beating up those six police officers. I was trying to get them off Manuel's back. I could have split and saved my own ass, but I knew we were in this together. These might be small examples, but magnify them.

There are several reasons why I immersed myself in the strike. At the risk of seeming egotistical, if we were to look at all the Asian Americans on campus at that time, who else would everybody have voted for? This wasn't about popularity. There was a historic need. By that time, I had an estrangement from the Black Panther Party. But I wasn't worried about the party. The year before, new leadership from SNCC was added. They were in good hands. What more could I add? But the Asian American Movement was just beginning and it seemed natural for me to help build this movement. Dolly Veale thinks that shift, which was sanctioned by Huey, was what saved my life because in the next year, things became bloodier than ever in the BPP.

Even after we won, I really didn't realize the significance of the victory. What I felt most was the release of the obligation: I had promised to stick it in through to the end and I did. I was never so glad when the strike was over. It was probably the most exhausting period in my whole life, physically, mentally, and emotionally. I didn't do a lot of introspection. I was on automatic pilot. Academically I was on my way to completing the requirements for my master's degree. Then the big split in the BPP hit. I'd been away from the party and I didn't see it coming. Then I had my personal life and personal plans.

I have to admit, at the beginning of the strike, I didn't think the cause was all that significant. After fighting hard on the streets of Oakland, the Berkeley strike seemed like a petit bourgeois struggle for upward mobility. I now see the importance of the strike. Number one, we practiced the idea of Third World solidarity. We hung in there tight, we hung in there tough. That's why we won. Second, we created a new revolutionary concept. Together with the San Francisco State strike victory, this was the first time Ethnic Studies was part of the education system. The strike itself wasn't a total victory, but it set up the framework for developing the Ethnic Studies Department. Third, in the long term, many of the students who participated in the strike returned to their communities as professionals. Those individuals set up programs and organizations, some of which have survived to this day. Fourth, the strike provided an inspiration to other student groups throughout the country and that continues to today. This wasn't just within the U.S. We inspired student movements worldwide. This was dialectical in nature because the revolutionary movements throughout the Third World were an inspiration to us. I was personally connected to some of the militants in Japan who were fighting the war in Vietnam and opposing the reemergence of Japanese militarism. Frantz Fanon as a radical intellectual certainly affected all our groups. The African American students ate him up, so did some of us in AAPA and MASC. The Cuban Revolution stood as a reference point for us. I remember being stunned when I heard that after the revolution, their big plan was education and literacy programs. I thought the first thing you do is make bigger guns to defend yourself. But many Cubans went into the countryside to teach the campesinos how to read and write. I didn't realize that creating a literate people is the best defense against oppression. So we too were doing something important in struggling for liberation through education.

THE REVOLUTIONARY POTENTIAL OF THE THIRD WORLD STRIKE

The Duality of Formal Education

"I didn't see the strike as that politically important." This is a surprising statement from one who provided tremendous leadership to the Third

World strike. Aoki's admission that he "wasn't paying too much attention" is revealing of his radical politics. In the 1960s, Richard saw formal schooling as having a dual function as a progressive and regressive force.[43] On one hand, Aoki made plans, beginning with his return to full-time studies at Merritt College, to use his education as a means to obtain personal economic mobility. On the other hand, he was developing a radical critique of the U.S. educational system. Aoki would have agreed with Troy Duster's analogy of the British colonial education system in India to warn against the co-optation of ethnic elites. In the *Daily Californian,* Duster recounted a debate in mid-nineteenth-century British-controlled India about the kind of education the Indian elite should receive. Lord Macaulay won the debate in favor of Western training. Duster, then a temporary instructor without security of employment, boldly stated: "The Academic Senate and the Regents will join to argue that there is only one kind of real education for the black elite, the Mexican-American elite, the Asian elite, or any ghetto elite. The Academic Senate follows Mccaulay *[sic].*"[44]

Aoki feared the U.S. minority elite, like the Indian elite, would use their education to discipline the protest and radical aspirations of the disenchanted majority. In the absence of a critical pedagogy and equal access to higher education, Aoki saw the mainstream curriculum as perpetuating the status quo by teaching a history of the privileged, by promoting notions of meritocracy, and by diminishing the power of institutionalized racism and class exploitation.[45]

Militaristic Strategies, Collective Organizing, and the Strike Victory

The duality of education produced in Aoki an ambivalence about the revolutionary potential of the struggle for Third World studies. But being at UC Berkeley, he nonetheless immersed himself in the strike, but did so in ways that reflected his preferred method of organizing. Noting that "most of us males were military veterans," he emphasized a unique perspective—that this was "probably the one single factor" that led to victory. He was less interested in, but still valued, the day-to-day organizing and the slow process of struggle through dialogue. When I questioned Aoki about important organizational decisions, such as AAPA's decision to "cool it" on the picket lines, he could barely recall that discussion or any AAPA meetings for that matter. No doubt Aoki was overwhelmingly busy during the strike, but he was also rather impatient with the dialogic process.[46] He got too angry and wanted to see action. To Aoki, action and people's experiences—not talking per se—are

Richard's mother, Toshiko, and her second husband, Albert Kaniye, 1980. After Richard's mother and his brother, David, both married in 1961, Richard too planned for marriage. He had several girlfriends, but never married. Collection of Richard Aoki.

Richard Aoki holds a sign stating "Yellow Peril Supports Black Power" as part of the Asian American Political Alliance's support for the Free Huey campaign, ca. 1968. Looking on at left is Richard's friend Douglas Daniels (in white T-shirt). Reprinted from Howard L. Bingham, *Black Panthers 1968*.

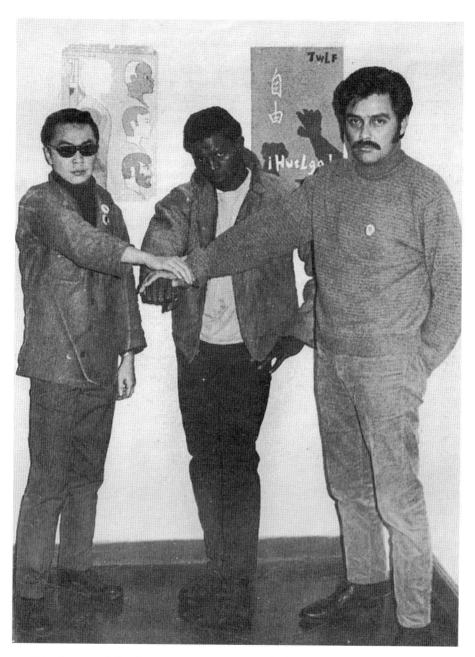

This photograph has become a preeminent symbol of Third World solidarity. First published in *Muhammad Speaks* on February 7, 1969, it features three leaders of UC Berkeley's Third World Liberation Front strike: Richard Aoki of the Asian American Political Alliance, Charles Brown of the Afro-American Students Union, and Manuel Delgado of the Mexican American Student Confederation.

Richard Aoki is arrested during the Third World strike at the Telegraph entrance to the University of California, Berkeley, February 18, 1969. Photograph by Lonnie Wilson/*Oakland Tribune.*

米国帝国主義打倒
CRUSH AMERICAN IMPERIALISM
RY OF PEOPLE'S WAR
LONG LIVE THE VICTO

Bea Tam, Richard Aoki, Patrick Hayashi, and William Lee with an Asian American student contingent from the University of California, Berkeley, protesting the U.S. invasion of Cambodia, 1970. Photograph by Nancy Park.

Richard Aoki *(sitting, at right)* was called to serve on internal security when Huey Newton, recently released from prison, spoke at Merritt College in October 1970. Collection of Richard Aoki.

Richard feeds a friend's baby, ca. 1970. Collection of Richard Aoki.

GRADUATION 1990: College
of ALAMEDA: FACULTY SENATE
PRESIDENT RICHARD AOKI AND
TEACHER of The YEAR Shirley Conner.
(PAST PRES U.C. ALUMNI ASSOC. FORMER
V.P. FACULTY SENATE)

TWO WINNERS
CONGRATULATIONS!
NL.

Richard Aoki, in his first of two terms as Academic Senate president, stands behind Teacher of the Year Shirley Conner at the College of Alameda's commencement ceremony, 1990. Photograph by Neal Lucas.

Richard reunites with Bobby Seale at the first Black Panther Party commemorative event, Oakland, 1990. The renewed focus on the Black Panthers, along with the twentieth-year reunion of Third World Liberation Front activists, sparked Richard's return to activism. Photograph by Harvey Dong.

Richard Aoki and Yuri Kochiyama, two of the foremost architects of Afro–Asian solidarity, 2003. Yuri, renowned for her work with Malcolm X, moved from Harlem to Oakland in 1999, and Richard began working with her on antiwar and Asian American organizing. Photograph by Diane Fujino.

Former members celebrate the fortieth anniversary of the founding of the Asian American Political Alliance at the University of California, Berkeley, Multicultural Center, 2008. Top row *(left to right)*: Miriam Ching Louie, Floyd Huen, Belvin Louie, Alvin Ja, Elaine Kim, Greg Jue, Frank Celada. Middle row: Victoria Wong, Jean Quan (elected mayor of Oakland in 2010), William Dere, Jeff Leong, Greg Mark, Bing Thom. Bottom row: Keith Kojimoto, Liz Del Sol, Richard Aoki, Harvey Dong, James Hsue, Emil DeGuzman. Collection of Harvey Dong.

In his later years, Richard connected with his extended family. The Aoki family at the Chapel of the Chimes, Oakland, ca. 2002. *Left to right*: Margaret Saito, Leo Saito, Hagumi Takizawa, Nobuji Kenneth Iyeki, May Iyeki, Anne Aoki, David Goi, Esther Asaka Aoki, James Tetsumi Aoki, Megumi Takizawa Goi, Richard Aoki, George Goi. Collection of Richard Aoki.

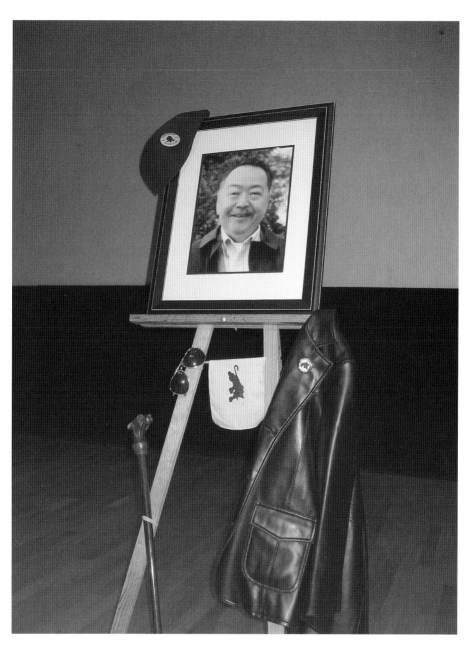

This display at Richard's memorial services in May 2009 showcases the symbols of his iconic image as an Asian American Black Panther. Photograph by Diane Fujino.

At Richard's memorial service, two U.S. Army color guards fold the American flag. Seen as symbolic of U.S. imperialism and militarism, the flag created a stir, but Richard's closest friends knew that among his few material possessions were two neatly pressed uniforms: his Black Panther leather jacket affixed with a Free Huey button and his U.S. Army uniform with an American flag in its pocket. Photograph by Diane Fujino.

what change political consciousness. Aoki agreed—"I knew which way the vote was going to go"—so after stating his opinion, he did not struggle to win people to his position. As he noted, "The way I see it, I'm not out to change anybody's mind, but reality speaks for itself."

Aoki's narrative is filled with vivid and detailed stories of confrontations with the police and other strike opponents. Beyond a personal penchant for military maneuvers, he articulated his rationale: it was the strike, and not primarily dialogue and negotiation, that imposed unbearable costs on the university—in terms of financial losses, threats to its reputation, and, with the closing of classes, the inability to function as a university—and forced the administration and faculty to concede to the establishment of the Department of Ethnic Studies, with some decision-making authority given to Third World faculty, students, and community. His stories of confrontation and escape also reveal a master organizer. Aoki approached the strike as a soldier would approach a battle. He helped develop creative strategies to undermine the power of the police and to strengthen the power of the student activists. He helped devise tactics for surrounding the police, mimicking the Black Panthers' police patrols. He articulated escape routes from potential police repression at meetings and at events. There was the use of force, if necessary, to diminish attacks against strikers. There were also strategic withdrawals to ensure the safety of participants. Aoki was bold and daring, but he was no individualist maverick. He believed in and practiced discipline and training and felt a responsibility as a TWLF leader for the well-being of participants. He felt a particular obligation to help those arrested or under police attack. When an AAPA member who had voted against the strike got arrested and the arrestee's own brother said, "He can rot [in jail]," Aoki stood by his principles in bailing out the student. Aoki used his own money to bail out numerous activists; he, in turn, was bailed out by fellow students. When Manuel Delgado was taking a police beating, Aoki fought alongside Delgado, risking injury and arrest. This was a collective struggle that required the "power of the people" to effect change, and Aoki acted in collective ways, across ethnic, racial, and gender differences.[47]

"Learning to Fly on the Way Down": The Courage to Defy Power

It takes courage and a certain audacity to defy powerful institutions. From today's vantage point, some will critique Aoki for displaying a macho bravado. But in the late 1960s, many gained the strength to fight for justice and risk their own safety from the bold defiance of a Malcolm X or a Huey Newton or a Richard Aoki. Men of color, in particular, displayed aggressive, insolent behavior as a means for contesting racism and asserting their manhood. Sometimes this cost them their lives, as seen in the brutal murder of Emmett Till, the Black teen who was killed not directly for whistling at a White woman in Mississippi in 1955 but rather for repeatedly refusing to submit to his White male confronters, who defended their protection of White femininity by demanding that Black men stay in their place.[48] Sometimes behaviors appear silly, as in Aoki's insistence on racializing the color of food by having red not white wine and chocolate not vanilla milkshakes. As Aoki explained, "During the strike, when I sensed things were lagging on the part of some of our people and I wanted to remind them what we're fighting for, I didn't have a chance to go into the subtleties of Marx, Lenin, or Mao. I had to get down to the nits and grits and say, 'Bam, this is it!' I know it sounds like a weak justification, but I'm standing behind that. . . . You have to understand that we were in the middle of a war."[49]

Indeed, Aoki and other sixties activists were developing strategies and learning to work together in the crucible of struggle. Things were moving fast, as Aoki frequently stated. As civil rights activist Chuck Jones put it, "Man, we just plain jumped off that cliff blind and learned to fly on the way down."[50] It's hard to convey the intensity of those times, with activists working night and day on projects they felt were just and winnable, with the violence of poverty and racism creating a sense of urgency, and with aggressive police and FBI repression resulting in activists getting arrested, killed, and forced underground. This context of struggle required, at times, the daring defiance and in-your-face opposition to the establishment that Aoki displayed in order to confront police brutality and the institutional power of the university.

Third World Solidarity

The strike's embodiment of Third World unity reveals similar strengths and weaknesses. In the shadow of Bandung, Aoki identified a strategy of "maximizing similarities and minimizing differences" among Third World organizations and activists. This belief enabled activists to see other people's struggles in their own and to be collective and generous when developing organizing goals and processes. It was also a necessary strategy among groups that represented a numeric minority of the campus community. But just as the Bandung conference ignored serious economic, religious, and other differences among delegate nations, Aoki's strategy also had its limitations. Whereas Aoki refused to reflect on intergroup tensions, TWLF and MASC leader Manuel Delgado was fairly candid:

> MASC was reluctant to join the strike. Generally speaking, prior to this time, minorities didn't go around backing each other up. Blacks didn't join the grape boycott or picket Safeway stores. Chicanos didn't march for Black civil rights and on campus we were competing for Educational Opportunity slots. . . . MASC was unwilling to be seen in a "supporting role" as Chicanos were at SF State. The perception of the strike there was that it was a Black Student Union strike supported by TWLF, the TWLF being the other minority groups on campus.[51]

Delgado became convinced of the importance of joining in the TWLF at UC Berkeley, after meeting with San Francisco State TWLF leader Roger Alvarado and Black Panther George Murray. To Delgado, "Murray's 'power over culture' rhetoric seemed to emphasize human rights over nationalism. And Roger Alvarado, well, Roger was one of us."[52] Still, during the strike, there continued to be problems, including, from Delgado's view, an AASU leader chilling in a suite while others put their bodies on the picket lines.[53]

Still, the very experience of struggling together also strengthened Third World unity. In the struggle for Black Studies at UC Santa Barbara in 1968, when someone sent food to the students occupying the North Hall computer center, a bunch of grapes came flying out the window. Black activists were rejecting the grapes boycotted by their fellow Chicano students, in solidarity with the farmworkers' strike.[54] Delgado himself recounted that prior to the strike, "we didn't know much about Asian Americans except that they 'kept to themselves and were non-confrontational,' an erroneous perception that would change during the course of the strike."[55] Thirty years later, Delgado proclaimed: "The heart and soul of the strike was the AAPA. They were the best organized, hardest working and most committed to the common struggle of the Third World."[56]

Self-Determination and the Primacy of Practice

Aoki, like most other student strikers, paints the UC Berkeley administration as oppositional to the TWLF. Yet, UC Berkeley's chancellor Roger Heyns was widely regarded as a liberal, who contrasted sharply with San Francisco State College's President S. I. Hayakawa. Hayakawa was seen as an entrenched conservative and theatrical administrator, remembered for his antic of jumping on top of a sound truck, pulling the amplifier plugs, and later exclaiming, "This has been the most exciting day of my life since my tenth birthday, when I rode a roller coaster for the first time!"[57] Heyns made great efforts to stress his commitment to racial equality. In an open letter to the university published in the *Daily Californian,* he claimed: "Within four months after coming to Berkeley, I initiated the Educational Opportunity Program in an effort to increase the number of minority and disadvantaged students."[58] In 1966, there were fifteen EOP students; by 1968, there were over eight hundred EOP students. Before the strike began, he relayed: "After analyzing the proposal and consulting with members of the staff and members of the Afro–American Students Union, I promised the group that I would work for the establishment of a Black Studies program. I made it clear to the group that before such a program could be instituted, there would have to be extensive discussions with Senate Committees and that their proposal might well be modified."[59] Because the university was already working to increase diversity, Heyns reasoned that "a strike is not warranted."[60]

So why have a strike? "What we're asking for is control," explained Manuel Delgado. "Heyns has already given us the ethnic group study. We want our own college, which we control."[61] The crux of the issue was self-determination and power. The students wanted to have decision-making power over the development of Ethnic Studies. This included not only gaining Ethnic Studies but also controlling the curriculum and hiring of faculty to maintain the original intentions of AASU's proposal for Black Studies.[62] The TWLF saw the administration offering a Macaulay-style education limited and controlled by the existing power structure. Although Heyns found it reasonable and appropriate to work through established university procedures, the TWLF wanted complete educational transformation. They wanted to change the content of the curriculum to include not only Ethnic Studies but also community-oriented courses that served the needs of working-class ethnic communities rather than corporations. Just as significantly, they wanted to change power relations and institutional structures and procedures so that students would have increased power to affect decision making at the university. A TWLF pamphlet stated, "We had made a mistake in relying on the administrators to grant us the power of self-determination. We recognize the racist power structure does not give up power willingly. . . . We now stand together to determine the educational hopes of our people."[63] This, as Aoki would later realize, was the revolutionary potential of the TWLF struggle.

Aoki is one to emphasize the primacy of practice in transforming people's consciousness; that "reality speaks for itself." While in 1969 he may not have articulated a revolutionary position on the struggle for Ethnic Studies, his immersion in this movement dramatically changed his life and solidified his commitment to Third World solidarity. As he burned out from the intensity of grassroots organizing, Asian American Studies offered him a professional career through which he could carry out his desire for racial and class equality. His reality speaks to how he resolved the duality of formal education. He went on to have a twenty-five-year career as an instructor, counselor, and occasional administrator in the East Bay community college system. He was proud of his work to bring marginalized students into higher education, to teach a critical pedagogy, and to connect students with the community. But before getting there, he would teach some of the first classes and serve as an early administrator in the newly formed Asian American Studies program at UC Berkeley.

9 "A Community-Oriented Academic Unit"

Creating Asian American Studies at UC Berkeley

After the strike ended, we had the task of setting up the Department of Ethnic Studies and the four divisions within it: Asian, Black, La Raza, and Native American Studies.[1] AAPA had taken the leading role among Asian Americans in the TWLF strike and now took the leading role in creating Asian American Studies. AAPA's two main goals, as I saw it, were to create "a community-oriented academic unit" and to do so with maximum "autonomy."[2] So now we had a big crisis. Who's going to run AAS? We understood that somebody with a professorial rank had to be in charge. There was a paucity of Asian American professors willing to undertake that. My first choice was Paul Takagi. He was my mentor, so I stopped by to see him. "This is a golden opportunity for you, Paul." He looked at me like, "I don't think so, Richard." Plus, he was a dean in the School of Criminology and couldn't head up another program.[3] My next choice was Yuji Ichioka. I do remember calling Yuji. He was in New York at the time, but he was not available. At UC Berkeley, there was a Chinese American doctoral graduate from the Sociology Department who did his dissertation on radical political activism. He had supported the strike from the sidelines, so he wasn't hostile. He seemed like a perfect candidate who the university could support and who we could support. But from day one, things started going wrong. In a graduate school paper that I wrote in June 1970, I explained, "The coordinator attempted to consolidate all the power governing policy into his own control. This was swiftly opposed by the entire teaching staff. A confrontation occurred. He was faced with the choice of losing his entire teaching staff which could not be easily replaced, or submitting his own resignation. He resigned." This lasted one month.[4]

After that, we set up a Governing Council, with a Graduate Student Council consisting of four members of the teaching staff, an administrative specialist, and an undergraduate student committee.[5] The Graduate Student Council consisted of the graduate students—all AAPA members—who taught the earliest AAS classes, including Wai-Kit Quon, Bing Thom, Alan Fong, and myself. I also became a coordinator of AAS in those early years. I was chosen because, on paper, I may have looked the most qualified. You have to remember at that time Bing was in architecture, Wai-Kit was in biochemistry, Alan was in folklore, Ling-Chi Wang was in Near Eastern Studies. I was in social work with an emphasis in public administration. But if you asked me what I did, I'd say coordinating what? I had no power. The council of eight students held the real power. Now who was doing what, or even what I was doing, I wasn't keeping notes. I was just going with the flow.[6]

Another early task was to select a chairman for the new Department of Ethnic Studies. The Central Committee of the TWLF had agreed upon Dr. Jack Forbes, a prominent scholar and one of the few Native Americans to have a PhD.[7] My argument was that Native Americans were the most oppressed, depressed, suppressed, repressed group, so they should head Ethnic Studies. The university administration also liked Jack Forbes. Initially Forbes was supportive of the idea, but he declined because another university gave him an offer he couldn't refuse.[8] So for that first year, we operated without a department chair. The coordinators of each of the four programs ran each division, but there was no overall chair to unify and coordinate activities.[9]

I was concerned about how we'd find a chairman because about that time, the relationships among the four groups was starting to get a little shaky. A number of candidates' names started getting submitted for consideration. One of the reasons I couldn't become chairman is that I didn't have a doctorate. Then the name Carl Mack Jr. came up. Carl Mack Jr., an African American classmate of mine at Berkeley High School, had just gotten his doctorate in sociology from UC Berkeley. During the Third World strike, he was chair of the Publicity Committee. So Carl Mack Jr. became the first chairman of Ethnic Studies. I thought Carl handled things well because he had diplomatic skills. You'd have to know Carl, his personality, his character—he worked very well with people. Then too, the fact that each program had a great deal of autonomy helped. That was a policy that I strictly adhered to. I had my program and I took care of that. I didn't stick my nose into other programs because I could get hooked. I thought I did a good job as a coordinator of Asian Studies.[10]

The Death of AAPA and the Birth of AAS

Simultaneous with starting AAS, Bryant Fong, the third and last chair of AAPA, was trying to keep AAPA alive. But numbers were dwindling. He was frustrated and talked about how the "general lack of interest and enthusiasm led the leaders to give up and the group stopped." He referred to himself as a "Chairman without anyone to chair!"[11] I'm just now realizing that AAPA's very success sped up its demise. Dialectically, you had the death of AAPA and the birth of AAS. With AAPA members getting rapidly politicized during the strike, they went into establishing AAS or working in the community. There was no longer a need for AAPA. After many attempts to revitalize AAPA, the group ended in September 1969.[12]

Over the years, I've been asked to talk about AAPA. I've distilled the four important principles of AAPA, the foundation of its political program, which I refer to as the "4 Ss." The first is the issue of "self-determination," that is, the power to name ourselves, transforming Orientals into Asian Americans. That in itself was revolutionary and part of the principle of the program because it somewhat settles the identity issue and once the identity issue is resolved then the political consciousness begins to come about.

Second is "service" to the community. The creation of AAS can be viewed as an alternative to the normal pathway of Asian Americans—education for the job, the 2.5 children and family out in the suburbs, and becoming either a nonentity or an apologist for the system. We've seen this mind-set among those who chose to ignore that their ancestors had to struggle for this opportunity and that they should return something, when they're able, to the community. That was one of the strongest principles that underscored AAPA because they not only recognized this but they actually operationalized it using AAS as an educational alternative to address social problems in the community. If you look at the names of the AAPA people in Yuji Ichioka's memorial booklet, you can see that virtually all have made meaningful contributions to society, so in retrospect this validates AAPA's program of serving the people.[13]

A third S is "solidarity." In contrast to cultural nationalism, this revolutionary nationalism goes outward; it is inclusionist. I use that term inclusionist to emphasize the support of other politically active nationalist groups, such as the Black Panther Party, Brown Berets, the Young Lords, and the American Indian Movement.

The fourth principle is "struggle." The gains did not come automatically, but power had to be wrested away from the establishment for progress to be made and the struggle is costly. It's costly in terms of human lives, not that AAPA people got killed in the revolution but nevertheless people got hurt in the struggle. I know of several Asian American students who were not able to finish their studies at Berkeley as a result of their involvement in the strike.

People who are politically committed are willing to give up their lives if the cause is just enough. I use the word struggle here to elongate the class struggle because it's not only a racial thing but it is a class issue that we're dealing with. This race and class struggle was one of the principles underlying AAPA.

Graduate School of Social Welfare

I was in graduate school during my escapades in AAPA, the TWLF strike, and AAS. So how did this West Oakland boy, who had the grades to go to Berkeley straight out of high school but almost didn't get there, go on to get an advanced graduate degree from the University of California, Berkeley? Well, a month after AAPA's first meeting, I graduated from UC Berkeley with a bachelor's degree in sociology. This was June 1968. I wasn't sure what I wanted to do. But two graduates of Berkeley's School of Social Work influenced me to go there. Ron Dellums graduated in the early 1960s. He's the nephew of C. L. Dellums, one of the main leaders of the Brotherhood of Sleeping Car Porters with A. Philip Randolph. Ron Dellums was a longtime U.S. congressman and the mayor of Oakland since 2007. Guess who graduated a couple of years after Ron—Melvin Newton, Huey's older brother. The Black Panther Party was starting to talk about survival programs. I talked with Huey, and I said "Now, Huey, I've been at Berkeley two years and I'm tired of this shit. Let's get it on!" He said, "We got this other thing, the survival programs. Of course, we're going to need someone to run them. So the School of Social Work is important for you to get into to get that knowledge."[14]

Berkeley's social work program was unique—a combined community organization, public administration, and social work graduate program.[15] Only three graduate schools in social work in the country offered it. The other two were back East—too cold. I was only interested in Berkeley, but I had heard that they don't accept their own undergrads. Douglas [Daniels] said, "Go for it. What have you got to lose?" So five minutes before the application closing time, he and I were there and I handed in my application. I forgot about it, not expecting to get in, until I got a letter saying, "You have been accepted." Oh, happy day. That's how I ended up in this two-year master's program.[16]

I had planned to keep my head low in graduate school. I had almost gotten kicked out of school earlier that year because of that Tri-Con incident and I wasn't about to tempt fate. But on the first day, they asked the incoming social work students, all 120 of us, "Why are you here?" I said, "I am here because I am from the community and I believe that after a fundamental economic, political, and social transformation of society, social work is going to be useful for about five years. We'll need skilled people to help others get housing, employment, health care. After that transition period, the whole institution will self-destruct because we'll then have a society where we won't need social welfare." The other 119 students looked at me. The professors looked at me. The dean leaned over and said, "Who are you?"

At the end of my first year, I was elected student body president of the School of Social Work while sitting in the Berkeley City Jail awaiting trial on the TWLF charges.[17] One of the reasons I was elected president was that my fellow students were sensitive to my unique needs. They used to bring the lecture notes and homework to me at whatever jail I was in at the time and told the professors that my absence was due to my serious engagement in the participant observer method of gathering data. One of my fellow students in the School of Social Work even paid my bail and got me out of jail. Here's what happened. In spring 1969, when the annual student government elections took place, one of my fellow students said, "Why don't you run for student body president?" I had just finished an intensive quarter—the Third World strike. I said, "I don't want to run for nothing. I'm tired. Let me rest." This person said, "We want you because you aren't wishy-washy. You're willing to take on the administration for the students." I also figured it would enhance my chances in court if it were known that I was a student body president. So I agreed to run. Then a curious thing happened. The elections came up. There's one other candidate besides me. At the last minute he pulled out and endorsed me. I found out the next year that he had gotten a visit and a suggestion that his health might be in jeopardy if he were to run. I told him I had nothing to do with that visit. I said, "No way. I don't do that type of thing, man." Here's the corker. The guy was African American. At that time nobody wanted to run and he didn't want a White to go for that position, so he ran. So after he found out I was running, he probably would have pulled out anyway.[18]

While running for president, I also negotiated with the conservative students in the school. They found out that the school had not updated their accreditation in years. They wanted to complain to the accreditation team about the liberal professors. I said, "I'll work on that." I did keep my promise. A year later, there was a big conference in Seattle. I was out on bail and couldn't leave California. So I sent the vice president, the treasurer, and the secretary of the student union to grapple with these powerful people: "We're students from the School of Social Work at UC Berkeley and we haven't had an accrediting visit in seventeen years."[19] Another thing I did as president was to rewrite the constitution, changing the name of the student group from "association" to "union" in order to strengthen, at least in the mental sense, the solidarity of students. Got to have a union, where you're one for all and all for one and not this individualistic stuff. One of the important changes was that this new constitution put students on the Admissions Committee. So the next year, I was able to get Jaime Solis, a Berkeley strike leader, into the School of Social Work.[20]

All first-year students in my program had to be placed in an internship in a community-based organization. I did my internship at the West Oakland Legal Switchboard. It somewhat grew out of the Black Panther Party, to the extent that if the cases were political they were probably linked to the Black Panther Party. Now there was another intern, Jim Nabors.[21] That's how Jim and I started knowing each other before the strike and that's when I found out that Jim was the West Coast consul general of the Republic of New Africa, the highest-ranking RNA official west of the Mississippi, and he's a student with us at Berkeley.[22] So Jimmy and I really got to know each other, had coffee together, stayed up late at night waiting for the police calls so we can go dashing out and do our little internship thing. It was easy for me because I was from the 'hood. Nobody knew I was a Panther. I was just playing it low key and didn't go down to the headquarters because this legal arm was so important.

My first year in graduate school was quite eventful. I had hit graduate school, made my mission known to the student body and the faculty and the administration on the first day, participated in the TWLF strike, and became student body president. Between the strike, classes, fieldwork, teaching, and being student body president, I don't know how I was able to graduate. But I finished, thanks to the support of certain professors.

So it's June 1970 and I'm faced with a monumental career decision. I acquired my master's degree in social work, now what am I going to do? Option number one was for me to return to the community right then. We knew that Huey was going to be sprung from prison soon. I was eager to get back into action. In a way I knew the stakes were much higher, because in '68 and '69 we lost so many of our people. Those we lost were giants who made significant contributions—that's why they were killed. I felt we needed to be carrying on the movement. My second option was to continue in graduate school and earn a doctorate in social work. The dean of the school called me into his office around graduation time and informed me that they had discovered money available for postgraduate scholarship. I was eligible for a three-year grant. He then added, the doctor of social welfare program was very rigorous and did not include time for me to be involved in campus or community activity. I had a third option. During and after the strike I worked closely with legal defense. Through my internship with the West Oakland Legal Switchboard I got to know the Boalt Hall law school. At that time they had an interim dean who seemed to like me and urged me to apply to the law school. He virtually guaranteed me admission under some sort of policy whereby the dean can admit a few candidates on a personal basis, no questions asked. Then too there were Asian American law students who were starting to become quite prominent like my attorney, Ken Kawaichi. I seriously thought over that option, but a voice within me said, "You already spent six years of booking. You want to spend another three years at a more intensive level?" Plus, why learn about all these bourgeois laws? My fourth option was to join AAS because there had to be somebody official to represent the program. Discussions started taking place in AAS and my name came up. Here I was just getting my master's degree in social work with a public administration major. I was a natural.

I was at a crossroads in my life, so what did I do? I went scurrying over to Professor Paul Takagi's office. I said, "I've been underqualified all my life, now I'm overqualified. Everybody wants me. But be that as it may, my heart says go back to the community right now. The community really needs me." Paul came back with, "If you do that, you'll probably get killed. The way you're going now, it's only a matter of time." He also told me that I was a natural at teaching. This was a point at which I was getting a little discouraged about where AAS was going and my role in it. He encouraged me to stay in AAS and in education primarily because due to my political set, it provided me with a greater venue in which to operate. I sure wouldn't have fit in a regular social work job, acting like a police officer. So he helped me out at a time when I was at a moment of crisis.[23]

Community Studies

I didn't want to be the sole coordinator for AAS, so I suggested having two coordinators. Alan Fong and I were given the responsibility for shepherding Asian American Studies through its most difficult early years. At the time, I was a full-time staff in the program, half-time administrator and half-time lecturer.[24] Alan and I got along fairly well, even though I was more militant than Alan. In fact, nobody in Asian American Studies during that period was more militant than me. Still, we never got into a conflict on policy. But as I mentioned, it was the student committee that was setting policy and running the program. That was based on the idea of participatory democracy. I saw Alan and myself as being complementary. Remember, Asian American Studies focused on two areas, the academic and the community. I was more oriented toward community programs because I'm street. Alan was a natural for handling the university end. His father was a professor at the university, his mother was a librarian, and Alan himself was in graduate school. He knew the ins and outs of the university.[25] At one point during the strike, we called for a meeting of the Asian American community to support us. His parents were the only ones who showed up. My mama sure wasn't at that meeting for her oldest son. When I was on TV being dragged off or being called an agitator in the newspapers, she was so glad that she had remarried and had a different last name. I felt a little hurt that she didn't recognize my community as well as my academic accomplishments. As an undergrad, when I informed her that I was majoring in sociology, her eyes rolled. She connected sociology with socialism, socialism with communism, and said, "It's true. Berkeley is turning you into a communist." A prophet is an outcast in his own country. What can I say? If my own mother felt that way, you could imagine how other members of my family must have felt.

AAPA was the main Asian American group in the TWLF strike and in initiating AAS. But with AAPA members graduating or going to work in the community, there became two groups creating AAS. There were those, such as myself, who were in the struggle from the beginning. Then there were others who came around because the university had put a stamp of legitimacy on Ethnic Studies. So from early on I sensed that we were going to lose the emphasis on the community. Now we understood that the mission of the university is research. But we wanted to emphasize "relevant research" geared to the needs of our community. The original intent was to have both an academic and a community orientation, symbiotically related, as integral components of AAS.

One of the first things I remember is working to get language courses in the curriculum. The students thought it was important to offer conversational language courses so students could communicate with people in the community, especially the seniors. When the students wanted a Cantonese language course, the subcommittee of the Academic Senate opposed this because they pointed out they're already offering Chinese. So we had to go meet with them and explain that most Chinese American immigrants spoke Cantonese and the university offered only Mandarin, the dialect of the elite. We got that Cantonese language course approved.[26]

Then the Filipino students came to my office. They wanted a conversational Filipino course. Now with the Filipinos there was a different twist. There were three different factions; one wanted Tagalog, another Ilocano, and a third wanted Visayan. I was at a loss. Then I realized that I needed to see a break-down of the most commonly spoken Filipino dialects in the United States. Being at Berkeley and having Filipino students there ready to give me the research, we discovered that Tagalog was the most common dialect spoken by Filipino immigrants and it was the official language of the Philippines. So I went with conversational Tagalog. Now where would we pick up somebody with a doctorate who could teach Tagalog? The students went and found somebody. But we discovered that that person had some connections to President Marcos of the Philippines and didn't muster up under our internal security system. So now we needed someone to teach Tagalog the next year. It turns out that the landlady at my apartment, the one who saw me and others leaving the apartment one day to go to the shooting range, was Filipina. She had blond hair and blue eyes, but her family had been in the Hukbalahap movement in the Philippines.[27] When I first moved in with my fiancée I was a little surprised that this White couple would rent to a mixed couple but I wasn't about to question it. Don't forget, interracial couples were considered scandalous in those days. As I got to know her, I found out that she had an advanced degree, so would meet the minimum qualifications for a lecturer at the university. So she became our Tagalog instructor.

I also did as much as I could to support the community-oriented classes and projects. These were projects to serve the community that our students developed through Asian American Studies courses.[28] We had a bunch of them. Every time I turned around there was a new one. The students worked in China-town and Manilatown, and the I-Hotel was one of the most important sites. The students helped start the Asian Community Center, located in the I-Hotel. The project I remember most was the East Bay Japanese for Action. When I was co-coordinator of AAS, a couple of students, Dennis Yotsuya and Grace Nagata, approached me about a community project to provide services for elderly Issei, or Japanese immigrants. Through one of our AAS courses, they conducted an initial survey and discovered that the regular social services agencies did not adequately address the needs of this particular group, either by not having services in Japanese or because of racism. I had to sign off for these two students to do further research and gave them some seed money to get started. The university jammed me on this. I had to explain that this is a valid research project. The School of Social Work would buy into this one; the School of Public Health probably would too. I remember in the Black community, senior citizens were apprehensive about cashing their Social Security checks at the local bank because local thugs would jump them. So the Black Panther Party started senior escort services. I haven't read much about this service, but young men from the party escorted these senior citizens from home to bank and home again. I said, "Right on!" The students organizing East Bay Japanese for Action then got matching funds from local, state, maybe even federal sources, and the organization eventually grew into Japanese American Services of the East Bay, which exists today. So this is a good example of how you can utilize resources, the expertise and the student energy of the university, to address problems in the community and still have academic rigor. To me academic rigor needs to involve academic relevance.[29]

Asian American Studies and Critical Pedagogy

For the three years I was in AAS at UC Berkeley, I was mostly teaching because that's what the program needed.[30] None of us had any training in AAS. We couldn't have. We had initiated a whole new field of scholarship. What helped me is that year I took with Dr. Yale Maxon at Merritt College on Far Eastern civilization. He was a master scholar and I was a bright young student that was just absorbing it all. So when I taught, I could begin with experiences in Asia before they immigrated to the U.S. Then too I was an omnivorous reader. I discovered that I had to search for books to read and to use in classes. There was nothing around! I'm proud that one of the major contributions of AAS was the resurrection of works that had been published but were no longer available. There was John Okada's book, No-No Boy.[31] We couldn't find it anywhere. I would also find references in readings and began to develop a more coherent set of readings. I would say, "There's a master's thesis on the Chinese in Mississippi that's worthy of reading." The student would come back and say, "I can't find that." These materials were virtually impossible to access. So I made it a point to get many of these books reproduced. That drained the departmental budget, but it was essential. I also strongly advocated the importance of the library fund.[32]

I felt there was a need to carry on the spirit of solidarity that we had engendered during the Third World strike. So we developed a proposal for a Third World Core course. I recently found the syllabus for the course, which explains, "The central purpose of the [course] will be to provide advanced students with an interdisciplinary approach to racial and ethnic relations. The interdisciplinary approach will combine elements of political, economic, philosophical, sociological and psychological theory to: (1) delineate the term 'Third World,' (2) to trace its origin and development in the United States, and (3) to identify the interaction between the national and international communities."[33] In fall

1969, the first quarter of the newly established Department of Ethnic Studies, there were three instructors for this course: Carl Mack Jr., Bill Vega, and myself. Some think Ethnic Studies is Mickey Mouse, but we were serious about teaching and demanded rigorous readings. The three books we required were Frantz Fanon's *Wretched of the Earth,* which was widely read at that time and has since become a classic study of colonialism, its psychological and sociological impact, and the importance of resistance; Irving Horowitz's *Three Worlds of Development;* and Ronald Segal's *The Race War.* We also recommended John Gerassi's *The Great Fear in Latin America,* Kwame Nkrumah's *Neo-Colonialism: The Last Stage of Imperialism,* and Vera Simone's *China in Revolution.* The next quarter, Don Davis, Lee Brightman, Richard Rodriquez, and I taught the Third World course, while Andrew Billingsley, a university administrator and supporter of Ethnic Studies, was the instructor on record. We developed an even longer list of more than thirty required and recommended readings, including books by Frantz Fanon, Carey McWilliams, Chinua Achebe, W. E. B. Du Bois, and Albert Memmi.[34]

Now there were strong cultural nationalist tendencies in all of these groups. So it wasn't necessarily going to be easy to teach a course like this. At one point, there was the issue of should we hire White professors. Those with more cultural nationalist tendencies said, "We're not going to hire any White people." I pointed out that the color of one's skin doesn't necessarily determine where they are on the race issue. Some of the best works on Asian American history were written by White people. What about Carey McWilliams and his study on prejudice against Japanese Americans and his classic work on Mexican farmworkers? What about Roger Daniels? In my own case I gained a rigorous lesson on Far Eastern history from a White professor.[35]

Another course I taught was on Hawaii. I'm minding my own business when a group of students come and say, "We have a special interest. We're from Hawaii and we want a class on Hawaii." So we agreed on a course on the history of Hawaii. Because I'm teaching it, we're going to talk all about the politics of Hawaii. At the time, I didn't know anything, but I'm a reader. The only good thing I'd ever read about Hawaii was James Michener's book *Hawaii.* The student told me, "Oh, no. Lawrence Fuchs just wrote a book on the social history of Hawaii." So I read the book. It was dynamite! So I used that as the textbook.[36] In developing a relevant education, AAS tried to be responsive to the needs of our students. I also taught a social theory course based on the theories of Marx, Freud, and Weber. We connected theory to practice, so this course offered students an analytic way of thinking about social problems.

There's something I have to say about the generosity and commitment of the early faculty. When the report came out that we didn't have enough money to fund all our courses, the AAS instructors voted to kick in part or all of their salaries. We were at this meeting and people were saying, "Let's kick back part of our salary." I was sitting there saying, "Am I hearing right?" I was really proud of the group. Now we made it a priority to always balance the books. In fact, on my watch, at the end of the fiscal year, there was a five-thousand-dollar discrepancy and I almost had a heart attack. Then it was discovered the university had made a mistake on some bills receivable or something. One of the other programs had a cost overrun for three years. I warned the coordinator: "This don't look good." At the end of three years, the administration called him in and asked for his resignation. But in AAS, by pooling our resources, we were able to hire more instructors and balance our books.[37]

So I was part of developing AAS at UC Berkeley during its important and tumultuous first three years. When I left in 1972, I could already see it moving away from our original focus on community studies. I left for the community colleges, where I felt my talents and political commitments would be put to better use.

THE BIRTH OF ASIAN AMERICAN STUDIES

The political milieu of the times demanded a radical restructuring of the educational system. The transformations that occurred within the university reflected the prevailing social movement's demands for racial equality, an economic leveling, and a focus on social justice and community responsibility rather than individual upward mobility and training for corporate America. Books like Paulo Freire's *Pedagogy of the Oppressed* and Robert Allen's *Black Awakening in Capitalist America* powerfully influenced Aoki and his fellow activists to rethink the purpose of education.[38] Allen's seminal book framed Black oppression as internal colonialism and argued for a model of liberation that critiqued capitalism, colonialism, and racism and demanded power to control social institutions. As stated in the foreword to the thirtieth anniversary edition of *Pedagogy of the Oppressed*: "There is no such thing as a *neutral* educational process. Education either functions as an instrument that is used to facilitate the integration of the younger generation into the logic of the present system and bring about conformity to it, *or* it becomes 'the practice of freedom,' the means by which men and women deal critically and creatively with reality and discover how to participate in the transformation of their world."[39] Aoki, as a TWLF strike leader and Asian American Studies program developer and instructor, sought to restructure higher education as, in Freire's words, "a practice of freedom."[40]

The process of transforming education was met with resistance and re-negotiations at every step. Aoki relayed that the teaching staff of AAS was "exhausted" during "the first year of its painful existence."[41] Indeed, they were creating an entirely new field, with scarcely any programmatic models to guide their work, few books and curricular resources to use in the class-room, and with instructors who were not academically trained in Ethnic Studies. On top of this, the young professors, graduate students, and even undergraduates developing AAS had to learn innumerable university pro-cedures, all of which were new to them and overwhelming. UC Berkeley's Ethnic Studies faculty recounted: "In its first year, recruiting faculty and sup-port staff, deciding on courses to be offered, gathering teaching materials, etc. occupied the time of every person in the Department."[42] The second year, though less chaotic, was still tough. The staff continued to be consumed with "basic matters—recruiting faculty, getting them approved, writing up course descriptions, getting them approved."[43]

The birthing process was indeed painful. But the times demanded it. The faculty and staff were willing to put in "60 to 80 hour weeks" because they believed they were developing an entirely new project and one that was a radical departure from business as usual.[44] UC Berkeley's and San Francisco State College's Third World strikes had inspired student struggles on other campuses nationwide that collectively built a new and interdisci-plinary academic field. Most obviously, Ethnic Studies sought to include the experiences and perspectives of marginalized people into the univer-sity curriculum and to increase the number of minority students and fac-ulty at the university. Still, their goals extended beyond changing the racial composition of the university or the racial components of the curriculum. "The guidelines for the department [of Ethnic Studies] had been developed in the spirit of the Third World," explained Andrew Billingsley, assistant chancellor for Academic Affairs and acting coordinator of Ethnic Studies.[45] In particular, "Students must play an active and decisive role in initiating and participating in the academic planning" and "academic programs must be made relevant to the specific needs of the ethnic minority communi-ties."[46] The Ethnic Studies project was thus part of the larger social move-ment to transform the purpose and scope of education and to democratize the university.[47]

The 1960 California Master Plan for Higher Education, passed by the California legislature in 1959, was created to coordinate the governance of the state's tripartite system of higher education: the University of California (UC) system, the state colleges, and the junior colleges.[48] The master plan was hailed for differentiating the functions of the three tiers and curtailing the explosion in college enrollment, brought about by the coming of age of the baby boom generation and the GI Bill making college within reach for ordinary Americans. By contrast, critics of the master plan asserted that it was a masterfully designed policy that attracted widespread support while catering to corporate needs in the postwar economy.[49] The crux of the master plan, critics contended, was to divert students away from the UCs and state colleges and into the junior colleges. It did so by raising admission criteria at the UCs and state colleges—a strategy that appealed to widely held beliefs in meritocracy and an objective education. This curbed the problem of overenrollment at the expensive UCs and created a major cost savings to the state, given that local taxes provided the major funding for junior colleges. But predictably enough, students of color and poorer students were disproportionately diverted to the community colleges. The drop in Black student enrollment San Francisco State College from 11 percent in 1960 to 3 percent in 1968 helped spark that campus's Third World strike.[50] The master plan also benefited the postwar industrial–technological economy. By channeling students to the junior colleges, the master plan facilitated the training of technicians, who were needed in much larger numbers than the professionals produced by the UCs. So when students like Aoki went on strike, they fought for both the establishment of Third World Studies and the development of a "relevant education" that prioritized the needs of working-class communities above the job-training needs of corporations and a curriculum that included the perspectives of racial minorities and women.[51]

Informed by the ideas of Third World revolutionaries like Mao, Fanon, Castro, and Guevara, and by U.S. radicals like Malcolm X, Huey Newton, and Robert Allen, student activists connected their struggles for educational transformation to global and domestic movements against racism and colonialism.[52] When it came to developing Ethnic Studies curriculum and practices, Paulo Freire's ideas were most relevant. Freire viewed education as the "practice of freedom," which in contrast with the "practice of domination," involved "neither abstract man nor the world without people, but people in their relations with the world."[53] Freire's concept of "praxis," or "reflection

and action upon the world in order to transform it," was particularly meaningful.[54] His emphasis on "dialogue" transformed the hierarchical teacher–
student relationship into one that involved mutual respect, listening, and
people talking and working with each other, as opposed to acting upon one
another. His focus on "naming the world" was critically important when
working with populations who traditionally had little voice and little power.[55]
In short, Freire viewed education as a dialectical process of theory and practice, involving a critical analysis of social problems connected with trust in
ordinary people to create and re-create their own world. These ideas help
explain why the originators of AAS emphasized the need for the oppressed,
including students and racial minorities, to engage in education as a practice of freedom, to empower students in building nonhierarchical relationships, and to connect their academic experiences to the betterment of their
communities.

Of the four Ethnic Studies units, AAS had the strongest community emphasis and student participation and, predictably enough, drew sharp criticism from the mainstream academy. The first academic review of Ethnic
Studies consisted of seven faculty members, one from each Ethnic Studies
division and three outside the department. Conducted in 1972, the Collins
Committee was to advise the university administration and budget committee about faculty hiring and budgetary matters. The committee viewed Ethnic
Studies as being "too heavily influenced by student participation" and favored
those Ethnic Studies divisions that hired stable and highly qualified faculty
and regularized administrative procedures.[56] The committee was particularly
disparaging of Contemporary Asian Studies, while giving generally favorable
assessments of Afro–American, Chicano, and Native American Studies. They
criticized AAS for offering too many lower-division courses, particularly the
less academic English composition and Asian language courses, and an un-
wieldy number of community projects that gave "rise to difficulties in supervision and coordination."[57] While recognizing that the cultural, linguistic,
and geographic diversity of Asian America required internships in Japantown,
Manilatown, and Chinatown, the committee concluded that AAS's eighteen
community projects were too many and found "some evidence that the field
work has, in many instances, not been well-organized and that students
frequently 'do their own thing' with little collective purpose."[58] In contrast,
they preferred Chicano Studies' model of two community projects or the
new Afro–American Studies coordinator's efforts to build "a rich curriculum emphasizing the humanities and social sciences and de-emphasizing

community projects."[59] In fact, the new coordinator of Afro–American Studies, whose appointment by the university administration sparked a Black student boycott of Afro–American Studies courses, viewed the primary focus of community involvement as "the intellectual growth of the student, not service to the community."[60]

Aoki remained critical throughout his life of AAS's and Ethnic Studies' turn away from community involvement and of what he viewed as the disempowerment of students. There were AAS students and staff who agreed with him and responded with strong words to the Collins Committee Report. They reaffirmed that "it is the main task of Asian American Studies to develop grassroots organizers and workers who will understand and know how to mobilize the larger community."[61] Even more emphatically, they asserted, "It is this educational philosophy, which refuses to view Asian students as mere commodities to be sold on the labor market upon graduation, that puts Asian American studies on the path of confrontation with the university."[62] Indeed, from early on, the university, with its greater power and resources, exerted substantial pressure for the Department of Ethnic Studies to conform to university practices. AAS insiders lamented: "In the first year, Ethnic Studies was given free reign [sic] on how it chose to educate Third World students. However, the following two years saw increased pressure from the university administration. It began to exercise more control over what courses should be offered, what programs may be considered academically 'legitimate,' who should be hired, and so forth."[63] As they feared, "Ethnic Studies began to change."[64] As the Collins Committee reviewed the department, Aoki left the university to work as a full-time counselor and instructor at Merritt College, where he worked against the closure of the campus that birthed the Black Panther Party.

10 "An Advocate for the Students"

Asian American Studies at Merritt College

I'm sitting in my office at UC Berkeley when a half dozen Merritt College students come to see me. This is around 1970. They wanted me to set up Asian American Studies at Merritt College, but my plate's full at Berkeley. So I said, "Let's do it this way. I'll teach one course and make it equivalent to the Introduction to Asian American Studies at Berkeley to make sure it's transferable." Students could then develop a plan for an Asian American Studies department. To teach at a community college in those days, you had to get credentials, so I filled out the forms and sent them to Sacramento. They hired about sixty part-timers for Merritt College and I was the only one to have a full committee evaluate me. Can you imagine—a full committee evaluation to teach a single course?! The usual procedures would be to have the department chair, or at the most, an assistant dean, make the appointment. The full committee included the dean of instruction, who happened to be my Merritt College German teacher, an anthropology instructor, and a Chinese American business professor. They must have figured, because he was Chinese, he should know something about Asian American Studies. But the field was so new, nobody knew what was going on. Not even Sacramento. This Chinese professor, who I believe had been associated with the Kuomintang, ended up endorsing me, which stunned a lot of people because the word hit the authorities that a Maoist from Berkeley was coming to take over Merritt College. But other Merritt faculty and administrators were excited to be getting somebody from Berkeley who's in the midst of developing this new field.[1]

So I taught the class. It was scheduled at eight in the morning in a portable two blocks from the main campus at the Bushrod Annex. Eight o'clock in the morning! At the Bushrod Annex! In a portable! Because my appointment had dragged on, that was all they had left at room reservations. But it turned out to be a blessing in disguise. I taught that class and then zipped over to Berkeley for the rest of the day. There were some interesting dynamics in that class. Before class even started, the dean of instruction told me, "You have at least one representative from the Oakland Police Department signed up for your class." That person was a Merritt student and had been critical of the Black Panther Party. Then the first week, I had students fill out a questionnaire—a habit I began at Berkeley. I discovered that one Japanese American student was a cadet with the Berkeley Police Department. He had graduated from Berkeley High School and UC Berkeley. That was curious—why would he take a community college class when he already had a bachelor's degree? I asked him about that. He could have said they didn't offer this course when I was in college. But he was very candid. He said the captain in charge of the cadets strongly suggested that he enroll in my class and give him a report. There was another student who seemed out of place. Now there were a number of Whites in the class, but this student was from Contra Costa County. So I asked him about his reason for taking the class. Turns out he was an officer in the Richmond Police Department. So I got three cops in my class of about thirty students. Meanwhile, I have eight Asian American students, almost street kids, from Oakland Chinatown. One of them volunteered to tape all my lectures in case there was an allegation that I was indoctrinating students into Marxism–Leninism–Maoism. He was sharp enough to realize that the police were in the class to document any inflammatory statements I might make. Of course, I never made inflammatory statements. What a homecoming!

One day, toward the end of the term, there was a blowup that could have been deadly. I got three law enforcement people sitting on one side of the room. I got eight Asian Americans sitting on the other side. In the middle are a bunch of students sweating it, wondering what's going to happen when the shooting starts. I did inform the Asian American students that if they wanted to go off on the opposition, don't do it in the classroom. If anything happened, they'd probably arrest me for instigating. But I made sure nothing happened in the classroom. Remember, I'm packing too. You're looking at me like you don't believe this. Well, UCLA was an idyllic campus. Who would have thought that Bunchy Carter and John Huggins would have gotten blown away there? There were enemies everywhere. But I diffused that situation and taught a righteous class. In fact, the representative from the Oakland Police department later became an ally of mine in some other struggles because she was impressed by my knowledge. She was one of those politically conservative people who wasn't racist, who really believe in right and wrong, but was coming at it from a different slant. I would say she was an ethical conservative. She was initially most vehement about my not teaching. But after the class, she became one of my strongest supporters.

As for developing Asian American Studies, I figured the students could form an Asian American club and use college hour to work on this because I've always been very religious about protecting the classroom for academic instruction. College hour was one or two hours during the week set aside for student government and student clubs to meet when no classes were scheduled. Now, the Department of African American Studies at Merritt College was officially approved by the board, and this paved the way for demands for Asian American Studies.[2] About this time, William Sato became available for appointment. He had just graduated from Cal State Hayward with a master's degree in history and had written his master's thesis on the Japanese American internment. I would run into Bill at movement activities, so I recommended him to the students as a full-time instructor to help develop Asian American Studies. Meanwhile, I continued to teach one class per semester at Merritt while I was still at Berkeley.[3]

Keeping Open the Birthplace of the Black Panther Party

Things began to change dramatically at Merritt College. The district decided to close the campus down because they wanted to move Merritt College, then at Fifty-Seventh and Grove Street, to the Oakland Hills. It created a storm of controversy because there would be no community college in the North Oakland–South Berkeley area.[4]

Dr. Ben Yerger was appointed the first college president. I was sitting in my office and I got a phone call from Dr. Yerger. He said, "You heard they are moving Merritt College up to the Oakland Hills? We don't want to lose the Grove Street campus. We don't want to lose accreditation." I agreed to meet him for lunch. Now there's no such thing as a free lunch. Ben asked me if I would consider going to work for him as special assistant to the president. He had been following my career since I left Merritt College as a student. It was his opinion that I'd served long enough at the university to be considered stable and suitable for appointment to the district. He even commented that I qualified for the three main credentials for employment in the community college system. Instructionally, I could be credentialed in a half dozen subject matter areas. I was eligible for a counseling credential because of my master's degree in social work. I was also qualified for an administrative credential based on my major of public administration. He even brought along the salary schedule and the benefits package for me to review.[5]

About the same time, I was having trouble getting my permanent lifetime credentials from Sacramento in instructing, counseling, and administration. Normally it takes ninety days to process the application, but more than a year had gone by and they still had not approved my application. That was due to the long arrest record I had to submit along with my application. The legal argument of my attorney, Dale Minami, was that because I was never convicted of anything, I should not be denied my credentials. Dr. Norvel Smith, the president of Merritt College, had written a nice letter of recommendation for me because it was under his watch that I was hired in the first place. I liked the way Dr. Smith attributed my trials and tribulations to my young rebellious days, as if those had occurred decades earlier, when it had only been a couple of years. So with the help of Ben, Dale, and Dr. Smith, approval for my credentials came through.[6]

The college at Fifty-Seventh and Grove changed names several times. First, the original Merritt College that I matriculated from was the birthplace of the BPP. After Merritt College was moved to the Hills in 1971, the college on Fifty-Seventh and Grove didn't have a name. It was called the old Merritt College as opposed to the new Merritt College. Then it became Grove Street College, which is what the students wanted. A year later, it became North Peralta Community College. I served at the original Merritt College in its final year and then as faculty when it became the unnamed Grove Street/North Peralta campus. We had to do a bit of administrative acrobatics to maintain accreditation since the accreditation of the old Merritt College was extended to the new Merritt College. This was very important. If you don't have accreditation, then the courses that are being offered and the programs that are being conducted don't mean jack. The life of that institution was short because by 1975, they closed it down, but I'm getting ahead of my story.[7]

That was an exciting period to be working at that place. You have to picture this: a new college is beginning and Richard's been hired, not without difficulty, but still, I was a little surprised. There were four presidents in as many years and I served as special assistant to all of them. First, Dr. Ben Yerger, an African American, was unceremoniously removed as president of that institution within six months of my appointment. Can you imagine that? I don't know what justification the chancellor and the board used, but I suddenly found myself as special assistant to the president without the president who hired me. The next president, Carl Mack Sr., also African American, was removed from office and demoted as well. The third president was Dr. Young Park, a Korean American and the first Asian American president of a community college in the state of California. It was during his presidency that the BPP reemerged on the campus. The party made a turn toward local electoral politics, with Bobby Seale, Elaine Brown, and Huey Newton running for public office. Now the good news was Young Park was more supportive of the BPP than most college presidents would have been. Ben Yerger and Carl Mack Sr. already knew Huey personally. Young Park was from out of town, so when he became aware of my background, he wanted an introduction to Huey. I got him an invite up to Huey's penthouse, though I never visited Huey there. After Young Park was removed from office and unceremoniously demoted, the last president was Nora Tucker, an African American.[8]

Throughout my whole career, my business card always listed counselor and instructor. That's how I saw myself, even though I was what we call a triple-threat person. I had the credentials in all three major areas—instruction, counseling, and administration—so that I could handle just about any problem that came along. I taught a variety of classes. I had an Ethnic Studies credential, which enabled me to teach to African American Studies, Latin/Mexican American Studies, Asian American Studies, and Native American Studies. I also came to recognize the importance of student services. After we won the battle to get our people into college, there was another struggle to provide the kinds of services to keep people there. What I did was different than the traditional model where someone has mainly one job—as a professor or counselor or administrator. But we weren't about tradition; we were about getting the job done. I could easily flow in and out of different jobs and I had a breadth of experiences that you really can't buy.[9]

At one point, I was made chair of the Departments of Social Sciences and Ethnic Studies. Being a small college we did not want to waste a lot of FTEs [full-time equivalent positions] on superfluous things. So, if we needed to fill in a department chair position, put Richard in charge. Most of the instructors were there to teach, not to build careers for themselves. So as department chair, my job was to ensure the department would function—hiring, class scheduling, whatever—so the instructors could attend to teaching. One of my first jobs was hiring the faculty. When the old Merritt College moved to the Hills, only a small core of dedicated faculty volunteered to stay and help Ben preserve that institution. So at one point, I recommended fifteen to twenty faculty appointments, full- and part-time. I had the mission before me. This was not a revolution but a job to set up the best educational institution of higher learning at the community college level. I worked to make sure that the most academically rigorous would be appointed for instruction. I generally hired graduate students from UC Berkeley, those with PhDs and with master's degrees because a master's degree was the minimal requirement for an instructional credential and for counseling as well.[10]

Now, of those fifteen to twenty personnel appointment forms I signed that term, only one came back from downtown. David Du Bois, the adopted stepson of W. E. B Du Bois, had recently returned from Africa, mainly Ghana, and agreed to be the editor of the BPP newspaper. I very quietly hired David Du Bois to teach at Merritt College. I was stunned that downtown questioned an appointment like Du Bois, who was eminently qualified to teach. The president of the college called me in and said, "I don't understand it, Richard. Why is this one being returned? They said he isn't qualified." I said, "That's bullshit. He's got two degrees. A master's from American University and a master's from the University of Cairo. He's being hired to teach African Civilization. He's been living in Africa for the last ten years." I didn't tell them he was going to be editor of the BPP newspaper. You talk about underground. Here I am, special assistant to the president. I'm hiring all this staff and I'm able to slip him in. I knew why he was being denied—because of who his father was and because he was so political. It's the only time I ever said, "If this don't go, I'm walking." I told him, "You go back downtown, talk to the head of personnel, and you tell him, 'The guy's qualified.' You don't want to hear nothing else. If you don't, I quit." At that time I was his right hand, he didn't need me walking out. David Du Bois got hired.[11]

In that period, I helped a number of party members. What happened was that in 1972, the party ordered members from throughout the country to come to Oakland to take over city politics. Bobby Seale was running for mayor and Elaine Brown for city council. That's how I began relations with the party again because where do you think one of the main campaign headquarters was? The college I was working at, the birthplace of the BPP and my alma mater. So there I was again in the right place. I'm special assistant to the president of the college. All of a sudden, "Richard, so-and-so needs a job." So I was finding jobs for Panthers coming in from out of town, or getting them admitted as students, or getting them financial aid. Not only that, but my office was a hotbed of activity during the campaign. I was doing behind-the-scenes things—raising money, making sure they had facilities, all the stuff of a normal campaign—and also making sure that I was not in violation of any college policy involving political activity. It helped that the college president at that time was supportive of the party, though he wasn't involved. Now, here is the funny part. There had been such a turnover of membership in the BPP that 90 percent of the party people who came through didn't know who the hell I was. All they know is that Bobby or Huey or David said, go to this guy's office. I enjoyed playing that role because there was no danger to me, although by that time, things was pretty quiet on the armed struggle front.[12]

Some may be surprised, but the party's decision to close the branch offices and consolidate work in Oakland made sense to me. The candidates ran as the BPP ticket in that election. You can always reopen branches at a later date, but you need all your cadre. And they came in. In fact, I was shocked that one of the former New York 21 Panthers came to Oakland.[13] I'm sitting there, I'm asking questions, I need to know who I'm dealing with. She said she was from New York, one of the New York 21. At that time, I wasn't in any position to make any judgments about the functioning of the party. It was also about that time that the drug situation within the party started getting out of control. That explained some of the contradictions I saw, but I didn't understand the extent of the problem because I was not in the loop. The bottom line is I'm still a party member and I'm ready when called.

I was also an adviser to various student groups. It was interesting to deal with a variety of politics. Eighty percent of the students were African American, but the White students there were radical.[14] In fact, there was even an Irish Republican Army student club on campus. That was discovered because the phone bill started to get out of control. In those days, I had to get a printout from the phone company and talk with the campus operators to place calls to figure this out. I found a common denominator—Belfast, Ireland. Then a second thing happened. Under my counseling duties there was a young lady from the Philippines whose father brought her into my office to help her adjust to American schools. Because she was not an American citizen and ineligible for financial aid, she was hired as a student helper in the duplicating room. One day, I got a call from the duplicating supervisor, who said, "These came out of my duplicating room and they're flyers announcing an event to raise funds for the IRA!" The college president hit the ceiling on that one: "That stuff is being printed in our duplicating machine with our money! I am going to fire her." But I said, "It's obvious she's a dupe. Some clown found out she was working in the duplicating room and must have asked her to run some stuff." She didn't get fired. Meanwhile, I talked with the club people and said, "Look this has got to cease and desist." I even went to the local gathering of the adult group. I took my life in my hands. "Hey, I support. However, you cannot use our facilities and personnel." This is a principle I've held in any managerial position, that this is taxpayers' money, the public's money, I'm just a trustee to make sure it is spent appropriately. Now it may be to my detriment that I never took advantage of my administrative position to amass great wealth or small wealth. I could account for every penny that came under my jurisdiction. That's something I have a great deal of sensitivity about because I have seen good programs destroyed by mismanagement.

As special assistant to the president, we had another problem. Black American veterans coming back from Vietnam wanted to start their own club, the Black Veterans Association. They could not find a faculty sponsor. They were puzzled why nobody would sponsor them, but they were one of the wildest groups I had ever encountered. Most of them came back from 'Nam, grubbed out, alcoholed out, and a source of embarrassment on the campus. When one their leaders passed out in the cafeteria, his gun fell out of his jacket and went sliding across the floor. A student dove into my office and said, "Mr. Aoki, so-and-so is passed out in the cafeteria and his gun is lying a couple of feet away. What do we do?" I jumped up and went to the cafeteria. I picked up the contraband and the guy and took him to my office to sober up. He was a veteran of 'Nam who had some serious problems. He allegedly torched his girlfriend's apartment. Heavens knows what happened to him in 'Nam. I never asked him why he had to pack all the time. I never asked him why he had to beat his woman all the time. When he was being arraigned for the arson job, he called my office since I happened to be the faculty sponsor of the club. So this dude was down meandering at the courthouse and said, "Wait till my friend Richard Aoki shows up." But little did he know that that was the worse thing he could have said because he had the same judge I beat when I went up for my big-time charges several years earlier. The judge leaned over and said, "Who did you say?" The student said, "Richard Aoki and he's here now," and pointed to me as the faculty sponsor. The judge slammed his gavel down and said, "I am revoking your bail. I'm remanding you to immediate custody. I will take a personal interest in the progress of your case!" To this day, I don't think that person realized that he said the wrong thing. He ended up serving time.[15]

When I was at North Peralta, we operated out of trailers scattered all over the campus. At one time, drug dealers became a very serious problem on campus. They were dealing outside the administration building portable. Since the district security seemed unable to deal with this problem, the campus's karate team, consisting of some Black Panthers and some members of the faculty, all ex-military, informed the dealers that selling drugs on campus was illegal. They could sell across the street, but we don't want to catch them selling on campus. When they realized who they were up against, the drug dealing ceased on campus and without any violence.[16] At one time the BPP was real strong on campus and some party members beat up a cultural nationalist instructor in the classroom. I had gotten feedback from students that this dude had heavily criticized the BPP. I support academic freedom, but you've got to be a little diplomatic. The college president, Carl Mack Sr., went with the guy to the hospital. So I had to put down the potential gunfight coming down because this instructor's friends had heard that he was attacked. As I was going to the classroom, I saw the security people running the other way. Then, two carloads of cultural nationalists drove up to the front gate. I said, "Turn around. There is nothing for you here." There were two groups of party people on campus that day: the group that attacked the instructor and then the more mature members who I notified to get off the campus fast. I was packing too and thinking, "Just try me, sucker. There's only two carloads of you. Where are the others?" You have to understand in those days, I was new to the field of higher education and had no couth. I called it in the way I saw it and did what needed to be done. I knew the outside elements should not disturb the tranquillity of our humble campus and I was the guardian for the moment, so they got to kill me to get by me. Of course, I realized I got no backup. The president is at the hospital. The security guards have left. The party people I could have relied on had to get off campus real fast too because the cops would be rounding up the Panthers. The alleged assailants withdrew from campus and disappeared. The main assailant was later seen as a homeless person in Oakland.[17]

In this period of time, I was so wrapped up with my work, I was the first to arrive on campus and the last to leave. At one point the personnel office called and said, "Richard, we need to reconcile the books, but you haven't cashed three months' worth of paychecks." When I got paid, I just threw the paychecks into the dresser drawer at home. I didn't have time to spend my money, except to drink my lunches at the surrounding bars. Then the last college president called me into her office and said two things. Number one, the car I had at the time was not bringing respect to the staff parking lot. It was an old clunker. I should get a new car. I started to say that I can't really afford a new car. Then she said, "I noticed you have put in a lot of overtime that you don't get compensated for. You're here morning, noon, and night. Why don't you turn in time sheets for the overtime?" So that night I went home, looked at my calendars, my schedule, my appointment book, and filled out those time sheets. I got the down payment for a 1975 Mustang with a V8 engine, body by Ghia, candy apple red with a white top—a bad car![18]

I also learned that I didn't need much money. So I got really cavalier about giving away thousands of dollars. My money went to political groups—nothing that I could declare on my income tax—and to students because I dealt with a lot of poor students. To many, a couple hundred dollars made the difference between whether they could complete the term or whether they had a roof over their head. Plus, my own expenses were minimal because my brother was a real estate broker and my landlord. He subsidized my rent because he felt I was making a contribution to society through teaching and he knew teachers didn't get paid what they deserved. Later, when I moved into the place I'm living in now, my stepfather told my mother, "The reason why we keep Richard's rent low is because he's a teacher."[19]

After four years, the board finally decided to close North Peralta Community College.[20] I have to give the chancellor credit for guts because he actually came to the campus to announce the closure. I was standing in the gymnasium and one student pulled a knife and was going for the chancellor. I stopped that student fast. Put a judo lock hold on him and escorted him outside the door informing him that it wouldn't do any good. But I can understand how raw emotions were because it was a tremendous defeat for the community. The community college is supposed to serve the local community. But there was nowhere to go until downtown Oakland with Laney College. Putting the new Merritt College at the top of the Oakland Hills only incited their anger and resentment.

The New Merritt College on the Hill

When the campus closed, my car was the last to leave. I was not a happy camper on that issue and made a big to-do about that. In fact, I had my resignation letter in my pocket. But a friend told me, "Don't do that, Richard." They knew how devoted I had been and encouraged me to think about it this way: in the four years that I was there, ten thousand students who would not have had the opportunity got a college education, whether academic or vocational. I ended up transferring to the new Merritt College on the counseling staff but also did some part-time teaching. What happened was that North Peralta faculty who had districtwide seniority could transfer to another Peralta District campus of their choice. I wanted to go to Laney College near Lake Merritt because I figured most of the North Peralta students would go there. But Kenn Waters, an African American counselor, and I were encouraged to go to the new Merritt College to help colorize the staff up there. They were getting a lot of static because the bulk of the faculty there were White. There was also a large number of White students at Merritt on the Hill, whereas North Peralta had very few White students. Plus, there were striking class differences. The African American students at North Peralta tended to be working class, whereas the African American students at Merritt were more middle class or well-established working class. A lot can be told from looking at the facilities and curriculum of the two schools. North Peralta was limited in its programmatic offering; classes were conducted out of portables; we lacked the capital investment in science modern lab facilities. But Merritt on the Hill had brand-new, state-of-the-art science labs and vocational shops.[21]

I got to be a real good reader of résumés just as I got to be an expert at transcript forwarding. I did make one mistake, however, in my professional career. One time a student came into my office. She was from out of state and had transcripts from five different schools. She needed to be evaluated to see if she met the associate degree course requirements and unit tally because half of the schools she went to were on the quarter system and the other half on the semester system. I told her she was good to go after taking these two classes. But after reconverting semester and quarter units, she ended up half a unit shy. It was the last week before graduation and by the time this error was caught, so she was not going to graduate. I called her: "I got some bad news. You aren't graduating." Now Richard does not make those mistakes! In fact, I prided myself on being the best. But Richard made a mistake. Now here's the corker. She was the wife of a military man and went with her husband all over the country. So she was not as uptight about graduating that particular year as most students would be. Also, she told me that most staff had given her the brush-off, so she was very thankful that I took the time to help her. I had made an error, but she forgave me.

I usually worked in the summer and that enabled me to help with fall registration. One time I was doing late registration and a Native American student walked in. He was from a southwestern state and his tribe and the Bureau of Indian Affairs had funded his educational expenses. In the sixties and seventies, one way the U.S. government tried to urbanize Native Americans was to encourage those on the reservations to attend urban colleges by underwriting their educational expenses. So I quickly got this guy's story. The BIA and tribe set him up for vocational education. But he had higher aspiration than to be a carpenter. He had good grades in high school and wanted to go on to a state college or UC Berkeley. I told him to take half his classes in the carpentry major and the other half in college prep—English, math, political science, U.S. history, and Ethnic Studies. Around Christmastime I got a call. He'd been arrested, was in the Oakland jail, and was going to be arraigned that afternoon. I have always had good relationships with my supervisors and they became accustomed to my unorthodox style. "Look, boss. I've got to go downtown for one of our students. Student's been arrested. Be gone a couple of hours. Kenn's willing to take over my classes." I got to the courtroom just before the guy was arraigned and got to talk with him. It was a misdemeanor. He was in downtown Oakland the night before. He was lonely, away from the reservation for the first time. There was this young lady that looked good. As soon as they agreed on a price, she whipped out a badge and he was arrested for solicitation. Now I knew the judge, whom I shall not name. I asked the clerk could I see the judge in his chambers. "My man, I'm glad it's you. Listen, this is the story. The next one coming up is a student at the college where I work. There must be a misunderstanding. He is such a nice young man, Native American, new to Oakland. He's not used to the ways of the big city." So the judge came out and read the charge: "I am changing the charge from solicitation to drunken disorder." I'm thinking, better than solicitation. The judge told him, "I'm putting you on one-year probation under the supervision of your college representative here. If you complete the one-year probation, I will seal your record." So he completed that one year, good student, excelled in his vocational major and went on to a state university in his home area and then went to the air force as an officer. His career would have been cut short had he been convicted of the original charge and word got back to the tribal elders and the BIA.

One time, I managed to get an associate degree for a student who had passed away. He was a White student, twenty-two or twenty-three years old, and was the Go champion of the city of Alameda.[22] He took my Asian American history class and I later became his permanent academic counselor. His goal was to transfer to Berkeley after acquiring his associate degree. One spring term, I got a phone call from the student's family telling me that he had passed away. I was stunned because he was so young, but it turned out that he had a congenital heart condition. He was slated to graduate in the next couple of months. So I went to my boss, the dean, showed him this student's letter of acceptance from UC Berkeley, and told him about my idea to give him a degree posthumously. The dean went through the president, the president went downtown to talk to the chancellor, the chancellor talked to the board, and they decided to approve it. I am glad I did that because it meant so much to this working-class family. They showed up for the graduation ceremony and thanked the college for their recognition of his work.

One of the plaques I've received at my retirement best summarizes what I tried to do during my professional career: be an advocate for the students. I found that in my professional career, about half of the serious problems students faced were institutionally derived. I got incensed about that. The social, economic, and political inequalities and injustices that took place outside the boundaries of the campus, I have no control over. You have to remember, the primary mission of the educational institution is education. I do stretch the word education, because there is formal schooling and then there is the learning-of-life aspect. Still, I realized that as a professional, I was constrained by rules and regulations. Don't get me wrong. I'm for rules and regulations if they are appropriate. But when people talk about law and order, give me a break. Law and order are human-made things. Just because someone breaks the law does not make them an outlaw. The law could be unjust. We've seen a period in American history, where separate but equal was the law of the land. To go along with that law meant you were a good citizen. To oppose that law meant you were an outlaw, an agitator, someone to be put in jail! The civil rights activists were morally justified in what they did, in going against a legal but morally wrong law. I'm not talking about bourgeois, Judeo-Christian morality. I am talking about the morality of what is right for the people![23]

This tension is the main reason why I never applied for a permanent managerial position. One of my colleagues—she was head of the union at one time and was looking over the personnel files for some research project—commented that I had held more interim managerial positions than anyone in the whole district. "Richard, you have been head of financial aid, director of Extended Opportunity Programs and Services, assistant dean, department chair, but never permanent." My response was I never wanted to become permanent because of those constraints. The more permanent and higher ranked I became, the more constrained I would be.

The Japanese American Redress Movement

During the time I was employed at Merritt College [1975–87], my political activity was very minimal mainly because of the downturn of the movement. So I threw myself into my professional work. Still, I kept abreast of historic events, though as a distant observer, and each glimpse was worse than the one before. I am referring to the resiliency of American capitalism, especially in the mid-1970s. I did some quasi-political stuff in the community, serving on the board of directors of several different Asian American social service groups.[24] I let my guard down a little bit when Mumia Abu-Jamal was arrested and accused of killing a cop in Philadelphia in the early 1980s. The Partisan Defense Committee approached me and asked if I would be one of the sponsors on their masthead. Normally I would not have lent my name, but I felt Abu-Jamal's case was part of the struggle for national liberation. Not to mention, he had been a Black Panther and a well-respected journalist, and his case represented the naked confrontation between the revolutionary movement and the state. So I said, "You can count on me to stand with Abu-Jamal." There weren't too many people stepping forward at that time, and that's another reason why I stepped forward. I just lent my name; that was about it.[25]

In the seventies, rumblings occurred in the Japanese American community about seeking justice for crimes against Japanese Americans who were interned in concentration camps during World War II. The redress movement was initiated by third-generation Japanese Americans, or Sanseis, as a carry-over from the student movement of the sixties.[26] It was a mystery to them because their parents didn't reveal the true scope of the injustice and the impact on their families. Don't forget, baby boomers were graduating from colleges and universities at the time, specializing in law and related fields, so they could use their skills to fight for redress. It might surprise some that my initial response to the redress movement was rather tepid, especially those who know how angry I still get about the injustice perpetrated upon our people. In fact, one of the few times I ever saw red was when Earl Warren refused to repudiate his role as California attorney general in the internment of our people.[27] I had confronted him when he came to Berkeley to receive a humanitarian award. But he adamantly refused to admit any wrongdoing and I almost went off on him. The position I should have taken was to put the United States on trial for crimes against humanity and to indict those responsible for the internment as war criminals. Didn't they try the people who set up and operated the concentration camps in Germany during World War II? Weren't the Nuremberg Trials devoted to making sure those who violated human decency should pay for the crimes they committed? The United States was as hypocritical as it got. My feeling was that we were one step away from extinction. Suppose the Japanese imperial army landed on the coast of California, how long do you think we would have lasted? But if the JACL was going to press forward through a legalistic approach, I was not going to get in the way. I did notice, however, that the National Coalition for Redress/Reparations seemed to be the most progressive group working for redress.

In the early 1980s, the redress movement gained a congressional commission to hold hearings in multiple cities.[28] A faction within the NCRR submitted my name to testify at the San Francisco hearing, scheduled for August 1981. For several weeks, I spent hours working on my presentation. There were two points I wanted to concentrate on. The first thing was recognition that the United States committed war crimes and should pay for it. The other was a direct response to S. I. Hayakawa.[29]

I made it quite clear that I would not kowtow before the commission, that I was going to tell it like it was, come hell or high water. The decades of outrage and anger had been bubbling underneath me and it started to come out. It surprised me that I was so emotional about the concentration camps, though I tried to remain unemotional. So in my few minutes, I leveled a variety of charges against the system. There were some six hundred people in the audience, mostly of Japanese ancestry, including members of my own family whom I had not seen for years. I stated, "On the question of Senator Hayakawa, if he felt we had an extended vacation during those four years in the camps, I would strongly advise him to take a vacation in one of those camps. His impression may change. If not that, he might revive an old Japanese custom. And if he doesn't have a sword, somebody may lend it to him. And if he needs someone to administer the coup de grâce, I'll be glad to volunteer."[30]

I wasn't sure how people would respond to my words, but people applauded. There is a quotation to the effect "He jests at scars who never felt wounds," and that is the way I felt about Hayakawa. He did not get hurt but our people got hurt and I was going to be the avenger for the people. Now I did feel a burst of gratification when I announced, "I'm prouder of my Japanese ancestry than I've ever been in my life."[31] That is when the audience applauded me the most and that's how I know our people got hurt. Senator Daniel Inouye is someone who visually represents that hurt because he lost an arm fighting in the U.S. Army in World War II. I say, for what? His people did not get respect. You're asking me what I think about the notion that the efforts of the Japanese American soldiers in time facilitated Japanese American acceptance into the American mainstream. I think it is a feeble attempt to justify the tragedy of those lost lives. The 442nd was replaced three times! Freedom, justice, and democracy are what they were supposed to be fighting for, but this government has a history of violating that. I think I got the best argument right now with the advent of 9/11. Who's catching hell like we did during World War II? Our Muslim brothers and sisters![32]

I know that the veterans of that period probably want a taste of me, but my real quarrel isn't with them. I'll stand on the side of the people because that is the way that it should be. That was one of the reasons that it was wise for me not to get too involved in the redress struggle because I would have been really frustrated when I got up there and spouted out my ideas. The people would have thought, "Oh my god. It is true. Richard is crazy." But if I am crazy, it was the camps that drove me crazy.

Strains and Pressures

You keep asking about the strains going on in my life in this period. The pressures compounded the personal relationships I had, maybe much more than I would like to admit. I don't want to go into the litany of how this economic system presents many, many barriers to healthy relationships. I won't go into that too much, although I have to thank Frederick Engels's *The Origin of the Family, Private Property, and the State* because that illuminated a lot of things for me intellectually.[33] But how do you practice this when you are in a capitalistic society? I didn't pay much heed to the more humanist philosophies, because I was more fixated on the political economy. I consider myself a dialectical materialist. Fred Ho was one of the few people I could carry on a deep discussion with about materialist and humanist aspects of Marxism.[34] What I'm saying is that to me, relationships are secondary to the mission at hand. If you can't get with the program [i.e., the revolutionary transformation of the political economy], I am sorry, it's not going to work. That accounts for my succession of "shack-up" relationships. This usually involved dating somebody, but we had separate apartments. In the mid-1980s, I got into a serious relationship with a woman who was half White, half Native American. We were introduced by mutual friends and we had things in common. She had been active in the sixties herself, but became professional in the business world. She had also been married before and had one grown child. I had twenty-five hundred dollars in the bank, my life savings. I talked to one of my friends about buying her an engagement ring with that. He jumped up and said, "Don't do it, man. You are crazy." This was a friend I had known about fifteen years. He knew me well and had always been critical of my female companions. He saved me twenty-five hundred dollars because that relationship didn't last.[35]

There were others that I lived with over the years. There was one woman, the blond in this photo. My mama was opposed to her; had never met her, but didn't like her. She thought she was after my money. "Mama, I ain't got no

money." I guess my mother objected for two reasons. One was that this woman
was White. My mother has this dream about my marrying a Japanese American—one of our people who can take good care of her son. Then too this
one here was a little too racy, too flashy for her son.[36] I remember one time, we
got caught in a traffic jam driving up to Sacramento. This was about 1997
or '98. My mama asked, "What do you see in her?" I said, "Sex." She said, "Sex
isn't everything." I said, "What else is there?" That shut her up, but I am sure
that all the female companions I had from 1966 to the present are well aware
that there is this political side of me that puts almost everything else secondary. You have to be that way. I said before that I have no regrets on the
political end, but on the personal end, I do have regrets. I ran this "woe is
me" thing by my friend a couple of weeks ago. He's married, has a kid, and is
quite levelheaded. He's seen me in these relationships on and off over the
years. He was a bit more philosophical and I expected that from him. "We can't
go back. This is the way it is and we got to learn to live with it." In other words,
just the thought of having regrets is useless.

I admit I got to drinking a bit. The breakups didn't help, but I blame it on
the movement. We're talking about the death throes of our organizations.
Boom boom boom—we were getting wiped out. My friends were going down
one by one. In the party alone, in a one-year span, Bunchy Carter and John
Huggins were killed off in LA and then Fred Hampton and Mark Clark in
Chicago. Not to mention what happened to Bobby Hutton, the first and the
youngest Panther to go down in police violence. Then the fratricide within
the party. During the whole period of time I was at Merritt, I drank. It was con-
venient to have a bar close to the campus. My drinking habits were kind of
weird. I usually didn't arrive to work drunk. What I would do is delay my alcohol consumption until I got home, unless there was a big party or something.
But being a professional, I had to make sure that my mind was clear. So I did
two things that were out of phase with a stereotypical drinker. I drank when I
got home, usually it was late because I often stayed overtime, and I drank
alone. I didn't go to any bars or nothing. On my way home, I'd stop by my
friendly ol' liquor store. They knew who I was and would have a bottle ready.
When I got home, I'd read through the *San Francisco Chronicle* and the *Oakland Tribune* for the local news and *Time, Newsweek,* and *U.S. News and World
Report* and occasionally the *Wall Street Journal* or the *New York Times* for
national and international news. One of the points of pride I had was keeping
on top of events so that I could understand what was impacting our students.
If they announced a big job layoff at the Oakland Army Base, then I would say,

we better think of getting programs here so that these laid-off workers could acquire skills to help them adjust to the new economy.[37]

Then 1987 came along. That was a bad year for me. My brother passed away at the beginning of the year. I broke up with somebody that I had been living with for a couple of years. Then my car engine blew out on me. Now that may not seem like a big deal, but there is a bit of irony regarding the car engine blowing out. What happened is I was at another friend's place and I was leaving about one or two in the morning. I said, "This horrible beginning to a new year has brought a few disastrous things on me. What else could go wrong?" On my way home, on the freeway, my car engine blew. I called my friend at four in the morning and said, "Remember when I said, what else could go wrong? Well, my car engine blew." But that wasn't the half of it. I got a March 15 letter saying that I might be laid off after sixteen years of faithful service to the community college district. I have to admit that I am a creature of habit; I was comfortable during those twelve years at Merritt College. I had myself a good job. I was getting paid to help people, mainly minority and working-class students, in a field I believed in. I was stunned to get that layoff letter. I had sixteen years in the district![38]

So these layoff notices went out because of the downturn in the state economy. Two major reasons for that. Number one was after Prop 13, the taxpayers' revolt, passed and funding became endangered for public education. When I was at North Peralta in the early 1970s, we had money. But after Prop 13, things started going downhill fast.[39] Number two would be corruption within the district itself emanating from the chancellor's office. In the spring of 1987, the district found itself with a projected budget shortfall of several million dollars. Various ideas were tossed around regarding how to meet that shortfall. There were places I saw could be cut to meet the deficit—like half the district office! I was tangential to those discussions because I didn't think anything bad would happen. But the chancellor made a mistake. He decided to balance the books by laying off instructors. This meant that forty-four of us were to be laid off. Now, I had sixteen years in the district and with a seniority system in place, how could I be on that list? Here's what happened. I had incurred the wrath of the chancellor the year before when he announced he was going to cut out a major program. Not a single faculty from that program would confront the chancellor. They were all on tenure track and didn't want to risk their jobs. So they approached me: "Richard, you know the situation. Would you be willing to appear at the next board meeting with a presentation for us?" When the chancellor announced his recommendations to cut this major program, I got up and said, "Yesterday in the newspaper, you said almost literally, hell would freeze over before you would give up that program. Now, what is the story?!"[40]

There were two other Japanese Americans on that layoff list. Two were Sansei, me and Bill Sato. Bill was the person who got me involved with the redress movement. The Nisei on that list, up to that point, had been pro-administration, was in the National Guard Reserve, and argued with Bill and myself about redress. Plus, he felt *shikataganai yo*.[41] But he got hit too. The interesting thing is that a couple of months later, I called his home for some other reason. He wasn't home, but his wife was glad to talk to me. She said, "My husband is a changed man." Before, he was for God, mother, and country, but now he couldn't do enough to help in the struggle to protect us from getting wiped out. This reflects how consciousness can change rapidly during a crisis. Once he realized he had been shafted, he became doubly loyal. So, the struggle was a mind bender for a lot of the people involved.[42]

That is when I had to roll up my sleeves because I was on that layoff list. I put in a lot of time and energy because to me, we were going to go to war. So I put together my plan A, B, and C. I passed the word out quickly in my networks. I did have job offers at other community colleges, but, if I transferred, I would have earned less because, in one case, they offered me only five years of seniority. Then comes Plan B. I was offered a job at a private industry, at beaucoup salary—I mean lucrative!—and in a field in which I was a natural. Now I was going to do it legally, get my license and whatever needs to be done, but this was very sensitive work. Plan C was to sue the district. I figured I'd use the University of California approach, so I researched things. I got documentation. I got testimonies from a bunch of sources. I had some of the best amateur legal minds working on this. I figured I'd take that lucrative job in private industry and also sue the district. Things started moving fast. The board made a decision to reverse the chancellor's layoff plan and wanted to call the forty-four of us back for the fall term. At this point, I already had the private industry offer and decided I'm not going back.[43]

Then Dr. Ben Yerger reentered my life. By that time he had quietly worked his way back up the ranks in the Peralta District and was a dean at the College of Alameda. He heard of my plight—everybody knew about the forty-four layoffs—and I got a phone call from Ben asking me to work for him again. I thought, a couple of months ago I was down in the dumps. Now I'm king of the world. I told Ben, "It's a funny thing. You're the only one in the whole district, at the managerial level, I would even pick up the phone for at this point.

I have a lucrative job offer and I'm getting ready to cut the deal soon. So if you're serious and if you can get the board to approve it at tomorrow night's board meeting, I'll be there the next morning." I didn't think there was a snowball's chance in hell that would happen. Several of my colleagues who were at the board meeting were stunned that this individual personnel action took place and the board all signed off. So that is the story of how I remained in the Peralta District. The bad news is, within six months of my employment at the College of Alameda, Ben got demoted again and was no longer the dean of students.[44]

The College of Alameda:
"The Most Productive Period of My Professional Life"

When I arrived in 1987, the College of Alameda had the highest percentage of White students among the four campuses in the Peralta District. The other campuses were Merritt College in the Oakland Hills; Laney College in downtown Oakland, the flagship of the district because it had the largest student enrollment; and Vista College in Berkeley.[45] The College of Alameda was also considered the most politically conservative of the four campuses. Its proximity to the Oakland army terminal across the estuary meant that the student population was heavily military. In fact, in 1990, when the Gulf War started, 122 of our students were called up for duty. I was able to get a motion passed through the Academic Senate that students not be penalized if they are called to active duty. Somewhere in Southern California, some liberal community college instructor who was against the war had penalized a student for being called off to active duty. I personally did not feel it was right. I didn't support the war, but I felt that it wasn't the fault of our students that were being called up. Instead, I believed they should have their grades frozen, get adjustments to their benefits, receive refunds on their enrollment fees, gets refunds on their books, and so forth. I said, "We'll set up a hotline." The students would say, "Mr. Aoki, I got called up" and I'd help them navigate through the college.[46]

Many of the faculty at the College of Alameda were also conservative World War II and Korean War veterans, many from reserve units like myself. In fact, during the Gulf War, I debated with the number one conservative faculty on the campus before the students regarding the pluses and minuses of the war. He was a top professor of economics. I sat in a few of his classes and talked to a bunch of his students when I realized I was going to be debating this guy. I talked to this one African American student. I asked, "Has he ever given you any cause to believe that he has a racist bone?" He said, "No, man. I was getting ready to flunk out. He took the time to tutor me and got me through that course." Though this professor was politically conservative, he wasn't a racist. That was one of the things I was sensitive about when dealing with my professional colleagues. My priority in judging them was based on their professional abilities, not on their politics.

The night of Rodney King riots, I was the most junior of the nine college administrators at the time. At the staff meeting that morning, word came down that we better brace ourselves for problems because the verdict was coming down and it didn't look good. All of a sudden, I'm administrator for the night. One of the other administrators said, "Richard, how's it feel? You know how to start riots. Now you're getting paid to stop one." As I'm listening to reports of the growing violence across the country, I called the district office and spoke to the head of security. I put in a formal request for two additional security officers, by name, because I knew who I could count on. These were dudes that were sharp and would enforce the law without getting excessively carried away. Nothing materialized on our campus, but there was a big demonstration at the Oakland police station. In Berkeley, there was rioting and looting on the south side of campus. My campus closed about ten o'clock and once I was assured the campus had been secured, I left. On my way home I drove by the police station and I could see a demonstration. I cruised by my old stomping grounds on the south side of Berkeley and I see it blocked off. But I was a community college manager and knew I shouldn't be out on a picket line. So I went home. It had been an eventful day. But I was pissed because I should have been out there demonstrating instead of trying to preserve the order. It was my duty to protect the students at our campus and I did it. In retrospect, the College of Alameda would probably be the last one to explode because of good relations there between students and faculty. Of course, most of the people were outraged by the verdict, but not to the point of going out and thrashing.[47]

I'm just getting to sleep about two o'clock when the phone rings. It was one of the college staff. Her son, a high school student, was busted for looting at Berkeley. I said, "Meet me at the college in the morning." There is nothing I could do that night. They had apparently arrested about thirty to forty people so it would take a couple of hours to process him. The next morning, I found out by calling the court what he was being charged with and that he was being arraigned at two o'clock. So I went into the president's office and said, "Your dean of students is going down to the Berkeley Police Department to take care of some business for a staff person." The president of the college was

understanding. So we bailed the guy out of jail. We didn't have to pay anything out of pocket. We used the OR method—got him out on his "own rec-
ognizance." The mother was so relieved that her son got out of jail. This was
horrible for her. She was a single parent trying to raise four kids in the projects.
That's why I dropped everything. Now, she is driving the van, I'm sitting in the
passenger seat, and the son is in the backseat. He's starting to realize that he is
in trouble now. Got himself and his mama in trouble. Embarrassed his mama.
His mama's boss is right there in the passenger seat. So he tries to get out of it.
He says, "Mama, they done abused me. I am victim of police brutality. Listen to
my story. There was a White boy grabbing up the jewelry like I was. But they
arrested me." She slammed on the brakes. If I didn't have a seatbelt on, I'd have
gone through the windshield. She did not say a word. She turned around and
looked at him as if to say, "Have I raised a fool for a son?" Everybody knows,
there is a White boy and a Black boy looting the jewelry store, who are the
cops going to arrest? The black boy. The situation ended pretty well in that
they dismissed the charges. After he graduated from high school, he became a
student at my campus and became a junior aide on the security staff, on my
recommendation.

In reviewing my experience at the College of Alameda [1987–98], I now
realize that it was probably the most productive period of my professional life.
By that time, I had gained a lot of experience in instruction, counseling, and
administration. I was in a new environment that allowed me to bring about
positive social changes from within an educational institution. I was quite comfortable with my contributions as an instructor and counselor. This included
establishing the first Asian American Studies class in the catalog and I made
sure it was transferable to the University of California. From the counseling
end, I started to get more involved in the student services special projects. I
was the director of Extended Opportunity Programs and Services, which originated at the UC about the time I was a student there. I had the good fortune
of being an apprentice to two of the academic founders of Berkeley's EOPS
program, both of whom ended up working at Merritt College. I was also able
to support students through my capacity as faculty adviser. When I was asked
to be the faculty sponsor of the Filipino Students Club, an uncle of one of the
students hit the roof: "What is a Jap doing sponsoring a Filipino students' club?"
He had been a member of the Philippine Constabulary, had been at Bataan
and Corregidor, and had been on the Bataan Death March during World War II
when Japan committed so many atrocities in the Philippines. But this student
defended me: "You were in that concentration camp in the Philippines with

the Japanese. Mr. Aoki was in a concentration camp here in the United States."
After Whites and then African Americans, the next largest group at Alameda
was Filipinos. Many of their parents were in the military at the naval air station
and the Oakland army terminal or in civil service.[48]

It may appear strange that less than two years after I arrived at the College
of Alameda I was elected president of the Academic Senate. But I had already
served as Faculty Senate vice president and treasurer at Merritt College, chair
of the Merritt Advisory Board, and was active at North Peralta before that.[49]
Plus there was a looming crisis at the college. We had to implement the Community College Reform Bill, AB1725. It mandated giving more power to the
faculty in the governance of the community college system. It was a needed
change. But somebody had to let the faculty know about their new rights
and to get the administration, the chancellor, the board, and the faculty to
move forward. In the Peralta District, the board was progressive and acknowledged most of the revisions of the reform bill. I was shocked that the boards
in other districts refused to go along. I was approached by the outgoing Academic Senate president, who felt that implementing that struggle would require somebody younger because he would have been the natural person to
lead the struggle. Meanwhile, since I had been at the college a year or so, the
faculty was able to get to know me better. I also had a base of support from
the faculty from the North Peralta period who transferred to the College of
Alameda when they closed North Peralta. I also had a connection with the
Vocational Education Department, including automotive, aviation, computer
science, and upholstery, because I always felt that the mission of the community colleges mandated their inclusion as full-fledged faculty. I ran for office
unopposed and was elected.[50]

This was the first time, as far as I know, in the history of the California community college system that the president of the college and the president of
the Faculty Senate were both Asian American. The college president, Ronald A.
Kong, came up through the ranks and understood the significance of the
reform bill. We worked well together and there wasn't a big struggle over
who's in charge. During my presidency, the implementation of that reform bill
took up all my time. We wanted to inform the faculty, make sure they knew
their rights, and answer questions about the impact of the bill, which I saw as
mostly positive.[51]

In 1996, I was elected Academic Senate president a second time at the College of Alameda. The previous Academic Senate president received an administrative appointment, and the vice president and other officers felt unable to

carry out the duties. So I was asked if I would consider running for president of the Academic Senate, with their support, so that we could get through the school year. I was opposed this time and the campaign involved some low-life tactics. I don't think it was my opponent, but the people around him circulated a warning to the faculty that I had been a member of the BPP and a radical at UC Berkeley. I had been causing trouble and would not make a good representative of the faculty. My victory on that election was one of the most personally satisfying moments of my life. I got three-quarters of the votes. It was obvious that the faculty overwhelmingly trusted me to shepherd the group through the leadership crisis.[52]

A year after I finished my second term as Academic Senate president, I ended up retiring. I wasn't planning to retire, but I changed my mind as more information became available about the financial status of the district and the state. As president of the faculty in 1996–97, I got to see how bad the situation was, with yet another budget deficit. They didn't want to lay off people after that one chancellor made that mistake. Instead, they reasoned that if enough of the senior faculty retired, they would be able to preserve the institutional integrity by hiring junior faculty at lower wages. So they sweetened up the retirement benefits and a lot of faculty retired between 1996 and 1998. I didn't make my decision in a vacuum. I made sure that at conferences I talked to others and compared notes. When I informed the college president that I was retiring, he was appalled. He had been my supervisor for most of my time at Merritt College and I felt that he respected me. The reason why he was so concerned is that downtown had notified him that they weren't going to fill the lost positions. Instead, they'd chop up each position and make them into something like one half-time and two quarter-time positions. This would save money in salaries and benefits. That did give me pause when the president of the college asked me to remain, but I realized these kinds of benefits wouldn't be around forever. I asked my secretary, who I trusted the most, for her thoughts. She said, "Quit while you're ahead, Richard. Right now everybody loves you." Several years earlier, we knew of a senior management person who retired but who was so disrespected there was no retirement party for him. She said, "Do you remember what happened to so-and-so. He stayed on beyond his time."[53]

Facing retirement is something that everybody goes through. When I was president of the faculty and entrusted with the responsibility of explaining retirement, I saw the effects of our work-oriented society on people, where occupation is almost a person's identity. Retirement is a scary thing to most people, even under the best of economic conditions. It's especially hard when people don't have anything to look forward to. I remember a guy who blew his brains out in a bar after he retired from the post office. This also has to do with the nature of our system where ageism is a factor. Then, there was also the personal part where my stepfather's health was beginning to deteriorate and since we were a small family, I knew I'd have to assume more responsibilities. I wasn't sure what I'd be doing, except to eat breakfast every morning at the University Café. But I knew this was probably the best retirement package I'd ever get. So I decided to retire at the end of the 1997–98 academic year.[54]

Things move in mysterious ways. After I retired, I started receiving more invitations to be a guest speaker. Almost every other week I was up at Berkeley or some other campus. There was a lot happening in the movement in the late 1990s and then after September 11, 2001, I got active with the antiwar movement. So retiring freed me up to do more activism at a time when the world was changing and political activities were intensifying.

I have fond memories of my experiences in the Peralta District because the institution, backward as it was in some areas, allowed me to achieve the goals and objectives along academic lines. The most rewarding for me was the chance to assist the students through teaching and counseling and from the administrative end, to establish and implement programs to further the progress of the students. I found that in a lot of cases, student problems were institutionally generated. Most frustrating to me was the continued financial erosion that hit higher education and the community colleges. It became harder to maintain special projects and programs, especially those that helped recruit and retain minority students and poor students. I have always been a believer in formal education. Not a believer in the system, but in education.

COUNSELOR, INSTRUCTOR, ADMINISTRATOR

In the early 1970s, after a decade of exhaustive activism, Aoki removed himself from overt political struggles and turned to the educational arena. Working in the community college system enabled him to channel his commitment to equality in more manageable ways, while sustaining himself physically, emotionally, and financially. He guided working-class and minority students toward pursuing higher education and broadening their life opportunities. He helped Black Panthers get jobs and into school. As Academic Senate president, he struggled against massive layoffs and worked to get a good retirement packet for his colleagues. He often worked in unorthodox ways, combining his street smarts and activist experiences with his professional expertise as a counselor and intermittent administrator. It was not uncommon for him to go to court to help defend a student or colleague. He used the performance of the gun to stop internecine fights on campus and to push drug dealers off campus. He gave away his own money—thousands as he recounts and which is quite plausible for one as generous as Aoki—to help students buy books and cover other necessary expenses. He recognized the significance of the original Merritt College as the birthplace of the BPP and an institution that facilitated the flowering of Black Power, and so worked in multiple capacities to keep that sinking ship afloat. He started or supported Asian American and Ethnic Studies at every college at which he worked. And he inspired many students to work hard and think expansively and imaginatively about their own lives and about broader issues of justice.

Many people would have been content with this record of professional accomplishment and service, and Aoki was. But his continuing radicalism also led him to question his political priorities. This occurs most vividly in relation to the public unrest that followed the police acquittals in the videotaped beating of Rodney King. When it became Aoki's responsibility to maintain order at the College of Alameda, one of his fellow administrators chided him: "Richard, how's it feel? You know how to start riots. Now you're getting paid to stop one." Aoki reasoned that it was his "duty to protect the students at our campus," but he was dismayed when he found himself avoiding the unrest in Berkeley because he was a "community college manager." In the late 1960s, he had been on the front lines protesting police brutality and demanding community control of education. In the early 1990s, he was acting as a manager to curb student protest. The contradiction angered him: "I should have been out there demonstrating instead of trying to preserve the order."

Even as Aoki strove for management positions within the community college system, his aspirations contained ambivalence: "I never wanted to become permanent. . . . The more permanent and higher ranked I became, the more constrained I would be."[55] Ever a Marxist, Aoki believed that managers function to maintain equilibrium in the capitalist system and, in doing so, suppressed the revolutionary strivings of ordinary people. But restricted by the neoconservative political climate since 1980, lacking a strong Left movement, and for personal reasons as well, many activists channeled their social justice work through professional careers, including prominent positions in government, social services, and academia. Paradoxically, Aoki, as a Third

World Leftist, separated from the grassroots movements at the moment when Asian American, Black, and Chicano activists were turning to Marxism–Leninism–Maoism.[56]

Aoki's work in the community college system in many ways appears to be a break from his radical work in the 1960s. But Aoki's political opposition toward working within the system always contained ambivalence. Even at the height of his Marxist activism, he sought mainstream educational credentials and held on to glimpses of the American Dream. When his work to establish Ethnic Studies placed him in proximity with the university power structure, he learned to follow standard protocol and procedures. These lessons became more salient after he moved to the new Merritt College in the Oakland Hills. He was now working in a fairly mainstream educational system and in a period of increasing conservatism. The times required new methods and Aoki grew to be more tactically flexible. He became more willing to see people in complex ways and less invested in making change through military strategies. At the community college, he was proud to be able to integrate his street smarts and administrative skills in his "uncouth" use of threats of firepower to thwart potential violence on campus.

Beyond a story of activism that waxes and wanes is the exploration of contradictory desires within many activists to dismantle an unequal system while simultaneously desiring mobility and/or inclusion within that system. I see in Aoki's narrative ambivalent desires about being recognized by the Japanese American community and by his professional colleagues. The applause for his testimonial at the redress hearings was so meaningful because it signaled an affirmation by the mainstream Japanese American community.[57] Aoki reflected on his winning the Academic Senate presidency in 1996: "My victory on that election was one of the most personally satisfying moments of my life. I got three-quarters of the votes. It was obvious that the faculty overwhelmingly trusted me to shepherd the group through the leadership crisis."[58] Significantly, Aoki's colleagues supported him despite the announcements of his radical past, suggesting that they either embraced his radicalism or saw it as irrelevant to his present work. Either way, they could see him as a whole and still view him as an admirable leader. He had gained the respect and recognition that most of us desire, in addition to receiving important feedback for one who felt marginalized throughout his life. This again points to the weakness of U.S. society and of U.S. social movements that offer uneven opportunities for sustainable contributions and community building. In this context, Aoki saw in the community colleges, more so than in the elite universities, opportunities to build just such alternative institutions and communities.

Through his quarter-century career in the community college system, Aoki resolved the duality of the educational system (discussed in chapter 8) by teaching about critical social issues, providing academic counseling to marginalized students, and providing leadership to his colleagues. He also found ways to work with people with diverse political beliefs and varied methods for creating change. While his radicalism created a certain unease with his professional work, in the end, he was quite proud of the ways he translated his strivings for freedom and justice toward enabling working-class youth, students of color, and the faculty and staff around him to achieve some measure of equality and fulfillment.

11 "At Least I Was There"

The Death of Huey Newton and
Birth of Panther Commemorations

Huey was murdered in August 1989 on the streets of Oakland.[1] His death was personally a very crushing blow to me. Even though Huey and I had drifted apart, we still occasionally crossed paths. It was painful seeing Huey in that period because his descent into the drug world was rather shocking. It was shocking because I respected him so much and because it was so public. One time, we ran into each other at the annual Black Filmmakers Festival at the Paramount Theater in Oakland, a real posh place. As my date and I were leaving, Huey and his entourage—a female and two bodyguards—were entering. It appeared as if he came floating in the door. He appeared to be heavily under the influence. At one point, he turned to the bodyguards and said, "This is the guy I've been telling you about. This is Richard Aoki. He carries a .357." The lobby was not very big and people were going in and out. He stood out because he was dressed to the max in a brand-new, long fur coat. It was obvious who he was. I shuddered because I was packing that night. I had a .45 on me and said, "I don't need this." My date was a little curious afterward. She was someone I had met professionally, an African American from Detroit, and didn't know anything about my past. This was in the early to mid-1980s.

Then there were other times when Huey and I would have a little time to chat, but nothing deep and profound. There was no basis for that. In April 1989, when he was serving time in the North County Jail in Oakland, he had a note smuggled out to me. I had been concerned about his continued activities in the drug world. I was glad that he wrote that note because I started looking into residential treatment programs for him once he got out of jail. I think Huey knew through the vine that I was trying to get him help. So I was looking forward to him getting released. However, after he got out, he didn't contact me.

Instead, he went back to the streets of West Oakland and that's where he was killed. When he died, it kind of shocked me, but it also didn't shock me.[2]

Events started moving fast after Huey's death. The founders of the *Commemorator,* a newspaper started by former Black Panthers, and others organized a big event at Bobby Hutton (DeFremery) Park in 1990. I was asked to speak. "It has come to the attention of the committee that you have made a major contribution to the Party. You were a personal friend of Huey as well. Bobby [Seale] is going to be there and a bunch of other Panthers. We want you to be in the group too." At first I was reluctant to accept the invitation because I had my professional career and it was starting to look good. I was just elected Academic Senate president at the College of Alameda and I didn't run on the basis of my radical political activities.[3] But I thought about it and said, "This is the first time that I will ever say publicly that I was a member of the party and be identified as a field marshal." Then I was asked to wear my uniform. The first issue of the *Commemorator* covers that particular event. Now I always felt that my contribution was modest and I'm not one of those that likes to see my picture in the front page because it's usually bad news. But I am glad in a way that Harvey took that picture of Bobby and me.[4]

My coming out of the closet at that event snowballed because two KQED public broadcasting producers, Ray Telles and Lewis Cohen, decided to do a documentary on the history of the Black Panther Party. The result was "Black Power, Black Panthers." When they contacted me, my first question was, "Who sent you?" It was David Hilliard. I figured if they were going to document the history, now that I'm officially out of the closet, what else have I got to lose? It had been twenty years since my party days. I researched the two producers and their reputations were impeccable. Ray Telles had gained a reputation for documenting the struggles of the farm workers. Lewis Cohen had a good spot in the African American area. So I agreed to that interview for their documentary. As we were figuring out a location for the interview, I thought maybe the college. I sure wasn't going to have it at my place, which in that period of time was a dump. Cohen volunteered his living room and that's where you see me getting interviewed. *Black Power, Black Panthers* aired on KQED television, a PBS affiliate. To this day, I think that documentary and Lee Lew-Lee's *All Power to the People* are the two best sources for the history of the BBP.[5]

The next morning after it aired, there was a Post-it on my desk asking me to see the president of the college as soon as I got to work. I thought this was a little unusual. When I became Academic Senate president, the college president, Ronald Kong, and I had set up a working relationship. We were both busy, so he kept a folder with my name on it and I had a folder with his name on it. Then we'd meet once a week and discuss the materials in our folders. The good news is that Ron and I had a good relationship. So I got my Coca-Cola, my beverage of choice in the morning at work, and sauntered over to the president's office, "What's up, my man!" He said: "There's something I don't understand about you, Richard. I got a phone call from the chancellor this morning before I came to work. Two board members called him last night saying they saw you in a documentary on the Black Panthers. What's going on?" I briefly told him that there was a documentary done on the BPP and I was asked to participate in the production. I didn't see anything outlandish or negative about it. I didn't even mention the college, although in the credits, I was identified as the president of the faculty at the College of Alameda. That was my undoing. But if you look at the tape, I didn't say anything about the college.[6]

So at the next board meeting, I showed up. I had to show up anyway since I was president of the faculty. I took a couple of copies of the documentary. At this meeting, I was minorly hostile because I thought they were making too big a deal out of my appearance. I was in the middle of a professional mission—to implement the educational reform bill—and I don't need side battles to take place. I said, "In the credits, I was listed as the president of the faculty at the College of Alameda. Don't you understand the importance of that?" They looked at me. I said, "In this period of declining enrollment and with our emphasis on outreach to the African American community, anybody that saw that documentary would say, 'If a former Black Panther could become the president of the faculty, then that's a school I want to send my child to.'" Now the African American student population at Alameda was the lowest of the four colleges in the district. So I threw that back in their faces and they had to chuckle about how quick I was on the uptake. Ron was over on the side, shaking his head: "I knew Richard was different. Everybody told me so. But they didn't tell me anything like this!" But I was cool with him and he was cool with me after that.

The Twentieth Anniversary of the Third World Liberation Front

The twentieth-anniversary reunion of the TWLF strike at Berkeley also took place in 1989, a few months before Huey's death. Sumi Cho, then a graduate student at UC Berkeley, did a good job in organizing the weeklong series of events. There was a lot of work put into dredging up old photographs and slogans and putting them on the flyers and programs to publicize the event. This was big time. That photo of Manuel Delgado, Charlie Brown, and myself represented the spirit of solidarity throughout the reunion. It was the main image used on the flyers and programs of the Commemoration Committee and in the newspaper coverage. The organizers were able to bring back most of the main TWLF leaders. I was excited about reuniting with those who also played a significant role in creating the Department of Ethnic Studies. The thirtieth TWLF anniversary sparked another strike. But the twentieth anniversary was about commemoration, remembering the 1969 strike and its legacy. My presentations were lightweight in that I had nothing profound to say. More than speech making, I was just happy to reunite with my colleagues and sit back and talk. We didn't have a tenth-anniversary reunion and I hadn't seen most of them in twenty years.[7]

You asked if this reunion sparked any desire in me to become politically active. Not really. By that time, I was pretty satisfied with my career, where I was getting respect. This reunion was frosting on the cake. But to a degree, things I avoided or ignored or didn't feel I had the time for suddenly became quite manifest. Now remember, even during my period of dormancy, I kept abreast of what was happening in the world. I saw that worldwide imperialism had much more regenerative powers than Marx, Lenin, or Mao had envisioned. When the Gulf War took place in 1991, I was approached by Jean Yonemura and Yuri Miyagawa, two Japanese American veteran activists, to oppose any possible internment of Arab Americans. They approached me and asked me if I would be part of the group organizing an event in Oakland, sponsored by the Unity Organizing Committee. I didn't do anything except show up at meetings and register my support. But what they did to show Japanese American solidarity for Arab Americans was important.[8]

Renewal: Black Panthers and Mumia Abu-Jamal

Meanwhile, I was approached by Steve McCutchen, who came out of the Baltimore BPP chapter, served with distinction, sided with the Newton faction when most of the East Coast went with Cleaver, and came to the Bay Area when Huey called all Panthers to help with local electoral work.[9] Steve maintained contact with the veterans. Steve was excited that I came out of the closet and had suspected way back in the 1970s that I was a member and a field marshal, although my identity wasn't that widely known by the rank and file, especially those who joined after '68. They started inviting me to make presentations at all these Black Panther commemoration events. At one event, Steve introduced me as "the unsung hero of the BPP." I almost fell off my chair because I didn't think that much of the role that I had played. Then Steve called me and asked me to serve on the Marshall Eddie Conway defense committee. I do believe in supporting our political prisoners, so I said, "Include me in." I didn't play an active role, but the fact that I even supported meant something because by then, around the early nineties, I thought things were far gone. We fought the great fight and we lost.[10]

Then in 1995, I got a call from Steve. Tom Ridge had been elected governor of Pennsylvania and set an execution date for Mumia Abu-Jamal, the famed U.S. political prisoner. This is when I really became active. Don't forget, I had gone on record as early as 1984 in support of Mumia. Mumia was a Black Panther and his case reminded me so much of Huey's: both were framed for killing a cop. The evidence supporting Mumia's innocence was mounting. My opinion was, Mumia is innocent. Free Mumia! I wasn't for any of this new trial stuff, but at the very least, we had to keep him from being executed. So I got involved in helping organize at least three or four activities for Mumia's defense. One event was a march from the BART MacArthur station in Oakland to the UC Berkeley campus. I did some of the security work. So I arrived really early to the BART station where the march would begin. I had never seen that many cops, riot cops, out there since the sixties. They had them four to a car. They had motorcycle cops. They had the BART K-9 core. What is going on? All we wanted was a march. So I called over a blond-haired, blue-eyed girl who was organizing with us to go across the street and find out why there's so many cops out here. So she went over there, chatted, came back, and told us that the reason was this march was in support of a cop killer. I thought I noticed that one of the cops happened to be the son of an officer killed by a member of the BPP. I said, "This is heavy. If somebody so much as sneezes badly, somebody's going to get hurt." So the word went down the line, cool it. When we're marching, stay on the sidewalks, don't block the traffic. They're waiting for an excuse to come after us. It was so important that I got one of my closest friends from high school who happened to live on the path of the march to join us. He wasn't political and wouldn't get involved, but I was willing to risk my friend getting hurt because we had to get the numbers out there. The march proceeded without incident until it hit the Berkeley campus and then a minor riot took place—a little fire in a trash bin. But it wasn't anything like what could've come down in Oakland.[11]

I was exhausted by that work. I hadn't been involved that way for years and it was an emotionally draining experience. My personal life was a little shaky too. My girlfriend at the time began to ask questions: "What are you doing? Where you going?" "Mumia." "When are you getting back?" "I don't know." If I had told her more, I would have gotten more static. "How come you're defending a cop killer?" I had a feeling that the ones I did talk with about my politics

thought I was crazy—crazy because I was so sure about my politics and so ada-
mant about my commitments. Others can say, "Richard's insensitive. Richard's
too much of a fanatic." But remember, I had a fiancée, we were going to get
married. Because I told her what I was doing, we didn't get married. You think
I'm going to play that same ol' broken record again?

"There's Nothing Else Left from the Struggle of the 60s": Affirmative Action

In 1996, Proposition 209 was introduced to ban affirmative action throughout
California. Even though Prop 209 affected me professionally and politically, I
didn't go all out against it because, to me, it was just another reformist issue. But
I was vice president of the faculty at the College of Alameda and a number of
ethnic minority faculty expressed concern. So I did what I could. At a state-
wide Academic Senate conference, a half dozen of us—all Senate presidents,
vice presidents, et cetera—caucused and wrote up a resolution. We lobbied like
hell and managed to get the floor. I remember what this one lobbyist said to our
group: "We're conducting our own polls. It's close now. So when you get back
to your constituents, make sure the vote gets out and we will win." But Prop 209
passed.[12] At the next convention, we cornered the guy and asked, "What happened?" He said, "It was that subconscious White vote." I just shook my head.
This guy is being paid big-time money and he didn't understand racism?

As the campaign to oppose 209 built up, my former student Dolly Veale
contacted me and pushed me to take a public stand against 209 based on my
political background. At that time I was reluctant to pimp on my Black Panther
background because I had put that long history to rest. But then I realized,
there's nothing else left from the struggle of the sixties. That's how far we had
lost ground: that we were reduced to defending affirmative action. So I accepted
Dolly's invitation to speak on a panel of Asian Americans opposing the repeal of
affirmative action here in Berkeley, sponsored by the Revolutionary Communist
Party.[13] Dolly was also insistent about getting my signature for a document
called "An Open Letter to Our Fellow Asian Brothers and Sisters: Join the Fight
to Defend and Expand Affirmative Action," published in *Hitting Critical Mass,* a
journal of the Asian American Studies program at UC Berkeley.[14] It was signed
by Steve Wong, an original AAPA member; Jeffrey Chan, professor of Asian
American Studies at San Francisco State; Dylan Rodriquez, then a graduate student in Ethnic Studies at UC Berkeley, as well as Dolly Veale and myself. I didn't
write the document, but I agreed to every word. I understand that there was
a fight on the editorial board about whether or not to print this document

because it was more political than academic. When I heard about the argument I almost fell on the floor. That a scholarly journal that represents the department born in the struggle even questions whether something like this should be included is beyond me.[15] I think those three items—my professional input, speaking on that panel, and signing off on that document—were enough. Like I said, that issue was so reformist, I sometimes felt ashamed that I was even associated with such a Mickey Mouse issue.

Writings about Richard Aoki

Then around the late 1990s, three things happened real fast. First, Dylan Rodríguez approached me to write an article on me. I had been interviewed before by undergraduate students at Berkeley a half dozen or so times for class papers. I was just a resource person to fill in background material on the concentration camps or whatever. Dylan had a different approach; he wanted to do a story on my life. Dylan was in graduate school, had cosigned that affirmative action document, and Harvey vouched for him, so I let him interview me. I didn't think much about it until I saw what he wrote. He titled the article "Thinking Solidarity Across 'Generations': Richard Aoki and the Relevance of Living Legacies," published in *Shades of Power,* newsletter of the Institute for Multi-Racial Justice. He said "living legacies," but I see it as my obituary; it's that good. His major contribution is that he dredged me out of obscurity. I also like the way he framed my life within the context of Frantz Fanon's ideology.

Second, Harvey approached me and said, "There are some people that want to interview you about the Asian American Movement, the Panthers, and the Third World strike." It was for a publication called *Giant Robot,* coedited by Martin Wong and Eric Nakamura. Before I agreed I checked out the publication because I had never heard of it. I was appalled. I had never seen anything like it. It's a hip-hop publication. Richard Aoki and hip-hop—we don't necessarily go to together. But sometimes when I have these initial reservations, I don't close things off automatically. Harvey said, "Go ahead and do it, Richard. What have you got to lose?" I said, "I could be the laughingstock of the movement." What I didn't know is that Nakamura and Wong were serious as a major heart attack. At first, I didn't think much of it, but then I found out, they're interviewing Yuri Kochiyama, Mo Nishida, Alex Hing, and others. I eagerly awaited that issue to see what it turned out like. I know that from an academic standpoint, it might appear superficial. But they had the audacity to connect the Black Panthers and Yellow Power. It was political dynamite, as far as I'm concerned. Thirty years had gone by since Asian American Studies was formed, and this was the first time that I saw a serious approach to the Black Panthers and Yellow Power.[16]

Third, Dolly Veale shows up in my face again. An anthology was being put together on the history of the Asian American radical movement, edited by Fred Ho, along with Diane Fujino and Steve Yip. They were trying to get written contributions or interviews with about thirty different members of the AAM going all the way back to the genesis. I said, "Good luck." It'd be a miracle to pull together all these strong individuals. I had known Steve Yip when he was a freshman at Berkeley working with AAPA. I had heard mixed things about Fred Ho, but found out he's politically serious. If they're solid politically, I can tolerate a lot on the other end. I had never heard of Diane Fujino, but I got reports that "she cool." I found out she was a professor at UC Santa Barbara and wondered if she was suicidal. I mean this could be a career bender for her to be associated with lowlifes like us. So I did my security check and everybody looked good. Meanwhile, Dolly got on my case until I consented. That's how the first lengthy interview about my life got into Legacy to Liberation.[17]

Those three publications made me feel like I did something. It may have not been that much, but the world now knows that I played a role in the movement. Opinions may vary about the significance of my contributions, but at least I was there.

The TWLF Thirtieth Anniversary Sparks a New TWLF Strike

Along comes late 1998—this is right after I retired—Harvey Dong, Douglas Daniels, and I were having coffee in Harvey's kitchen. At that time, Harvey had entered the doctoral program in Ethnic Studies at Berkeley. It was ironic that Harvey, being one of the founders of the department, was now an active graduate student. Harvey dropped this idea, "What do you guys think about a thirtieth-anniversary reunion of the TWLF?" Douglas and I looked at him like graduate school must be hard, so hard that Harvey's starting to his lose his marbles. The twentieth anniversary was a good-time thing and if it wasn't for Sumi Cho, that wouldn't have happened. Next thing we know, Harvey managed to get the seal of approval from the Ethnic Studies Department and started to secure funding for a reunion. So along comes the reunion in April 1999. I had just had major surgery and I was really physically weak. But since I had my signature on the invitation, I had to be at the first session. Harvey and Douglas practically carried me into the event. Over the weekend, a bunch of us veterans got to talking with the students and we were shocked to discover how much ground the department had lost over the last thirty years. Still, I didn't think much more about it. We had a good time and it was good to talk with the students. So I was shocked when, the following week, the students took over Barrows Hall and I saw on TV the same students I'd been talking with a couple of days earlier. That lifted my spirits, as I recovered from surgery.[18]

The first night of the strike, there's a big rally in the back of California Hall, which houses the chancellor's office. I'm standing minding my own business, then all of a sudden the speaker says, "We have Richard Aoki in the audience." Harvey was laughing because I wasn't prepared to speak. So I introduced myself. Now I needed a title. Just like in the TWLF strike, it was important to have a title. So on the spot, I said, "I'm the provisional representative of the Third World strikers of 1969. As the spokesperson for that class, I'm here to tell you, we support you 100 percent." After it was over, Harvey nudged me and laughed, "I don't recall us having a meeting electing you the provisional representative." The reason why I felt bold enough to make that statement was that we had just met over the weekend and I was tuned in with the TWLF veterans. It was one of those times when the students needed to hear those words of encouragement.[19]

I didn't play a major role; however, I was there from the beginning to the end, watching it unfold and culminate in a victory for the students. I made a number of speeches to offer moral support to the students from the veterans. I have two observations. First, I'm convinced that Ethnic Studies was saved by the '99 student strike. Second, the leadership of the two strikes was very different. The '69 strike leadership was mostly men and many veterans. The '99 strike leadership was primarily women, Asians, Africans, and Latinas.

The students voted to have a hunger strike to put more pressure on the university. I remember one student asked me, "Mr. Aoki, how did you guys decide on tactics?" I bit my tongue when they talked about bringing this mighty university to a close through a hunger strike. But I felt I had to be there. So every night those hunger strikers were out there, I was out there giving my support and it's cold and I'm recovering from surgery. I saw this as the continuation of our strike, which we didn't end in 1969, but declared a moratorium. Now I had predicted that they'd lose that hunger strike. But history moves in strange ways. Chancellor Berdahl's order to arrest the hunger strikers was the worst move he could have made. When the students got arrested, there were ten times as many there at the noon rally the next day. The campus and community support increased and the student negotiators managed to secure from the university eight faculty positions, restoration of funds for the Department of Ethnic Studies, a student center, and money for support programs. I couldn't believe it. Any one would have been a major victory, and they got four![20]

9/11 and Its Aftermath: Organizing in Vulnerable Times

Between 1999 and 2001, because I was retired, I started making more and more public appearances, mostly guest lecturing in courses at local colleges and universities about the period of the sixties, the struggle for national liberation, and the creation of Ethnic Studies at Berkeley. I also began speaking more and more at community-based events, mostly in the African American community on the history of the BPP and Mumia Abu-Jamal. So I was bibbity-bopping along at a moderate pace until September 11, 2001.

I will admit that I was shocked and awed by the enormity of that historic event. The ironic thing is that about six months earlier I made a presentation at Revolution Bookstore where I almost predicted this type of event. In my presentation, I developed how twenty-first-century globalism was twentieth-century neocolonialism, which was nineteenth-century imperialism, which was eighteenth-century capitalism. If you look at the major social and economic problems that exist in the world today, you can trace them to the economic political system of capitalism and its mutated varieties. Capitalism is a system that places property rights over human rights, that produces for greed instead of need, that places profits before people. Lenin in his work *Imperialism: The Highest Stage of Capitalism* points out that the basic elements of capitalism/imperialism consist of four components: resources, labor, finance capital, and markets. The Third World provides an overseas source of raw materials like oil, lumber, agriculture, and in some cases cultural goods. The second component is cheap labor. We've seen that manifested by the importing of immigrant labor and now the outsourcing of jobs and manufacturing. Labor overseas is much cheaper and allows capitalists to increase their productivity and their profit at the expense of the United States working class. This is straightforward Marxist theory: that the bourgeoisie tries to extract as much blood as it can from the international proletariat. We see that the drive of capitalists for higher productivity and higher profits means more misery and more suffering for the workers.[21] This is a very tragic consequence of globalism. The third component of this new world order has to do with the need for capitalism to continually expand, especially in finance capital, so you see economic penetration taking place into even the most remote sections of the Third World. The fourth component is a bit more insidious. It's about developing a market to dump not only surplus commodities but also dangerous commodities as well.

So what's my Marxist analysis of September 11 and the U.S. invasions of Afghanistan and Iraq? As I said, I wasn't entirely surprised by 9/11. As the system of globalism took a great leap forward, especially after the fall of the Soviet

Union in the early 1990s, the world changed dramatically because dialectically the Soviet Union ceased to be the U.S.'s opponent. The United States' world dominance grew in the absence of the Soviet Union. One just has to look at how people who have been oppressed in the past have reacted to their oppression. They didn't just pray their way into freedom, some shot their way into freedom. That's what happened with 9/11. Just look at the targets—the Pentagon representing U.S. military domination and the World Trade Center representing the seat of global finance capital. So that's why I say I wasn't totally surprised. As Malcolm X said, chickens be coming home to roost. Then too the U.S. was motivated by controlling the oil in that region. So I do see these wars as a continuation of the United States' efforts to maintain its global dominance as the major imperial power.[22]

Shortly after 9/11, Yuri Kochiyama connected with me. Yuri and I, up to that point, had interacted only superficially after her relocation from Harlem to Oakland, primarily due to her physical limitations and the fact that I was just coasting along. Within a couple of months of 9/11, Yuri launched a series of meetings and other activities to protest U.S. terrorism. We formed an All People's Coalition, which became the People's United Front (PUF). Our first event was to have a community speak-out on the war on terrorism on December 8, 2001. Our position was that the United States is the biggest terrorist internationally and at home. Our flyer stated, "The war on terrorism is a war on all people from Oakland to Kabul." The crowd was fairly small, but I was actually heartened by the turnout for a number of reasons. In that climate of repression and anxiety, those who showed up represented the die-hards. We had a strong turnout of individuals and organizations from the Black movement, the prisoner and political prisoner movements, Palestinians and Arabs, and the general Left. I'm also convinced that our small numbers protected us from being arrested or hassled by the police. I have to be candid, had I still been employed, I may not have spoken at the event. Think about the hell I caught in my professional life just for speaking out against a bourgeois reformist issue, Clinton's welfare reform. Think how much worse it would be to accuse the United States of being a terrorist in that stiflingly patriotic climate.[23]

We attempted to hammer out a solid political program. We had a broad spectrum of individuals and organizations, all Left of center and mostly anti-imperialist and Third World. We used the case of Mumia Abu-Jamal as a domestic example of what we stood for. In fact, at our first event, the main speaker was Mumia's attorney, Eliot Grossman. Then, we began having a series of meetings with Jack Heyman, executive board of the International Longshore and

Warehouse Union Local 10; Gerald Sanders, a longshoreman and former Black Panther; the Labor Action Committee to Free Mumia Abu-Jamal; and PUF. If you recall, the ILWU shut down the ports on the entire West Coast in 1999. Jack was one of the key people in getting the union to officially support Mumia and in initiating the work stoppage. During these meetings, we agreed that the defense of Mumia Abu-Jamal was important, that we needed to connect U.S. domestic and foreign policies. So here I was, connecting labor and Black revolutionary nationalism, two of the biggest struggles I worked on in the 1960s.[24]

We organized a series of other events, including more community speakouts. We also set up a speakers bureau because the various college and university campuses in the Bay Area were thirsting for alternative views. About fifteen to twenty of us in PUF, myself included, became members of the speakers bureau. Over a three- to four-month period, we spoke at virtually all the college and university campuses in the larger Bay Area, from Sacramento State, to San Francisco State, to San José. I took the responsibility for appearing at UC Berkeley and the Peralta community colleges. Over time, more organizations and more individuals came forward to express their discontent with the U.S. system. Our work culminated in an All People's Tribunal to charge the U.S. government with ethnic cleansing, terrorism, and genocide. Gerald Sanders and Mel Mason and myself, all former Black Panthers, were invited to speak. Other speakers were Russell Redner of the American Indian Movement (AIM), Curly Estremera of the Black Liberation Army and Young Lords, and Kawal Ulanday of the Committee for Human Rights in the Philippines.[25]

So PUF's chugging along and then in 2003, the issue of the imminent invasion of Iraq comes along. It was fortunate that PUF got off the ground soon after 9/11, so we were a substantive political organization by 2003. As PUF was doing its activities, we begin to discuss how best to oppose the war. Now Yuri and I had already signed off on the initial call for action by Not in Our Name.[26] We agreed with NION's principles. There was a broad spectrum of opposition, ranging from clergy to liberals to radicals. The mass demonstrations were effective to a degree, but I've always thought that it was the militant segments of the antiwar movement that kept up the pressure. In the sixties, though there were those who tried to stop the troop train, mostly what I saw was a lot of marches and demonstrations. That's what I saw coming down pre-Iraq, people running around, waving signs, and showing their disapproval of the imminent U.S. invasion of Iraq. I will say, I was surprised and inspired by the huge demonstrations that took place around the world, even before the U.S. invaded Iraq. In PUF, we were developing our strategy about the U.S. invasion. Of course, we took the anti-imperialist position. This is different from liberals' hands-off Iraq thing that's about saving their sons and daughters from going off to fight some damn war. Our position was that the United States wasn't doing this to save the world from terrorism. In fact, the U.S. was the biggest terrorist and was going to war to maintain U.S. world dominance. PUF operated on two levels. On one level, we supported the calls for mass demonstrations and participated in them. On the second level, we thought the two major antiwar groups, NION and ANSWER [Act Now to Stop War and End Racism], weren't going far enough. That's when one of the PUF people came up with this bright idea: a national general strike to be held on the day the U.S. invades Iraq. By that time, it became apparent that the United States was not wavering in its course toward the invasion, despite having the flimsiest of all pretexts and being opposed by the United Nations and most of the world. Our plan for a general strike came from the history of general strikes to achieve social and political changes and also from our collaboration with the Labor Action Committee. The idea was to show the power of labor and of consumers to shut down business as usual. We felt a general strike would be earth shattering, but wondered if we could pull it off. We worked hard to communicate our position and found isolated pockets of concurrence, but the strike never happened. There has been a lot of self-criticism regarding our inability to pull this off. My own opinion is that we lacked the strong organizational base to swing this; in other words, we had too few resources, too few people, too little money, and too little time.[27]

As expected, the U.S. invaded Iraq. This was March 20, 2003. On the day of the invasion, I got really involved. In the morning, I was trying to stop traffic on the freeway. In the afternoon, I zipped up to UC Berkeley to protest and almost got arrested with 126 students and others that were arrested. In the evening, I was in the financial district, cheering the team on as they were visiting Starbucks and Citicorp bank and making external renovations to the front of those business. I am confident that the U.S. invasion and occupation of Iraq will go down in history as one of the brashest acts of globalism in the twenty-first century. It has also launched widespread pessimism about the promises of freedom and democracy in the United States.[28]

Awards and Recognition

Very shortly thereafter, I collapsed and ended up in the hospital. The second day I was there, I got a phone call from Yuri chiding me for overextending myself and suggesting I be grounded for a little while to get my health back. I have to be candid, the combination of old age and lack of physical activity contributed to my hospitalization. After my brief hospital stay, I bounced back into some unexpected events. In fact, my hospitalization precluded me from attending an event at Fresno State, where I was a recipient of a Kwame Ture Lifetime Achievement Award. There were two students from UC Davis that I had been mentoring, Mike Cheng and Ben Wang, who accepted the award on my behalf. At the time, Mike and Ben were working on a documentary about my life.[29] I was flabbergasted when I was informed that I was receiving the award. I've had respect for Kwame Ture from way back when he was known as Stokely Carmichael of SNCC and made the call for Black Power. Then I was honored to be included among the other recipients: Yuri Kochiyama; David Brothers, a founding member of the New York BPP and a close comrade of Kwame Ture in SNCC and the All-African People's Revolutionary Party; Chief Ernie Longwalker; the Big Mountain Grandmothers in their struggles for Native Americans; and Dolores Huerta of the farmworkers movement.[30]

Six months later, I received an invitation to participate in an event sponsored by the Japanese American Citizens League, Berkeley chapter. The event was part of the Berkeley JACL's East Bay Living History Project, this time to honor Japanese Americans who contributed to the early AAM. Now to be invited by the JACL was especially surprising to me. I received the invitation from Eugene Tomine, who I met in the late 1960s or early 1970s when he and other Asian Americans at UC Berkeley's Boalt Law School got involved in defending political activists like myself. I initially declined. To understand why, we have to review the history of the JACL.

At the program that night, I said, "It's a little awkward to be on this panel because I don't really belong to this group that is so accomplished and so squeaky clean. I'm also ambivalent about my feelings to the JACL because of its past history."[31] I showed the picture of me and my brother inside Topaz and said, "I was not a happy camper. When I found out about the JACL's role in encouraging the Japanese Americans to comply with evacuation, I was more unhappy."[32] I had been highly critical of the JACL not only for their collaborationist role with the U.S. government during World War II, but also because during the Civil Rights period I didn't see them step forward actively to support the struggle of African Americans for freedom, justice, and equality.[33] Then, during the struggle for redress and reparations, JACL, as I recall, was initially reluctant to step into that battle.[34] I explained my reservations about the JACL to Eugene so that there would be no misunderstanding of about where I stood. However, 9/11, being a defining moment, helped redefine the JACL in my own mind. The JACL as an organization, especially in the Bay Area, leaped forward to declare solidarity with our Muslim brothers and sisters and to speak out against any possible internment of Muslims. While the past history of the JACL seem politically thwarted, more recent events show JACL making a positive contribution.[35] So I agreed to participate in the program.

Ironically, most of the people who were honored at this event were individuals I had worked with during the sixties, including Ken Kawaichi and Dale Minami. They both came out of that group of Asian American Boalt Law School students in the late sixties and early seventies. I publicly thanked Ken and Dale for stepping forward and saying, "We will defend Richard." Ken represented me in my TWLF strike arrests and Dale represented me when I had those problems getting my community college credentials. I also received a handcrafted Japanese plate recognizing my activism and community service.[36]

I brought up the two events that occurred in 2003, the Kwame Ture and the JACL awards, because they were unusual. Throughout my political life, these types of recognition didn't seem to be plentiful. Getting the JACL award was especially a mind bender. I mean, this is *the* mainstream Japanese American organization. So I'm pleased now that I didn't boycott the event. While those of us that participated in the struggle didn't do it for a lifetime recognition award, I did interpret this as, "Well, I didn't waste forty years of my life."

A REBIRTH IN ACTIVISM

The Black Panther Party presented Aoki with one of the greatest politically and personally gratifying experiences of his life. It is thus apropos that Aoki's return to grassroots organizing in the early 1990s, his coming home to meaningful work that matched his radical politics, was sparked by the death of BPP cofounder Huey Newton. With the passage of time, former Panthers could seek to understand the significance of an organization that longtime FBI director J. Edgar Hoover dubbed "the greatest threat to the internal security of the country" and that historian Clayborne Carson said best "inspired discontented urban African Americans to liberate themselves from oppressive conditions."[37] Brought together by Newton's death, former Panthers began to organize commemorations to honor the legacy of the BPP, and Aoki, for the first time, "came out" publicly as a Panther.

Simultaneously, another embodiment of Third World radicalism, the twentieth- anniversary celebrations of the TWLF strike, further spurred Aoki's activist reengagement. Aoki quite enjoyed the collegial interactions at these commemorations and the remembrances of his involvement with causes larger than himself. Still, he only gradually returned to activism, as is seen in his minimal support for political prisoner Marshall "Eddie" Conway; Aoki did not even write to Conway. Still, as Aoki stated, "The fact that I even supported meant something because by then, around the early nineties, I thought things were far gone. We fought the great fight and we lost." Aoki had lost his faith in the movement and in the efficacy of ordinary people to collectively create meaningful social change.[38] But he had not lost his desire for "freedom, justice, and equality" or his radical analysis of social problems.

By the early 1990s, through two decades of work in higher education, Aoki came to see the value of working in tactically flexible ways and how the need for alliances could make strange bedfellows. The vast majority of his colleagues were not radicals but caring people facing a multitude of their own problems while trying to help working-class youth of color. Although he never completely lost his ambivalence toward formal education, he saw it as his professional job to help students succeed in school and to ease the pipeline from community college to the university, even in the absence of explicit critiques of capitalist schooling. While never simplistic in his thinking, he grew to more fully appreciate the complexity of people's political and personal concerns, such as recognizing the ways a conservative, pro-war colleague extended help to an African American student. These changes reflected personal development as well as a way to respond to the political conservativeness of the times. In the face of constricted social movements, Aoki came to see social change as taking place through small gains in individual's lives. His life was made meaningful by helping a Native American student stay in college, supporting a colleague whose son seemed to be racially targeted by police, and helping any number of students live out their dreams.

Still, because Aoki, as a sociologist, social worker, and radical, continued to see a need for the far-reaching transformation of social structures, he was energized by the possibilities presented to him, especially after 9/11, to engage in activist work no longer "too reformist" for his political proclivities. While continuing his Marxist analysis of war and imperialism, Aoki's experiences in the intervening two and a half decades left him with a more flexible approach to social change. In contrast with his self-acknowledged "hard-liner" position against ending the 1969 Third World strike, three decades later, he viewed the hard-core strikers as being "adventurist" in their dismissal of important gains made in the 1999 strike.

In the 1990s, Aoki began to gain public recognition for his political contributions in the 1960s and early '70s. For one whose work as a "samurai among Panthers" and in the grossly underrecognized Asian American Movement obscured his public prominence, it felt good to gain visibility as a noteworthy activist. Even in the late 1960s and early 1970s, when Aoki was revered as a movement leader and iconic figure, there was little public attention on him, except for brief mention in newspaper articles or photographs or in Seale's book, *Seize the Time*.[39] So to be the focus of three published articles, in 1998 and 2000, signaled his political and historic significance to the next generation as well as to himself. While Aoki felt rather ambivalent about the spotlight, it was gratifying to be appreciated and admired in a period when Aoki, though only age sixty, faced serious health problems that sped up his desire to reflect on the meaning of his life. Aoki's comment that "those three publications made me feel like I did something" points to the "looking-glass self" phenomenon. As discussed in the introduction, we construct our sense of self through the social meanings reflected back by others, and what Aoki saw marked his life as historically significant and personally fulfilling.

Epilogue

Reflecting on a Movement Icon

Of Black Panthers and U.S. Soldiers

A processional of old guard Black Panther Party members marched down the aisle of Wheeler Auditorium on the UC Berkeley campus. While their graying hair betrayed their age, they carried the spirit of the party in the large banner they held featuring a black panther over a red star, pronouncing Richard Aoki to be a "People's Warrior," and in the black leather jackets, light blue shirts, and black berets they wore. Thus began the weekend filled with memorial services for Richard Aoki. More than five hundred people attended this service on Saturday, May 2, 2009, in UC Berkeley's largest auditorium. The extensive program featured speakers from across Aoki's life, with particular attention to the activist period of the 1960s–1970s. Bobby Seale, Tarika Lewis, Ericka Huggins, and Mike Tagawa spoke as former Black Panthers. Famed Japanese American activist Yuri Kochiyama was a cherished speaker. A host of others spoke about Aoki's activism in the Asian American Political Alliance and Third World Liberation Front, his professional work in the educational arena, and his recent life. There were musical performances, a martial arts demonstration, and clips from the documentary on his life, making for a lengthy, four-hour program. Aoki would have chuckled at the irony of his memorial being held in Wheeler Auditorium, the same building that burned at the beginning of the Third World strike forty years earlier.[1]

The next day, some two hundred people crowded into the Chapel of the Chimes crematorium and columbarium in Oakland, where part of Aoki's ashes remain, alongside his father's and other Aoki relatives.[2] This more solemn service, while still featuring many activist speakers, focused more on Aoki's personal life with remarks by childhood friends and family members. A lifelong friend since high school, who was on the phone with Aoki three to four times a week for years, talked about their childhood love of Ping-Pong, their frequent escapades to Sweets Ballroom, and their current sports team betting and annual vacations to Reno. A young Asian brother, himself from West Oakland, spoke about a time when Aoki came to guest lecture in his community college class. He was expecting another boring speaker but was surprised by the dynamism of Aoki's talk, which kept him engaged for an hour. He commented on Aoki's ability to see people's potential at a time when he needed a second chance. A former professor and father figure to Aoki disclosed that after his wife died, Aoki took him to the shooting range. He wondered why it was important to Aoki to teach him self-defense, but saw it as Aoki's effort to protect him. The main speaker, a woman minister who met Aoki thirty years earlier, saw Aoki as a compassionate and untiring fighter for justice as well as a rather traditional person in mannerism and in his high regard for order and respect. A young activist relayed how Aoki could sell an event like no other. After a call from Aoki, you thought the event was the most important in the world. Toward the end of the program, two U.S. Army color guards, one Asian American, the other Latino, dressed in formal uniforms complete with white gloves, fastidiously unfolded and re-folded the American flag before a large portrait of Aoki, as "Taps" played. Following the formal program, a long line of speakers gathered for the open mike segment, in which a former Panther led the audience in reciting the BPP slogan, "All Power to the People."[3]

Predictably enough, some in the largely activist audience, most of whom came of age during or after the Vietnam era, were surprised and offended by the presence of the U.S. flag and "Taps" ceremony at Aoki's memorial. They saw Aoki's politics in opposition to U.S. imperialism and militarism, symbolized by the U.S. flag. But the memorial organizers recognized that in Aoki's closet, among the few material possessions kept all these years, hung two neatly maintained uniforms—his Black Panther leather jacket affixed with a Free Huey button and his U.S. Army uniform with an American flag in its pocket.[4] At both memorials, Richard's work in the BPP, AAPA, and TWLF were emphasized, and his BPP uniform hung on Aoki's large portrait with no army uniform in sight. At the Chapel of the Chimes memorial service, anticipated for an audience of family and friends, the organizers wanted to acknowledge the centrality of Aoki's military experiences in his life and to give him a soldier's honoring. Rather than seeing it as an affront to Aoki's politics, they "saw a final irony in the military having to honor a Third World revolutionary."[5]

On Social Death and Revolutionary Dying

On Sunday morning, March 15, 2009, Richard Aoki, at age seventy, passed away. This was the same weekend as the TWLF fortieth anniversary events and the annual Asian Pacific Islander Issues conference that drew many TWLF and AAPA veterans, as well as younger activists and students, to the UC Berkeley campus. Ten days earlier, Aoki had collapsed and was taken to the hospital and days before he died, his kidneys shut down. When I spoke to him during the dozen days he spent in the hospital, he told me that he "wasn't going anywhere." Aoki was not able to attend the TWLF commemoration, but his presence was palpable in the room. Veteran activists repeatedly invoked his name. They spoke about his dedication, his Afro–Asian solidarities, his bad-ass image, his militancy, and his contributions to the TWLF strike and victory. Toward the beginning of his hospitalization, Aoki felt well enough to receive visitors, but by that weekend, he barely spoke by phone other than to his closest friends. As I sat in the San Francisco airport awaiting my flight home, I received a phone call and learned that he had died.[6]

Richard Aoki died "due to complications from longstanding medical problems," stated the widely circulated e-mail announcing his death.[7] If all narratives, rather than containing a single truth, require interpretation and the construction of social meaning, as Norman Denzin contends, then certainly all obituaries, created by design to highlight people's best selves, contain elements of truths and falsehoods.[8] It is true that Aoki had a long history of medical complications. A decade before he died, he had surgery to remove the plaque, or fatty material, from his carotid arteries, located on either side of the neck. Though this procedure opens up the carotid arteries, Aoki still suffered a major stroke. Years later, while sitting at the University Cafe in Berkeley, probably dining on fish, Aoki lamented about how he had planned his retirement around eating greasy bacon and sausage, eggs sunny side up, hash brown potatoes, English muffins dripping with butter, and other artery-clogging foods every morning at this working-class diner. He was profoundly disappointed when his doctor told him that he needed to change his diet. Throughout the next decade, Aoki was hospitalized several times for heart problems and renal failure, among other ailments, and was on a steady dose of medications. He also had diabetes, but still drank ten to twelve cans of Dr Pepper a day—regular, not diet, which tastes terrible, protested Aoki. On the day he was discharged from the hospital in 2003, Aoki told me that he felt like one of the *ronin,* or masterless samurai, in the epic Japanese story of the forty-seven *ronin.* At one point, a mortally wounded samurai picked up his sword and dragged himself to battle, fighting to the end.[9] Aoki had a way of feeling like he was always in battle. But his last years struggling with severe health problems were especially hard. By the last week of his life, "Richard's body couldn't tolerate even his first run of dialysis. When they tried again, on his second run, his heart stopped momentarily and still he continued to lose fluids."[10]

Thus, he did indeed die from long-standing medical problems, but not as the immediate cause of death. Aoki's death certificate identified the most proximal cause: a "bullet wound of the abdomen."[11] The day he died, the phone lines of Aoki's friends were abuzz about his method of death. Was it an accident? Was it suicide? "Richard knows his weapons. He don't make mistakes like that," some of his comrades were saying. My thoughts coincided, but for a somewhat different reason. Those facing terminal illness and an incurably deteriorating body often express a desire to die with dignity, rather than to live with pain and dependency. Significantly, Aoki's elderly mother had passed away two months earlier and his father and brother were already gone, leaving him free from the familial obligations inscribed in the bushido code. This wasn't about being socially isolated. Aoki had a wide circle of friends who called him daily, transported him to appointments, and provided food and sustenance. This was rather a release from the social obligations of caring for those dependent on him.

Aoki's closest friends made a deliberate decision not to disclose how he died. In American culture, suicide is often equated with psychological factors, with weakness and emotional instability, rather than, as Durkheim contends, with social causes.[12] On the one-year anniversary of Aoki's death, the Richard Aoki Memorial Committee released a statement: "During the immediate aftermath of Richard's passing, Richard's friends and comrades focused on a public honoring of Richard's legacy while respecting his personal privacy."[13] They wanted to focus on "what his life meant and not on how he died."[14] There was also a concern that some might copy Aoki's method, especially in this period of economic crisis and generalized anxiety.[15] But suicide can also be viewed as strength—an exertion of control over one's body and life. Afflicted by an incurable illness and a rapidly declining body, Aoki chose to end his life on his own terms. He chose his time and his method. He left no suicide note or sense of premeditation. The method is not surprising given Aoki's lifelong fascination with guns and their ready availability in his home. His method, as opposed to the pills often taken by women, also marked his manliness.[16]

Aoki's death can be understood in terms of Huey Newton's idea of "revolutionary suicide," which is also the title of Newton's autobiography. Newton cited Durkheim to argue for a social contextualization of suicide: "The primary cause of suicide is not individual temperament, but forces in the social environment. In other words, suicide is caused primarily by external factors, not internal ones."[17] "Reactionary suicide" also has a social context; it was, as Newton put it, a succumbing to "self-murder" as a result of a life bound by racism, economic exploitation, daily harassments and humiliations, and a relative lack of control over one's circumstances. By contrast, Newton's concept of "revolutionary suicide" both incorporated and resisted social death. The revolutionary remained affected by conditions of domination. A close friend of Aoki's joked, "Richard you are Black. You got diabetes. You got hypertension. You got heart problems. You Black."[18] Indeed, Aoki's health problems reflected the stress and strain associated with the social conditions of Black life. But the revolutionary also chose to fight back, to infuse "hope and dignity" into his or her struggles. This required a willingness to sacrifice one's own life in an effort to create a new world. Newton explained: "Above all, it demanded that the revolutionary see his death and life as one piece. Chairman Mao says that death comes to all of us, but it varies in its significance: to die for the reactionary is lighter than a feather; to die for the revolution is heavier than Mount Tai."[19] Aoki's self-inflicted gunshot wound represents both the vulnerability and fear that makes his act so human and the honor, courage, and dignity he embodied throughout his life.

Cold War Paradox and Cold War Masculinities

The 1950s are widely viewed as a period of unprecedented material prosperity for the United States. The nation had emerged the victor in World War II, a war that restructured forms of global power, undermining Old World colonialism and developing the indirect, neocolonial ascendancy that enabled the United States, as a latecomer to international capitalism, to compete for global hegemony. Indeed in the postwar period, the United States emerged out of the Great Depression and the Second World War as the dominant world power. "From 1946 to 1964, the United States underwent the most sustained period of economic growth in world history, effectively tripling the average income of Americans."[20] The benefits were many: "Any white high-school graduate could reasonably expect to support a family with his paycheck, to own a home, a car, and plenty of other goods, and to send his children to college."[21] The use of "his" in this sentence is indeed correct.

The establishment of the "family wage" was a gendered enterprise, linking masculinity to the breadwinner ideal and femininity to domesticity.[22] Moreover, alongside this newly acquired material prosperity simmered new fears and new worries. Such was the paradox of the Cold War: anxiety amid abundance. Disrupting the carefully manicured suburban lawn was the bomb shelter, stocked with rows and rows of canned goods, to ensure a family's physical safety in the event of a nuclear attack. But more than providing any substantive safety, the craze for bomb shelters created fears in the general populace, fears of nuclear blowback for the sins of Hiroshima and other atrocities against civilian populations and of Communist threats to the nation's newly acquired power and affluence.[23]

Aoki's story reveals the racial, economic, and gendered fault lines just under the surface of the American good life. The nation's unparalleled consumer prosperity was not doled out equally across divisions of race, class, and gender. Aoki understood this, living as he was in the 1950s with his working-class, single mother in a tiny Berkeley apartment, sharing a bedroom with his brother while his mother slept on the couch in the living room. Jim Crow segregation, de jure and de facto, restricted job and residential mobility for people of color and undermined their ability to build personal wealth through homeownership and enhanced educational opportunities. Japanese Americans, newly out of the concentration camps, faced a mixed reception, symbolized by Richard's father's disillusionment with U.S. democracy and run-ins with the law and by his uncle Shigeo's faith in the model of citizenship whereby "this wonderful country [offers] the best opportunity in the world to accomplish these dreams," though it required working hard from "2–3 a.m. till 9 p.m." to achieve such entrepreneurial success.[24] Even for those on the margins, "the values of the white middle class shaped the dominant political and economic institutions that affected all Americans," such that "there were no groups . . . for whom these norms were irrelevant."[25]

Aoki's life was profoundly shaped by the Cold War milieu. He came of age in postwar America, where Americans wanted "secure jobs, secure homes, and secure marriages in a secure country."[26] The omnipresent shadow of the Great Depression reminded people that their own (and the nation's) present prosperity could vanish quickly. The United States rose to world power through the atomic bomb, and that meant others too might rise up through military maneuvers.[27] Threats to U.S. hegemony—from the Soviet Union, Third World anticolonial wars, domestic Civil Rights struggles, and women's demands for equality—seemed ubiquitous. In this context, U.S. security became equated with a rugged, hard-bodied masculinity, and President-elect Kennedy chastised "soft Americans" as a menace to the "vitality of the nation."[28] It is not surprising that Aoki developed a rather conventional masculinity that embodied "physical strength, bravado, exclusive heterosexuality, stoicism, authority, and independence."[29]

While Aoki was excluded from "hegemonic masculinity," R. W. Connell's term referring to the socially dominant masculinity in a particular historical context, he was, along with most men and women, nonetheless "complicit" with maintaining the gendered order as well as the postwar world order, with the United States as the new hegemonic global power.[30] Straight out of high school, he eagerly joined the army "to be a man." He had been fascinated by guns since childhood and dreamed of becoming an air force fighter pilot. His narrative is filled with military conquests, whether fighting fraternity boys on the picket lines of the Third World strike or beating back the cops in Berkeley and Oakland. The Aoki figure in the Hollywood film *The Panthers* is shown supplying the Panthers with guns. It is easy to read Aoki as a macho warrior. But Aoki's sense of manhood is at once muscular and nurturing, conventional and transgressive.

It was in the tension between complicity with power and marginalization from power that Aoki developed complex (and at times contradictory) forms of masculinities. In the Cold War era, adulthood meant marriage and work, maturity and responsibility.[31] Richard, like his grandfathers and paternal uncles, performed the expectations for masculine responsibility through school, work, and the military. But in the same decade—the 1950s—that saw marriage rates rise to new heights, men were already expressing a masculine mystique, or a boredom with conventional expectations, a full decade before Betty Friedan coined the term "feminine mystique."[32] Some, like Richard's father and maternal uncle, played the playboy as a way to escape the hard work of marriage, while still exerting a heterosexual manhood.[33] Even as Richard exhibited manly maturity in the workplace, he fell short of a significant marker of manhood in the 1950s—that of marriage and family. As Aoki expressed it, social justice came first and personal relationships second. A certain distancing from intimacy is also readily apparent in his narrative, influenced no doubt by his parents' hostile separation as well as his own experiences with parental abandonment. So Aoki made jokes, equating marriage to a "three-ring circus": "First there's the engagement ring. Then there's the wedding ring. Then there's the suffering." He also quipped: "I have a friend who said he didn't know what true happiness was until he got married. Then it was too late." Beyond showcasing his wit, Aoki expressed ambivalence toward marriage. He rejected the loss of personal freedom, feared the intimacy, but also desired the closeness, companionship, and achievement of manhood through marriage.[34] In his words, not getting married may well have been the "greatest personal mistake I ever made." But, or rather because, being a nonplayboy bachelor raises questions in the U.S. mainstream of homosexuality, Aoki told me numerous stories about his (hetero)sexual escapades. He wanted it known that he was not gay, which to Aoki, continued to carry connotations of failed manhood, even as he grew to support gay rights.[35]

In other ways, Richard adapted the flexible masculinities enacted by his father. While Shozo Aoki was a single parent and homeschool teacher, Richard went into the field of social work, a profession associated with "women's work." But, as Christine Williams observed in her study of work and gender, men entering traditionally feminine professions, like nursing, teaching, and social work, do not abandon their gender identities, nor do they necessarily forgo male privilege. Instead, they negotiate the meaning of their masculinity through the workplace. Richard's stories about following prominent men of color into Berkeley's School of Social Welfare and about entering the field to provide leadership to the Black Panthers' survival programs were assertions of masculinity. That Aoki rose to numerous leadership positions in the School of Social Welfare, in Berkeley's Asian American Studies program, and in the Peralta Community College District buttresses Williams's contention that even in predominantly female professions, men tend to hold positions of power. Of course, masculinity is not fixed but rather repeatedly negotiated in interactions and in social institutions.[36] By working as a professional counselor, Richard found ways to express a complex masculinity, one that allowed him to nurture students and to fight against race and class inequalities, to do the mundane work of checking units and to physically protect colleagues and students from potential violence and the rulings of elite courtrooms, and to provide frontline counseling services and to serve as Academic Senate president creating and implementing policy decisions.

In the activist arena as well, Aoki held contradictory tendencies in tension.[37] Even in his obviously muscular fixation on weaponry, the gun symbolized much more than power grabbing or macho posturing. Aoki's activism went far beyond the gun, seeking to empower ordinary people and to build alternative institutions. In the next two sections, I explore further the complicated masculinities that Aoki embodied, at once conventional (as protector of community, nation, and women and children) and potentially transgressive (as a promoter of alternative ways of being).

The Performative Power of the Gun

The gun is the predominant image of the Black Panther Party, elevated to near singular proportions by the mainstream media. The Panthers themselves also promoted this image. But their rhetoric of "picking up the gun" and "offing the pigs" was part of a larger program for liberation, which included community service activities (e.g., free breakfast and clothing programs, escorts for seniors, health clinics), the call for human rights (e.g., full employment, decent housing), and ultimately, the desire for "freedom" and "land, bread, education, clothing, justice and peace," as stated in the first and last points of their Ten-Point Program. In point seven, the party invoked the U.S. Constitution and the Second Amendment right to bear arms as a strategy to end police brutality. Like the Zapatistas twenty-five years later, theirs was a carefully crafted strategy to contest state violence and not a call to armed struggle per se. They were, after all, a grossly unequal military challenge to the organized violence of the state.

Still, the Panthers posed a serious threat to establishment power in at least two significant ways.[38] First, like the guerrilla fighters in Vietnam and the insurrectionists in current-day Iraq, a smaller physical force can achieve a strategic victory, whether or not they actually win the military battle, by disrupting the image of invincibility of a mighty military command and by showing the falsehood behind the stability the outsiders allegedly produce. Second, while the Panthers often invoked Mao's statement that "political power grows out of the barrel of a gun," they also knew that sometimes "power is at the end of the shadow or image of a gun."[39] As Nikhil Singh cogently argues, the Panthers used the power of performance to fight off the dominance of the state.[40] This was most famously displayed in Sacramento when a few carloads of Panthers, visibly armed, marched into the California state capitol. They didn't shoot anyone, but rather used the performative power of the gun to draw national attention to the Mulford Bill, which sought to repeal the law that allowed the public carrying of loaded weapons (as long as they were displayed) in an effort to eliminate the Panther model of police patrolling.

By policing the police, the Panthers represented a largely unacknowledged danger, that is, observes Singh, "the eruption of a non-state identity into the everyday life of the state."[41] By substituting themselves for the performance of the state, the Panthers not only confronted the government's "monopoly on physical violence" but, more significantly, challenged the notion that the state is the only legitimate arbitrator of violence. Moreover, by speaking and acting against the state, the Panthers disrupted the populace's unspoken consent to be ruled. This work is crucial in the struggle to confront U.S. hegemony, domestically and globally. Hegemonic power is, after all, achieved through the development of widespread consensus and belief in the ruling ideology and institutions, even when they are not in the best interest of the nation's majority. And violence and the threat of violence by the state (the stick), in conjunction with ideological institutions like the media (the carrot), are instrumental in manufacturing such hegemonic domination and subjugation.[42]

Like the Panthers, Aoki also engaged a performative use of the gun. By this, I do not mean that the real threat of armed power didn't exist; it did and was used. But Aoki believed as Frederick Douglass did that "if there is no struggle, there is no progress. . . . This struggle may be a moral one, or it may be a physical one, and it may be both moral and physical, but it must be a struggle. Power concedes nothing without a demand."[43] And he believed as Lenin did that the ruling class would not concede power except though "a violent revolution."[44] So he was willing and prepared, following the example of Cuba and Vietnam and many others, to use violence to gain liberation, if necessary. This readiness to use whatever means necessary, whether actually applied or not, is what was important in the contestation of hegemonic power. This is the performative power of the gun. In fact, rather than engaging in much combat in the movement or in the army, Aoki was like a "gun with the safety on."[45] Aoki himself stated, "I pushed the spirit of self-defense . . . [as] a tool to help stop the violence." In his weapons classes, his first emphasis was on gun safety. In the Third World strike at UC Berkeley, Aoki terminated strategies to take power from the police when his assessment spelled danger for student strikers. When serving on internal security during a talk by Huey Newton at Merritt College, Aoki assured the college president that he would "do my utmost in preserving the peace" because "that's why I was there." Following a disturbance in the audience, while Aoki asserted a menacing stance—"I was getting ready to Freddie there; that dude was history in my eyes"—his primary role, as he himself stated, was to avoid bloodshed or any embarrassment to the Black Panthers or the college. Instead of the trigger, Aoki was the safety on the gun, using the symbolic power of violence to stop violence.

In addition to viewing self-defense as a method to resist state violence and hegemonic power, Aoki embraced Frantz Fanon's thesis on the psychology of revolutionary violence. In his widely influential book *The Wretched of the Earth,* Fanon wrote: "At the individual level, violence is a cleansing force. It rids the colonized of their inferiority complex, of their passive and despairing attitude. It emboldens then, and restores their self-confidence."[46] The Mexican and Filipino farmworkers associated with Cesar Chavez's movement articulated a similar ideological decolonizing process, a lifting of the fear when they dared to cross the boundaries of "their place" in the 340-mile march (or pilgrimage) from Delano to Sacramento or when they performed the part of the bosses in the street theater of El Teatro Campesino.[47] By contrast to the BPP, the farmworkers movement embodied the teachings of Gandhi, King, and "nonviolent resistance." Through such resistance, argues King, "the attack is directed against forces of evil rather than against persons who are caught in those forces" and thus seeks to "win his friendship and understanding," rather than seeking "to defeat or humiliate the opponent." Moreover, such resistance "avoids not only external physical violence, but also internal violence of spirit." Nonviolent resistance strengthens the human dignity of the oppressed and of the oppressor. It manifests "agape" love, or the "redeeming good will for all men, an overflowing love which seeks nothing in return."[48]

Even as Fanon advocated revolutionary violence as a "cleansing force," he also recognized that there were costs in the use of such force. The psychiatrist describes in agonizing detail the psychological and physical damage inflicted on individuals, not only as the targets but also as the perpetrators of violence. But Fanon was careful to locate the individual acts in the context of the brutality of colonialism, of poverty and starvation, of limited self-determination and self-power, and of indignity. It was the violence in service to ending colonialism, and not the violence of oppression, that had the potential to be a "cleansing force."[49]

Although there were costs to using violence, Aoki would also agree with Malcolm X and Robert Williams that there were also costs to not using violence in the face of brutal oppression. In his famous "Message to the Grass Roots" speech in 1963, he asked, "How are you going to be nonviolent in Mississippi, as violent as you were in Korea? How can you justify being nonviolent in Mississippi and when your churches are being bombed, and your little girls are being murdered?"[50] Malcolm X was particularly disturbed by the hypocrisy contained in the debate on violence. He questioned why nonviolence was obligatory for the oppressed, while the state could use violence with legal and moral impunity. Even worse, the oppressed were asked to participate in the violence of the state while being asked to denounce the use of violence to gain their own rights and freedom. He proclaimed: "If violence is wrong in America, violence is wrong abroad. If it is wrong to be violent defending black women and black children and black babies and black men, then it is wrong for America to draft us and make us violent abroad in defense of her. And if it is right for America to draft us and teach us how to be violent in defense of her, then it is right for you and me to do whatever is necessary to defend our own people right here in this country."[51]

Robert Williams focused the debate on individual White racists, reinforced by the power of the state. Williams's widely publicized statement, "We must meet violence with violence," made in 1959 in Monroe, North Carolina, was actually a simplification of his views.[52] He explained: "I do not advocate violence for its own sake, or for the sake of reprisals against whites. Nor am I against the passive resistance advocated by the Reverend Martin Luther King and others. My only difference with Dr. King is that I believe in flexibility in the freedom struggle. This means I believe in nonviolent tactics where feasible. . . . But where there is a breakdown of the law, the individual citizen has a right to protect his person, his family, his home and his property."[53] He stressed: "When an oppressed people show a willingness to defend themselves, the enemy, who is a moral weakling and coward is more willing to grant concessions and work for a respectable compromise. Psychologically, moreover, racists consider themselves superior beings and they are not willing to exchange their superior lives for our inferior ones. They are most vicious and violent when they can practice violence with impunity."[54] To Williams, self-defense was a strategy to challenge individual and societal acts of violence and, ultimately, to reduce racist violence and gain equality.

In his advocacy of a mix of methods that might include violent resistance, Williams reflected the ideas of the famous abolitionist Frederick Douglass: "The limits of tyrants are prescribed by the endurance of those whom they oppress. . . . Men may not get all they pay for in this world; but they must certainly pay for all they get. If we ever get free from the oppressions and wrongs heaped upon us, we must pay for their removal. We must do this by labor, by suffering, by sacrifice, and if needs be, by our lives and the lives of others."[55] By 1967, Martin Luther King Jr. had joined the voices against the "destruction of Vietnam." While remaining an advocate of nonviolent resistance, he acknowledged the historical and social context in which violence emerges. While quoting John F. Kennedy of all people, King sounded a lot like Robert Williams: "Those who make peaceful revolution impossible will make violent revolution inevitable."[56]

Aoki understood the performative power of the gun as a strategy to challenge the hegemonic power of the state and the violence of racism, capitalism, and imperialism. Although the masculine method of the gun looms large in his public persona, his political practice overwhelmingly centered on grassroots organizing, radical pedagogy, and the creation of educational opportunities.

On Top–Down Leadership and Participatory Democracy

While Aoki embraced the hierarchical chain-of-command leadership style of the army and some political groups, he also enacted a democratic and flexible practice. In 1999, when the Berkeley hunger strikers asked him what he thought about their strategy, Aoki, wincing as he relayed the story to me, said he had to "bite my tongue." While he saw a hunger strike as an ineffective tactic against the power of "this mighty university," he respected the students' need to determine for themselves the proper goals and methods of their struggle. He also noted with surprise that the hunger strike worked, as the students won many of their demands. Aoki has long displayed a healthy respect for democratic processes, collective organizing, and alliance building. As early as November 1961, while some in the Berkeley Young Socialist Alliance, based in the Trotsky–Stalin split, denounced Fidel Castro as "a traitor to socialism" for accepting Soviet aid, Aoki was among the YSA members who defended the Cuban Revolution and Castro as revolutionary.[57] When working with the Vietnam Day Committee, Aoki helped to pull together a booklet remarkable for its inclusion of political essays by ten liberal-to-Left groups with diverse and at times conflicting ideologies.[58] When, at a national antiwar convention in Washington, D.C., in 1965, "a major struggle developed . . . between the Stalinists and Trotskyists," Aoki apparently sided with the VDC in promoting a united-front practice of bringing together diverse groups to work against the war in Vietnam.[59] From inside the Tri-Continental Students Committee in 1967, Aoki worked to generate support for the Huey Newton Defense Committee and to "produce fraternal relationships" with the Afro–American Student Union.[60] While in the Asian American Political Alliance, Aoki worked to develop both pan-Asian and Third World solidarities. And of course, during the Third World strike, Aoki insisted on collective leadership and equal decision-making powers among the four racial groups comprising the TWLF.

Perhaps most surprising is that Aoki, a hardcore militant, regularly took a compromising position, defending ostracized members, even those on the wrong side of his politics, and working for unity rather than polarizing issues. When the first coordinator of Asian American Studies was ousted for having a fairly authoritative leadership style, allying with the university, and undermining student power, Aoki, if the FBI report is accurate, was one of the few who supported the coordinator.[61] Aoki similarly argued that AAPA needed to organizationally defend a Third World strike arrestee who had voted against the strike, when the arrestee's own brother advocated throwing him to the wolves. Despite being more radical than most and having some ultra-Left tendencies, Aoki was able to see the complexity of human choices as well as to subordinate his own ideas to the collective.

Aoki told me a story that revealed his views on social change and on his own ability to learn and grow. In the late 1960s and 1970s, he participated little in the decadelong struggle to save the International Hotel in San Francisco. The campaign, which drew widespread support from multiple community and activist sectors, sought to secure affordable housing for elderly, working-class Filipino and Chinese men; to promote housing as a human right, rather than a property right; and to oppose a gentrification process that privileged corporate America and undermined the existence of community residences and mom-and-pop businesses. The hotel was also important as a social movement hub, housing several Asian American Movement organizations.[62] Aoki viewed antigentrification struggles as losing battles and thus unworthy of his time. True to his prediction, I-Hotel residents were evicted in 1977 and the building was later demolished. But Aoki came to change his assessment of that struggle. His good friend Harvey Dong, an active participant in the I-Hotel campaign, convinced Aoki that more than focusing only on a single outcome (the eviction), the I-Hotel struggle raised political consciousness, connected students with community members and community issues, and, significantly, developed a mass-based movement. Dong argues that "the only source of power and strength has to be the community itself" and that the "most important contribution" of the late 1960s and 1970s was "the willingness of the youth to go to the masses and learn from them."[63] While Aoki might disagree with Dong's emphasis, he did come to see the value of struggle in changing people's consciousness and in building an activist infrastructure, even when activists lose important battles. The I-Hotel campaign also achieved some material victories: it took a nine-year battle to evict the tenants; the land sat empty for some twenty-five years; and in 2005, community activists, including those who fought the evictions, succeeded, like a phoenix rising from the ashes, in resurrecting a new building on the site of the old, providing low-income senior housing and the International Hotel Manilatown Center to keep alive the memories of the I-Hotel movement.[64] The I-Hotel struggle visibly represented Aoki's desire to empower ordinary people to determine their own lives and, as a materialist, to see utility in the work to change political consciousness.

Antonio Gramsci's concepts of "war of maneuver" and "war of position" are instructive here. Aoki favored a war of maneuver, with efforts at quick combat victories and armed attempts to seize state power. He enjoyed telling stories of developing strategies to outmaneuver the police, of small Asian American men beating burly police officers and fraternity boys, and of moments of solidarity in which activists supported one another physically and politically. But he also recognized the need for a war of position, based on protracted struggle involving ideological and cultural, in addition to economic and political, resistance. This political activity was important in undermining the legitimacy of establishment power and prefiguring a new society, and thereby destabilizing hegemonic power. Aoki objected to participating in the I-Hotel struggle because it could not be won through a war of maneuver, but he worked through war-of-position strategies throughout most of his life. Through the TWLF strike and establishment of Asian American Studies, Aoki sought to develop new ways of thinking about the goals and purposes of education, linking the university to critical analysis and social responsibility. As an educator and activist, he sought to build community institutions to enable people to live with their material human needs met and with dignity and the power to control their own lives. He understood the importance of language and metaphor and of militant style and dress to create a cultural image of manly defiance, in the face of dominant ideology's disempowerment and subordination of ordinary people. And as a counselor in the community colleges, he provided academic guidance, mentorship that strengthened the self-worth of marginalized students, and, though unorthodox, offered financial and legal aide to students and colleagues alike. From the Black Panthers to the community colleges, he worked through the war of position to build civil society, which as Gramsci posits, shapes the ideological consciousness and political engagement of ordinary people and thus changes the conditions that make possible a war of maneuver to seize state power.[65]

In two other areas, Aoki's life represents seeming contradictions. The first explores the planned and random nature of activism. The second centers on racialized differences and solidarities among Asian Americans and African Americans.

"The Wrong Place at the Wrong Time": The Accidental and Intentional Nature of Struggle

A weakness of chronological biographies is their vulnerability to imposing a teleological clarity and logical consistency on individual human development that did not exist at the time. Aoki himself imposes a certain coherency on his political development, from the concentration camps, to West Oakland, to the army, to labor struggles, to Marxism–Leninism, to Black Power and Third World radicalism. But he also remarks on, time and time again, the sometimes aleatory nature of struggle. Aoki was fond of saying about his activist development, "I was in the right place at the right time" or, depending on how you look at it, "the wrong place at the wrong time." By accident of timing and location, his politics developed in a particular way. Through unforeseen circumstances, he grew up in West Oakland instead of San Leandro, the predominantly White community where he was born, or Berkeley, where his mother grew up and relocated after the war. Had he gone straight to UC Berkeley, he might have continued in the predominantly White Left and "missed out on the greatest political opportunity of my career." But he went to Merritt College, "A Campus Where Black Power Won," blared a *Wall Street Journal* headline.[66] Aoki underestimated the significance of the Third World strike, but he got involved because he happened to be at UC Berkeley when the strike started.

To be sure, these are interlocking sets of arbitrary and deliberate interventions. The Berkeley Third World strike did not unexpectedly emerge in January 1969, but Aoki and activists like him collectively created the conditions that erupted in worldwide student activism in that fateful year of 1968.[67] Indeed, the dialectical relationship between the forces of history and human agency explain Aoki's political development. By accident of birth, he grew up in Black West Oakland and ended up at Merritt College in the midst of Black Power upsurges. But he made choices—to give guns to the BPP and thereby, in retrospect, joined the party; to take a stance against the Vietnam War while still in the military reserves; to provide leadership to AAPA during the strike—that turned his life from pursuing the American Dream to dreams of freedom. Even here, freedom dreams never fully replaced his desire for a nuclear family formation and other trappings of the American Dream, but, in his choosing the BPP over his fiancée, his life took a particular turn, made through an interaction of accidental and intentional choices.

Afro–Asian Solidarities

While it may seem redundant to state that Aoki was one of the foremost architects of Afro–Asian unity, the actual task was both harder and easier than it appears. It was easier in that Aoki was building on a history of Afro–Asian solidarities, connecting him to the work of W. E. B. Du Bois, Richard Wright, Robert F. Williams, Malcolm X, Grace Lee Boggs, Yuri Kochiyama, and of course, the Afro–Asian conference in Bandung. Huey Newton deliberately linked the "enslavement of Black people" with the "dropping of atomic bombs on Hiroshima and Nagasaki" and "the cowardly massacre in Vietnam."[68] Panther leaders looked to revolutions in China, Korea, and Vietnam as models of resistance to imperialism, racism, and global capitalism. But the rise of the model minority image of Asian Americans in the same auspicious year that birthed the Black Panther Party created obstacles to Afro–Asian unity. Many Blacks viewed Asian Americans as immune from U.S. racism and the U.S. historic amnesia rendered Asian American activism invisible to most.

So the work that Aoki did, through the International Secretariat of the Vietnam Day Committee, the Tri-Continental student organization, the TWLF strike, the AAPA, and the BPP, were significant on-the-ground practices linking Asian American and Black oppression and resistance. As early as 1965, Aoki worked with the Vietnam Day Committee in its antiwar organizing. As part of the International Days of Protest in October 1965, he helped create a booklet showcasing global opposition to the Vietnam War, including protests in Japan. Aoki's work helped to magnify an international gaze through which to view and strengthen the nascent U.S. antiwar movement. At a time when little was known about Japanese American internment, Aoki spoke out about his experiences in the concentration camps. In doing so at BPP meetings and later in teaching Asian American Studies, Aoki raised awareness about the ways U.S. racism affected Asian Americans and framed a common subjugation of Blacks and Asian Americans. He also brought the analysis, methods, and issues of Black Power to the Asian American Movement. While many AAM activists already embraced Black struggles, Aoki's connections to Black Power organizations and his style of Black militancy embodied in dress, language, and mannerism made visible

the Afro–Asian solidarities forged in a shared oppression and a shared opposition to racism, colonialism, and capitalism.

Confronting Hegemonic Power:
A Materialist's Radical Imagination

Even as Aoki worked to provide the kinds of social services to build civil
society and to challenge the dominant ideology, he was critical of Gramsci.
He did not fully articulate his criticism, but it likely arose from Gramsci's
stress on the role of cultural representation and ideological frameworks in
indoctrinating ordinary people to support capitalist structures, even when
it went against their class's own self-interest. Aoki, as a hard-core materialist, would have seen this as a misplaced Marxist adaptation, emphasizing
superstructure over the economic base. But Aoki was also a warrior–scholar
who believed that class struggle involved changing not only material conditions but also ideas. He read widely because he believed political theory
ought to guide activist strategies. Aoki stressed: "Although Mao said, 'political power grows out of the barrel of a gun,' it has to be understood that the
politics guide the gun." In his self-defense classes, Aoki denounced "commandism," or as he put it, "an overly militaristic approach that affects personality to the extent that politics becomes secondary to the military side."[69]
Aoki's desire for "freedom, justice, and equality" involved both the achievement of material needs and a radical vision of a liberatory society that
inspired hope and dignity. John Holloway, in discussing the Zapatista movement, sought to give substance to the abstract concept of dignity in revolutionary thought. While dignity incorporates the inspiring, yet nontangible
concepts of "refus[ing] to accept humiliation and dehumanization," "self-
creativity," "self-emancipation," and "democracy in struggle," Holloway is
careful to argue for a materialist basis for dignity:[70] "Dignity is a class concept, not a humanistic one."[71] Even as the Zapatistas themselves do not use
the vocabulary of class struggle, and in many ways reside outside the capitalist market, theirs is a struggle against subordination and for the right
to control their land, food, shelter, and other aspects of material existence.
Jackson Lears contends that Gramsci too "remained faithful to the Marxist tradition in granting causal priority to the economic sphere under most
conditions."[72]

So I would daresay that Aoki, ever a self-avowed materialist and Marxist,
embraced the idealist notion of "freedom dreams," which, as Robin Kelley
articulates, inspire one to imagine a world free of oppression and to see life

as possibility: "Progressive social movements . . . the best ones do what great poetry always does: transport us to another place, compel us to relive horrors, and more importantly, enable us to imagine a new society."[73] Through his vibrant and dynamic storytelling, Aoki was able to transport us to a different place, to empathize with the Other, and to develop a radical vision that inspired hope and a sense of efficacy, that together we can create the world we want to live in. In this way, Aoki also exhibited what Kelley calls "poetic knowledge," or the realization that conditions can change, an ability to imagine a different and better world, to engage "that effort to see the future in the present."[74]

Aoki had dreams of freedom, dreams that extended beyond incorporation into the good life or assimilation into the mainstream. He dreamed of a world where, as Martin Luther King Jr. famously stated in 1963, "sons of former slaves and sons of former slave owners will be able to sit down together at the table of brotherhood" and where "my four little children will one day live in a nation where they will not be judged by the color of their skin but by the content of their character."[75] Despite the obvious appeal (and easy co-optation) of King's "I Have a Dream" speech, Aoki's freedom dreams resonated more with the radical vision that King had by 1967. In a daring speech titled "A Time to Break Silence," King vowed to "break the betrayal of my own silences and speak from the burnings of my own heart."[76] It was an admittedly difficult speech to give, to condemn the U.S. role in Vietnam and to call for a sense of "brotherhood" with the Vietnamese people, but it was one that "my conscience leaves me no other choice."[77] While Christian preachers regularly spoke of the Good Samaritan, of doing good on life's road, King, by 1967, stressed that "the whole Jericho road must be transformed so that men and women will not be constantly beaten and robbed as they make their journey on life's highway."[78] He asserted that "true compassion is more than flinging a coin to a beggar; it is not haphazard and superficial. It comes to see that an edifice which produces beggars needs restructuring."[79] The solution was no longer as idealistic as the "sons of former slaves and sons of former slave owners . . . sit[ting] down together at the table of brotherhood,"as King put it in his "I Have a Dream" speech; the whole table needed restructuring. In "A Time to Break Silence," King called for a "radical revolution of values," the transformation from a "thing-oriented" society to a "person-oriented" society: "When machines and computers, profit motives and property rights are considered more important than people, the giant triplets of racism, materialism, and militarism are incapable of being conquered."[80] He spoke with urgency: "A true revolution of values will soon look uneasily on the glaring contrast of poverty and wealth. With righteous indignation, it will look across the sea and see individual capitalists of the West investing huge sums of money in Asia, Africa, and South America, only to take the profits out with no concern for the social betterment of the countries and say, 'This is not just.'"[81]

When Aoki emphatically stated, "I never left the Black Panther Party," he indeed held steadfast to the ideas, programs, and revolutionary dreams of the party. This was about wanting "freedom" and the "power to determine the destiny of our Black Community," and about wanting jobs, housing, quality education, fairness in the legal system, and an end to police brutality for all peoples.[82] This was about, as AAPA stated, "support[ing] all oppressed peoples and their struggles for Liberation."[83] Aoki's own radical imagination coincided with the momentous social movements of the 1960s and 1970s and enabled an ordinary person to make extraordinary choices, involving him in the creation of new societies and new histories.

Acknowledgments

The writing of a book, while solitary, is never an individual act. On the contrary, research, teaching, and knowledge production come through the sharing of ideas and resources, the creation of a social good. A great number of people, too many to acknowledge here, made the research for and writing of this book not only possible but joyful and deeply satisfying. My first acknowledgment goes to the activists of the Asian American Political Alliance, the Black Panther Party, and the Third World Liberation Front, whose efforts to create a just world enabled Richard Aoki's political contributions and historic significance. My gratitude goes to Richard Aoki, for placing trust in me to write his story. To Fred Ho for introducing me to Richard in the late 1990s while working on *Legacy to Liberation: Politics and Culture of Revolutionary Asian Pacific America.* To Dolly Veale, who successfully gained Richard's participation in his first lengthy interview (published in *Legacy to Liberation*) and who accompanied me to my first interview with Richard. To Douglas Daniels, whose positive endorsement got me through Richard's security procedures. To Yuri Kochiyama, whose life and biography inspired Richard to invite me to write his story.

I am grateful to all those who shared stories and insights about Richard through interviews and extended conversations, many of whom graciously opened their homes to me: Debbie Aoki, James T. Aoki, Anne Aoki, Brenda Wong Aoki, Shoshana Arai, Pam Lee Burnett, Kathleen Cleaver, Douglas Daniels, Liz Del Sol, Lillian Fabros Bando, Alan Fong, Bryant Fong, Sherwin Forte, Patrick Hayashi, Carol (Shelly) Hayden, David Hilliard, Alex Hing, Elbert "Big Man" Howard, Floyd Huen, Mark Izu, Lee Lew-Lee, Earl Napper, Mo Nishida, Leo Saito, Tom Sanders, Bill Sato, Bobby Seale, Mike Tagawa, Paul Takagi, Dolly Veale, LaNada (Means) War Jack, and Kenn Waters. Others shared valuable archival and other materials, including James T. Aoki, Mike Cheng, Patrick Hayashi, Jeffrey Heyman, and Ben Wang. I especially thank Harvey Dong, whose interviews, documents, and many discussions were indispensable and whose scholarship on Asian American activism illuminated my own work.

I thank the librarians and archivists, whose magnificent work, often under the radar, was invaluable to this project, including those at the Special Collections and Ethnic Studies Collections at the University of California, Santa Barbara (Gary Colmenar, Sal Guerrena); Ethnic Studies Library and Bancroft Special Collections of the University of California, Berkeley (Wei-Chi Poon); Asian American Studies Library at the University of California, Los Angeles (Marjorie Lee); Oakland Public Library (Steven Lavoie); Berkeley Public Library; Merritt College; College of Alameda; Berkeley High School; the Moorland–Spingarn Research Center of Howard University; It's About Time/BPP archives (Billy X Jennings); and the Hirasaki National Resource Center of the Japanese American National Museum. Funding from Melvin Oliver of the Division of Social Sciences, the Interdisciplinary Humanities Center, the Academic Senate, and the Institute for Social, Behavioral, and Economic Research as well as California taxpayers and (ever increasing) student fees enabled this research.

My appreciation goes to George Lipsitz and Douglas Daniels for reviewing the entire manuscript and for multiple stimulating discussions. George is a foremost model of a committed activist–scholar, brilliant, intellectually generous, and politically engaged. Douglas offers his unique and witty insights and critical feedback. James T. Aoki, Shoshana Arai, Harvey Dong, Fred Ho, Mo Nishida, and two anonymous reviewers for the Press provided feedback that pushed me to produce a better manuscript. My work draws from a wealth of incredible scholars, including Nikhil Singh, Robin Kelley, Bill Mullen, Laura Pulido, Jeanne Theoharis, Komozi Woodard, James Smethurst, Barbara Ransby, Timothy Tyson, Peniel Joseph, and Glenda Gilmore. I am particularly grateful to scholars and activists engaged in the study of the Asian American Movement, including Fred Ho, Mo Nishida, Daryl Maeda, May Fu, Harvey Dong, Glenn Omatsu, Steve Louie, Estella Habal, Michael Liu, Kim Geron, Tracy Lai, Judy Wu, Jason Ferreira, Mary Gao, Karen Ishizuka, Karen Umemoto, Susie Ling, and Megan White. For providing a generative and supportive place to work, I thank my colleagues in the Department of Asian American Studies at the University of California, Santa Barbara: Xiaojian Zhao, John Park, erin Ninh, Celine Parrenas Shimizu, Sameer Pandya, Ben Zulueta, Ambi Harsha, Jeff Sheng, Arlene Phillips, Elizabeth Guerrero,

James Lee, Jon Cruz, and Sucheng Chan. I further benefited in multiple ways from conversations with Ralph Armbruster-Sandoval, Jeffrey Stewart, Paul Spickard, Karen Leong, Chela Sandoval, Howie Winant, Eileen Boris, Claudine Michel, Sharon Hoshida, Zaveeni Khan-Marcus, Viviana Marsano, and colleagues at the Japanese American National Museum.

The work of several research assistants was important to this project, including Megan White, Hillary Nakano, Jamie Luu, Jeff Liang, Leigh Saito, Yvonne Tran, Derek Lum, Tony Samara, Marcelino Sepulveda, Carol Chiu, and particularly Lindsey Quock. Students, some now professors in their own right, inspired my intellectual and political endeavors, including Helene Lee, Tony Samara, Nadia Kim, Jessica Taft, Gabriel Cohn, Manisha Lal, Daniel Magpali, Jordan Camp, John Munro, Daniel Olmos, Tara Villalba, and Tomas Carrasco. My thanks go to the fabulous group at the University of Minnesota Press, especially Richard Morrison, Erin Warholm-Wohlenhaus, Laura Westlund, and Mary Byers. I am honored that this book adds to the Press's growing collection of Asian American radicalism and Afro–Asian scholarship.

My gratitude goes to my parents, May and the late Yasuo Fujino, for allowing a sometimes rebellious daughter the freedom and unconditional love to explore her own ideas. To my sister Robyn, for being a paragon of thoughtfulness, generosity, and wit. To my brother Don and sister Wendy, for the questioning of scientists that expands all our minds and for scrumptious meals. To my family, the late Matilda Barker, Linbrook Barker, Sandee, Lori, Jaden, Azriel, Bev, and Aunt Marcia for showing a lived practice of community, hospitality, education, and spirituality. To the Osugis, Nakamuras, Cisneroses, Fujinos, and Barkers for nurturing family relationships. I'm grateful to the grassroots communities in which I am embedded that show the power of the commons, namely, Open Alternative School, Grace Community Church, and our local and national activist communities—people precious to me for their vision, values, and life in service to others and to environmental sustainability. To Janet, Elaine, Ellen, Karina, Nancy, Lia, Marcelino, Zaveeni, Zeina, Raquel, Beth, Sean, and their wonderful families, for friendship and perspective. I thank my children, Kano and Seku, for creating a vibrant, artistic, affectionate, and compassionate center of my life: Kano warms me with his humor, kindness, and social sensitivity, and Seku, our capoeiraista, with his tenderness, determination, and intensity. To Matef, a fierce fighter and gentle humanist, for making this life's journey deeply meaningful and for being the biggest supporter of this book, critiquing and editing every page, while sharing in the reproductive work at home and the activist work in community to make it all possible. To these three, I owe my daily sustenance filled with great joy, delightful wonder, and the kinds of challenges that make life real. To the Almighty Creator, for love, hope, and grace.

Notes

INTRODUCTION

1. Che Guevara, captured in a photograph by Alberto Korda, is arguably the most famous image in popular culture throughout the world. Although he was a Marxist revolutionary and controversial figure in life, in death his captivating image has come to symbolize a generic struggle against injustice (Casey, *Che's Afterlife*; Kakutani, "Brand Che").

2. Pete Bellencourt created the banner, sponsored by It's About Time/BPP Alumni; see http://www.itsabouttimebpp.com. The Third World Liberation Front at UC Berkeley sought to restructure education and establish Third World Studies at UC Berkeley in the late 1960s.

3. Seale references Aoki three times, twice by name (spelled as "Iokey"). Seale, *Seize the Time*, 72; also 79, 81.

4. "Understanding AAPA," AAPA newspaper, summer 1969.

5. Espiritu, *Asian American Panethnicity*, 32, 34.

6. Wei, *The Asian American Movement*, 19–21, 24–26, 213; Ho, *Legacy to Liberation*, 399; Yip, "Serve the People"; Asian Community Center Archive Group, *STAND UP*; Umemoto, "'On Strike!'"

7. In part because of the success of the racial movements, there has been a neoconservative backlash and the rise of colorblindness (Omi and Winant, *Racial Formation*; Bonilla-Silva, *Racism without Racists*). As I wrote, the state of Arizona signed a bill to ban the teaching of Ethnic Studies (*Los Angeles Times*, May 12, 2010). A month earlier, Arizona passed the nation's harshest immigration bill, requiring the police to check documents of anyone they have "reasonable suspicion" to believe might have illegal status. In response, several city councils voted for economic boycotts of Arizona, President Obama criticized the bill, the Phoenix Suns wore "Los Suns" on their jerseys in nationally televised games, and a call was made to ban the National Baseball League's All-Star game from Arizona, costing an estimated $40 million, among countless other protests (*Los Angeles Times*, April 14, 30, 2010, and May 2, 6, 13, 2010; see also related reports on *Democracy Now*, May 6, 2010; http://www.democracynow.org/shows/2010/5/6).

8. The power of words, our own and those of others, can alter our own memories and others' views of our lived experiences. "Our knowledge about the past is always

already mediated through narratives," state Fujitani, White, and Yoneyama (*Perilous Memories,* 16). Paulo Freire famously wrote, "If it is in speaking their word that people, by naming the world, transform it, dialogue imposes itself as the way by which they achieve significance as human beings" (*Pedagogy of the Oppressed,* 88).

9. I thank Mo Nishida for insisting on a careful and critical discussion of the samurai.

10. Gordon, *A Modern History of Japan,* 10; Jansen, *The Making of Modern Japan,* 101. Because samurai were virtually all men, I use masculine pronouns when referring to the samurai.

11. James Aoki, interview; Harvey Dong, conversation with author, July 1, 2009. See chapter 1 for more on the Aokis' samurai lineage.

12. Takagi interview.

13. Nitobe, *Bushido,* 5.

14. Ibid.; Jansen, *The Making of Modern Japan,* 101–11; Turnbull, *Samurai.*

15. Reprinted in Turnbull, *Samurai,* 6.

16. The early samurai, recognized by historians as early as the tenth century, were regional warriors individually serving aristocratic families or at times the imperial court. In the Tokugawa period, the most elite samurai, now warrior–administrators, and their military lords, the *daimyo,* became political rulers with power equal to, or even surpassing, the hegemonic power of the aristocracy (Gordon, *A Modern History of Japan,* 3, 9–11; Jansen, *The Making of Modern Japan,* 103–7; Duus, *Modern Japan,* 29–31).

17. Daniels interview; Seale interview.

18. In practice, of course, not all samurai lived by the noble bushido code. Some remained loyal to their lord only when he protected them and provided rewards, others ran away from a losing battle, and still others sold their services to the highest bidder (McClain, *Japan,* 78). While "master" was used in the feudal period of the samurai, Aoki would not have used this word so associated with slavery and oppression.

19. Jansen, *The Making of Modern Japan,* 106; also Duus, *Modern Japan,* 6–9.

20. Hayashi interview.

21. Fujino, "Race, Place, Space, and Political Development."

22. Ichioka, *The Issei.*

23. Kublin, *Asian Revolutionary;* Fowler, *Japanese and Chinese Immigrant Activists;* Ichioka, "A Buried Past"; Yoneda, *Ganbatte;* Thomas and Nishimoto, *The Spoilage;* Hohri, *Resistance.*

24. Azuma astutely shows how the Japanese immigrant elite sought to control the poor and "inferior" elements of the immigrant community through the politics of assimilationism (*Between Two Empires,* 35–60, 89–110).

25. Chapter 5 elaborates on these ideas.

26. Arnesen, "Civil Rights Historiography," 31.

27. Jacquelyn Dowd Hall most prominently advanced the "Long Civil Rights Movement" framework (2005), but its basic idea emerged earlier; see Korstad and Lichtenstein, "Opportunities Found and Lost" (1988). I borrow Cha-Jua and Lang's

analysis term "Long Movement" to counter collapsing Black Power politics under a civil rights rubric ("The 'Long Movement' as Vampire"). To extend the time frame of Black Power, Peniel Joseph uses the term "long Black Power movement" (see *The Black Power Movement, 7*). In *The World the 60s Made,* Gosse and Moser contest a declensionist interpretation of the death by the end of that decade of the movements of the 1960s.

28. Biondi, *To Stand and Fight;* Bush, *We Are Not What We Seem;* Dudziak, *Cold War Civil Rights;* Gaines, "The Historiography of the Struggle for Black Equality since 1945"; Gilmore, *Defying Dixie;* Gosse, *Rethinking the New Left;* Horne, *Black and Red;* Kelley, *Hammer and Hoe;* Plummer, *Rising Wind;* Ransby, *Ella Baker;* Singh, *Black Is a Country;* Von Eschen, *Race against Empire.*

29. Hall, "The Long Civil Rights Movement," 1245.

30. Arnesen, "Civil Rights Historiography"; Cha-Jua and Lang, "The 'Long Movement' as Vampire."

31. Dittmer, *Local People,* 47, 285–86.

32. Payne, *Groundwork,* xi.

33. Kelley, "'But a Local Phase of a World Problem.'"

34. Von Eschen, *Race against Empire,* 97, 111–12.

35. Radicalism continued in the works of W. E. B. Du Bois, Richard Wright, Esther Cooper Jackson, Jack O'Dell, and others; see Munro, "The Anticolonial Front"; McDuffie, "'No Small Amount of Change Could Do'"; O'Dell, *Climbin' Jacob's Ladder.*

36. Fujino, "The Global Cold War and Asian American Activism"; Kotani, *The Japanese in Hawaii;* FBI file of Sak Ishihara (copy in author's possession); Bahr, *The Unquiet Nisei;* Holmes, *The Specter of Communism in Hawaii;* Martha Nakagawa, "Rebels with a Just Cause" and "Sakae Ishihara: A Marked Man," *Rafu Shimpo,* December 11 and 12, 1997; Robinson, "Nisei in Gotham."

37. Joseph, "Black Liberation without Apology," *The Black Power Movement,* "The Black Power Movement," *Waiting 'til the Midnight Hour,* and "Waiting till the Midnight Hour"; Ahmad, *We Will Return in the Whirlwind;* Johnson, *Revolutionaries to Race Leaders;* Ogbar, *Black Power;* Smethurst, *The Black Arts Movement;* Tyson, *Radio Free Dixie;* Woodard, *A Nation within a Nation.*

38. Gosse, "A Movement of Movements," 292.

39. Ibid., 285.

40. Dittmer, *Local People;* Payne, *I've Got the Light of Freedom;* Theoharis and Woodard, *Freedom North* and *Groundwork.*

41. Lawson, "Freedom Then, Freedom Now"; Crawford, Rouse, and Woods, *Women in the Civil Rights Movement;* Gore, Theoharis, and Woodard, *Want to Start a Revolution?*

42. For a historiography of Asian American Movement studies, see Fujino, "Who Studies the Asian American Movement?" Also see Fujino, *Heartbeat of Struggle,* "Black Militants and Asian American Model Minorities," and "Grassroots Leadership and Afro-Asian Solidarities"; Habal, *San Francisco's International Hotel;* Ho, *Legacy to Liberation* and *Wicked Theory, Naked Practice;* Liu, Geron, and Lai, *The*

Snake Dance of Asian American Activism; Louie and Omatsu, *Asian Americans;* Maeda, *Chains of Babylon;* Pulido, *Black, Brown, Yellow, and Left;* as well as dissertations by Dong, "The Origins and Trajectory of Asian American Political Activism"; Ferreira, "All Power to the People"; and Fu, "Keeping Close to the Ground."

43. *Eyes on the Prize II: The Time Has Come,* 1989.

44. With Seale's permission, I gave Aoki the transcript of my interview. This is something I wouldn't normally do, but it seemed to provide Aoki with an important affirmation of his role in the party and his place in history.

45. Veale, "Interview with Richard Aoki," 326–27.

46. Denzin, *Interpretive Biography,* 24.

47. Portelli, *The Death of Luigi Trastulli.*

48. Ransby, *Ella Baker;* Payne, "Men Led, but Women Organized."

49. Blumer, *Symbolic Interactionism;* Cooley, *Human Nature and the Social Order.*

50. Aoki, telephone call to Fujino, November 7, 2002; Fujino, letter to Aoki, November 10, 2002 (author's collection).

51. Fujino, *Heartbeat of Struggle.*

52. In a quite successful approach, Maurice Isserman interspersed archival documents throughout Dorothy Healey's narrative (Healey and Isserman, *California Red*).

53. Chuck Jones, cited in Carmichael, *Ready for Revolution,* 298.

1. "My Happy Childhood That I Don't Remember"

1. Richard Masato Aoki was born on November 20, 1938, in San Leandro, California (Certificate of Birth, Alameda County). His parents, Shozo Aoki and Toshiko Nakazawa, married on Tuesday, May 3, 1938, in Carson City, Nevada (Certificate of Marriage, Ormsby County, Nevada). Richard's cousin remembers her uncle, the husband of Shozo's sister, sitting her down to inform her that Shozo had suddenly gotten married. There was no wedding for the family to attend (Aoki's cousin, anonymity requested). Others recall Shozo as being a "ladies' man" and driving a nice car when few Nisei could afford any car (Saito interview).

2. Given gendered constructions about controlling women's bodies and women's chastity, and the ways masculinity is achieved through the protection of women, it is not surprising that the woman's family—with her father's masculinity being the most threatened—would be more distressed than the man's about an out-of-wedlock pregnancy. That Aoki did not mention this explanation reflects the more accepting attitudes toward out-of-wedlock pregnancy in the culture and times in which he was socialized, as well as the looming presence of his father as both a rake to be admired and an irresponsible father to be despised.

3. When Richard was born, his father identified his work as "laundry help" and his mother as "housewife." David was born on February 18, 1940, in Berkeley, also with the assistance of a midwife. His father was a "delivery man" in a laundry for one and a half years and his mother was a "housewife" for two years. David died at age forty-six in December 1986 (David Aoki, Certificate of Birth, County of Alameda; David Aoki, Certificate of Death, County of Alameda). Shozo and Shigeo Aoki

attended UC Berkeley (UC Berkeley transcripts for Shigeo Aoki, 1924, and Shozo Aoki, 1938).

4. Davis McEntire's influential book, *Residence and Race,* was sponsored by the Commission on Race and Housing, formed in 1955 to discuss the social problem of racial segregation. A number of renowned social scientists, including Gordon Allport and Robert Merton, sat on the commission's Research Advisory Committee. The book shows the extent of residential segregation by examining geographic housing patterns of Whites and non-Whites, particularly "Negroes," but also has information on the Chinese, Japanese, Mexicans, and Puerto Ricans in numerous cities throughout the United States. The material on the Japanese would have drawn Aoki's attention and thus shaped his memory, inflating the book's focus on Japanese Americans.

5. The majority of Japanese laborers, predominantly male, traveled to the West Coast as manual laborers between 1891 and 1908, when the Gentlemen's Agreement between the United States and Japan ended the immigration of laborers. Students began arriving in large numbers in the mid-1880s, and large numbers of women immigrated after the Gentlemen's Agreement permitted wives of U.S. residents to immigrate. Japanese immigration ended when the 1924 Immigration Act banned the entry of "aliens ineligible for citizenship" (Ichioka, *The Issei*).

6. When Shozo was born on March 24, 1914, his father, age forty-one, was a "merchant" and his mother, age forty-two, was a "housewife" (Shozo Aoki, Certificate of Birth, County of Alameda). The first three Aoki children were born in Japan: Sadae circa 1891, Minoru circa 1901, and Shigeo in November 1902 (U.S. Census, 1910, 1920, 1930; Shigeo Aoki, UC Berkeley transcripts). The three youngest, including Shozo, were born in the East Bay: Riuzo was born on November 26, 1908, and Haruko on September 2, 1911 (for each, Certificate of Birth, County of Alameda).

7. Shizuka Nakazawa, Richard's maternal grandmother, immigrated through San Francisco on October 14, 1912, en route to Oakland to join her husband, Tatsumi Nakazawa, who had immigrated in 1908. Tatsumi Nakazawa, born in 1884, and Shizuka Nakazawa, born in 1891, had four children, all U.S.-born: Hideo, born October 18, 1913; Yoshiko, born June 10, 1915; Toshiko, born September 29, 1916; and Hideko, called Decky or Deki, born September 24, 1917. When Richard's mother, Toshiko, was born, her father, age thirty-one, was in the "cleaning and dyeing" business and her mother, age twenty-five, was a "housewife." See Shizuka Nakazawa, Immigration/Passenger Records; Tatsumi Nakazawa, Hideo Nakazawa, Yoshiko (Nakazawa) Takei, Form WRA 26; Tatsumi and Hideo Nakazawa, Final Accountability Roster, all obtained from the Japanese American National Museum (JANM), Los Angeles; Tatsumi Nakazawa, Certificate of Death, County of Alameda; Shizuka Nakazawa, Certificate of Death, County of Alameda.

8. As Japanese immigrants settled on land and gained a hold in the California agricultural market, California passed the 1913 Alien Land Law, which targeted Japanese by prohibiting "aliens ineligible for citizenship" from purchasing agricultural land. But Japanese American land holdings continued to rise, in part because of the agricultural boom during World War I, and many purchased land in the name of

their U.S.-born children, as did the Aokis. Japanese agricultural holdings declined when the 1920 Alien Land Law closed such loopholes. The Japanese American community protested, but their court cases were met with defeat (Ichioka, *The Issei,* 153–56, 226–43). On the Aoki family's property, see chapter 3.

9. Since then, the property was transformed into a hip-hop club (Aoki, telephone interview, October 4, 2005) and then became artists' lofts (Fujino, observation of the site, circa 2007).

10. This photograph is dated 1937.

11. Working as a self-employed gardener was one of the most common jobs for Japanese American men prior to World War II (Tsuchida, "Japanese Gardeners"). Japanese immigrant women often worked as domestic servants (Glenn, *Issei, Nisei, War Bride*).

12. It was common in Japan, with its collective notions of family, for Issei laborers to send their children to Japan to be raised by grandparents, while they labored for the family's livelihood in the United States. Kibei refers to a subgroup of Japanese Americans born in the United States, but raised and educated in Japan, who returned to the United States usually as teenagers or young adults. Those educated in Japan in the 1920s and early '30s were influenced by Japan's more liberal policies. But those educated in the mid- to late 1930s were influenced by the highly militaristic and imperialist policies of Japan (Takahashi, *Nisei Sansei*).

13. Jitsuji Aoki's immigration to the United States in 1902 (Jitsuji Aoki, immigration card, 1921, JANM; War Relocation Authority [WRA] Form 26, JANM; U.S. Census, 1910, 1930; *Oakland Tribune,* March 3, 1939; Shigeo Joseph Aoki, interview by Ann Yabusaki) is more credible than the 1897 date stated on the 1920 U.S. Census.

14. For excellent accounts of Japanese American history, see Ichioka, *The Issei;* Azuma, *Between Two Empires.*

15. Even though there were few Christians in Japan, there were apparently "no special restrictions on Christian beliefs and rites of worship" (Wakatsuki, "Japanese Emigration," 418). In 1930, 18 percent of the Issei in California were Christian, while 77 percent were Buddhist (Strong, *Japanese in California,* 169).

16. I. Aoki and K. Aoki, "Descendants of Reverend Peter Chojiro Aoki"; Gleason, "Summary of Aoki Family Geneology"; James T. Aoki interview. That Chojiro's and Jitsuji's families were Methodist Episcopal is not surprising. In the prewar period, the Methodist Episcopal Church had, by far, the largest representation of Japanese in the continental United States of any Christian denomination (Hayashi, *"For the Sake of Our Japanese Brethren,"* 3–4).

17. Ichioka, *The Issei,* 164–68.

18. Fusa Aoki and her son Shigeo arrived at the port of Seattle on October 8, 1907 (List or Manifest of Alien Passengers for the United States, 1907–17, JANM); daughter Sadae also immigrated in 1907 (U.S. Census, 1930), as did daughter Minoru (WRA Form 26). Jitsuji's mother, Tase or Tosey Aoki, then age sixty-eight, was living with Jitsuji's family in Oakland at the time of the 1910 Census, but not in 1920.

19. *Oakland Tribune,* August 10, 1930.

20. It was rare for Japanese immigrants to begin a manufacturing facility, even a small one, as early as 1903. Even in 1929, of the 257 Japanese American businesses in California, only three were in food manufacturing (Ichihashi, *Japanese in the United States,* 126–27; also 116–36).

21. *Oakland Tribune,* April 15, 1927; May 11, 1930; June 1, 1930.

22. See, among others, *Oakland Tribune,* May 20, 1916; June 3, 1916; April 13, 1930; August 10, 1930.

23. B. Aoki, *Uncle Gunjiro's Girlfriend.*

24. *San Francisco Chronicle,* November 11, 1933; also *Oakland Tribune,* March 19, 1909.

25. The most fundamental social division in early-nineteenth-century Japan was between samurai and commoners, a distinction marked primarily by birthright in a society of limited social mobility. When the Meiji government rose to power in 1868, it rapidly transformed feudal Japan into a modern, capitalist economy. The samurai, more than any other class, lost their economic and social status. With the advent of a modern military system, there was no longer a need for the samurai, or the "warrior elite ruling class" (Duus, *Modern Japan,* 6). The stipends given the samurai were an overwhelming financial drain on the new government. So in 1869, a year after the Meiji ascendency, the new government convinced the *daimyo,* or regional military lords, to surrender their lands to the emperor. This reinforced emperor rule over all lands and the government soon began collecting land taxes. In 1873, taxes were imposed on the samurai stipends and in 1876, the right to wear swords, long established as the sole right of the samurai, was reserved only for soldiers and police officers. Within a decade of the rise of the Meiji government, the samurai as a class were stripped of their economic position and social privileges. Still, because virtually all samurai were educated, they rose to power in the new government's civilian structure (Duus, *Modern Japan,* 6–9, 93–95; Gordon, *A Modern History of Japan,* 62–67). Jitsuji Aoki, for example, worked as a postal officer in Japan before immigrating (James T. Aoki interview).

26. See the Introduction for more on the Aoki family's swords.

27. Spickard, *Mixed Blood,* 42–46, 70–73, 374–75.

28. Ibid., 374–75.

29. *Oakland Tribune,* March 25, 1909. At the time, the newspaper's use of "jiu jitsu" would have orientalized Gunjiro Aoki—in opposition to the Occident—in the eyes of the readership, as well as signaled a possible yellow peril threat.

30. *New York Times,* March 26, 1909.

31. Ibid.

32. *New York Times,* March 28, 1909.

33. Ibid. At the time, interracial marriage involving a Japanese spouse was so unusual that the Immigration Commission commented: "They are of interest chiefly in connection with the strong protests which are called forth and given expression through the press" (Ichihashi, *Japanese in the United States,* 217; also Steiner, *The Japanese Invasion,* 149–74). Although highly atypical, there were a few interracial unions in California as early as the 1870s, including the German–Japanese and

Japanese–Black intermarriages in the Wakamatsu tea and silk colony (Spickard, *Japanese Americans*, 11–12).

34. *San Francisco Chronicle*, March 16, 1909.

35. B. Aoki, *Uncle Gunjiro's Girlfriend*.

36. *Oakland Tribune*, March 25, 1909.

37. Ibid.

38. Ibid.

39. Helen Gladys Aoki became a citizen of Japan upon marrying Gunjiro (*Los Angeles Times*, March 30, 1909). In 1933, a year after Gunjiro died, Helen successfully regained her U.S. citizenship and legally changed her last name to "Oakey," "Oakie," or "Okei" (*Los Angeles Times*, November 11, 1933; *San Francisco Chronicle*, November 11, 1933; *Oakland Tribune*, November 11, 1933). The 1922 Cable Act provided that "any woman citizen who marries an alien ineligible to citizenship" forfeited her U.S. citizenship. The Cable Act was amended in 1931 to allow women to recover U.S. citizenship (Ichihashi, *Japanese in the United States*, 324–25).

40. *Oakland Tribune*, December 23 and 26, 1909; *Los Angeles Times*, June 14, 1910.

41. Mrs. Sophronia Emery moved in with Gunjiro and Helen; they named their first child after her (*Oakland Tribune*, July 25, 1909; Gunjiro Aoki, 1920 U.S. Census; B. Aoki, *Uncle Gunjiro's Girlfriend*).

42. B. Aoki, *Uncle Gunjiro's Girlfriend*; *Oakland Tribune*, December 23 and 26, 1909; *Los Angeles Times*, June 14, 1910.

43. Helen Gladys Aoki, 1930 U.S. Census; *Los Angeles Times*, November 11, 1933; *San Francisco Chronicle*, November 11, 1933; "Descendants of Gunjiro Aoki," family document. It is surprising that the newspapers did not condemn parents for a child conceived outside marriage, merely announcing the birth of Gunjiro and Helen's first child in July 1909 (*Oakland Tribune*, July 25, 1909).

44. *Daily Northwestern* (Oshkosh, Wis.), January 15, 1923; *Nebraska State Journal* (Lincoln), January 10, 1923. Phelan and the Exclusion League notoriously pushed for Japanese exclusion (Ichioka, *The Issei*, 136, 143, 173, 252–53).

45. *Nichibei Times*, August 1, 1998; September 12, 1998; *Los Angeles Times*, April 30, 2000; http://www.brendawongaoki.com.

46. Brenda Wong Aoki, conversation with author, May 3, 2009, Oakland, Calif.

47. Shigeo Aoki was in his mother's womb when his father emigrated in 1902 and first met his father when Shigeo arrived in the United States in 1907. Shigeo experienced an emotional distance from his father and felt that his father favored the two sons with whom he had bonded since birth, Riuzo and Shozo ("Background of Joseph Shigeo Aoki—His Words," April 23, 2005; Shigeo Joseph Aoki, interview by Ann Yabusaki). Others too noticed this conflict. Shigeo's nephew from New York apologized for not visiting when he was in Oakland: "I stayed at Ojiisan's [Grandfather's] . . . and since there has been a rift between you and the family, I thought it best not to go over to your place" (Ken Iyeki, letter to Shigeo Aoki, September 3, 1947). At two church events, Shigeo Aoki, as speaker, recounted: "When I was a child in Oakland, all parents worked hard. There was no television; few people had radios.

So we children went to church and raised a lot of fuss, especially in Sunday school. How I loved that Sunday school!" (Shigeo Aoki, for the one hundredth anniversary of West Tenth Street Methodist Church, October 18, 1987). He also disclosed: "I was supposed to be the *itazura kozo* [incorrigible boy] of the Sunday school, so usually it got to my parents' ears and I 'got it'" (Shigeo Aoki, "Oldest Memories of West 10th," *The Plowshare: Newsletter of Lake Park Church,* January 31, 1982). On Shigeo's citizenship, see the end-of-chapter commentary in chapter 3.

2. "Protecting the Japanese"

1. There is now a voluminous literature on the Japanese American internment experience. For an overview, see Daniels, *Prisoners without Trial.* On the rationale behind the decision for mass removal, see Daniels, *Decision to Relocate;* Robinson, *By Order of the President.* For an extended bibliography, see Spickard, *Japanese Americans,* 192–95, 203–6.

2. Richard's family lived at 2844 California Street in Berkeley, two blocks from his maternal grandparents, who were at 1623 Stuart Street (David Aoki, Certificate of Birth, Alameda County; Tatsumi Nakazawa, *Polk-Husted City Directory,* 1941).

3. For information on and a scholarly interpretation of the Topaz camp, see Taylor, *Jewel of the Desert.*

4. The Utah State Hospital, which began as a Territorial Insane Asylum, continues to provide mental health services (http://www.ush.utah.gov/history.htm).

5. Artists, scholars, and writers from San Francisco and Berkeley were among the internees who documented their experience at Tanforan and Topaz, including artist Miné Okubo *(Citizen 13660),* writers Toshio Mori (e.g., *The Chauvinist*) and Yoshiko Uchida (e.g., *Desert Exile*), and UC professor and artist Chiura Obata, who taught art classes in Tanforan and Topaz (see Hill, *Topaz Moon,* which presents Obata's work from the internment period); see also the Topaz Museum at http://topazmuseum.org.

6. Okubo depicts this potbelly stove in her drawings and text of life in Topaz (*Citizen 13660,* 146–47). A potbelly stove and a bit of "winterizing" of the wooden barracks by lining inner walls were all the Topaz internees had to stave off the freezing cold. Internees began arriving September 11, 1942, and by late October, the temperatures had dropped to well below freezing—10 degrees in one report. Schools were open only from 1:00 to 5:00 p.m. because it was "too cold in the morning." The shortage of coal to fuel these stoves was the cause of major concern in Topaz (John Baker, "Notes on Central Utah," October 31, November 1, 1942, Japanese American Evacuation and Resettlement Records [JERS] Reel 131; E. B. Marks Jr., "Central Utah," November 27, 1942, JERS Reel 131; *Topaz Times,* October 27, 1942).

7. Pieces of lumber such as Aoki describes would have been plentiful at Topaz at the beginning of their stay. When internees first arrived, construction was still under way in the Topaz camp, which was designed to house some nine thousand people in a one-square-mile area, at a cost of $5 million, making it the fifth-largest city in Utah (Taylor, *Jewel of the Desert,* 89–97). The *Topaz Times* assured internees: "Since sufficient wood is available, there will be no necessity for hoarding or nocturnal

commando raids" (*Topaz Times,* ca. September 22, 1942). The hostilities between pro-U.S. and pro-Japan factions—the latter included Black Dragon Society members—inside the camps have been widely discussed. Inside the Manzanar and Poston camps, the conflict rose to the level of violence, with the beatings of pro-U.S. JACL leaders; see Hansen and Hacker, "The Manzanar Riot"; Kurashige, *Japanese American Celebration and Conflict,* 75–110; Okihiro, "Japanese Resistance"; Ueno, *Manzanar Martyr;* Yoneda, *Ganbatte.*

8. Taylor, *Jewel of the Desert,* 121, 128.

9. Aoki has told this story many times; see, for example, Veale, "Interview with Richard Aoki," 320. Leo Saito, Shozo's childhood friend, laughed when he heard this story and commented: "Sounds like Sho-y [for Shozo]" (Saito interview).

10. Yoshiko Uchida makes clear how important culinary treats were to those who were deprived of physical comforts: "I wrote to my non-Japanese friends in Berkeley shamelessly asking them to send us food" (*Desert Exile,* 77). Later, in Topaz, limited treats were available in the canteen.

11. Monthly wages in the camps ranged from twelve to nineteen dollars (Daniels, *Prisoners without Trial,* 66), though others also recall receiving as low as eight dollars a month (Uchida, *Desert Exile,* 88; Fujino, *Heartbeat of Struggle,* 47). Less was spent on feeding internees (thirty-eight cents/day) than on feeding soldiers (fifty cents/day). U.S. Army soldiers also got substantially higher wages at fifty dollars/month (previously twelve dollars/month), plus room and board. One group—conscientious objectors at five dollars/month—were the lowest paid of all inside the camps (Taylor, *Jewel of the Desert,* 99, 158; Daniels, *Prisoners without Trial,* 67).

12. Certified White teachers were scarce, so internees—many with college degrees, but even some without—taught classes in Topaz. White teachers earned $150–$200/month, while internees earned the $19/month paid to professionals (Taylor, *Jewel of the Desert,* 119–33).

13. Democracy—and its ambivalent meanings—was a common subject in Topaz schools (Taylor, *Jewel of the Desert,* 81, 126). It is reasonable to assume that Shozo had some degree of patriotic spirit when he joined the ROTC in high school in the early 1930s (*Oakland Tribune,* September 27, 1931). But inside Topaz, childhood friend Leo Saito remembers Shozo as being not very patriotic, likely spurred by the racism and politics of incarceration (Saito interview).

14. On April 11, 1943, James Wakasa, a sixty-three-year-old Issei who had lived for forty years in the United States, was shot and killed by a military police sentry in guard tower number eight. The sentry claimed that Wakasa was "climbing through the fence" and had been warned four times. But the coroner found that Wakasa was shot in the chest, facing the guard; the blood on the ground indicated that he was some five feet inside the fence. Most internees did not think Wakasa was trying to escape. The internees quickly organized and raised questions such as what should be the penalty even if an internee tries to escape? Certainly not death. Because Topaz was run by the War Relocation Authority, a civilian agency, what authority did the military have, especially to exclude the WRA from its investigation? The internees responded in two major ways. First, they organized a large funeral for

Wakasa. Second, they engaged in widespread work stoppages on the day of Wakasa's funeral; whether intentional or not, they defied the WRA administration's refusal to make the day a holiday. Although the *Topaz Times* speculated that the sentry would be court-martialed, in the end, he was exonerated of all charges (*Topaz Times*, April 12 and 13, 1943; R. A. Bankson, "The Wakasa Incident," May 10, 1943, JERS Reel 119; Resolution by Resident Representative and Councilmen, circa September 1943, JERS Reel 119). Referring to the Wakasa incident, Taylor noted, "The point had been made: Topaz was an armed concentration camp." Although there was no other killing in Topaz, the incident traumatized the internees, signifying their vulnerability (Taylor, *Jewel of the Desert*, 144, 136–47). This sense of fear and danger is conveyed throughout Aoki's story.

15. Aoki was under the impression that his father was a "no-no boy" and that status made him a draft resister (Veale, "Interview with Richard Aoki," 321). But this is unlikely. Aoki is conflating two separate incidents. In February 1943, the WRA and the Selective Service administered what has become known as the loyalty registration. Those answering no to two key questions—on their willingness to serve in combat duty wherever ordered and to forswear allegiance to the Japanese emperor— came to be known as "no-no boys." These so-called disloyals were sent to the Tule Lake concentration camp in Northern California. The registration caused innumerable problems (Thomas and Nishimoto, *The Spoilage*; Drinnon, *Keeper of Concentration Camps*, 78–80; Weglyn, *Years of Infamy*, 134–51). A year later, in January 1944, the U.S. Army reinstituted the draft for Japanese Americans. Over three hundred internees were arrested and convicted of violating the Selective Service order; in Heart Mountain, Wyoming, one in nine draft-eligible men refused to comply. The vast majority of draft resisters were not "no-no boys" (Nelson, *Heart Mountain*; Muller, *Free to Die for Their Country*; Mackey, *A Matter of Conscience*; Abe, *Conscience and the Constitution*; and Omori, *Rabbit in the Moon*). Shozo Aoki may well have opposed the racism of incarceration and of segregated army units, but he was neither a draft resister nor a no-no boy. His age (thirty in 1944) and marital status would have made him a distant draft pick, with men over thirty, and possibly even down to age twenty-six, unlikely to get drafted (*Topaz Times*, May 17, 1944).

16. The JACL perspective on internment dominated Japanese American historiography until the Asian American Movement of the late 1960s and 1970s and particularly the redress movement of the 1980s revised this history. The JACL's views are presented in Hosokawa, *JACL*; Masaoka, *They Call Me Moses Masaoka*. On critiques of the JACL's wartime positions, see Lim, "Lim Report"; Spickard, "The Nisei Assume Power."

17. The Nazi–Soviet Non-Aggression Pact, signed in August 1939, provided a buffer zone for the Soviet Union. But this secret pact enabled Germany's aggressive expansion in Europe and ultimately did not safeguard the Soviet Union from German invasion in June 1941.

18. Two major radical organizations, the Socialist Party and the Socialist Workers Party, opposed evacuation. Norman Thomas of the Socialist Party has been called "the only national political figure to take a public position against Executive Order

9066" (Robinson, "Norman Thomas and the Struggle against Internment," 420). The SWP newspaper denounced the "evacuation" as "racial terrorism," arguing that agribusiness and banking interests seized on an opportunity to confiscate Japanese American farmlands and eliminate competition. A major concern was that the incarceration "establishes one of the most dangerous precedents for the usurpation of civil liberties" (*Militant*, March 7, 1942, May 30, 1942). By contrast, the Communist Party of the United States of America aligned itself with President Roosevelt and the fight against fascism, to the exclusion of any critical analysis of the war or of U.S. or European militarism. Shortly after the bombing of Pearl Harbor, the CPUSA suspended all its American-born Japanese members and any non-Japanese spouses of Japanese members for the duration of the war. The rationale, according to Japanese American CPUSA member Karl Yoneda, was that CPUSA leader Earl Browder believed "the best place for any Japanese fifth columnist to hide is within the Communist Party ranks and consequently no Japanese American should be kept in the Party while the war against Japan is going on" (Yoneda, *Ganbatte*, 115–16; see also Foster, *History*, 383–407).

19. Some kind treatment was shown toward Japanese Americans, usually by individuals, but also by a few organizations. Overwhelmingly, however, virtually every sector of American society—from the executive, legislative, and judicial branches to the military, the media, agribusiness, White supremacist groups, and the public at large—held anti-Japanese sentiments and/or failed to oppose incarceration (Grozdins, *Americans Betrayed*; Daniels, *Prisoners without Trial* and *Politics of Prejudice*).

20. Aoki showed me a photograph of a Japanese American man on a bucking horse, signed "To Sho Aoki" from "Mac Komatsu, Topaz, Utah, 1945."

21. Cameras were banned in camp. But in a now widely known story, Toyo Miyatake, internee and famed photographer of Little Tokyo in Los Angeles, snuck camera parts into the Manzanar concentration camp and assembled a camera hidden inside a wooden box (Alinder, *Moving Images*, 77). Two famous photographers were invited to photograph Manzanar. Ansel Adams, the celebrated landscape photographer, often showed happier moments and images of Americanized internees. Dorothea Lange, best known for her photographs of the Depression era for the Farm Security Administration, took haunting photographs that captured the angst and humanity of Tanforan and Manzanar internees (Nakamura, *Toyo Miyatake*; Adams, *Born Free and Equal*; on Lange, see Gordon and Okihiro, *Impounded*).

22. At Topaz, Dave Tatsuno, with help from a supportive camp official, obtained a movie camera, and while taking regular leaves to make purchases for the consumer cooperative, smuggled film into camp. Tatsuno's 8-mm film on life in Topaz was the second home movie placed on the National Film Registry (Taylor, *Jewel of the Desert*, 158; *New York Times*, February 13, 2006).

23. Aoki's analysis of Japan draws from Paul Baran's *The Political Economy of Growth* and Lenin's *Imperialism*. Baran argues that Japan's rapid capitalist development was facilitated by its being the only country in Asia, or Africa or Latin America for that matter, to escape Western colonialism, primarily because Japan lacked natural resources (156; also 151–62). Aoki remarked: "Baran was a Marxist economist professor at Stanford. I read his book and was stunned because, pardon

my ego, his theory of the primitive accumulation of capital in Japan during the Tokugawa shogunate paralleled my own independent thoughts and development. That's
when I said, 'Marxism is where it's at.'" Japan colonized Manchuria to gain resources
and land and Southeast Asia for its markets and raw materials, including rubber;
"the move was needed economically (Japan faced rationing and threats of unrest),
and strategically (Indochina could be a springboard for assaults on its mineral-rich
neighbors" (LaFeber, *The Clash*, 197; also 191–93). For a sophisticated study of Japanese immigration to the United States, see Azuma, *Between Two Empires.*

24. The Monroe Doctrine, introduced in 1823 at a time when Latin American
countries were dismantling Spanish colonialism, asserted the United States' claim to
the entire Western Hemisphere; any European colonial project in the hemisphere
would be viewed as an act of aggression. The United States, in turn, would respect
the boundaries of European colonies and not interfere with the internal affairs
of European countries. Similarly, Japan fashioned its own Monroe Doctrine. The
"Greater East Asia Co-Prosperity Sphere" declared pan-Asianism as a solution to
liberate Asia from Western colonialism and White supremacy, but, of course, under
the domination of Japan. Despite this clash of empire building, LaFeber convincingly
argues that war between the United States and Japan was not inevitable. Other
options were possible, including the creation of boundaries to separate their colonial projects, especially because both countries were strongly interdependent trading
partners (LaFeber, *The Clash,* 174–97). Dower, in *War without Mercy,* cogently
frames the Pacific war as a "race war," in addition to being a struggle for resources
and empire building. Racism, on the part of the United States and Japan, as well as
images of the Orient and Occident as oppositional and incompatible, fueled the war
and made the Pacific war particularly vicious. On the Nanking massacre, see Chang,
The Rape of Nanking. On U.S. and Japanese empire building, see also Iriye, *Pacific
Estrangement* and *Power and Culture;* Dower, *Embracing Defeat.*

25. On U.S. military and CIA intervention, see Blum, *Killing Hope;* Johnson,
Blowback and *Sorrows of Empire.* Aoki added: "Just look at why the U.S. is in Iraq
today. Bringing democracy to the Iraqis was not the name of the game. Finding
weapons of mass destruction was not the name of the game. Oil is what the game is
all about."

26. Because the United States had broken the Japanese codes, as early as September 1940, U.S. officials knew on December 6, 1941, that Japan had planned a major
intervention. A thirteen-part intercept was before the president that night and U.S.
intelligence decoded it by 5:30 a.m. on December 7. Fearing the Japanese had inter-
cepted their scrambler phone, the army chief of staff sent his message warning the
U.S. military in Hawaii by radio dispatch and then, when transmission was delayed
by poor weather conditions, by Western Union telegram. The military authorities
in Honolulu finally received the warning message two hours *after* the first bombs
dropped (LaFeber, *The Clash,* 197, 211).

27. Layton, *And I Was There.* Secretary of War Henry Stimson explains of his
discussions with President Roosevelt and his top advisers, "The question was how
we should maneuver them [the Japanese] into the position of firing the first shot

without allowing too much danger to ourselves" (Stimson diary, cited in LaFeber, *The Clash,* 209). The U.S. ban on scrap iron and scrap steel and the oil embargo, as well as the imposition of nonnegotiable demands, particularly Secretary of State Cordell Hull's November 16, 1941, demand for Japan's withdrawal from China and Indochina, effectively forced Japan's hand. Japan attacked Pearl Harbor, knowing it could not gain a military victory. LaFeber observes: "The problem at the center of the Japanese policy was that if Japan did not go to war, it would collapse internally [from lack of oil and other resources] and lose everything it had shed blood for (Manchukuo, parts of China, Indochina) quite soon; if it did go to war, it could lose everything later" (208).

28. Tatsumi Nakazawa, Richard's paternal grandfather, died at age sixty on July 2, 1945, one week after he returned to Berkeley (Certificate of Death, County of Alameda).

29. *Children of the Camps* documentary; Nagata, *Legacy of Injustice.*

30. *Personal Justice Denied* contains the findings and recommendations of the Congressional Commission on Wartime Relocation and Internment of Civilians, which conducted research and heard testimonies from more than 750 witnesses, mainly former internees, but also scholars and government and military officials. The book-length report contains stories of significant physical illness, psychological impairment, economic deprivation, and education and work losses, and concluded that incarceration resulted from "race prejudice, war hysteria, and a failure of political leadership," and not the government's long-standing claim of military necessity (459). See also Taylor, "Evacuation and Economic Loss"; Daniels, Taylor, and Kitano, *Japanese Americans.*

31. Inside Topaz or shortly after their release, Shigeo Aoki apparently proposed a plan "by which the old Oakland Food Products might resume business again" (Shigeo Aoki, letter to Minoru Iyeki, February 28, 1946).

32. Another severe illness inside Topaz forced this aunt to quit her job (Minoru Iyeki, Coordinator of M & O, "Narrative Report of M & O," November 1942–August 1944, JERS Reel 131; Minoru Iyeki, "Narrative Report," July 24, 1945, Topaz, Utah, JERS Reel 131). Even after camp, she continued to have "sick spell[s]"—"That's me all the time," she commented (Minoru Iyeki, letter to Shigeo Aoki, January 29, 1946).

33. Iyeki, "Narrative Report of M & O."

34. The lack of privacy resulting from barrack living, where every word of private conversations could be overheard through the flimsy wooden planks, has been widely documented; see, for example, Fujino, *Heartbeat of Struggle,* 41; Taylor, *Jewel of the Desert,* 92–95.

35. Kitano, *Japanese Americans,* 41–42, 110; Taylor, *Jewel of the Desert,* 84–85.

36. A. L. Strauss, "Preliminary Sizing-up of Topaz Psychology," n.d., JERS Reel 131.

37. Shozo Aoki and his sons, Richard and David, left Topaz on October 11, 1945, destined for Oakland. Richard's mother, Toshiko Aoki, left Topaz on August 26, 1945, destined for Berkeley (War Relocation Authority, Final Departure Form, obtained from the Japanese American National Museum, Los Angeles).

38. Kikumura, *Through Harsh Winters,* 8–9.

39. James Aoki interview; also Aoki's cousin's interview and letter to author, September 6, 2005; anonymity requested.

40. *Topaz Times,* ca. September 22, 1942; Taylor, *Jewel of the Desert,* 97.

41. The promotion of Japanese Americans as model minorities who gained achievement through assimilation and hard work was long embraced by liberal Whites and Japanese Americans themselves as a response to racism, and popularized in Petersen's *New York Times Magazine* article in 1966.

42. *Oakland Tribune,* August 8, 1915; also January 5, 1928.

43. *Oakland Tribune,* August 8, 1915.

44. *Oakland Tribune,* April 23, 1933; March 11, 1934; May 5, 1935; March 19, 1937. Riuzo Aoki also participated on the Berkeley YMCA judo team (*Oakland Tribune,* May 19, 1954).

45. West Tenth Methodist Church, seventy-fifth anniversary, 1887–1962, program, October 6–7, 1962; Shigeo Aoki, "Personal Reflections," in *The Plowshare: News of Lake Park Church,* October 6, 1987.

46. *Oakland Tribune,* September 13, 1954.

47. *Oakland Tribune,* November 7, 1926; September 27, 1931; October 16, 1932.

48. Inside the concentration camps, many Japanese Americans expressed anger, disillusionment, and a sense of abandonment by the U.S. government. In *The Spoilage,* Thomas and Nishimoto document the pervasive frustrations and resentments of internees, particularly focusing on those who refused to state their loyalty to the United States on a government-administered questionnaire and were transferred to the camp in Tule Lake, Calif.

49. Shozo Aoki, UC Berkeley transcript, 1934–38.

50. Minoru Iyeki, letter to Shigeo Aoki, January 29, 1946. While *ojisan* means "uncle" in Japanese, it is clear from the context that the intended referent is *ojiisan,* or "grandfather."

51. Shigeo Aoki, letter to Minoru Iyeki, February 28, 1946.

52. Ibid.

53. Jameson, *Political Unconscious,* 102.

54. Homer, "Narratives of History," 79.

55. Sturken, "Absent Images of Memory," 34, 36. Many internees destroyed their remembrances—photographs, letters, Japanese books; the Aoki family buried their samurai swords—in an attempt to erase their cultural linkage to an enemy nation.

56. Ibid., 38.

57. Gordon and Okihiro, *Impounded.*

58. Adams, *Born Equal and Free,* 70.

59. Daniels, *Concentration Camps USA,* 112–13.

60. Creef notes that Adams's photographs reinscribe the Japanese American faces as an "iconographic sign for American citizenship," as heroic figures for the "white American gaze" (*Imaging Japanese America,* 19). By contrast, Lange's photographs present a humanizing face that captures the anguish and complexity of incarceration and seeks to "anchor her subjects to a particular historical and political context" (39). Also see Alinder, *Moving Images;* Nakamura, *Toyo Miyatake.*

61. Ricoeur, "On Interpretation"; cited in Homer, "Narratives of History," 78.

62. Homer, "Narratives of History," 82.

63. Ibid., 84.

64. Jameson, *Political Unconscious,* 102.

65. Derald Sue and colleagues use the term "racial microaggressions" to refer to "brief and commonplace daily verbal, behavioral, and environmental indignities, whether intentional or unintentional, that communicate hostile, derogatory, or negative racial slights and insults to the target person or group." Microaggressions have a negative impact on people of color "by sapping psychic and spiritual energy" and on society "by creating inequalities" ("Racial Microaggressions in Everyday Life," 273). Here I do not limit my discussion of trauma and microaggression to racial events, though there are clear racial injuries in Aoki's narrative.

66. I am grateful to George Lipsitz for this discussion of the effects of history and ungrieved traumas, which he elaborates on in *Rainbow at Midnight,* 33–39.

67. Jameson, *Political Unconscious,* 102.

3. "Learning to Do the West Oakland Dip"

1. Aoki identified their traveling companions by name. However, a search of the National Archives online database on Japanese American internment by the family's surname revealed no such family, with children around Richard and David's age, who hailed from the Bay Area, in the Topaz, Utah, concentration camp; http://aad.archives.gov/aad.

2. On the histories of West Oakland, see Bagwell, *Oakland;* Johnson, *The Second Gold Rush;* Olmsted and Olmsted, "History of West Oakland"; Praetzellis and Praetzellis, *Putting the "There" There;* Rhomberg, *No There There;* Self, *American Babylon.* On C. L. Dellums, see R. V. Dellums and Halterman, *Lying Down with the Lions;* Olmsted and Olmsted, "History of West Oakland," 211–21.

3. A chapter of the Ku Klux Klan formed in Oakland in 1922 and by 1924 had at least two thousand members and claimed a following in the thousands. The Oakland Klan's membership base was concentrated in the middle class and included clergy, professionals, and managers, skilled workers, public employees, and even the son of a U.S. congressperson (Rhomberg, *No There There,* 1–2, 57–62).

4. McEntire, *Residence and Race;* Rhomberg, *No There There,* 29–30, 81–82; Self, *American Babylon,* 104.

5. In the early 1940s, Oakland's population and economy were dramatically transformed in what the *San Francisco Chronicle* dubbed "the second gold rush." Enticed by the construction of two new military installations in the East Bay in 1938—the Naval Supply Base in Oakland and the nearby Alameda Naval Air Station—as well as shipbuilding and other defense industries, the Bay Area's population expanded by over half a million, or 26 percent, from 1940 to 1945, while its Black population skyrocketed from 19,759 to 64,680, or 227 percent, in the same period. Most Black migrants came from the South, especially Louisiana, Texas, Oklahoma, and Arkansas, and settled in West Oakland and North Richmond. In West Oakland, the Black population swelled from just over 8,000, or 16.2 percent of the area's

population, in 1940 to 42,335, or 61.5 percent, by 1950. Blacks were forced into racially segregated communities, disproportionately resided in public housing, and created their own West Oakland Black culture, centered on Seventh Street's commercial district and jazz scene. Oakland and Los Angeles became the major centers of Black resettlement during this massive interstate migration to California during World War II. See *San Francisco Chronicle,* series of articles, April 25–May 20, 1943; Johnson, *The Second Gold Rush,* 17, 30–34, 51–59, 83–112; Self, *American Babylon,* 47, 50–54; Olmsted and Olmsted, "History of West Oakland," 169; also Weaver, *The Negro Ghetto.*

6. Residential racial segregation was widespread in the postwar years (McEntire, *Residence and Race;* Massey and Denton, *American Apartheid*). Despite the U.S. Supreme Court's ban on restrictive covenants in 1948, the Federal Housing Authority, realtors, and bankers continued discriminatory housing practices (Lipsitz, *The Possessive Investment in Whiteness,* 25–33).

7. According to Aoki, the Lower Bottom area of West Oakland was bordered on the north by DeFremery Park, on the west by the railroad tracks, on the east by Broadway, and on the south by Oakland Army Terminal. The Dog Town area stretched north from DeFremery Park up to around Thirtieth Street, with Market Street on the east and the railroads on the west. The Ghost Town area stretched from about Thirtieth on the south to Emeryville at the Oakland border on the north; the west side was again the railroad tracks; and the east side was around Grove Street, now known as Martin Luther King Way.

8. Though Richard does not say this, the children teasing and fighting him were mainly Black.

9. *Jujitsu* is a Japanese martial art evolved from the samurai of feudal Japan. It is considered a soft art in which one uses the force or aggression of an opponent against him or her and includes *tomoenage* (circle throw or stomach throw) and *koshinage* (hip throw).

10. Pseudonyms were used for this family.

11. The house at 2603 Union Street appears to have been first leased to Jitsuji Aoki in 1922 and purchased by Riuzo Aoki in 1937 (Deed of Indenture from P. Q. Rothrock and Minnie Rothrock to Riuzo Aoki, August 21, 1925; Deed of Trust, with Riuzo Aoki as Trustee, May 5, 1937). California's 1913 Alien Land Law prohibited "aliens ineligible to citizenship," including all Japanese immigrants until 1952, from purchasing "real property." Because the 1911 treaty with Japan protected the rights of Japanese nationals to own residential and business property, the 1913 law in effect prohibited the purchase of *agricultural land.* The 1920 Alien Land Law closed most of the loopholes of the 1913 act and effectively reduced Japanese American landholdings. See California Alien Land Law, approved May 19, 1913; Ferguson, "The California Alien Land Law and the Fourteenth Amendment"; Ichihashi, *Japanese in the United States,* 192; Ichioka, *The Issei,* 153–56, 226–43.

12. Jitsuji Aoki's business was apparently quite lucrative, with "more than a ton [of noodles] manufactured daily to supply the ever increasing demand and the products are shipped from coast to coast" (*Oakland Tribune,* August 10, 1930). By 1921

Jitsuji had established the Oakland Noodle Factory at 2531 Union Street, located near Union and Twenty-Sixth Street (*Polk–Husted City Directory for Oakland, Berkeley, and Alameda,* 1921). There was no listing for the Oakland Noodle Factory before 1921, though directories were not published in 1919 or 1920. By 1927, the factory moved to 1255 Twenty-Sixth Street (Deed of Indenture, Dorothy Christine Kinne to Riuzo Aoki, February 26, 1927). Jitsuji and Fusa Aoki's children lived nearby. In 1935, for example, Haruko, Riuzo (misspelled as Rinzo), and Shozo (Richard's father) were "roomers" at the main family home at 2603 Union, and Shigeo was the "householder" at 2611 Union (*Polk–Husted City Directory for Oakland, Berkeley, and Alameda,* 1935). The noodle factory was later named Oakland Food Products Company.

13. Richard later moved into the parlor: "They were kind of cramping my style." His father and brother continued to shared the bedroom until David was about twelve or thirteen years old, when the two brothers moved to their mother's home. When I asked, "Was it typical for parents and children to share a bedroom?" Richard brushed off the question.

14. *The Book of Knowledge: The Children's Encyclopedia; The Book of History: A History of All Nations from the Earliest Times to the Present,* vol. 2: *The Far East.*

15. From the development of the modern school system in the period of industrialization until relatively recently, it was uncommon for American, including Japanese American, parents to homeschool their children. While American agrarian life was centered on the family, it was not until the 1960s, and particularly since the mid-1980s, that homeschooling became a recognized alternative to public schooling. Being homeschooled in the 1940s and '50s was highly unusual; to have a male instructor was even more exceptional.

16. While Richard remembered his brother having no interest in art, David apparently learned to draw. David was selected to sketch illustrations depicting the life of the school principal Elwood Hess for a booklet created by his junior high English class (*Oakland Tribune,* March 28, 1954). Richard's drawings are well proportioned and detailed pencil sketches of military airplanes on "Army Air Force" letterhead signed by "AOKI" and dated March 1952. In the 1960s, Richard sketched various political events unfolding around him (Wang and Cheng, *AOKI,* preview screening, May 30, 2008, Oakland), and was an illustrator for the journal *Black Politics.*

17. Aoki's maternal grandmother, deeply religious according to Aoki, gave him a Bible for his seventeenth birthday. Although not religious himself, Richard has kept this gift, which he showed me, to the present.

18. The Japanese Methodist Episcopal Church in Oakland was first organized in 1887. The building of the church the Aokis attended at 795 Tenth Street, at Clay Street, was completed in 1916 at the cost of $10,000. A second Japanese Methodist Episcopal Church was located at 289 Sixth Street (Hinkel and McCann, *Oakland 1852–1938,* 422–23, 447).

19. The Japanese word *dorobo* refers to a troublemaker, robber, or thief.

20. In the 1950s, the vast majority of Japanese Americans dated coethnics. While a few Japanese Americans dated Whites, fewer married interracially, and even fewer dated or married African Americans.

21. Job discrimination was rampant for the Nisei or second-generation Japanese Americans like Richard's father, uncles, and aunts. Even those with college degrees often found themselves employed in the ethnic enclaves (e.g., in the fruit and vegetable stands in Little Tokyo), having been shut out of professional jobs (Kurashige, *Japanese American Celebration and Conflict*, 26–34). One Issei man lamented: "How many sons of ours with a beautiful bachelor's degree are accepted into American life? Name me one young man who is now working in an American firm on equal terms with his white colleagues. Our Nisei engineers push lawn mowers. Men with degrees in chemistry and physics do research in the fruit stands of the public market. And they all rot away inside" (Sone, *Nisei Daughter*, 121).

22. Jack Johnson was said have to spread rumors that he threw that fight, but it's widely recognized that he was worn down by his much younger and larger opponent. See Ken Burns's documentary *Unforgivable Blackness*, based on the book of the same name by Geoffrey Ward. Hietala uses the lens of race to analyze the significance of Jack Johnson's brazen mocking of racial hierarchies in his victories over White boxing champions and his relations with White women *(The Fight of the Century)*. In popular culture, jazz greats Miles Davis and Wynton Marsalis paid musical homage to Jack Johnson: Miles Davis, *A Tribute to Jack Johnson* (Columbia, 1971), the original score for the Academy Award–nominated film *Jack Johnson* (1970); Miles Davis, *The Complete Jack Johnson Sessions* (Columbia, 2003); Wynton Marsalis, *Unforgivable Blackness* (Blue Note, 2004), the original score for Ken Burns's documentary. The movie *The Great White Hope* (1970), starring James Earl Jones, is based on Johnson's life.

23. A search of police records, FBI files, court records, and newspapers revealed only one criminal charge against Shozo Aoki (the shooting of his "wife," *Oakland Tribune*, October 24, 1954). It is hard to assess whether Richard inflated the severity of his father's criminal behavior when any such records most likely have been destroyed. The Oakland Police Department will release arrest information from the 1940s–1950s only if a charge resulted in a conviction and if one can provide arrest dates and other specific information obtained from an FBI "rap sheet," which is created when a person is fingerprinted. The FBI in its search did not find any record on Shozo Aoki, nor would they have because all criminal and civil fingerprint records for people born before 1929 were destroyed under the bureau's record destruction policy. I found no criminal records for Shozo Aoki at the Criminal Records Division of Alameda County; however, if a felony had been reduced to a misdemeanor or if a charge was settled out of court, there would be no record. Still, others do collaborate this robbery and other criminal activities of Shozo Aoki (Debbie Aoki interview).

24. This drinking of soda pop became a lifelong habit. Despite having diabetes, Aoki did not reduce his consumption of about ten cans of Dr Pepper a day or switch to diet soda.

25. If Aoki's memory of twenty-five cents per hour is correct, then he was grossly underpaid. California minimum wage was sixty-five cents per hour (1947–52) and federal minimum wage was forty cents per hour (1945–50). But for many youngsters, twenty-five cents an hour would have seemed like "good money."

26. The *Oakland Post-Enquirer* folded in September 1950, when Aoki was eleven years old, leaving the *Oakland Tribune* as the sole daily in Oakland (*Time*, "Final Edition," September 11, 1950). Aoki must have stopped delivering papers a few years before he began junior high school in early 1953.

27. John H. Johnson, founder of Johnson Publishing, published magazines directed at an African American audience: *Negro Digest* (patterned after *Reader's Digest*) began in 1942, *Ebony* (patterned after *Life*) in 1945, and *Jet* in 1951. That Aoki recalls *Negro Digest* being published last reflects the order in which he became introduced to these magazines. Unlike the middlebrow, entertainment-oriented material of *Ebony* and *Jet, Negro Digest* was political; the January 1967 issue featured an article titled "On Racism, Exploitation and the White Liberal"; the May 1968 issue features an article by Frantz Fanon. On how middlebrow productions like *Reader's Digest* generated popular enthusiasm for an Orientalist gaze toward Asia in the Cold War period, see Klein, *Cold War Orientalism.*

28. Emmett Till wasn't killed only for whistling at a White woman in Mississippi in 1955, but also for refusing to subordinate himself to the demands of White men for an apology (Huie, "The Shocking Story of Approved Killing in Mississippi").

29. There was no record of this event, nor would there be because records for misdemeanor charges are deleted from the system after seven years.

30. A well-known contemporary example is that of George Jackson, who in 1960 stole seventy dollars and got a one-year-to-life sentence. In prison, Jackson grew in political consciousness, joined the Black Panther Party, and became the preeminent symbol of the prison liberation movement before being killed by prison guards on August 21, 1971. His death is commemorated yearly in Black August activities. See Wald and Churchill, "Remembering the Real Dragon"; Jackson, *Soledad Brother* and *Blood in My Eye*; Davis, *If They Come in the Morning.* Also Engels, *The Condition of the Working Class in England in 1844*; Hugo, *Les Misérables* and the Broadway hit musical that opened in 1987; Thompson, *The Making of the English Working Class*; and the classic novels of Charles Dickens.

31. This death was not reported in the *Oakland Tribune,* but coverage was racially uneven in this newspaper owned by the conservative Knowland family. Whatever the accuracy of Aoki's memory of this incident, its meaning to him centers on the dangers involved in children's play when recreational facilities are distributed unequally by race and class.

32. On the Stanford-Binet intelligence test, administered in June 1953, Richard (fourteen years six months) and David (thirteen years four months) performed at the "genius" level, denoted by scores of 140 and above. Richard yielded an IQ of 144 (mental age of twenty years two months). David scored even higher, with an extraordinary IQ of 157 (mental age of twenty years ten months). Six months earlier, on the Stanford Achievement Tests, Richard had a stellar reading performance level of

over fifteen years eleven months and an average arithmetic performance age of thirteen years six months; David had a reading performance level of fifteen years nine months and arithmetic performance level of thirteen years nine months (Richard Aoki and David Aoki, transcripts, Herbert Hoover Junior High School).

33. BPP leader David Hilliard commented that "being a traffic boy" was the "'in' thing" at his elementary school in Oakland. He recounts being "so proud of my new station and responsibility" because "every student wants to wear the rust orange jacket and yellow, peaked soldier's cap" and he could "control the traffic!" (Hilliard and Cole, *This Side of Glory,* 73). Aoki was fairly active during his one year in junior high school, participating in projector crew, student council, and traffic, as well as being awarded several Certificates for Good Scholarship and a Certificate for Good American Citizenship (Richard Aoki, report cards, June 12, 1953; January 29, 1954; student transcript). Elwood V. Hess, affectionately known as "Doc," was a well-liked and respected principal at Herbert Hoover Junior High School (1947–55) and later at McClymonds High School (*Oakland Tribune,* March 28, 1954; May 20, 1956).

34. David Hilliard says he attended Herbert Hoover Junior High School. Huey Newton says he started junior high school with Hilliard at Woodrow Wilson, but acknowledges attending "almost every grammar and junior high school in the city of Oakland" because his family "moved around a lot." See Hilliard and Cole, *This Side of Glory,* 77; Newton, *Revolutionary Suicide,* 18, 24–25. Though I found no documentation of Herbert Hoover Junior High School's mascot, the Panther Junior Hi-Y Club was located at Herbert Hoover Junior High (*Oakland Tribune,* March 24, 1957).

35. Aoki certainly was a good student in junior high school, but his grades are inflated in his own memory. Based on his report cards and student transcripts, he received two As and two Bs in core subjects (English, science, Spanish, and algebra, respectively) in his first semester, and three As and one B in core subjects (English, social studies, Spanish, and algebra, respectively) in his second semester. This is in addition to As in "homeroom" and electives and Bs in physical education in both semesters. Reflecting his adjustment and impressive work transitioning to his first year in the formal education system, his science teacher wrote, "Richard has not only done excellent work in science but is making a fine adjustment to a new situation. This was difficult for him at first and he often seemed discouraged but I'm sure he is on the right track now. I have thoroughly enjoyed knowing him" (Richard Aoki, Herbert Hoover Junior High School transcript).

36. I found no records to verify Aoki that was covaledictorian. Herbert Hoover has since closed and the only records dating to the 1950s are student transcripts (Microfilm Department, Oakland Unified School District).

37. The *Oakland Tribune* reported an incident in which a student struck the McClymonds High School principal and vice principal, but it occurred a full year after Aoki started at Berkeley High School (March 5, 1955). There may have been another incident on Aoki's first day, or Aoki's attendance at Berkeley High School may have been precipitated by his move to Berkeley in early 1953 to live with his mother. His father's troubles with the law were likely the primary motivator for

Richard and David's move to their mother's home, after living with their father for almost a decade. There was no mention of any other racial strife in that period, but it would not be unusual for the *Oakland Tribune* to minimize such problems. While Aoki alludes to having observed the attacks on the administrators, he relayed his story with rather vague descriptions.

38. Berkeley High School, with its higher property values and proximity to the prestigious University of California campus, was considered more academically rigorous than schools in Oakland. But Aoki's figures about Berkeley High's academic distinction are exaggerated. Neither local newspapers nor Berkeley High School records make any noteworthy remarks about the school's academic success historically or today. The rankings of high schools by *Newsweek, U.S. News and World Report,* and Public School Ranking began in the last decade. In 1999, Berkeley High ranked 135 out of California's 834 public high schools (http://www.psk12.com).

39. To place Aoki's mother's wages in context, when Aoki was in high school, the California minimum wage was seventy-five cents an hour (1954–57). The federal minimum wage was seventy-five cents an hour until March 1956, when it jumped to one dollar an hour. Aoki's high school grades tended to be split between As and Bs, with a scattering of Cs and even one D, with a GPA of 3.1 in his academic classes. His second semester, however, was exceptional, with his earning all As (three in academic subjects and one in typing) (Richard Aoki, transcript, Berkeley High School).

40. David Aoki got married in December 1961 at age twenty-one and had a child in August 1962, when he was a twenty-two-year-old student at the university (David Aoki and Debbie Sasahara, Marriage Certificate, County of San Francisco; Michael Aoki, Certificate of Live Birth, County of Alameda). David graduated from UC Berkeley in June 1965, a year before Richard began UC Berkeley. Richard and David's grades were quite comparable in junior high and high school, but by university, David's grades had deteriorated significantly (he got several Cs and Ds), while Richard had a B average (David Aoki and Richard Aoki, transcripts, Herbert Hoover Junior High School, Berkeley High School, UC Berkeley).

41. Aoki has two black-and-white photographs of himself in his oversized Saints jacket, one by himself and one among five young men in Saints jackets: Richard, his brother, David, and three African Americans.

42. Berkeley High School does not have records of student disciplinary actions dating back to the 1950s.

43. Abortion was illegal in the United States until the 1973 *Roe v. Wade* U.S. Supreme Court decision determined that the Constitution protects a woman's decision to terminate her pregnancy, although in 1967, several states allowed abortions under various conditions.

44. Richard's mother left the Topaz concentration camp on August 26, 1945, separately from her children and husband, and separately from her own father and brother (War Relocation Authority, Final Departure Form, obtained from the Japanese American National Museum, Los Angeles). Richard's mother lived at 1519 Stuart Street in Berkeley (Richard Aoki, transcript, Herbert Hoover Junior High

School, 1954), a block from her pre- and postwar family home at 1623 Stuart Street (*Oakland–Berkeley–Alameda City Directory,* 1941).

45. Berkeley is adjacent to and north of Oakland. His mother's home in Berkeley was less than three miles from his father's home in Oakland. More than geographic distance, Aoki's comment about "living in different worlds" speaks to the huge social, psychological, and emotional divide that he felt between him and his mother during this period.

46. William Shinji Tsuchida's *Wear It Proudly* discusses his experiences as a soldier in the integrated Seventy-First Infantry in France and Germany from September 1944 to July 1945. These letters offer a detailed narrative of Tsuchida's life in the trenches, despite his awareness of army censorship requirements. Missing from the book is even a brief biography of Tsuchida and his life in Berkeley. A Tsuchida family owned College Cleaners before the war, and a College Cleaning and Dye Works was located at the same address, 2942 College in Berkeley, in the postwar period (*Oakland–Berkeley–Alameda City Directory,* 1939; *Oakland–Berkeley Telephone Directory,* 1946).

47. A newspaper article about an incident between Shozo Aoki and his "wife" indicated that they lived in an empty warehouse at 1255 Twenty-Sixth Street, at the corner of Union Street, which in the 1930s was the location of the Aoki's noodle company (*Oakland Tribune,* October 24, 1954; *Oakland–Berkeley–Alameda City Directory,* 1934, 1940). Although the newspaper reported the woman as Shozo's wife, there is no record of their marriage, at least not in Alameda County (Certification of No Records, County of Alameda) and others stated that they did not marry (Debbie Aoki interview).

48. Richard and David were living with their mother in January 1953, at the time she enrolled them in junior high school (Richard Aoki, transcript, Herbert Hoover Junior High School). Richard speaks sparingly about his parents' separation and divorce. The circumstances surrounding his parents' relationship remain shrouded in mystery; his mother had advanced dementia, his father and brother were deceased, those few family members with whom I spoke expressed knowing nothing about the subject, and I respected Richard's request not to inquire about this issue with other extended family members. Toshiko Aoki's request for a divorce was heard before the Superior Court judge in November 1954. The sparse court record states that Richard's parents separated around August 23, 1945, which would have been three days before Toshiko left the Topaz concentration camp, though it seems they had separated even earlier inside the camp. Toshiko's statement was that Shozo treated her in a "cruel manner and has wrongfully and without cause inflicted upon plaintiff great and grievous mental suffering" (Complaint for Divorce, November 19, 1954). Although Shozo had been summoned, he did not appear in court; he may have left town by then. The court awarded Toshiko the divorce, custody of the children, and "a reasonable sum of money" for the divorce suit and child support (Summons, November 19, 1954; Final Judgment of Divorce, December 30, 1955; both County of Alameda).

49. Earl Napper remembers the tiny size of Richard's mother's apartment and Richard's mom giving her bedroom to her sons (Napper interview).

50. From Aoki's home in Berkeley, off Stuart and Sacramento Streets, Herbert Hoover Junior High School, at 890 Brockhurst Street in Oakland, was less than 2.5 miles away, going straight down Sacramento Street, which becomes Market Street.

51. Despite having different personalities and styles, Earl Napper and Richard became close friends at Berkeley High School. They shared activities with the Saints at the YMCA and an interest in girls. Earl recalls teaching Richard to dance and sharing local table tennis championships with David (Napper interview; *Oakland Tribune,* February 19, 1956; March 31, 1957). They were lifelong friends, although less connected during the height of Richard's political activities in the 1960s and early '70s.

52. Richard was in the Stamp and Coin Club, almost all of whose members were White, for most of his time in high school and was elected president twice, in fall 1955 and fall 1956. He was also in the Latin Club, the Honor Society, and the California Scholarship Federation (Berkeley High School yearbooks, spring 1954 to fall 1956).

53. Napper reported Richard's mother telling him, "You're the only one, when Richard goes with you, I know he's safe" (Napper interview).

54. Famous Black entertainers like Ray Charles, Dorothy Dandridge, Ella Fitzgerald, Jimi Hendrix, Billie Holiday, Lena Horne, Richard Pryor, and Ike and Tina Turner performed on the Chitlin' Circuit at venues such as the Cotton Club and the Apollo in Harlem, the Victory Grill in Austin, and the Howard Theater in Washington, D.C.

55. By the 1920s, Oakland became a blues mecca, with Seventh Street as the center of local Black culture. Seventh Street thrived throughout the 1940s and '50s, until urban development projects displaced the physical sites of the music scene (Goldman, "7th Street Blues").

56. Charles Brown (1922–99) was a popular blues singer–pianist with some two dozen hits on the R&B charts from 1946 to 1952. Aoki's narrative generally matches the published materials on Brown. The "mama" who insisted on his studying piano refers to Brown's maternal grandmother; she and his grandfather, "Papa," raised him after his mother's death early in his life. In 1997 Brown was awarded a National Heritage Fellowship by the National Endowment for the Arts at a White House ceremony. In 1999 he was inducted posthumously into the Rock and Roll Hall of Fame, with Bonnie Raitt as presenter. See Deffaa, *"Charles Brown"*; http://www.rockhall .com; http://www.nea.gov; http://www.allaboutjazz.com.

57. Tempest Storm, one of the highest-paid burlesque performers, had her professional debut at the El Rey Theater in Oakland in 1951. After appearing onstage there numerous times, she helped to close the El Rey's doors in 1957, when the building was taken over by freeway construction. Aoki was twenty years old when Storm and Herb Jeffries married in 1959 (*Oakland Tribune,* May 15, 1953; June 24, 1957; May 22, 1959).

58. Debbie Aoki also mentioned the foreclosure on the family home following Hideo Nakazawa's purchase of a Jaguar for his girlfriend (Debbie Aoki interview).

59. Richard interacted with his grandparents in Japanese cultural ways, calling his grandmother *Obaasan* and taking her a small gift or *omiage* so as to never visit empty handed.

60. When Richard's father died in 2002, he was living at the low-income Miyako Gardens Apartment in Little Tokyo, Los Angeles, on Central Avenue between Second and Third Streets (Shozo Aoki, Certificate of Death, County of Los Angeles). He had been living there for years, including when he visited David in the hospital in 1986 (Debbie Aoki interview).

61. *Oakland Tribune,* October 24, 1954.

62. Richard identified his cousin and aunt by name, but this cousin requested anonymity. She was one of the few relatives to keep in touch with Shozo, reconnecting with him to inform him of Riuzo's death. She has fond, but sparse, memories of Shozo, Richard, and David.

63. David Aoki died on December 27, 1986, at age forty-six, of "hepatic failure" and "alcoholic cirrhosis," the latter of which he had for years. Richard's paternal grandfather, Jijitsu Aoki, died at age seventy-seven in 1950. His paternal grandmother, Fusa Aoki, died at age ninety-five in 1967 (Certificate of Death, County of Alameda, for all three).

64. *Oakland Tribune,* August 8, 1915.

65. Hantover, "The Boy Scouts and the Validation of Masculinity"; Kimmel, *Manhood in America,* 112–13. The latter source provides an important history of the shifts in American middle-class masculinities as a result of political-economic and cultural-ideological transformations.

66. *Oakland Tribune,* January 5, 1928; April 23, 1933; March 11, 1934; May 5, 1935. Hata's advocacy efforts were not strong enough to offset racial discrimination and a separate, rather than integrated, Boy Scout troop was formed in Oakland.

67. Shozo was in the Japanese American Boy Scout Troop 63, with Riuzo as scoutmaster (*Oakland Tribune,* November 7, 1926; September 27, 1931; October 16, 1932).

68. Connell, *Masculinities,* 76–78.

69. Kimmel, *Manhood in America,* 105.

70. The Nisei were viewed as "quiet" and "conventional" and indeed had among the lowest rates of criminality of any ethnic group (Kitano, *Japanese Americans,* 143–50). Earl Warren, California attorney general (1939–43) and U.S. Supreme Court Justice (1953–69), remarked in his memoirs that "although we had a sizable Japanese population [in California], neither the young nor the old violated the law" (Warren, *Memoirs,* 149). Shozo Aoki represented what Paul Spickard called the Nisei "underclass," referring to those "Nisei whose resistance to racial oppression was neither organized nor self-conscious." While Richard too exhibited some "deviant" behaviors, his political consciousness differentiated him from the "underclass" (Spickard, "Not Just the Quiet People," 82).

71. Kimmel argues that acceptance through the "male gaze" is crucial to proving one's manhood, to showing one's separation from the feminine and homosexual ("Masculinity as Homophobia").

72. Shigeo Aoki's life was indeed not easy; among other difficulties, he experienced estrangement from his father, racist taunting from schoolmates, the death of his young son, internment as a young father and budding entrepreneur, and

"working—from 2–3 am til 9 pm" only to have his tofu factory burn ("Background of Joseph Shigeo Aoki—His Words," April 23, 2005; Shigeo Joseph Aoki, interview by Ann Yabusaki; Asaka Aoki, "My Life's Journey," October 18, 1998). On Shigeo Aoki's accomplishments, see *Oakland Tribune*, April 20, 1929; December 26, 1931. On the academic, athletic, and leadership accomplishments of Shigeo's sons, see *Oakland Tribune*, January 11, 1953; March 29, 1953; August 20, 1955; December 26, 1956; March 24, 1957; August 13, 1958; and May 13, 1959, among others.

73. Not surprisingly given its pro-American display and Knowland's presence, the *Oakland Tribune*'s coverage of Citizens Day was disproportionate to the numbers of new citizens involved (September 13, 1954; also September 8, 10, and 12, 1954).

74. Smiles's *Self-Help* is discussed in Kinmonth, *The Self-Made Man in Meiji Japanese Thought*, 9–43; also see Connell, *Masculinities*, 180–81.

75. The single-paragraph newspaper blurb stated: "A 32-year-old Oakland woman was in serious condition . . . with a gunshot wound in the abdomen. Police held her husband for investigation of assault with a deadly weapon." The husband of "Mrs. Nellie Oaki" (misspelling of Aoki), identified as Sho, age forty, told the police that she "accidentally shot herself." But "police said the position of the wound indicated this was impossible" ("Woman Shot, Husband Held," *Oakland Tribune*, October 24, 1954). Nellie was most likely Shozo's girlfriend, not his wife.

4. "I Was a Man by the Standards of the 'Hood"

1. Through 1964, any student meeting UC eligibility was admitted to the Berkeley campus. Aoki was included in this group of UC-eligible students. See *Oakland Tribune*, January 24, 1957; Committee on Admissions and Enrollment, *Freshman Admissions at Berkeley*.

2. Ted Williams would have impressed Aoki. Not only was he one of the greatest hitters in the history of baseball, he also served as a Marine Corps pilot during the Korean War.

3. In this narrative, after resolving to enter the army rather than the air force, Aoki returns to his dream of becoming an airman. Military historian Michael S. Sherry argues that the allure of aerial warfare was captured in the imagination as much as in reality. Postwar America was fascinated with the recent advances in aviation technology, the frightening and reassuring destruction of aerial bombings (consider the massive devastation by U.S. firebombings of Tokyo during World War II), and the power of the nuclear bomb (*The Rise of American Air Power*). To Aoki in the 1950s, Ben Kuroki, much heralded in the mainstream press and segments of the Japanese American community, was indeed an American war hero. Kuroki garnered multiple medals for courageous service in a remarkable fifty-eight combat missions during World War II. Shortly after the draft was reinstated for Japanese Americans, Kuroki was featured in *Time* magazine (February 7, 1944) as a shining example of the patriotism of this vilified and suspect group. The government sent Kuroki to visit Topaz, Utah, and two other concentration camps to recruit Japanese American soldiers. Although Aoki remembers none of this, Sgt. Kuroki was celebrated as a

"Nisei Hero" by the editors of the Topaz camp newspaper (*Topaz Times,* May 13, 19, 24, 1944). The 442nd Regimental Combat Team, an all-Japanese army unit, became renowned for its sacrifice and bravery; it was the most decorated unit of its size in U.S. military history.

4. Universal military training, passed by the U.S. Congress in 1951 and modified in 1955, required men ages eighteen to twenty-eight to serve in active duty for a period of six months, followed by seven and a half years of reserve service in the armed forces. It was expected that nearly every young man in the United States would participate. Compulsory military service, or the draft, was also in effect at the time (1940–72), but between the Korean War and the Vietnam War buildup, it attracted little attention. See House Committee on Armed Services, *Universal Military Training,* 1–5; House Committee on Armed Services, *Reserve Forces Act of 1955,* 1–8; Griffith, *The U.S. Army's Transition to the All-Volunteer Force,* 8–10.

5. The USSR invaded Hungary on November 4, 1956, in response to a spontaneous national uprising on October 23 against Stalinist rule in Hungary. Although President Eisenhower, the United Nations, and many in the West, including Western Marxists, quickly denounced the Soviet invasion, the call was for diplomatic and economic measures and not U.S. military intervention (*New York Times,* November 6, 9, 10, 1956). Still, that a young Aoki might see possibilities for military involvement is reasonable. At the time, the U.S. State Department threatened that any USSR invasion of Austria would be "a grave threat to the peace" (*New York Times,* November 6, 1956), and, of course, Germany's invasion of Poland had sparked World War II in 1939.

6. On Tsuchida's wartime experiences, see *Wear It Proudly.*

7. The Reserve Forces Act of 1955 stipulated that a person could be called to active duty for training when he graduated, stopped pursuing high school, or reached twenty years of age, whichever came first (House Committee on Armed Services, *Reserve Forces Act of 1955,* 5).

8. Featured in military uniform on the cover of *Life* magazine (July 16, 1945), Audie Murphy was propelled to national fame. His autobiography, *To Hell and Back,* a gripping story of American soldiers at war, became a best seller and was later made into a top-grossing motion picture of the same title, featuring Audie Murphy as himself (Universal International, 1955).

9. A letter to Aoki from the Reserve Forces Act Regiment headquarters at Fort Ord, March 14, 1957, and Aoki's honorable discharge papers, March 31, 1964, indicate that he enlisted under the Reserve Forces Act of 1955 and completed his eight-year enlistment. I could find no other records of Aoki's military service, perhaps because "the record may have been lost before we introduced the computerized registry" (Dana Netherton, archives technician, National Personnel Records, letter to Diane Fujino, May 25, 2009). Although Aoki falls outside this period, there was also a fire in 1973 that "destroyed approximately 80 percent of military personnel records for Army veterans who were discharged between 1912 and 1960" (Netherton, letter to Fujino, April 27, 2009). Fort Ord, on Monterey Bay, is about 110 miles south of Oakland. Established in 1917, Fort Ord was considered an ideal geographic location

for military training, using its shoreline for amphibious maneuvers. It closed in 1994 and is currently the site of California State University, Monterey Bay (U.S. Army Corps of Engineers, *Fort Ord: A Place in History*).

10. Life insurance of ten thousand dollars was given for UMT personnel (House Committee on Armed Services, *Universal Military Training*, 4).

11. Aoki's military experiences held meaning for him, as evidenced by his accurately remembering his military number forty years after separating from the army (Aoki, Honorable Discharge certificate, October 31, 1964).

12. During World War II, the huge increase in noncommissioned officers, from 20 percent of the enlisted ranks at the beginning of the war to 50 percent by June 1945, greatly diminished the prestige and meaning of enlisted combat leaders. In the postwar period, the army worked to strengthen the selection process and training of NCOs, but by the early 1960s, the results were uneven (Fisher, *Guardians of the Republic*).

13. The Warner Bros. movie *Darby's Rangers*, starring James Garner, was released in 1958, a year after Aoki's reported fight with his sergeant. But Aoki, with his interest in and knowledge of military history, would have known about Darby's Rangers, famous for their daring World War II maneuvers and specialized training. Several books have been published about Darby's Rangers, including one posthumously by its commander Major William Orlando Darby, *Darby's Rangers: We Led the Way.*

14. The army established Fort Sam Houston, in Texas, as its principal medical training facility at the end of World War II. One of three twentieth-century influenza pandemics occurred in 1957–58.

15. This is the entirety of the brief letter from Lewis Maness, Colonel, Infantry, Commanding, to Private Aoki, March 14, 1957, on RFA Regiment letterhead, Headquarters Reserve Forces Act Regiment, Fort Ord, California.

16. If Aoki mastered physics concepts in his two semesters of high school physics, it was not reflected in his grades—a C and B (Richard Aoki, transcript, Berkeley High School).

17. *Fragging* was a term introduced in the Vietnam War era to refer to the killing of an authoritative, aggressive, or inept officer by someone in his own unit, usually with a fragmentation grenade, hence the term. Fragging was rather common in Vietnam. According to U.S. Army records, 300 fraggings occurred in 1969–70; by 1972, there were 551 incidents. Others estimate 800 to 1,000 fragging attempts using explosives alone. A Department of Defense source speculated that more officers were killed by fragging by gunfire than by grenades. See Moser, *The New Winter Soldiers*, 48–51; Bibby, *Hearts and Minds*, 126.

18. Aoki discussed his views on homosexuality in 2003, a crucial time in the struggle for same-sex marriage and heightened visibility of the gay movement. The life of the first openly gay elected official in California, Harvey Milk, has captured the imagination of filmmakers in Oscar-winning films *The Times of Harvey Milk* (1985) and *Milk* (2009), and of several book authors. Milk and San Francisco mayor George Moscone were both assassinated on November 27, 1978, by former city supervisor

Dan White. The 1969 Stonewall riots in New York City came to symbolize the beginnings of the U.S. gay rights movement.

19. The 1955 Reserve Forces Act amended the 1951 Universal Military Service and Training Act by doubling the size of the Ready Reserve and by continually providing training since "the Reserve Forces [were] becoming more of a pool of personnel than an organized military force" (House Committee on Armed Services, *Reserve Forces Act of 1955,* 1). After three to six months of active duty, one could transfer to the Ready Reserve, subject to active duty in the event of war or a national emergency declared by the president or Congress. After five years of active service and Ready Reserve service, one could transfer to Standby Reserve, considered the second line of reserves subject to active duty after Ready Reserves and only in time of war or a national emergency declared by Congress. Aoki was honorably discharged from the Standby Reserves in October 1964 (Aoki, Honorable Discharge certificate). See note 4, this chapter.

20. Both California and federal minimum wage was $1.00 per hour at this time; both rose to $1.25 an hour in 1963.

21. Aoki is referring to Malcolm X's famous "Message to the Grass Roots" speech (1963; in Malcolm X, *Malcolm X Speaks,* 10–12).

22. In a rare moment, Aoki got choked up and teary-eyed as he discussed *The Grapes of Wrath,* both the widely read novel (Viking, 1939) and the immensely popular film (20th Century–Fox, 1940), known for its heart-wrenching, poignant scenes of human suffering caused by capitalist exploitation. John Steinbeck (1902–68) won a Pulitzer Prize for this novel and later a Nobel Prize in Literature. The film, with more socialist themes and optimism about the possibilities for social change than the novel, ends with Tom Joad telling his mother before his forced departure, "I'll be ever'where—wherever you can look. Wherever there's a fight so hungry people can eat, I'll be there. Wherever there's a cop beatin' up a guy, I'll be there. I'll be in the way guys yell when they're mad—I'll be in the way kids laugh when they're hungry an' they know supper's ready. An' when the people are eatin' the stuff they raise, and livin' in the houses they build, I'll be there, too." After untold hardships, his mother, in the film's final scene, proclaims, "That's what makes us tough. Rich fellas come up an' they die an' their kids ain't no good, an' they die out. But we keep a-comin'. We're the people that live. They can't wipe us out. They can't lick us. And we'll go on forever, Pa . . . 'cause . . . we're the people" (http://www.filmsite.org/grap3.html).

23. The writings of Carey McWilliams (1905–80) on social issues, racism, and farm laborers helped shape the nation's views on racial and economic inequalities. *Grapes of Wrath* and *Factories in the Fields,* two masterpieces published months apart in 1939, along with Dorothea Lange's stirring photographs of the Depression era, focused sympathetic attention on the plight of migrant farmworkers and offered scathing critiques of large-scale agribusiness. The difference in genre (the fictionalized drama of Steinbeck versus the journalistic writings of McWilliams), in addition to its different racial subjects, account for the wider popular appeal of *Grapes of Wrath.* See also McWilliams, *Brothers Under the Skin* and *Prejudice;* Lange and Taylor, *An American Exodus.*

24. When Aoki first voted in 1960, the minimum voting age was twenty-one. In 1971, in response to student antiwar activism, the voting age was lowered to eighteen via the Voting Rights Act Amendment of 1970 and the Twenty-Sixth Amendment to the U.S. Constitution.

25. Kennedy, of course, was hardly pro-Communist. In an effort to "contain communism," his administration was embroiled in the Bay of Pigs invasion of Cuba (1961), the Cuban Missile Crisis (1962), and the Vietnam War.

26. It is hard to create a precise timeline for the development of Aoki's political consciousness. Given the uneven process of political development, it is possible that Aoki began reading Steinbeck, McWilliams, and others before the 1960 election. Certainly by the time Aoki joined the YSA/SWP, he would not vote for a Republican candidate, and likely not for a Democrat either. But in 1960, regardless of any budding working-class consciousness, Aoki's rage about the Japanese American incarceration could singularly explain his voting choice.

27. Balmer and Wylie, *When Worlds Collide,* was made into a movie, of the same title (Paramount Pictures, 1951).

28. Aoki admired Debs's courage and convictions. In court for violating the 1917 Espionage Act, Debs boldly proclaimed, "Your Honor, years ago I recognized my kinship with all living beings, and I made up my mind that I was not one bit better than the meanest on earth. I said then, and I say now, that while there is a lower class, I am in it, and while there is a criminal element I am of it, and while there is a soul in prison, I am not free" (Debs, *Writings and Speeches of Eugene V. Debs,* 437). Aoki was also drawn to Debs's advocacy of cross-racial union organizing. "The class struggle is colorless," said Debs (65), which contrasted with the AFL's racially exclusionary policies.

29. Aoki showed me his inscribed copy of Preis, *Labor's Giant Step.*

30. Solidarity strikes sprouted up across the country in support of a major newspaper strike in New York City that shut down the city's nine major dailies, including the *Times* (*New York Times,* December 10, 18, 1962). This may be the strike to which Aoki refers.

31. In fall 1965, Aoki earned an A in a two-unit Paint Tech course at Oakland Junior College (Richard Aoki, transcript, Peralta Community College District).

32. Richard M. Aoki, Honorable Discharge certificate, October 31, 1964.

33. Kimmel, "The Contemporary 'Crisis' of Masculinity" and *Manhood in America.*

34. In contrast with the western fantasies of White men, for Asian American men the frontier represented violence, racism, and labor exploitation. This was particularly the case for Chinese immigrants who came to the western United States beginning in the mid-1800s. By the late 1800s, when Japanese began immigrating, the frontier was closing and Japanese immigrants had some measure of protection from racist violence from an increasingly powerful homeland. On racial, economic, and state violence against Chinese immigrants, see Saxton, *The Indispensable Enemy.* On anti-Japanese hostility as well as on the Japanese government's tenuous safeguarding of its citizens abroad, see Daniels, *The Politics of Prejudice;* Ichioka, *The Issei;* McWilliams, *Prejudice.*

35. Gaddis, *The Cold War*; McCormick, *America's Half-Century*; Shrecker, *Many Are the Crimes*; Sherry, *In the Shadow of War*, 123–44.

36. LaFeber, *America, Russia, and the Cold War, 1945–2002*; Westad, *The Global Cold War*.

37. House Committee on Armed Services, *Universal Military Training* and *Reserve Forces Act of 1955*.

38. McCormick, *America's Half-Century*; Klein, *Cold War Orientalism*; Brooks, *Alien Neighbors, Foreign Friends*; Fujino, "The Global Cold War and Asian American Activism."

39. Theodor Reik quoted in Schlesinger, "The Crisis of American Masculinity," 240.

40. Schlesinger, "The Crisis of American Masculinity," 237–38.

41. Dean, *Imperial Brotherhood*, 169–99; Griswold, "The 'Flabby American,' the Body, and the Cold War."

42. Kennedy, "The Soft American"; Dean, "Masculinity as Ideology," 50.

43. Nguyen, "The Remasculinization of Chinese America."

44. May, *Homeward Bound*.

45. Debs, *Writings and Speeches of Eugene V. Debs*, 189–90.

46. Ibid., 224. In the best seller *Fast Food Nation*, Eric Schlosser tells numerous stories of worker alienation, of the lack of ownership of one's body, even of dismemberment of the working body—all driving the rising profits in the fast-food industry. Kenny, a tough, powerfully built midwesterner, worked in the meatpacking industry. After being stitched and bandaged, he kept returning to the slaughterhouse, sustaining one injury after another in this dangerous profession. When Kenny suffered "injuries that would've killed weaker men," including having his lungs burned by hazardous chemical solvents, the company fired him. After sixteen years on the job and with no pension, Kenny, age forty-five, said, "They used me to the point where I had no body parts left to give. Then they just tossed me into the trash can" (190).

47. Schlesinger, "Crisis of American Masculinity," 238.

48. Kinsey, Pomeroy, and Martin found that at least 37 percent of American men had had at least one same-sex experience "to the point of orgasm" (*Sexual Behavior in the Human Male*, 623).

49. May, *Homeward Bound*, 82–86, 103; also Dean, *Imperial Brotherhood*; Epstein, "Anti-Communism, Homophobia, and the Construction of Masculinity."

50. Cited in Cuordileone, "'Politics in an Age of Anxiety,'" 532.

51. Ibid., 538.

5. "My Identification Went with the Aspirations of the Masses"

1. David Aoki married in December 1961 and had a child in August 1962 (Certificate of Marriage, County of San Francisco; Michael Aoki, Certificate of Live Birth, County of Alameda). David attended UC Berkeley as a full-time student from fall 1962 until he graduated with a BA in psychology in June 1965 (UC Berkeley transcripts). Earlier in 1961, Richard's mother, Toshiko, married Albert Kaniye (Marriage Certificate, County of Washoe, Nev., July 19, 1961).

2. Karl Yoneda was a longtime member of the International Longshoremen's Association and the Communist Party; see Yoneda, *Ganbatte*.

3. Katsiaficas, *The Imagination of the New Left*.

4. Aoki and SNCC staff exchanged letters in February 1963. Aoki wrote: "Today I read in *Jet Magazine* that James Forman was critically ill. . . . Although I cannot donate blood myself due to being underweight, several friends . . . would donate their blood." Norma Collins, office secretary, SNCC, Atlanta, Ga., acknowledges receipt of a sixteen-dollar money order sent by Aoki and raised by Aoki and friends to, as Aoki explained, "aid SNCC in carrying on its heroic struggle" (Richard M. Aoki to Charles McDew, chairman, SNCC, Atlanta, Ga., February 3, 1963; Ruby Doris Smith, executive committee, SNCC, Atlanta, Ga., to Richard M. Aoki, February 6, 1963; Richard M. Aoki, to Ruby Doris Smith, February 10, 1963; Norma Collins, to Richard Aoki, February 15, 1963).

5. Frazier, *The Black Bourgeoisie*.

6. In their influential book, *Black Power,* Stokely Carmichael and Charles V. Hamilton wrote, "Integration . . . is based on complete acceptance of the fact that in order to have a decent house or education, Black people must move into a white neighborhood or send their children to a white school. This reinforces . . . the idea that 'white' is automatically superior and 'black' is by definition inferior. For this reason, 'integration' is a subterfuge for the maintenance of white supremacy" (54–55).

7. Sociologist Robert E. Park introduced the concept of "marginal man" to refer to those at the margins of two cultures, but accepted by neither. Park's theories on race, developed in the 1920s, promoted assimilationism as a solution to race problems (Park, "Human Migration and the Marginal Man"; Park, *Race and Culture*). By the 1960s, what was once a progressive response to biological theories of White racial superiority was strongly critiqued for ignoring issues of power and promoting unilateral movement from minority to dominant culture (Carmichael and Hamilton, *Black Power;* Omi and Winant, *Racial Formation*). For an excellent study of the Chicago sociologists' influence on academic and popular thinking about Asian Americans, see Yu, *Thinking Orientals*.

8. On the historical genealogy and splits among various Left organizations from a SWP perspective, see Sheppard, *The Party*, 19–28.

9. In allying with the USSR and under the influence of Browder, the CPUSA gave uncritical support to President Roosevelt's policies and failed to oppose the forced incarceration of Japanese Americans. The CP likewise either "suspended entirely" (Howe and Coser, *The American Communist Party,* 416) or "forced . . . into narrow channels" (Isserman, *Which Side Were You On?,* 141; see also 143–45) the struggles for Black rights during the war, which they saw as separate from and subordinate to the international struggle against fascism. See also Foster, *History of the Communist Party of the United States of America,* 383–407; Yoneda, *Ganbatte,* 111–65.

10. In Manzanar, in December 1942, internee anger toward pro-U.S. Japanese Americans turned violent with internees beating a JACL leader and the camp police killing an internee in a crowd of protestors. Camp administrators, fearing reprisals, snuck out, under cover of darkness, several pro-U.S. JACL and CP leaders, including

Yoneda. On the Manzanar Riot, see Hansen and Hacker, "The Manzanar Riot"; Okihiro, "Japanese Resistance in America's Concentration Camps"; Yoneda, *Ganbatte*, 112–24, 132–44; Takagi interview.

11. *Militant,* March 7, 1942; May 30, 1942.

12. Marx and Engels's *The Communist Manifesto* is one of the most widely read political documents; also Hegel, *The Phenomenology of Mind.* Aoki earned Bs in the two German language courses he took in fall 1958 and spring 1959 at Oakland City College (Richard Aoki, transcript, Peralta Community College District).

13. Writing during World War I, Rosa Luxemburg feared that the war pitted the nationalist interests against the class interests of the proletariat, but in the end she argued that the "nationalist interests and international solidarity of the proletariat" are in "complete harmony" (199). She implored workers to strive for a "speedy peace" and "to utilize the industrial and political crisis to accomplish the awakening of the people, thus hastening the overthrow of capitalist class rule" (180), urging "Proletarians of all countries, unite!" (217); see Luxemburg, "The Junius Pamphlet."

14. Lenin's *Imperialism* strongly influenced theoretically minded activists like Aoki in framing their opposition to imperialism, under which system, according to Lenin, "(1) production and capital concentration have developed to such an extent that economic life is dominated by monopoly organization; (2) banking capital and manufacturing capital have merged, and a financial oligarchy has emerged on the basis of this 'financial capital'; (3) capital export, as distinct from commodity export, assumes special significance; (4) an international monopoly alliance has been formed; and (5) the most powerful capitalist powers have dismembered the territories of the world." Aoki, like other radicals, viewed imperialism as one of the key sources of oppression. Sivanandan, in "New Circuits of Imperialism," maintains that "imperialism is still the highest stage of capitalism," though the "circuits of imperialism" have changed with capitalist development. In particular, capital is less dependent on labor and production, but works more through multinational corporations and banks, international agencies like the International Monetary Fund and World Bank, culture and war, and has shifted the brunt of exploitation from the core to the periphery, i.e., workers in the Third World.

15. Aoki took a two-part series on Marxism in winter and spring 1968, several years after he adopted socialism (Richard Aoki, transcript, University of California, Berkeley).

16. Carol (Shelly) Hayden, a close comrade of Aoki's in the SWP, recalls there being regular SWP political education study groups that she assumes Aoki would have attended (Hayden interview). Still, university professor Douglas Daniels proclaims that Aoki is more widely read than just about anyone he knows (Hayden interview). That Aoki does not recall attending SWP study groups reflects, at least in part, his ability to learn independently of formal or informal educational institutions.

17. James P. Cannon is a prolific and influential writer on American Trotskyism; see, for example, Cannon, *The History of American Trotskyism.*

18. The SWP newspaper, the *Militant,* gave extensive coverage to Malcolm X's travels, news, and speeches as well as Breitman's commentaries on Malcolm X.

Breitman's widely read edited volume *Malcolm X Speaks* and *The Last Year of Malcolm X* generated anticapitalist and pro-socialist interpretations of Malcolm's ideas in the last year of Malcolm's life.

19. Malcolm X represents the most famous Nation of Islam redemption story. Manning Marable observes that by overstating the severity of his criminal activity in his autobiography, Malcolm X emphasized the themes of salvation and deliverance through the Nation of Islam (Marable, "Rediscovering Malcolm's Life"; also Dyson, *Making Malcolm,* 134). Despite the numerous controversies surrounding the Nation of Islam, there is widespread agreement that the organization has enabled numerous people with drug addictions and other problems to lead sober, productive, and self-disciplined lives.

20. The leaflet *In Defense of the Los Angeles Black Muslims* (June 16, 1963) reports on the police murder of one Black Muslim and beating of six others, all unarmed. It denounces the fact that "the innocent victims were placed on trial instead of the savage white officers." The *Militant* gave sympathetic coverage to the Black Muslims in their reporting of the killing and the trial of fourteen Black Muslims accused of "felony assault" and "resisting arrest" in the same incident (*Militant,* May 14, 1962; April 22, 1963; June 10 and 17, 1963). In sharp contrast, the *Los Angeles Times* blamed the Black Muslims for starting the "riot" that injured eight police officers and called the "super-secret Muslim" organization an "anti-white, anti-integration, anti-Christian cult." The day after the killing, the *Los Angeles Times*'s front-page headline announced, "'Muslims' Riot: Cultist Killed, Policeman Shot" (*Los Angeles Times,* April 28, 1962; May 7, 1962; April 7 and 30, 1963). It would take another thirty years and a widely broadcast videotaped police beating of another Black man, Rodney King, to alert mainstream America to the existence of police brutality.

21. Apparently unbeknownst to Aoki, as early as 1957, Army Intelligence viewed him as connected to Left organizing, though peripherally. In the meager army files I received on Aoki (see chapter 4, note 9), Army Intelligence reported that "Aoki has been associated with the Labor Youth League" (May 29, 1957). The Labor Youth League was the youth wing of the Communist Party. Aoki received his honorary discharge in October 1964 (certificate), but at other times, Aoki believed he joined the YSA and SWP around 1963. The FBI reports that on October 1, 1961, "Richard Aoki was accepted as a new member of the BYSA [Berkeley YSA]" (FBI report, December 13, 1961) and by December 20, 1962, Aoki was a member of the Berkeley SWP (FBI report, January 18, 1963). In October 1961, Aoki was already representing the BYSA at public events, including a lecture series on communism at Berkeley High School, sponsored by the Berkeley Board of Education (FBI report, December 13, 1961; Bureau File 100-427226-352). SWP comrade Carol (Shelly) Hayden distinctly remembers Aoki being in the YSA in May 1962, when she and her husband moved to the Bay Area (Hayden interview).

22. In July 1953, the Oakland Board of Education merged Laney Trade and Technical Institute and Merritt School of Business to form Oakland Junior College, renamed Oakland City College in October 1958 ("History of the College," Oakland City College Catalog, 1963–64).

23. Aoki first enrolled at Oakland City College in fall 1958 as a premed major. After two semesters as a full-time student earning average grades, he withdrew in fall 1959. From fall 1963 to fall 1965, he enrolled as a full-time student for three semesters (Richard Aoki, transcript, Peralta Community College District).

24. The main reason, it seems, that an independent group was established at Oakland City College (OCC), rather than a YSA chapter, was that YSA and Bay Area Progressive Labor (BAPL) agreed to work as a united front at OCC. In a series of meetings in January 1964, Berkeley YSA, with Aoki as its representative in this work, and BAPL deliberately opposed an "isolationist tendency" and created an "issues oriented" group at OCC. The FBI reported that the YSA and BAPL would retain their "organizational integrity" and concentrate on, in language resembling Aoki's, "minimizing the differences and maximizing the similarities of their respective programs" (FBI report, August 24, 1964). In addition, the FBI certainly targeted the SWP with a vengeance (Churchill and Vander Wall, *The COINTELPRO Papers*, 49–62). An independent student group, however radical its name, would have seemed less threatening than a long-standing, nationwide organization like the SWP.

25. Yale Candee Maxon, obituaries, *Stanford* magazine, January–February 2000; *Oakland Tribune*, October 23, 1958.

26. Aoki's undergraduate paper is interesting for a number of reasons. First, he is clearly writing about himself and his brother when discussing gifted students whose achievements were thwarted by their social, economic, and familial circumstances. Major themes center on the negative impact of "a broken home" and on teachers and school counselors who failed to show interest in disadvantaged students or to inquire about their home lives. One interviewee, a Mr. D. F., so closely resembled Aoki, including graduating from Berkeley High School in 1957 and having an IQ of 140, that Aoki was likely writing about his own life. Aoki concluded: "A troubled home life resulted from the divorce or separation of the child's parents, or an impaired child–parent relationship, often turns the child to 'the streets' for his social life." Second, Aoki's solution rested on the coordination of the professions of social work and education to guide the gifted student. These ideas anticipated Aoki's entry, years later, into both fields. Finally, Aoki withdrew the first time he enrolled in History 19A (Asian Civilization) and did not retake the course until fall 1963. Yet, Maxon invited Aoki to participate in this project in 1961, likely reflecting Maxon's own commitments to the gifted student from the lower socioeconomic structure and a potential he saw in Aoki (Aoki, transcript, Oakland Junior College). See Aoki, "Major Problems of Gifted Students from the Lower Socio-economic Structure and a Possible Solution," edited by Yale Candee Maxon, Ph.D., March 12, 1961. Aoki presented his research at a discussion group of the California State Employees Association, Public Health Chapter 132, in Berkeley, in December 1961 (schedule of "The Noon Discussion Group"; "Noon Discussion Group," newsletter of California State Employees Association, February 1, 1962).

27. Judie Hart, "'Revolutionary Socialist' Leads New Club," *Tower*, published by the Associated Students of Oakland City College, February 26, 1964. The article began: "Richard Aoki, who calls himself a 'revolutionary socialist,' was elected temporary

chairman of the new Socialist Discussion Club last week." The article revealed the political differences between the organization's chair and faculty adviser: "Dr. Yale Maxon . . . defined Britain as a democratic socialist society. He noted that public ownership there included not only the mails, but railroads and bus lines also. . . . Dr. Maxon said that a revolutionary socialist, rather than using appealing propaganda and rational argument as a democratic Socialist does, believes that it is hopeless to reason with the population and is usually involved in or in favor of a conspiratorial setup." Aoki believed, as argued by Lenin in *The State and Revolution,* that the ruling class will not relinquish power without violent overthrow, though educational and "rational argument" methods were also necessary.

28. Bobby Seale and Huey Newton were among the leaders of the Soul Students Advisory Council, but disagreed with the cultural nationalist politics of the group. After they left, Newton and Seale formed the Black Panther Party in 1966 (Seale, *Seize the Time,* 24–34). Seale concurs that there were exchanges between the Soul Students Advisory Council and Socialist Discussion Club (Seale interview).

29. Baldwin, *The Fire Next Time;* Wright, *Uncle Tom's Children* and *Native Son;* Malcolm X, *Malcolm X Speaks;* Breitman, *The Last Year of Malcolm;* Zinn, *SNCC;* Herskovits, *Myth of the Negro Past;* Aptheker, *American Negro Slave Revolts.*

30. As early as 1962, Vietnam became a focus of the long-standing peace movement, including some five hundred at a peace rally in San Francisco and a few hundred people protesting the visit of Madame Ngo Dinh Nhu of South Vietnam to San Francisco and Berkeley (*Militant,* January 8, 1962; *San Francisco Chronicle,* October 28 and 30, 1963; *Oakland Tribune,* October 27, 1963; Halstead, *Out Now!,* 33, 35–36). The *Militant* was giving critical coverage to the Vietnam War even earlier; a February 19, 1962, article opposed President Kennedy's decision to "plunge deeper into the South Vietnamese civil war" and asked, "Is there any good reason why GI's should die for the Diem dictatorship?"

31. Aoki consistently remembers joining the Vietnam Day Committee while in the Army Reserves. Given that the VDC began in 1965, his memories might be of antiwar protests anticipating the VDC's formation. The VDC dates its origins to May 1965, when it organized a thirty-five-hour antiwar teach-in that brought some fifty thousand people to UC Berkeley. See various flyers on Vietnam Day community meeting, May 21–22, 1965; Prof. Stephen Smale and Jerry Rubin, cochairs of the Bay Area Vietnam Day Committee, letter to "Dear Friend," June 18, 1965; VDC, Minutes of Action Committee, April 3, 1966, all from SPC, box 2, folder 17; Rorabaugh, *Berkeley at War,* 91–100. The antiwar teach-in at the University of Michigan at Ann Arbor, two months earlier, launched the widespread use of the teach-in format (Manashe and Radosh, *Teach-Ins: USA,* 8-13; Halstead, *Out Now!,* 62–80).

32. The Gulf of Tonkin incident in August 1964 provoked the first large-scale deployment of U.S. troops to Vietnam. President Lyndon Johnson and Secretary of Defense Robert McNamara told the American public that North Vietnam attacked American destroyers in the Gulf of Tonkin. The U.S. Congress, with unanimous support in the House and only two dissenting votes in the Senate, authorized the president to take military action in Southeast Asia as he saw fit, enabling him to initiate

conflict without a formal declaration of war by Congress. The government immediately deployed American troops into Vietnam and began bombing North Vietnam. Since then researchers, including National Security Agency historian Robert J. Hanyok, have uncovered evidence that the attack was fictitious (*New York Times*, October 31, 2005). On the Vietnam War and the U.S. antiwar movement, see Herring, *America's Longest War;* Gettleman, *Vietnam and America;* DeBenedetti, *An American Ordeal;* Small and Hoover, *Give Peace a Chance;* Zaroulis and Sullivan, *Who Spoke Up?;* Morgan, *The 60s Experience;* Davis, *Assault on the Left;* Zinn, *A People's History of the United States.*

33. *Did You Vote for War?*, a twenty-four-page booklet published by the Bay Area VDC in 1965, was designed to counter the silencing of radical antiwar voices in the mainstream media. The booklet is remarkable for its inclusion of two-page essays by ten liberal-to-Left groups with diverse and at times conflicting ideologies, including the SWP, CPUSA, IWW, Spartacist League, Progressive Labor, Young Democrats, and independent socialist groups. According to VDC cofounder Jerry Rubin, the VDC in Berkeley managed to keep sectarian conflict to a minimum because the independent radicals disengaged from the ideological "Stalin–Trotsky conflict" (Halstead, *Out Now!,* 153). By early 1966, the VDC split into two factions over prioritizing radical electoral politics or militant grassroots organizing. After one faction focused on the congressional campaign of VDC leader Robert Scheer, the VDC, according to Rorabaugh, "fell under the control of the Trotskyists [particularly the YSA] and then slowly disintegrated" (*Berkeley at War*, 98–99). On the various Left groups in Berkeley in the early 1960s, see Freeman, *At Berkeley in the '60s*, 24–27.

34. The VDC gained widespread publicity for its multiple efforts to stop trains filled with U.S. soldiers, presumably headed for Vietnam, at the Santa Fe station in Berkeley. At the last minute protesters jumped off the tracks and the trains continued forward unimpeded, but the symbolic importance of the issue was established (*New York Times*, August 7 and 24, 1965; *Stop the Troop Train*, VDC leaflet, SPC, box 2, folder 17).

35. The FBI identified Aoki as the "chairman of the International Committee of the Vietnam Day Committee" (FBI report, October 12, 1966).

36. The Berkeley VDC initiated the International Days of Protest Against the War in Vietnam on October 15–16, 1965. The U.S. media reported the event, but tended to focus on the alleged failures of the planned seven-mile march from UC Berkeley to the Oakland army terminal and the two-day teach-in. The California attorney general threatened criminal charges against anyone who used civil disobedience to protest American foreign policy; the cities of Berkeley and Oakland denied parade permits; a group of UC Berkeley faculty denounced the VDC; the police blocked the marchers from reaching the army terminal; and members of the Hell's Angels motorcycle club attacked the marchers (*Los Angeles Times*, October 8, 15, and 16, 1965; *New York Times*, October 16 and 17, 1965; *San Mateo Times*, October 16, 1965; VDC, "October 15–16 International Days of Protest against American Military Intervention," various leaflets and programs, 1965, SPC, box 2, folder 17; also Rorabaugh, *Berkeley at War*, 95–98). By contrast, the U.S. media barely registered

that antiwar protests were held concurrently in some eighty U.S. cities as well as in Europe, Asia, Latin America, and Africa (Berkeley VDC, *International Committee Newsletter,* vol. 1, no. 1, October 31, 1965, SPC, box 2, folder 17; *Los Angeles Times,* October 13, 1965; *New York Times,* October 16, 1965). Aoki says little about this event or the significance of the VDC in shaping the early antiwar movement. He acknowledges that the International Days of Protest were "big for the VDC," but "no big deal" to him. In 1965, he was getting "overwhelmed" by the Black nationalism movement and was immersed in organizing with the Socialist Discussion Club at Merritt College. His fiancée, who worked at UC Berkeley, attended many VDC meetings and updated him on VDC events. Aoki made his contribution with the International Committee of the Berkeley VDC. Formed in 1965, the International Committee sought to "establish contact with organizations and individuals abroad and to publicize among them the forthcoming international protest. Hundreds of letters were sent out, including 'international calls' which were prepared and printed in seven languages" (the International Secretariat of the National Committee to End the War in Vietnam and the Vietnam Day Committee, *The International Protest Movement against American Intervention in the War in Vietnam,* ca. late 1965, i–ii).

37. *The International Protest Movement against American Intervention in the War in Vietnam* (1965) was a forty-two-page, single-spaced document that highlighted the activities of antiwar movements worldwide. By emphasizing the "duty of citizens to voice their protest loudly and courageously when they feel that their own government is following a dangerous and immoral policy," the publication targeted an American audience as its primary goal. A secondary goal was to unite the international antiwar movements by creating information about widespread antiwar protests, especially as a corrective to the limited U.S. press coverage.

38. Aoki wrote a letter on behalf of the Asian Section of the International Committee of the Vietnam Day Committee, to Zendentsu, the All-Japan Telecommunications Workers Union, dated December 13, 1965, updating them on events of the U.S. antiwar movement, particularly a twenty-thousand-strong march in Berkeley on November 20, 1965, and an antiwar convention in Washington, D.C., on Thanksgiving weekend 1965. The FBI secured a copy of this letter from "a usually reliable source" in Tokyo. The FBI indicated that Zendentsu is "located within the rightwing of the leftist-oriented General Council of Trade Unions of Japan (Sohyo) but is one of the leading proponents of Sohyo's anti-American campaign centering on the Vietnamese issue in Japan" (FBI report, March 15, 1966).

39. This was one of the few times that Aoki left the Bay Area. SWP was actively involved in organizing the first SDS-led antiwar rally in Washington, D.C., on April 17, 1965, and also participated in the November 27, 1965, antiwar rally in Washington (*New York Times,* April 18, 1965; November 28, 1965; Halstead, *Out Now!,* 48–61; Barber, *Marching on Washington*). Aoki, in a letter from the VDC to the All-Japan Telecommunications Workers Union, dated December 13, 1965, indicated that "a major struggle developed during the course of the convention [in Washington, D.C., in November 1965] between the Stalinists and the Trotskyists. The issue concerned the formation of a broadly based, non-exclusive membership, national

anti-war organization." The VDC had a "united front" character and thus worked to unify major political tendencies (FBI report, March 15, 1966). On SWP's work in the antiwar movement, see Halstead, *Out Now!*

40. Three VDC members were slightly injured in the April 1965 midnight bombing of the VDC office (*Syracuse Herald-American,* April 10, 1966; *Post-Register* [Idaho Falls, Idaho], April 10, 1966; *Brazosport Facts* [Freeport, Tex.], April 10, 1966). In August 1966, VDC members, along with other antiwar activists, were called to testify about their activities before the House Un-American Activities Committee (*Los Angeles Times,* August 5, 14, and 20, 1966; *New York Times,* August 17–19, 1966).

41. Richard M. Aoki, letter to Robert F. Williams, September 12, 1965, sent by letter from Aoki to Vernel Olson, September 25, 1965.

42. Aoki interview in Ho, *Legacy to Liberation,* 328–29. Although rarely mentioned in histories of the Civil Rights Movement today, Williams was one of the foremost Black radicals in the 1960s, on a par with Malcolm X. Aoki would have been drawn to Williams's audacious advocacy and practice of self-defense in the 1950s Dixie South (Williams, *Negroes with Guns;* Nelson, *People with Strength;* Cohen, *Black Crusader;* Tyson, *Radio Free Dixie*). Vernel Olson was the national chairman of the FPCC of Canada; he and his wife were distributors of the *Crusader* in Canada and the United States (*Crusader,* February 1964, 8).

43. Williams sent Aoki at least one letter from Cuba in April 1966; the year stamped on the envelope is illegible, but likely is 1966, given that Williams was responding to Aoki's September 1965 letter and Williams moved to China in July 1966 (Cohen, *Black Crusader,* 318; Ahmad, "Robert Franklin ('Rob') Williams"; "In Memory of Robert Williams"). Williams sent several letters to Aoki from China in 1967 and 1968.

44. It's important to Aoki to see himself in the radical Afro–Asian tradition of Yuri Kochiyama (Fujino, *Heartbeat of Struggle*). On Black influences on Asian American radicalism, see Boggs, *Living for Change;* Fujino, "Black Liberation Movement and Japanese American Activism"; Fujino, "Race, Place, Space, and Political Development"; Prashad, *Everybody Was Kung Fu Fighting;* Louie, "'Yellow, Brown, & Red.'" On Asian influences on the Black freedom movement, see Kelley and Esch, "Black Like Mao." On Afro–Asian political and cultural collaborations, see Ho and Mullen, *Afro Asia;* Ho, *Wicked Theory, Naked Practice;* Raphael-Hernandez and Steen, *AfroAsian Encounters.*

45. The *Militant* gave extensive coverage of the Sino–Soviet split. The SWP extended critical support to China, despite China's denunciation of Trotsky and its bureaucratic adherence to Stalinism, primarily because China "advocates a far more aggressive class-struggle," urges the dismantling of imperialism and capitalism, and gives stronger support to Third World anticolonial movements, which contrasted with Khrushchev's "peaceful co-existence" with capitalist powers (*Militant,* December 24, 1962; March 25, 1963; April 1, 1963; among others). Luthi, in *The Sino-Soviet Split,* argues that ideological differences, spurred by Mao's sharp Left turn in 1957, was the single largest contributor to the Sino–Soviet split. Third World movements in the United States and globally generally aligned with China in condemning

Krushchev's retreat from Marxism–Leninism, as seen in his policy of peaceful co-existence with the United States and Western imperialism and departure from class struggle. Robert F. Williams elicited from Mao two statements in support of Black liberation (1963, 1968), which were published in the *Militant* (September 2, 1963; reprinted in Ho and Mullen, *Afro Asia,* 91–96). On Mao's influence on the U.S. Third World Left, see Kelley and Esch, "Black Like Mao"; Elbaum, *Revolution in the Air;* Ho, "The Inspiration of Mao."

46. The FPCC, with heavy SWP/YSA membership, published Fidel Castro's speech "History Will Absolve Me." Castro gave this five-hour speech, without the benefit of any notes, at his trial in October 1953, on charges of conspiracy and armed insurrection at the Moncada Barracks on July 26, 1953. While in prison, Castro painstakingly recorded his speech from memory using lime juice to create an invisible document. He could only write some twenty minutes each day at sunset, when the sun shone on the paper at the right angle to make the letters discernible. In the speech, Castro used the ideas of liberal philosophers like John Milton and John Locke as well as U.S. and French declarations of independence to argue that it is the duty of a people to overthrow a tyrannical and unjust government such as the Batista dicta-torship. In doing so, he sought to undermine the charges of subversion and terrorism against him and the 167 Moncada rebels under his leadership. For an SWP interpre-tation of the Cuban revolution, see Hansen, *Dynamics of the Cuban Revolution.*

47. "The Third World was not a place. It was a project," writes Vijay Prashad in *The Darker Nations* (xv). It was a project of colonized peoples against colonialism and for dignity and material equality. Albert Sauvy introduced the term "Third World" in his August 14, 1952, *L'Observateur* article, "Trois mondes, une planète," to refer to the Western capitalist, the socialist, and the colonized spheres. In 1960 French intellectuals founded the journal *Tiers-Monde* to focus on Third World issues. Peter Worsley's *The Third World* (1964) popularized the term in English. Meanwhile, the global Third World movement was launched by the 1955 Afro-Asian Conference in Bandung, the initiation of the Non-Aligned Movement in Belgrade in 1961, and the Tricontinental Conference in Havana in 1966. OSPAAAL was founded in January 1966, out of the Tricontinental Conference, and publishes the magazine *Tricontinental.* Together these Third World countries created an important, though flawed, movement seeking to create an egalitarian world based in anticolonial national liberation struggles that created an "internationalist national-ism" (Prashad, *The Darker Nations,* 6–15).

48. The Third World radical movement and ideas developing in the 1960s had an immense influence on Aoki. In 1955, while Aoki was in high school, eagerly antici-pating the day he could join the army, twenty-nine newly independent nations met at the Afro–Asian Conference in Bandung, Indonesia, to advance their "common detestation of colonialism and . . . racialism" and "peace in the world" (President Sukarno, "Speech at the Opening of the Afro-Asian Conference," 43; also see Wright, *The Color Curtain*). "Let us remember," cautioned the host president Ahmed Sukarno, "that the stature of all mankind is diminished so long as nations or parts of nations are still unfree. Let us remember that the highest purpose of man is the

liberation of man from his bonds of fear, his bonds of poverty, the liberation of man from the physical, spiritual and intellectual bonds which have for long stunted the development of humanity's majority" (Sukarno, "Speech," 51). In the aftermath of numerous postwar national liberation victories, newly independent nations forged a Non-Aligned Movement to resist the pressure to take sides in the Cold War and to advance an alternative method opposed to imperialism and racism. Representing the most revolutionary wing of the Non-Aligned Movement, Che Guevara stated on the floor of the United Nations General Assembly in 1964, "Peaceful coexistence cannot be limited to the powerful countries if we want to ensure world peace. . . . As Marxists we maintain that peaceful coexistence does not include coexistence between exploiters and exploited, between oppressors and the oppressed. [We want] the right to full independence from all forms of colonial oppression"(Guevara, "At the United Nations," 322–23). The Non-Aligned Movement, from the Bandung conference on, encompassed diverse strategies and goals for anticolonial struggles. But by January 1966, when the First Solidarity Conference of the Peoples of Africa, Asia, and Latin America was held in Havana, Cuba, Aoki would have been drawn to the growing advocacy of armed struggle to overthrow colonial rule. The shocking defiance of Vietnam inspired Third World resistance and advanced the call to armed action. Aoki was influenced by Keith Buchanan's essay "The Third World," published in the *New Left Review* in 1963, which was critical of "clientele–sovereignty" conditions, or "fake independence," what Kwame Nkrumah referred to as "the practice of granting a sort of independence by the metropolitan power, with the concealed intention of making the liberated country a client-state and controlling it effectively by means other than political ones" (Nkrumah, *I Speak of Freedom,* 265; cited in Buchanan, "The Third World," 8). Aoki would have endorsed Amílcar Cabral's view, delivered at the 1966 Havana conference, that "there is not, and cannot be, national liberation without the use of liberating violence by the nationalist forces, to answer the criminal violence of the agents of imperialism" (Cabral, "The Weapon of Theory," 107). Given the Non-Aligned Movement's emphasis on anticolonial, antiracist politics and its growing commitment to armed struggle, by 1966, Aoki rather easily incorporated Third World radicalism into his politics.

49. Aoki consistently remembers joining the Tri-Continental Student Committee as soon as he hit Berkeley in fall 1966. By February 1967, the FBI revealed that Aoki was elected to the Steering Committee of the Tri-Continental Progressive Student Committee (FBI report, May 29, 1967; also see *Daily Californian,* April 24, 1967; *Berkeley Daily Gazette,* April 1, 1968).

50. Peter Camejo ran on the Green Party ticket for California governor in 2002, 2003, and 2006, and as the vice presidential running mate of Ralph Nader in 2004. FBI files indicate that Aoki was one of the three or four leading members of Tri-Con and through Tri-Con had developed relations with the Afro–American Student Union from at least November 1967 (FBI reports, May 29, 1967; July 21, 1967; May 28, 1868).

51. Tri-Continental Student Committee, "Mass Meeting in Support of the National Liberation Front of Vietnam," flyer, n.d.

52. *Berkeley Daily Gazette,* April 1, 1968.

53. Ibid. According to the FBI, the provocative statements announcing the National Liberation Front event by a spokesperson for the off-campus Friends of the Tri-Continental Progressive Students Committee created dissension between on-campus and off-campus Tri-Con groups. The on-campus group denounced the off-campus group's statements as "irresponsible" and accused the off-campus group of "ultra-leftism." The off-campus group claimed the students were "making a deal" with the campus administration. Apparently so, as an FBI source indicated that on March 31, 1968, "five separate meetings were called" between 11:00 a.m. and 10:45 p.m. to discuss the issue. No doubt Aoki, as the one summoned to the vice-chancellor's office, was involved in these meetings and had apparently recommended canceling the entire affair, but was narrowly defeated (FBI report, July 22, 1968).

54. *Berkeley Daily Gazette,* April 1, 1968.

55. William Boyd, vice-chancellor, letter to Mr. Aoki, March 31, 1968.

56. *Daily Californian,* April 2, 1968.

57. Drawing on ideas of Cruse in *Rebellion or Revolution?* and Carmichael and Hamilton in *Black Power,* Blauner further developed the idea of internal colonialism in his influential book *Racial Oppression in America.*

58. Aoki refers to Marx's statement: "The philosophers have only interpreted the world, in various ways; the point is to change it" (Marx, "Theses on Feuerbach"). Aoki took a two-part series on Marxism in winter and spring 1968 (Richard Aoki, transcript, University of California, Berkeley).

59. *Los Angeles Times,* April 28, 1962.

60. FBI report, June 22, 1962.

61. As discussed in this book's introduction, recent Black Power studies extend Black Power back in time and/or complicate the political differences between the Civil Rights Movement and the Black Power Movement.

62. *Commentary,* April 1961.

63. *Militant,* May 14, 1962.

64. *Militant,* January 8 and 22, 1962; March 12, 1962; also see Dudziak, *Cold War Civil Rights.*

65. *Militant,* September 9, 1963.

66. The march leaders, who met with President Kennedy shortly before the march, wanted to maintain good relations with the president in their efforts to gain civil rights legislation (*New York Times,* August 29, 1963).

67. *Militant,* September 9, 1963.

68. The "Big Six" leaders were Dr. Martin Luther King Jr. (SCLC), James Farmer (CORE), John Lewis (SNCC), A. Philip Randolph (founder of the Brotherhood of Sleeping Car Porters and cofounder of the Leadership Conference of Civil Rights), Roy Wilkins (NAACP), and Whitney Young (National Urban League). On the March on Washington, Malcolm X stated, "It's just like when you've got some coffee that's too black, which means it's too strong. What do you do? You integrate it with cream, you make it weak. . . . [A]s they took it over, it lost its militancy. It ceased to be angry, it ceased to be hot, it ceased to be uncompromising. Why it even ceased

to be a march. It became a picnic, a circus" (Malcolm X, "Message to the Grass Roots," *Malcolm X Speaks*, 16; also *Militant*, September 30, 1963). By contrast, the organizers of the march stated, "[The march] will be orderly, but not subservient. It will be proud, but not arrogant. It will be non-violent, but not timid" (*New York Times*, August 26, 1963). The *New York Times* reported the march, with its unprecedented two hundred thousand participants, was "orderly" with an atmosphere of "courtesy and restraint" (*New York Times*, August 29, 1963).

69. *Militant*, September 9, 1963.

70. Ibid.

71. *Militant*, March 12, 1962.

72. *Liberation*, September 1959; reprinted in Carson et al., *Eyes on the Prize*, 110.

73. Williams, *Negroes with Guns*, 5.

74. *Militant*, October 7, 1963.

75. *Militant*, June 29, 1964.

76. *Militant*, January 21, 1963.

77. *Militant*, June 29, 1964.

78. *Militant*, June 8, 1964. These speeches are also in *Malcolm X Speaks*.

79. Ibid.

80. Malcolm X, *Malcolm X Speaks*.

81. *Militant*, November 5, 1962.

82. *Militant*, May 11, 1964.

83. *Militant*, December 3, 1962, emphasis in original; Socialist Workers Party, "Freedom Now."

84. Socialist Workers Party, "Freedom Now," 3, 9, 22.

85. Ibid., 10. The SWP offered long-standing support for Black self-determination. In 1939, the SWP, only one year old, unanimously adopted the following convention resolution: "The American Negroes, for centuries the most oppressed section of American society and the most discriminated against, are potentially the most revolutionary elements of the population. . . . The SWP must recognize that its attitude to the Negro question is crucial for its future development." Moreover, "the awakening political consciousness of the Negro not unnaturally takes the form of a desire for independent action uncontrolled by whites. . . . Such a desire is legitimate and must be vigorously supported" (James, "The Socialist Workers Party and Negro Work"; *Militant*, September 14, 1964). See also Trotsky, *Leon Trotsky on Black Nationalism and Self-Determination*; Socialist Workers Party, "The Case for an Independent Black Political Party," 1967 convention resolution, and, "A Transitional Program for Black Liberation," 1969 convention resolution.

86. Socialist Workers Party, "Freedom Now," 22–23.

87. Ibid.

88. *Militant*, August 5, 1963.

89. Gosse, *Where the Boys Are*, 6–8. "Cuba Libre" is the title of LeRoi Jones's award-winning essay in which he discusses his travels to Cuba in July 1960 with a delegation of Black Americans organized by the Fair Play for Cuba Committee. The essay signaled his transformation from a Beat poet to a prominent figure in the Black

Arts movement and anticipated his later radicalization to Black nationalism and then to Marxism–Leninism.

90. Gosse, *Where the Boys Are,* 1–12.

91. On the FPCC, see ibid., 137–73.

92. Ibid., 146.

93. Ibid.

94. Tyson, *Radio Free Dixie,* 235.

95. Gosse, *Where the Boys Are,* 146.

96. *Militant,* January 15, 1962; January 7, 1963; March 4, 1963.

97. *New York Times,* April 6, 1960; Gosse, *Where the Boys Are,* 6–8, 141; *Baltimore Afro-American,* April 22, 1961.

98. *Militant,* May 7, 1962; January 21, 1963; among others. See also Joseph, *Waiting 'til the Midnight Hour,* 45–50.

99. *Baltimore Afro-American,* April 22, 1961; reprinted in Mealy, *Fidel and Malcolm X,* 79–80.

100. Moore, *Castro, the Blacks, and Africa,* cited in Tyson, *Radio Free Dixie,* 242.

101. Tyson, *Radio Free Dixie,* 226, 236.

102. Hayden interview.

103. In July 1962, three months *before* the Cuban Missile Crisis, the Berkeley YSA showed pro-Cuban films on the UC Berkeley campus and issued a leaflet in September 1962 stating that "the Cuban Revolution represented the greatest gains the Latin American people had ever made . . . and that the possible new invasion of Cuba by the United States should be opposed by determined protest" (FBI report, January 18, 1963).

104. FBI report, June 22, 1962.

105. See, e.g., Cruse, "Marxism and the Negro."

106. Ibid., 153. DeBerry's candidacy was announced in the *New York Times,* January 14, 1964.

107. Cruse, "Marxism and the Negro," 140, 148.

108. Ibid., 140; emphasis added.

109. *Militant,* September 7, 1964.

110. Ibid.

111. Ibid.

112. Cruse, "Revolutionary Nationalism and the Afro-American."

113. Cruse, "Marxism and the Negro," 153.

114. *Militant,* August 24, 1964.

115. Ibid.

6. "The Greatest Political Opportunity of My Life"

1. Aoki uses the terms "Black Panther Party," "Panthers," and "party" interchangeably.

2. Merritt College gained national attention (or notoriety) for its revolutionary activities, as in the title of a *Wall Street Journal* article, "A Campus Where Black Power Won" (November 18, 1969).

3. The Afro–American Association, started in 1962 in the Bay Area, was, according to Warden, "probably the first Black Student Union in the United States." Warden asserts that they were among the first to use the term "Afro–American," to exclude Whites from their organization, and to "really talk about Black is beautiful" (Don Warden interview). Seale concurred that the Afro–American Association was "developing the first black nationalist philosophy on the West Coast" (*Seize the Time*, 14). On Newton's criticisms of Warden, see Newton, *Revolutionary Suicide*, 66–70; also Seale, *Seize the Time*, 21–22.

4. On RAM, see Stanford, "Revolutionary Action Movement"; Ahmad, *We Will Return in the Whirlwind*. On Seale joining RAM, see Seale, *Seize the Time*, 24–25.

5. By contrast to Aoki, virtually all accounts of BPP history, including Seale's own, regard Newton as the more intellectual and theoretically advanced of the two cofounders. But BPP leader Elbert "Big Man" Howard also discussed Seale's acumen at leading BPP study sessions (Howard interview).

6. Newton discusses his embarrassment at being "a functional illiterate" and the process by which he painstakingly taught himself to read in his last year of high school and later developed a love of books and ideas (Newton, *Revolutionary Suicide*, 47–49, 57–59, 72–78).

7. Seale, *Seize the Time*, 15–18.

8. Newton served as his own attorney on several occasions (Newton, *Revolutionary Suicide*, 84–98).

9. Aoki also told this story in Veale, "Interview with Richard Aoki," 325.

10. Aoki's narrative is based on his report to the Socialist Workers Party, "Nationalism, S.F. Black Power Conference, and the SWP," October 8, 1966. At several points during our conversation, he read verbatim from his report.

11. Unlike Aoki, Seale remembers little about the conference (Seale interview).

12. R. Aoki, "Nationalism, S.F. Black Power Conference, and the SWP."

13. Ibid.

14. Aoki's account that the name "Black Panther" originated at this conference counters conventional Panther history. Newton explained that in spring 1966, months before the conference, he and Seale "asked the people if they would be interested in forming the Black Panther Party for Self-Defense." The black panther symbol came from the Lowndes County (Alabama) Freedom Organization, which adopted it because a panther does not attack but will defend itself fiercely when backed in a corner (Newton, *Revolutionary Suicide*, 126–27; Foner, *Black Panthers Speak*, xv). The Lowndes County Freedom Organization also used the name Black Panther Party (http://www.blackpast.org/?q=aah/lowndes-county-freedom-organization).

15. Muhammad Ali famously refused induction into the army in 1966, stating, "I ain't got no quarrel with them Viet Cong" (*New York Times*, January 11, 1967). He's widely remembered for asserting, "They never called me nigger" (*Jet*, April 28, 1967; May, 2 1994). At the height of his boxing career, the world heavyweight champion had his title and boxing license revoked. In explaining his position, which was both religious and political, Ali asked, "Why should they ask me, another so-called Negro, to put on a uniform and go 10,000 miles from home and drop bombs and

bullets on brown people in Vietnam while so-called Negro people in Louisville are treated like dogs and denied simple human rights?" (*New York Times,* April 21, 1967).

16. Aoki and other Asian American activists would later fight against the continued use of concentration camps under Title II of the 1950 Internal Security Act (*AAPA Newspaper,* November–December 1968, 3; Okamura, "Background and History of the Repeal Campaign").

17. R. Aoki, "Nationalism, S.F. Black Power Conference, and the SWP."

18. Ibid. The resolution he quotes is from James, "The Socialist Workers Party and Negro Work."

19. R. Aoki, "Nationalism, S.F. Black Power Conference, and the SWP." The first three sentences of this paragraph are taken verbatim from the SWP's 1963 convention resolution, "Freedom Now" (21), but with "Black" replacing "Negro" and "Black liberation struggle" replacing "Negro movement" in Aoki's report. The rest of the paragraph paraphrases the same SWP document.

20. Months before the birth of the BPP, Aoki apparently had plans to work with Seale and Newton. Around February 1966, Tom Sanders invited Aoki to travel to Nicaragua with him, but Aoki declined because, according to Sanders, "some old friends of his wanted to organize something to fight police brutality . . . a few months later they organized the Panthers" (Sanders interview). Months before establishing the BPP, Newton and Seale proposed a program of armed self-defense to the Soul Students Advisory Council and later to RAM; both groups rejected their proposal, according to Newton (*Revolutionary Suicide,* 119–29).

21. "What Muslims Want," a ten-point list of the Nation of Islam's political demands, including "end to the police brutality," "equal education," and "freedom," anticipated the BPP's program. The BPP combined "What We Want" and "What We Believe" into a single political document, whereas "What Muslims Believe" focused primarily on religious beliefs. Malcolm X created *Muhammad Speaks,* the Nation of Islam's newspaper, in 1959. See Marsh, *From Black Muslims to Muslims,* 61–64.

22. Like many others at the time, Newton read the Nation of Islam newspaper and was greatly influenced by the speeches and ideas of Malcolm X (Newton, *Revolutionary Suicide,* 77, 125).

23. Seale, *Seize the Time,* 59–69; Newton, *Revolutionary Suicide,* 128–32.

24. During the course of our interviews, Aoki corrected the misconception that he had helped to write the Ten-Point Platform, an implication he made in a published interview (Veale, "Interview with Richard Aoki," 326–27). He explained to me: "I didn't have anything to do with the substantive part of the program. Maybe they asked me some minor questions about some reference thing, but I didn't put anything in there that I could say was my unique contribution to the program" (Aoki interview, July 30–August 1, 2003). Still, "Big Man" Howard agreed that Aoki influenced Newton's and Seale's politics, recalling that Seale, Newton, Aoki, and Howard participated in political education rap sessions even before the party began, which helped shape the BPP program (Howard interview; Seale interview).

25. In an often-repeated story, Seale claims that he and Huey flipped a coin to determine the two positions. Elsewhere, it's written that they each picked their own title or Newton nonchalantly picked their positions (Newton, *Revolutionary Suicide*, 132; Seale, *Seize the Time*, 62; Seale in Lew-Lee, *All Power to the People*; Seale interview). Aoki's less flippant interpretation does not necessarily contradict Seale's and Newton's versions: "All I know is, when the decision was made, I concurred 100 percent based on personal knowledge of both of their characters."

26. Seale memorialized the connection between Aoki and the Panthers' first guns in *Seize the Time*: "Richard Iokey *[sic]* came in—the Japanese brother who gave Huey and me the M-1 and 9 mm—and he got to talking about how he had a .357 Magnum. We got the .357 Magnum from him and a couple more pistols" (79). "Late in November 1966, we went to a Third World brother we knew, a Japanese radical cat. He had guns for a motherfucker: .357 Magnum, 22's, 9mms, what have you. . . . We told him that if he was a real revolutionary he'd better go on and give them up to us" (72–73). In an interview with me, Seale explained Aoki's role in more detail and with less bravado: "Huey and I liked Richard. Richard was good theoretically with ironing out, debating, and discussing revolutionary principles of our liberation. So, one of those nights [after finishing the Ten-Point Platform] we went over to Richard's and got his approval [or rather advice]. He said, 'This is fantastic.' And then told him what we was getting ready to do. We said, 'We need two guns.' 'Two guns?' Richard is a gun collector. He says, 'You gonna do what?' 'We're gonna go patrol the police.' He says, 'You guys are gonna get fuckin' killed!' We discussed this thing, and Huey [says] that as long as the weapon is not concealed it's not illegal. So I think we went back and then the next night picked the guns up and something, or went back and discussed it with him some more and he gave them to us. But my point is, that night, after [finishing] the Ten-Point Platform and Program, Richard and I and Huey, at Richard's apartment, we were drinking wine and cheese and discussing political shit, socialist stuff" (Seale interview).

27. Seale, "History of the BPP," http://www.bobbyseale.com, accessed August 27, 2003. Aoki had a BPP membership card, which he showed to select friends (Daniels interview; Takagi interview), but Aoki's difficulty in identifying when he joined illustrates the often-contested nature of organizational membership. Within a month or so of the BPP formation, Aoki was attending meetings and doing party work. Sherwin Forte, an original Panther, recounted seeing Aoki at a BPP meeting, shortly after the party formed, at which Newton asked Aoki to speak about the Japanese American incarceration. At that time, Forte considered Aoki a BPP member (Forte interview). Seale recounted that Newton and Aoki wrangled over Aoki's membership: "It was something about Huey saying, 'Are you officially in the party or not?' Richard say, 'Well, do you want me to be in the party? You don't want me to be in the party?' I said, 'What are you talking about?! Richard helped us do all kinds of stuff. He's just like a person that's working in the party!' But Huey says, 'I'm trying to get him to say whether or not he's officially in the party.'" To Seale, there was no dispute: "Richard was in the party because he was working and he was coming to the office more than a hell of a lot of other people was even though he had studies and

other things to do. I'm telling Huey that as far as I'm concerned Richard's a member of the BPP" (Seale interview).

28. The "Intake Application Form for Membership," BPP for Self-Defense (n.d.), included the questions: "Have you ever been convicted of a felony where you used a fire arm of some kind?" and "Do you believe in self defense? If answer is *no* then why?" The form did not ask about military service (Bay Area Black Panther Party Collection, box 1, file 9).

29. On patrolling the police, see Newton, *Revolutionary Suicide,* 127–42.

30. Aoki recalled participating on occasion as a driver: "We didn't have that many cars. I had a car." Seale remembered Aoki patrolling the police a few times, but did not think they stopped the police when Aoki was with them (Seale interview). Others have no memory of Aoki on patrol, but assume he did this (Howard interview; Forte interview).

31. Newton apparently read Mao before starting the BPP. In a chapter of his book, located chronologically prior to the BPP formation, Newton wrote, "The transformation from a nationalist to a socialist was a slow one, although I was around a lot of Marxists. . . . My conversion was complete when I read the four volumes of Mao Tse-tung to learn more about the Chinese Revolution. It was my life plus independent reading that made me a socialist—nothing else" (Newton, *Revolutionary Suicide,* 75; also 123, 128).

32. In August 1970, Newton made a progressive statement on homosexuality, in which he supported gay rights and denounced using gay terminology to refer to "enemies of the people," such as calling Nixon a faggot. He also stated, "And maybe I'm now injecting some of my prejudice by saying that 'even a homosexual can be a revolutionary.' Quite the contrary, maybe a homosexual could be the most revolutionary" (*To Die for the People,* 152–55). Upon inquiry, Aoki reported endorsing Newton's statement "100 percent" at the time it was made.

33. These include pay fairly for what you buy; return everything you borrow; do not hit or swear at people; do not take liberties with women; if we ever have to take captives do not ill-treat them; obey orders in all your actions; do not take a single needle or a piece of thread from the poor and oppressed masses. These also appear in Nkrumah's *Handbook of Revolutionary Warfare.*

34. Aoki's comment is a corrective to misinformation in a published interview. After relaying that he was the "first minister of education" for the BPP, Aoki allegedly added, "and there ain't been one since that time." Certainly the latter statement is incorrect and was not in the original interview transcript that Aoki showed me. Both the interviewer and the editor of that volume are unclear how that phrase ended up in the book (Veale, "Interview with Richard Aoki," 331; author's separate conversations with Dolly Veale and Fred Ho, ca. 2003; Aoki interviews, July 16–18, 2003; July 30–August 1, 2003).

35. The FBI reported that Aoki was branch captain in Berkeley and minister of education for the BPP (FBI report, July 23, 1969).

36. On January 28, 1968, Aoki spoke on the role of White tutors in the Black community at UC Berkeley in a series of workshops on education sponsored by the

Associated Students Community Projects. In the typed notes of his speech, Aoki disclosed that he had been appointed the minister of education of the Black Panther Party for Self-Defense in January 1967 (Workshop Series 1: Education, flyer, n.d.; Jane E. Schiesel, coordinator, Community Projects, letter to Richard Aoki, February 2, 1968; typed notes for speech).

37. Seale credits Aoki with being the Panther most well versed in Marxism–Leninism in the earliest years of the party. But, recounted Seale, "even Richard did not necessarily put as much emphasis on Marxism and Leninism as he put on the Ten-Point Platform and Program of the BPP. That's what he rapped about." The FBI proffered that only Aoki, Newton, and Seale "were fully informed on the political philosophies of the organization" (FBI report, November 30, 1967) and that Aoki was "a scholar of classic writings on revolution by such former black militants as Frantz Fanon, Marcus Garvey, Malcolm X Little, and W. E. B. Du Bois" (FBI report, November 16, 1967). By mid-1968, when Ray "Masai" Hewitt became the minister of education, Seale viewed Hewitt as, by far, the most knowledgeable person he knew on Marxism–Leninism and particularly Maoism. It was at this time that the party began to study the "full works of Mao." Seale's memory coincides with Aoki's that Aoki did not teach Mao in BPP study sessions (Seale interview).

38. Veale, "Interview with Richard Aoki," 328.

39. Seale's narration in *Seize the Time* implies that the Panthers' Red Book sales were primarily economically motivated, to generate funds to purchase guns. Seale's third and last reference to Aoki in *Seize the Time* is in connection to the Red Book: "Richard Iokey [sic] walked up around the time that we first got there and told us to make sure that we didn't go on campus with the books because those agents were standing all around waiting to bust us" (81).

40. If Hutton was born on April 21, 1950, as identified in the BPP newspaper tribute to the fallen martyr, then he was sixteen when he joined the party. That issue also identified Hutton as BPP treasurer (May 15, 1967).

41. Elbert "Big Man" Howard explained that the day before Hutton was murdered on April 6, 1968, Hutton asked Howard for a weapon to go on police patrol and Howard gave him one of his own shotguns (Howard, *Panther on the Prowl*, 30–31; Howard interview). Before that, Hutton carried a shotgun at the May 1967 Sacramento incident, captured in a famous photograph on the front page of the *Black Panther* newspaper on May 15, 1967. According to Seale, the party gave Hutton the M-1 carbine rifle that Aoki gave to Newton when the BPP first started (Seale interview).

42. A substantial portion of the BPP newspaper was devoted to covering the police shootout, the arrests of Eldridge Cleaver and other Panthers, Hutton's funeral, and tributes to Hutton (*Black Panther*, May 15, 1967; also Hilliard and Cole, *This Side of Glory*, 187–95). The *Commemorator* and *It's About Time* (http://www.its abouttimeBPP.com), two publications started by BPP veterans to commemorate the Panther legacy, both organize and report on events honoring Bobby Hutton. The homage to Hutton stems from his martyr status, his youthful age, and his dedication to the BPP.

43. Seale, "History of the Black Panther Party"; Howard interview; Forte interview.

44. Chris Booker offers an insightful analysis of the role of the lumpen in the BPP ("Lumpenization"); also Cleaver, "On Lumpen Ideology."

45. Aoki showed me a picture of him with his fiancée. The FBI interviewed this woman in July 1968 and reported that she had "dated and lived with [Richard Aoki] for two years beginning about October or November, 1964." Based on her desire of "not wanting to see people hurt, hungry, or unable to find jobs," she worked with the Vietnam Day Committee and "began going to Young Socialist Alliance (YSA) functions in early fall of 1964." She expressed regret about her involvement in YSA and with Aoki, indicating that he was "irrational"; because "she became frightened of Aoki," it took a year to break up with him, quit her job, and leave Berkeley (FBI report, September 23, 1968, Bureau File 100-447047; quoted material comes from the FBI report, but is paraphrased from the interview). As expected, this woman's name was deleted from the FBI report sent to the author. Aoki's sister-in-law, who was in the family at the time, did not recall Aoki ever being engaged, nor did she recall this woman (Debbie Aoki interview). When asked whether, as Black nationalism grew, racial politics affected his relationship with his White fiancée, Aoki replied, "It didn't to me." He also denied ever being chided about dating White women. But it was important to Aoki to emphasize that his fiancée was Basque, an oppressed group in Spain and one with darker features (Aoki interview, July 30–August 1, 2003). Seale relayed an incident when, in the BPP's early days, a Panther prevented Mark Comfort's wife, a White woman, from entering the BPP office. Seale told him, "Are you stupid? Let her in that office." To Seale, if Mark Comfort was a Panther, so was his wife, and it didn't matter whether she was White or otherwise (Seale interview).

46. It seems that Aoki had long prioritized the political above the personal. According to FBI reports, Aoki sided with the majority within Berkeley YSA, who believed that YSA members should "sacrifice everything for the cause of Socialism maintaining few personal effects and being available to respond to SWP orders." They contrasted with the minority within BYSA, who advocated "a more liberal interpretation of Marxist-Lenin [sic] doctrine. . . . These individuals would like to work themselves into positions of respectability insofar as their organizations and living conditions are concerned" (FBI report, January 18, 1963).

47. The Panthers first tried to work through the system, but when the Oakland City Council moved slowly, the Panthers decided to direct traffic themselves until a street light was installed (Seale, *Seize the Time,* 99–106). That Aoki would relay the tactical part of this campaign is not surprising. He tended not to participate in negotiations with the Establishment, but rather in more militaristic tactical strategies. Their use of guns contrasts with a Civil Rights Movement tactic such as laying down one's body to block traffic (e.g., Fujino, *Heartbeat of Struggle,* 119, 124).

48. Tom Sanders recalled Aoki telling him back in the 1960s that he was captain of the Berkeley branch, with a membership of one (Sanders interview; also see FBI report, November 16, 1967).

49. By July 1967, an FBI informant reported that the BPP had branches in North Oakland, North Richmond, East Oakland, San Francisco, and Berkeley; the latter was headed by Aoki (FBI report, July 23, 1969).

50. Mark Comfort had both integrationist and self-defense beliefs, somewhat akin to Robert F. Williams (Comfort interview with Robert Wright).

51. In a different incident, Comfort was arrested in an Oakland bar in December 1966 on charges of carrying a concealed weapon (*Oakland Tribune,* December 29, 1966) but later acquitted (*Oakland Tribune,* June 14, 1967; *Black Panther,* May 15, 1967).

52. In April 1967, Comfort invited the Panthers to North Richmond to protest the police killing of Denzil Dowell, and in May 1967, Comfort and other ODAC members went with the Panthers to Sacramento (*Black Panther,* April 25, 1967; *Oakland Tribune,* May 3, 1967). Comfort apparently joined the BPP (Seale, *Seize the Time,* 134; *Black Panther,* May 15, 1967; *Oakland Tribune,* December 17, 1976), though Pearson asserts otherwise (*The Shadow of the Panther,* 121, 128, 130). Comfort himself indicates that ODAC "more or less worked with [the BPP] to help them get started," suggesting that ODAC as an organization did not merge with the BPP (Comfort interview with Robert Wright).

53. The Panthers covered Dowell's killing and protests throughout the entire four pages of the first issue of the BPP newspaper. One article reported on the North Richmond rally, secured by "15 Black Brothers, most of them armed," showcasing the power and constitutional rights achieved through armed self-defense (*Black Panther,* April 25, 1967).

54. Seale remembered Aoki, with a .44 Magnum strapped to his side, organizing four guys to hold down one street at a Richmond rally for Dowell (Seale interview). At the second Dowell rally, Newton pointed to the helicopter circling overhead and made his famous statement: "The spirit of the people is greater than man's technology" (Newton, *Revolutionary Suicide,* 153–61; Seale, *Seize the Time,* 134–49).

55. One might question Aoki's failure to anticipate the state's response to some twenty-six militant Black men and a half dozen woman entering the legislature, visibly armed. Sherwin Forte, for example, feared being killed: "I kind of had not really planned to come back" (Forte interview). But to Aoki, "Everything was legal. So what else could happen? Trust me, we had done this on a number of occasions already. We did the shotgun patrol, rallies, demonstrations already." The Panthers had, for example, gone armed to a meeting with the Richmond district attorney about the Dowell murder (*Black Panther,* May 15, 1967). In fact, the Panthers did not get arrested at the state capitol, but when they made a strategic mistake, stopping at a gas station in Sacramento rather than leaving town (Seale, *Seize the Time,* 153–66; Newton, *Revolutionary Suicide,* 162–68).

56. The boldness of the Panthers' action in Sacramento and the widespread media coverage put the BPP on the national map (*New York Times,* May 3, 1967; *Los Angeles Times,* May 3, 1967). Party membership increased most rapidly after the killings of Martin Luther King—and with him, the hope of a nonviolent revolution—and Bobby Hutton, within days of each other in April 1968. According to Seale, Party membership peaked at five thousand in some forty chapters in late 1968 and early 1969, though many academics and journalists estimate two thousand members in that period. By the 1970s, there were BPP chapters in every major city in the United

States (*Black Panther,* May 9, 1970; Johnson, "Explaining the Demise of the BPP," 391–93, 410).

57. SWP as a legal organization was apparently alarmed that its own standing could be jeopardized if one of its members associated with the BPP, whose threats of violence contesting state power were likely to provoke further state repression and violence. Former SWP member Carol (Shelly) Hayden remembers the SWP asking Aoki to choose between the two organizations (Hayden interview). By contrast, the FBI reports that the BPP "discouraged dual membership," especially seeking to dissociate from Communist and Socialist organizations (November 16, 1967).

58. A discussion between Newton and Aoki over whether Aoki was a formal member of the BPP may have occurred around this time (see note 27, this chapter). Seale associates this memory with recruiting Aoki to provide security for the Denzil Dowell rally, which took place in April 1967. If this were the case, then Aoki may have left the SWP a couple of months later than he remembers, or the process of leaving the SWP may have occurred over a period of weeks. Around that time, some in the BPP were growing increasingly critical of White Leftists. The July 20, 1967, issue of the *Black Panther* published a hard-hitting editorial, "White 'Mother Country' Radicals," by Eldridge Cleaver, asserting that the Communist Party, the Socialist Workers Party, and other White Leftists "pretend to be the friend of black people when in fact they are opportunistic conspirators against the best interests of the black people. . . . From now on, the Socialist Workers Party and the Communist Party should not be allowed to function in the black community at all." Later, as before this time, the BPP would work with White Leftists, notably running Black Panthers on electoral campaigns with the Peace and Freedom Party and organizing the United Front Against Fascism conference, held in Oakland in July 1969, with the Communist Party (*Black Panther,* June 21, 1969). The FBI reported that Aoki resigned from the SWP in spring 1967 (FBI report, November 16, 1967).

59. On Newton's arrest, trial, and defense campaign, see Newton, *Revolutionary Suicide,* 190–302; *New York Times,* October 29, 1967; *Los Angeles Times,* October 29, 1967; Cleaver conversation. A photo of Aoki holding the "Yellow Peril Supports Black Power" sign is in Bingham, *Black Panthers 1968,* n.p. Aoki's reference is to a different photo, also of AAPA members at a Free Huey rally, in Louie and Omatsu, *Asian Americans,* 249.

60. On Huey's birthday event and the short-lived, contentious BPP–SNCC "merger," see the *Black Panther,* February 11, 1968; March 16, 1968; Seale, *Seize the Time,* 211–22; Hilliard and Cole, *This Side of Glory,* 171–75; Newton, *Revolutionary Suicide,* 218–19; Newton, "Huey Newton Talks to the Movement." On SNCC's views of the BPP–SNCC "alliance" and divisions within SNCC, see Forman, *The Making of Black Revolutionaries,* 522–43; Carmichael, *Ready for Revolution,* 659–72; Sellers, *The River of No Return,* 246–52, 659–72. For an astute academic analysis, see Carson, *In Struggle,* 278–85.

61. "Big Man" Howard was aware back in the 1960s that Newton made Aoki a field marshal—perhaps the first one—probably in late 1966 or early 1967. Unlike Aoki, who asserts there were only six field marshals in BPP history, Howard

explained that a field marshal was attached to every branch. The field marshals associated with the national headquarters like Don Cox or Geronimo ji-Jaga Pratt were top BPP leaders and served on the central committtcc; others were deputy field marshals. Howard understood that field marshals were weapons experts, though their specific duties, as well as Aoki's work as field marshal, were vague to him (Howard interview).

62. In the same breath, Aoki said, "Berkeley headquarters was getting started and logically I should have been made the branch captain."

63. More than any other Asian American group, the Red Guard Party, formed in 1969 by San Francisco Chinatown–based street youth, emulated the BPP in its revolutionary ideology, lumpenproletariat membership, and emphasis on military tactics and community service. The BPP strongly influenced the formation of the Red Guard and invited Red Guard members to study groups with BPP leader Eldridge Cleaver. Hing remembers Aoki making "a strong impression" on the young Red Guards because of his use of Black street lingo, militant dress, and sunglasses and gloves, even at night. While Hing and Aoki meet from time to time, Aoki remained a "mystique," always speaking obliquely about his political activities (Hing interview). In 1971, the Red Guard Party merged with the New York–based I Wor Kuen (IWK) to form the first national revolutionary Asian American organization. That the new formation took on the name IWK reflected its criticism of Red Guard's "ultra-military line" ("A History of the Red Guard," Getting Together, http://www.aamovement.org). Instead, IWK focused on mass-based community organizing, while adopting socialist and later Marxist–Leninist ideology. On the Red Guard Party, see Lyman, "Red Guard on Grant Avenue"; Maeda, "Black Panthers, Red Guards, and Chinamen"; Red Guard newspapers.

64. There were at least seven Asian American BPP members, including three men in Seattle (Dixon, "Memoirs of a Black Panther," 111).

65. Geographic proximity and segregation were significant factors in the development of political consciousness, especially for Japanese Americans, who, more than other Asian Americans, lived in communities coterminous with Black populations (Fujino, "Race, Place, Space, and Political Development"; Morris and Braine, "Social Movements and Oppositional Consciousness").

66. On Guy Kurose, see Martin Wong, Art Ishii, and Guy Kurose interview; Fitzgerald, "Guy Kurose Devoted Life to Helping Youth"; Seattle Times, November 9, 2003; Northwest Asian Weekly, November 2, 2002. Mike Tagawa talks openly about his experiences as a Japanese American Panther in Seattle (Seattle Civil Rights and Labor History Project, http://depts.washington.edu/civilr/tagawa.htm); Lum, "Overshadowed"; Richard Aoki memorial website (http://ramemorial.blogspot.com); Tagawa conversation.

67. Fujino, telephone conversation with Lew-Lee; Wong, "Lee Lew-Lee Interview." On All Power to the People, see http://www.engnetwork.com.

68. The latter woman helped produce Black Politics with Aoki and has a daughter active in revolutionary politics (Reiko Redmonde, conversation with author, May 2, 2009; Sanders interview).

69. The advent of the Asian American and the Chicano movements, both in the late 1960s, meant that there was less need for the BPP to accept non-Blacks. In addition, in response to the growing nationalism in the Black movement, the party may well have closed its membership as a strategic move to recruit Blacks, even as the party vigorously defended alliances with Whites and repudiated cultural nationalism.

70. This widely quoted statement was made by anti-Nazi activist Pastor Martin Niemöller.

71. When writing about the first members, Seale stated, "two females named Kathy and Matalaba [sic] . . . were members for only three months" (http://www.bobbyseale.com). Tarika Lewis, also known as Matilaba, is recognized as the first woman to join the Party; "she quickly advanced beyond the rank and file and assumed various leadership positions" (LeBlanc-Ernest, "'The Most Qualified Person,'" 307).

72. The BPP has been criticized for its predominance of male leadership, masculinist rhetoric and images, and sexist practices. But the Panthers also supported women's equality and rights. By 1968, "when paramilitary functions of the organization were less prominent," women comprised over half the BPP membership (see Matthews's astute gendered analysis, "'No One Ever Asks,'" 267–304) and the Panthers provided unusual opportunities for the development of women's leadership (Pulido, *Black, Brown, Yellow, and Left,* 186–94). On women in the party, see Shakur, *Assata;* Brown, *A Taste of Power;* Cleaver, "Women, Power, and Revolution"; Jennings, "Why I Joined the Party"; LeBlanc-Ernest, "'The Most Qualified Person.'"

73. The SWP, for example, published a newspaper, the *Militant,* and a theoretical magazine, *New International.*

74. Eight issues of *Black Politics* came out from January 1968 (vol. 1, no. 1) until sometime in 1969 (no month; vol. 2, no. 13–14). The *San Francisco Chronicle* on August 5, 1970, reported the publication ended in April 1969. Listed as a "monthly journal" from the start, the first three issues came out monthly and then less frequently thereafter, often combining two or more months in a single issue. The stated purpose of *Black Politics* was to "provide a forum for vanguard theories and ideas that deal with currently crucial issues," including support for Vietnam and Black liberation. The articles tended to focus on self-defense—rationale for supporting armed self-defense and detailed, technical "how-to" articles, at times accompanied by illustrations. Tom Sanders explained the magazine's main purpose was to disseminate detailed and explicit information on self-defense (the George Prosser articles) and secondarily to analyze Black history (Sanders interview). There were a number of articles on the BPP and a reprinted article from the Asian American Political Alliance titled "Concentration Camps USA."

75. My interview with Tom Sanders generally supports this description by Aoki, with one major exception. Sanders remembers leaving the SWP in March 1966, when he went to Nicaragua to provide direct support to the Sandinistas. His actions, he said, contradicted SWP's view of guerrilla warfare. If correct, Sanders would have left the SWP a full year before Aoki's departure (Sanders interview).

76. The *Oakland Tribune* identified Jim Nabors as the western regional vice president of the Republic of New Africa (February 11, 1972). Douglas Daniels remembered Aoki initiating conversations with Black students, including himself, when Daniels was a new graduate student at UC Berkeley in the late 1960s (Daniels interview).

77. While high-ranking leaders of the BPP (Elbert "Big Man" Howard) and of the RNA (Jim Nabors) worked on *Black Politics,* as did a Japanese–White woman member of the Berkeley BPP chapter, it's unclear whether the BPP or RNA offered any *organizational* support (Howard interview; United States Congress, *Riots, Civil and Criminal Disorders,* 896). Tom Sanders explained that there was none and despite the listing of three to five editors, he and Aoki—and at the end, mainly Sanders—did the bulk of the work to produce and distribute the magazine. If true, this does not undercut Aoki's main point that members of different groups worked together on this publication despite organizational differences. Moreover, that the editorial board was multiracial—Asian, White, and Black—reflected, at least in part, a belief stated in a *Black Politics* editorial: "Malcolm X . . . was willing to work with any group, regardless of its color or political, economic, or social philosophy, as long as it was determined to fight the injustices done to black people" (*Black Politics,* February 1968, 2; Sanders interview).

78. The decision to use fictitious names was made before the first issue of *Black Politics* appeared in January 1968. Thus, the Tri-Con incident, which occurred in April 1968, would not have been a determining factor. But the point remains: Aoki was aware of state repression and did not want to risk his safety by using his real name. Richard Assegai, Aoki's nom de plume, was listed on the editorial board for all the issues, except the last one. A congressional report investigating 1960s activism discusses *Black Politics* and reveals names (United States Congress, *Riots, Civil and Criminal Disorders,* 874, 895–96).

79. While Aoki remembers a "printing press," Douglas Daniels distinctly remembers obtaining a three-hundred-dollar loan from the Co-op to buy a "mimeograph machine" and Tom Sanders recalls purchasing a "Gestetner duplicator," which is "similar to a mimeograph, but much better." Either of the latter two would have been far easier to use (Daniels, e-mail to author, March 3, 2010; Daniels, conversation with author, March 15, 2010; Sanders interview). That they invested in purchasing a duplicating machine reveals a considerable level of dedication to producing *Black Politics.*

80. One of the reasons for starting *Black Politics* was to impart technical knowledge of self-defense tactics to Black Panthers and other Black militants, but Aoki did not know whether the BPP formally studied *Black Politics:* "By that time, I was too far removed from David [Hilliard] and the operations of the party to know." But a *Black Politics* editorial suggested that at least by their fifth issue, they had already made an impact. Articles were broadcast on radio stations and had been reprinted in California (several in UC Berkeley's *Daily Californian*), North Carolina, and Brazil (*Black Politics,* Summer 1968, 38–39). Sanders recalled the print run being about 1,500 (Sanders interview).

81. There is evidence that the FBI COINTELPRO's underhanded tactics succeeded in provoking and exacerbating tensions between the BPP and US Organization, culminating in the killings of two Panthers on January 17, 1969 (Churchill and Vander Wall, *The COINTELPRO Papers*, 133–35; Brown, *A Taste of Power*, 156–70).

82. The expulsion of Karenga at an RNA meeting in Detroit on April 5, 1969, was reported in the *Black Panther* (May 11, 1969).

83. Sanders recalls Aoki recruiting most of the editors and contributors to *Black Politics* (Sanders interview).

84. In a letter to the RNA, Newton noted that although the BPP did not advocate RNA's separate "nation within a nation" position, and believed that a separate nation or territory would further isolate the Black community at a time when alliances were urgently needed, the BPP did not oppose a Black Nation and, in fact, called for a plebiscite for the Black people to determine their future, as contained in Point 10 of the Ten-Point Program. Thus, concluded Newton, "we don't have any contradiction" between the positions of the two groups and encouraged the two groups to work together, especially given their common internal colonial analyses (Newton, letter to RNA, September 1969; printed in the *Black Panther*, December 6, 1969).

85. On Tijerina, see Tijerina, *Mi lucha por la tierra*, English translation by Gutiérrez, *They Called Me "King Tiger"*; Maciel and Peña, "La Reconquista"; Mariscal, *Brown-Eyed Children of the Sun*, 185–202.

86. Congressional hearings on the topic of riots and civil and criminal disorders were held from November 1, 1967, through August 6, 1970. The U.S. government investigated *Black Politics*, along with publications of the BPP, Weathermen, and others, because of their descriptions of how to make Molotov cocktails and other explicit "terrorism and sabotage" tactics. The congressional committee was particularly focused on determining the identity of George Prosser, a pseudonym for the author of several *Black Politics* articles, complete with pictures and diagrams. At some point, a "reliable source" identified George Prosser as Tom Sanders, but a staff investigator stated, "We could not locate Mr. Prosser or any record of Mr. Prosser" (United States Congress, *Riots, Civil and Criminal Disorders*, 874–96, 5585–90; *San Francisco Chronicle*, August 5, 1970).

87. Aoki was an instructor and co-coordinator of Asian American Studies at UC Berkeley (Hayashi, "Contemporary Asian Studies Division Report"); see chapter 9, this book.

88. Newton was released on August 5, 1970, after thirty-three months in prison. On October 13, 1970, he spoke at Merritt College, with over a thousand people in attendance, wearing the same white shirt and with the same background as in the photo with Aoki on security (*Merritt College Reporter*, October 15, 1970; flyer announcing Newton's talk, Merritt College archives).

89. David Hilliard also "loved Huey through the end," despite the "profound personal betrayals" and craziness, because as Hilliard put it, "with him I felt I was near greatness" (*Nation*, September 6, 1993).

90. Newton earned a PhD in history of consciousness at UC Santa Cruz, completing his dissertation, "War Against the Panthers: A Study of Repression in America,"

in June 1980. His dissertation was published posthumously in 1996. J. Herman Blake interviewed Aoki when putting together Newton's autobiography, *Revolutionary Suicide* (Blake, letter to Aoki, November 6, 1970).

91. Aoki distinctly remembers Bakunin's "Catechism of a Revolutionist" on the front page of the Black Panther newspaper. Bakunin's essay, though not in the BPP newspaper, was reprinted as an official BPP publication, *Perspectives in Black Liberation #1,* with an introduction by the BPP minister of information (Eldridge Cleaver). Also in the *Black Panther* (April 11, 1970), in response to the interviewer's questioning about adventurism, Cleaver referenced Bakunin: "People used to say that we were provoking the power structure into coming down prematurely when people weren't prepared, but . . . it's always time to move if you're willing to face the consequences. . . . You recall the first phrase in The Catechism of a Revolutionist by Bakunin says that a Revolutionary is a doomed man, so all these people who are concerned about survival and who want to carry out a revolution without suffering any consequences, I think that they don't really want to carry out a revolution. . . . [P]eople in the United States talked about police brutality for about 50 years. . . . But it wasn't until the BPP got out into the street with guns and confronted the cops on the street at great loss and at great suffering that we have been able to do something to create a climate and an awareness, where the pigs are uptight. All the talking in the world didn't do anything about it. [I]t took the type of action that we [do], which they call adventurist, and which we accept."

92. Newton invited Cleaver to appear with him on a San Francisco television show on February 26, 1971. But on the show, Cleaver, by telephone from Algeria, demanded that Newton reinstate the New York 21 and expel David Hilliard. After the show, Newton phoned Cleaver and the two argued and expelled each other from the party (Newton, *Revolutionary Suicide,* 337–40; Pearson, *The Shadow of the Panther,* 230–32). The FBI fomented this conflict by sending Cleaver a series of forged letters about Newton's erratic behavior and by promoting Cleaver's leadership (Newton, *War Against the Panthers,* 65–71).

93. Newton best articulated his theory of intercommunalism in a series of public conversations with Erik Erickson held at Yale University in February 1971. Grounded in the Marxist method of dialectical materialism, Newton explained that "the United States is no longer a nation. . . . We call it an empire, . . . a nation-state that has transformed itself into a power controlling *all* the world's lands and people. . . . [W]hat happens when the raw materials are extracted and labor is exploited within a territory dispersed over the entire globe? . . . Then the people and the economy are so integrated into the imperialist empire that it's impossible to 'decolonize,' to return to the former conditions of existence. . . . We say that the world today is a dispersed collection of communities. . . . And we say further that the struggle in the world today is between the small circle that administers and profits from the empire of the United States, and the peoples of the world who want to determine their own destinies. We call this situation intercommunalism." He went on to distinguish "revolutionary intercommunalism" (globalization from below) from "reactionary intercommunalism" or rule by the powerful (globalization from above). He also acknowledged

that communism "is an even higher stage than revolutionary intercommunalism" (Erikson and Newton, *In Search of Common Ground*, 30–31, 33). In many ways, Newton's intercommunalism anticipated current theories of globalization.

94. Aoki's discussion of anarchism coincides with critiques of focoism, a guerrilla strategy inspired by Che Guevara and rooted in the idea that small military actions can catalyze an armed insurrection of the people and create revolutionary change. While Cleaver seemed to promote focoist strategy, Newton, without using the term, argued against this: "[N]o party or organization can make the revolution, only the people can. . . . You must establish your organization aboveground so that the people can relate to it in a way that will be positive and progressive for them" (Newton, "On the Defection of Eldridge Cleaver" and "The Correct Handling of a Revolution"). Focoism was theorized by Régis Debray in *Revolution in the Revolution?*

95. The widespread association of anarchism with violence seems unfair. Some nonanarchist Leftists also believe that the ruling class will not concede power except through violent revolution, as discussed by Lenin in *The State and Revolution.* More important, the theory of spontaneous order characterizes anarchism more than does any promotion of violence per se. Ward explained that this is "the theory that, given a common need, a collection of people will, by trial and error, by improvisation and experiment, evolve order out of the situation—this order being more durable and more closely related to their needs than any kind of externally imposed authority could provide" (*Anarchy in Action*, 28). See Kropotkin, *Selected Writings on Anarchism and Revolution;* Bukharin, "Anarchy and Scientific Communism"; Lenin, *The State and Revolution.*

96. Hing was the minister of defense of the Red Guard. Aoki claims being minister of defense for AAPA before the TWLF strike. While Aoki served this role in AAPA, there's no evidence that AAPA formally developed this position (Aoki interview, May 18–21, 2003).

97. Rather than any bitterness about this nonpayment, there's sarcasm and particularly pride in Aoki's tone.

98. Hing recalls talking on occasion to Cleaver in Algeria, but has only a vague memory of this event (Hing interview). Kathleen Cleaver remembers Hing and Eldridge being on good terms, including during Cleaver's exile in Algeria (Cleaver conversation).

99. Aoki's ideas echo Newton, who contended: "If these imposters would investigate the history of revolution, they would see that the vanguard group always starts out above ground and is later driven underground by the aggressor" (*Black Panther,* May 18, 1968).

100. Aoki's ideas were influenced by the SWP's urging of an independent Black political party (Socialist Workers Party, "The Case for an Independent Black Political Party"). In an article Aoki wrote for *Black Politics,* he urged its readership to "vote Black Panther." He stated his rationale for participating in electoral politics as follows: "In general, we cannot get any real or fundamental changes in this election; the real change will take place on the streets. . . . Vote for the Party as a gesture of protest against the white and Uncle Tom candidates of the Republican and Democratic

parties. . . . [A]fter you cast your vote for the BPP, go out and get involved in the liberation struggle" (September–October 1968, 10).

101. The party newspaper stated that "the Free Breakfast for Children program is a socialistic program, designed to serve the people. All institutions in a society should be designed to serve the masses, not just a 'chosen few'" (*Black Panther,* October 4, 1969). Newton explained: "We call them survival programs, meaning survival pending revolution. We say that the survival program . . . is like the survival kit of a sailor stranded on a raft. It helps him to sustain himself until he can get completely out of that situation. So the survival programs are not answers or solutions, but they will help us to organize the community around a true analysis and understanding of their situation. When the consciousness and understanding is raised to a high level then the community will seize the time and deliver themselves from the boot of their oppressors" (Newton, *To Die for the People,* 104).

102. Some contend that the BPP dropped its revolutionary program by 1971, when, after the party split, the BPP mainly engaged in electoral politics or serve-the-people programs. By contrast, Umoja argues that the revolutionary activities of the BPP went underground in the form of the Black Liberation Army ("Repression Breeds Resistance," 3–4). After the Seale–Brown electoral defeat in late 1973 and Seale's resignation in July 1974, there were only about two hundred party members, down from the peak of a claimed five thousand. Some state that the BPP existed, though barely a shell of its former self, until 1982, when the last party program, the Oakland Community School, closed. See Hopkins, "The Deradicalization of the Black Panther Party"; Johnson, "Explaining the Demise of the Black Panther Party," 392–94; LeBlanc-Ernest, "'The Most Qualified Person.'"

103. In August 1967, the FBI officially launched its notorious COINTELPRO operations against the BPP. By September 1968, FBI director J. Edgar Hoover dubbed the BPP "the greatest threat to the internal security of the country." In 1969 alone, the police killed twenty-eight Panthers, according to BPP lawyer Charles Garry. The FBI also bombed Panther offices, wiretapped phones, mailed forged letters, leaked false news to the media, sent in infiltrators and agent provocateurs, made multiple arrests, and so forth, to "neutralize" the party. On FBI and police repression of the BPP, see Churchill and Vander Wall, *Agents of Repression* and *The COINTELPRO Papers;* Newton, *War Against the Panthers.*

104. The party's internecine fighting turned deadly, with the killings of Black Panthers Robert Web and Sam Napier, allegedly by Panthers on the other side of the split (Cox, "The Split in the Party").

105. In siding with Newton, Aoki knew that he was vulnerable to attacks by Eldridge's faction: "It got to the point where the ones who were siding with Huey would be the ones I trusted." But Aoki wasn't sure whom he could trust and who trusted him—on either side. This is consistent with the intense distrust that existed within the party, fomented, in part, by COINTELPRO operations.

106. See the "Alliances and Coalitions" section in Foner's *The Black Panthers Speak;* the "Coalition Politics" section in Lazerow and Williams, *In Search of the Black Panther Party;* Heath's *The Black Panther Leaders Speak,* 79–97.

107. Cleaver and Katsiaficas, *Liberation, Imagination, and the Black Panther Party*; Heath, *The Black Panther Leaders Speak*, 98–120.

108. Newton explained: "The original vision of the Party was to develop a lifeline to the people, by serving their needs and defending them against their oppressors. . . . We knew that this strategy would raise the consciousness of the people and also give us their support" (*Black Panther*, April 17, 1971). Indeed, at a time when the majority of Black people believed in working through the existing system, that so many supported the BPP is somewhat surprising. A national poll of Black Americans, taken by Market Dynamics, Inc., for ABC-TV in 1970 found that the BPP ranked third, after the NAACP and the Southern Christian Leadership Conference, as having done the most for Black people over the past two years. Sixty-two percent of those polled admired the work of the BPP (Foner, *The Black Panthers Speak*, xiv).

109. Neil helped start the first BPP Free Breakfast Program and was considered the Panther's religious adviser (*Black Panther*, July 26, 1969). Small founded the BPP Sickle Cell Anemia Foundation (*Commemorator*, May 13, 2005; *Revolutionary Worker*, February 17, 2002). Villa worked with the Free Breakfast Program and other BPP programs and was awarded Woman of the Year in 1994 by Assemblywoman Barbara Lee (*It's About Time*, Fall 2000).

110. See note 103, this chapter.

111. Aoki recounted: "From prison, Huey got the word to me. We need leadership publicly. The primary and secondary leadership has been wiped out—in prison, in exile. We need someone to run the party for a little while. David [Hilliard] would be ideal. There was a brief instant where my name came up and that was quashed real fast, by me. I knew that if I publicly took over the party, especially as a Japanese American, I would have been killed. So in the middle of the night, I'm at the back door at David's home. Let me in. I got a message from Huey. We up against the wall. Huey is willing to make you deputy chief of staff." Hilliard denies that Aoki helped convince him to join the BPP or become chief of staff. Hilliard's autobiography indicates that shortly after writing the Ten-Point Program and after Aoki gave them their first two guns, Newton and Seale introduced the party to Hilliard and took him on one of the first police patrols. When Hilliard acted courageously following the police shooting of Newton in October 1967, Cleaver made Hilliard the captain of the national headquarters, which signified to Hilliard, "I've become a member of the Party." Following the police killing of Bobby Hutton in April 1968, and with the growing conflict between Cleaver and Newton, Newton appointed Hilliard the chief of staff. The point here is that Aoki realized that despite bringing trouble, the party brought profound meaning to people's lives (Hilliard conversation; Hilliard and Cole, *This Side of Glory*, 115–18, 130–35, 195; Aoki interview, January 11–12, 2003; August 21–26, 2003). Pat Hilliard died in 2000, so I was unable to verify Aoki's conversation with her (*It's About Time*, Spring 2000).

112. While Cleaver does not recall any specifics, she remarked that this sounded like a conversation they would have had (Cleaver conversation).

113. The FBI, in fact, viewed Aoki as the "only non-Negro known to be affiliated with the BPPSD" (FBI report, November 16, 1967).

114. Seale interview.

115. Okihiro, *Margins and Mainstreams;* Prashad, *Everyone Was Kung Fu Fighting;* Mullen, *Afro-Orientalism;* Raphael-Hernandez and Steen, *AfroAsian Encounters;* Ho and Mullen, *Afro Asia.*

116. Prashad, *The Darker Nations.*

117. Newton, *Revolutionary Suicide,* 359; also Brown, *A Taste of Power,* 217–40, 295–304; Heath, *The Black Panther Leaders Speak,* 62–72; Cleaver, "Back to Africa"; Kelley and Esch, "Black Like Mao." Cleaver was particularly impressed with Kim Il-sung's concept of *Juche* or self-reliance (*Black Panther,* April 11, 1970), and Cleaver's delegation included Asian Americans Alex Hing and Pat Sumi (Ho and Yip, "Interview with Alex Hing"; Yokota, "Interview with Pat Sumi"). Around mid-April 1970, Aoki was invited to travel to North Korea, it seems by a Leftist activist in Japan who was showing the film *Red Army of Japan* during a visit with the Asian Americans for Action in New York City. Aoki apparently declined the invitation "due to other commitments" (FBI report, April 2, 1970; June 5, 1970).

118. Howard, *Panther on the Prowl,* 42, 38–48.

119. Forte interview.

120. The statement included: "At the same time that the American government is waging a racist war of genocide in Vietnam, the concentration camps in which Japanese-Americans were interned during World War II are being renovated and expanded. Since America has historically reserved its most barbaric treatment for non-white people, we are forced to conclude that these concentration camps are being prepared for Black people who are determined to gain their freedom by any means necessary" (BPP, "Executive Mandate No. 1," May 2, 1967).

121. Petersen, "Success Story, Japanese-American Style"; "Success Story of One Minority Group in U.S."

122. Park, *Race and Culture;* Yu, *Thinking Orientals.*

123. Carmichael and Hamilton, *Black Power.*

124. Pulido, *Black, Brown, Yellow, and Left,* 156.

125. Newton, letter to RNA, September 1969, in the *Black Panther,* December 6, 1969.

126. This debate was exacerbated by differences in the class-based politics of the West Coast national headquarters and the nationalism of the New York Panthers; the increasingly highly centralized, authoritarian command of Newton and Hilliard; and the erratic and violent behavior of both Newton and Cleaver (Johnson, "Explaining the Demise of the Black Panther Party"; Cleaver, "Back to Africa"; Brown, *A Taste of Power*).

127. Newton, "On the Defection of Eldridge Cleaver" and *Revolutionary Suicide,* 366–70.

128. Hopkins, "The Deradicalization of the Black Panther Party"; Cleaver, "Back to Africa," 239.

129. As another example, while most accounts of BPP history explain that Newton and Seale flipped a coin to determine the two positions (Newton, *Revolutionary Suicide,* 132; Seale, *Seize the Time,* 62; Seale in Lew-Lee, *All Power to the People;* Seale

interview), Aoki's narrative creates a more logical context for this decision. Seale's strength as an organizer and orator and Newton's as a street fighter and legal mind made the choice of chairman and minister of defense, respectively, most appropriate, even if the selection was made inadvertently.

7. "Support All Oppressed Peoples"

1. When referring to the 1960s, Aoki used the vocabulary of the time, "Oriental." The term "Asian American" emerged only in 1968 through AAPA organizing (see note 7, this chapter).

2. Gee played a leadership role far beyond being a gracious host; see commentary at the end of this chapter.

3. On the historiography of the AAM, see Fujino, "Who Studies the Asian American Movement?"

4. Hayashi, "Contemporary Asian Studies Division Report"; Vicci Wong, TWLF panel, Professor Carlos Muñoz's class, UC Berkeley, October 26, 1995; Dong interview; Alan Fong interview; Bryant Fong interview; Huen interview. On Filipino farmworker organizing, see Scharlin and Villanueva, *Philip Vera Cruz.*

5. Louie, "'Yellow, Brown & Red'"; Fujino, *Heartbeat of Struggle;* Boggs, *Living for Change.*

6. On Japanese Americans in the Communist Party USA, see Yoneda, *Ganbatte;* Oda, *Heroic Struggles of Japanese Americans;* Fowler, *Japanese and Chinese Immigrant Activists.*

7. AAPA was one of the earliest groups to refer to themselves as "Asian Americans." The new term was an act of self-naming that countered the imposition of "Oriental"—a term seen in opposition and inferiority to the Occident and developed, as Edward Said argues, in the context of imperialism (Said, *Orientalism*). Yuji Ichioka, in the context of AAPA, is credited with coining the term "Asian America" (Espiritu, *Asian American Panethnicity,* 32, 34). Aoki could not recall any specific details, but defended the attribution to Ichioka and AAPA (Aoki interview; also Alan Fong interview). Others remember the discussion, but credit the collective rather than a single individual for developing the term (Bryant Fong interview; Huen interview).

8. Aoki was a member of the Nisei Student Club (Nikkei Student Club Roster, 1968–69). On the Chinese Students Club and Chinese Student Association, see *CSC Monsoon Mercury,* July 28, 1968; Dong, "Origins and Trajectory of Asian American Political Activism," 41–44. While Aoki added that "there was PACE [Pilipino American Collegiate Endeavor] for the Filipinos students," he may have been referring to the organization on San Francisco State's campus.

9. The layout of the flyer, with the organization's name and logo comprising the top two-thirds of the paper, suggests that the event was organized to showcase AAPA (AAPA flyer for July 28 event). AAPA's speaker was not listed, but other speakers revealed AAPA's pan-Asian (Professor Masao Miyoshi, George Woo, PACE representative) and Third World emphases (Bobby Seale of the BPP, Antonio Mondragon of Alianza). If this was AAPA's coming out, as Aoki asserts, it is curious why a largely

campus group would do so in the summer. Still, other UC Berkeley groups had some summer activities (*CSC Monsoon Mercury,* July 28, 1968).

10. There is little evidence that Aoki was elected AAPA's official spokesperson when he was asked to represent the group at the July 28, 1968, event. Given AAPA's collective leadership style, there was little reason to have a single spokesperson. Moreover, the July 28 event was not mentioned in Aoki's graduate student paper and holds no particular significance for other AAPA members (Dong interview; Alan Fong interview; Bryant Fong interview; Huen interview). Why has the July 28 program taken on such great importance for Aoki? A teleological reinterpretation appears to be occurring as Aoki struggles to locate his place in history within a social movement with virtually no visible leaders.

11. Aoki read from a typed outline of his speech, while adding his own present-day commentary ("AAPA rally, July, 28, 1968" was added in Aoki's handwriting, no author, no title). His speech was closely based on AAPA's program, "AAPA Perspectives" (first known as the "General Philosophy Statement," June 1968), with one minor difference: Aoki emphasized and criticized the accommodationist approach. There was a strong current within the AAM to denounce assimilationism; see Uyematsu, "The Emergence of Yellow Power in America."

12. The use of the word "before" seems to imply a two-step process: first, gaining self-control, then struggling to end oppression. But I have found nothing in AAPA's written materials or activities to suggest such a process; instead, AAPA worked simultaneously for self-determination and against structural oppression.

13. From November–December 1968 to December 1969, AAPA published nine volumes of its newspaper, which is located at the Ethnic Studies and Bancroft Libraries, UC Berkeley, and in the Steve Louie Collection, UCLA. "AAPA Perspectives" first appeared in the fifth issue (Summer 1969) and ran in two other issues: October 1969 and November 1969. This statement is most accessible in *Roots,* though mistitled as "Understanding AAPA."

14. The November 1969 issue had Seale's photo on the front page and Kochiyama's "Rob Williams" on page 2, reprinted from *Asian Americans for Action* newsletter (Asian Americans for Action was a New York–based organization), October 1969, 4, 8.

15. "Third World Power," *AAPA* newspaper, February 1969, 1, 4; "Third World Roots: Bandung," *AAPA* newspaper, March–April 1969, 1, 4. Two of the six sentences of "AAPA Perspectives" captured the importance of Third World solidarity: "We Asian Americans support all oppressed peoples and their struggles for Liberation and believe that Third World People must have complete control over the political, economic, and educational institutions within their communities" and "We Asian Americans refuse to cooperate with the White Racism in this society which exploits us as well as other Third World people and affirm the right of Self-Determination" (capitalization as in original document).

16. Aoki is referring to a photo in Louie and Omatsu, *Asian Americans,* 249. There is also a photo of Aoki holding a "Yellow Peril Supports Black Power" sign in Bingham, *Black Panthers 1968* (n.p.).

17. At a Black Panther rally, Aoki delivered a polemical speech before the Oakland City Council expressing AAPA's demands for "an investigation of the murder of Bobby Hutton" and for "our two so-called Oriental representatives [to explain] what they have done, are doing, and will do about the problem of racism in Oakland and the harassment of the Black Panthers" (typed speech, with "Huey Newton defense rally, DeFremery Park, Oakland, July 14, 1968" handwritten on the flyer).

18. Bryant Fong developed into a "master teacher" in Wu Shu martial arts, studied and certified in China (Bryant Fong interview; also *CSC Monsoon Mercury,* July 1968).

19. AAPA's newspaper highlighted a quotation on the tactical use of violence by, of all people, Mahatma Gandhi: "Where the choice is set between cowardice and violence, I would advise violence. I praise and extol the serene courage of dying without killing. Yet I desire that those who have not this courage should rather cultivate the art of killing and being killed, than basely to avoid the danger. This is because he who runs away commits mental violence. . . . I would a thousand times prefer violence than the emasculation of a whole race. I prefer to use arms in defence of honour rather than remain the vile witness of dishonour" (*AAPA* newspaper, November 1969, 1; also M. K. Gandhi, "The Doctrine of the Sword").

20. The *Washington Post* (September 23, 1968) broke the "fat Jap" comment in an article on Agnew's campaign travels, forcing Agnew to offer excuses, then apologies. On September 19, 1996, following Agnew's death, William Safire wrote in the *New York Times* that the incident was "unfairly blown up as a racial slur" after Agnew gave a "cheery 'How's the fat Jap?'" to a reporter widely known as "the fat Jap." But that reporter's daughter felt otherwise: "My father [Gene Oishi] never accepted the comment as anything but an insulting slur. . . . [D]uring World War II . . . [p]hrases like 'a Jap is a Jap' and 'a good Jap is a dead Jap' were common parlance, often repeated and printed to rationalize the existence of the [concentration] camps" (Eve Oishi, letter to editor, *New York Times,* September 27, 1996).

21. Aoki's statement comes from AAPA, "Nixon/Agnew Report," September 26, 1968; no author cited, but Aoki presented the statement and identified himself as the author.

22. The *Hokubei* reported: "At the conclusion of Aoki's remarks, all of the members of the Asian American Political Alliance dramatically got up and walked out of the building. The audience was reduced to one half after the AAPA walk-out." The ethnic and mainstream presses gave more coverage to Aoki's speech than to the comments of JACL leaders Ray Okamura and Yukio Kawamura (*Hokubei Mainichi,* September 30, 1968; *San Francisco Chronicle,* September 27, 1968).

23. Okamura, note to Aoki, September 27, 1968.

24. On the Title II campaign, see Ichioka, "Would You Believe Concentration Camps for Americans?" *AAPA* newspaper, November–December 1968, 3, with typos corrected, as per "Concentration Camps U.S.A.," issued by AAPA, SPC, Bancroft Library, box 18; Okamura, "Background and History of the Repeal Campaign"; Izumi, "Prohibiting 'American Concentration Camps'"; "Infamous Concentration Camp Bill: Title II-Emergency Detention Act," *Asian Americans for Action* newsletter, October 1970, 8.

25. A 1969 AAPA newspaper article explained: "The background for the treaty goes back to 1945 . . . [when] General Douglas MacArthur . . . forbade the rebuilding of the Japanese military machine." In 1952, at the end of the formal U.S. occupation of Japan, the U.S.–Japan Security Treaty authorized the United States to maintain land, air, and sea forces in and about Japan and its territory of Okinawa. Okinawa is particularly important to U.S. military interests: On a mere 1 percent of Japan's land base, Okinawa houses 75 percent of U.S. bases in Japan. The AAPA article continued: "In 1960 this treaty was superceded by the Treaty for Mutual Cooperation and Security. Under the terms of the 1960 treaty, the U.S. can step in militarily, after prior consultation with Japan, when it feels that 'the security of Japan or international peace and security in the Far East is threatened.' The U.S. can maintain air and naval forces in Japan . . . The treaty is effective [for] ten years and will be renewed automatically unless one of the parties dissents." Note that "when [this treaty was] signed on June 23, 1960, [it] caused such a stir in Japan that then Prime Minister Kishi and his entire cabinet resigned" (*AAPA* newspaper, Summer 1969, 2; also Johnson, *Blowback*, 34–64; Bello, "From American Lake to a People's Pacific"). Aoki denounced the treaty in an AAPA newspaper article. With his political and class analysis trumping ethnic unity, he accused the Japanese government of being "a running dog of the U.S. aggression in Vietnam" and "extend[ing] its own nefarious neo-colonialist tentacles into the Third World." He wrote: "[The Japanese government] profits from the war in exchange for [U.S.] political support. The basis for this unholy alliance is the U.S.–Japan Treaty which allows the U.S. to store nuclear weapons and nerve gas on Okinawa" ("Running Dogs Meet Their Masters," *AAPA* newspaper, Summer 1969, 2, 7).

26. "Japan Week," "Security Treaty," and "Running Dogs Meet Their Masters," *AAPA* newspaper, Summer 1969, 2.

27. "AAPA Perspectives."

28. The Vietnam War was featured prominently in AAPA's newspaper. Like many radical Third Worldist groups at the time, AAPA viewed the war as one of U.S. imperialist aggression and advocated self-determination for the Vietnamese people. AAPA's position on Vietnam stated, "America is conducting a war of technological genocide in Vietnam. . . . The Vietnamese people, struggling for independence, democracy, peace, and neutrality, are resolved to drive out any imperialist forces from Viet Nam." It was bold, but not surprising that AAPA printed a full-page political statement of the National Liberation Front and a statement by Ho Chi Minh. This contrasted with AAPA's "dissatisfaction with the current Anti-War Movement and its orientation toward saving American lives, instead of Vietnamese lives." In calling for Asian Americans to "put themselves on the line" in opposing "genocide on Asian peoples," AAPA helped organize or publicize Asian-specific protest marches, draft counseling, and educational and political forums on Vietnam, "so that people, particularly Asians, can better understand the complexities of the Vietnam War and how it relate to American industry, military, and government policies." See *AAPA* newspaper, November–December 1968, 1, 4; January 1969, 2, 3, 4; Summer 1969, 7; October 1969, 1; November 1969, 1, 2, 3; December–February 1969–70, 5.

29. Aoki, speech, in outline form, given at the SDS Western Regional Conference, Richmond, Calif., late spring/early summer 1969. Also, AAPA worked with the Asian Coalition, SDS, and Los Siete de la Raza to oppose the "Japan Week" activities in September 1969. Los Siete de la Raza formed in 1969 to defend seven Latinos, active with the Chicano movement, against charges of killing a police officer. The organization was Third Worldist in orientation and drew support from the BPP and Asian American activists (Ferreira, "'All Power to the People,'" 297–305).

30. While written in a dramatic style, Wolfe's *Esquire* article did not report that AAPA was running gun-training sessions. Wolfe gained fame with his books, including *Radical Chic and Mau-Mauing the Flak Catchers,* a satirical social commentary on the 1960s, the BPP, and Leonard Bernstein.

31. *AAPA* newspaper, Summer 1969, 4–5.

32. Today, it is often former AAPA women who speak on panels on AAPA and the TWLF: Vicci Wong, TWLF panel, Professor Carlos Muñoz's class, UC Berkeley, October 26, 1995; Vicci Wong, TWLF plenary session, thirtieth anniversary of TWLF strike, UC Berkeley, April 9, 1999; Lillian Fabros, TWLF panel, thirtieth anniversary of TWLF strike, UC Berkeley, April 10, 1999; Vicci Wong, TWLF strike, fortieth TWLF strike commemorative dinner, UC Berkeley, March 13, 2009; Lillian Fabros Brando and Liz Del Sol, TWLF panel, API Issues Conference, UC Berkeley, March 14, 2009.

33. Gordon Hirabayashi was one of three test cases opposing the evacuation of Japanese Americans heard before the U.S. Supreme Court during World War II.

34. Jerry Enomoto of National JACL expressed support for Asian Studies 100X, noting that it was a project "most worthy of JACL support." Of the $2,000 requested from the Japanese and Chinese communities, JACL was considering giving $200–$300 (Jerry Enomoto, letter to Ray Okamura, on National JACL letterhead, January 1, 1969). The university paid for the instructor and teaching assistants, while private monies were raised to support guest lecturers (Leonard Machlis, assistant chancellor for educational development, UC Berkeley, letter to Paul Takagi, December 12, 1968).

35. Two Japanese American newspapers announced that Asian Studies 100X, "sponsored by AAPA and initiated by students," was the first course at UC Berkeley to focus extensively on Japanese American history (*Nichi Bei Times,* December 19, 1968; *Hokubei Mainichi,* December 20, 1968). The AAPA newspaper explained that the first section covered conditions in "China and Japan from whence the first emigrants emerged"; the second section covered Asian experiences in the United States; and the third section would "pursue feelings of Asian students relative to their situation in America" (*AAPA* newspaper, January 1969, 1, 2; November–December 1968, 1). To Aoki, the most important section focused on the nature of imperialism—the "relationship of Britain to China" and "America to Japan."

36. The students spent more time in discussion sections (ninety minutes twice a week) than in lecture (Tuesdays and Thursdays, 7–8 p.m.). See *AAPA* newspaper, January 1969, 1; Asian Studies 100X syllabus, Winter 1969; flyer for Asian Studies 100X, n.d.; Machlis, letter to Takagi, December 12, 1968.

37. Espiritu, *Asian American Panethnicity,* 20; based on Hayano, "Ethnic Identification and Disidentification," 162.

38. Espiritu's *Asian American Panethnicity* provided the first comprehensive discussion of pan-Asian formation.

39. Maeda, *Chains of Babylon.*

40. Dong, "The Origins and Trajectory of Asian American Political Activism," 51–53; Espiritu, *Asian American Panethnicity,* 34–35; Wei, *The Asian American Movement,* 1926, 207–17; Ho, *Legacy to Liberation,* 399; Yip, "Serve the People"; Umemoto, "'On Strike!'" Wei noted that AAPA was the most militant and actively involved of the three Asian American groups in the San Francisco State strike (*The Asian American Movement,* 19). According to an FBI investigation, the strongest AAPA chapters were at UC Berkeley, San Francisco State, and San José State. Although the "outlook for AAPA was bleak at [Cal State University] Hayward" due to the campus's "conservative" climate, efforts at UCLA, Merritt College, and elsewhere to start AAPA chapters signaled the importance of this organization (FBI reports, n.d., ca. 1968 and 1969).

41. R. Aoki, "The Asian American Political Alliance"; "AAPA's Financial Communique No. 1," from "R.A.," May 6, 1969; "AAPA's Financial Communique No. 2," from "R.A.," July 28, 1969; AAPA's EASTer Symposium program, April 4–6, 1969, San José; FBI report, January 29, 1970.

42. On the performance of Black manhood, see Maeda, "Black Panthers, Red Guards, and Chinamen."

43. Among the AAPA activists with whom I spoke, many saw Aoki's militancy as positive. But there were others who viewed the BPP and others as hooligans whom they disrespected for being excessively rhetorical and also for using the gun to intimidate fellow activists.

44. Bryant Fong interview; R. Aoki, "The Asian American Political Alliance."

45. *AAPA* newspaper, Summer 1969, 2, 7. On Japan's importance to U.S. Cold War interests, see Johnson, *Blowback,* and McCormick, *America's Half-Century.*

46. AAPA, "General Philosophy Statement," June 1968, quoted in AAPA, "Fact Sheet," September 17, 1968; emphasis in original.

47. "aapa is," *AAPA* newspaper, November–December 1968, 4.

48. "How AAPA Works," *AAPA* newspaper, November–December 1968, 4.

49. Fong and Huen, "An Understanding of AAPA."

50. R. Aoki, "The Asian American Political Alliance." In August 1969, an internal document proposed a clearly delineated structure for the group. The central committee, consisting of the chair of each of nine work-groups and the AAPA chair, would be the "central decision making body of AAPA," empowered to "make general policy for AAPA, including position statements, as delegated by the mass meeting, fiscal matters, and major political actions." AAPA's chair would be responsible for "day to day positions." Still, the majority of the organization's work took place in "work-groups," a title that suggests an open structure where those willing to work were given decision-making powers for specific areas. Moreover, mass meetings would be held monthly and it was only at mass meetings that any changes to

AAPA's program or philosophy, organizational structure, or membership criteria could take place ("some notes about AAPA," typed document, with "Floyd [Huen], August 7, 1969" handwritten on the document).

51. Quoted in Ransby, *Ella Baker,* 188. On grassroots leadership, see Ransby's discussion of the contrasting leadership models of Ella Baker and Martin Luther King Jr. (*Ella Baker,* 189–92); Payne, "Men Led, but Women Organized"; Bernal, "Grassroots Leadership Reconceptualized."

52. R. Aoki, "The Asian American Political Alliance"; Aoki interview, August 21–26, 2003.

53. Dong interview.

54. Sen, *Stir It Up.*

55. I Wor Kuen's "12 Point Platform and Program" contained as point number four: "We want an end to male chauvinism and sexual exploitation" (Ho, *Legacy to Liberation,* 406). The Young Lords Party offers a striking example of how gendered consciousness changed over time. Women members successfully argued that machismo cannot be revolutionary and prompted the group to change its 13-Point Platform and Program from point number 10: "We want equality for women. Machismo must be revolutionary . . . not oppressive" (October 1969) to point number five: "We want equality for women. Down with machismo and male chauvinism" (revised May 1970). See Melendez, *We Took the Streets,* 236, 239; ¡*Palante, Siempre Palante!,* documentary.

56. "AAPA Perspectives."

57. For a nuanced racial comparative analysis of gender politics in the Third World Left, see Pulido, *Black, Brown, Yellow, and Left,* 180–214; also Cade, *Black Women;* "Combahee River Collective Statement"; Gore, Theoharis, and Woodard, *Want to Start a Revolution?* On gender politics in the AAM, see Ling, "The Mountain Movers"; Wei, *The Asian American Movement,* 72–100.

58. G. L., "Notes on Women's Liberation," *AAPA* newspaper, Summer 1969, 4–5.

59. Ibid.

60. Ibid.

61. Ling, "The Mountain Movers."

62. For a discussion of these and other anthologies, see Fujino, "Who Studies the Asian American Movement?"

63. Sacks, "Gender and Grassroots Leadership" and *Caring by the Hour.* On Asian American women's leadership, see Fujino, "Grassroots Leadership and Afro-Asian Solidarities."

8. "It Was about Taking Care of the Collective"

1. Nine months after their proposal for an Ethnic Studies Department was submitted to Chancellor Roger W. Heyns, the Afro-American Student Union (AASU) presented an ultimatum, setting Friday, January 17, 1969, as the deadline for "some decision regarding this matter" (*Daily Californian,* January 15, 1969). They did not specify any action, but with the San Francisco State College strike occurring across the Bay, the possibility of a strike at UC Berkeley was obvious.

2. In August 1968, Mexican American Student Confederation members met with Vice-Chancellor Campbell to request that the university stop purchasing table grapes in support of the renowned United Farm Workers Union (UFW) grape strike and boycott. While a couple of senior administrators gave their verbal approval to stop grape purchases, California governor Ronald Reagan, accompanied by a tele-vised image of him eating grapes, strongly denounced the UFW strike, and UC pres-ident Charles Hitch directed all nine UC campuses not to refuse the purchase of any food products (TWLF, "Strike 1969," pamphlet, ca. March 1969).

3. Dong discusses two key meetings that generated Asian American support for the TWLF strike. First, at the "Asian Experience in America—Yellow Identity" symposium, held at UC Berkeley on January 11–12, 1969, students from numerous campuses throughout California discussed whether to support the San Francisco State strike. Some students were opposed, reflecting in part their view that Asian Americans did not face racial oppression akin to that affecting African Americans and Chicanos. In the end, the attendees passed a resolution supporting the SF State strike and the general movement for Ethnic Studies on campuses. They also voted to establish themselves as AAPA chapters. This conference took place the day after AASU publicly began to discuss the need for action, including a possible strike, and initiated efforts to form a TWLF at UC Berkeley. Second, during the first week of Asian Studies 100X in January 1969, AAPA called an after-class meeting to discuss the possibility of joining AASU and MASC in a strike for Ethnic Studies. See Dong, "The Origins and Trajectory of Asian American Political Activism," 50–51, 57; *Berkeley Barb,* January 24–30, 1969. An FBI informant similarly noted that on Janu-ary 16, 1969, Third World leaders, including Aoki, met to determine whether AAPA, MASC, and AASU would unite in a strike. On January 20, 1969, Aoki presided over an AAPA steering committee meeting at which he and a couple of others were selected as "temporary AAPA representatives to the TWLF Central Committee" (FBI report, January 29, 1970).

4. There apparently was equal representation in the TWLF, but Manuel Delgado recalls there being two representatives from each of the four racial groups (http://www.manuelrdelgado.com/twlfstrike).

5. Jim Nabors, identified as the western regional vice president of the Republic of New Africa (*Oakland Tribune,* February 11, 1972), was known for his militant, even inflammatory, rhetoric and run-ins with the law (*Oakland Tribune,* March 5, 1970; February 24, 1972).

6. Manuel Delgado himself does not claim to have been the main MASC leader. On the contrary, Delgado credits Ysidro Macias with calling the first MASC meeting. In the first MASC elections, Macias was elected president and Delgado, vice presi-dent (http://www.manuelrdelgado.com/mascucberkeley1.html).

7. Aoki is widely recognized as a TWLF leader and was considered the Asian American representative in negotiations between Chancellor Heyns and the Third World Faculty and Administration Alliance (TWFAA). One student representative from each of the four groups was copied on letters: Richard Aoki of AAPA, Charles Brown of AASU, Manuel Delgado of MASC, and LaNada Means of United Native

Americans (TWFAA, letter to Heyns, March 29, 1969; Heyns, letter to Troy Duster of TWFAA Executive, April 2, 1969). Elsewhere the emphasis was on collective leadership, rather than a single leader; the FBI notes that it is "extremely difficult to pinpoint any particular leader," though the bureau did identify the most visible, including Aoki, who represented AAPA on the TWLF Central Committee (FBI report, February 27, 1969). The UC Berkeley newspaper, the *Daily Californian,* throughout its coverage of the strike, identified a number of individuals as "TWLF spokesmen" or implied their TWLF leadership, including AAPA leaders Richard Aoki, Floyd Huen, Jeffrey Leong, Alan Fong, and Ron Miyamura; AASU leaders Charles Brown, Jim Nabors, Charles Jackson, Don Davis, and Carl Mack; and MASC leaders Manuel Delgado, Ysidro Macias, Jaime (Jim) Solis, Fernando Garcia, and Rich Rodriquez. United Native Americans leader LaNada Means was also a TWLF leader though rarely mentioned in the *Daily Californian.* At one event, Floyd Huen and Manuel Delgado spoke as representatives of the Third World Negotiating Team, while Richard Aoki, LaNada Means, Ysidro Macias, and Carl Mack spoke as Third World students ("Third World Solidarity Day!" March 12, 1969, leaflet).

8. From early on, segments of the faculty supported the strike. Even before the strike began, eighteen faculty in the School of Social Welfare announced their support of the strike (*Daily Californian,* January 22, 1969). The day the strike began, the majority of Social Welfare faculty were supporting the strike, though not necessarily striking themselves (*Daily Californian,* January 23, 1969). The faculty union (AFT local 1474), librarians union (AFT local 1795), the progressive Berkeley Faculty Alliance, minority faculty, and especially the teaching assistants union (AFT local 1570) were early supporters of the strike (*Daily Californian,* January 23 and 28, 1969). In time, more and more faculty, from a variety of departments, including history, sociology, rhetoric, and design, expressed support for the strike in the pages of the *Daily Californian.* Chancellor Heyns sought to fire at least one junior faculty, Professor Ronald Yank, because of his activism, including allegedly participating in a moving picket line, not holding class in support of the strike, and speaking at a rally using "unauthorized sound amplification" (*Daily Californian,* April 28, 1969).

9. Takagi interview; *Daily Californian,* January 24, 28, and 30, 1969.

10. After a week of "informational" picketing, with picket lines of some three hundred strikers, the TWLF changed tactics and began to physically prevent people from crossing the picket lines. Police presence and repression escalated, as did university disciplinary action. On January 28, one hundred police, including thirty Highway Patrol and thirty Alameda County sheriffs, entered campus (*Daily Californian,* January 28 and 29, 1969).

11. TWLF, "Police Riot," leaflet (n.d.); reprinted in TWLF, *Strike 1969,* ca. March 1969. In a press release, the TWLF Central Committee denounced offensive violence but asserted its right to self-defense: "Because of the tense situation that has developed, the Third World has exercised every precaution to prevent violence or confrontation, but if violently acted upon, we will defend ourselves by any means necessary" (press release, no title, n.d.).

12. TWLF, "Police Riot."

13. In 1968, Blacks comprised 2.8 percent, Hispanics 1.3 percent, and Asians 10 percent of Berkeley's twenty-seven thousand students (Academic Senate, Berkeley Division, "Freshman Admissions at Berkeley: A Policy for the 1990s and Beyond," May 19, 1989, at http://academic~senate.berkeley.edu/archives/karabel.html, accessed October 24, 2008; *AAPA* newspaper, November–December 1968, 1). In 1966, a survey revealed there were only 236 Negroes, 68 Mexican Americans, and 36 American Indians (Somerville, "Can Selective Colleges Accommodate the Disadvantaged?," 5). In 1966, Chinese Americans comprised 2.7 percent and Japanese Americans 2.5 percent of the twenty-six thousand UC Berkeley students (Academic Senate, Berkeley Division, "Freshman Admissions at Berkeley").

14. On day two of the strike, some fraternity men tried to break through the picket line at Dwinelle Hall, but "force was met with force and they were noisily extracted from the circle" (*Daily Californian,* January 24, 1969). There were intragroup differences. A student wrote a letter to the editor mildly encouraging his fraternity brothers to consider supporting the strike, "regardless of the inaction of IFC or Panhellenic" or "the majority opinion in your house" (*Daily Californian,* January 30, 1969).

15. The *Daily Californian* reported: "Some picketers used force to deter nonstrikers from passing through the lines. Several of the people in the line carried heavy wooden sticks marked, 'Student Power'" (January 29, 1969).

16. Cordell Abercrombie was visible to the police as a strike captain on the picket line. Still, he states that it was a case of mistaken identity: "I was taken to the bottom of Sproul Hall and all the time they were taking me down I heard them hollerin', 'This is the one we've been looking for—for the last three days. We've got him. We've got him.'" The police proceeded to hold down his legs and arms, while "they all came down on me and beat me. They beat me with their billy clubs" (speech at TWLF strike convocation, UC Berkeley, 1969, cited in Dong, "Origins and Trajectory of Asian American Political Activism," 65–67).

17. The *Daily Californian* does not cover any such attack on the police. To demonstrate the effectiveness of fighting back, Aoki actually stated that no further beating by the police of arrestees took place. I added "at least for a while." After the police beat Abercrombie on February 4, they continued to beat other TWLF leaders, including Jim Nabors and Ysidro Macias, as well as nonstrikers. One White male nonstriker, Eric Davidson, was on his way to class when he witnessed the police beating Black radio reporter Clifford Vaughs so severely that he felt a moral obligation to try to stop it. When the police ignored Davidson's shouts to stop, Davidson kicked one of the police officers in an attempt to get him to stop. The police then took Davidson to the Sproul basement, where they beat him into semiconsciousness and knocked out his two front teeth (*Daily Californian,* February 6, 19, and 28, 1969; TWLF, "The State of the Campus," leaflet, February 26, 1969).

18. On the night of January 22, after the first day of strike activities, Wheeler Auditorium, with its intricately carved wooden ceiling, was burned, resulting in $500,000 damage to the building. The *Daily Californian* quoted Jim Soliz (Jaime Solis) of the TWLF: "It is our intention not to destroy public property, but rather to

open up the University to all people, especially to members of the Third World community." The fire engendered sharp condemnation from many quarters and, among
those who believed student strikers were responsible, it heightened criticism of the
strike (*Daily Californian,* January 23, 24, and 27, 1969). The *Berkeley Barb* profile on
Aoki contained his quote (February 14–21, 1969).

19. Aoki was elected in spring 1969 to serve as president of the Berkeley Social
Welfare Student Union in 1969–70 (Milton Chernin, dean, letter to Richard Aoki,
president, Berkeley Social Welfare Student Union, October 6, 1969; Aoki, president,
"Welcome to Hallowed Haviland Halls," Fall 1969).

20. During the strike, the *Daily Californian* regularly reported incidents of vandalism and window breaking and the use of cherry bombs and stink bombs. The
newspaper condemned vandalism by strike supporters, but even more harshly, condemned "police terror" (*Daily Californian,* February 18 and 19, 1969).

21. This was among the strike chants directed at the police (*Daily Californian,*
February 6, 1969). The *Daily Californian* reported a "watermelon-eating crowd of 200
seated on Sproul Plaza at the conclusion of yesterday's picketing" (March 6, 1969).

22. Committee of Cadres, Asian-American Political Alliance, "To Brothers and
Sisters," leaflet (n.d.).

23. A Chinese American undergraduate in French was among the twenty
arrestees on a day in which "violence and arrests reached a new peak." Although he
was identified by name, I leave him anonymous per Aoki's request (*Daily Californian,* February 5, 1969).

24. By February 28, there had been 145 arrests since the strike started (*Daily Californian,* February 29, 1969).

25. On February 18, the day Jim Nabors was arrested and beaten, twelve others
were arrested, including TWLF leaders Richard Aoki, Manuel Delgado, and Charles
Jackson (*Daily Californian,* February 19, 1969; *San Francisco Chronicle,* February
19, 1969). Beyond this, it's difficult to verify the number of times Aoki was arrested
during the strike. No other arrests of Aoki are mentioned in local newspapers. Mis-
demeanors remain on the court records for only seven years; plus, Aoki indicated
that his criminal records were sealed. No felonies were listed under his name in the
Alameda County court records. See also note 27.

26. Aoki was to be arraigned on March 12, 1969, for "resisting arrest"; bail was set
at five hundred dollars (*Berkeley Daily Gazette,* March 1, 1969).

27. The UC Berkeley Committee on Student Conduct charged Aoki with
"wrestl[ing] with several police officers in an attempt to free a prisoner" (Willis A.
Shotwell, memo to Committee on Student Conduct, May 12, 1969). If this was Aoki's
only arrest it would have occurred on February 18 (Arleigh Williams, dean of students, letter to Richard Aoki, June 12, 1969). In his interview with me, however, Aoki
implied that this occurred during the February 27 police beating of Ysidro Macias,
who required hospitalization. In response, strikers broke windows, including those
of the chancellor's office. Heyns, in turn, cancelled his 2:00 p.m. meeting with TWLF
leaders, relaying in a prepared statement: "As I was waiting for that meeting with student leaders of the strike, their supporters standing outside my office threw chunks

of concrete through my windows. . . . [I] could not meet with them under the present conditions of siege" (*Daily Californian,* February 28, 1969). Under the UC Regents' new ruling of February 21, students violating university rules would immediately be placed on interim suspension and barred from entering the campus before being given a hearing (*Daily Californian,* February 24, 1969). By the time of Macias's beating, fifty-three students had been placed on interim suspension for strike activities. TWLF leaders Manuel Delgado, LaNada Means, and Fernando Garcia—but not Aoki—were listed among arrestees on February 27 (*Daily Californian,* February 28, 1969).

28. The university charged Aoki "with violation of the University Standard of Conduct . . . for participating in activities involving conduct which threatened or endangered the health and safety of persons" (Willis A. Shotwell, letter to Richard Aoki, April 11, 1969).

29. Ken M. Kawaichi, letter to Richard M. Aoki, from the Law Offices of Yone-mura & Yasaki, March 20, 1969; form letter to "Rich Aoki" stating that the Attorneys Committee of the TWLF Legal Defense Committee assigned "Ken Kewachi" (i.e., Kawaichi) as his lawyer (n.d.). Based on his experiences defending TWLF strikers and teaching a law course in UC Berkeley's Asian American Studies program, Kawaichi cofounded the Asian Law Caucus in 1972 as a nonprofit legal aid organization (Minami, "Asian Law Caucus").

30. Willis A. Shotwell, coordinator of facilities and regulations, in a May 12, 1969, letter to the Committee on Student Conduct explained that Aoki "is a first year graduate student in the School of Social Welfare" with a "cumulative grade point average of 3.84." The committee merely stated that it found "evidence insufficient to make a finding of guilty—no penalty" (Arleigh Williams, letter to Richard Aoki, June 11, 1969).

31. Ken Kawaichi recalled the juror stating something to the effect that "it's okay this time. But don't do it again," indicating a belief in Aoki's guilt (East Bay Living History Project: Genesis of the Asian American Movement, Activism Then and Now, September 18, 2003, UC Berkeley, videotape of program).

32. Manuel Delgado, Ysidro Macias, and four others were arrested at the time Macias was beaten. But in total, thirteen were arrested that day, suggesting that there was a second group of arrestees (*Daily Californian,* February 18, 1969).

33. These committees are listed on "TWLF Communications People" (typed document, n.d.) and "Committee Heads" (handwritten document, n.d.).

34. On February 20, 1969, AAPA held an emergency meeting in response to the mounting conflict between strikers and the unprecedented police presence on campus. Indeed, that day, "Violence Hits a New High in Strike," reported the *Daily Californian* (February 21, 1969). AAPA's debate lasted late into the night and polarized positions between "softliners" and "hardliners." Harvey Dong explained: "The softliners felt that the violence had gotten out of hand. The strike was being taken over by 'crazy white radicals,' and was no longer controlled by Third World people. They feared that the ongoing negotiation process between the TWLF and the chancellor's office would be replaced by military martial law. The hardliners felt there was the need to intensify the protests and that the only basis for negotiations was the

mass pressure on strike lines. One hardliner argued that it was not just a question of fighting for a Third World College but rather one of defeating a power structure that was responsible for the slaughter in Vietnam" (Dong, "Origins and Trajectory of Asian American Political Activism," 71). AAPA members voted twenty to seven to "cool it." The next day, a TWLF communiqué issued the following guidelines to strikers: "*be cool*"; "*no* violence initiated by our side"; "all picket lines will remain peaceful and *legal* at all times"; "*no* rock throwing"; and "*obey* the TWLF monitors." Their goal was to "refuse to be provoked and intimidated by the police" and to "not give Reagan the excuse" to call in the National Guard (TWLF, "On Strike—Be Cool, Avoid the Police Riot," February 21, 1969, emphasis in original). On February 22, a three-thousand-strong demonstration outside a UC regents meeting attended by Governor Reagan turned out to be unusually peaceful.

35. The *Berkeley Daily Gazette* reported that police responded to a three-thousand-strong student strike and rally at UC Berkeley with "the largest display of organized law enforcement in Berkeley's history." There were some six hundred baton-wielding officers from over twenty law enforcement agencies across the Bay Area, in addition to one thousand National Guard troops encamped at a military facility in nearby Alameda (February 22, 1969).

36. On March 5, 1969, the *Daily Californian* reported: "With only four dissenting votes, the Academic Senate yesterday went on record as favoring the establishment of an Ethnic Studies Department, reporting directly to the Chancellor, which could eventually evolve into a College of Ethnic Studies." The vote was 550–4 (*Daily Californian*, March 5, 1969; Ling-chi Wang, "Chronology of the Third World Liberation Front Strike at U.C. Berkeley"; http://www.manuelrdelgado.com/twlf1.html).

37. *Oakland Tribune*, October 15, 1970.

38. List of arrestees in *Berkeley Daily Gazette*, March 1, 1969.

39. In an analysis of the political forces that moved beyond a simplistic "us" vs. "them" dichotomy, Craig Murphy discussed the complexity of motivations for ending the strike. He viewed Governor Reagan as gaining votes for his law-and-order stance against campus unrest; Chancellor Heyns, as a liberal, desired to reach any settlement "that i[s] not open to strong attack at the [Regents'] meeting"; and the faculty as "reluctant to support the strike demands because of 'academic tradition,'" but willing to do so in order to "save Heyns" (*Daily Californian*, March 5, 1969).

40. *Muhammad Speaks*, February 7, 1969.

41. *Sun Reporter*, February 8, 1969.

42. The cover of *Ramparts* shows a photo of LaNada Means with "Better Red Than Dead" in red spray paint on a wall behind her (*Ramparts*, February 1970, 26–38). Means rose to prominence as a leader of the eighteen-month takeover of Alcatraz Island in the San Francisco Bay that began in November 1969 (Smith and Warrior, *Like a Hurricane*). LaNada (Means) War Jack recalls Aoki as a principled and dedicated TWLF leader (War Jack interview).

43. Even before he gained a critical consciousness, Aoki had an ambivalent relationship with the formal school system. His father's unusual choice to homeschool his sons flowed, at least in part, from his distrust of U.S. institutions.

44. *Daily Californian,* February 20, 1969. A key faculty advocate for the TWLF, Troy Duster stated, "My grandmother [famed antilynching leader Ida B. Wells] probably would think I'm not militant enough" (*New York Times,* October 18, 2005). Duster has since gained a national and international reputation as a distinguished sociologist and served as president of the American Sociological Association.

45. Robert Allen wrote, "It is the educated and trained blacks who are slated to become the new managers of the ghetto. . . . It is assumed that these educated blacks will identify with the values and aspirations of white society, and, therefore, will become the willing (and well-rewarded) agents of the corporate power structure" (*Black Awakening in Capitalist America,* 262). Edna Bonacich similarly argues that the schools produce middle-class administrators who manage and reproduce economic inequalities ("Inequality in America," 106–9). Samuel Bowles and Herbert Gintis, in *Schooling in Capitalist America,* critique the widespread notion of schooling as the great equalizer.

46. Dong interview. Renowned educator Paulo Freire emphasizes the dialogic process, stressing "reflection and action," or praxis, as crucial to creating social change. "Dialogue," he writes, "is the encounter between men, mediated by the world, in order to name the world" (*Pedagogy of the Oppressed,* 87–88).

47. Manuel Delgado recalled Aoki's contributions: "We chose January 30, 1969, as the day the pickets would lock arms and prevent non-strikers from passing through. I was given the assignment to carry out the plan, Richard Aoki would direct the action on the street" (http://www.manuelrdelgado.com/twlfstrike2.html).

48. Huie, "The Shocking Story of Approved Killing in Mississippi"; http://www.pbs.org/wgbh/amex/till/sfeature/sf_look.html.

49. In criticizing the political dilution of the famed 1963 March on Washington, Malcolm X stated, "It's just like when you've got some coffee that's too black, which means it's too strong. What do you do? You integrate it with cream, you make it weak" (Malcolm X, "Message to the Grass Roots," 16).

50. Quoted in Carmichael, *Ready for Revolution,* 298.

51. Delgado, "The TWLF Strike," http://www.manuelrdelgado.com/twlfstrike1.html.

52. Delgado, "30 Year Commemoration," speech, April 9, 1999.

53. Delgado, "The TWLF Strike," http://www.manuelrdelgado.com/twlfstrike3.html.

54. Cynthia George, former North Hall striker, "1968: A Year of Student Driven Change" conference, UC Santa Barbara, November 20, 2008; *El Gaucho,* October 15, 1968.

55. Delgado, "The TWLF Strike," http://www.manuelrdelgado.com/twlfstrike1.html.

56. Delgado, "The TWLF Strike," http://www.manuelrdelgado.com/twlfstrike4.html.

57. Barlow and Shapiro, *An End to Silence,* 258, 262.

58. Chancellor Roger W. Heyns, open letter to "Students, Staff, Faculty, and Friends of the University," dated January 21, 1969, printed in the *Daily Californian* on the first day of the strike, January 22, 1969.

59. Ibid.

60. Ibid.

61. *Daily Californian,* January 22, 1969.

62. Afro–American Student Union, "Proposal for Establishing a Black Studies Program," UC Berkeley, spring 1968.

63. TWLF, "The Real Reasons behind the Strike," ca. January 18–21, 1969.

9. "A Community-Oriented Academic Unit"

1. *Daily Californian,* October 15, 1970.

2. R. Aoki, "Asian American Studies Division."

3. At the time, UC Berkeley's School of Criminology was embroiled in a battle for its very survival. Paul Takagi was then associate dean of the School of Criminology and a leading scholar in radical criminology. The school was closed in 1976. See "Editorial: Berkeley's School of Criminology, 1950–1976"; Shank, "Paul T. Takagi, Honored"; *Daily Californian,* August 2, 2007; Platt and Takagi, *Punishment and Penal Discipline.*

4. R. Aoki, "Asian American Studies Division," 3. Several former AAPA members concurred that this first coordinator exhibited a fairly authoritative leadership style, allied with the university administration, and did not defer to student power. They requested that he remain anonymous because he later changed and became supportive of Asian American progressive issues (Dong interview; Bryant Fong interview; Huen interview; also Hayashi, "Contemporary Asian Studies Division Report"; UC Berkeley, Department of Sociology, Alumni Archive, http://sociology.berkeley.edu/alumni2). It is surprising that, at least according to an FBI informant, Aoki was one of the few who supported the ousted chair (FBI report, January 29, 1970).

5. In his 1970 graduate student paper, Aoki identified three organizational structures governing AAS in the "first year of its painful existence": (a) a coordinator to be advised by a committee of teaching staff and students, which lasted one month; (b) a Graduate Student Council and a group of undergraduates, which lasted six months; and (c) an executive council of eight people that allowed for the separation of teaching from administrative duties, at a time when AAS leaders were "exhausted" (R. Aoki, "The Asian American Studies Division"). In reference to this third form, Aoki's memory did not match his writings of three decades earlier (Aoki interview, September 8–10, 2003). So I discuss only the first two forms that are supported by other sources. Corresponding with Aoki's second form, a 1969 Asian Studies Division report indicated that the coordinating council was composed of an administrative custodian (Floyd Huen), four instructors (Richard Aoki, Alan Fong, Wai-Kit Quon, and Bing Thom), a research coordinator (Bruce Quan), and an advisory chairman (Paul Takagi); the Student Standing Committee included Pam Lee, Bruce Occena, Mark Hayamizu, Bryant Fong, Norman Wong, and Carl Kuwata (Asian Studies Division, Proposal [partial], 1969; also Paul Wong, memo to Chancellor Roger Heyns, July 9, 1969; Hayashi, "Contemporary Asian Studies Division Report"; Burnett interview; Dong interview).

6. Aoki recalled being the main coordinator of Asian Studies during its initial two or three years, with the exception of the first coordinator, who lasted only one month.

Aoki's résumé, dated 1995, reports that he was acting coordinator (1969–70) and coordinator (1970–72) of AAS at UC Berkeley. By contrast, Hayashi's 1972 "Contemporary Asian Studies Division Report" identified the coordinators of Asian Studies as Floyd Huen (1969–70), Richard Aoki and Alan Fong (1970–71), and Patrick Hayashi and Ken Kawaichi (1971–72) (also Alan Fong interview; Huen interview).

7. The *Daily Californian* referred to anthropologist Forbes as "an eminent scholar in the field of minority relations" (May 12, 1969).

8. In declining to chair Ethnic Studies, Forbes stated that the university had failed to commit the resources necessary to create a viable department, allocating only "15 to 25 percent" of the estimated $1 million needed to establish a new department in a new field. Forbes did not mince words: "The total system should be sacrificing new buildings and other programs and projects in order to find the millions of dollars needed to make up for 100 years of racism and cultural chauvinism" (*Daily Californian*, May 12, 1969). In 1969, Forbes became one of three founding faculty in the Native American Studies program at UC Davis, which in 1993 became the first Department of Native American Studies in the nation; Forbes remained at UC Davis until retirement (http://nas.ucdavis.edu/Forbes/bio.html; http://nas.ucdavis.edu/site/history.html).

9. In the absence of a department chair that first year, signature authority was given to Professor Paul Takagi and Andrew Billingsley, assistant chancellor for academic affairs (L.A. Doyle, memo to John Raleigh and Andrew Billingsley, October 10, 1969; Request for Approval of a Course, for ES 100, September 15, 1969).

10. In October 1970, a *Daily Californian* front-page article announced that Carl Mack, pictured with a full afro and a Malcolm X button, became the first chair of Ethnic Studies, coordinating four divisions: La Raza, Native American, Black, and Asian Studies. Aoki, identified as a friend of Mack's for fifteen years, described Mack as a "brilliant, committed humanitarian [who is] academically, administratively, and professionally qualified for the position" (*Daily Californian*, October 15, 1970; also *Oakland Tribune*, October 15, 1970; May 31, 1973).

11. R. Aoki, "The Asian American Political Alliance."

12. Bryant Fong's analysis of the end of AAPA, while similar to Aoki's, stresses the importance of resources for social movement success: "AAPA didn't have any resources, the Asian Studies department did. So in a sense, Asian Studies became an arm of AAPA and eventually Asian Studies grew bigger than AAPA . . . [and] AAPA outlived its use." He added that "AAPA should have been independent of Asian Studies so that it could keep a check on it" (Bryant Fong interview).

13. Harvey Dong wrote the "Statement Commemorating AAPA Founder Yuji Ichioka (1936–2002) by Former Members of the Asian American Political Alliance (AAPA)" and gathered most of the twenty-eight AAPA signatories (Yuji Ichioka's Forty-Ninth Day Memorial Program, UCLA, October 19, 2002).

14. Ron Dellums graduated from UC Berkeley's Graduate School of Social Welfare in 1962 and Melvin Newton in 1967 (*Social Welfare at Berkeley*, 37; *San Francisco Chronicle*, January 3, 2007; Dellums and Halterman, *Lying Down with the Lions*, 25–27).

15. UC Berkeley's School of Social Welfare established a separate master's in social welfare) specialization in community organization in the mid-1960s, responding to the demands of the Civil Rights Movement and the War on Poverty. From its inception, tensions existed over whether to emphasize the more traditional focus on administration and planning or to stress "social change, community power, and citizen participation." The community organization program introduced new methods of field teaching by hiring "roving supervisors" to oversee student work in a wide range of community settings (*Social Welfare at Berkeley*, 25, 35, 37, 41).

16. Aoki enrolled in the Graduate School in Social Welfare in fall 1968 and graduated with a master's degree in social welfare in June 1970 (Richard Aoki, transcript, UC Berkeley).

17. Elected in spring 1969, Aoki served as president of the Berkeley Social Welfare Student Union in 1969–70 (Milton Chernin, dean, letter to Richard Aoki, president, Berkeley Social Welfare Student Union, October 6, 1969; Aoki, president, "Welcome to Hallowed Haviland Halls," Fall 1969).

18. That there was widespread support for a radical activist like Aoki is not entirely surprising. In the politically charged late 1960s, the School of Social Welfare was caught between forces trying to establish the field as a rigorous, research-oriented endeavor and forces focusing on community relevance, student empowerment, and the democratization of the university. The Social Welfare faculty saw itself as progressive, with little reason to feel threatened by the student activism that nearly paralyzed the university in the 1960s. The school had more minority students, greater student participation, a focus on ameliorating poverty and oppression, and was "the center of organization for the students who organized the Third World Strike in 1969" (*Social Welfare at Berkeley*, 6). But student activists and non–tenure track faculty vented strong criticism against the school. They denounced the school for, among other issues, its underrepresentation of minority students and faculty; its hierarchical structure, which severely limited the decision-making power of lower-ranking faculty; and being an agent of the establishment by regulating the poor, rather than transforming social consciousness to change an unjust social order (essays in *Social Welfare at Berkeley* by social welfare professors Harry Specht, 4–6, and Henry Miller, 38–40; also 36–37). In this context, there was strong student support for a leader of the Third World strike like Aoki.

19. The School of Social Welfare experienced a tumultuous period from 1968 to 1971. In 1971, reports critical of the school came from the profession (Golden Gate chapter of the National Association of Social Workers; NASW), an accreditation panel (Council on Social Work Education; CSWE), and the University Graduate Division. The accreditation panel found "high tension . . . and mistrust among students, faculty, administration, field agencies, and professional associations" (*Social Welfare at Berkeley*, 43). The NASW report cited a "serious underrepresentation of minority faculty" and a need for senior faculty to share in the decision-making process (*Oakland Tribune*, October 15, 1971). Earlier that year, Chicano students attending the Seattle Council on Social Work filed a complaint of "institutional racism" against the school. Chancellor Bowker stated that while he was not

recommending closing the school, "it was one of the possible options" (*Social Welfare at Berkeley,* 37). The CSWE did accredit the school in 1972, only for eighteen months, but extended accreditation to the standard ten years in 1973 (*Social Welfare at Berkeley,* 35).

20. The Associated Students of the School of Social Welfare, established in 1953, changed its name to the Berkeley Social Welfare Student Union in 1969 (General Catalog, UC Berkeley, 1970–71, 115; *Social Welfare at Berkeley,* 18, 35). In 1968, student participation became part of the formal decision-making process, with students sitting on most faculty committees (*Social Welfare at Berkeley,* 37). Jaime Solis graduated from the Graduate School of Social Welfare (Amanda Reiman, School of Social Welfare, UC Berkeley, e-mail to author, March 30, 2009).

21. James Nabors was a youth leader at the West Oakland Legal Switchboard in summer 1969 (*Rosenberg Foundation Annual Report,* 1969).

22. *Oakland Tribune,* February 11, 1972.

23. This conversation held no particular significance for Takagi, a professor who has dispensed advice to hundreds of students. Still, Aoki was a student who stood out to Takagi for his militancy, intensity, and commitment to justice. Aoki, who viewed Takagi as a mentor and father figure, had visited Takagi's home on a number of occasions (Takagi interview).

24. In 1970–71, co-coordinators Aoki and Fong were both paid as half-time coordinators and half-time instructors; Fong taught five courses that year and Aoki taught three. That same year, Ken Kawaichi was hired as the first tenure-track professor at the rank of Assistant Professor I (Hayashi, "Contemporary Asian Studies Division Report"; Carl Mack Jr., memo to Coordinator's Council, March 8, 1971).

25. Alan Fong too viewed their relationship as cooperative and complementary (Alan Fong interview).

26. Hayashi, "Contemporary Asian Studies Division Report."

27. The Hukbalahap, or "People's Army to Fight Japan," was formed in 1942. Many of its leaders were in the Communist Party, but the Huks was a mass-based organization to oppose Japanese colonialism in the Philippines (Schirmer and Shalom, *The Philippines Reader,* 69–77).

28. The Asian Studies Division had as many as eighteen community projects in 1972–73 (Collins Committee Report, 12). For a list of community projects, see Hayashi, "Contemporary Asian Studies Division Report," 5–8.

29. The East Bay Japanese for Action (EBJA), started by a group of Bay Area college students and incorporated in 1971, was a nonprofit, multiservice agency providing transportation, escort, translation, home maintenance, and information and referral services to Japanese elderly in Alameda and Contra Costa Counties. In 1976, Grace Yotsuya was chair of the board of directors and Dennis Yotsuya was on the Eden Community Advisory Board of the EBJA (Bay Area Social Planning Council, Evaluation of East Bay Japanese for Action, Inc., March 5, 1976). In 1986, EBJA and East Bay Issei Housing merged to form the Japanese American Services of East Bay, which today operates a senior center and a one-hundred-unit senior residence (http://www.jaseb.org).

30. During his tenure in Asian American Studies at UC Berkeley, Aoki taught three different courses across five quarters: Third World Core (fall 1969, winter 1970); Social Theory and Contemporary Social Problems (fall 1970, winter 1971); and Hawaii (fall 1970, winter 1971, winter 1972). See Asian Studies course catalog, fall 1970, winter 1971; Hayashi, "Contemporary Asian Studies Division Report." Neither Asian Studies nor Ethnic Studies was listed in the UC Berkeley general catalog in this period (1969–72).

31. In the introduction to the 1976 edition of *No-No Boy,* Lawson Inada discusses a similar process of "discovering" the 1957 original edition, which was all but ignored until the Asian American Movement discovered it and eagerly consumed it. Inada and coeditors of *Aiiieeeee!* reprinted excerpts of the novel, which culminated in its republication in 1976. Okada's *No-No Boy,* considered a classic novel on the Japanese American incarceration experience, continues to be widely studied in Asian American literature courses.

32. The Asian Studies library, established in 1969, was viewed as a vital component of Asian Studies. There were more than a thousand volumes in the library collection by 1972, and more than two thousand by 1974 (Hayashi, "Contemporary Asian Studies Division Report," 31; Ethnic Studies Committee, "A Proposal for the Establishment of the College of Third World Studies," 1974, A22). Particularly noteworthy was the library's "valuable archival materials" (Review of the Department of Ethnic Studies, 1992, 17–19).

33. Asian Studies 198/Ethnic Studies 100: Third World Core Course syllabus, fall 1969.

34. Asian Studies 198/Ethnic Studies 100 syllabus, fall 1969; Ethnic Studies syllabus, Winter 1970; Ethnic Studies 100 Book List, n.d.

35. Carey McWilliams prefigured the establishment of Ethnic Studies with *Factories in the Field* (1939) and *Prejudice* (1944). Roger Daniels's scholarship grew alongside the development of Ethnic Studies, though his *The Politics of Prejudice* (1962) would have influenced Aoki as he began to teach Asian American Studies.

36. Fuchs, *Hawaii Pono.* Christina Klein argues that in the Cold War period, cultural productions like Michener's *Hawaii* served to create the image of the United States as a leading defender of democracy, equality, and inclusion, thereby countering assertions of U.S. imperial motives *(Cold War Orientalism).*

37. Alan Fong concurs that by collectivizing salaries, Asian American Studies hired additional instructors and paid unofficial teaching assistants and others, including undergraduates, who otherwise would not have been paid by the university (Fong interview).

38. Although Allen's *Black Awakening in Capitalist America* and Freire's *Pedagogy of the Oppressed* were published shortly after the TWLF strike, my point is that these authors' ideas resonated with the goals and practices of the TWLF's Ethnic Studies project.

39. Richard Shaull, foreword to Freire, *Pedagogy of the Oppressed,* 34.

40. Freire, *Pedagogy of the Oppressed,* 81.

41. R. Aoki, "The Asian American Studies Division," 3.

42. Ethnic Studies Committee, "Proposal for the Establishment of the College of Third World Studies," 18.

43. Ibid. Reflecting the program's commitment to participatory democracy and non-elitism as well as the lack of human resources, an undergraduate student, Bryant Fong, was apparently the first personnel director in the Asian Studies Division, a position not officially recognized or paid by the university (Bryant Fong interview).

44. Ethnic Studies Committee, "Proposal for the Establishment of the College of Third World Studies," 18.

45. Billingsley, Davidson, and Loya, "Ethnic Studies at Berkeley," 15.

46. Ibid.

47. On the transformational goals of the Third World strikes, see Barlow and Shapiro, *An End to Silence;* Karagueuzian, *Blow It Up!;* Orrick, *Shut It Down!;* Smith, Axen, and Pentony, *By Any Means Necessary;* Umemoto, "'On Strike!'"; *San Francisco State: On Strike,* documentary; Dong, "Origins and Trajectory of Asian American Political Activism," 28–79; Ferreira, "'All Power to the People.'" On the San Francisco State Strike archival collection, see http://www.library.sfsu.edu/about/col lections/strike.

48. *A Master Plan for Higher Education in California, 1960–1975* (http://www .ucop.edu/acadinit/mastplan/MasterPlan1960.pdf).

49. Barlow and Shapiro, *An End to Silence,* 19–32; *San Francisco State: On Strike,* documentary; Umemoto, "'On Strike!'"

50. *San Francisco State: On Strike,* documentary.

51. AAS at UC Berkeley and San Francisco State College explicitly prioritized Community Studies and academic learning and internships in service to working-class communities (Asian Studies Division, "Proposal," 1969; Hayashi, "Contemporary Asian Studies Division Report"; Umemoto, "'On Strike!'").

52. Dong, "Origins and Trajectory of Asian American Political Activism"; Ferreira, "'All Power to the People'"; Katsiaficas, *The Imagination of the New Left.*

53. Freire, *Pedagogy of the Oppressed,* 81.

54. Ibid., 51.

55. Ibid., 88–89.

56. Collins Committee Report, 4.

57. Ibid., 12.

58. Ibid., 18.

59. Ibid., 15.

60. William Banks, letter to Provost and Dean Roderic Park, June 20, 1974.

61. Asian American Studies, *Library Newsletter* 2, no. 1 (December 1973): 3.

62. Ibid. Robert Allen observed that the new Black Studies Department at San Francisco State College "could not be modeled after other departments and accept the constraints imposed on them, because one function of these departments is to socialize students into a racist and oppressive society. The function of black studies must be to create enemies of racism, enemies of oppression, enemies of exploitation. This is a revolutionary task which necessarily required that the Black Studies

Department be fully autonomous and self-governing" (*Black Awakening in Capitalist America*, 262).

63. Asian American Studies, *Library Newsletter* 2, no. 1 (December 1973): 2.

64. Ibid.

10. "An Advocate for the Students"

1. Merritt College students invited Aoki to teach their first Asian American Studies class, which would have been in the 1970–71 academic year (Connie Chan, Aoki's memorial, Oakland, May 3, 2009). At the beginning of the academic year, Aoki gained a "Standard Teaching Credential with a Specialization in Junior College Teaching" from the California State Board of Education, September 8, 1970. Asian American Studies courses were first listed in the catalog of Grove Street College, as Merritt was then named, in 1971–72. At that time, eight courses were listed, including Communities, History, Community Research, and Reading and Composition.

2. Merritt College asserts that it was the first community college in California to offer an associated arts degree in African American Studies (*Peralta Colleges Bulletin*, December 8, 1967) and among the first Departments of African American Studies in the nation. African American Studies courses were first offered at Merritt College as early as fall 1964. By fall 1968, departmental status was approved by the college's president, Norvel Smith, the Faculty Senate, and the Ad Hoc Committee of Faculty Concerned: Afro-American Studies Program. The department began in winter 1969, at a time when San Francisco State College and UC Berkeley students were on strike to gain Ethnic Studies (Norvel Smith, memo to Merritt Council, October 23, 1968; *Merritt College Reporter*, November 21, 1968; Ad Hoc Committee, memo to Faculty, n.d.; *Peralta Colleges Bulletin*, January 24, 1969; Sid Walton, memo to Instructional Council members and Other Interested Persons, regarding development of a Black Curriculum and AA degree, ca. May or June 1967).

3. Aoki was teaching part-time at Merritt College when Bill Sato was hired as a full-time instructor in 1971. In 1971–72, Sato became the division chair of Social and Behavioral Sciences and Aoki began working as a full-time counselor soon thereafter (William Sato, letter to Faculty, Behavioral and Social Sciences Division, September 14, 1971; catalog, Grove Street College, 1971–72; catalog, North Peralta Community College, 1973–74; Sato interview).

4. Relocating Merritt College to the posh Oakland Hills was nothing if not contentious. The Peralta Community College District administrators saw in the $47 million bond passed in 1965 an opportunity to "meet [local students'] growing demand for higher education" by refashioning itself into a four-campus district, with new campuses in the Oakland Hills, downtown Oakland, and Alameda; a fourth campus was to be built later in Berkeley (Linda Berry-Camara, vice president of instruction, Merritt College, "Merritt College: Institutional History," October 2002; *Oakland Tribune*, January 29, 1967; September 13, 1967). By building a new campus in the Oakland Hills, the district could ameliorate the overcrowded and dilapidated conditions at the Grove Street campus. But many viewed the move, without any plan for a replacement campus in the flatlands, as an attempt to remove a vital resource from

the working-class Black community and undermine the militant Black student movement. Students argued that after building costs were overrun, there were no funds left to build a flatlands campus (Black Student Union, Merritt College, *Lumpen,* Revolutionary Student News Service, October 29, 1970). The *Oakland Tribune,* owned by the conservative and powerful Knowland family, regularly ran articles and letters to the editor fueling fears of Black Power militancy, including "Police Expect Urban Guerilla Warfare" (January 27, 1970) and "Merritt Students Gripped by Fear" (May 5, 1969). In a seven-part series in the *Oakland Tribune,* reporter Ernie Cox painted a picture of Merritt College as a "racially tense" and "chaotic" campus in the "flatlands ghetto," where "blackboard jungle bullies" held captive the Faculty Senate for four hours and in other ways made faculty "scared stiff" (*Oakland Tribune,* May 5–10 and 22, 1969). Indeed, militant activism had arrived at Merritt, following its birth of the BPP in 1966. In April 1969, students stole (or liberated, depending on one's perspective) an alleged $7,200 worth of books and supplies and distributed them free of charge to needy students. The Black Student Union claimed this was an effort to redistribute resources and meet the needs of the poor, not unlike Robin Hood or in a culturally closer model, the BPP. Student militancy at Merritt captured the nation's eye, with a *Wall Street Journal* article dubbing it "A Campus Where Black Power Won" (*Wall Street Journal,* November 18, 1969; Black Student Union, Merritt College, *Lumpen,* October 29, 1970; November 7, 1970; "Merritt College: Home of the Black Panthers"). Indeed, Black Power activists achieved a fair degree of campus power at Merritt. In 1968, the Black Student Union swept the Associated Students elections and held virtually every AS office. In October 1970, at a district board meeting, a broad coalition of students forming the People's Committee for Defense of Merritt succeeded in getting the board to keep open the Grove Street campus until a permanent flatlands college would be built, with full funding and community control of the campus. Two weeks before Merritt College's move to the Oakland Hills in spring 1971, militant students seized four administrative offices and demanded community control of the Grove Street campus, while other students barricaded campus gates to prevent equipment from being moved to the new Merritt College (*Oakland Tribune,* May 7, 1969; March 16–17, 1971; April 20, 1971; Black Student Union, Merritt College, *Lumpen,* October 29, 1970).

5. Benjamin Yerger was appointed "acting president" of the Grove Street campus in spring 1971, when Merritt College and its president, Norvel Smith, transferred to the Oakland Hills campus (*Oakland Tribune,* April 20, 1971). Less than four months later, Carl Mack Sr. was serving as "chief administrator" rather than "president" (*Oakland Tribune,* August 17, 1971; Grove Street College catalog, 1971–72). Aoki would have been offered the job during Yerger's short tenure as acting president and was a "full time Counselor at the Peralta Community College District from 1971–98" (verification of Aoki's employment record, Doris H. Kogo, Human Resources, Peralta Community College District, August 31, 2009). In 1971–72, Aoki served as interim director of student personnel as well as counselor (Annual Performance Evaluation of Aoki, February 9, 1973; also note 40, this chapter). Aoki's résumés and job applications, however, consistently indicate that he began full-time

at Merritt in June 1972, after leaving UC Berkeley, and was hired as a counselor and only "unofficially" as "Assistant to the Administrative Dean" (Aoki, résumés, 1983–95; Aoki, application for ACE Fellows Program in Academic Administration, January 12, 1979; Aoki, application for EOPS director, College of Alameda, June 15, 1987).

6. After getting his teaching credential in September 1970 (note 1, this chapter), it was not until March 18, 1971, that he received his "Community College Counselor Credential" (valid for life) and "Community College Instructor Credential" (in Ethnic Studies, Public Services and Administration, Sociology, valid for life). Aoki publicly thanked Minami for his legal representation on this case when both sat on a panel sponsored by the Berkeley JACL (East Bay Living History Project: Genesis of the Asian American Movement, Activism Then and Now, September 18, 2003, UC Berkeley, videotape).

7. The original campus, at 5714 Grove Street, was known as Oakland City College when Aoki attended in the early 1960s and became Merritt College by 1965. The campus was called Grove Street College in spring 1971, when Merritt College was relocated to the Oakland Hills, and then changed to North Peralta Community College in September 1972. The latter name seemed to have been selected to appease those wanting a community college in the northern Peralta district, but critics argued that it "fail[ed] to provide a sense of identity" with the local community (*Oakland Tribune*, August 3, 1971; September 6, 1972; catalogs, Merritt campus, 1960–61, 1965–66, 1971–72, 1972–73, 1973–74).

8. On Yerger and Mack, see note 5, this chapter. Carl Mack Sr. served as interim "administrator" for a year, until Dr. Young Park, the first Asian American to head a California community college, was named the college president in June 1972. When the chancellor sought to close North Peralta and establish the Berkeley Learning Center in its stead, Young was appointed as president of the new campus (*Oakland Tribune*, May 19, 1974) and later became the assistant to the chancellor, per Park's request and for "personal reasons" (*Oakland Tribune*, May 15, 1975). Norma Tucker had the official titles of dean and chief administrative officer, rather than president, at North Peralta Community College and president at Merritt College in the Oakland Hills (*Oakland Tribune*, May 19, 1974; *Merritt College Reporter*, March 5, 1987).

9. While Aoki found personal fulfillment in being a counselor, it seems he desired to become an administrator (Aoki, application for ACE Fellows Program in Academic Administration, January 12, 1979) and later in his career he wanted to "return to a full-time or part-time" teaching (Aoki, Tenured Faculty Evaluation, Self-evaluation Form, June 1994).

10. On a small campus and one in transition, and given Aoki's skills and ambitions, he served in multiple capacities simultaneous with his job as counselor. He was interim director of student personnel in 1971–72 during his first year as a full-time campus employee as well as the school's first year of operation (Annual Performance Evaluation of Aoki, February 9, 1973). During the 1972–73 academic year, Aoki assumed full responsibility as the division chair of Social and Behavioral Sciences when the previous chair had an "untimely accident" (Annual Performance Evaluation of

Aoki, February 9, 1973). In 1973–74, Aoki also served as assistant to the Office of Instruction for Social Sciences and English/Foreign Languages (Annual Performance Evaluation of Aoki, February 13, 1974). To give a sense of the size of the campus, in 1973–74, thirty-five faculty were listed, which at the community college included instructors, counselors, librarians, and administrators (catalog, North Peralta Community College, 1973–74).

11. As department chair of Ethnic Studies, Aoki gave Du Bois a stellar teaching evaluation of his African American history course (Evaluation of David Du Bois by Richard Aoki, Class Visitation Form, North Peralta Community College, December 20, 1973). Du Bois was editor of the BPP newspaper from August 1972 to December 1976 (Du Bois, "Understanding the Legacy of W. E. B. Du Bois"; David Graham Du Bois, article for thirty-fifth anniversary of the Black Panther Party, http://www .itsabouttimeBPP.com/our_stories/chapter1/35th_Anniv_BPP.html).

12. In 1972, the BPP Central Committee, on Newton's recommendation, closed virtually every branch and ordered members to Oakland to organize Seale and Brown's electoral campaigns. Many Panthers opposed this move because it ended their work in the local community, including free breakfast and other survival programs, their campaigns to support imprisoned comrades, and their efforts to build a national mass base. Seale also opposed this decision, but agreed to it as a temporary measure. While the move resulted in an even sharper turn to reformism—some call this the end of the BPP's revolutionary period—it did enhance women's participation in the BPP, running electoral campaigns and working in the survival programs, as well as on the party newspaper. See various essays in Jones, *Black Panther Party Reconsidered*, especially Johnson, "Explaining the Demise of the Black Panther Party," 403–6, and LeBlanc-Ernest, "'The Most Qualified Person'").

13. Because the New York Panthers sided with Cleaver in the split, it was surprising to find that this person heeded Newton's call to move to Oakland. The New York 21, all of whom were BPP members, were arrested in 1969 and charged with 156 counts of conspiracy to bomb. Although they were acquitted on all counts, their excessively high bails and resulting two years in jail awaiting trial effectively eliminated the New York BPP chapter.

14. White radicals from the Students for a Democratic Society initiated "Revolutionary Studies" at Merritt College. Despite efforts to begin by fall 1969, it was first in the catalog in 1972–73. The area focused on Marxism, comparative revolutionary societies, U.S. political economy, and the women's movement (Don Kaiper, "Rationale for a Revolutionary Studies Department at Merritt College," April 15, 1969; petition for Revolutionary Studies Department, ca. spring 1969; Student Advisory Committee Statement on the Revolutionary Studies Department; catalog, Grove Street College, 1972–73).

15. The Black Veterans Association was a student organization in 1972 (Policies Relating to Students and Student Affairs, Grove Street College, 1972).

16. At the Grove Street campus, where the BPP inspired a culture of self-defense, karate was one of three major team sports. Black faculty like Kenn Waters studied under Kenny Youn, who headed the campus's karate team (Policies Relating to

Students and Student Affairs, Grove Street College, 1972; Waters interview). Black Power militants and urban youth held a keen interest in Asian martial arts. Beyond the desire to learn self-defense, martial arts films, best represented by Bruce Lee, showed small Asian men "kickin' the asses" of formidable White men—a metaphor for the powerless defeating the powerful in worldwide struggles against colonialism and racism (Ho, "Kickin' the White Man's Ass"). Moreover, martial artists embodied inner fortitude, confidence, and respect (Prashad, *Everybody Was Kung Fu Fighting*, 132–33), and martial arts aesthetics parallel not just Asian but also Black culture (Hewitt, "Martial Arts Is Nothing if Not Cool").

17. On the beating of the instructor Fritz Pointer, see *Oakland Tribune*, February 10, 1973; also Sato interview; Waters interview.

18. Aoki's work performance evaluations noted his "willingness to be called upon at any time" and his being a "tireless performer" who "always made himself available to students well beyond scheduled hours." It was also noted that "at times this generous attitude has prevailed on his health" (Annual Performance Evaluation, February 14, 1975; Summary of Evaluation of Contract Instructors, February 16, 1980; Summary of Evaluation of Counselor, April 1, 1982). Today, ritzy Mercedes-Benzes and BMWs sit in the parking spaces reserved for senior administrators and the Academic Senate president at Merritt College (author's observation, July 1, 2009).

19. Richard's sister-in-law remembered Richard renting from his brother and stepfather (Debbie Aoki interview).

20. By summer 1974, it was clear that after a period of "phasing out," North Peralta Community College would soon be closed. But not without a fight, including a lawsuit filed by NPCC students, U.S. representative Ronald Dellums, Berkeley mayor Warren Widener, and two city council members. The lawsuit argued that among the four campuses in the Peralta District, one was to serve students in North Oakland and Berkeley. In October 1975, a Superior Court ruled that the district was "not contractually bound" to provide a campus in that area. See *Oakland Tribune*, May 19, 1974; August 11, 1974; September 10, 1974; October 9, 1975.

21. Aoki transferred to the counseling staff at Merritt College in the Oakland Hills by fall 1975 (Evaluation of Contract Instructors, Merritt College, December 18, 1975). Grove Street College served a "large low-income and minority constituency" (*Faculty Handbook*, Grover Street College, 1972, 2; also Sato interview; Waters interview).

22. Go is a popular Japanese game requiring skill and strategy to capture territory on the board through the use of black and white stones.

23. Throughout his twenty-five-year-plus career as a counselor, instructor, and administrator in the Peralta Community College District, Aoki consistently received glowing evaluations. He was viewed as an "excellent" and "highly motivated" counselor who developed exceptional "rapport with students" and "is forever extending both himself and his time to students." His counseling style viewed the student as "a total human being," demonstrated cultural sensitivity, and was "as positive about the transfer student as the student having difficulty" (Summary Evaluation of Contract Instructors, February 6, 1978; Summary Evaluation of Counselor, April 1, 1982; Tenured Faculty Summary Report Form, Counselor, spring 1994).

24. Aoki served for over a decade on the board of directors of Asians for Job Opportunities in Berkeley, Inc. (AJOB), including as vice president, secretary, and treasurer; on the board of directors of East Bay Asian Youth Center; and was active with the Asian American Community Mental Health Training Center in San Francisco (staff newsletter, College of Alameda, September 11, 1995; Aoki, Year End Report, Self-evaluation, June 8, 1994; Training Center Council Membership, 1979).

25. On Aoki's later involvement in Mumia Abu-Jamal's defense, see chapter 11.

26. The social movement for redress and reparations began in the political milieu of the Asian American Movement, though a few individuals sought monetary compensation as early as the 1940s. In 1970, Edison Uno's resolution seeking monetary compensation was passed at the Japanese American Citizens League national convention. In the late 1970s, the JACL, primarily working through legislative channels, heeded Senator Daniel Inouye's suggestion for a congressional hearing, what became the Commission on Wartime Relocation and Internment of Civilians (CWRIC). The Seattle JACL chapter and William Hohri of the Chicago JACL split from the national JACL, arguing that the hearings asked the victims to tell their tales of woe, but had no power of enforcement even if the commission recommended reparations. They formed the National Council on Japanese American Redress (NCJAR) and brought a $27.5 billion class action lawsuit against the U.S. government. A third national group, the National Coalition for Redress/Reparations (NCRR), formed primarily by Sansei activists, engaged heavily in grassroots organizing. On the JACL, see Hatamiya, *Righting a Wrong*. On the NCJAR, Hohri, *Repairing America*. On the NCRR, see Kitayama, "Japanese Americans and the Movement for Redress." On the redress movement, see Maki, Kitano, and Berthold, *Achieving the Impossible Dream;* Takezawa, *Breaking the Silence;* Murray, *Historical Memories.*

27. Late in his life, Earl Warren acknowledged deeply regretting his prominent role as California's attorney general in advocating the incarceration of Japanese Americans. He claimed to have had "no prejudice against the Japanese," but recognized that "when fear, get-tough military psychology, propaganda, and racial antagonism combine with one's responsibility for public security," they produce "the cruelty of war" (Warren, *The Memoirs of Earl Warren,* 149; also *Oakland Tribune,* July 10, 1974).

28. From July to December 1981, over 750 people, mostly former internees, but also noted scholars and government officials, testified before the CWRIC in ten locations. Based on the CWRIC recommendations, Congress passed the Civil Liberties Act in 1988, awarding monetary compensation, a public apology, and a public education fund. The movement continues to the present, seeking redress for various constituencies, most notably Japanese Latin Americans. For the congressional report, see Commission on Wartime Relocation and Internment of Civilians, *Personal Justice Denied.* On testimonies at the Los Angeles CWRIC hearing, see *Speak Out for Justice!* On the redress campaign for Japanese Latin Americans, see the video *Hidden Internment: The Art Shibayama Story* (http://www.campaignforjusticejla.org/resources/video.html).

29. A week before the San Francisco hearings, S. I. Hayakawa, then a Republican senator from California, stated publicly that his "flesh crawls with shame and

embarrassment" at the demand for redress and reparation movement. He voiced that the camps "turned out to be a three-year vacation from long years of unremitting work" for many Japanese immigrants. This outraged the Japanese American community all the more because Hayakawa, safely in Chicago during World War II, escaped removal to a concentration camp. Hayakawa's testimony before the CRWIC in Los Angeles is in *Speak Out for Justice!;* also *Los Angeles Times,* August 5, 1981; Maki, Kitano, and Berthold, *Achieving the Impossible Dream,* 76, 104.

30. Beyond the political injustice, the injuries of incarceration were deeply personal. In his testimony, Aoki did not say that his parents separated inside the camps and that he rarely saw his mother for the next eight years. Instead he focused on his family's health problems, apparently triggered by the forced removal and confinement (Richard Aoki, testimony, CWRIC hearing, San Francisco, August 13, 1981, transcript; Katrina Shores, letter to Richard Aoki, January 11, 1982).

31. Richard Aoki, testimony, CWRIC hearing, San Francisco, August 13, 1981, transcript; audiotape of Aoki's testimony.

32. For its heavy casualties, the 100th/442nd became the most highly decorated unit of its size in U.S. military history, earning more than fifteen thousand medals for a unit of three thousand men (Chang, *"I Can Never Forget,"* 59; Tanaka, *Go for Broke,* 99).

33. Frederick Engels's influential text *The Origin of the Family, Private Property, and the State,* widely read on the Left, uses a historical materialist approach to examine family formation and the subjugation of women. He argues that the rise of private property and the overthrow of mother-right led to the rise of class-based societies and the change from group to monogamous marriage, both newly controlled by men, leading to "the world historical defeat of the female sex" (68).

34. On Ho's political ideas and musical innovations, see Ho, *Wicked Theory, Naked Practice.*

35. Aoki showed me a picture of himself with this woman, taken in a photo booth at Pier 39 at the San Francisco wharf.

36. Aoki showed me a photo of this woman, a buxom blond, heavily made up, with lots of leg showing.

37. Many people have discussed Aoki's heavy alcohol consumption, dating back to at least the late 1960s (my interviews with Debbie Aoki, Daniels, Dong, Napper, Sanders, Sato, Takagi, and Waters). There were concerns about his brandishing guns and his driving while drunk. There was even a story about his hitting a police car while driving drunk. Most stated that he drank alone or in social settings, but a few indicated that at times he drank first thing in the morning and also on the job. Aoki himself made an off-hand remark about "drink[ing] my lunches at the surrounding bars" during the workweek. His brother had "guzzled" alcohol for years and died at age forty-six of "alcoholic cirrhosis" (David Aoki, Certificate of Death). His father too, it seems, drank heavily.

38. Aoki began full-time employment with the Peralta Community College District in 1971, giving him sixteen years with the district at the time of his layoff. His brother died two days after Christmas in 1986 (David Aoki, Certificate of Death, December 27, 1986).

39. Proposition 13, passed by California voters in 1978, capped property taxes at 1 percent of the assessed value of the home. It also required a two-thirds majority in both houses to increase state taxes. The reduced revenue to the state resulted in drastic reductions in funding for public education, public libraries, fire departments, and other social services. California public schools fell dramatically from having high national rankings in student achievement in the 1960s to the state's current location at third from the bottom—forty-seventh in funding per pupil and dismal student achievement ratings (*Education Week,* 2009; http://www.edweek.org/ew/qc/2009/17src.h28.html).

40. At its March 3, 1987, meeting, the Peralta board of trustees voted four to three to approve faculty layoffs. An earlier proposal sought to lay off nearly eighty employees, including one-third of the Merritt College counseling staff. There were many alternative suggestions to meet the $7 million projected budget deficit, including cutting management positions, rescheduling counselor workloads, and eliminating trustee travel. In May the board decided to lay off forty faculty, a category at the community colleges that includes instructors, counselors, and librarians, and about seventy-one support staff. Aoki was among the seven faculty laid off at Merritt College (*Merritt College Reporter,* March 5, March 19, April 23, and May 28, 1987). Chancellor Donald Godbold resigned in June 1987, following sharp criticism of his handling of the budget deficit, including criticism from several trustees (*Merritt College Reporter,* September 24, 1987).

41. A Japanese expression meaning "it can't be helped" or "nothing can be done about it."

42. Bill Sato, with seventeen years of seniority, was also laid off. At the time, he taught the district's only Asian American Studies courses. After the local Asian community protested, the Asian American Studies courses and Sato's job were reinstated, though it might well have been Sato's seniority that saved his job (*East/West News,* August 20, 1987; *Monclarion,* August 18, 1987; Sato interview).

43. Of the forty-five faculty positions eliminated, thirty-six were rehired by September (*Merritt College Reporter,* September 24, 1987). Aoki, the only Asian American in the district who lost his job, was offered a position in the district's Feather River campus, three hundred miles away, which he declined (*East/West News,* August 20, 1987). The president of the Peralta Federation of Teachers threatened the district with a lawsuit that would make the $2 million lawsuit filed by part-time instructors "look like petty cash." That lawsuit, which left the district with no reserves, along with Proposition 13, which undermined the local funding base, were among the nine causes of the budget deficit identified by the board vice president (*Merritt College Reporter,* March 19 and May 28, 1987).

44. Benjamin Yerger was dean of students (College of Alameda catalog, 1985–87), but a couple of years later he was no longer listed as an administrator (College of Alameda catalog, 1989–90/1990–91).

45. Feather River Community College was also part of the Peralta district, though its geographic distance, some three hundred miles away, created controversy about its placement in the East Bay district.

46. Throughout his life, Aoki felt an affinity for soldiers and veterans. He was also on the three-member Crisis Team activated to provide support for students experiencing anxieties resulting from the Gulf War crisis (staff newsletter, College of Alameda, January 22, 1991).

47. At the time of the Rodney King verdict, Aoki was acting assistant dean of student services, appointed in February 1992 (staff newsletter, College of Alameda, February 24, 1992). The nine college administrators included the president, the dean of instructional services and three assistant deans, the dean of student services and two assistants, and a business officer (Catalog, College of Alameda, 1989–90/1990–91).

48. The first Asian American Studies course was offered at the College of Alameda in fall 1989, with Aoki as instructor (Schedule of Classes, College of Alameda, fall 1989; catalog, College of Alameda, 1989–90/1990–91). EOPS offers a variety of services, including counseling, priority registration, tutorial services, and cultural enrichment activities, to low-income students with educational challenges (http://alameda .peralta.edu/apps/comm.asp?$1=20085). Aoki served as faculty sponsor for the campus group Pilipino American League (Aoki, Self-evaluation, Tenured Faculty Evaluation, April 1994).

49. Because counselors and librarians are considered faculty at the community colleges, Aoki was eligible to run for a Faculty Senate office; he was elected Academic Senate president for the 1989–90 term (staff newsletter, College of Alameda, September 25, 1989). He also served as Merritt Advisory Board chair (Christmas holiday celebration program, Merritt College, December 13, 1984), among other positions (Aoki résumé, 1987).

50. At the College of Alameda, meetings to explain AB1725 began by 1990, under Aoki's tenure as Academic Senate president (1989–90). By 1995, the Academic Senate passed a resolution to implement AB1725. AB1725 increased the power of the faculty and reduced the role of the state in community college governance by mandating that faculty regulate qualifications and responsibilities, including establishing a peer review system to determine teaching qualifications (thus ending the state's role in granting credentials), hiring, promotion criteria, and dismissal procedures and establishing regular faculty meetings to discuss curriculum and other departmental business. The community college thus began operating more like a university and less like a high school (staff newsletter, College of Alameda, February 26, 1990, April 10, 1995).

51. Ronald Kong ended his tenure as president of the College of Alameda in June 1991 to become the chancellor of the San José–Evergreen Community College District (staff newsletter, College of Alameda, June 10, 1991).

52. Aoki was elected president of the College of Alameda Academic Senate in October 1996; his opponent was a fellow counselor (staff newsletter, College of Alameda, October 14, 1996). By that time, Aoki's involvement with the Black Panther Party and the Asian American Movement had already been publicized in the "People in the News" section of the staff newsletter (staff newsletter, College of Alameda, September 21, 1992; October 11, 1993). After completing his one-year term as faculty president, Aoki was elected president of the Peralta Association

of Pacific Asian Americans, the districtwide organization for the Asian American employees (1997–98).

53. George Herring was president of the College of Alameda when Aoki retired in spring 1998 (staff newsletter, May 11, 1998). Herring had served as chair of the committee in the annual evaluation of Aoki's work at Merritt College (Summary Evaluation of Contract Instructors, December 18, 1975; February 6, 1978).

54. Aoki retired in 1998 (verification of Aoki's employment record, Doris H. Kogo, Human Resources, Peralta Community College District, August 31, 2009).

55. As early as 1979, Aoki had applied for and was one of the Peralta district's nominees for an academic administration fellowship (Aoki, application for ACE Fellows Program in Academic Administration, January 12, 1979). An annual employment evaluation stated, "Mr. Aoki is ambitious and perhaps sees a future in some managerial position" (Management Evaluation of Counselor/Nurse, evaluation of Aoki, Merritt College, April 1, 1982). A former colleague in UC Berkeley's Asian American Studies program who later served as an administrator at UC Berkeley noted that every time they ran into each other, Aoki spoke with pride about his being the president of the Academic Senate.

56. Elbaum, *Revolution in the Air;* Pulido, *Black, Brown, Yellow, and Left.*

57. Similarly, among the few documents retained over the years, Aoki kept a brief note of thanks from JACL leader Raymond Okamura, commending him on his remarks against Agnew's "fat Jap" comment (Okamura, note to Aoki, September 27, 1968).

58. Aoki interview, December 21–23, 2003.

11. "At Least I Was There"

1. Newton was killed in a drug deal in Oakland on August 22, 1989 (Pearson, *The Shadow of the Panther,* 311–15). Newton's death made front-page headlines news in the most prominent newspapers around the country (*New York Times,* August 23, 26, 27, 1989; *Los Angeles Times,* August 22, 23, 1989; *Washington Post,* August 23, 1989), but was not covered by the *Oakland Tribune.*

2. Newton's note to "Hi Aoki," reads in full: "I was here talking about the old days with [blacked out by Aoki]—I hope you are doing well" (April 28, 1989). There is nothing in this brief note to indicate that Newton knew about or wanted Aoki's help with a drug treatment program, but Aoki interpreted Newton's acknowledgment of him as a green light to offer help.

3. Aoki served as Academic Senate president in 1989–90 (staff newsletter, College of Alameda, September 25, 1989).

4. In the *Commemorator's* coverage of the "unity rally" in commemoration of Huey Newton, Richard Aoki is identified as a speaker and his photo is featured, dressed in his "Panther uniform": a black leather jacket, light blue shirt, and beret (*Commemorator,* November 1990, Oakland, Calif., 1–3). That Aoki's speech focused on Newton's dual education, at the university and on the streets, reflects Aoki's philosophy of learning: "Dr. Huey P. Newton . . . had a Ph.D. from the University of California at Santa Cruz. He also had his Ph.D. from the streets of West Oakland. He was 'bad'!"

5. *Black Power, Black Panthers,* produced by Ray Telles and Lewis Cohen, aired on PBS-affiliate KQED on May 30, 31, and June 1, 1990 (*TV Guide,* San Francisco metropolitan edition). Among Emmy Award–winning producer Telles's thirty documentaries is *The Fight in the Fields: Cesar Chavez and the Farmworkers' Struggle.* Lee Lew-Lee's award-winning documentary *All Power to the People!* was broadcast in twenty-four countries.

6. In *Black Power, Black Panthers,* Aoki spoke about the BPP police patrols. He was identified in the credits as president of the Faculty Senate, College of Alameda.

7. Aoki spoke at two programs during the weeklong events organized by the twenty-year Commemoration Committee, a group of UC Berkeley students of color who formed to recognize the TWLF strike for its critical role in establishing the Department of Ethnic Studies and launching "major institutional changes in the undergraduate admissions policy" (Sumi K. Cho, letter to Richard Aoki, March 18, 1989; also "Open It Up or Shut It Down," flyer for the TWLF events, April 11–15, 1989). The photo of Third World unity featuring Aoki, Brown, and Delgado, originally in *Muhammad Speaks,* February 7, 1969, was reprinted on the commemoration flyers and programs and in newspapers (*East Bay Express,* April 7, 1989; *Hokubei Mainichi,* April 4, 1989).

8. The 1991 Day of Remembrance event, commemorating Executive Order 9066 and the incarceration of Japanese Americans, was titled "1942: Japanese Americans Were Incarcerated—1991: Are Arab Americans Next?" (flyer, February 23, 1991, Oakland, Calif., sponsored by UNITY Organizing Committee; cosponsored by National Coalition for Redress/Reparations and the Bay Area Palestine Coordinating Committee; *Daily Californian,* February 25, 1991). Jean Yonemura was editor, and Yuri Miyagawa, a staff photographer, both for *Unity,* published by Getting Together Publications.

9. See McCutchen, "Selections from a Panther Diary."

10. Aoki is listed on the "Advisory Team" and not the "Support Team" of the Bay Area Support Committee for Marshall E. Conway, suggesting that he was important enough to be listed alongside prominent Black Panthers Geronimo ji-Jaga Pratt, David Hilliard, and Emory Douglas, but was not expected to do any actual organizing (flyer, n.d.). Conway, now in prison forty years, was a member of the BPP Baltimore chapter and allegedly killed a police officer in 1970. Conway asserts his innocence and his supporters state he was framed as part of the FBI's COINTELPRO efforts to neutralize the BPP (http://www.freeeddieconway.org).

11. In June 1995, newly elected Pennsylvania governor Tom Ridge signed an execution warrant for Mumia Abu-Jamal, sparking massive worldwide protest. Ten days before the execution date of August 17, 1995, Judge Albert Sabo did the unlikely— reversed his own ruling in the original trial to grant an indefinite stay of execution (*New York Times,* June 3, 1995; August 8, 1995).

12. California voters, with 54 percent in favor, passed Proposition 209 in November 1996 (*Los Angeles Times,* November 6, 1996).

13. Aoki was listed as a panelist for "Asians Speak Out for Affirmative Action," October 17, 1995, held at Revolution Books in Berkeley (flyer, n.d.; video recording of program; *Sing Tao* newspaper, October 18, 1995).

14. The initial signatories to "An Open Letter" were Steve Wong, Richard Aoki, Dolly Lumsdaine Veale, Jeffery Chan, and Dylan Rodríguez.

15. The theme for that issue of *Hitting Critical Mass* was "struggles of consciousness, consciousness in struggle," and the majority of editors voted to publish "An Open Letter." The editors did acknowledge, however, that "some editors felt that the topical nature and intended general audience of the letter appeared more suitable for media like newspapers; its lack of documentation for cited statistics presented a problem for the journal; and the signatory status of one of the editors might represent a conflict of interest" (134). Aoki lamented: "By the time it was published in 1997, the elections were over and Prop 209 had passed. Disappointment in that field went a little more in my heart." That issue was intended to be published in spring 1996, as vol. 3, no. 2 (as indicated on the title page and in the editors' note stating "looking ahead, the Spring 1997 issue . . ."), but Aoki insists it was published in spring 1997, as volume 3, no. 2, which coincides with the information on the journal's cover.

16. The Asian American pop culture zine, *Giant Robot,* embarked on a new area with its coverage of political activism in fifteen fairly superficial interviews with 1960s–1970s AAM activists ("Yellow Power," spring 1998). The issue sparked popular and scholarly interest in Asian American activism, as noted in a historiography of the AAM (Fujino, "Who Studies the Asian American Movement?").

17. See Veale, "Interview with Richard Aoki."

18. The thirtieth-anniversary reunion was transformed into a two-day conference with two foci: commemoration of the TWLF strike and "radical politics beyond the schooling industrial complex." The conference, held April 9–10, 1999, at UC Berkeley, had over fifty panels, workshops, roundtables, or performances ("Crossing Over: Ethnic Studies and Radical Politics Beyond the Schooling Industrial Complex," conference program; Harvey Dong, "Some Panels on Third World Strike Commemoration/Crossing Over Events," ca. April 1999).

19. Aoki is featured as a 1969 striker and 1999 supporter in the documentary *On Strike! Ethnic Studies, 1969–1999.*

20. The student-led "non-violent take-over" of Barrows Hall and hunger strike began on April 14, 1999, in response to what the Ethnic Studies Graduate Group called "death by attrition" (Ethnic Studies Graduate Group, e-mail to Chancellor Robert Berdahl, May 3, 1999). Around midnight of May 7, 1999, Chancellor Berdahl, Academic Senate chair Robert Brentano, and Ethnic Studies Department chair Ling-chi Wang issued an agreement offering eight FTE searches to replace current and anticipated *vacancies* over the next five years; funding to maintain the current curricular offerings; seed money of $100,000 per year for five years to establish the long-sought-after Institute of Race and Gender Studies; outreach funding; temporary space for a multicultural student center; space for a mural; and the dropping of charges, with a mere letter of admonishment, to students with no more than two charges (May 7 agreement, signed by Berdahl, Brentano, and Wang; Ling-chi Wang, e-mail, May 8, 1999). Some condemned "weak-kneed administrators" for caving in to the demands of protesters (Eric Langborgh, "Berkeley Administration to Protestors: You're in

Charge," Accuracy in Academia website, http://www.academia.org, February 2000). But Chancellor Berdahl insisted that "the administration did not capitulate to the protest" because "the agreement could have been reached without a sit-in, a hunger strike, or an illegal encampment" and the concessions, including the dropping of charges against protesters with no more than two citations, abided by the normal review processes of the university (Berhahl, *San Francisco Chronicle,* May 19, 1999). Three UC Berkeley graduate students blasted the agreement as a "Struggle for Nothing at All." They argued that they gained no *new* faculty positions when they had asked for twenty and, most important, they failed to gain full amnesty for arrested students. At least eighty protesters were arrested on day six of the hunger strike (Frank Wilderson III, Jared Sexton, and Dylan Rodríguez, e-mail, ca. May 11, 1999; *Los Angeles Times,* May 5, 1999; UC Berkeley Ethnic Studies petition, circulated via e-mail). Aoki viewed the three graduate students as being "adventuristic" in their dismissal of any gains, as reflecting a schism between the mainly female undergraduate and the mainly male graduate student leadership, and for mistakenly airing dirty laundry.

21. Marx, *Das Kapital.* A vast literature captures the economic and psychological struggles of the poor and low-waged workers, exacerbated by race and gender oppression, including the novels of Charles Dickens, Richard Wright's powerful novel *Native Son,* and Barbara Ehrenreich's *Nickel and Dimed.*

22. Using the "chickens come home to roost" metaphor to argue that U.S. violence toward others provokes violence against the U.S. government has resulted in the disciplining of the speaker. When Malcolm X used this statement during a question-and-answer period in November 1963, he was suspended from the Nation of Islam for raising any criticism of President Kennedy days after Kennedy's assassination. Shortly after September 11, 2001, Ward Churchill, professor of Ethnic Studies at the University of Colorado, Boulder, wrote an essay titled "'Some People Push Back': On the Justice of Roosting Chickens," in which he asserted that American foreign policies engendered the attacks and described the "technocratic corps at the very heart of America's global financial empire" in the World Trade Center as "little Eichmanns." In 2005, this essay was widely publicized and led to a university investigation into Churchill's research and his subsequent firing. Aoki was among those who strongly defended Churchill. See Ward Churchill, "'Some People Push Back': On the Justice of Roosting Chickens" (http://www.kersplebedeb.com/mystuff/s11/churchill .html); Churchill, *On the Justice of Roosting Chickens.*

23. "Community Speak out on the War on Terrorism" (December 8, 2001, Oakland, flyer).

24. Aoki was a featured speaker at an event supporting Mumia Abu-Jamal, along with widely known Mumia supporters Pam Africa, Jack Heyman, and Mumia's attorneys Eliot Grossman and Marlene Kamish (flyer, August 2, 2002, Oakland). The ILWU voted to shut down shipping ports all along the West Coast on April 24, 1999, to coincide with nationwide protests on Mumia's birthday. On the same day, a three-hundred-member IWLU contingent led twenty-five thousand marchers down the streets of San Francisco with slogans of "Stop the Execution!" and "Free Mumia!" (Jeff Mackler, "ILWU Leads April 24 March for Mumia Abu-Jamal in San Francisco,"

Socialist Action newsletter, May 1999; ILWU resolution in support of Mumia, April 1999, archive.ilwu.org/0499/ieb_sops_0499.htm; *Los Angeles Times,* April 24, 1999).

25. "All People's Tribunal to Charge the United States Government for Ethnic Cleansing, Terrorism, and Genocide" (flyer, April 13, 2002, Oakland); also, "A People's Tribunal" to "charge George W. Bush and the US Government for the Crimes of Terrorism, White Supremacy, Slavery, Ethnic Cleansing, and Genocide!" (flyer, January 26, 2003, Oakland). Many of the same people spoke at both tribunals, including Aoki (Aoki's speeches, handwritten notes, April 13, 2002, and January 23, 2003; program, January 26, 2003; flyer, April 2002). Mel Mason is one of the main organizers working to free Romaine "Chip" Fitzgerald, a former Black Panther from Los Angeles and one of the longest-held political prisoners, incarcerated since 1969; see http://freechip.org.

26. Aoki was among the hundreds of people who signed on to Not in Our Name's (NION) statement against the war, which called for "no more transfusions of blood for oil" (http://freeamericausaweb.com/backers.html). NION's Pledge of Resistance became a rallying cry of the post–9/11 antiwar movement (http://www.notinourname.net).

27. A month before the United States bombed Iraq, several million people in some 350 cities around the world, from London, to South Africa, to Tokyo, to San Francisco and New York, protested the anticipated invasion (*New York Times,* February 16, 2003). While many were inspired by the magnitude of the protests initiated prior to the invasion, numerous people, including Aoki, were also disheartened that significant worldwide opposition from the United Nations, to heads of nations across the globe, to ordinary people on the streets, could not stop the United States and Britain's unilateral actions.

28. The United States spearheaded the bombing of Iraq, backed primarily by Britain, on March 20, 2003. The bombing was necessary, according to then-president George W. Bush, to "disarm Iraq of weapons of mass destruction" and because of Saddam Hussein's alleged ties to Osama bin Laden (White House press release, March 22, 2003; georgewbush-whitehouse.archives.gov/news/releases). From the start, the legality of the war was called into question. United Nations secretary-general Kofi Annan stated that the U.S. invasion of Iraq was "illegal" because it proceeded without approval from the "UN Charter" or "broader support from the international community" (interview with BBC, September 19, 2004). France, Germany, Russia, China, and growing numbers of countries opposed the U.S. attack on Iraq (*New York Times,* February 17, 2003). Undermining a major rationale for bombing Iraq, the director of the International Atomic Energy Agency charged with weapons inspection made public statements that Iraq's nuclear program had been "neutralized" by 1998, and that to date, there was no evidence of Iraq reviving its nuclear program and that the IAEA expected to complete their investigation in the near future, indicating that the U.S. bombings of Iraq were, at best, premature (http://www.iaea.org/NewsCenter/Statements, February 13, 2003; March 7, 2003). By 2005, the CIA's top weapons inspectors concluded that they had completed their investigations and found no weapons of mass destruction (http://www.msnbc.msn.com, April 25, 2005).

29. The film premiered at the Grand Lake Theater in Oakland on November 12, 2009 (*AOKI: A Documentary Film;* see http://www.aokifilm.com).

30. The Kwame Ture Lifetime Achievement Awards were initiated by Warrior Woman to honor elders in Third World communities, including her husband, Ernie Longwalker (program, April 12, 2003, Fresno).

31. East Bay Living History Project: Genesis of the Asian American Movement, Activism Then and Now, September 18, 2003, UC Berkeley, videotape.

32. Ibid. For critiques of the JACL's wartime policies, see Lim, "Lim Report"; Spickard, "The Nisei Assume Power"; Takahashi, *Nisei Sansei,* 53–65, 85–112; Kurashige, *Japanese American Celebration and Conflict,* 75–116.

33. JACL's own historical timeline shows limited work for social justice in the 1950s–1960s, with most of the work focusing on gaining rights for Japanese Americans (http://www.jacl.org/about/jacl-history). My review of the JACL's major publication, the *Pacific Citizen,* from 1959 to 1963, shows moderate coverage of civil rights issues, especially housing, employment practices, and media images. The JACL did issue a "Civil Rights Statement," adopted on July 21, 1963, saying that the organization "endorses intensified participation in responsible and constructive activities to obtain civil equality, social justice and full economic and educational opportunities as a matter of fundamental right for all Americans regardless of race, color, creed or national origin. To this end, we accelerate our continuing program in seeking legislative, judicial and executive fulfillment of constitutional guarantees of human rights for all Americans" (*Pacific Citizen,* July 26, 1963). This statement suggests a politic of integrationism and routine establishment methods of contestation, quite different from Aoki's.

34. Although the national JACL was slow to work actively for redress, certain JACL chapters, especially Seattle, were among the earliest advocates of redress and reparations (Takezawa, *Breaking the Silence*).

35. Spurred by the redress movement and victory, JACL's civil rights activities broadened. By 1990, the JACL was an early supporter of same-sex marriages and after 9/11, immediately denounced any discrimination or detention of Arabs or Muslims, opposed the USA PATRIOT Act, opposed the government's proposal to establish detention camps for "enemy combatants," and defended Lt. Ehren Watada in his case refusing deployment to Iraq based on the illegality of the Iraq War (http://www.jacl.org/about/jacl-history; http://www.pdxjacl.org/newsletter/October/october; http://www.icfresno.org/programs/03b; Zia, *Asian American Dreams*). Others in the Japanese American community, particularly Nikkei for Civil Rights and Redress (NCRR), were also active in fighting for civil rights (http://ncrr-la.org). On Watada, see *Nation,* May 19, 2009; October 26, 2009.

36. Inscribed on the beautiful decorative plate is, "In recognition of your activism and service to the community, Richard Aoki, East Bay Living History Project, September 18th 2003, UC Berkeley, JACL."

37. Churchill and Vander Wall, *The COINTELPRO Papers,* 123; Carson, foreword to *The Black Panthers Speak,* ix.

38. Social movement theorists argue for the critical role of interpretation in activist engagement. When people view their demands as legitimate and hold a belief

that collective agency can effect social change, people gain "cognitive liberation"—a necessary precondition to activism, posits scholar Doug McAdam *(Political Process and the Development of Black Insurgency)*.

39. A profile on Aoki in the *Berkeley Barb* (February 14–21, 1969), a local alternative newspaper, appears to be the only article focused solely on Aoki before the late 1990s.

EPILOGUE

1. Following the Berkeley memorial was a reception at UC Berkeley's Multicultural Center with impromptu speakers, artwork featuring silk-screened T-shirts of Aoki's iconic image, and a community alter built by the Eastside Arts Alliance. The second memorial, an activist remembrance at Little Bobby Hutton (DeFremery) Park in West Oakland organized by former Black Panthers and Asian American activists, got rained out and canceled. For more information, see Aoki's memorial website: http://ramemorial.blogspot.com; Richard Aoki memorial program, May 2, 2009, Berkeley; "Statement on the Anniversary of Richard Aoki's Passing," March 15, 2010, posted at http://ramemorial.blogspot.com.

2. The other half of Aoki's ashes were sprinkled out at sea, joining those of his mother.

3. Richard Aoki memorial program, May 3, 2009, Oakland; Earl Napper, Mike Sheng, Paul Takagi, Naomi Southard, and Ben Wang, speakers.

4. Harvey Dong, e-mail to author, March 10, 2010.

5. Ibid. The memorial organizers publicly stated: "While some attendees were critical of this show of respect, the majority in attendance were not lost to the irony of this military veteran's recognition from a government he fought against for civil and human rights" ("Statement on the Anniversary of Richard Aoki's Passing").

6. I thank Shaka At-Thinin for this phone call.

7. Also on http://ramemorial.blogspot.com.

8. I discuss Denzin's ideas of narrative as fiction in the introduction.

9. Aoki, conversation with author, April 4, 2003, author's notes. The forty-seven *ronin* were not simply fighting to win a battle. They were the forty-seven most courageous and honorable of their master's samurai, making painful personal sacrifices to avenge the dishonor and death of their master (*The 47 Ronin,* film, Kenji Mizoguchi, 1941; Benedict, *The Chrysanthemum and the Sword,* 200–205). Aoki too tried to live out his life in honor to his mentors and his vision of justice.

10. "Statement on the Anniversary of Richard Aoki's Passing."

11. After the autopsy was performed, the coroner ruled Aoki's death a "suicide" in that he "shot self with a handgun" at 5:45 a.m. on March 15, 2009 (Certificate of Death, County of Alameda, March 17, 2009).

12. Durkheim, *Suicide.*

13. The "Statement on the Anniversary of Richard Aoki's Passing," also signed by former Asian American Political Alliance members, Serve the People, and Friends of Richard Aoki, disclosed his suicide and explained "the medical conditions that led to Richard's death."

14. Harvey Dong, e-mails to author, February 5 and March 10, 2010; Harvey Dong, conversation with author, July 1, 2009.

15. In the ten weeks following Aoki's death, three other prominent leaders of Asian American Studies and the early Asian American Movement died in the San Francisco Bay Area: internationally renowned scholar Ronald Takaki, historian and archivist Him Mark Lai, and poet and activist Al Robles (*Los Angeles Times,* May 29, 2009; *San Francisco Chronicle,* May 29, 2009; *Hyphen,* May 2, 2009). After Takaki's family announced his death by suicide, some felt even more convinced that publicizing the suicides of two Japanese American leaders might provoke copycat behaviors.

16. Men are four times more likely to commit suicide than women. Suicide is the seventh leading cause of death for men. Men most often commit suicide with firearms and women through self-poisoning (data for 2006, http://www.cdc.gov/ViolencePrevention/pdf/Suicide-DataSheet-a.pdf).

17. Newton, *Revolutionary Suicide,* 1–2; Durkheim, *Suicide.*

18. Aoki relayed this to me.

19. Newton, *Revolutionary Suicide,* 6.

20. Gosse, *Where the Boys Are,* 10.

21. Ibid.

22. Ehrenreich, *The Hearts of Men,* 7.

23. Szasz, *Shopping Our Way to Safety,* 15–55; Johnson, *Blowback.*

24. *Oakland Tribune,* September 13, 1954; Joseph Shigeo Aoki, "Background of Joseph Shigeo Aoki (his words)," typed from handwritten notes, April 23, 2005.

25. May, *Homeward Bound,* xxiv.

26. Ibid.

27. I take literary license here in using the bombings of Hiroshima and Nagasaki as a symbol for the United States' global ascent. Some scholars argue that the atomic bombings were not necessary because Japan was already prepared to surrender; instead this muscular assertion signaled the United States' hegemonic position to the Soviet Union (Takaki, *Hiroshima*).

28. Kennedy, "The Soft American," 16.

29. Williams, *Still a Man's World,* 188.

30. According to Connell, hegenomic masculinity was not necessarily embodied by the most powerful men, but often by movie stars, fantasy figures, and other symbols of power. Like Gramsci's term *hegemony,* hegemonic masculinity was not a "fixed character type" but "always contestable" and changing in response to current constructions of masculinities and femininities (Connell, *Masculinities,* 76–81).

31. Ehrenreich, *The Hearts of Men,* 17.

32. May, *Homeward Bound,* xi–xvii; Ehrenreich, *The Hearts of Men,* 30; Friedan, *The Feminine Mystique.*

33. Ehrenrich, *The Hearts of Men,* 42–51.

34. In *The Way We Never Were,* Stephanie Coontz shows that few families ever resembled the "traditional family," with the "breadwinner father and stay-at-home mother," and that those that did were supported by massive government subsidies and policies, from federal housing loans to the GI Bill. But the ideology of the nuclear

family continues to shape normative constructions of masculinity and femininity, as seen in Aoki's narrative, and to fuel public policy debates.

35. Kimmel, "Masculinity as Homophobia."

36. West and Zimmerman, "Doing Gender."

37. I thank an anonymous reviewer for this vivid phrasing, "contradictory tendencies in tension."

38. Newton defined the establishment as "the power structure, based on the economic infrastructure, propped up and reinforced by the media and all secondary educational and cultural institutions" (*Revolutionary Suicide*, 3).

39. Genet, *Prisoner of Love,* cited in Singh, *Black Is a Country,* 202.

40. Singh, *Black Is a Country,* 202–3.

41. Ibid., 204–5.

42. Ibid. On hegemony, see Gramsci, *Selections from the Prison Notebooks.* The media, argues Noam Chomsky in *Manufacturing Consent,* is a primary institution for manufacturing the public's consent to be ruled.

43. Douglass, "The Significance of Emancipation in the West Indies."

44. Lenin, *The State and Revolution,* 25.

45. Douglas Daniels, conversation with author, March 15, 2010, Santa Barbara, Calif.

46. Fanon, *The Wretched of the Earth,* 51.

47. *The Fight in the Fields* (documentary, 1997); *The Struggle in the Fields* (documentary, 1996). Paulo Freire discusses a "fear of freedom" adopted by the oppressed, whereby especially in the initial stages of struggle, being fearful of freedom, they tend to imitate their oppressors. But through the resolution of this contradiction between the desire for and fear of freedom, oppression can give way to liberation (*Pedagogy of the Oppressed,* 45–48).

48. King, "Nonviolence and Racial Justice," 7–8. Smith, in *Conjuring Culture,* offers a complex discussion of the use of nonviolence, forgiveness, and reconciliation to bring healing to the victims and the victimizers.

49. See especially the chapter titled "Colonial War and Mental Disorders" in Fanon, *The Wretched of the Earth.*

50. Malcolm X, "Message to the Grass Roots," 7–8.

51. Ibid., 8.

52. Williams made this statement after two juries, within a day of each other, separately acquitted a White man charged with the attempted rape of a Black woman and a White man charged with kicking a Black hotel maid down a flight of stairs. His anger was compounded by his own sense of failure at having naively misled the Black community into relying on the courts for justice (Williams, *Negroes with Guns,* 61–64).

53. Ibid., 4

54. Ibid., 40; Robert F. Williams, "The Resistant Spirit: Why Do I Speak From Exile?," in Revolutionary Action Movement, *Black America,* 1965, 11, Social Protest Collection, Bancroft Library, University of California, Berkeley, box 18, folder 21.

55. Douglass, "The Significance of Emancipation in the West Indies."

56. King, "A Time to Break Silence," 240.

57. FBI report, June 22, 1962.

58. Vietnam Day Committee, "Did You Vote for War?"

59. Aoki, letter from VDC to Zendentsu, All-Japan Telecommunications Workers Union, December 13, 1965, in Aoki's FBI files.

60. FBI report, May 24, 1968.

61. FBI report, January 29, 1970.

62. Habal, *San Francisco's International Hotel; The Fall of the I Hotel* (documentary).

63. Dong, "Transforming Student Elites," 193, 203. These ideas resonate with Mao's writings: "Where do correct ideas comes from? Do they drop from the sky? No. Are they innate in the mind? No. They come from social practice, and from it alone; they come from three kinds of social practice, the struggle for production, the class struggle, and scientific experiment" (Mao, "Where Do Correct Ideas Come From?" and "On Practice"). While some may disagree with Mao's seemingly dogmatic approach, the point is that ideas have a material basis; ideas develop in particular social contexts, notably in political struggle.

64. Habal, *San Francisco's International Hotel,* 171.

65. Gramsci, *Selections from the Prison Notebook,* 5–14, 229–39.

66. *Wall Street Journal,* November 18, 1969.

67. Katsiaficas, *The Imagination of the New Left.*

68. Black Panther Party, "Executive Mandate No. 1," May 2, 1967.

69. In *Philippine Society and Revolution,* the "bible" of the Philippine revolution, Amado Guerrero similarly condemns "adventurism," or a strategy "to seize political power" in a short time period "through a series of military offensives . . . without regard for laying down the political base of popular mass support" (227).

70. Holloway, "Dignity's Revolt," 160, 165.

71. Ibid, 180.

72. Lears, "The Concept of Cultural Hegemony," 571.

73. Kelley, *Freedom Dreams,* 9. The use of poetic narration and images in "The Fourth World War" enables this documentary to powerfully "transport us to another place," to almost feel the pain of neoliberalism and war as well as the people's resistance to global capitalism.

74. Ibid., 9–11.

75. King, "I Have a Dream," 219.

76. King, "A Time to Break Silence," 232. This speech is sometimes referenced as "Beyond Vietnam."

77. Ibid., 231.

78. Ibid., 241.

79. Ibid.

80. Ibid., 240.

81. Ibid., 241.

82. Black Panther Party, "Ten-Point Program and Platform."

83. "AAPA Perspectives."

Bibliography

ARCHIVAL MATERIALS

Asian American Political Alliance newspapers, Special Collections, San Francisco State University

Bay Area Black Panther Party Collection, 1963–2000. Special Collections, University of California, Santa Barbara

Black Panther Party Collection. Merritt College, Oakland

College of Alameda History, College of Alameda, Alameda

Educational Systems in Oakland, Oakland Public Library

Ethnic Studies Collection, Ethnic Studies Library, University of California, Berkeley

High School Yearbooks, Berkeley High School

History of Berkeley, Berkeley Public Library

History of Oakland, Oakland Public Library

Japanese American Evacuation and Resettlement (JERS) Records, Bancroft Library, University of California, Berkeley

Japanese American History, Oakland Public Library

Yuri Kochiyama Collection, University of California, Los Angeles

Steve Louie Collection, University of California, Los Angeles

Merritt College History Collection, Merritt College, Oakland

Peralta Community College District Archives, Merritt College, Oakland

Social Protest Collection (SPC), Bancroft Library, University of California, Berkeley

Social Welfare archives, School of Social Welfare, University of California, Berkeley

World War II Collections, Japanese American National Museum, Los Angeles

INTERVIEWS CONDUCTED BY DIANE FUJINO

Aoki, Debbie, July 2, 2009, Emeryville, California

Aoki, James T., June 8, 2009, Oakland, California

Aoki, Richard, all in Berkeley, California: November 7, 1999; January 11–12, 2003; May 10–11, 2003; May 18–21, 2003; June 16–20, 2003; July 16–18, 2003; July 30–August 1, 2003; August 21–26 2003; September 8–10, 2003; December 21–23, 2003; January 6, 2004; January 18–19, 2004; March 14–16, 2004; October 4, 2005

Aoki, Richard's cousin, telephone interview, August 14, 2005; anonymity requested

Burnett, Pam Lee, November 23, 2005, Davis, California

Cleaver, Kathleen, conversation, October 24, 2005, Santa Barbara, California
Daniels, Douglas, September 7, 2006, Santa Barbara, California
Dong, Harvey, May 11 and 20, 2003, Berkeley, California
Fong, Alan, January 20, 2004, Berkeley, California
Fong, Bryant, January 19, 2004, San Francisco, California
Forte, Sherwin, December 30, 2003, Los Angeles, California
Hayashi, Patrick, June 9, 2009, Oakland, California
Hayden, Carol (Shelly), November 21, 2005, Albany, Calfornia
Hilliard, David, telephone conversation, August 4, 2003
Hing, Alex, November 9, 2005, New York City
Howard, Elbert "Big Man," November 18, 2005, Forestville, California
Huen, Floyd, May 30, 2008, Oakland, California
Lew-Lee, Lee, telephone conversation, ca. November 2005
Napper, Earl, July 1, 2009, Emeryville, California
Redmonde, Reiko, conversation, May 2, 2009, Berkeley, California
Saito, Leo, September 8, 2005, Oakland, California
Sanders, Tom, September 9, 2005, Berkeley, California
Sato, Bill, June 8, 2009, El Cerrito, California
Seale, Bobby, September 2, 2003, Oakland, California
Tagawa, Mike, telephone conversation, ca. February 2007
Takagi, Paul, September 9, 2005, Oakland, California
Veale, Dolly, February 19, 2007, Los Angeles, California
War Jack, LaNada (Means), March 14, 2009, Berkeley, California
Waters, Kenn, November 22, 2005, Fremont, California

Oral Histories

Shigeo Joseph Aoki, interview with Ann Yabusaki, January 2, 1987, Oakland, California

Mark Comfort, interview with Robert Wright, November 16, 1968, Moorland-Spingarn Research Center, Howard University, Washington, D.C.

Don Warden, interview with Robert E. Martin, July 25, 1969, Moorland-Spingarn Research Center, Howard University, Washington, D.C.

Published and Unpublished Sources

Adams, Ansel. *Born Free and Equal: The Story of Loyal Japanese Americans.* 1944. Reprint, Bishop, Calif.: Spotted Dog, 2001.

Ahmad, Muhammad (Maxwell Stanford Jr.). "Robert Franklin ('Rob') Williams, 1925–1996." *Bulletin in Defense of Marxism,* 1997, 43–44.

———. *We Will Return in the Whirlwind: Black Radical Organizations, 1960–1975.* Chicago: Charles H. Kerr, 2007.

Alinder, Jasmine. *Moving Images: Photography and the Japanese American Incarceration.* Urbana: University of Illinois Press, 2009.

All Power to the People. Film by Lee Lew-Lee. Electronic News Group, 1996.

Allen, Robert L. *Black Awakening in Capitalist America: An Analytic History.* Garden City, N.Y.: Doubleday Anchor Book, 1969.

"American Topics: Rare Look at Internment Camp." *New York Times,* January 27, 1997.

AOKI: A Documentary Film. By Ben Wang and Michael Cheng. 2009.

Aoki, Brenda Wong. *Uncle Gunjiro's Girlfriend,* April 1, 2006, at http://www.historylink.org/index.cfm?DisplayPage=output.cfm&file_id=7716.

Aoki, Isamu, and Kathy Aoki. "Descendants of Reverend Peter Chojiro Aoki." Unpublished manuscript, 2007.

Aoki, Richard M. "The Asian American Political Alliance: A Study of Organizational Death." Graduate student paper for Professor R. Biller, June 9, 1970.

———. "The Asian American Studies Division: A Study in Administrative Behavior." Graduate student paper for Professor R. Biller, June 10, 1970.

———. "Nationalism, S.F. Black Power Conference, and the SWP." Report to the Socialist Workers Party, October 8, 1966.

Aptheker, Herbert. *American Negro Slave Revolts.* New York: Columbia University Press, 1943.

Arnesen, Eric. "Civil Rights Historiography: Two Perspectives." *Historically Speaking* 10 (2009): 31–34.

Asian Community Center Archive Group. *STAND UP: An Archive Collection of the Bay Area Asian American Movement, 1968–1974.* Berkeley, Calif.: Eastwind Books, 2009.

Asian Studies Division, Ethnic Studies Department. Proposal (partial), 1969–70, for the Asian Studies Conference, September 20–21, 1969.

Asian Women. 1971. Reprint, Los Angeles: Asian American Studies Center, UCLA, 1975.

Azuma, Eiichiro. *Between Two Empires: Race, History, and Transnationalism in Japanese America.* New York: Oxford University Press, 2005.

Bagwell, Beth. *Oakland: The Story of a City.* Novato, Calif.: Presidio Press, 1982.

Bahr, Diana Meyers. *The Unquiet Nisei: An Oral History of the Life of Sue Kunitomi Embrey.* New York: Palgrave, 2007.

Bakunin, Mikhail Alexandrovich. *The Catechism of the Revolutionist.* Pamphlet published by Black Panther Party for Self-Defense, n.d.

Baldwin, James. *The Fire Next Time.* New York: Dial Press, 1963.

Balmer, Edwin, and Philip Wylie. *When Worlds Collide.* New York: A. L. Burt, 1933.

Baran, Paul A. *The Political Economy of Growth.* New York: Monthly Review, 1957.

Barber, Lucy G. *Marching on Washington: The Forging of an American Political Tradition.* Berkeley: University of California Press, 2002.

Barlow, William, and Peter Shapiro. *An End to Silence: The San Francisco State College Student Movement in the '60s.* New York: Pegasus, 1971.

Bello, Waldo. "From American Lake to a People's Pacific." In *Let the Good Times Roll: Prostitution and the US Military in Asia,* edited by Saundra Pollock Sturdevant and Brenda Stoltzfus, 4–16. New York: New Press, 1992.

Benedict, Ruth. *The Chrysanthemum and the Sword: Patterns of Japanese Culture.* Boston: Houghton Mifflin, 1946.

Bernal, Dolores Delgado. "Grassroots Leadership Reconceptualized: Chicana Oral Histories and the 1968 East Los Angeles Blowouts." *Frontiers* 19 (1998): 113–42.

Bibby, Michael. *Hearts and Minds: Bodies, Poetry, and Resistance in the Vietnam Era.* New Brunswick, N.J.: Rutgers University Press, 1996.

Billingsley, Andrew, Douglas Davidson, and Theresa Loya. "Ethnic Studies at Berkeley." *California Monthly*, June–July 1970, 13–20.

Bingham, Howard L. *Black Panthers 1968.* Pasadena, Calif.: AMMO Books, 2009.

Biondi, Martha. *To Stand and Fight: The Struggle for Civil Rights in Postwar New York City.* Cambridge, Mass.: Harvard University Press, 2003.

Black Power, Black Panthers. By Ray Telles and Lewis Cohen. KQED, 1990.

Blauner, Robert. *Racial Oppression in America.* New York: Harper and Row, 1972.

Blum, William. *Killing Hope: U.S. Military and CIA Intervention since World War II.* Monroe, Maine: Common Courage Press, 1995.

Blumer, Herbert. *Symbolic Interactionism.* Berkeley: University of California Press, 1998.

Boggs, Grace Lee. *Living for Change: An Autobiography.* Minneapolis: University of Minnesota Press, 1998.

Bonacich, Edna. "Inequality in America: The Failure of the American System for People of Color." In *Race, Class, and Gender: An Anthology,* edited by Margaret Andersen and Patricia Hill Collins, 96–110. Belmont, Calif.: Wadsworth, 1992.

Bonilla-Silva, Eduardo. *Racism without Racists: Color-Blind Racism and the Persistence of Racial Inequality in the United States.* Lanham, Md.: Rowman and Littlefield, 2003.

Booker, Chris. "Lumpenization: A Critical Error of the Black Panther Party." In *The Black Panther Party Reconsidered,* edited by Charles E. Jones, 337–62. Baltimore: Black Classic Press, 1998.

Bowles, Samuel, and Herbert Gintis. *Schooling in Capitalist America: Educational Reform and the Contradictions of Economic Life.* New York: Basic Books: 1976.

Breitman, George. *The Last Year of Malcolm X: The Evolution of a Revolutionary.* New York: Merit Publishers, 1967.

———, ed. *Leon Trotsky on Black Nationalism and Self-Determination.* New York: Merit Publishers, 1967.

Brooks, Charlotte. *Alien Neighbors, Foreign Friends: Asian Americans, Housing, and the Transformation of Urban California.* Chicago: University of Chicago Press, 2009.

Brown, Elaine. *A Taste of Power: A Black Woman's Story.* New York: Anchor Books, 1992.

Bryce, James, Holland Thompson, and Flinders Petrie, eds. *The Book of History: A History of All Nations from the Earliest Times to the Present.* Volume 2, *The Far East.* New York: Grolier Society; London: Educational Book Company, 1915.

Buchanan, Keith. "The Third World." *New Left Review* 18 (1963): 5–23.

Bukharin, Nikolai. "Anarchy and Scientific Communism." In *The Poverty of Statism: Anarchism vs. Marxism; A Debate.* Sanday, Orkney, UK: Cienfuegos Press, 1981.

Bush, Rod. *We Are Not What We Seem: Black Nationalism and Class Struggle in the American Century.* New York: New York University Press, 1999.

Cabral, Amílcar. "The Weapon of Theory." In *Revolution in Guinea: Selected Texts by Amílcar Cabral,* translated and edited by Richard Handyside. New York: Monthly Review Press, 1969.

Cade, Toni. *Black Women.* New York: New American Library, 1970.

Cannon, James P. *The History of American Trotskyism.* New York: Pathfinder Press, 1972.

Carmichael, Stokely. *Stokely Speaks: From Black Power to Pan-Africanism.* 1971. Reprint, Chicago: Lawrence Hill Books, 2007.

———, and Charles V. Hamilton. *Black Power: The Politics of Liberation in America.* New York: Vintage, 1967.

———, with Ekwueme Michael Thelwell. *Ready for Revolution: The Life and Struggles of Stokely Carmichael [Kwame Ture].* New York: Scribner, 2003.

Carson, Clayborne. Foreword to *The Black Panthers Speak,* edited by Philip S. Foner, ix–xviii. 1970. Reprint, New York: Da Capo, 1995.

———. *In Struggle: SNCC and the Black Awakening of the 1960s.* Cambridge, Mass.: Harvard University Press, 1981.

———, David J. Garrow, Gerald Gill, Vincent Harding, and Darlene Clark Hine, eds. *The Eyes on the Prize Civil Rights Reader: Documents, Speeches, and Firsthand Accounts from the Black Freedom Struggle.* New York: Penguin, 1991.

Casey, Michael. *Che's Afterlife: The Legacy of an Image.* New York: Random House, 2009.

Castro, Fidel. "History Will Absolve Me!" Speech, October 16, 1953. Reprinted in English as booklet, New York: Fair Play for Cuba Committee, 1961.

Cha-Jua, Sundiata Keith, and Clarence Lang. "The 'Long Movement' as Vampire: Temporal and Spatial Fallacies in Recent Black Freedom Studies." *Journal of African American History* 92 (2007): 265–88.

Chang, Iris. *The Rape of Nanking: The Forgotten Holocaust of World War II.* New York: Basic Books, 1997.

Chang, Thelma. *"I Can Never Forget": Men of the 100th/442nd.* Honolulu: Sigi Productions, 1991.

Children of the Camps: A Documentary and Educational Project. By Satsuki Ina. San Francisco: National Asian American Telecommunications Association, 1999.

Chin, Frank, Jeffrey Paul Chan, Lawson Fusao Inada, and Shawn Wong, eds. *Aiiieeeee! An Anthology of Asian-American Writers.* Washington, D.C.: Howard University Press, 1974.

Churchill, Ward. *On the Justice of Roosting Chickens.* Oakland, Calif.: AK Press, 2003.

———, and Jim Vander Wall. *Agents of Repression: The FBI's Secret War against the Black Panther Party and the American Indian Movement.* Boston: South End Press, 1988.

———. *The COINTELPRO Papers: Documents from the FBI's Secret Wars Against Dissent in the United States.* Boston: South End Press, 1990.

Cleaver, Eldridge. "On Lumpen Ideology." *Black Scholar,* 1972, 2–10.

Cleaver, Kathleen. "Back to Africa: The Evolution of the International Section of the Black Panther Party (1969–1972)." In *Black Panther Party Reconsidered,* edited by Charles E. Jones, 211–54. Baltimore, Md.: Black Classic Press, 1998.

———. "Women, Power, and Revolution." In Cleaver and Katsiaficas, *Liberation, Imagination, and the Black Panther Party,* 123–27.

———, and George Katsiaficas, eds. *Liberation, Imagination, and the Black Panther Party: A New Look at the Panthers and Their Legacy.* New York: Routledge, 2001.

Cohen, Robert Carl. *Black Crusader: A Biography of Robert Franklin Williams.* Secaucus, N.J.: Lyle Stuart, 1972.

Collins Committee. *Report of the Committee Appointed to Review the Department of Ethnic Studies, UC Berkeley.* July 1973. Ethnic Studies Library, University of California, Berkeley.

Color of Honor, The. By Loni Ding. Berkeley, Calif.: Center for Educational Telecommunications, 1987.

"Combahee River Collective Statement" (1977). In *This Bridge Called My Back: Writings by Radical Women of Color,* edited by Cherríe Moraga and Gloria E. Anzaldúa. New York: Kitchen Table: Women of Color Press, 1984.

Commission on Wartime Relocation and Internment of Civilians. *Personal Justice Denied.* Washington, D.C.: The Civil Liberties Public Education Fund; Seattle: University of Washington Press, 1997.

Committee on Admissions and Enrollment. *Freshman Admissions at Berkeley: A Policy for the 1990s and Beyond.* Report to UC Berkeley Academic Senate, 1989, known as "Karabel Report."

Connell, R. W. *Masculinities.* 2nd ed. Berkeley: University of California Press, 2005.

Conscience and the Constitution. By Frank Abe. Transit Media, 2000.

Cooley, Charles Horton. *Human Nature and the Social Order.* 1902. Reprint, New York: Schocken Books, 1964.

Coontz, Stephanie. *The Way We Never Were: American Families and the Nostalgia Trap.* New York: Basic Books, 1992.

Cox, Don. "The Split in the Party." In Cleaver and Katsiaficas, *Liberation, Imagination, and the Black Panther Party,* 118–22.

Crawford, Vicki L., Jacqueline Anne Rouse, and Barbara Woods, eds. *Women in the Civil Rights Movement: Trailblazers and Torchbearers, 1941–1965.* Brooklyn, N.Y.: Carlson, 1990.

Creef, Elena Tajima. *Imaging Japanese America: The Visual Construction of Citizenship, Nation, and the Body.* New York: New York University Press, 2004.

Cruse, Harold. "Marxism and the Negro." In *Rebellion or Revolution?,* 139–55.

———. *Rebellion or Revolution?* New York: William Morrow, 1968.

———. "Revolutionary Nationalism and the Afro-American." In *Rebellion or Revolution?,* 74–96.

Cuordileone, K. A. "'Politics in an Age of Anxiety': Cold War Political Culture and the Crisis of American Masculinity, 1949–1960." *Journal of American History* 87 (2000): 515–45.

Daniels, Roger. *Concentration Camps USA: Japanese Americans and World War II.* Hinsdale, Ill.: Dyden Press, 1971.

———. *The Decision to Relocate the Japanese Americans.* Philadelphia: J. B. Lippincott, 1975.

———. *The Politics of Prejudice: The Anti-Japanese Movement in California and the Struggle for Japanese Exclusion.* Berkeley: University of California Press, 1962.

———. *Prisoners without Trial: Japanese Americans in World War II.* New York: Hill and Wang, 1993.

———, Sandra C. Taylor, and Harry H. L. Kitano, eds. *Japanese Americans: From Relocation to Redress.* Seattle: University of Washington Press, 1991.

Darby, William O., with William Henry Baumer. *Darby's Rangers: We Led the Way.* San Rafael, Calif.: Presidio Books, 1980.

Darby's Rangers. By William A. Wellman. Warner Bros., 1958.

Davis, Angela Y. *If They Come in the Morning: Voices of Resistance.* New York: Third Press, 1971.

Davis, James Kirkpatrick. *Assault on the Left: The FBI and Sixties Antiwar Movement.* Westport, Conn.: Praeger, 1997.

Dean, Robert D. *Imperial Brotherhood: Gender and the Making of Cold War Foreign Policy.* Amherst: University of Massachusetts Press, 2001.

———. "Masculinity as Ideology: John F. Kennedy and the Domestic Politics of Foreign Policy." *Diplomatic History* 22 (1998): 29–62.

DeBenedetti, Charles. *An American Ordeal: The Antiwar Movement of the Vietnam Era.* Syracuse, N.Y.: Syracuse University Press, 1990.

Debray, Régis. *Revolution in the Revolution? Armed Struggle and Political Struggle in Latin America.* New York: Monthly Review Press, 1967.

Debs, Eugene V. *Writings and Speeches of Eugene V. Debs.* New York: Hermitage Press, 1948.

Deffaa, Chip. "Charles Brown." In *Blue Rhythms: Six Lives in Rhythm and Blues.* Urbana: University of Illinois Press, 1996.

Dellums, Ronald V., and H. Lee Halterman. *Lying Down with the Lions: A Public Life from the Streets of Oakland to the Halls of Power.* Boston: Beacon Press, 2000.

Denzin, Norman K. *Interpretive Biography.* Newbury Park, Calif.: Sage, 1989.

Dittmer, John. *Local People: The Struggle for Civil Rights in Mississippi.* Urbana: University of Illinois Press, 1995.

Dixon, Aaron. "Memoirs of a Black Panther." Unpublished manuscript; http://www.itsabouttimebpp.com/Chapter_History.

Dong, Harvey C. "The Origins and Trajectory of Asian American Political Activism in the San Francisco Bay Area, 1968–1978." PhD diss., University of California, Berkeley, 2002.

———. "Transforming Student Elites into Community Activists: A Legacy of Asian American Activism." In *Asian Americans: The Movement and the Moment,* edited by Steve Louie and Glenn K. Omatsu, 187–204. Los Angeles: UCLA Asian American Studies Center Press, 2001.

Douglass, Frederick. "The Significance of Emancipation in the West Indies." In *The Frederick Douglass Papers,* vol. 3, edited by John W. Blassingame, 1885–63. New Haven, Conn.: Yale University Press, 1985.

Dower, John W. *Embracing Defeat: Japan in the Wake of World War II.* New York: W. W. Norton, 1999.

———. *War without Mercy: Race and Power in the Pacific War.* New York: Pantheon, 1986.

Drinnon, Richard. *Keeper of Concentration Camps: Dillion S. Myer and American Racism.* Berkeley: University of California Press, 1987.

Du Bois, David. "Understanding the Legacy of W. E. B. Du Bois." *Emerge,* October 1993.

Dudziak, Mary. *Cold War Civil Rights: Race and the Image of American Democracy.* Princeton, N.J.: Princeton University Press, 2000.

Durkheim, Emile. *Suicide: A Study in Sociology.* Edited and translated by George Simpson. New York: Free Press, 1951.

Duus, Masayo Umezawa. *Unlikely Liberators: The Men of the 100th and 442nd.* Honolulu: University of Hawai'i Press, 1987.

Duus, Peter. *Modern Japan.* 2nd ed. Boston: Houghton Mifflin, 1998.

Dyson, Michael Eric. *Making Malcolm: The Myth and Meaning of Malcolm X.* New York: Oxford University Press, 1995.

"Editorial: Berkeley's School of Criminology, 1950–1976." *Crime and Social Justice* 6 (1976).

Ehrenreich, Barbara. *The Hearts of Men: American Dreams and the Flight from Commitment.* Garden City, N.Y.: Anchor Press/Doubleday, 1983.

———. *Nickel and Dimed: On (Not) Getting By in America.* New York: Henry Holt, 2001.

Elbaum, Max. *Revolution in the Air: Radicals Turn to Lenin, Mao, and Che.* London: Verso, 2002.

Emi, Frank. "Draft Resistance at the Heart Mountain Concentration Camp and the Fair Play Committee." In *Frontiers of Asian American Studies,* edited by Gail Nomura, Russell Endo, Steve Sumida, and Russell Leong, 41–48. Pullman: Washington State Press, 1989.

Engels, Frederick. *The Condition of the Working Class in England in 1844.* Translated by Florence Kelley Wischnewetsky. New York: J. W. Lovell, 1887.

———. *The Origin of the Family, Private Property, and the State.* New York: Pathfinder Press, 1972.

Epstein, Barbara. "Anti-Communism, Homophobia, and the Construction of Masculinity in the Postwar US." *Critical Sociology* 20 (1994): 21–44.

Erikson, Erik H., and Huey P. Newton. *In Search of Common Ground: Conversations with Erik H. Erikson and Huey P. Newton.* New York: W. W. Norton, 1973.

Espiritu, Yen Le. *Asian American Panethnicity.* Philadelphia: Temple University Press, 1992.

Ethnic Studies Committee of the Department of Ethnic Studies. *A Proposal for the Establishment of the College of Third World Studies.* Submitted to Provost Roderic Park, September 18, 1974.

Eyes on the Prize II: America at the Racial Crossroads, 1965–1985. PBS Video, 1989.

Eyes on the Prize II: Episode 1, *The Time Has Come.* PBS Video, 1989.

Fall of the I Hotel, The. By Curtis Choy. NAATA Distributors, 1995.

Fanon, Frantz. *Black Skin, White Masks.* New York: Grove Press, 1967.

———. *The Wretched of the Earth.* New York: Grove Press, 2004.

Ferguson, Edwin E. "The California Alien Land Law and the Fourteenth Amendment." *California Law Review* 35 (1947): 61–90.

Ferreira, Jason Michael. "'All Power to the People': A Comparative History of Third World Radicalism in San Francisco, 1968-1974." PhD diss., University of California, Berkeley, 2003.

Fight in the Fields, The: Cesar Chavez and the Farmworkers' Struggle. By Ray Telles and Rick Tejada-Flores. Paradigm Productions, 1997.

Fisher, Ernest F., Jr. *Guardians of the Republic: A History of the Noncommissioned Officer Corp of the U.S. Army.* New York: Ballantine Books, 1994.

Fitzgerald, Dennis. "Guy Kurose Devoted Life to Helping Youth"; http://www.its abouttimebpp.com/Memorials/Guy_Kurose_Devoted_Life.html.

Foner, Philip S., ed. *The Black Panthers Speak.* New York: Da Capo Press, 1970.

Fong, Bryant, and Floyd Huen. "An Understanding of AAPA." Unpublished manuscript, August 24, 1968.

Forman, James. *The Making of Black Revolutionaries.* Seattle, Wash.: Open Hand Publishing, 1985.

47 Ronin, The. By Kenji Mizoguchi. Image Entertainment, 1941.

Foster, William Z. *History of the Communist Party of the United States.* New York: International Publishers, 1952.

Fourth World War. By Jacqueline Soohen and Richard Rowley. Big Noise Films, 2004.

Fowler, Josephine. *Japanese and Chinese Immigrant Activists: Organizing in American and International Communist Movements, 1919–1933.* New Brunswick, N.J.: Rutgers University Press, 2007.

Frazier, Edward Franklin. *The Black Bourgeoisie.* New York: Free Press, 1957.

Freeman, Jo. *At Berkeley in the '60s: The Education of an Activist, 1961–1965.* Bloomington: Indiana University Press, 2004.

Freire, Paulo. *Pedagogy of the Oppressed.* New York: Continuum, 2007.

Friedan, Betty. *The Feminine Mystique.* New York: Dell, 1963.

Fu, May. "Keeping Close to the Ground: Politics and Coalition in Asian American Community Organizing, 1969–1977." PhD diss., University of California, San Diego, 2005.

Fuchs, Lawrence H. *Hawaii Pono: A Social History.* New York: Harcourt, Brace & World, 1961.

Fujino, Diane C. "Black Liberation Movement and Japanese American Activism: The Radical Activism of Richard Aoki and Yuri Kochiyama." In *Afro Asia,* edited by Fred Ho and Bill V. Mullen, 165–97. Durham, N.C.: Duke University Press, 2008.

———. "Black Militants and Asian American Model Minorities: Contesting Oppositional Representations, or on Afro-Asian Solidarities." *Kalfou* (forthcoming).

———. "The Global Cold War and Asian American Activism." Under review.

———. "Grassroots Leadership and Afro-Asian Solidarities: Yuri Kochiyama's Humanizing Radicalism." In Gore, Theoharis, and Woodard, *Want to Start a Revolution?,* 294–316.

———. *Heartbeat of Struggle: The Revolutionary Life of Yuri Kochiyama.* Minneapolis: University of Minnesota Press, 2005.

———. "Race, Place, Space, and Political Development: Japanese American Radicalism in the 'Pre-Movement' 1960s." *Social Justice* 35, no. 2 (2008–9): 57–79.

———. "Who Studies the Asian American Movement? A Historiographical Analysis." *Journal of Asian American Studies* 11 (2008): 127–69.

Fujitani, Takashi, Geoffrey M. White, and Lisa Yoneyama, eds. *Perilous Memories: The Asia-Pacific War(s).* Durham, N.C.: Duke University Press, 2001.

Gaddis, John Lewis. *The Cold War: A New History.* London: Penguin, 1995.

———. *We Now Know: Rethinking Cold War History.* Oxford: Oxford University Press, 1997.

Gaines, Kevin. "The Historiography of the Struggle for Black Equality since 1945." In *A Companion to Post-1945 America,* edited by Jean-Christophe Agnew and Roy Rosenzweig, 211–34. Malden, Mass.: Blackwell, 2002.

Galbraith, John Kenneth. *The Affluent Society.* London: Hamish Hamilton, 1958.

Gandhi, M. K. "The Doctrine of the Sword." *Young India,* August 11, 1920, 3–5.

Gee, Emma, ed. *Counterpoint: Perspectives on Asian America.* Los Angeles: University of California, Asian American Studies Center, 1976.

Gettleman, Marvin E., ed. *Vietnam and America: A Documented History.* New York: Grove Press, 1985.

Gilmore, Glenda Elizabeth. *Defying Dixie: The Radical Roots of Civil Rights, 1919–1950.* New York: W. W. Norton, 2008.

Gleason, Alan. "Summary of Aoki Family Geneology." Unpublished manuscript, 1998.

Glenn, Evelyn Nakano. *Issei, Nisei, War Bride.* Philadelphia: Temple University Press, 1986.

Goldman, Justin. "7th Street Blues." *Diablo,* June 2007.

Gordon, Andrew. *A Modern History of Japan: From Tokugawa Times to the Present.* New York: Oxford University Press, 2003.

Gordon, Linda, and Gary Y. Okihiro, eds. *Impounded: Dorothea Lange and the Censored Images of Japanese American Internment.* New York: W. W. Norton, 2006.

Gore, Dayo F., Jeanne Theoharis, and Komozi Woodard, eds. *Want to Start a Revolution? Radical Women in the Black Freedom Movement.* New York: New York University Press, 2009.

Gosse, Van. "A Movement of Movements: The Definition and Periodization of the New Left." In *A Companion to Post-1945 America,* edited by Jean-Christophe Agnew and Roy Rosenzweig, 277–302. Malden, Mass.: Blackwell, 2002.

———. *Rethinking the New Left: An Interpretive History.* New York: Palgrave Macmillan, 2005.

———. *Where the Boys Are: Cuba, Cold War America, and the Making of a New Left.* London: Verso, 1993.

———, and Richard Moser, eds. *The World the 60s Made: Politics and Culture in Recent America.* Philadelphia: Temple University Press, 2003.

Gramsci, Antonio. *Selections from the Prison Notebooks.* New York: International Publishers, 1971.

Grapes of Wrath, The. By John Ford. Film, 20th Century–Fox, 1940.

Griffith, Robert K. *The U.S. Army's Transition to the All-Volunteer Force, 1968–1974.* Washington, D.C.: Center of Military History, U.S. Army, 1997.

Griswold, Robert L. "The 'Flabby American,' the Body, and the Cold War." In *A Shared Experience: Men, Women, and the History of Gender,* edited by Laura McCall and Donald Yacovone, 323–67. New York: New York University Press, 1998.

Grodzins, Morton. *Americans Betrayed: Politics and the Japanese Evacuation.* Chicago: University of Chicago Press, 1949.

Guerrero, Amado. *Philippine Society and Revolution.* Hayward, Calif.: Philippine Information Network Service, 1996/1970.

Guevara, Che. "At the United Nations" speech, December 11, 1964. In *Che Guevara and the Cuban Revolution: Writings and Speeches of Ernesto Che Guevara,* edited by David Deutschmann, 321–36. Sydney: Pathfinder, 1987.

Habal, Estella. *San Francisco's International Hotel: Mobilizing the Filipino American Community in the Anti-Eviction Movement.* Philadelphia: Temple University Press, 2007.

Hall, Jacquelyn Dowd. "The Long Civil Rights Movement and the Political Uses of the Past." *Journal of American History* 91 (2005): 1233–63.

Halstead, Fred. *Out Now! A Participant's Account of the Movement in the U.S. Against the Vietnam War.* New York: Pathfinder, 1978.

Hansen, Arthur A., and David A. Hacker. "The Manzanar Riot: An Ethnic Perspective." *Amerasia Journal* 2 (1974): 112–57.

Hansen, Joseph. *Dynamics of the Cuban Revolution: A Marxist Appreciation.* New York: Pathfinder Press, 1978.

Hantover, Jeffrey P. "The Boy Scouts and the Validation of Masculinity." In *Men's Lives.* 3rd ed. Edited by Michael S. Kimmel and Michael A. Messner. Boston: Allyn and Bacon, 1995.

Harrington, Michael. *The Other America: Poverty in the United States.* New York: Macmillan, 1962.

Hatamiya, Leslie T. *Righting a Wrong: Japanese Americans and the Passage of the Civil Liberties Act of 1988*. Stanford, Calif.: Stanford University Press, 1993.

Hayano, David M. "Ethnic Identification and Disidentification: Japanese-American Views of Chinese-Americans." Unpublished manuscript, n.d.

Hayashi, Brian Masaru. *"For the Sake of Our Japanese Brethren": Assimilation, Nationalism, and Protestantism among the Japanese of Los Angeles, 1895–1942*. Stanford, Calif.: Stanford University Press, 1995.

Hayashi, Patrick. *Contemporary Asian Studies Division Report*. Department of Ethnic Studies, University of California, Berkeley, March 1972.

Healey, Dorothy Ray, and Maurice Isserman. *California Red: A Life in the American Communist Party*. Urbana: University of Illinois Press, 1993.

Heath, G. Louis. *The Black Panther Leaders Speak*. Metuchen, N.J.: Scarecrow Press, 1976.

Hegel, Georg Wilhelm Friedrich. *The Phenomenology of Mind*. 2nd ed. Translated by J. B. Baillie. New York: Macmillan, 1931.

Herring, George. *America's Longest War: The United States and Vietnam, 1950–1975*. New York: Wiley, 1979.

Herskovits, Melville J. *Myth of the Negro Past*. New York: Harper and Brothers, 1941.

Hewitt, Kim. "Martial Arts Is Nothing if Not Cool: Speculation on the Intersection between Martial Arts and African American Expressive Culture." In *Afro Asia: Revolutionary Political and Cultural Connections between African Americans and Asian Americans*, edited by Fred Ho and Bill V. Mullen, 263–84. Durham, N.C.: Duke University Press, 2008.

Hidden Internment: The Art Shibayama Story. By Casey Peek. Peek Media, 2004.

Hietala, Thomas R. *The Fight of the Century: Jack Johnson, Joe Louis, and the Struggle for Racial Equality*. Armonk, N.Y.: M. E. Sharpe, 2002.

Hill, Kimi Kodani, ed. *Topaz Moon: Chiura Obata's Art of the Internment*. Berkeley, Calif.: Heyday Books, 2000.

Hilliard, David, and Lewis Cole. *This Side of Glory: The Autobiography of David Hilliard and the Story of the Black Panther Party*. Boston: Little, Brown, 1993.

Himes, Chester. *If He Hollers Let Him Go*. 1945. Reprint, New York: Da Capo Press, 1986.

Hinkel, Edgar J., and William E. McCann, eds. *Oakland 1852–1938: Some Phases of the Social, Political and Economic History of Oakland, California*. Oakland: Oakland Public Library, 1939.

Ho, Fred. "The Inspiration of Mao and the Chinese Revolution on the Black Liberation Movement and the Asian Movement on the East Coast." In Ho, *Wicked Theory, Naked Practice*, 283–92.

———. "Kickin' the White Man's Ass: Black Power, Aesthetics, and the Asian Martial Arts." In Raphael-Hernandez and Steen, *AfroAsian Encounters*, 295–312.

———. *Wicked Theory, Naked Practice: A Fred Ho Reader*. Edited by Diane C. Fujino. Minneapolis: University of Minnesota Press, 2009.

——, Carolyn Antonio, Diane C. Fujino, and Steve Yip, eds. *Legacy to Liberation: Politics and Culture of Revolutionary Asian Pacific America.* San Francisco: AK Press, 2000.

——, and Bill V. Mullen, eds. *Afro Asia: Revolutionary Political and Cultural Connections between African and Asian Americans.* Durham, N.C.: Duke University Press, 2008.

——, and Steve Yip. "Interview with Alex Hing." In Ho et al., *Legacy to Liberation,* 279–96.

Hohri, William Minoru. *Repairing America: An Account of the Movement for Japanese-American Redress.* Pullman: Washington State University Press, 1988.

——, with Mits Koshiyama, Yosh Kuromiya, Takashi Hoshizaki, and Frank Seishi Emi. *Resistance: Challenging America's Wartime Internment of Japanese-Americans.* Kearney, Neb.: Morris, 2001.

Holloway, John. "Dignity's Revolt." In *Zapatista! Reinventing Revolution in Mexico,* ed. John Holloway and Eloína Peláez, 159–98. London: Pluto, 1998.

Holmes, T. Michael. *The Specter of Communism in Hawaii.* Honolulu: University of Hawai'i Press, 1994.

Homer, Sean. "Narratives of History, Narratives of Time." In *On Jameson: From Postmodernism to Globalization,* edited by Caren Irr and Ian Buchanan, 71–91. Albany: State University of New York Press, 2006.

Hopkins, Charles. "The Deradicalization of the Black Panther Party, 1967–1973." PhD diss., University of North Carolina, Chapel Hill, 1978.

Horne, Gerald. *Black and Red: W. E. B. Du Bois and the African American Response to the Cold War, 1944–1963.* Albany: State University of New York Press, 1986.

Hosokawa, Bill. *JACL: In Quest of Justice; The History of the Japanese American Citizens League.* New York: Morrow, 1982.

House Committee on Armed Services, U.S. Congress. *Reserve Forces Act of 1955.* Washington, D.C.: U.S. Government Printing Office, 1955.

——. *Universal Military Training.* Washington, D.C.: U.S. Government Printing Office, 1952.

Howard, Elbert "Big Man." *Panther on the Prowl.* Baltimore: BCP Digital Printing, 2002.

Howe, Irving, and Lewis A. Coser. *The American Communist Party: A Critical History.* New York: Praeger, 1962.

Hugo, Victor. *Les Misérables.* London: Hurst and Blackett, 1862.

Huie, William Bradford. "The Shocking Story of Approved Killing in Mississippi." *Look,* January 24, 1956.

Ichihashi, Yamato. *Japanese in the United States.* Stanford, Calif.: Stanford University Press, 1932.

Ichioka, Yuji. "A Buried Past: Early Issei Socialists and the Japanese Community." *Amerasia Journal* 1 (1973): 1–25.

——. *The Issei: The World of the First Generation Japanese Immigrants, 1885–1924.* New York: Free Press, 1988.

Iijima, Kazu. "Brief History of AAA and the NY Asian Movement." Speech, n.d.

"In Memory of Robert Williams: A Voice for Armed Self-Defense and Black Liberation." *Revolutionary Worker,* November 17, 1996.

Iriye, Akira. *Pacific Estrangement: Japanese and American Expasion, 1897–1911.*
Chicago: Imprint Publications, 1994.

———. *Power and Culture: The Japanese–American War, 1941–45.* Cambridge, Mass.:
Harvard University Press, 1981.

Isserman, Maurice. *Which Side Were You On? The American Communist Party during the Second World War.* Urbana: University of Illinois Press, 1993.

Izumi, Masumi. "Prohibiting 'American Concentration Camps': Repeal of the Emergency Detention Act and the Public Historical Memory of the Japanese American
Internment." *Pacific Historical Review* 74 (2005): 165–93.

Jackson, George. *Blood in My Eye.* Baltimore, Md.: Black Classic Press, 1971.

———. *Soledad Brother: The Prison Letters of George Jackson.* New York: Bantam,
1970.

James, C. L. R. "The Socialist Workers Party and Negro Work." Resolution adopted
at the 1939 SWP convention. In *Leon Trotsky on Black Nationalism and Self-
Determination,* edited by George Breitman, 49–55. New York: Pathfinder Press,
1970.

Jameson, Fredric. *The Political Unconscious: Narrative as a Socially Symbolic Act.*
Ithaca, N.Y.: Cornell University Press, 1981.

Jansen, Marius B. *The Making of Modern Japan.* Cambridge, Mass.: Harvard University Press, 2000.

Jennings, Regina. "Why I Joined the Party." In Jones, *The Black Panther Party Reconsidered,* 257–65.

Johnson, Cedric. *Revolutionaries to Race Leaders: Black Power and the Making of
African American Politics.* Minneapolis: University of Minnesota Press, 2007.

Johnson, Chalmers. *Blowback: The Costs and Consequences of American Empire.* 2nd
ed. New York: Henry Holt, 2004.

———. *The Sorrows of Empire: Militarism, Secrecy, and the End of the Republic.* New
York: Metropolitan Books, 2004.

Johnson, Marilynn S. *The Second Gold Rush: Oakland and the East Bay in World War
II.* Berkeley: University of California Press, 1993.

Johnson, Ollie A. "Explaining the Demise of the Black Panther Party: The Role of
Internal Factors." In Jones, *The Black Panther Party Reconsidered,* 391–414.

Jones, Charles E., ed. *The Black Panther Party Reconsidered.* Baltimore, Md.: Black
Classic Press, 1998.

Jones, LeRoi. "Cuba Libre." In *The LeRoi Jones/Amiri Baraka Reader,* edited by William J. Harris with Amiri Baraka, 125–60. New York: Thunder's Mouth Press, 1991.

Joseph, Peniel E. "Black Liberation without Apology: Reconceptualizing the Black
Power Movement." *Black Scholar* 31 (2001): 3–19.

———. "The Black Power Movement: A State of the Field." *Journal of American History* 96 (December 2009): 751–76.

———. "Introduction: Toward a Historiography of the Black Power Movement." In *The Black Power Movement: Rethinking the Civil Rights–Black Power Era,* edited by Peniel E. Joseph, 1–25. New York: Routledge, 2006.

———. *Waiting 'til the Midnight Hour: A Narrative History of Black Power in America.* New York: Henry Holt, 2006.

———. "Waiting till the Midnight Hour: Reconceptualizing the Heroic Period of the Civil Rights Movement, 1954–1965." *Souls* 2 (2000): 6–17.

Kahin, George McTurnan. *The Asian-African Conference.* Ithaca, N.Y.: Cornell University Press, 1956.

Kakutani, Michiko. "Brand Che: Revolutionary as Marketer's Dream." *New York Times,* April 20, 2009.

Karagueuzian, Dikran. *Blow It Up! The Black Student Revolt at San Francisco State College and the Emergence of Dr. Hayakawa.* Boston: Gambit, 1971.

Katsiaficas, George. *The Imagination of the New Left: A Global Analysis of 1968.* Boston: South End Press, 1987.

Kelley, Robin D. G. "'But a Local Phase of a World Problem': Black History's Global Vision, 1883–1950." *Journal of American History* 86 (1999): 1045–77.

———. *Freedom Dreams: The Black Radical Imagination.* Boston: Beacon Press, 2002.

———. *Hammer and Hoe: Alabama Communists during the Great Depression.* Chapel Hill: University of North Carolina Press, 1990.

———, and Betsy Esch. "Black like Mao: Red China and Black Revolution." *SOULS: A Critical Journal of Black Politics, Culture, and Society* 1 (1999): 6–41.

Kennedy, John F. "The Soft American." *Sports Illustrated,* December 26, 1960.

Kikumura, Akemi. *Through Harsh Winters: The Life of a Japanese Immigrant Woman.* Novato, Calif.: Chandler and Sharp, 1981.

Kimmel, Michael S. "The Contemporary 'Crisis' of Masculinity in Historical Perspective." In *The Making of Masculinities: The New Men's Studies,* edited by Harry Brod, 121–53. Boston: Allen and Unwin, 1987.

———. *Manhood in America: A Cultural History.* Oxford: Oxford University Press, 2006.

———. "Masculinity as Homophobia: Fear, Shame, and Silence in the Construction of Gender Identity." In *Theorizing Masculinities,* edited by Harry Brod and Michael Kaufman, 119–41. Thousand Oaks, Calif.: Sage, 1994.

King, Martin Luther, Jr. "I Have a Dream" (1963). In *A Testament of Hope: The Essential Writings of Martin Luther King, Jr.,* edited by James M. Washington, 217–20. San Francisco: Harper and Row, 1986.

———. "Nonviolence and Racial Justice." In King, *A Testament of Hope,* 5–9.

———. "A Time to Break Silence." In King, *A Testament of Hope,* 231–44.

Kinmonth, Earl H. *The Self-Made Man in Meiji Japanese Thought: From Samurai to Salary Man.* Berkeley: University of California Press, 1981.

Kinsey, Alfred C., Wardell B. Pomeroy, and Clyde E. Martin. *Sexual Behavior in the Human Male.* Philadelphia: W. B. Saunders, 1948.

Kitano, Harry H. L. *Japanese Americans: The Evolution of a Subculture.* 2nd ed. Englewood Cliffs, N.J.: Prentice-Hall, 1976.

Kitayama, Glen Ikuo. "Japanese Americans and the Movement for Redress: A Case Study of Grassroots Activism in the Los Angeles Chapter of the National Coalition for Redress/Reparations." MA thesis, University of California, Los Angeles, 1993.

Klein, Christina. *Cold War Orientalism: Asia in the Middlebrow Imagination, 1945–1961.* Berkeley: University of California Press, 2003.

Korstad, Robert, and Nelson Lichtenstein. "Opportunities Found and Lost." *Journal of American History* 75 (1988): 786–811.

Kotani, Roland, *The Japanese in Hawaii: A Century of Struggle.* Honolulu: Hawaii Hochi, 1985.

Kropotkin, P. A. *Selected Writings on Anarchism and Revolution,* edited by Martin A. Miller. Cambridge, Mass.: MIT Press, 1970.

Kublin, Hyman. *Asian Revolutionary: The Life of Sen Katayama.* Princeton, N.J.: Princeton University Press, 1964.

Kurashige, Lon. *Japanese American Celebration and Conflict: A History of Ethnic Identity and Festival in Los Angeles, 1934–1990.* Berkeley: University of California Press, 2002.

LaFeber, Walter. *America, Russia, and the Cold War, 1945–2002.* 9th ed. Boston: McGraw-Hill, 2004.

———. *The Clash: U.S.–Japan Relations throughout History.* New York: W. W. Norton, 1997.

Lai, Him Mark. "A Historical Survey of the Chinese Left in America." *Bulletin of Concerned Asian Scholars,* Fall 1972.

Lange, Dorothea, and Paul Schuster Taylor. *An American Exodus: A Record of Human Erosion.* New York: Reynal and Hitchcock, 1939.

Lawson, Steven F. "Freedom Then, Freedom Now: The Historiography of the Civil Rights Movement." *American Historical Review* 96 (1991): 456–71.

Layton, Edwin T. *And I Was There: Pearl Harbor and Midway—Breaking the Secrets.* New York: Morrow, 1985.

Lazerow, Jama, and Yohuru Williams, eds. *In Search of the Black Panther Party: New Perspectives on a Revolutionary Movement.* Durham, N.C.: Duke University Press, 2006.

Lears, T. J. Jackson, "The Concept of Cultural Hegemony: Problems and Possibilities." *American Historical Review* 90 (1985): 567–93.

LeBlanc-Ernest, Angela. "'The Most Qualified Person to Handle the Job': Black Panther Party Women, 1966–1982," In Jones, *The Black Panther Party Reconsidered,* 305–34.

Lenin, V. I. *Imperialism: The Highest Stage of Capitalism.* Moscow: Progressive Publishers, 1975.

———. *The State and Revolution.* Peking: Foreign Language Press, 1973.

Lent, Henry. *Bombardier: Tom Dixon Wins His Wings with the Bomber Command.* New York: Macmillan, 1943.

Lim, Deborah. "Lim Report." Unpublished report on the JACL's wartime activities; http://www.resisters.com/lim_report.

Ling, Susie. "The Mountain Movers: Asian American Women's Movement in Los Angeles." *Amerasia Journal* 15 (1989): 51–67.

Lipsitz, George. *The Possessive Investment in Whiteness: How White People Profit from Identity Politics.* Philadelphia: Temple University Press, 1998.

———. *Rainbow at Midnight: Labor and Culture in the 1940s.* Urbana: University of Illinois Press, 1994.

Liu, Michael, Kim Geron, and Tracy Lai. *The Snake Dance of Asian American Activism: Community, Vision, and Power.* Lanham, Md.: Lexington Books, 2008.

Louie, Miriam Ching. "'Yellow, Brown, & Red': Towards an Appraisal of Marxist Influences on the Asian American Movement." Unpublished manuscript, 1991.

Louie, Steve, and Glenn Omatsu, eds. *Asian Americans: The Movement and the Moment.* Los Angeles: UCLA Asian American Studies Center Press, 2001.

Lum, Lydia. "Overshadowed." *Diverse Issues in Higher Education,* February 8, 2007.

Luthi, Lorenz M. *The Sino-Soviet Split: Cold War in the Communist World.* Princeton, N.J.: Princeton University Press, 2008.

Luxemburg, Rosa. "The Junius Pamphlet" (1906). In *The Mass Strike, the Political Party, and the Trade Unions.* New York: Harper and Row, 1971.

Lyman, Stanford M. "Red Guard on Grant Avenue." In *Culture and Civility in San Francisco,* edited by Howard S. Becker, 20–52. Chicago: Transaction Books, 1971.

Maciel, David R., and Juan José Peña. "La Reconquista: The Chicano Movement in New Mexico." In *The Contested Homeland: A Chicano History of New Mexico,* edited by Erlinda Gonzales-Berry and David R. Maciel, 269–301. Albuquerque: University of New Mexico Press, 2000.

Mackey, Mike, ed. *A Matter of Conscience: Essays on the World War II Heart Mountain Draft Resistance Movement.* Powell, Wyo.: Western History Publications, 2002.

Maeda, Daryl J. "Black Panthers, Red Guards, and Chinamen: Constructing Asian American Identity through Performing Blackness, 1969–1972." *American Quarterly* 57 (2005): 1079–1103.

———. *Chains of Babylon: The Rise of Asian America.* Minneapolis: University of Minnesota Press, 2009.

Maki, Mitchell T., Harry H. L. Kitano, and S. Megan Berthold. *Achieving the Impossible Dream.* Urbana: University of Illinois Press, 1999.

Malcolm X. *Malcolm X Speaks.* Edited by George Breitman. New York: Grove Press, 1965.

———. "Message to the Grass Roots." In *Malcolm X Speaks,* 3–17.

Manashe, Louis, and Ronald Radosh, eds. *Teach-ins, USA: Reports, Opinions, Documents.* New York: Praeger, 1967.

Manufacturing Consent: Noam Chomsky and the Media. Documentary. Directed by Peter Wintonick and Mark Achbar. New York: Zeitgeist Films, 1992.

Mao Tse-tung. "On Practice" In *Selected Readings from the Works of Mao Tsetung,* edited by the Editorial Committee for Selected Readings from the Works of Mao Tse-tung, 65–84. Peking: Foreign Language Press, 1971.

———. "Where Do Correct Ideas Come From?" In *Mao Tse-tung: An Anthology of His Writings,* edited by Anne Fremantle, 301–2. New York: Mentor Books, 1971.

Marable, Manning. "Rediscovering Malcolm's Life: A Historian's Adventures in Living History." *SOULS: A Critical Journal of Black Politics, Culture, and Society* 7, no. 1 (2005): 21–35.

Mariscal, George. *Brown-Eyed Children of the Sun: Lessons from the Chicano Movement, 1965–75.* Albuquerque: University of New Mexico Press, 2005.

Marsh, Clifton E. *From Black Muslims to Muslims: The Transition from Separatism to Islam, 1930–1980.* Metuchen, N.J.: Scarecrow Press, 1984.

Marx, Karl. *Das Kapital.* Edited by Frederick Engels. New York: International Publishers, 1970.

———. "Theses on Feuerbach." In *The German Ideology.* Amherst, N.Y.: Prometheus Books, 1998.

———, and Frederick Engels. *The Communist Manifesto.* New York: Pathfinder Press, 1990/1848.

Masaoka, Mike, with Bill Hosokawa. *They Call Me Moses Masaoka.* New York: Morrow, 1987.

Massey, Douglas S., and Nancy A. Denton. *American Apartheid: Segregation and the Making of the Underclass.* Cambridge, Mass.: Harvard University Press, 1993.

Master Plan for Higher Education in California, 1960–1975, A. Sacramento: California State Department of Education, 1960; http://www.ucop.edu/acadinit/mastplan/MasterPlan1960.pdf.

Matthews, Tracye. "'No One Ever Asks, What a Man's Place in the Revolution Is': Gender and the Politics of the Black Panther Party, 1966–1971." In Jones, *The Black Panther Party Reconsidered,* 267–304.

May, Elaine Tyler. *Homeward Bound: American Families in the Cold War Era.* New York: Basic Books, 1999.

McAdam, Doug. *Political Process and the Development of Black Insurgency, 1930–1970.* Chicago: University of Chicago Press, 1982.

McClain, James L. *Japan: A Modern History.* New York: W. W. Norton, 2002.

McCormick, Thomas J. *America's Half-Century: United States Foreign Policy in the Cold War and After.* Baltimore: The Johns Hopkins University Press, 1995.

McCutchen, Steve D. "Selections from a Panther Diary." In Jones, *The Black Panther Party Reconsidered,* 115–33.

McDuffie, Erik S. "'No Small Amount of Change Could Do': Esther Cooper Jackson and the Making of a Black Left Feminism." In Gore, Theoharis, and Woodard, *Want to Start a Revolution?,* 25–46.

McEntire, Davis. *Residence and Race.* Berkeley: University of California Press, 1960.

McWilliams, Carey. *Brothers Under the Skin: African-Americans and Other Minorities.* Boston: Little, Brown, 1943.

———. *Factories in the Field: The Story of Migratory Farm Labor in California.* Boston: Little, Brown, 1939.

———. *Prejudice: Japanese-Americans, Symbol of Racial Intolerance.* Boston: Little, Brown, 1944.

Mealy, Rosemari. *Fidel and Malcolm X: Memories of a Meeting.* Melbourne, Australia: Ocean Press, 1993.

Melendez, Miguel. *We Took the Streets: Fighting for Latino Rights with the Young Lords.* New York: St. Martin's Press, 2003.

Merritt College: Home of the Black Panthers. By Jeffrey Heyman and Michelle Lee. Peralta TV, 2008.

Michener, James A. *Hawaii.* New York: Random House, 1959.

Milk. By Gus Van Sant. Universal Pictures, 2009.

Minami, Dale. "Asian Law Caucus." *Amerasia Journal* 3 (1975): 28–39.

Morales, Sylvia. "The Struggle in the Fields." Part one in the PBS series *Chicano! The History of the Mexican American Civil Rights Movement.* PBS, 1996.

Morgan, Edward. *The 60s Experience: Hard Lessons about Modern America.* Philadelphia: Temple University Press, 1991.

Mori, Toshio. *The Chauvinist and Other Stories.* Los Angeles: UCLA, Asian American Studies Center, 1979.

———. *Unfinished Message: Selected Works of Toshio Mori.* Berkeley, Calif.: Heyday Books, 2000.

———. *Yokohama, California.* 1949. Reprint, Seattle: University of Washington Press, 1985.

Morris, Aldon, and Naomi Braine. "Social Movements and Oppositional Consciousness." In *Oppositional Consciousness: The Subjective Roots of Social Protest,* edited by Jane Mansbridge and Aldon Morris, 20–37. Chicago: University of Chicago Press, 2001.

Moser, Richard. *The New Winter Soldiers: GI and Veteran Dissent during the Vietnam Era.* New Brunswick, N.J.: Rutgers University Press, 1996.

Mullen, Bill V. *Afro-Orientalism.* Minneapolis: University of Minnesota Press, 2004.

Muller, Eric L. *Free to Die for Their Country: The Story of the Japanese American Draft Resisters of World War II.* Chicago: University of Chicago Press, 2001.

Munro, John J. "The Anticolonial Front: Cold War Imperialism and the Struggle against Global White Supremacy, 1945–1960." PhD diss., University of California, Santa Barbara, 2009.

Murphy, Audie. *To Hell and Back.* New York: Holt, 1949.

Murray, Alice Yang. *Historical Memories of the Japanese American Internment and the Struggle for Redress.* Stanford, Calif.: Stanford University Press, 2008.

Nagata, Donna K. *Legacy of Injustice: Exploring the Cross-Generational Impact of the Japanese American Internment.* New York: Plenum Press, 1993.

Nelson, Douglas. *Heart Mountain: The History of an American Concentration Camp.* Madison: State Historical Society of Wisconsin, 1976.

Nelson, Truman. *People with Strength: The Story of Monroe, N.C.* Monroe, N.C.: Committee to Aid the Monroe Defendants, 1962.

Newton, Huey P. "Huey Newton Talks to the Movement about the Black Panther Party, Cultural Nationalism, SNCC, Liberals and White Revolutionaries." In Foner, *The Black Panthers Speak*, 55–66.

———. "On the Defection of Eldridge Cleaver from the Black Panther Party and the Defection of the Black Panther Party from the Black Community." In Foner, *The Black Panthers Speak*, 272–78.

———. *Revolutionary Suicide.* New York: Ballantine, 1973.

———. *To Die for the People.* Edited by Toni Morrison. New York: Writers and Readers, 1995.

———. *War Against the Panthers: A Study of Repression in America.* New York: Harlem River Press, 1996.

Nguyen, Viet Thanh. "The Remasculinization of Chinese America: Race, Violence, and the Novel." *American Literary History* 12 (2000): 130–57.

Nietzsche, Friedrich. *Beyond Good and Evil.* Edinburgh: T. N. Foulis, 1909.

Nisei Soldier. By Loni Ding. Berkeley, Calif.: Center for Educational Telecommunications, 1983.

Nitobe, Inazo. *Bushido: The Soul of Japan.* 1905. Reprint, Rutland, Vt.: Charles E. Tuttle, 1973.

Nkrumah, Kwame. *Handbook of Revolutionary Warfare.* London: Panaf Books, 1980.

———. *I Speak of Freedom.* New York: Panaf Books, 1961.

Oda, James. *Heroic Struggles of Japanese Americans: Partisan Fighters from America's Concentration Camps.* North Hollywood, Calif.: KNI, 1980.

O'Dell, Jack. *Climbin' Jacob's Ladder: The Black Freedom Movement Writings of Jack O'Dell.* Edited by Nikhil Pal Singh. Berkeley: University of California Press, 2010.

Ogbar, Jeffrey O. G. *Black Power: Radical Politics and African American Identity.* Baltimore: The Johns Hopkins University Press, 2004.

Okada, John. *No-No Boy.* 1957. Reprint, Seattle: Combined Asian American Resources Project, 1976.

Okamura, Raymond. "Background and History of the Repeal Campaign." *Amerasia Journal* 2 (1974): 74–94.

Okihiro, Gary. "Japanese Resistance in America's Concentration Camps: A Reevaluation." *Amerasia Journal* 2 (1973): 20–33.

———. *Margins and Mainstreams: Asians in American History and Culture.* Seattle: University of Washington Press, 1994.

Okubo, Miné. *Citizen 13660.* 1946. Reprint, Seattle: University of Washington Press, 1983.

Olmsted, Nancy, and Roger W. Olmsted. "History of West Oakland." In *West Oakland—a Place to Start From,* edited by Mary Praetzellis, 9–223. Rohnert Park, Calif.: Anthropology Studies Center, Sonoma State University Academic Foundation, 1994–95.

Omi, Michael, and Howard Winant. *Racial Formation in the United States.* 2nd ed. New York: Routledge, 1994.

On Strike! Ethnic Studies, 1969–1999. By Irum Shiekh. Progressive Films, 1999.

"Open Letter to Our Fellow Asian Brothers and Sisters, An: Join the Fight to Defend and Expand Affirmative Action." *Hitting Critical Mass: A Journal of Asian American Cultural Criticism* 3, no. 2 (Spring 1997): 135–40.

Orrick, William H. *Shut It Down! A College in Crisis: San Francisco State College, October 1968–April 1969.* Washington, D.C.: U. S. Government Printing Office, 1969.

¡Palante, Siempre Palante! The Young Lords. By Iris Morales. Latino Education Network Service, 1996.

Panther. By Mario Van Peebles. Gramercy Pictures, 1995.

Park, Robert E. *The Collected Papers of Robert Park.* Vol. 1, *Race and Culture.* Glencoe, Ill.: Free Press, 1950.

———. "Human Migration and the Marginal Man." *American Journal of Sociology* 33 (1928): 881–93.

Payne, Charles M. Foreword to *Groundwork: Local Black Freedom Movements in America,* edited by Jeanne Theoharis and Komozi Woodard, ix–xv. New York: New York University Press, 2005.

———. *I've Got the Light of Freedom: The Organizing Tradition and the Mississippi Freedom Struggle.* Berkeley: University of California Press, 1995.

———. "Men Led, but Women Organized: Movement Participation of Women in the Mississippi Delta." In Crawford, Rouse, and Woods, *Women in the Civil Rights Movement,* 1–13.

Pearson, Hugh. *The Shadow of the Panther.* Reading, Mass.: Addison-Wesley, 1994.

Petersen, William. "Success Story, Japanese-American Style." *New York Times Magazine,* January 9, 1966.

Platt, Tony, and Paul Takagi. *Punishment and Penal Discipline: Essays on the Prison and the Prisoners' Movement.* Folsom, Calif.: Crime and Social Justice Associates, 1980.

Plummer, Brenda Gayle. *Rising Wind: Black American and U.S. Foreign Affairs, 1935–1960.* Chapel Hill: University of North Carolina Press, 1996.

Portelli, Alessandro. *The Death of Luigi Trastulli and Other Stories: Form and Meaning in Oral History.* Albany: State University of New York Press, 1990.

Praetzellis, Mary, and Adrian Praetzellis, eds. *Putting the "There" There: Historical Archaeologies of West Oakland.* California Department of Transportation, 2004.

Prashad, Vijay. *The Darker Nations: A People's History of the Third World.* New York: New Press, 2007.

———. *Everybody Was Kung Fu Fighting: Afro-Asian Connections and the Myth of Cultural Purity.* Boston: Beacon, 2001.

Preis, Art. *Labor's Giant Step.* New York: Pathfinder Press, 1964.

Pulido, Laura. *Black, Brown, Yellow, and Left: Radical Activism in Los Angeles.* Berkeley: University of California Press, 2006.

Rabbit in the Moon. By Emiko Omori. A Wabi-Sabi Production, 1999.

Ransby, Barbara. *Ella Baker and the Black Freedom Movement.* Chapel Hill: University of North Carolina Press, 2003.

Raphael-Hernandez, Heiki, and Shannon Steen, eds. *AfroAsian Encounters: Culture, History, Politics.* New York: New York University Press, 2006.

Rhomberg, Chris. *No There There: Race, Class, and Political Community in Oakland.* Berkeley: University of California Press, 2004.

Robinson, Greg. *By Order of the President: FDR and the Internment of Japanese Americans.* Cambridge, Mass.: Harvard University Press, 2001.

———. "Nisei in Gotham: The JACD and Japanese Americans in 1940s New York." *Prospects* 30 (2005): 581–95.

———. "Norman Thomas and the Struggle against Internment." *Prospects* 29 (2005): 419–34.

Rodríguez, Dylan. "Thinking Solidarity Across 'Generations': Richard Aoki and the Relevance of Living Legacies." *Shades of Power* 1, no. 2 (Summer 1998): 10–11, 14.

Rorabaugh, W. J. *Berkeley at War: The 1960s.* New York: Oxford University Press, 1989.

Sacks, Karen Brodkin. *Caring by the Hour: Women, Work, and Organizing at Duke Medical Center.* Urbana: University of Illinois Press, 1988.

———. "Gender and Grassroots Leadership." In *Women and the Politics of Empowerment,* edited by Ann Bookman and Sandra Morgen, 77–94. Philadelphia: Temple University Press, 1988.

Said, Edward. *Orientalism.* New York: Pantheon Books, 1978.

San Francisco State: On Strike. Documentary, San Francisco: California Newsreel, 1969.

Saxton, Alexander. *The Indispensable Enemy: Labor and the Anti-Chinese Movement in California.* Berkeley: University of California Press, 1995.

Scharlin, Craig, and Lilia V. Villanueva. *Philip Vera Cruz: A Personal History of Filipino Immigrants and the Farmworkers Movement.* Los Angeles: UCLA Labor Center and UCLA Asian American Studies Center, 1992.

Schirmer, Daniel B., and Stephen Rosskamm Shalom. *The Philippines Reader: A History of Colonialism, Neocolonialism, Dictatorship, and Resistance.* Boston: South End Press, 1987.

Schlesinger, Arthur M. "The Crisis of American Masculinity" (1958). In *The Politics of Hope.* Boston: Houghton Mifflin, 1963.

Schlosser, Eric. *Fast Food Nation.* Boston: Houghton Mifflin, 2001.

Schrecker, Ellen. *Many Are the Crimes: McCarthyism in America.* Boston: Little, Brown, 1998.

Seale, Bobby. "History of the Black Panther Party." http://www.bobbyseale.com, accessed August 27, 2003.

———. *Seize the Time: The Story of the Black Panther Party and Huey P. Newton.* 1968. Reprint, Baltimore: Black Classic Press, 1991.

Self, Robert O. *American Babylon: Race and the Struggle for Postwar Oakland.* Princeton, N.J.: Princeton University Press, 2003.

Sellers, Cleveland. *The River of No Return.* Jackson: University Press of Mississippi, 1990.

Sen, Rinku. *Stir It Up: Lessons in Community Organizing and Advocacy.* San Francisco: Jossey-Bass, 2003.

Shakur, Assata. *Assata: An Autobiography.* Chicago: Lawrence Hill Books, 1987.

Shank, Gregory. "Paul T. Takagi, Honored." *Social Justice* 35 (2008).

Shaull, Richard. Foreword to Paulo Freire, *Pedagogy of the Oppressed,* 29–34. New York: Continuum, 2007.

Sheppard, Barry. *The Party: The Socialist Workers Party, 1960–1988.* Chippendale, N.S.W., Australia: Resistance Books, 2005.

Sherry, Michael S. *In the Shadow of War: The United States since the 1930s.* New Haven, Conn.: Yale University Press, 1995.

———. *The Rise of American Air Power: The Creation of Armageddon.* New Haven, Conn.: Yale University Press, 1987.

Shibutani, Tamotsu. *The Derelicts of Company K: A Sociological Study of Demoralization.* Berkeley: University of California Press, 1978.

Singh, Nikhil Pal. *Black Is a Country: Race and the Unfinished Struggle for Democracy.* Cambridge, Mass.: Harvard University Press, 2004.

———. "The Black Panthers and the 'Underdeveloped Country' of the Left." In Jones, *The Black Panther Party Reconsidered,* 57–105.

Sivanandan, A. "New Circuits of Imperialism." *Race and Class* 30, no. 4 (1989): 1–19.

Small, Melvin, and William Hoover. *Give Peace a Chance: Exploring the Vietnam Antiwar Movement.* Syracuse, N.Y.: Syracuse University Press, 1992.

Smethurst, James Edward. *The Black Arts Movement: Literary Nationalism in the 1960s and 1970s.* Chapel Hill: University of North Carolina Press, 2005.

Smith, Lillian. *Strange Fruit.* New York: Grosset and Dunlap, 1944.

Smith, Paul Chaat, and Robert Allen Warrior. *Like a Hurricane: The Indian Movement from Alcatraz to Wounded Knee.* New York: New Press, 1996.

Smith, Robert, Richard Axen, and DeVere Pentony. *By Any Means Necessary: The Revolutionary Struggle at San Francisco State.* San Francisco: Jossey-Bass, 1970.

Smith, Theophus H. *Conjuring Culture: Biblical Formations of Black America.* New York: Oxford University Press, 1994.

Social Welfare at Berkeley 6, no. 1 (Fall 1994).

Socialist Workers Party. "The Case for an Independent Black Political Party." Resolution adopted at the 1967 SWP convention. New York: Merit Publishers, 1968.

———. "Freedom Now: New Stage in the Struggle for Negro Emancipation." Resolution adopted at the 1963 Socialist Workers Party convention. Reprinted in *International Socialist Review,* Fall 1963.

———. "A Transitional Program for Black Liberation." Resolution adopted at the 1969 SWP convention. *Internationalist Socialist Review* 30 (Nov.–Dec. 1969): 50–60.

Somerville, Bill. "Can Selective Colleges Accommodate the Disadvantaged? Berkeley Says 'Yes.'" *College Board Review* 65 (Fall 1967): 5.

Sone, Monica. *Nisei Daughter.* Seattle: University of Washington Press, 1953.

Speak Out for Justice! The Los Angeles Hearings of the Commission on Wartime Relocation and Internment of Civilians. Video recording by National Coalition for Redress/Reparations. Visual Communications, 1988.

Spickard, Paul R. *Japanese Americans: The Formation and Transformation of an Ethnic Group.* 2nd ed. New Brunswick, N.J.: Rutgers University Press, 2009.

———. *Mixed Blood: Intermarriage and Ethnic Identity in Twentieth-Century America.* Madison: University of Wisconsin Press, 1989.

———. "The Nisei Assume Power: The Japanese American Citizens League, 1941–1942." *Pacific Historical Review* 52 (1983): 147–74.

———. "Not Just the Quiet People: The Nisei Underclass." *Pacific Historical Review* 68 (1999): 78–94.

Stanford, Max. "Revolutionary Action Movement: A Case Study of an Urban Revolutionary Movement in Western Capitalist Society." MA thesis, Atlanta University, 1986.

"Statement on the Anniversary of Richard Aoki's Passing." March 15, 2010, signed by Richard Aoki Memorial Committee, former Asian American Political Alliance members, Serve the People, and Friends of Richard Aoki; posted at http://ra memorial.blogspot.com, accessed March 2010.

Steinbeck, John. *The Grapes of Wrath.* New York: Viking, 1939.

———. *In Dubious Battle.* New York: Modern Library, 1936.

———. *Travels with Charley: In Search of America.* New York: Viking, 1962.

Steiner, Jesse Frederick. *The Japanese Invasion: A Study of the Psychology of Interracial Contacts.* 1917. Reprint, New York: Arno Press, 1978.

Strong, Edward K. *Japanese in California.* Stanford, Calif.: Stanford University Press, 1933.

Sturken, Marita. "Absent Images of Memory: Remembering and Reenacting the Japanese Internment." In *Perilous Memories: The Asia-Pacific War(s),* edited by Takashi Fujitani, Geoffrey M. White, and Lisa Yoneyama, 33–49. Durham, N.C.: Duke University Press, 2001.

"Success Story of One Minority Group in U.S." *U.S. News and World Report,* December 26, 1966.

Sue, Derald Wing, Christina M. Capodilupo, Gina C. Torina, Jennifer M. Bucceri, Aisha M. B. Holder, Kevin L. Nadal, and Marta Esquilin. "Racial Microaggression in Everyday Life." *American Psychologist* 62 (2007): 271–86.

Sukarno. "Speech at the Opening of the Afro-Asian Conference April 18, 1955." In *The Asian-African Conference,* by George McTurnan Kahin, 39–51. Ithaca, N.Y.: Cornell University Press, 1956.

Szasz, Andrew. *Shopping Our Way to Safety: How We Changed from Protecting the Environment to Protecting Ourselves.* Minneapolis: University of Minnesota Press, 2007.

Takahashi, Jere. *Nisei Sansei: Shifting Japanese American Identities and Politics.* Philadelphia: Temple University Press, 1997.

Takaki, Ronald. *Hiroshima: Why America Dropped the Atomic Bomb.* Boston: Little, Brown, 1995.

Takezawa, Yasuko I. *Breaking the Silence: Redress and Japanese American Ethnicity.* Ithaca, N.Y.: Cornell University Press, 1995.

Tanaka, Chester. *Go for Broke: A Pictorial History of the Japanese American 100th Infantry Battalion and 442nd Regimental Combat Team.* Richmond, Calif.: Go For Broke, 1982.

Taylor, Sandra C. "Evacuation and Economic Loss: Questions and Perspectives." In *Japanese Americans: From Relocation to Redress,* edited by Roger Daniels, Sandra C. Taylor, and Harry H. L. Kitano, 63–67. Seattle: University of Washington Press, 1991.

———. *Jewel of the Desert: Japanese American Internment at Topaz.* Berkeley: University of California Press, 1993.

Theoharis, Jeanne F., and Komozi Woodard, eds. *Freedom North: Black Freedom Struggles Outside the South, 1940–1980.* New York: Palgrave Macmillan, 2003.

———. *Groundwork: Local Black Freedom Movements in America.* New York: New York University Press, 2005.

Thomas, Dorothy S., and Richard Nishimoto. *The Spoilage: Japanese-American Evacuation and Resettlement during World War II.* 1946. Reprint, Berkeley: University of California Press, 1969.

Thompson, E. P. *The Making of the English Working Class.* New York: Pantheon Books, 1966.

Thompson, Holland, and Arthur Mee, eds. *The Book of Knowledge: The Children's Encyclopedia.* London: Educational Book Company, 1910; New York: Grolier, 1912.

Tijerina, Reies López. *Mi lucha por la tierra.* Mexico City: Fondo de Cultura Económica, 1978. Translation by José Angel Gutiérrez. *They Called Me "King Tiger": My Struggle for the Land and Our Rights.* Houston: Arte Público Press, 2000.

Times of Harvey Milk, The. By Rob Epstein. New Yorker Films, 1985.

To Hell and Back. By Jesse Hibbs. Universal International, 1955.

Toyo Miyatake: Infinite Shades of Gray. By Robert A. Nakamura. Los Angeles: Japanese American National Museum, Frank H. Watase Media Arts Center, 2001.

Trotsky, Leon. *Leon Trotsky on Black Nationalism and Self-Determination.* Edited by George Breitman. New York: Pathfinder Press, 1970.

Tsuchida, Nobuya. "Japanese Gardeners in Southern California, 1900–1941." In *Labor Immigration under Capitalism: Asian Workers before World War II,* edited by Lucie Cheng and Edna Bonacich, 435–69. Berkeley: University of California Press, 1984.

Tsuchida, William Shinji. *Wear It Proudly.* Berkeley: University of California Press, 1947.

Turnbull, Stephen. *Samurai: The World of the Warrior.* Oxford: Osprey, 2003.

Tyson, Timothy. *Radio Free Dixie: Robert F. Williams and the Roots of Black Power.* Chapel Hill: University of North Carolina Press, 1999.

Uchida, Yoshiko. *Desert Exile: The Uprooting of a Japanese-American Family.* Seattle: University of Washington Press, 1982.

———. *Journey to Topaz.* New York: Scribner, 1971.

Ueno, Harry Y. *Manzanar Martyr: An Interview with Harry Y. Ueno.* Edited by Sue Kunitomi Embrey, Arthur A. Hansen, and Betty Kulberg Mitson. Fullerton, Calif.: Oral History Program, California State University, 1986.

Umemoto, Karen. "'On Strike!' San Francisco State College Strike, 1968–69: The Role of Asian American Students." *Amerasia Journal* 15 (1989): 3–41.

Umoja, Akinyele Omowale. "Repression Breeds Resistance: The Black Liberation Army and the Radical Legacy of the Black Panther Party." In Cleaver and Katsiaficas, *Liberation, Imagination, and the Black Panther Party,* 3–19.

Unforgivable Blackness: The Rise and Fall of Jack Johnson. By Ken Burns. PBS Home Video, 2005.

United States Army Corps of Engineers. *Fort Ord: A Place in History.* Documentary, ca. 1995.

United States Congress, Permanent Subcommittee on Investigations of the Committee on Government Operations. *Riots, Civil and Criminal Disorders.* Washington D.C.: Government Printing Office, 1970.

Uyematsu, Amy. "The Emergence of Yellow Power in America." In *Roots: An Asian American Reader,* edited by Amy Tachiki, Eddie Wong, Franklin Odo, and Buck Wong, 9–13. Los Angeles: University of California, Asian American Studies Center, 1971.

Veale, Dolly. "Interview with Richard Aoki." In Ho, *Legacy to Liberation,* 319–34.

Von Eschen, Penny M. *Race against Empire: Black Americans and Anticolonialism, 1937–1957.* Ithaca, N.Y.: Cornell University Press, 1997.

Wakatsuki, Yasuo. "Japanese Emigration to the United States, 1866–1924." *Perspectives in American History* 12 (1979): 389–516.

Wald, Karen, and Ward Churchill. "Remembering the Real Dragon: An Interview with George Jackson." In *Cages of Steel: The Politics of Imprisonment in the United States,* edited by Ward Churchill and J. J. Vander Wall, 174–93. Washington, D.C.: Maisonneuve Press, 1992.

Ward, Colin. *Anarchy in Action.* London: George Allen and Unwin, 1973.

Warren, Earl. *The Memoirs of Earl Warren.* New York: Doubleday, 1977.

Weaver, Robert C. *The Negro Ghetto.* New York: Harcourt, Brace, 1948.

Weglyn, Michi. *Years of Infamy: The Untold Story of America's Concentration Camps.* New York: Morrow, 1976.

Wei, William. *The Asian American Movement.* Philadelphia: Temple University Press, 1993.

West, Candace, and Don H. Zimmerman. "Doing Gender." In *Doing Gender, Doing Difference,* edited by Sarah Fenstermaker and Candace West, 3–23. New York: Routledge, 2002.

Westad, Odd Arne. *The Global Cold War.* Cambridge: Cambridge University Press, 2007.

When Worlds Collide. By Rudolph Mate. Paramount Pictures, 1951.

Williams, Christine L. *Still a Man's World: Men Who Do "Women's Work."* Berkeley: University of California Press, 1995.

Williams, Robert F. *Negroes with Guns.* New York: Marzani and Munsell, 1962.

Wolfe, Tom. "The New Yellow Peril." *Esquire,* December 1969, 190–99, 322.

———. *Radical Chic and Mau-Mauing the Flak Catchers.* New York: Farrar, Straus and Giroux, 1970.

Woodard, Komozi. *A Nation within a Nation: Amiri Baraka (LeRoi Jones) and Black Power Politics.* Chapel Hill: University of North Carolina Press, 1999.

Worsley, Peter. *The Third World.* London: Weidenfeld and Nicolson, 1964.

Wright, Richard. *The Color Curtain: A Report on the Bandung Conference.* Cleveland: World Publishing, 1956.

———. *Native Son.* New York: Harper, 1940.

———. *Uncle Tom's Children.* New York: Harper, 1938.

Wylie, Philip. *Generation of Vipers: In Which the Author Rails against Congress, the President, Professors, Motherhood, Businessmen, and Other Matters American.* Champaign, Ill.: Dalkey Archive Press, 1942.

Yamada, Robert T. *The Berkeley Legacy, 1895–1995.* Berkeley: Berkeley Historical Society, 1995.

"Yellow Power." *Giant Robot* 10 (Spring 1998): 61–81.

Yerby, Frank. *The Foxes of Harrow.* New York: Dial Press, 1946.

Yip, Steve. "Serve the People—Yesterday and Today: The Legacy of Wei Min She." In Ho, *Legacy to Liberation,* 15–30.

Yokota, Ryan Masaaki. "Interview with Pat Sumi." In *Asian Americans: The Movement and the Moment,* ed. Steve Louie and Glenn Omatsu, 16–31. Los Angeles: UCLA Asian American Studies Center Press, 2001.

Yoneda, Karl. *Ganbatte: Sixty-Year Struggle of a Kibei Worker.* Los Angeles: UCLA Asian American Studies Center, 1983.

Yu, Henry. *Thinking Orientals: Migration, Contact, and Exoticism in Modern America.* Oxford: Oxford University Press, 2004.

Zaroulis, Nancy, and Gerald Sullivan. *Who Spoke Up? American Protest against the War in Vietnam, 1963–75.* New York: Doubleday, 1984.

Zia, Helen. *Asian American Dreams: The Emergence of an American People.* New York: Farrar, Straus, and Giroux, 2000.

Zinn, Howard. *A People's History of the United States, 1492–Present.* New York: Harper Perennial, 1995.

———. *SNCC: The New Abolitionists.* Boston: Beacon Press, 1964.

Index

DIANE C. FUJINO is associate professor and chair of Asian American Studies at the University of California, Santa Barbara. She has published two other books with the University of Minnesota Press, *Heartbeat of Struggle: The Revolutionary Life of Yuri Kochiyama* (2005) and *Wicked Theory, Naked Practice: A Fred Ho Reader* (2009).